MVS JCL
& UTILITIES

Second Edition

MVS JCL & UTILITIES

A Comprehensive Treatment

Michael Trombetta
Queensborough Community College

Sue Carolyn Finkelstein
IBM Corporation

 Addison-Wesley Publishing Company

Reading, Massachusetts • Menlo Park, California • New York
Don Mills, Ontario • Wokingham, England • Amsterdam • Bonn
Sydney • Singapore • Tokyo • Madrid • San Juan

Keith Wollman: Sponsoring Editor
Karen Myer: Production Supervisor
Lifland et al., Bookmakers: Packager
Marshall Henrichs: Cover Designer
Hugh Crawford: Manufacturing Supervisor

Many of the designations used by manufacturers and sellers to distinguish their products are claimed as trademarks. Where those designations appear in this book, and Addison-Wesley was aware of a trademark claim, the designations have been printed in initial caps or all caps.

The programs and applications presented in this book have been included for their instructional value. They have been tested with care, but are not guaranteed for any particular purpose. The publisher does not offer any warranties or representations, nor does it accept any liabilities with respect to the programs or applications.

Library of Congress Cataloging-in-Publication Data

Trombetta, Michael.
    MVS JCL and utilities : a comprehensive treatment / by Michael
  Trombetta, Sue Carolyn Finkelstein. -- 2nd ed.
      p.   cm.
  Rev. ed. of: OS JCL and utilities. 1984.
  Bibliography: p.
  Includes index.
  ISBN 0-201-08318-3
    1. MVS (Computer system)   2. Job Control Language (Computer
program language)   3. Utilities (Computer programs)
I. Finkelstein, Sue Carolyn. II. Trombetta, Michael. OS JCL and
utilities. III. Title.
QA76.6.T76 1989   88-10893
005.4'429--dc19   CIP

Reprinted with corrections October, 1989

CDEFGHIJ-DO-89

To Angela
  If they asked me I could write a different book

                                 MT

To my mother Yetta Klieger, who made this book possible,
  and my daughter Marla Rose Diamond, who made it necessary

                                 SCF

Preface

The widespread acceptance of the first edition of our book convinced us to retain the same approach in this second edition. That approach is to teach JCL as a programming language. By that we mean two things: first, students must see statements used in the context of complete programs (job streams), and second, students must execute solutions to programming assignments.

So as to show students complete job streams as soon as possible, we use IBM utility programs in our examples. This has the extra benefit that students learn how to use the utilities while they are learning JCL. For example, in Chapter 2 we present a job stream that uses `IEBGENER` to list instream data. In Chapter 3 `IEBGENER` is used to create disk and tape data sets. Chapter 4 introduces `IEBPTPCH` and a two-step job stream. In Chapter 5 libraries and the utilities used with them are discussed. In every case, the job streams presented are based on actual computer-produced listings, so the student can be sure that they do not contain errors. The programming assignments at the end of each chapter ask the student to code job streams similar to those in the chapter.

Changes in This Edition

The most substantial change in this edition is the addition of a new chapter (Chapter 15) on JES. As networks have become more common, it has become necessary for programmers to understand JES services and how to request them, in order to obtain the precise control over input and output processing that can be achieved only by using JES control statements. In keeping with the comprehensive character of the rest of the book, Chapter 15 contains detailed discussions about every JES parameter that the application programmer is likely to use.

Also new in this edition is a discussion of the `OUTPUT` statement and the `OUTPUT` parameter (Chapter 10) and of the recently introduced `SORT` control statements, `INCLUDE`, `OMIT`, `INREC`, and `OUTREC` (Chapter 9).

The parameter most students have the most trouble with is COND. For this edition we have substantially revised the discussion of the COND parameter both in Chapter 4, where it is used with programs, and in Chapter 8, where it is used with procedures.

In response to the high interest in VSAM, we have revised the discussion of the IDCAMS DEFINE CLUSTER, DEFINE ALTERNATEINDEX, and SET commands. We have also included a discussion of implications of operating under ICF.

Although we have changed the title from *OS JCL* to *MVS JCL*, we have been careful throughout to point out the statements and commands that are not available in VS1, the other version of OS that is currently in use.

Pedagogical Features

One of the most useful pedagogical features of this text is the presentation and explanation of the output produced when a job executes. Included are some jobs that contain errors and therefore do not execute properly. This output helps students to understand their output and error messages and to learn how to correct their errors.

Because students have told us that they find the learning objectives, vocabulary terms, and chapter summaries helpful, we have retained them from the first edition. The vocabulary terms are printed in bold the first time they appear, and all are defined in the glossary at the end of the book. As in the first edition, we have paid particular attention to the relationship between JCL and the programming languages COBOL, PL/I, FORTRAN, and assembler.

In order to execute the programming assignments, students need some information about their computer center. They must know their account number, the job classes they may use, the serial numbers of the volumes they may use, and so on. The inside front cover has been designed to help students organize this information.

Course Outline

We have tried to live up to the subtitle "A Comprehensive Treatment" by including everything an application programmer is likely to need to know about JCL, JES, and utilities. As a result, the book contains more material than can be covered in the usual course. We leave it up to the instructor to choose whatever seems most valuable to his or her class.

There is a certain amount of core material that must be covered if later chapters are to be understandable. Chapter 1 should be covered completely, with the possible exception of the section of data storage. Chapters 2, 3, and 4 also contain fundamental material that should be covered completely. The instructor may choose to omit some of the material on utility control statements, however.

The material in the remaining chapters is basically independent; the instructor may select material according to the needs and interests of the students and the dictates of time. For instance, in Chapter 5 it is not necessary to learn all the utilities that process libraries (`IEBGENER`, `IEBPTPCH`, `IEBUPDTE`, `IEBCOPY`, `IEHLIST`, and `IEHPROGM`) or all of the control statements of the utilities that are studied. The material on generation data groups in Chapter 6 and on the linkage editor in Chapter 7 is not required to understand the later chapters. It is not necessary to cover both Chapter 11 on ISAM and Chapter 12 on VSAM. The discussions of the sort in Chapter 9, of advanced JCL features in Chapter 10, and of the various utilities in Chapter 13 are completely independent.

The Instructor's Guide contains a suggested course outline. It also contains the answers to all the exercises and programming assignments, as well as a disk with all the program listings and Appendixes C and D. The Guide is available to instructors from the publisher: Addison-Wesley Publishing Company, Route 128, Reading, MA 01867.

Acknowledgments

It is a pleasure to acknowledge the assistance we received while preparing this second edition. John Zipfel of Queensborough Community College, who taught from the first edition, made several helpful suggestions. Netiva Caftori of Northeastern Illinois University kindly sent her course outline and class notes, which were helpful. James Coleman suggested the technique discussed in Chapter 12 for making an alternate index unique, for which we thank him. We are also grateful to the following reviewers for their comments and suggestions: Lincoln G. Andrews (Miami-Dade Community College), Robert P. Behlendorf (DeVry Institute of Technology — City of Industry), Roland J. Couture (Southern Connecticut State University), and Tom Taylor (Mercer County Community College). Finally, we would also like to acknowledge the respondents to the user survey: Ron Bierman, Delaware Technical and Community College; Neil A. Blum, County College of Morris; Laurie A. Bosu, Southern Ohio College N.E.; C. T. Cadenhead, Richland College; John Chapman, Johnson County Community College; Janet P. Dunford, Central Virginia Community College; John K. Gotwals, Purdue University; Russell Griemsmann, New York City Technical College; T. Sherwood Jernigan, Nash Community College; Ulysses T. Johnson, Watterson College; James R. McBriar, Madison Area Technical College; Gerald P. Marquis, Walsh College; Linda Watson Metcalf, Trident Technical College; Dr. Josephine F. Morecroft, Virginia Commonwealth University; John A. Morris, CPA, Lincoln Land

Community College; Patti Loika Nunnally, John Tyler Community College; Professor Ramakrishna, Avila College; Dieter Schmidt, University of Cincinnati; Perry W. Ustick, University of West Florida; Patricia A. Weikerth, San Antonio College; and Len Weiner, Texas Tech University.

Bayside, New York   M.T.
May 1988   S.C.F.

Contents

Chapter 6 **Generation Data Groups**   171

Chapter 9   **Sorting and Merging**   273

Chapter 10   **Advanced JCL Features**   293

Chapter 12   VSAM Data Sets   365

Chapter 13   **Utilities**   435

Introduction

In this chapter you will learn

- what job control language (JCL) is
- what an operating system is
- what the components of a computer system are
- what the components of an operating system are
- what versions of the operating system have been and are currently available
- how a job is processed by the operating system
- how data are represented in storage
- the notation used to describe the syntax of JCL statements

One objective of this book is to teach you **JCL.** You might well ask, "What is JCL and why do I need it?" JCL stands for **job control language,** which is the language you use to communicate with the computer's operating system. That answer just raises another question: "What is an operating system and why do I want to communicate with it?" An **operating system** is a collection of programs that control a computer system. To have the computer execute your program, you use JCL to tell the operating system which computer resources the program requires. Before we can discuss the resources your program requires, however, you have to learn more about computer systems and operating systems.

Components of a Computer System

A modern computer system consists of several interconnected units. At the heart of the computer system is the **central processing unit,** or **CPU.** Instructions are executed in the CPU.

Another unit is the **main storage** unit, where programs and data are stored while they are being processed. The size of main storage is measured in bytes, each of which can store one letter or one digit. (Bytes are discussed in more detail later in this chapter.) Because main storage units can contain millions of bytes, abbreviations are generally used to specify the number of bytes. **K** stands for kilobyte, which is 1024 bytes, and **M** stands for megabyte, which is 1024 kilobytes. So you might say that a program requires 320K or that a computer's main storage has 3M.

Main storage is temporary in the sense that after processing is complete, the programs and data are replaced by the next set of programs and data to be processed. Programs and data are permanently stored on **auxiliary storage** such as magnetic tape, disk, and mass storage. For reasons that will be explained later in this chapter, magnetic disks are called **direct access storage devices,** abbreviated DASD. You will learn more about magnetic tape and disk in Chapter 3 and about mass storage in Chapter 14.

Until the early 1970s, programs and data were punched on cards and entered into the computer using a card reader. Today a terminal is more commonly used both to enter programs and data and to receive the results of program execution. A **terminal** consists of a typewriterlike keyboard and a televisionlike display screen. Many terminals may be used at the same time, in a type of operation known as **time sharing.**

If a small computer such as a personal computer, or even a medium-size computer such as a Model 36 or 38, is used to submit programs and data to and receive results from a large computer, the small computer is frequently called a **workstation.** The difference between a terminal and a workstation is that a terminal can only interact with a large computer, whereas a workstation can function independently. For example, with a terminal you usually transmit one line at a time to the large computer, but with a workstation you can enter your whole program and then, after it has been completely entered, you can transmit the complete program to the large computer.

Although cards are rarely used today, their influence is still felt. For example, just as cards contain 80 columns, most terminals display 80 characters on a line. Similarly, JCL statements and data entered with a program may not extend beyond 80 columns.

Printers and, rarely, card punches are used to record the results of program execution. Card readers, punches, and printers are called **unit record devices.**

Frequently terminals and printers are miles from the central computer and are connected by communication lines, often supplied by the telephone company. This arrangement makes it possible for you to enter programs and data and receive answers at a remote site just as though you were at the central site.

Supervising the whole computer system is the computer operator. The operator's console includes a keyboard and a display screen which are used to enter commands to the computer and receive messages from the computer. You might think that the operator, who runs the whole computer system, would be very busy. Sometimes he or she is, but one of the main functions of the operating system is to increase the efficiency of a computer system by automating the operation of the computer and relieving the operator of many routine tasks.

Components of an Operating System

The programs that make up the operating system may be classified into two categories: control programs and processing programs. Control programs schedule and supervise work done by the computer. Users do not communicate directly with control programs. Instead the user codes JCL statements indicating the computer resources the program requires. The control programs interpret the JCL statements and make those resources available.

You might be wondering what kind of resources your programs will need. At this point in your studies, you do not have the necessary background to understand completely the resources you will request. In fact, one of the things you will learn from this book is what resources you need and how to request them. Perhaps two simple examples will give you an idea of what is meant by resources. Suppose your program needs five minutes of computer time to execute; you must request those five minutes. Or suppose your program prints a report; you must request that a printer be made available to your program.

The second category of operating system programs consists of processing programs. There are three categories of processing programs: language translators, service programs, and utility programs. In contrast to the situation with control programs, when you want to use one of the processing programs you must explicitly ask for it. Let us briefly look at the three categories.

Language translators are used to translate programs into machine language. They include the assemblers, which translate programs written in assembler language, and the compilers, which translate programs written in higher-level languages such as COBOL, FORTRAN, and PL/I. Computers understand only machine language, so before a program written in one of these other languages can be executed it must be translated into machine language. You will learn how to use the language translators in Chapter 7.

Service programs include the linkage editor, the loader, and the sort/merge program. The linkage editor and the loader are used with the language translators; you will learn how to use them in Chapter 7. The sort/merge program is used to sort or merge records; its use is explained in Chapter 9.

Utility programs perform commonly required tasks such as copying data from one storage device to another. Teaching you how to use utility programs is a major objective of this book. In all, 21 utility programs are discussed. Throughout the book utility programs are used to illustrate the elements of JCL. In addition, Chapter 13 is devoted to utility programs.

Versions of Operating Systems

Every computer needs an operating system in order to function. The operating systems we will be studying are those that have been developed by IBM and that have the family name of OS, which stands for operating system. OS is used on the System/360, System/370, 303X, 308X, 3090, and 43XX main-frame computers. An operating system named DOS is used on IBM's smaller main-frame computers. The JCL for DOS is completely different from the JCL for OS, and we will not discuss it in this book. If you have used an IBM PC, you may be familiar with PC–DOS. PC–DOS is a relatively simple operating system and does not use JCL.

The MFT and MVT Operating Systems

There have been a number of operating systems in the OS family. One of the first was **MFT,** which stands for Multiprogramming with a Fixed number of Tasks. The control unit can execute only one instruction at a time. Thus **multiprogramming** is actually a means of alternating among programs, to take advantage of the fact that **I/O** (input/output) instructions are executed thousands of times more slowly than internally executed instructions, such as arithmetic instructions. In a multiprogramming system several programs are stored in the main storage unit simultaneously. When the currently executing program begins to carry out an I/O instruction, it is put into a "wait" state, and another program is executed. This means that instead of waiting until the slow I/O instruction is executed, the CPU can keep busy.

In an MFT system a portion of main storage is reserved for the operating system programs, and the rest is divided into a fixed number of partitions. A **partition** is simply a region of main storage in which a program is executed. The number and sizes of the partitions are decided when the operating system is installed on the computer (the operator may modify them during execution). Installing the operating system is called generating the system or, more commonly, **sysgen.** Thus you could say that the number of partitions is established at sysgen time.

An MFT system may sometimes be inefficient because the available partitions are too small to hold any of the programs waiting to be executed. Those partitions will not be used until programs that they can hold are submitted for execution. To eliminate this source of inefficiency, IBM introduced the **MVT** operating system. MVT stands for multiprogramming with a variable number of tasks. In an MVT operating system, a portion of main storage is reserved for operating system programs, and the rest is available in one large pool to be used by jobs. The user specifies how much main storage a program needs, and a region of storage is allocated to that program.

MFT and MVT were early operating systems and are no longer supported by IBM. They have both been replaced by virtual storage operating systems.

Virtual Storage Operating Systems

Virtual storage operating systems permit a program to use more main storage than is actually available. This sounds impossible, but it is done by treating auxiliary storage as an extension of main storage. When virtual systems are discussed, it is customary to call main storage **real storage,** to distinguish it from **virtual**—that is, auxiliary—**storage.** To understand how it is possible to use more storage than is actually available, you must realize that it is necessary to keep in main storage only the instructions that are currently being executed and the data that are currently being processed. The rest of the program and data are kept on auxiliary storage. A virtual operating system divides a program into small sections called **pages,** some of which are in real storage and the rest of which are on auxiliary storage. When instructions or data that are not in real storage are needed, a page of the program is written to auxiliary storage and the required page is read into real storage. This process is called **paging.** Because paging must be done quickly, the auxiliary storage used must be DASD.

The programmer does not have to be concerned with the fact that the program will be divided into pages and that these pages will be paged between real and auxiliary storage. We describe this situation by saying that paging is **transparent** to the user.

There were originally two versions of virtual operating systems: VS1 and VS2. VS1 is a virtual version of MFT, and VS2 is a virtual version of MVT. VS2 developed into **MVS,** which stands for **multiple virtual storage.** MVS allows programs to use 16M of storage. The latest version of MVS is called **MVS/XA,** where the XA stands for extended architecture. In an MVS/XA system programs can use 2 billion bytes of storage. Remember that because these are virtual operating systems, the computer does not need to have 2 billion bytes or even 16M of real storage.

Although operating systems have changed, the JCL that is used to communicate with them has not changed very much. Most of the JCL that you will be studying is valid for all versions of the operating systems. You will be told when a feature that is being discussed is not valid for all versions of the operating systems.

Executing a Job

It may seem to you that an operating system is extremely complicated, and indeed it is. Fortunately, to learn how to use an operating system you do not need a detailed understanding of how it works. A general understanding, however, will make your study of JCL more meaningful.

When a programmer wants to use a computer, he or she uses a terminal to create a file of 80-column card images. This file, called a job stream, is made up of one or more jobs. A **job** is a unit of work the computer is to perform. A **job stream** consists of JCL statements, programs that are to be executed, and data that are to be processed. The data included in the job stream are called **input stream data.** The system is able to distinguish JCL statements from the other statements in the job stream because JCL statements have two slashes,//, or a slash and an asterisk,/*, in columns 1 and 2. A job stream is shown in Figure 1.1.

The first statement in a job stream must be a JOB statement. The main function of the JOB statement is to identify the job to the system. The JOB statement is usually followed by an EXEC (execute) statement. The EXEC statement names the program or the procedure that is to be executed. (Procedures are discussed in Chapter 7, so for now assume that you will only

▬ Figure 1.1 ▬

A Typical Job Stream

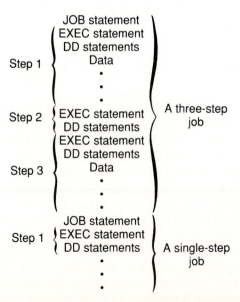

Figure 1.2

Progress of a Job Through a Computer System

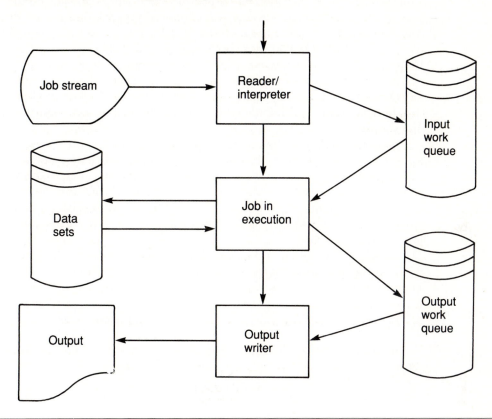

execute programs.) Following the EXEC statement are the DD (data definition) statements. The DD statements describe the data used by the program. An EXEC statement and its DD statements make up a **job step.** A job may consist of any number of job steps. Figure 1.1 shows a job stream that contains a three-step job followed by a one-step job.

The JOB, EXEC, and DD statements are the most important JCL statements. The others are the delimiter, null, and comment statements, which you will study in Chapter 2; the PROC and PEND statements, which you will study in Chapters 7 and 8; and the OUTPUT statement, which you will study in Chapter 10.

Figure 1.2 uses standard system flowchart symbols (which are explained in Appendix A) to illustrate a job being processed by a computer system. The job stream is entered into the computer via a terminal. Once the job has been submitted, there is no further interaction between the programmer and the computer. This type of operation, in which programs and their data are submitted as a unit, is called **batch processing.** If you have used an IBM PC, you may be familiar with another way of operating called interactive processing, in which the programmer interacts with the computer while a program is executing. Under OS you may develop your job stream by using an editor interactively, but jobs are executed in batch mode.

The first part of the operating system the job encounters is the **job entry subsystem.** The job entry subsystem reads jobs into the system, schedules jobs for execution, and handles the output produced by jobs. VS1 uses a job entry system named **JES,** and MVS uses either **JES2** or **JES3.***

A portion of the job entry system known as the reader/interpreter (sometimes called the converter/interpreter) reads the job stream and checks the coding of the JCL statements. If it finds an error, it prints a message and then stops further processing of the job. If there are no errors, the job stream is written to a direct access device, where it joins other jobs waiting to be executed in what is known as the **input work queue.** A **queue** is just a list of jobs awaiting service.

There are actually several input work queues. To balance the computer's workload, computer centers establish job classes. For example, one class might be for jobs that have high I/O requirements, whereas another might be for jobs that require a lot of time. The programmer is told to which class to assign his or her job. You will learn how jobs are assigned to classes in Chapter 2. A separate input work queue is established for each job class.

Writing the job stream to a direct access device is known as **spooling.** The word "spool" has become such an integral part of the data processing vocabulary that most people have no idea what it stands for — simultaneous peripheral operation on-line. Spooling is also done on output. When a program creates output that is to be printed or punched, it is not usually sent directly to a printer or punch. Rather, it is written to the **output work queue** on a disk. After a job terminates, a part of the job entry subsystem called the output writer sends the output to a printer or punch. The purpose of spooling is to isolate the CPU from the relatively slow card readers, punches, and printers. Spooling is transparent to the programmer, so programs may be written as though they read card data and write to a printer when actually they are reading and writing spooled files.

The job waits in the input work queue for its turn to be executed. Jobs may be assigned priorities, so the order in which they are executed is not necessarily the order in which they entered the system. When it's a job's turn to be executed, execution is started by a program named the initiator. Job steps within a job are executed separately in the order in which they appear in the

---

* The job entry subsystems used with MFT and MVT were ASP and HASP.

job stream. Before the initiator starts a job step, it makes sure that any input and output devices required by the job step are available. A program in executable form and the data it needs are called a **task.**

Although we have been following one job through the system, keep in mind that several jobs are executed concurrently.

Data Sets

You may be familiar with the concept of a file, which is defined as a collection of related records. In JCL terminology a file is called a **data set.** Data sets can be classified according to the way their records are organized, as follows: sequential data sets (discussed in Chapters 2, 3, and 4); partitioned data sets (also called libraries and discussed in Chapter 5); direct data sets (briefly discussed in Chapter 11); indexed sequential data sets (discussed in Chapter 11); and **virtual storage access method (VSAM)** data sets (discussed in Chapter 12).

Sequential data sets may be stored on either magnetic tape, magnetic disk, or mass storage devices. The other types of data sets must be stored on magnetic disk or mass storage devices.

No matter how a data set is organized, it may be accessed sequentially. Sequential access means that records are processed in the order in which they physically occur in the data set. Direct, indexed sequential, and VSAM data sets may also be accessed directly. **Direct access** means that the computer can process a desired record without having to process all the preceding records. Because magnetic disks permit direct access, they are called direct access storage devices, or **DASD.**

When a program executes an I/O instruction, control is turned over to an access method to perform the actual I/O. The particular access method used will depend on the organization of the data set and whether it is being accessed sequentially or directly. There are two categories of access methods: basic and queued. Basic access methods are used when a data set is accessed directly. So, for example, direct data sets are processed by means of an access method named BDAM, for basic direct access method. Queued access methods are used when a data set is accessed sequentially, in which case the system can anticipate the next record that will be processed. Sequential data sets are usually processed by means of an access method called QSAM, for queued sequential access method. Indexed sequential data sets can be processed either sequentially or directly, so two access methods are used: BISAM and QISAM. VSAM provides both basic and queued processing of VSAM data sets.

Sometimes the type of data set is indicated by giving the name of the access method used to access it, as in VSAM data sets. Similarly, indexed sequential data sets are frequently called **ISAM (indexed sequential access method)** data sets, and sequential data sets are sometimes called **SAM (sequential access method)** data sets.

Data Storage

You can understand about 95 percent of the following chapters without knowing how data are stored in main and auxiliary storage. But to understand the remaining 5 percent, you must know a little about data storage.

Main storage is made up of several million electronic components called **bits.** Bits may be in one of two states: on or off. These two states are represented by the digits 0 and 1. On auxiliary storage, magnetic spots are used to represent the 0 and 1 states. A group of eight bits is called a **byte.** To specify the contents of a byte, you must specify the states of the eight bits. For example, you might say that a byte contains 11010100.

Writing all those zeros and ones is time consuming and conducive to error, so a code was developed to permit the contents of a byte to be specified with only two characters. The code is the hexadecimal number system. The **hexadecimal number system** is a real number system in which it is possible to do arithmetic, but for your purposes you can consider it to be just a code that represents the state of four bits with one character. The code is shown in Table 1.1.

To use this code to represent the contents of a byte, you separate the eight bits into two groups of four bits each and use a hexadecimal digit to represent each set of four bits. For example, to find the hexadecimal representation for the byte that contains 11010100, you separate it into 1101 and 0100. Using the table, you find that 1101 is represented by D and 0100 by 4, so the contents of the byte may be written as D4.

Table 1.1

The Hexadecimal Number System

Bits	Hexadecimal Digit	Bits	Hexadecimal Digit
0000	0	1000	8
0001	1	1001	9
0010	2	1010	A
0011	3	1011	B
0100	4	1100	C
0101	5	1101	D
0110	6	1110	E
0111	7	1111	F

The EBCDIC Code

The code used in IBM computers to represent characters is called the **EBCDIC code.*** In the EBCDIC code a character occupies a byte. Starting from 00 and going through FF, there are 256 different values that may be stored in a byte. So the EBCDIC code could represent 256 characters, but not all the values are used to represent characters. The code for commonly used characters is shown in Table 1.2. As you can see, both upper-case and lower-case letters, digits, and special characters are represented.

If the letters CAT are entered on a terminal and those data are read into main or auxiliary storage, they will occupy three consecutive bytes, which will contain C3 C1 E3. Similarly, if three consecutive bytes containing C4 D6 C7 are sent to a printer, the printer will print DOG.

Numeric Data

Numeric data may be stored in several different forms. When numbers are stored in character form, the EBCDIC code is used. So the number 724 would appear in storage as F7 F2 F4. The left digit of the rightmost byte is used to represent the sign of the number. If the number is unsigned, as in our example, that digit is an F. If the number has a positive sign, the left digit of the rightmost byte is a C. So +628 would appear as F6 F2 C8. If the number has a negative sign, the left digit of the rightmost byte is a D. So −459 would appear as F4 F5 D9.

Numeric data may also be represented in packed format. In **packed format** two decimal digits are stored in each byte except for the rightmost byte, which contains one decimal digit and the sign of the number. The sign of the number is represented by the right digit of the rightmost byte (recall that it is the left digit of the rightmost byte that represents the sign when the number is stored in character form). So +628 would appear as 62 8C, and −459 would appear as 45 9D.

What would happen if you tried to print the packed number 62 8C? Table 1.2 shows that neither 62 nor 8C represents a printable character. When presented with a byte that does not represent a printable character, most printers don't print anything. Either nothing or meaningless characters will be printed if you try to print a packed number. Before a packed number may be printed, it must be converted to character form by a process known as **unpacking.**

Numeric data may also be stored in binary form and in floating point form, a discussion of which would take us too far afield. It is important to know,

---

* In the IBM PC a different code, called ASCII, is used.

Table 1.2
The EBCDIC Code

Hexadecimal Code	Character	Hexadecimal Code	Character	Hexadecimal Code	Character
40	space	84	d	C8	H
4A	¢	85	e	C9	I
4B	.	86	f	D1	J
4C	<	87	g	D2	K
4D	(	88	h	D3	L
4E	+	89	i	D4	M
4F	|	91	j	D5	N
50	&	92	k	D6	O
5A	!	93	l	D7	P
5B	$	94	m	D8	Q
5C	*	95	n	D9	R
5D	)	96	o	E2	S
5E	;	97	p	E3	T
5F	¬	98	q	E4	U
60	–	99	r	E5	V
61	/	A2	s	E6	W
6B	,	A3	t	E7	X
6C	%	A4	u	E8	Y
6D	—	A5	v	E9	Z
6E	>	A6	w	F0	0
6F	?	A7	x	F1	1
7A	:	A8	y	F2	2
7B	#	A9	z	F3	3
7C	@	C1	A	F4	4
7D	'	C2	B	F5	5
7E	=	C3	C	F6	6
7F	"	C4	D	F7	7
81	a	C5	E	F8	8
82	b	C6	F	F9	9
83	c	C7	G		

however, that, like numbers in packed form, numbers in binary and floating point form must be converted to character form before they can be printed.

Notation Used to Describe Syntax

Almost all of what you will learn in this book will work at your computer center, but there are slight differences in the way statements are coded and utilities are used, depending on which version of the operation system and of JES is used. The final authorities are the IBM JCL and utility manuals. Your computer center should have a complete set of manuals for your installation. In addition, the Bibliography lists the important manuals with their order numbers.

These manuals use an excellent notation, which clearly and succinctly shows the rules you must follow when you code a statement. These rules are known as the **syntax** of the statement. Because of its usefulness, this notation will be employed in this book. Appendix B uses this notation to show the syntax of JCL statements for both VS1 systems and MVS systems.

In this notation upper-case letters are used to distinguish JCL words from values that you must supply. You code upper-case letters and words exactly as they appear, and you substitute values for lower-case letters and words. For example, the format for the CLASS parameter, which you will study in Chapter 2, is

```
CLASS=jobclass
```

This means that you must code the word CLASS, but substitute a value for jobclass.

Braces ({ }) are used to group related items and to indicate that you must code one of the items. Two different methods are used to list the items from which you must choose. Because one purpose of this book is to prepare you to read the IBM manuals on your own, both methods will be used. In the JCL manuals the items from which you must select are listed in a column. For example, part of the format of the SPACE parameter, which you will study in Chapter 3, is

$$
\begin{Bmatrix} \texttt{TRK} \\ \texttt{CYL} \\ \texttt{blocksize} \end{Bmatrix}
$$

This means that you must code either TRK or CYL or you must substitute a value for blocksize.

In the utilities manuals the items from which you must select are written in a row, separated by a vertical line. For example, part of the format of the FIELD parameter for IEBGENER, which you will study in Chapter 4, is

```
{input-location|'literal'}
```

In this case you would substitute a value for either input-location or literal.

Brackets ([ ]) are used to enclose an optional item or items. As in the case of braces, if you may choose one of several items, they will be listed either in a column or in a row, separated by a vertical line. Sometimes showing both braces and brackets can make the description confusing. In this book the text will specify that the items are optional and the brackets will not be shown.

Ellipses, or three consecutive periods (. . .), indicate that the preceding item may be repeated. For example, the format of the COND parameter, which you will study in Chapter 4, is

```
COND=((code,operator), . . . )
```

The ellipses mean that (code,operator) may be repeated.

Differences Among Computer Centers

In your study of JCL you will occasionally have to code values that depend on conventions established at your computer center. For example, as previously mentioned, each computer center establishes its own job classes. Similarly, tape reels, cartridges, and disk packs are given serial numbers which are chosen by each computer center. Because these values are different in different computer centers, someone familiar with your computer center will have to tell you what values to code. If you are studying this book as part of a course, your instructor will give you this information. If you are studying this book on your own, your supervisor or perhaps a coworker will give you this information. Throughout this book the person who will give you this information is called your advisor.

When one of these variable values is discussed, you will have to ask your advisor what value to use at your computer center. The inside front cover of this book has been designed to permit you to enter these values, so that they will be available in one convenient place. You can start now by asking your advisor the names of the operating system and the job entry subsystem used at your computer center. Enter these names in the place provided on the inside front cover.

Summary

In this chapter you have learned

—what job control language (JCL) is and what it is used for

—what an operating system is

—the functions of the CPU, main storage, auxiliary storage, and operator's console

—in what ways the MFT, MVT, VS1, and MVS operating systems are similar and in what ways they are different

—how virtual storage operating systems permit programmers to use more storage than is really available

—the functions of the JOB, EXEC, and DD statements

—the functions of the reader/interpreter, initiator, and output writer

—how and why spooling is done

—how data sets may be organized and accessed

—how data are stored in main and auxiliary storage

—how the contents of storage may be represented using the hexadecimal number system

—the notation used to describe the syntax of JCL and utility control statements

Vocabulary

In this chapter you have been introduced to the meanings of the following terms:

access method	MVS/XA
auxiliary storage	MVT
batch processing	operating system
bit	output work queue
byte	packed format
central processing unit (CPU)	page
data set	paging
direct access	partition
direct access storage device (DASD)	queue
EBCDIC code	real storage
hexadecimal number system	sequential access method (SAM)
indexed sequential access method (ISAM)	spooling
	syntax
input stream data	sysgen
input work queue	task
I/O	terminal
job	time sharing
job control language (JCL)	transparent
job entry subsystem (JES, JES2, JES3)	unit record device
	unpacking
job step	utility program
job stream	virtual storage
K	virtual storage access method (VSAM)
M	
main storage	virtual storage operating system (VS1)
MFT	
multiple virtual storage (MVS)	workstation
multiprogramming	

Exercises

1. What is an operating system?
2. What is JCL used for?
3. What are the functions of the CPU, main storage, auxiliary storage, and the operator's console?
4. What devices are used for auxiliary storage?
5. What are the three unit record devices?
6. What is a workstation?
7. What is a language translator?
8. What is a utility program?
9. What is multiprogramming?
10. What is a virtual operating system?
11. What are the names of the virtual operating systems?
12. What is a job stream?
13. What is a job step?
14. What are the names of the JCL statements?
15. Describe briefly the functions of the JOB, EXEC, and DD statements.
16. What are the functions of the job entry subsystem? What are the names of the job entry subsystems used by VS1 and MVS?
17. What is spooling and why is it done?
18. What does it mean to say that spooling is transparent to the programmer?
19. What are the ways in which a data set may be organized?
20. What are the ways in which a data set may be accessed?
21. What kind of data set organization does magnetic tape support?
22. What is the meaning of DASD? Give an example of DASD.
23. What is an access method?
24. What is a bit?
25. What is a byte?
26. A byte contains 10011110. Express the contents in hexadecimal form.
27. Three consecutive bytes contain the characters JCL. Express the contents in hexadecimal form.
28. How would the number +505 appear if it were stored in packed format? What would be printed if this value were sent to a printer without being unpacked?
29. The syntax of the MSGCLASS parameter is

    ```
    [MSGCLASS=output-class]
    ```

    Explain.
30. The syntax of the BURST parameter is

$$[\,\text{BURST}=\left\{\begin{matrix} \text{Y} \\ \text{N} \end{matrix}\right\}\,]$$

    Explain.

2

Listing Input Stream Data

In this chapter you will learn

- how to use the utility program IEBGENER to list input stream data

- how to code simple versions of the JOB, EXEC, and DD statements

- how to code the comment, delimiter, and null statements

- how to read the system messages produced when a job is executed

In this chapter you will see your first examples of JCL statements. The problem posed will be to list input stream data on a high-speed printer. This problem will be solved by developing all the JCL statements required to use the IBM utility program IEBGENER to list the input stream data.

Using IEBGENER to List Input Stream Data

The processing we want to do is shown in the system flowchart in Figure 2.1. System flowcharts are useful because they clearly show the relationships between the data sets and the programs that are used to process them. Figure 2.1 shows that input stream data is the input data set, that the program named IEBGENER will be executed, and that a listing of the input stream data is the

Figure 2.1

System Flowchart to List Input Stream Data

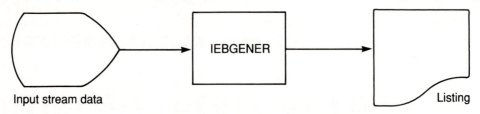

output data set. (This statement of the problem assumes that you are using a terminal system. If you are using a card system, you may assume that the data we want to list are in the form of a card deck.) IEBGENER is an IBM utility program that is used to copy sequential data sets. In this problem we are using IEBGENER to copy the input stream data to the printer listing.

Figure 2.2 shows the job stream to list input stream data. The job stream consists of a JOB statement, three comment statements, an EXEC statement, four DD statements, a delimiter statement, a null statement, and the input stream data we want to list. The same input stream data will be used in examples throughout the text. Although you can understand everything in this chapter without knowing the meaning of the various fields in the data, if you would like to know what they mean you can find them explained in Appendix C. Let us now examine the job stream in detail.

Format of the JOB, EXEC, and DD Statements

The JOB, EXEC, and DD statements have a common format which is shown below:

```
//name operation operand comments
```

The two slashes must be in columns 1 and 2. They are followed by the **name field,** which must start in column 3. The name field is the only field that must start in a specific column. Notice that there must not be a blank between the second slash and the name.

The name may consist of from one to eight characters. The permitted characters are the letters A through Z, the digits 0 through 9, and the three characters #, @, and $, which are called **national characters.** The first character of the name must be a letter or a national character; thus ABCDEFG, @TEST, and JOB123 are valid names. Listed below are several invalid names, with the reasons they are invalid.

■ Figure 2.2 ■

Job Stream to List Input Stream Data

```
//JCLQB001 JOB (14155,000000001),
//              'J. C. LEWIS',
//              CLASS=A,                              JOB statement
//              MSGLEVEL=(1,1)
//*
//* USING IEBGENER TO LIST INPUT STREAM DATA   Comment statement
//*
//LIST      EXEC PGM=IEBGENER              EXEC statement
//SYSPRINT DD SYSOUT=A
//SYSIN    DD DUMMY                    3 DD statements
//SYSUT1   DD *
13009REED,TINA               A0842000426072100        74
15174HANDJANY,HAIDEH         H0229000220022900        71
17337BUTERO,MAURICE          H0501000434050100        63
19499LAFER,BRUCE             A0706000819050000        52
21661LEE,SUI                 A0390170303030017        76
23821COOPER,LUCY             L0745000730070000        64
25980NELSON,LAWRENCE         L0513000217051300        78
28138KRUKIS,SONIA            A0346000510034600        59
30295CHEN,YIN                H0295000514010000        81
32451SIMPKINS,KEVIN          L0388000321038806        76
34605PORTER,MICHELE          A0627500128042700        65
36759DECICCO,RICHARD         A0255000619010000        71
38912ABREU,JUANITA           H0732001030070000        80
41063HIGH,CAROL              L0311000521031100        82
43214ENGLISH,REYNOLDS        A0443000228043300        82
45363LEE,BOHYON              A0515000214050000        79
47512THOMPSON,STANLEY        H0640750307064075        66
49659VALDEZ,FABIO            L0706000430070600        71
51805AMATO,ROBERT            A0466000417015000        63
53950RIZZUTO,JAMES           A0693000822000000        81
56094SCHWARTZ,MICHAEL        H1037000605050000        67
58238RUFINO,CARLOS           L0673000520047300        64
60380MORLEY,JOHN             A0786000514078600        71
62521BREVIL,JAMES            H0812000314081200        55
64660FALCONER,EDWARD         L1080000227008000        74
66799MARTIN,KATHLEEN         L0895000129089500        65
68937YEUNG,SUK               A0517000816050000        49
71074PAUL,MARINA             A0441000414034100        80
73210FRADIN,SHIRLEY          L0668000728066800        56
75344BURNS,JEFFREY           L0706000226070000        57
/*
//SYSUT2   DD SYSOUT=A         DD statement
//                     Null statement
              Delimiter statement
```

Input stream data to be listed

Name	Reason
GOOD NAME	A name may not contain a space.
123JOB	A name may not start with a digit.
VERYLONGNAME	A name may not contain more than eight characters.

JCL and JES keywords may not be used as names. A list of JCL and JES keywords may be found in Appendix B.

The letters and digits together are called the **alphameric characters.** Any characters other than alphameric and national characters used in coding JCL statements are known as **special characters.** The comma, period, and blank, for example, are special characters.

The name field is followed by the **operation field.** In the operation field you specify the kind of statement you are coding, either JOB, EXEC, or DD. There must be at least one blank between the name field and the operation field, although you can have as many blanks as you want. Not much more need be said about the name and operation fields; the rest of this book is mostly devoted to discussing the operand field.

The **operand field** follows the operation field. There must be at least one blank between the operation field and the operand field, and, again, you can have as many blanks as you want. The operand field consists of a single parameter or a series of parameters. The **parameters** provide detailed information about the job, the program being executed, and the data sets being used. The parameters are separated by commas; there must not be blanks within the operand field.

The operand field may not extend beyond column 71.* If all the parameters will not fit within the first 71 columns, the statement must be continued onto the next line. Even if the parameters would fit in the first 71 columns, the programmer may choose to interrupt a statement before column 71 and continue on the next line.

When a JCL statement is continued, these rules must be followed:

Interrupt the statement after a parameter or subparameter and the comma that follows it anywhere you like before column 71.

Begin the next line with // in columns 1 and 2 and a blank in column 3.

Start coding the next parameter or subparameter on the new line anywhere between columns 4 and 16.

---

* The reason the operand may not extend beyond column 71 is rooted in history. When JCL was punched on cards, sequence numbers were usually punched in columns 72 through 80. Then, if a card deck was dropped, the sequence numbers could be used to reassemble the deck in the correct order.

You will see applications of these rules shortly.

The operand field is followed by the **comments field.** Again, one or more blanks must separate the operand field and the comments field. (Now you can see why the operand field must not contain a blank. If it did, the system would interpret the blank as the end of the operand field and treat the remaining parameters as comments.) The comments field is optional. Rather than use the comments field, most programmers use the comment statement to include comments in a job stream. None of the statements in Figure 2.2 uses the comments field.

Although the operand field may not extend beyond column 71, the comments field may extend out through column 80. There are special rules for continuing a comments field, but instead of remembering the special rules the easiest thing to do is to make the next line a comment statement. If you do that, the statement technically is not being continued, so you do not have to follow any special rules.

Coding Conventions

This book uses conventions similar to those many businesses have adopted for coding JCL statements. If these conventions are followed, the JCL rules will automatically be obeyed, and in addition the JCL will be easy to read. Having JCL that is easy to read is a big advantage because it allows you to find and correct errors more readily.

The first convention is to begin the operation fields, JOB, EXEC, and DD, in column 12. This ensures that even a name containing eight characters will be separated from the operation by a space. (In Chapter 7 you will learn that the name on a DD statement may be longer than eight characters. In those cases it will be necessary to begin DD in a later column.)

Leave one space after the operation field and then start the first parameter of the operand field. Code only one parameter on a line. When a line is continued, start the parameter on the next line in column 16.

These are useful conventions for you to follow; you should realize, however, that they are only conventions and are not required by the rules of JCL.

The JOB Statement

Let us now examine the JOB statement in detail. For convenience the JOB statement in Figure 2.2 is repeated here:

```
//JCLQB001 JOB (14155,000000001),
//              'J. C. LEWIS',
//              CLASS=A,
//              MSGLEVEL=(1,1)
```

The main functions of the JOB statement are to indicate the beginning of a job and to assign a name to the job.

The Jobname

The name that is coded on the JOB statement, JCLQB001, is known as the **jobname,** and it is usually printed in large block letters on the first and last pages of the output produced by the job. When you invent a jobname, you must, of course, follow the rules for names we discussed earlier—a name must consist of one to eight alphameric and national characters, with the first character a letter or a national character. To ensure that jobs submitted at the same time have different jobnames, individual computer centers often impose additional rules regarding which jobnames may be used. Otherwise several users might submit jobs with names like TEST at the same time. ✓

At the City University of New York (CUNY) Computer Center, where the programs in this book were run, it is suggested that a jobname consist of three initials to identify the user, two letters to identify the user's school, and three digits to number the job. For the purposes of this book, a user whose name is J. C. Lewis (and whose initials just happen to be JCL) and whose school identification is QB (which stands for Queensborough Community College) was created. The job shown in Figure 2.2 is the first job that student ran, so the three-digit number 001 was added to the user's initials and the school identification to create the jobname JCLQB001. Your computer center may or may not have rules for forming jobnames. If it does, your advisor will tell you what they are, and you should write them in the space provided on the inside front cover.

Some systems will automatically add a valid jobname to your JOB statement; all you have to do is leave one or more spaces between the two slashes and the operand JOB. Your advisor will tell you whether your system automatically adds a jobname to your JOB statement.

Positional and Keyword Parameters

As required, there is a space between the jobname and the operation (JOB), and then another space between the operation and the beginning of the operand field. There are two kinds of parameters in the operand field: **positional parameters** and **keyword parameters.** The operating system recognizes positional parameters by their position in the operand field. They must be coded in a specific order before any keyword parameters. In the example, the first two parameters

```
(14155,000000001)
```

and

```
'J. C. LEWIS'
```

are positional parameters, which will be discussed in detail shortly. The other parameters, CLASS and MSGLEVEL, are keyword parameters. The keyword —for example, CLASS and MSGLEVEL— is followed by an equal sign and the value you want to assign to that keyword parameter. In the example we assign the value A to the keyword parameter CLASS and the value (1,1) to the keyword parameter MSGLEVEL. (What this all means will be explained shortly.) In contrast to positional parameters, which must be coded in a specified order, keyword parameters may be coded in any order.

The Accounting Information Parameter. The first parameter in the operand field is the accounting information parameter, which in Figure 2.2 is (14155,000000001). The accounting information parameter is a positional parameter, and it must be the first parameter in the operand field if it is coded. The accounting information parameter, however, is optional; some computer centers do not require accounting information, whereas others obtain it from a JES statement. Your advisor will tell you whether accounting information is required at your computer center and, if it is, how it is specified and what your account number is. You should write this information in the place provided on the inside front cover.

The form that the accounting information parameter takes is determined by the computer center. At the CUNY Computer Center, it consists of two subparameters: a five-digit number and a nine-digit number. Notice how the two subparameters are separated by a comma and how the whole accounting information parameter is enclosed in parentheses. That is a general rule for all parameters:

> If a parameter consists of more than one subparameter, the individual subparameters are separated by commas and the whole subparameter list is enclosed in parentheses.

A second general rule is the following:

> If the parameter list coded consists of just one subparameter with no commas, the enclosing parentheses may be omitted.

This means that if the accounting information parameter consists of a single subparameter—say XHB4702—then it would be legal to code it as

```
//JCLQB001 JOB XHB4702,
```

without the parentheses.

Because it is so variable, the accounting information parameter tends to be somewhat confusing. As you will see, the other parameters are not as variable or as confusing.

The Programmer's Name Parameter. Following the conventions discussed earlier, we code a comma after the accounting information and continue the JOB statement onto the next line. On the next line we code a // in columns 1 and 2 and begin the programmer's name parameter in column 16. In Figure 2.2 the programmer's name parameter is 'J. C. LEWIS'. It is the first apostrophe (not the J) that is coded in column 16. The programmer's name is printed on the first and last pages of the output produced by the job.

Like the accounting information parameter, the programmer's name parameter is a positional parameter and is theoretically optional, although some computer centers may require it. If it is coded, it must immediately follow the accounting information parameter. A programmer's name must consist of no more than 20 characters. It may contain any characters you like, but if it contains special characters (and remember that a blank is a special character), it must be enclosed in apostrophes. (Under certain circumstances a programmer's name may contain special characters and not require the apostrophes, but it is easier to type the apostrophes than to remember the specific circumstances.)

To code an apostrophe in a programmer's name, you must use two consecutive apostrophes. So if a programmer's name were O'Neill, you would code it as 'O''NEILL'.

Omitting Positional Parameters. As you know, positional parameters must be coded in the specified order. On the JOB statement this means that the accounting information must precede the programmer's name. But that raises a question: If you want to omit the accounting information, how can accounting information precede the programmer's name? Three rules govern omitting positional parameters. The first rule is as follows:

> If a positional parameter or subparameter is omitted, you must code a comma in its place.

Suppose we wanted to omit the accounting information from the JOB statement in Figure 2.2. The first line of the JOB statement could be written as

```
//JCLQB001 JOB ,'J. C. LEWIS',
```

When the system encounters the comma before 'J. C. LEWIS', it knows that accounting information has been omitted.

Suppose we wanted to include accounting information, but omit the programmer's name. Following the rule we could write the first two lines of the JOB statement as

```
//JCLQB001 JOB (14151,000000001),,
//               CLASS=A
```

Notice that we code two consecutive commas. One comma stands for the missing programmer's name, and the second is the usual comma separating parameters.

This coding is correct, but a second rule permits us to simplify it. This rule is as follows:

> If the omitted positional parameter is the last one, or if all the later positional parameters are also omitted, you do not have to code replacing commas.

This rule means that the last example could also be coded as

```
//JCLQB001 JOB (14155,000000001),
//              CLASS=A
```

Notice that the comma that stood for the missing programmer's name is gone, but the comma that separates the accounting information and CLASS parameters remains.

Finally, consider what happens if both positional parameters are omitted. Following the rule we could write

```
//JCLQB001 JOB ,,CLASS=A
```

A third rule, however, allows us to simplify this statement:

> If all the positional parameters are omitted, you do not have to code the replacing commas.

This rule means that the last example could also be coded as

```
//JCLQB001 JOB CLASS=A
```

Although these three rules have been illustrated by the accounting information and programmer's name parameters, they apply to all positional parameters and also to positional subparameters, which we will encounter shortly.

The CLASS Parameter.   The third parameter

```
CLASS=A
```

is a keyword parameter that specifies the class of the job. In Chapter 1 you learned that computer centers establish a number of job classes to indicate the resources the job requires. Your advisor will tell you the class you must use on your jobs, which you should write in the place provided on the inside front cover.

Default Values.   The CLASS parameter is optional; if you do not code it, the class for your job will be assigned a default value. A **default value** is the value that is automatically assigned to a parameter. For example, a computer center may decide that any job that does not have a CLASS parameter coded on the JOB statement will be assigned a job class of P. For that computer center P is the default job class. If your job should be run under class P, you do not have to code the CLASS parameter; you get it automatically. Your advisor will tell you the default value for the CLASS parameter at your computer center. If the default value is the value you should use, you do not have to code the CLASS parameter.

Default values are widely used in JCL. Sometimes, as in the case of the CLASS parameter, the default value is assigned by the computer center, and in other cases the default value is assigned by the operating system. In both cases the purpose of default values is to save programming effort. Making the commonly used values the default values saves the programmer the trouble of coding them. You will meet many examples of default values as you continue to study JCL.

The MSGLEVEL Parameter.   The fourth parameter

```
MSGLEVEL=(1,1)
```

specifies which JCL statements and system messages you want printed when the job is executed. MSGLEVEL is a keyword parameter that consists of two positional subparameters:

```
MSGLEVEL=(statements,messages)
```

The statements subparameter may be assigned the value 0, 1, or 2. The meanings of these values are shown below:

Value	Meaning
0	Print only the JOB statement
1	Print all the input JCL and the JCL from cataloged procedures*
2	Print only the input JCL

* Cataloged procedures will be discussed in Chapter 7.

A value of 1 for the statements subparameter says essentially, "Print everything." Because you want everything printed during testing, all the examples in this book use a value of 1 for the statements subparameter.

The messages subparameter controls the printing of allocation messages. Allocation messages show which physical devices are allocated to the data sets used in a job and what the system did with the data sets at the end of the job. The `messages` subparameter may be assigned the value 0 or 1. The meanings of these values are shown below:

Value	Meaning
0	Print allocation messages only if the job abnormally terminates
1	Print all allocation messages

Notice that if you code 0 for the `messages` subparameter, the allocation messages are printed only if the job abnormally terminates. Abnormal termination occurs when an error condition for which no provision has been made in the program causes the program to stop executing. When a program abnormally terminates, it is said to **abend,** which is the abbreviation for abnormal end. We shall see several examples of programs that abend. As in the case of the JCL statements, during testing you want everything printed, so the examples in this book use a value of 1 for the `messages` subparameter.

If you do not code the `MSGLEVEL` parameter or if you code only one subparameter, default values are supplied. The default values are determined by the computer center, so your advisor will have to tell you what they are at your computer center. You should write them in the place provided on the inside front cover. If the default values for the `MSGLEVEL` parameter are (1,1), you do not have to code it.

Omitting Positional Parameters—A Review. The `MSGLEVEL` parameter provides a convenient example for reviewing what you have learned about the use of parentheses and commas with positional parameters or subparameters. Suppose you were willing to accept the default value for the `statements` subparameter, but wanted to specify a value of 1 for the `messages` subparameter. You would code

```
MSGLEVEL=(,1)
```

Notice that you must include the comma to indicate the missing first positional subparameter.

If the situation were reversed and you wanted to specify a 1 for the `statements` subparameter and accept the default value for the `messages` subparameter, you could code

```
MSGLEVEL=(1,)
```

Using the rule that when the last positional parameter is omitted the comma is not required, you could write this as

```
MSGLEVEL=(1)
```

Finally, using the rule that if only one subparameter with no commas is coded the enclosing parentheses may be omitted, this could be written as

```
MSGLEVEL=1
```

Order of Keyword Parameters. Because CLASS and MSGLEVEL are keyword parameters that may be coded in any order, you might wonder which order to use. In general, the order does not matter. (I coded CLASS before MSGLEVEL because I wanted to discuss the CLASS parameter before I discussed the MSGLEVEL parameter.) Sometimes, for one reason or another, one order seems preferable. In Chapter 3 you will see the order I use on complex DD statements and why I prefer that order. You should understand, however, that that is only a personal preference and that keyword parameters may be coded in any order.

Additional Parameters. Several other parameters may be coded on the JOB statement. We do not need any of the additional parameters to solve the current problem, however, and to discuss them now would just be confusing. The complete format of all the JCL statements is shown in Appendix B. As you proceed through this book, you will be shown only what you need to know to solve the current problem. This procedure will allow complications to be introduced gradually. If your curiosity gets the better of you, remember that you can always find the full format of any JCL statement in Appendix B and the location of additional information in the index.

The Comment Statement

For convenience, the comment statements in Figure 2.2 are repeated here.

```
//*
//* USING IEBGENER TO LIST INPUT STREAM DATA
//*
```

Two blank comment statements are used so that the real comment stands out. The comment statement must start with the characters //* in columns 1, 2, and 3. The comment itself may start in column 4, unless you have JES3, in which case it is wiser to start the comment in column 5 to prevent the system from confusing your comment with a JES3 statement. The comment may extend through column 80 and may contain any character you can type at your keyboard. You may have as many comment statements as you want, and you may place them anywhere you want after the JOB statement. If a comment won't fit on one comment statement, don't continue the comment statement; simply use additional comment statements. The JCL in Figure 2.2 might have included the following comment statements:

```
//*
//* THIS IS AN EXAMPLE OF A JOB STREAM THAT SHOWS HOW
//* TO USE IEBGENER TO LIST INPUT STREAM DATA
//*
```

You should use comment statements to document your JCL statements for the same reason you would document any program you write — so that anyone who has to read your coding can understand what you have done.

The EXEC Statement

For convenience the EXEC statement in Figure 2.2 is repeated here.

```
//LIST     EXEC PGM=IEBGENER
```

The EXEC statement names the program that is to be executed.*

The Stepname

The name that is coded on the EXEC statement is called the **stepname**. It is optional, but you should code it. When you invent a stepname, you must, of course, follow the rules we have already discussed for forming names, but in addition you should create names that are meaningful. Because the purpose of the job stream in Figure 2.2 is to list input stream data, LIST was chosen as the stepname. There are rarely any computer center restrictions on permissible stepnames, the way there are on permissible jobnames.

The PGM Parameter

There are several parameters that may be coded on the EXEC statement, but for now all we need is the PGM parameter. The PGM parameter is a positional parameter that identifies the program to be executed. In Figure 2.2 the name of the program to be executed is IEBGENER.

The PGM parameter and the PROC parameter, which we will study in Chapter 7, are the only two positional parameters that use an equal sign. When you see an equal sign used with any other parameter, you know that parameter is a keyword parameter.

* In Chapter 7 you will learn that procedures may also be executed.

The DD Statement

Figure 2.2 contains four DD statements, which are repeated here.

```
//SYSPRINT DD  SYSOUT=A
//SYSIN    DD  DUMMY
//SYSUT1   DD  *
//SYSUT2   DD  SYSOUT=A
```

The DD statements describe the data sets used by the program, and there must be a DD statement for each one. Because Figure 2.2 contains four DD statements, you know that the program IEBGENER uses four data sets. The DD statements may be in any order, but when I use IEBGENER, I usually code the DD statements in the order shown in Figure 2.2.

The name on a DD statement is called the **ddname.** The rules for ddnames are the same as the rules for jobnames and stepnames, which we discussed above. There are some ddnames, however, that invoke special facilities and thus should be used only when you want to use those facilities. These names are

JOBCAT	SYSCHK
JOBLIB	SYSCKEOV
STEPCAT	SYSIN
STEPLIB	SYSMDUMP
SYSABEND	SYSUDUMP

The following names have special meaning to JES3 and should not be used as ddnames in JES3 systems:

JCBIN	JESJCL
JCBLOCK	JESMSG
JCBTAB	JOURNAL
JCLIN	JST
JESInnnn	SYSMSG

The IEBGENER DD Statements

SYSPRINT is the ddname of the data set that IEBGENER uses to write messages to you. For example, it might write a message that an error occurred during execution, or more optimistically, that your job ran successfully. SYSIN is the ddname of the data set that contains the control statements to tell IEBGENER how the input data set should be modified while it is being copied. SYSUT1 is the ddname of the input data set that IEBGENER is to copy, and SYSUT2 is the ddname of the output data set that is to be created.

Let us study the parameters coded on these four DD statements.

The SYSOUT Parameter

The SYSPRINT and SYSUT2 DD statements both have as their only parameter

    SYSOUT=A

SYSOUT is a keyword parameter that assigns a data set to an output class. In this example the output class is A. The output classes are defined by the computer center, but most computer centers use class A to mean that the data set should be printed on a high-speed printer and class B to mean the data set should be punched on cards. Other letters and numbers are used by computer centers to define output classes that meet their needs. For example, one class may designate low-priority output and another class high-priority output. Other classes may indicate special printer forms.

Recall that SYSPRINT is the ddname of the data set that IEBGENER uses to write messages to you. By coding SYSOUT=A on that DD statement, we specify that we want those messages printed. Similarly, recall that SYSUT2 is the ddname of the data set that IEBGENER creates. By coding SYSOUT=A on that DD statement, we specify that we want that data set printed.

It is important to understand that coding SYSOUT=A merely directs a data set to the printer; it has nothing to do with the program that is being executed. It happens that in Figure 2.2 the program being executed is IEBGENER, but you would still code SYSOUT=A to direct a data set to the printer if you were executing a COBOL, PL/I, FORTRAN, or assembler program or a different utility program.

The DUMMY Parameter

The SYSIN DD statement in Figure 2.2 contains the parameter DUMMY. DUMMY is a positional parameter that indicates that the data set is not to be processed. DUMMY may be coded on DD statements for both input and output data sets. When DUMMY is specified for an input data set, the first read of that data set causes an end-of-file to be recognized. When DUMMY is specified for an output data set, write statements to the data set are executed, but no data are actually transmitted. That is a convenient way to suppress output that you do not wish to have produced. Suppose, for example, a program produces several reports, and for a particular execution of that program you do not want one of the reports printed. You can suppress printing of that report by coding DUMMY on the DD statement for that report, without affecting the rest of the program.

Why was DUMMY coded for the SYSIN DD statement in Figure 2.2? Recall that the SYSIN data set (strictly speaking, the proper expression is "the data set whose ddname is SYSIN," but "the SYSIN data set" is more convenient and just as clear, so generally the shorter expression is used) contains the control statements that tell IEBGENER how the input data set is to be modified while it is being copied. In this program we do not want any modifications made to the input data set, and therefore we do not need any control statements. But we may not simply omit the SYSIN DD statement! IEBGENER expects to find a SYSIN DD statement, and if we leave it out the program will not run. One way to include a SYSIN DD statement but to have the data set empty is to DUMMY the DD statement.

The * Parameter

The SYSUT1 DD statement in Figure 2.2 contains the positional parameter *. The * parameter indicates that input stream data follow immediately after the DD statement. As you can see in Figure 2.2, the input stream data to be listed are placed immediately behind the SYSUT1 DD statement.

Specifying Ddnames in a Program

The ddnames are selected by the person who writes the program. The method used within a program to specify a ddname varies depending on the language in which the program is written. For example, in an assembler program the ddname is specified in the DCB instruction:

```
SALEFILE DCB DDNAME=SALES,  . . .
```

In a COBOL program the ddname is specified in the ASSIGN clause:

```
SELECT SALEFILE
        ASSIGN TO SALES.
```

In a PL/I program the ddname is specified in a DECLARE statement:

```
DECLARE SALES FILE . . .
```

These three programs would use the same ddname,

```
//SALES   DD . . .
```

In a FORTRAN program the ddname is selected differently; the file number specified in a READ or WRITE statement is used to construct the ddname. For example, the statement

```
WRITE (6,1000) . . .
```

results in the ddname FT06F001, so the DD statement would be

```
//FT06F001 DD . . .
```

If you are going to use a program written by someone else, the author of the program must supply documentation specifying the ddnames that must be used and their meanings. In the case of IEBGENER, the IBM utilities manual specifies the four ddnames: SYSPRINT, SYSIN, SYSUT1, and SYSUT2.

The Delimiter (/*) Statement

The delimiter statement, which has /* in columns 1 and 2, indicates the end of input stream data. In Figure 2.2 the SYSUT1 DD statement marks the beginning of the input data set, and the /* statement marks its end.

Strictly speaking, the delimiter statement in Figure 2.2 is not required, because the end of input stream data may be marked not only by a delimiter statement but also by any other JCL statement. In Figure 2.2, if the delimiter statement were omitted, the system would know it had come to the end of the input stream data when it encountered the SYSUT2 DD statement, which is the next JCL statement. Nevertheless, it is good practice to include a delimiter statement to mark the end of all input stream data, and all the examples in this book will use one.

The Null (//) Statement

The null statement marks the end of the job. It must have two slashes in columns 1 and 2, and the rest of the statement must be blank. The null statement is not absolutely necessary. When the system reads your last statement, it knows it has come to the end of your job. Nevertheless, it is good practice to include a null statement as the last statement in a job stream, and all the examples in this book have one. (Null statements are more important with card systems, where not coding a null statement might cause your job to get mixed up with the following job.)

Executing the Job Stream

The job stream in Figure 2.2 was executed, and the output produced is shown in Figure 2.3. (The first and last pages of the output, which contain only identifying information, are not shown.) The exact output produced when a job is executed depends on which operating system is used. The programs in this book were run on a computer operating under MVS and JES3. If your computer uses a different operating system, the output you get will be slightly different. The important parts of the output are similar, however, so even if your computer uses a different operating system, this discussion of my output will help you understand your output.

The output shown in Figure 2.3 was originally printed on five pages, but to save space it is compressed. The solid lines indicate the original page boundaries. The first three pages contain system messages, which you must learn to interpret. In Figure 2.3 the first page consists of just four lines, which indicate the time at which the job started and ended. For this output this first page is not very important, but as you will see in the next example, if your JCL

Figure 2.3

Output Produced by Executing the Job Stream in Figure 2.2

```
IAT6140 JOB ORIGIN FROM GROUP=LOCAL   , DSP=IJP, DEVICE=INTRDR   , 000
15:57:34 IAT2000 JOB 1744 JCLQB001 SELECTED M2         GRP=BATCH
15:57:39 M2 R= JCLQB001 IEF403I JCLQB001 - STARTED
15:57:39 M2 R= JCLQB001 IEF404I JCLQB001 - ENDED
```

```
//JCLQB001 JOB (14155,000000001),                              **
//         'J.C. LEWIS',                                       **
//         CLASS=A,
//         MSGLEVEL=(1,1)
//*
//* USING IEBGENER TO LIST INPUT STREAM DATA
//*
//LIST     EXEC PGM=IEBGENER
//SYSPRINT DD SYSOUT=A
//SYSIN    DD DUMMY
//SYSUT1   DD *
/*
//SYSUT2   DD SYSOUT=A
//
```

```
     1    //JCLQB001 JOB (14155,000000001),
          //         'J.C. LEWIS',                             **
          //         CLASS=A,                                  **
          //         MSGLEVEL=(1,1)
          //*
          //* USING IEBGENER TO LIST INPUT STREAM DATA
          //*
     2    //LIST     EXEC PGM=IEBGENER
     3    //SYSPRINT DD SYSOUT=A
     4    //SYSIN    DD DUMMY
     5    //SYSUT1   DD *,DCB=BLKSIZE=80
     6    //SYSUT2   DD SYSOUT=A
          //
```

```
IEF236I ALLOC. FOR JCLQB001 LIST
IEF237I JES3 ALLOCATED TO SYSPRINT
IEF237I DMY ALLOCATED TO SYSIN
IEF237I JES3 ALLOCATED TO SYSUT1
IEF237I JES3 ALLOCATED TO SYSUT2
IEF142I JCLQB001 LIST - STEP WAS EXECUTED - COND CODE 0000    (A)
IEF285I    LIST.SYSPRINT                              SYSOUT
IEF285I    JESIO001                                   SYSIN
IEF285I    LIST.SYSUT2                                SYSOUT
```

```
** START - STEP=LIST   JOB=JCLQB001 DATE=10/23/81 CLOCK=15.57.35 PGM=IEBGENER REGION USED= 36K OF 192K **   (B)
** END -               DATE=10/23/81 CLOCK=15.57.38 CPU TIME = 0 MIN 0.06 SEC   CC= 0 **
** I/O COUNTS - DISK=  0,   SPOOL/OTHER=  5,   TAPE=  0,   VIO=  0; TOTAL=  5 **
```

34

```
DDNAME      I/O COUNT
SYSPRINT:   SPOOL/DMY
SYSIN   :   SPOOL/DMY
SYSUT1  :   SPOOL/DMY
SYSUT2  :   SPOOL/DMY

** START - JOB=JCLQB001    DATE=10/23/81    CLOCK=15.57.35
** END   -                 DATE=10/23/81    CLOCK=15.57.38    CPU TIME =    0 MIN    0.06 SEC    **
```

DATA SET UTILITY - GENERATE

IEB352I WARNING : OUTPUT RECFM/LRECL/BLKSIZE COPIED FROM INPUT

PROCESSING ENDED AT EOD

```
13009REED,TINA                    A0842000426072100    74
15174HANDJANY,HAIDEH              H0229000220022900    71
17337BUTERO,MAURICE              A0501000434050100    63
19499LAFER,BRUCE                 A0706000819050000    52
21661LEE,SUI                     A0390170303030017    76
23821COOPER,LUCY                 L0745000730070000    64
25980NELSON,LAWRENCE             L0513000217051300    78
28138KRUKIS,SONIA                A0346000510034600    59
30295CHEN,YIN                    H0295000514010000    81
32451SIMPKINS,KEVIN              L0388000321038806    76
34605PORTER,MICHELE              A0627500128042700    65
36759DECICCO,RICHARD             A0255000619010000    71
38912ABREU,JUANITA               H0732001030070000    80
41063HIGH,CAROL                  L0311000521031100    82
43214ENGLISH,REYNOLDS            A0443000228043300    82
45363LEE,BOHYON                  A0515000214050000    79
47512THOMPSON,STANLEY            H0640750307064075    66
49659VALDEZ,FABIO                L0706000430070600    71
51805AMATO,ROBERT                A0466000417015000    63
53950RIZZUTO,JAMES               A0693000822000000    81
56094SCHWARTZ,MICHAEL            H1037000605050000    67
58238RUFINO,CARLOS               L0673000520047300    64
60380MORLEY,JOHN                 A0786000514078600    71
62521BREVIL,JAMES                H0812000314081200    55
64660FALCONER,EDWARD             L1080000227008000    74
66799MARTIN,KATHLEEN             L0895000129089500    65
68937YEUNG,SUK                   A0517000816050000    49
71074PAUL,MARINA                 A0441000414034100    80
73210FRADIN,SHIRLEY              L0668000728066800    56
75344BURNS,JEFFREY               L0706000226070000    57
```

contains an error, an error message will be printed on the first page. Therefore it is a good idea always to check the messages on the first page.

The JCL Listing

The second page of output in Figure 2.3 contains two copies of the JCL. The first copy of the JCL is produced by JES3 automatically. It is an exact copy of the original JCL except that an asterisk has been added to column 72 of the continued lines of the JOB statement and the parameters have been moved so that they now start in column 4. Your system may or may not produce this copy of the input JCL, and if it does it may not make these slight changes.

The second copy of the JCL is controlled by the statements subparameter of the MSGLEVEL parameter. If the statements subparameter had been 0, only the JOB statement would have been printed. Because it was 1, all the JCL was printed. This second copy of the JCL looks a lot like the first copy, but when we get to Chapter 7 you will see that the two copies can look quite different. Even here you can see that the two copies are not identical. In the second copy the comment statements have three asterisks in columns 1 through 3 and the SYSUT1 DD statement contains a DCB parameter. In the system that executed this JCL, a DCB parameter is automatically added to all DD * statements. (The DCB parameter will be discussed in Chapter 3.) The statement numbers to the left of the JCL are used by the system to identify statements that contain errors. You will see an example of that in Figure 2.4. Notice that statement number 1 refers to all four lines of the JOB statement and that the comment statements are not numbered.

Allocation Messages

The third page of output contains mostly allocation messages. Most of these messages would be suppressed if the messages subparameter of the MSGLEVEL parameter were assigned the value 0. In this output the allocation messages are not particularly interesting; in Chapter 3 you will see that allocation messages sometimes contain important information.

Return Codes

The most important line on the third page is indicated by Ⓐ. It says that for the job JCLQB001 the step named LIST (recall that LIST is the stepname on the EXEC statement) was executed and gave a condition code (COND CODE) of 0000. The **condition code**, which is more commonly called the **return code**, provides a way for a program to inform the operating system about the results of an execution. The program does this by assigning a numerical value to the return code. For the IBM utilities and compilers, a return code of 0 means that the program ran successfully. Generally, a return code of 4 means that only

minor errors were encountered, whereas return codes of 8 , 12 , and 16 indicate that progressively more severe errors were encountered.

Setting Return Codes Within a Program.   Although the utility programs use
return codes of 0 , 4 , 8 , 12 , and 16 , you as a programmer can set the return
code of your program to any value from 0 to 4095, giving it any meaning you
wish.

   If your program is written in assembly language, the return code is set by
storing the desired value in register 15 immediately prior to the program's end
of execution. In PL/I the return code is set using PLIRETC, for example,

```
CALL PLIRETC (IERR);
```

where the variable IERR contains the desired return code value. In COBOL
the return code is set by moving a value into the special register RETURN-
CODE.

   In Chapter 4 you will see how you can use a return code set in a program.

Region Used

The second most important piece of information on the third page is indicated
by Ⓑ: REGION USED= 36K OF 192K. This message refers to the amount of
main storage that was used by the job. As you may recall from Chapter 1, main
storage is measured in terms of bytes and K stands for 1024 bytes. The message
means that the job was allocated 192K (roughly 192,000 bytes) but only 36K
were required. As you will see in Chapter 3, you can make use of that information.

Program Messages and Results

The rest of the output appears on the fourth and fifth pages in Figure 2.3. The
fourth page contains messages from IEBGENER. These are the messages
mentioned earlier, when the need for the SYSPRINT DD statement was explained. The warning message means that because we did not specify the
record format (RECFM) or logical record length (LRECL) or blocksize
(BLKSIZE) that we wanted for the output file, these characteristics were
copied from the input file. RECFM, LRECL, and BLKSIZE are subparameters
of the DCB parameter, which will be explained in Chapter 3. For now all you
have to know is that for this problem, which is to list input stream data,
having IEBGENER copy these characteristics is satisfactory.

   The second message from IEBGENER says PROCESSING ENDED AT EOD.
EOD means end of data, and the message means that IEBGENER stopped
executing when it came to the end of the input data. This is the message you
will see if the program runs successfully.

The fifth page contains the actual listing of the input stream data. The data appear here exactly as they appear in the input stream in Figure 2.2.

All the output in Figure 2.3 was printed on one printer. You might have expected records of the two printed data sets, SYSPRINT and SYSUT2, to be intermixed. This is where spooling comes in. While the job is executing, records for the two data sets are actually written to two different spool data sets. When the job finishes executing, the output writer separately writes each spool data set to the printer.

Syntax Errors

Errors were deliberately introduced into the job stream in Figure 2.2, and the job was rerun. The output, shown in Figure 2.4, was originally printed on three pages. On the first page, at Ⓐ, is the message JOB FAILED WITH CON-VERTER/INTERPRETER JCL ERROR. This is the kind of error message you will get if your job stream contains statements that violate JCL rules. Such statements are said to contain **syntax errors**. For example, you might have left out a space where one is required, or inserted a space where one is illegal, or misspelled a keyword, or left out a comma. You will learn from experience that there are many different ways you can make JCL syntax errors. What is important is that you learn how to correct them.

The second page of the output, as usual, simply contains two copies of the input JCL, but the third page is really helpful because it contains specific error messages. The error messages consist of a statement number, which refers to the numbered JCL statements on the second page, an error number (IEF something), and a short explanation of the error. If you can't correct the error based on the short explanation, you can look up the error number in the IBM *System Messages* manual for your system (see Bibliography). There you will sometimes find a longer explanation of the error, which may be more helpful.

The first error message says that statement 1 contains an UNIDENTIFIED KEYWORD IN THE CLASS FIELD. Careful examination shows that there is nothing wrong with the CLASS field. The error is in the following keyword, where MSGLEVEL is misspelled. You will find that often the error messages are not as clear as you would like and it takes experience and imagination to interpret them properly.

The second error message says that statement 2 contains an UNIDENTI-FIED OPERATION FIELD. Here is another error message whose meaning is not immediately clear. What happened in statement 2 was that the system took the stepname to be LISTEXEC because the required space between the stepname, LIST, and the operation field, EXEC, was left out. Then the system tried to interpret PGM=IEBGENER as the operation field. When this didn't make sense as an operation field, it gave up on the statement and

■ Figure 2.4 ■

Execution of a Job Stream That Contains Syntax Errors

```
IAT6140 JOB ORIGIN FROM GROUP=LOCAL    , DSP=IJP, DEVICE=INTRDR   , 000   First page
16:46:31 IAT4204   JOB FAILED WITH CONVERTER/INTERPRETER JCL ERROR ←—(A)
16:46:31 IAT4801 JOB JCLQB002 (9268) EXPRESS CANCELED BY INTERPRETER DSP
```

```
//JCLQB002 JOB (14155,000000001),                                    * Second page
// 'J. C. LEWIS',                                                     *
// CLASS=A,                                                           *
// MSGLEVL=(1,1)
//*
//* USING IEBGENER TO LIST INPUT STREAM DATA
//*
//LISTEXEC PGM=IEBGENER
//SYSPRINT DD SYSOT=A
//SYSIN    DD DUMMY
//SYSUT1   DD *
/*
//SYSUT2   DD SYSOUT=A
//
     1      //JCLQB002 JOB (14155,000000001),                             *
            // 'J. C. LEWIS',                                             *
            // CLASS=A,                                                   *
            // MSGLEVL=(1,1)
            ***
            *** USING IEBGENER TO LIST INPUT STREAM DATA
            ***
     2      //LISTEXEC PGM=IEBGENER
     3      //SYSPRINT DD SYSOT=A
     4      //SYSIN    DD DUMMY
     5      //SYSUT1   DD *,DCB=BLKSIZE=80
     6      //SYSUT2   DD SYSOUT=A
            //
```

```
STMT NO. MESSAGE                                                     Third page

    1     IEF630I UNIDENTIFIED KEYWORD IN THE CLASS FIELD
    2     IEF605I UNIDENTIFIED OPERATION FIELD
    3     IEF630I UNIDENTIFIED KEYWORD ON THE DD STATEMENT
    6     IEF607I JOB HAS NO STEPS
```

printed the message UNIDENTIFIED OPERATION FIELD. The way to correct that statement is to insert the required space between LIST and EXEC.

The third error message refers to statement 3. This error is much easier to fix, so it is left to you. The last error message refers to statement 6 and says JOB HAS NO STEPS. What happened here was that the system did not find the EXEC statement because of the error in statement 2. A job stream without an EXEC statement has no steps, makes no sense, and is illegal. The error message was associated with statement 6 because that is the last numbered statement in the job stream; there is nothing wrong with statement 6. When we correct statement 2, this error message will disappear.

Figure 2.5

Execution of a Job Stream That Contains a Logic Error

First page

```
17:00:16 IAT2000 JOB 9770 JCLQB003 SELECTED M1        GRP=BATCH
17:00:22 M1 R= JCLQB003 IEF403I JCLQB003 - STARTED
17:00:58 M1 R= JCLQB003 IEF404I JCLQB003 - ENDED
```

Second page

```
//JCLQB003 JOB (14155,000000001),                                   *
// 'J. C. LEWIS',                                                   *
// CLASS=A,                                                         *
// MSGLEVEL=(1,1)
//*
//* USING IEBGENER TO LIST INPUT STREAM DATA
//*
//LIST      EXEC PGM=IEBGENER
//SYSPRINT DD SYSOUT=A
//SYSIN     DD DUMMY
//SYSUT1    DD *
/*
//SYSIN DD *                                                         JES3GEN
//SYSUT2    DD SYSOUT=A
//
    1     //JCLQB003 JOB (14155,000000001),                                   *
          // 'J. C. LEWIS',                                                   *
          // CLASS=A,                                                         *
          // MSGLEVEL=(1,1)
          ***
          *** USING IEBGENER TO LIST INPUT STREAM DATA
          ***
    2     //LIST      EXEC PGM=IEBGENER
    3     //SYSPRINT DD SYSOUT=A
    4     //SYSIN     DD DUMMY
    5     //SYSUT1    DD *,DCB=BLKSIZE=80
    6     //SYSIN DD *,DCB=BLKSIZE=80                                          JES3GEN
    7     //SYSUT2    DD SYSOUT=A
          //
```

```
IEF236I ALLOC. FOR JCLQB003 LIST
IEF237I JES3 ALLOCATED TO SYSPRINT
IEF237I DMY  ALLOCATED TO SYSIN
IEF237I JES3 ALLOCATED TO SYSUT1
IEF237I JES3 ALLOCATED TO SYSIN
IEF237I JES3 ALLOCATED TO SYSUT2
IEF142I JCLQB003 LIST - STEP WAS EXECUTED - COND CODE 0000
IEF285I    LIST.SYSPRINT                          SYSOUT
IEF285I    JESI0001                               SYSIN
IEF285I    JESI0002                               SYSIN
IEF285I    LIST.SYSUT2                            SYSOUT

** START - STEP=LIST   JOB=JCLQB003 DATE=10/26/81 CLOCK=17.00.03 PGM=IEBGENER REGION USED= 36K OF 192K **
** END -                           DATE=10/26/81 CLOCK=17.00.39 CPU TIME = 0 MIN 0.08 SEC   CC=   0 **
** I/O COUNTS - DISK=      0,   SPOOL/OTHER=    4,  TAPE=    0,  VIO=    0; TOTAL=    4 **

** START - JOB=JCLQB003    DATE=10/26/81    CLOCK=17.00.03
** END -                   DATE=10/26/81    CLOCK=17.00.39    CPU TIME =    0 MIN   0.08 SEC   **
```

```
DATA SET UTILITY - GENERATE

IEB352I WARNING : OUTPUT RECFM/LRECL/BLKSIZE COPIED FROM INPUT

PROCESSING ENDED AT EOD
```

41

Logic Errors

Unfortunately, syntax errors are not the only kind of errors you can make. A second kind of error you can (and will!) make is a **logic error**. A job stream contains a logic error when it executes but gives incorrect results. An example of a job stream that contains a logic error is shown in Figure 2.5. Notice that there are no JCL syntax errors, that the condition code is 0, and that the message from IEBGENER says PROCESSING ENDED AT EOD. All that sounds good, but no output was produced!

The clue to what happened here can be found on the second page. There you can see that an extra SYSIN DD statement has been added to the job stream. The extra statement has the word JES3GEN in columns 73 through 79. JES3GEN indicates that this statement was generated by JES3; it was not part of the original job stream.

To understand why JES3 generated this statement you have to realize that a job stream consists of only two kinds of statements: JCL or JES statements and data statements. Any statement that has a // or a /* in columns 1 and 2 is a JCL or JES statement. All the other statements are data statements. If you are used to writing programs, this definition of data statements may be surprising. It includes not only those statements that contain the data your program will process, which you usually think of as data statements, but also the program statements themselves. The assembler, COBOL, FORTRAN, and PL/I statements are considered data statements for the simple reason that they don't contain either a // or a /* in columns 1 and 2.

Now, data statements can only occur immediately behind a DD * statement. If the operating system scans your job stream and finds any data statements that are not immediately behind a DD * statement, it inserts a SYSIN DD * statement just in front of those data statements. So that you will know that a statement was inserted, the inserted statement contains the word JES3GEN (in your system it might be a different but similar word) starting in column 73.

What error caused the system to insert the SYSIN DD statement? The input stream data was put behind the delimiter statement, instead of in front of it. Because these misplaced data statements were not immediately behind a DD * statement, the system inserted a SYSIN DD * statement just in front of them. Remember that as far as IEBGENER is concerned, the input data set consists of all those statements between the SYSUT1 DD statement and the delimiter statement. There were no statements between the SYSUT1 DD statement and the delimiter statement, so the input data set was empty. That is why IEBGENER produced no output. IEBGENER does not consider an empty input data set to be an error, so it did not print any error message.

Summary

In this chapter you have learned

— how to use IEBGENER to list input stream data

— the format of the JOB, EXEC, and DD statements

—how to code the comment, delimiter, and null statements

—the rules for forming jobnames, stepnames, and ddnames

—the rules for coding positional and keyword parameters

—the rule for continuing JCL statements

—how to read the system messages produced when a job is executed

—how to read the error messages produced when a job that contains a JCL syntax error is executed

—how to code the accounting information, programmer's name, CLASS, MSGLEVEL, PGM, DUMMY, *, and SYSOUT parameters

Vocabulary

In this chapter you have been introduced to the meanings of the following terms:

abend	name field
alphameric characters	national characters
comments field	operand field
condition code	operation field
ddname	parameter
default values	positional parameter
EOD	return code
jobname	special characters
keyword parameter	stepname
logic error	syntax error

Exercises

1. Name, in order, the four fields on the JOB, EXEC, and DD statements.
2. Which are the national characters?
3. Which are the special characters?
4. Which of the following are valid names?
   a. VALIDNAME
   b. GOODNAME
   c. BADNAME
   d. TEST-JOB
   e. JOB#1
   f. #1JOB
   g. STEP ONE
   h. 123JOB
5. How many blanks may there be between the name field and the operation field?
6. What are the rules for continuing a JCL statement?
7. What are the two categories of parameters?

8. What must you do if you omit a positional parameter?
9. What must you do if you omit a keyword parameter?
10. Why are parentheses required when you code MSGLEVEL=(1,1) but not when you code MSGLEVEL=1?
11. What is a default value? What is the purpose of default values?
12. What is the default value for CLASS at your computer center?
13. What are the functions of the two subparameters of the MSGLEVEL parameter?
14. Which of the following are legal? Which of the following are equivalent to each other?
   a. MSGLEVEL=(0,0)
   b. MSGLEVEL=(1)
   c. MSGLEVEL=(1,)
   d. MSGLEVEL=(,2)
   e. MSGLEVEL=(,1)
   f. MSGLEVEL=2
15. Correct any errors you find in the following JOB statements. (Assume that there are no computer center restrictions on jobnames and that 12345 is a valid account number.)

   a. ```
      //MYJOB   JOB 12345
      //   'SNOOPY',
      //   CLASS=A,
                        MSGLEVEL=(1,1)
      ```
   b. ```
      //YOURJOB JOB MSGLEVEL=(2,2)
      //             CLASS=P
      ```
   c. ```
      //HISJOB   JOB CLASS=F,
      //   'WOODSTOCK'
      ```
   d. ```
      //HERJOB    JOB 12345
      //                'LUCY',
      //                CLASS=B,
      //                MSGLEVEL=(0,1),
      ```

16. a. Code a JOB statement that uses default values for the CLASS and MSGLEVEL parameters and omits accounting information. Use your name for the programmer's name.
    b. Code a JOB statement that omits accounting information and the programmer's name, assigns the job to class W, and requests that only the job card be printed and system messages be suppressed.
17. What is an abend?
18. How many comment statements may a job contain?
19. The name on a JOB statement is called the jobname, and the name on a DD statement is called the ddname. What is the name on an EXEC statement called?
20. Code the EXEC statement to execute the program named BLUE. The stepname should be COLOR.

21. What are the names and purposes of the four DD statements used by IEBGENER?
22. In what order must you code the DD statements?
23. How do you direct a data set to the printer?
24. What are input stream data? How do you include input stream data in a job stream?
25. What is the function of the delimiter statement?
26. What is the function of the null statement?
27. Show how you would change the job stream in Figure 2.2 if
    a. you wanted to suppress the IEBGENER messages.
    b. you wanted to punch the input stream data rather than list them.
28. What is a return code? What does a return code of 0 usually mean?
29. Correct the error in statement 3 in Figure 2.4.
30. Correct the errors in the following job stream. (Assume that there are no computer center restrictions on jobnames and that 12345 is a valid account number.)

```
//THEIRJOB JOB  12345,
//                'CHARLIE BROWN,'
//                CLASS=A,
//                MSGLEVEL=1,
//PRINT    EXEC IEBGENER
//SYSOUT   DD SYSPRINT=A
//SYSIN    DD DUMMY,
//SYS1     DD *
/*
//SYS2     DD SYSPRINT=A
```

31. Assume that your computer center is about to replace IEBGENER with a newly purchased program named COPY, which uses much more sensible ddnames. COPY writes its messages to a data set whose ddname is MESSAGES, gets its input from a data set whose ddname is INPUT, and writes its output to a data set whose ddname is OUTPUT. COPY does not use control statements. Code the job stream to use COPY to list input stream data.

Programming Assignment

Write and execute a job stream to use IEBGENER to list input stream data. You may use the data listed in Appendix D or any other data your advisor suggests.

3

Creating Sequential Data Sets on Tape and Disk

In this chapter you will learn

- the characteristics of magnetic tape and magnetic disk

- how to create a sequential data set on tape and disk

- how to use the parameters

```
DSN (DSNAME)     VOL (VOLUME)
DISP             REGION
UNIT             SPACE
                 DCB
```

Magnetic tape and disk are widely employed for auxiliary storage, so it is important that you understand how to use them. In this chapter you will study the characteristics of tape and disk and learn how to create a sequential data set and store it on a tape or a disk.

Characteristics of Magnetic Tape and Disk*

Magnetic Tape

The magnetic tape used with computers comes on both reels and cartridges. The reels, which have been in use for many years, contain 2400 feet of half-inch-wide tape. The cartridges, which were introduced in the early 1980s, are more convenient and more reliable than the reels.

Each reel or cartridge is called a **volume.** When a new reel or cartridge is received at a computer center, it is assigned a unique **serial number,** which is used to identify it. A paper label containing the serial number is pasted to the outside of the reel or cartridge. In addition, the IBM utility program IEHIN-ITT, which you will study in Chapter 13, may be used to write the serial number magnetically on the tape in an area of the tape known as the **volume label.** The tape is then stored in a tape library with the computer center's other tapes. Tapes stored in the tape library are said to be **off-line,** meaning that they are not immediately available to be processed by a computer.

When a job is to be run, the tapes it requires are retrieved from the tape library and mounted on tape drives. The system reads the volume labels to verify that the correct volumes are mounted.

Label Records.   When a data set is stored on a tape, you can have the system automatically write header label records in front of the data set and trailer label records in back of it. These **label records** are similar to the volume label records discussed earlier, but they contain information about the data set, such as the date it was created and its size.

Data sets that have system-written header and trailer label records are said to have standard labels. Alternatively, data sets may also have user-written label records or no label records at all. If a data set has no labels, it is called, naturally enough, an unlabeled data set.

Magnetic Disk

There are a number of different models of disks available, with different storage capacities, data retrieval speeds, and costs. Because the IBM 3330 Disk Storage Facility is widely used, it will serve as an example. The characteristics of other disks are given in Appendix E.

The 3330 Disk Storage Facility uses a disk pack called the 3336 Disk Pack. The 3336 Disk Pack consists of 11 metallic coated disks mounted on a common shaft, as shown in Figure 3.1. Data are recorded on the surfaces of these

---

* This section discusses the basic principles of magnetic tape and disk. If you are familiar with these media, you may skip this section.

Figure 3.1

A 3336 Disk Pack

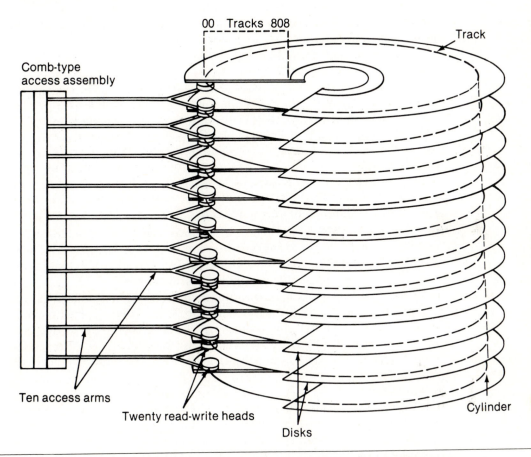

Reprinted by permission from *Introduction to IBM Direct-Access Storage Devices and Organization Methods.* © 1974 by International Business Machines Corporation.

disks. The exterior surfaces are not used for recording data, and one interior surface is used by the disk drive for system functions, so each pack has 19 surfaces that may be used by the programmer to record data. Each recording surface is divided into 808 concentric circles, called **tracks,** on which data are recorded. In addition there are several alternative tracks that may be used if any of the 808 tracks become unusable. Although the tracks get smaller toward the center of the disk, all the tracks can hold the same amount of data.

As Figure 3.1 shows, each recording surface has its own read/write head. All the read/write heads move together. So if, for example, you wanted to read data on track 158 of the sixth recording surface, the access mechanism would position all 20 read/write heads over track 158 of their respective surfaces. All the data that can be read (or written) without moving the read/write heads is called a **cylinder.** The concept of a cylinder is important because, whereas it takes a relatively long time to move the read/write heads, all the data in a cylinder can be accessed quickly.

A disk pack is called a **volume.** Like a new tape reel or cartridge, a new disk pack is assigned a serial number when it is received at a computer center. A paper label containing the serial number is pasted to the plastic housing of the disk pack, and an IBM utility program, which you will study in Chapter 13, is used to write the serial number magnetically on the volume label.

Unlike tapes, many disk packs remain permanently mounted in a disk drive; they are **on-line.** When a job requests a disk volume that is on-line, the computer can begin processing immediately without waiting for the requested disk volume to be retrieved and mounted.

Timing.   The total time involved in reading or writing a record on a disk can be divided into three parts: access arm motion time, rotational delay time, and data transfer time. Access arm motion time is the time needed for the access arm to reach the desired cylinder. This is the operation that takes the most time — typically about 30 milliseconds. Rotational delay time is the time required for the desired record to rotate to the read/write head. A typical value is 8 milliseconds. Data transfer time is the time required for data to move between the disk and primary storage. A 1000-byte record can be transferred in about 1 millisecond. The large contribution of the first component to the total time shows why it is desirable to minimize access arm motion.

The VTOC.   A disk pack usually contains many data sets. To permit the system to keep track of where each data set is and where the unused tracks are, stored on each disk is a volume table of contents **(VTOC),** which is automatically maintained by the system. The VTOC contains the name of each data set stored on the disk (how a data set gets a name is explained later in this chapter) and where the data set is. For example, if a disk pack contained a data set named PAYROLL that started at track 764, surface 6, that information would be stored in the VTOC. The VTOC also contains other information about each data set stored on the disk pack, such as the date it was created and its size, similar to the data stored in header and trailer labels on tape.

Besides information on the data sets on the disk pack, the VTOC contains information on the unused tracks. Usually the unused tracks are not all together in one place, but scattered throughout the pack. Tracks that are in the same cylinder and cylinders that are next to each other are said to be **contiguous.** A group of contiguous tracks, all of which are either used by a data set or available, make up an **extent.** The VTOC contains information on the location and size of the unused extents. It is not necessary that a data set occupy only one extent. A data set can be spread out over as many as 16 extents. The system does all the work, remembering where on the disk pack each portion of a data set is stored. Generally the user is not even aware that the data set is not stored in one extent.

Additional information about magnetic tape and disks appears in Appendix E.

Record Formats

When data are stored on tape or disk, the area occupied by the data is called a **block.** Each block is separated from its neighbors by a gap called the **interblock gap.** The length of the gap depends on the model tape or disk drive used. On many tape drives it is 0.6 inch.

Records may be stored on tape and disk in several formats. Two record formats used with sequential data sets are shown in Figure 3.2. (The term RECFM, which appears in Figure 3.2, means record format; it is explained later in this chapter.) Additional record formats used with sequential data sets and with ISAM data sets are discussed in Appendix E.

Figure 3.2

Record Formats Used with Sequential Data Sets on Tape and Disk

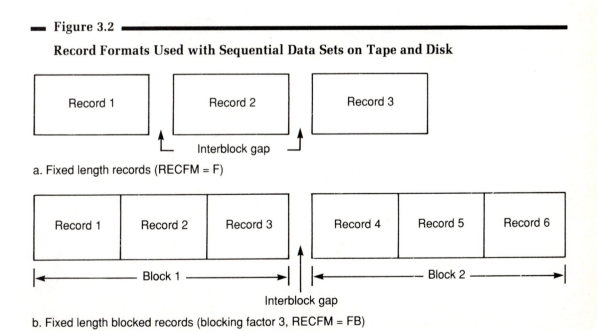

a. Fixed length records (RECFM = F)

b. Fixed length blocked records (blocking factor 3, RECFM = FB)

Fixed Length Records

Figure 3.2a shows the simplest record format, which is called fixed length. All the records are the same size, and each block consists of one record.

As you learned in Chapter 1, when data are stored in the computer's storage unit or recorded on tape or disk, each letter or special character occupies one byte. When numbers are stored in character form, each digit requires a byte. When numbers are stored in packed form, two digits occupy each byte except the last one, which contains one digit and the sign of the number. The number of bytes of data in a record is called the **logical record length.** The number of bytes of data in a block is called the **blocksize.** For fixed length records the logical record length and the blocksize are equal, because each block contains one record. So if the records were created by copying input stream data to tape, the logical record length and the blocksize would both be 80 bytes.

The length of a block on tape depends on the blocksize and the recording density. The **recording density** is the number of bytes recorded per inch of tape, and the value depends on the particular model tape drive used. Common values of recording density are 800, 1600, and 6250 bytes per inch. Some tape drives, called dual-density drives, can record and read at two densities; for example, 800 and 1600 or 1600 and 6250 bytes per inch.

If records with a logical record length and blocksize of 80 bytes were recorded at a density of 800 bytes per inch, the length of a block would be 80 bytes/800 bytes per inch = 0.1 inch. Because the interblock gap is 0.6 inch, six times as much tape would be wasted as would be used. Similar considerations apply to disk.

Blocking

To permit tape and disk to be used more efficiently, records are frequently blocked. Figure 3.2b shows how fixed length records look when they are blocked. Blocking involves storing a number of records together in one block. The number of records in a block is called the **blocking factor.** The blocking factor in Figure 3.2b is 3. Suppose the 80-byte records in the previous example were blocked using a blocking factor of 10. Then the blocksize would be $10 \times 80 = 800$ bytes, and the length of a block would be 800 bytes/800 bytes per inch = 1 inch. The gap would remain the same size it was before—0.6 inch—so almost twice as much tape would be used as would be wasted.

In addition to increasing the efficiency with which data are stored, blocking reduces the time required to read or write a data set. The time is reduced because the tape drive reads (or writes) a complete block and then stops the tape. When the next block is required, the drive starts the tape again. When the data set is blocked, there are fewer gaps and fewer stops and starts, and therefore less time is required to process the data set. Blocking also reduces processing time for data sets on disk.

If we repeated our previous analysis using a blocking factor of 100 instead of 10, we would find that the data set occupied less space and was processed faster with a blocking factor of 100 than with a blocking factor of 10. In general, the larger the blocking factor, the less space the data set occupies and the faster it can be processed. So, you might wonder, why stop? Why not increase the blocking factor until the whole data set is one giant block? One reason is that the maximum blocksize permitted by the access methods is 32,760 bytes, but there is a second reason. Because a whole block is read at one time, there has to be enough room in main storage to accommodate it. If the blocking factor is too large, there may not be enough space in main storage to accept a block.

Selecting the best blocking factor in any particular case involves a tradeoff between, on the one hand, the efficient use of tape and disk and faster processing (which are improved by large blocking factors) and, on the other hand, the demand on main storage (which is reduced by low blocking factors). As main storage has become less expensive, there has been a tendency to use larger blocking factors. Usually a systems analyst selects the blocking factor. Additional information about blocking appears in Appendix E.

We have discussed how large a block may be; we must also consider how small a block may be. The minimum blocksize is 18 bytes. Blocks smaller than 18 bytes may be confused with background noise and not read.

Creating a Sequential Data Set on a Disk

Assume you have input stream data that you want to use to create a sequential data set and store it on a disk. The processing you want to do is shown in the system flowchart in Figure 3.3, with the ddnames SYSUT1 and SYSUT2 on

Figure 3.3

System Flowchart to Create a Sequential Data Set on Disk

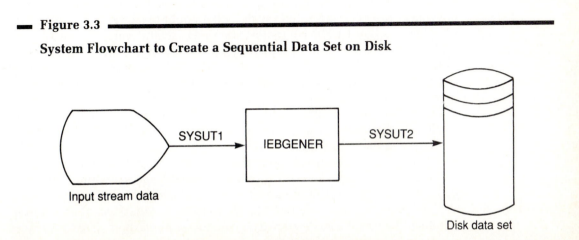

the flowlines. (From the discussion in Chapter 2 you know that IEBGENER requires two additional data sets with the ddnames SYSIN and SYSPRINT. These two data sets are not important to the processing being done, however, and are therefore not shown in Figure 3.3.) Throughout this book illustrations will always show the ddnames on the flowlines connecting the data set and the program symbols.

Figure 3.4 shows a job stream to use IEBGENER to create a sequential data set and store it on a disk. Some changes have been made to the JOB statement and the SYSUT2 DD statement contains some new entries, but the other statements should be familiar to you from Chapter 2.

The JOB Statement

The accounting information and the CLASS and MSGLEVEL parameters have been eliminated from the JOB statement, and the REGION parameter has been added. The CUNY computer system obtains accounting information from a JES3 accounting statement, which is automatically added to the job stream, so it is not necessary to specify accounting information on the JOB statement. At the CUNY computer center the default values for CLASS and MSGLEVEL are CLASS=A and MSGLEVEL=(1,1). Because these are the values desired, they need not be coded on the JOB statement. (They were included in the examples in Chapter 2 to show you how they are coded.)

The REGION Parameter.   REGION is used in MVS systems to request main storage. REGION has meaning in VS1 systems only in the unusual situation in which you request that your program not be paged.

The REGION parameter

```
REGION=40K
```

was added to the JOB statement to request 40K of main storage. If REGION is not coded, the job is allocated the default amount of storage. As you saw in Chapter 2, at the CUNY computer center the default value for REGION is 192K. (Examine the output produced by your solution to the Programming Assignment in Chapter 2 to determine the default value of REGION at your computer center.) This JCL requests 40K instead of the 36K required to execute IEBGENER, because the actual amount of main storage required depends on the characteristics of the data sets being processed, and it is good practice to request a little extra space as a safety margin. In MVS/XA systems an M may be used to request storage in terms of megabytes. For example, REGION=3M requests three megabytes. If you request storage using K, the value you code on the REGION parameter should be an even number; if you code an odd number, the system rounds up to the next even number.

You should always code the REGION parameter unless your job requires the default amount of main storage. If your job requires more than the default

Figure 3.4

Job Stream to Create a Sequential Data Set on Disk

```
//JCLQB010 JOB ,'J. C. LEWIS',
//              REGION=40K
//*
//* USING IEBGENER TO CREATE A SEQUENTIAL DATA SET ON A DISK
//*
//CREATE EXEC PGM=IEBGENER
//SYSPRINT DD SYSOUT=A
//SYSIN    DD DUMMY
//SYSUT1   DD *
13009REED,TINA               A0842000426072100      74
15174HANDJANY,HAIDEH         H0229000220022900      71
17337BUTERO,MAURICE          H0501000434050100      63
19499LAFER,BRUCE             A0706000819050000      52
21661LEE,SUI                 A0390170303030017      76
23821COOPER,LUCY             L0745000730070000      64
25980NELSON,LAWRENCE         L0513000217051300      78
28138KRUKIS,SONIA            A0346000510034600      59
30295CHEN,YIN                H0295000514010000      81
32451SIMPKINS,KEVIN          L0388000321038806      76
34605PORTER,MICHELE          A0627500128042700      65
36759DECICCO,RICHARD         A0255000619010000      71
38912ABREU,JUANITA           H0732001030070000      80
41063HIGH,CAROL              L0311000521031100      82
43214ENGLISH,REYNOLDS        A0443000228043300      82
45363LEE,BOHYON              A0515000214050000      79
47512THOMPSON,STANLEY        H0640750307064075      66
49659VALDEZ,FABIO            L0706000430070600      71
51805AMATO,ROBERT            A0466000417015000      63
53950RIZZUTO,JAMES           A0693000822000000      81
56094SCHWARTZ,MICHAEL        H1037000605050000      67
58238RUFINO,CARLOS           L0673000520047300      64
60380MORLEY,JOHN             A0786000514078600      71
62521BREVIL,JAMES            H0812000314081200      55
64660FALCONER,EDWARD         L1080000227008000      74
66799MARTIN,KATHLEEN         L0895000129089500      65
68937YEUNG,SUK               A0517000816050000      49
71074PAUL,MARINA             A0441000414034100      80
73210FRADIN,SHIRLEY          L0668000728066800      56
75344BURNS,JEFFREY           L0706000226070000      57
/*
//SYSUT2    DD DSN=WYL.QB.JCL.POLYFILE,
//              DISP=(NEW,KEEP,DELETE),
//              UNIT=DISK,
//              VOL=SER=WYL002,
//              SPACE=(TRK,5),
//              DCB=(RECFM=FB,LRECL=80,BLKSIZE=800)
//
```

amount of main storage and you don't request the amount you need, your job may not run. On the other hand, if your job requires less than the default amount of main storage and you don't request the amount you need, your job may not run as quickly as it could. This is because the operating system will have to wait until the default amount of storage is available, instead of starting execution of your job as soon as the smaller amount of storage that it actually requires becomes available. Virtual systems usually have a large amount of main storage, so competition among jobs is not as important as it was in nonvirtual systems.

The SYSUT2 DD Statement

The SYSUT2 DD statement directs the output from IEBGENER to a disk. It is important to understand that the SYSUT2 DD statement in Figure 3.4 shows how to create a sequential data set on disk. It happens that the program being executed in Figure 3.4 is IEBGENER, but you would code the same DD parameters if you were executing a COBOL, PL/I, FORTRAN, or assembler program or a different utility program to create a sequential data set on disk. Only the ddname would be different, for it would have to be the one the program required.

Let us now discuss the parameters on the SYSUT2 DD statement in turn.

Naming the Data Set — The DSN Parameter.   The first parameter

```
DSN=WYL.QB.JCL.POLYFILE
```

assigns a name to the data set. DSN, which is an abbreviation for DSNAME, is a keyword parameter that stands for data set name. The name assigned by this entry, WYL.QB.JCL.POLYFILE, is the name entered into the VTOC of the disk pack. If later we want to use this data set, we must use the name WYL.QB.JCL.POLYFILE to refer to it.

Qualified and Unqualified Names.   The rules you must follow when you invent a data set name are a little complicated. **Data set names** may be either **unqualified** or **qualified.** The rules for an unqualified data set name are similar to the rules you learned in Chapter 2 for jobnames, stepnames, and ddnames: Names must consist of from one to eight characters, the first character must be alphabetic or national, and the remaining characters must be alphameric or national. In addition to these characters, a data set name may contain a hyphen after the first character.

Now that you know what an unqualified data set name is, understanding what a qualified data set name is is easy. A qualified data set name consists of two or more unqualified data set names connected by periods. The only new rule is that the total length of a qualified data set name, including the periods, cannot be greater than 44 characters. So PLANT1.PAYROLL and JULY.SALES are valid qualified data set names, but JULY.TOTALSALES is invalid because TOTALSALES contains more than eight characters. JULY.1987.SALES is also invalid because 1987 begins with a digit.

The name used here, WYL.QB.JCL.POLYFILE, is a valid qualified data set name, but it looks so strange you might wonder how it was invented. A data set name has to satisfy the requirements that have been established at the computer center where the job is run. Recall that the data set name is entered into the VTOC of the disk pack. The operating system will not allow two data sets stored on a particular disk pack to have the same data set name; if it did, it would have no way of knowing which of the two you wanted when you tried to refer to one of them. (Notice that there is nothing wrong with having data sets with the same data set name on different disk packs, for each disk pack has its own VTOC.) If each programmer were allowed to use any data set name he or she wanted, several might decide that MASTER.FILE was a good name, and this would lead to problems. Therefore, most computer centers establish rules for naming data sets.

At the CUNY computer center, data set names must begin with the three letters WYL (except for special data sets established by center personnel and VSAM data sets, which are described in Chapter 12), followed by a two-letter code identifying the programmer's school (QB stands for Queensborough Community College). Next comes a three-letter code that uniquely identifies a particular programmer at a school. You may remember that for this book a student whose initials are JCL was created. This scheme uses 11 characters (remember to count the periods), leaving the user the option of using up to 33 characters to name his or her data sets. POLYFILE was chosen for the last part of the name because the data set contains policy information. Most likely your computer center has its own data set–naming rules. Your advisor will tell you what they are, and you should write them in the place provided on the inside front cover.

Specifying the Data Set's Status and Disposition — The DISP Parameter. The second parameter

```
DISP=(NEW,KEEP,DELETE)
```

defines the data set's status and disposition. DISP is a keyword parameter that consists of three positional subparameters:

```
DISP=(status,normal-disposition,abnormal-disposition)
```

The values that may be coded for the positional subparameters are listed in Table 3.1.

The status subparameter indicates the status of the data set at the start of the job step. NEW means that the data set did not formerly exist and is being created during this step. OLD means that the data set existed before this step, and that while your job is using the data set no other job may use it. SHR,

■ Table 3.1 ■
Valid Values for the DISP Subparameters

status	normal-disposition	abnormal-disposition
NEW	DELETE	DELETE
OLD	KEEP	KEEP
SHR	PASS	CATLG
MOD	CATLG	UNCATLG
	UNCATLG	

which stands for share, also means that the data set existed before this step, but it indicates that other jobs can use the data set while your job is using it. You will see examples of the use of SHR in Chapter 5. Like OLD and SHR, MOD, which stands for modify, signifies that the data set existed before this step, but in addition it means that new records are going to be added to the end of the data set. You will see an example of the use of MOD in Chapter 4.

The normal-disposition subparameter indicates what is to be done with the data set when the current step finishes normally. DELETE means that the data set is to be deleted. The system deletes a data set from a disk by deleting the data set's entry from the disk's VTOC. KEEP means that the data set is to be kept. The remaining values, PASS, CATLG (which stands for catalog), and UNCATLG (which stands for uncatalog), will be explained in Chapter 4.*

The abnormal-disposition subparameter indicates what is to be done with the data set if the current step terminates abnormally. Except for PASS, the same values may be coded as for the normal-disposition subparameter, and they have the same meanings.

Default Values.   There are a few additional rules you should know about coding the DISP parameter. If the abnormal-disposition subparameter is not coded, the default value is the value coded for the normal-disposition subparameter. This means that

```
DISP=(NEW,KEEP,KEEP)
```

and

```
DISP=(NEW,KEEP)
```

are equivalent.

If PASS is coded for the normal-disposition, the default value for the abnormal-disposition is KEEP for data sets that existed before the step and DELETE for data sets that did not exist before the step.

---

* In some systems, if KEEP is specified for a data set, the data set is automatically cataloged.

If neither a `normal-disposition` nor an `abnormal-disposition` subparameter is coded, the following rule applies: Data sets that existed before the step are kept, and data sets that did not exist before the step are deleted. This means that

```
DISP=(NEW,DELETE)
```

and

```
DISP=(NEW)
```

are equivalent, and that

```
DISP=(OLD,KEEP)
```

and

```
DISP=(OLD)
```

are also equivalent. If only the first subparameter is coded the parentheses may be omitted, so this last example may be written as

```
DISP=OLD
```

If the `status` subparameter is not coded, the default value is `NEW`. So instead of

```
DISP=(NEW,KEEP)
```

you will sometimes see the equivalent coding

```
DISP=(,KEEP)
```

Notice that you must code a comma to indicate that the status subparameter was omitted, because the subparameters are positional. Finally, if `DISP` is completely omitted, the default is

```
DISP=(NEW,DELETE)
```

This means that if the data set is created and deleted in the same step you do not have to code `DISP`. In Chapter 5 you will see examples of data sets for which `DISP` is not coded.

Specifying the Device — The UNIT Parameter.   The third parameter

```
UNIT=DISK
```

specifies the type of physical device the data set uses. `UNIT` is a keyword parameter that may be coded as follows:

$$
UNIT = \begin{cases} \text{address} \\ \text{device type} \\ \text{group name} \end{cases}
$$

One way to specify a unit is to code a group name. In Figure 3.4 the JCL used a group name of DISK to request any disk drive that is available. Group names are established by the computer center and vary from one center to another. Typical names include TAPE to specify a tape drive and SYSDA and DISK to specify any direct access device. Your advisor will tell you the valid group names at your computer center, which you should write on the inside front cover.

You can also specify a unit by coding a device type. For example, a device type of 3330 requests a model 3330 disk drive. Other valid device types are 2400 to request a model 2400 tape drive and 3380 to request a model 3380 disk drive. Clearly the device types you are permitted to code will depend on which models of disk and tape drives are available at your computer center. Your advisor will tell you the valid device types at your center and their meanings, which you should write on the inside front cover.

Finally, you can specify a unit by coding an address, which is a three-digit number such as 472. When you code an address, you are requesting a particular physical device. Unless there is a good reason for specifying a particular device, this is not good practice. If that particular device is being used by another job, your job will not run until the other job ends. If that particular device is being repaired, your job will not run at all.

Generally speaking, you should use a group name when you code the UNIT parameter. If you specify UNIT=3330 and the model 3330 disk drives are replaced by model 3380's, you must change your JCL. If, however, you specify UNIT=DISK, then when the 3330's are replaced by 3380's, the system programmer need only change the meaning of DISK from 3330 to 3380.

Specifying the Volume — The VOL Parameter.   The fourth parameter

```
VOL=SER=WYL002
```

specifies the serial number of the volume on which the data set is to be written. VOL, which is an abbreviation for VOLUME, is a keyword parameter, and SER is a keyword subparameter. In Figure 3.4 the JCL requested that the data set be placed on the volume whose serial number is WYL002. Each computer center creates its own serial numbers, which programmers must use. Your advisor will tell you the serial numbers you may use, which you should write on the inside front cover.

It is not necessary to specify the volume you want to use. If you do not specify the volume, the system will select a volume for you. The allocation messages printed when your job runs will tell you the serial number of the volume selected. When a data set on disk is to be kept, it is usual to specify the volume. When the data set is to be deleted, the volume is usually not specified.

Requesting Space — The SPACE Parameter.   The fifth parameter

```
SPACE=(TRK,5)
```

requests space for the data set. SPACE is a keyword parameter, and the format shown here has two positional subparameters:

```
SPACE=(units,quantity)
```

The units subparameter specifies the units in which space should be allocated, and the quantity subparameter specifies the amount of space you want. In Figure 3.4 five tracks are requested. To request space in units of cylinders, code CYL for the units subparameter. The following entry requests three cylinders:

```
SPACE=(CYL,3)
```

which on a 3336 Disk Pack would be $3 \times 19 = 57$ tracks.

Appendix E shows how to calculate how much space a data set requires.

You can also request space in units of blocks. So, for example, if the blocksize of your data set is 800 bytes and the data set will contain 500 blocks, you can request space by coding

```
SPACE=(800,500)
```

This means that your data set needs enough space to hold 500 blocks, each of which is 800 bytes long. The system will calculate for you the number of tracks your data set requires. Space is always allocated in terms of full tracks, so if the system calculates that your data set requires 26.3 tracks, it will allocate 27 tracks.

Besides saving you the trouble of calculating the number of tracks your data set requires, requesting space in terms of blocks has the second advantage of making your space request device-independent. This means that if your computer center installs new disks, the system will calculate the number of tracks your data set needs based on the characteristics of the new disks. You may get fewer or more tracks on the new disks than you got on the old disks, but you will always get the right number of tracks to hold your data set.

Secondary Allocation.   Sometimes you don't know the exact number of records in a data set and therefore cannot exactly calculate the amount of space it needs. The solution to this problem is to use the full version of the quantity subparameter, which is itself made up of subparameters which allow you to request a **primary allocation** and a **secondary allocation** as follows:

```
SPACE=(TRK,(5,2))
```

The syntax of this statement is a little tricky. Notice that the whole `quantity` subparameter is enclosed in parentheses and is separated from the `units` subparameter by a comma. This entry requests a primary allocation of five tracks, but if that is not enough to hold the data set, a secondary allocation of two tracks is to be made. If the seven tracks is still not enough to hold the data set, a second secondary allocation of two tracks is to be made. How many times can the secondary allocation be made? To answer that question requires that we consider extents.

You may recall that an extent is a group of contiguous tracks all of which either are used by a data set or are available. As mentioned earlier, a data set may consist of up to 16 extents. Usually the primary allocation is one extent, and each secondary allocation is one extent. Under these circumstances the secondary allocation can be made 15 times. If, however, the available space on the disk is broken into many small extents and/or you request a large amount of space, the primary allocation and each secondary allocation may consist of up to five extents. Under these extreme circumstances the secondary allocation can take place only twice. If the system cannot allocate the primary or secondary allocation in five or fewer extents, the job is terminated.

Secondary allocations may also be requested when space is specified in units of cylinders or blocks. So both of the following entries are valid:

```
SPACE=(CYL,(3,1))
```

and

```
SPACE=(800,(500,100))
```

The first example requests a primary allocation of three cylinders and a secondary allocation of one cylinder, and the second example requests a primary allocation of 500 800-byte blocks and a secondary allocation of 100 800-byte blocks.

The RLSE Subparameter. The secondary allocation allows you to increase the size of a data set if your estimate for the primary allocation is too small. But what happens if your estimate for the primary allocation is too large? It does not seem reasonable that the extra space not needed by your data set should be wasted. You can request that any unused space be released by coding the `RLSE` subparameter,

```
SPACE=(TRK,(5,2,),RLSE)
```

Notice the comma between the `quantity` subparameter and the word `RLSE`.

There is no contradiction between coding `RLSE` and requesting secondary allocation. If, when the data set is created, not all of the primary allocation is used, the unused space will be released. Later, if records are added to the data set, the system will make a secondary allocation to increase the size of the data set. RLSE can also be coded when space is requested in units of cylinders or blocksize.

Defining Record Characteristics.   The final parameter

```
DCB=(RECFM=FB,LRECL=80,BLKSIZE=800)
```

specifies some characteristics of the records in the data set. DCB is a keyword parameter and consists of many keyword subparameters, only three of which are shown here. DCB stands for data control block and refers to the information the system assembles about every data set. In Figure 3.4 RECFM=FB is specified, which means that the record format is fixed length blocked. RECFM can also be F, for fixed length unblocked; V, for variable length unblocked; VB, for variable length blocked; VS, for variable length spanned; VBS, for variable length blocked spanned; and U, for undefined.*

Adding the letter A to these record formats (as in FBA) indicates that the first byte of the record contains a character used to control printer spacing or to select a stacker for a card punch.

The record format may also be specified in an assembler, PL/I, or COBOL program. Assembler programmers specify the record format by coding the RECFM operand in the DCB instruction in their program. PL/I programmers specify the record format by including the value (F, FB, VB, etc.) in the ENVIRONMENT option. COBOL programmers specify the record format indirectly. If the RECORD CONTAINS clause specifies one number, for example,

```
RECORD CONTAINS 120 CHARACTERS
```

the records are fixed length. If the RECORD CONTAINS clause specifies two numbers, for example,

```
RECORD CONTAINS 100 to 150 CHARACTERS
```

the records are variable length. In addition, if the BLOCK CONTAINS clause is coded, the record format is blocked; if it is not coded, the record format is unblocked.

The DCB parameter in Figure 3.4 also specifies that the logical record length, LRECL, is 80 bytes and that the blocksize, BLKSIZE, is 800 bytes. Because the input data set consists of input stream data, its logical record length and blocksize are both 80 bytes. Notice how easily IEBGENER permits you to change the blocksize when the data set is copied. IEBGENER also permits you to change the logical record length, but that is a more complicated process, which you will learn about in Chapter 4. When fixed length records are blocked, BLKSIZE must be an integral multiple of LRECL. In Figure 3.4 BLKSIZE is ten times LRECL.

---

* These record formats are discussed in Appendix E.

Figure 3.5

Output Produced by Executing the Job Stream in Figure 3.4

First page

```
IAT6140 JOB ORIGIN FROM GROUP=LOCAL       , DSP=IJP, DEVICE=INTRDR , 000
15:56:17 IAT5110 JOB 6476 (JCLQB010)  USES D WYL002 WYL.QB.JCL.POLYFILE
15:56:20 IAT5200 JOB 6476 (JCLQB010)  IN SETUP ON MAIN=M1
15:56:20 IAT5210 SYSUT2  USING D WYL002 ON 377    WYL.QB.JCL.POLYFILE
15:56:23 IATXXXX JOB 6476 (JCLQB010)  SETUP COMPLETED ON MAIN=M1
15:56:27 IAT2000 JOB 6476 JCLQB010 SELECTED M1     GRP=BATCH
15:56:35 M1 R= JCLQB010 IEF403I JCLQB010 - STARTED
15:57:14 M1 R= JCLQB010 IEF404I JCLQB010 - ENDED
15:57:23 IAT5400 JOB 6476 (JCLQB010) IN BREAKDOWN
```

Second page

```
                                                     *
//JCLQB010 JOB ,'J. C. LEWIS',
//  REGION=40K
//*
//* USING IEBGENER TO CREATE A SEQUENTIAL DATA SET ON A DISK
//*
//CREATE EXEC PGM=IEBGENER
//SYSPRINT DD SYSOUT=A
//SYSIN    DD DUMMY
//SYSUT1   DD *
/*
//SYSUT2   DD DSN=WYL.QB.JCL.POLYFILE,
//            DISP=(NEW,KEEP,DELETE),
//            UNIT=DISK,
//            VOL=SER=WYL002,
//            SPACE=(TRK,5),
//            DCB=(RECFM=FB,LRECL=80,BLKSIZE=800)

                                          *
1      //JCLQB010 JOB ,'J. C. LEWIS',
       //  REGION=40K
       //***
       //*** USING IEBGENER TO CREATE A SEQUENTIAL DATA SET ON A DISK
       //***
2      //CREATE EXEC PGM=IEBGENER
3      //SYSPRINT DD SYSOUT=A
4      //SYSIN    DD DUMMY
5      //SYSUT1   DD *,DCB=BLKSIZE=80
6      //SYSUT2   DD DSN=WYL.QB.JCL.POLYFILE,
       //            DISP=(NEW,KEEP,DELETE),
       //            UNIT=DISK,
       //            VOL=SER=WYL002,
       //            SPACE=(TRK,5),
       //            DCB=(RECFM=FB,LRECL=80,BLKSIZE=800)
```

64

```
IEF236I ALLOC. FOR JCLQB010 CREATE
IEF237I JES3 ALLOCATED TO SYSPRINT
IEF237I DMY  ALLOCATED TO SYSIN
IEF237I JES3 ALLOCATED TO SYSUT1
IEF237I 377  ALLOCATED TO SYSUT2
IEF142I JCLQB010 CREATE - STEP WAS EXECUTED - COND CODE 0000
IEF285I     CREATE.SYSPRINT                          SYSOUT
IEF285I     JESI0001                                 SYSIN
IEF285I     WYL.QB.JCL.POLYFILE                       KEPT   ◀── The data set was KEPT
IEF285I     VOL SER NOS= WYL002.  ◀── The data set is on WYL002
```

** START - STEP=CREATE JOB=JCLQB010 DATE=10/30/81 CLOCK=15.56.23 PGM=IEBGENER REGION USED= 36K OF 40K ** ◀── 40K allocated
** END -   DATE=10/30/81 CLOCK=15.57.02 CPU TIME = 0 MIN 0.08 SEC CC= 0 **
** I/O COUNTS - DISK=   3, SPOOL/OTHER=   11, TAPE=   0, VIO=   0; TOTAL=   14 **

DATA SET UTILITY - GENERATE

PROCESSING ENDED AT EOD

As explained in Appendix E, for variable length records LRECL must be equal to the length of the largest record plus 4. So if the largest record has a length of 150 bytes, LRECL will be set equal to 154. Appendix E also explains that for variable length records the BLKSIZE must be equal to *at least* LRECL plus 4. So for this example BLKSIZE could be as small as 158, but larger values would be valid too.

Generally the size of a record is determined by the problem being solved. Certain data must be included in the record, and those data require a particular logical record length. But the blocksize is under the control of the programmer. When a data set is created by an assembler, PL/I, or COBOL program, the blocksize may be specified either within the program or in the DCB parameter. (In a FORTRAN program the blocksize must be specified in the DCB parameter.)

Assembler programmers can specify blocksize in the DCB parameter by simply omitting BLKSIZE in the DCB instruction in their program. Similarly, PL/I programmers omit BLKSIZE in the ENVIRONMENT option. COBOL programmers must include the statement

```
BLOCK CONTAINS 0 RECORDS
```

as part of the FD entry.

The advantage of specifying the blocksize in the DCB parameter is that the blocksize can be changed without recompiling the program. Because of this advantage, some computer centers require that blocksize be specified in the DCB parameter. Nevertheless, it is common for the blocksize to be specified within the program and for the DCB parameter to be omitted entirely from the DD statement. If the DCB parameter is omitted when IEBGENER is used, IEBGENER copies the record characteristics from the input data set. This is what the message

```
WARNING : OUTPUT RECFM/LRECL/BLKSIZE COPIED FROM INPUT
```

in Figure 2.3 means.

If the same DCB subparameters are assigned different values within a program and on a DD statement, the values assigned in the program are used. So, for example, if you specify a blocksize of 2000 bytes in the program and 1000 bytes on a DD statement, the blocksize actually used will be 2000 bytes.

Order of Parameters

Because DSN, DISP, UNIT, VOL, SPACE, and DCB are keyword parameters, they may be coded in any order. I code them in what I consider to be the most logical order. The most important characteristic of a data set is its name, so DSN is coded first. As you will learn in Chapter 4, the only parameters you must code to access an existing data set that is cataloged are DSN and DISP, so DISP is coded second. As you will also learn in Chapter 4, to access an existing data set that is not cataloged you must code UNIT and VOL as well as DSN and DISP, so these two parameters are coded next. Finally, you need the SPACE and DCB parameters only when you create a data set, so these two parameters are coded last.

You should realize that you do not have to follow this order; you may use any order that appeals to you. But if you choose some order and stick to it, you will be less likely to accidentally leave out a parameter.

Executing the Job Stream

Figure 3.5 shows the output produced by executing the job stream in Figure 3.4. The output was originally on four pages. The first two pages are similar to the output we obtained in Chapter 2. On the third page notice the allocation message, which indicates that the data set WYL.QB.JCL.POLYFILE was KEPT and that the serial number of the volume it was kept on is WYL002, just as we requested. Notice also that, as we requested, 40K of storage were allocated for the job. Finally, notice the message printed by IEBGENER indicating that processing ended at end of data (EOD). This message tells us that the complete input data set was written onto the disk.

Creating a Sequential Data Set on Tape

Figure 3.6 shows the output produced by executing a job stream that uses IEBGENER to create a sequential data set on tape. The output was originally on four pages. The original job stream is shown on the second page. The only differences between the coding in Figures 3.4 and 3.6 are in the SYSUT2 DD statement. First, the UNIT parameter specifies a tape drive rather than a disk drive. Second, the VOL parameter is not coded. When you are using tape, it is better to let the operator mount any available tape. If you specify a tape volume, you run the risk that the particular volume is already in use or that it was in such poor condition that it has been replaced. The allocation message on the third page tells you the tape serial number actually used was QBT010. Third, the SPACE parameter is not coded. The SPACE parameter is not specified for tape; it is specified only for direct access devices such as disks.

The DEN Subparameter

Finally, the DEN subparameter of the DCB parameter is coded. DEN specifies the recording density to be used for the data set and is sometimes coded when data sets are created on tape using a dual-density tape drive. The values that DEN may have and the corresponding recording densities are shown in Table 3.2. If DEN is not coded, however, the recording density actually used

Figure 3.6

Output Produced by a Job Stream That Creates as Data Set on Tape

```
IAT6140 JOB ORIGIN FROM GROUP=LOCAL      ,   DSP=IJP, DEVICE=INTRDR    ,   000
16:30:56 IAT5110 JOB 7357 (JCLQB015)  GET T QBT010 ,SL WYL.QB.JCL.POLYFILE
16:30:56 IAT5200 JOB 7357 (JCLQB015)  IN SETUP ON MAIN=M2
16:30:56 IAT5210 SYSUT2   MOUNT T QBT010 ON 48A    ,SL,RING   WYL.QB.JCL.POLYFILE
16:32:19 IATXXXX JOB 7357 (JCLQB015)  SETUP COMPLETED ON MAIN=M2
16:32:19 IAT2000 JOB 7357 JCLQB015 SELECTED M1       GRP=BATCH
16:32:19 M1 R= JCLQB015 IEF403I JCLQB015 - STARTED
16:33:42 M1 R= JCLQB015 IEF234E K 68A,QBT010,PVT,JCLQB015,CREATE
16:33:43 M1 R= JCLQB015 IEF471E FOLLOWING VOLUMES NO LONGER NEEDED BY JCLQB015
16:33:43 M1 R= JCLQB015          QBT010.
16:33:43 M1 R= JCLQB015 IEF404I JCLQB015 - ENDED
16:33:44 IAT5410 KEEP     T QBT010 ON 48A,M2
16:33:45 IAT5400 JOB 7357 (JCLQB015) IN BREAKDOWN
```

```
   //JCLQB015 JOB ,'J. C. LEWIS',
   // REGION=40K
   //*
   //* USING IEBGENER TO CREATE A DATA SET ON A TAPE
   //*
   //CREATE EXEC PGM=IEBGENER
   //SYSPRINT DD SYSOUT=A
   //SYSIN    DD DUMMY
   //SYSUT1   DD *
   //*
   //SYSUT2   DD DSN=WYL.QB.JCL.POLYFILE,
   //         DISP=(NEW,KEEP,DELETE),
   //         UNIT=TAPE,
   //         DCB=(RECFM=FB,LRECL=80,BLKSIZE=800,DEN=4)
1  //JCLQB015 JOB ,'J. C. LEWIS',
   // REGION=40K
   //***
   //*** USING IEBGENER TO CREATE A DATA SET ON A TAPE
   //***
2  //CREATE EXEC PGM=IEBGENER
3  //SYSPRINT DD SYSOUT=A
4  //SYSIN    DD DUMMY
5  //SYSUT1   DD *,DCB=BLKSIZE=80
6  //SYSUT2   DD DSN=WYL.QB.JCL.POLYFILE,
   //         DISP=(NEW,KEEP,DELETE),
   //         UNIT=TAPE,
   //         DCB=(RECFM=FB,LRECL=80,BLKSIZE=800,DEN=4)
```

68

```
IEF236I ALLOC. FOR JCLQB015 CREATE
IEF237I JES3 ALLOCATED TO SYSPRINT
IEF237I DMY  ALLOCATED TO SYSIN
IEF237I JES3 ALLOCATED TO SYSUT1
IEF237I 68A  ALLOCATED TO SYSUT2
IEF142I JCLQB015 CREATE - STEP WAS EXECUTED - COND CODE 0000
IEF285I   CREATE.SYSPRINT                      SYSOUT
IEF285I   JESI0001                             SYSIN
IEF285I   WYL.QB.JCL.POLYFILE                  KEPT
IEF285I   VOL SER NOS= QBT010.
```

(The data set is on QBT010.)   (The data set was KEPT)

```
** START - STEP=CREATE JOB=JCLQB015 DATE=10/30/81 CLOCK=16.32.08 PGM=IEBGENER REGION USED= 36K OF 40K **
** END -                              DATE=10/30/81 CLOCK=16.33.30 CPU TIME = 0 MIN 0.10 SEC  CC= 0 **
** I/O COUNTS - DISK=    0,  SPOOL/OTHER=   52,  TAPE=   3,  VIO=   0; TOTAL=   55 **
```

DATA SET UTILITY - GENERATE

PROCESSING ENDED AT EOD

Table 3.2
Values of DEN and Corresponding
Recording Densities

Value of DEN	Recording Density (bytes per inch)
0	200
1	556
2	800
3	1600
4	6250

will be the highest value of which the tape drive is capable. Because recording at the highest possible density is generally desirable, it is customary to omit the DEN subparameter. Execution of the job stream in Figure 3.6 would have produced exactly the same results if the DEN subparameter had been omitted.

It is important to understand that the SYSUT2 DD statement in Figure 3.6 shows how a sequential data set is created on tape. Although the program executed in Figure 3.6 is IEBGENER, you would code the same DD parameters if you were using a COBOL, PL/I, FORTRAN, or assembler program to create a sequential data set on tape. Only the ddname would be different, for it would have to be changed to the ddname the program required.

The DISP Parameter for Tape

The DISP parameter works a little differently for tapes than it does for disks. When you code NEW for the status of your data set, the data are written on the tape; any data that were originally on the tape are simply erased. When you code KEEP for the disposition, the tape is rewound and unloaded from the tape drive at the end of the job. The system issues a message to the operator that the tape volume is to be kept, and the operator sends the tape volume to the library. (On the next-to-last line of the first page in Figure 3.6, you can see the message to the operator to KEEP tape QBT010.) When you code DELETE for the disposition, the tape is rewound and unloaded at the end of the job, but this time the system issues a message to the operator that the tape volume may be used. The operator sends the tape volume to be stored with the other tapes that are available to be used by any job that needs a tape.

Errors

Figure 3.7 shows the output produced by a job stream that contains a syntax error. Although there are three error messages, there is only one error. The

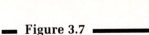
■ **Figure 3.7** ■■

Execution of a Job Stream That Contains a Syntax Error

```
IAT6140 JOB ORIGIN FROM GROUP=LOCAL    , DSP=IJP, DEVICE=INTRDR  , 000     First page
16:23:52 IAT4204  JOB FAILED WITH CONVERTER/INTERPRETER JCL ERROR
16:23:52 IAT4801 JOB JCLQB016 (7172) EXPRESS CANCELED BY INTERPRETER DSP
```

```
//JCLQB016 JOB ,'J. C. LEWIS',                                    * Second page
// REGION=40K
//*
//* USING IEBGENER TO CREATE A SEQUENTIAL DATA SET ON A DISK
//*
//CREATE EXEC PGM=IEBGENER
//SYSPRINT DD SYSOUT=A
//SYSIN    DD DUMMY
//SYSUT1   DD *
/*
//SYSUT2   DD DSN=WYL.QB.JCL.POLYFILE,
//            DISP=(NEW,KEEP,DELETE),
//            UNIT=DISK,
//            VOL=SER=WYL002,
//             SPACE=(TRK,5),
//            DCB=(RECFM=FB,LRECL=80,BLKSIZE=800)
//
     1      //JCLQB016 JOB ,'J. C. LEWIS',                              *
            // REGION=40K
            ***
            *** USING IEBGENER TO CREATE A SEQUENTIAL DATA SET ON A DISK
            ***
     2      //CREATE EXEC PGM=IEBGENER
     3      //SYSPRINT DD SYSOUT=A
     4      //SYSIN    DD DUMMY
     5      //SYSUT1   DD *,DCB=BLKSIZE=80
     6      //SYSUT2   DD DSN=WYL.QB.JCL.POLYFILE,
            //            DISP=(NEW,KEEP,DELETE),
            //            UNIT=DISK,
            //            VOL=SER=WYL002,
     7      //*           SPACE=(TRK,5),
     8      //            DCB=(RECFM=FB,LRECL=80,BLKSIZE=800)
            //
```

```
STMT NO. MESSAGE                                              Third page

     6      IEF621I EXPECTED CONTINUATION NOT RECEIVED
     7      IEF605I UNIDENTIFIED OPERATION FIELD
     8      IEF605I UNIDENTIFIED OPERATION FIELD
```

error is that the SPACE parameter begins in column 17. Recall that when a JCL statement is continued, the continuation statement must have two slashes in columns 1 and 2 and the coding must resume between columns 4 and 16.

Because of the comma after WYL002, the system expected the statement to be continued on the next line, but because SPACE begins in column 17, the SPACE line was not recognized as a continuation line. The system therefore

■ **Figure 3.8** ■

Execution of a Job Stream That Contains a Logic Error

```
IAT6140 JOB ORIGIN FROM GROUP=LOCAL    , DSP=IJP, DEVICE=INTRDR  , 000    First page
16:42:35 IAT5110 JOB 7607 (JCLQB020) USES D WYL002 WYL.QB.JCL.POLYFILE
16:42:35 IAT5200 JOB 7607 (JCLQB020) IN SETUP ON MAIN=M1
16:42:35 IAT5210 SYSUT2   USING D WYL002 ON 377   WYL.QB.JCL.POLYFILE
16:42:35 IATXXXX JOB 7607 (JCLQB020) SETUP COMPLETED ON MAIN=M1
16:42:35 IAT2000 JOB 7607 JCLQB020 SELECTED M2       GRP=BATCH
16:42:36 M2 R= JCLQB020 IEF403I JCLQB020 - STARTED
16:42:37 M2 R= JCLQB020 IEF453I JCLQB020 - JOB FAILED - JCL ERROR
16:42:38 IAT5400 JOB 7607 (JCLQB020) IN BREAKDOWN
```

```
//JCLQB020 JOB ,'J. C. LEWIS',                              * Second page
// REGION=40K
//*
//* USING IEBGENER TO CREATE A SEQUENTIAL DATA SET ON A DISK
//*
//CREATE EXEC PGM=IEBGENER
//SYSPRINT DD SYSOUT=A
//SYSIN    DD DUMMY
//SYSUT1   DD *
/*
//SYSUT2   DD DSN=WYL.QB.JCL.POLYFILE,
//            DISP=(NEW,KEEP,DELETE),
//            UNIT=DISK,
//            VOL=SER=WYL002,
//            SPACE=(TRK,5),
//            DCB=(RECFM=FB,LRECL=80,BLKSIZE=800)
//
      1     //JCLQB020 JOB ,'J. C. LEWIS',                        *
            // REGION=40K
            ***
            *** USING IEBGENER TO CREATE A SEQUENTIAL DATA SET ON A DISK
            ***
      2     //CREATE EXEC PGM=IEBGENER
      3     //SYSPRINT DD SYSOUT=A
      4     //SYSIN    DD DUMMY
      5     //SYSUT1   DD *,DCB=BLKSIZE=80
      6     //SYSUT2   DD DSN=WYL.QB.JCL.POLYFILE,
            //            DISP=(NEW,KEEP,DELETE),
            //            UNIT=DISK,
            //            VOL=SER=WYL002,
            //            SPACE=(TRK,5),
            //            DCB=(RECFM=FB,LRECL=80,BLKSIZE=800)
            //
```

```
IEF253I JCLQB020 CREATE SYSUT2 - DUPLICATE NAME ON DIRECT ACCESS VOLUME   Third page
IEF272I JCLQB020 CREATE - STEP WAS NOT EXECUTED.
IEF285I    CREATE.SYSPRINT                        SYSOUT
IEF285I    JESI0001                               SYSIN
```

printed the error message EXPECTED CONTINUATION NOT RECEIVED and printed an asterisk in column 3 of the SPACE line, treating that line as a comment. The system then tried to interpret the SPACE and DCB statements as independent JCL statements, but it couldn't recognize them so it printed the error message UNIDENTIFIED OPERATION FIELD. To fix the error all you would have to do is retype the SPACE line, starting SPACE between columns 4 and 16.

Figure 3.8 illustrates an error people often make when creating a data set on a disk. Typically, this error comes about in the following way. A job is executed but does not run perfectly. The space is allocated, however, and the data set name is entered in the disk pack's VTOC. Unfortunately, the programmer does not read the allocation messages for the job, which show that the data set was kept, and therefore does not realize that the data set name has been entered into the VTOC. The programmer therefore corrects the program and reruns the job. The second job also fails, and the system prints the error message shown on the third page in Figure 3.8,

DUPLICATE NAME ON DIRECT ACCESS VOLUME

What this message means is that when the system saw the disposition NEW, it tried to enter the data set name in the VTOC. Because the exact same name was already in the VTOC, however, and data set names in the VTOC must be unique, the system printed the error message and the job was terminated.

The easiest way to correct this error is change the DISP parameter to

DISP=(OLD,KEEP,DELETE)

As the error message implies, this kind of error cannot occur with tape, for only direct access volumes have VTOCs.

Summary

In this chapter you have learned

—the characteristics of magnetic tape and magnetic disk

—the parameters used to create a sequential data set on tape or disk:

DSN: to assign a name to a data set

DISP: to specify a status and disposition

UNIT: to specify the type of physical device

VOL: to specify a particular volume

SPACE: to request space in terms of tracks, cylinders, or blocks on a disk volume

DCB: to assign a data set characteristics of record format, logical record length, blocksize, and recording density

—the rules for forming qualified and unqualified data set names

Vocabulary

In this chapter you have been introduced to the meanings of the following terms:

allocation, primary and secondary	label records
block	logical record length
blocking factor	off-line
blocksize	on-line
contiguous	recording density
cylinder	serial number
data set name, qualified and unqualified	track
	volume
extent	volume label
interblock gap	VTOC

Exercises

1. What is the purpose of assigning serial numbers to tape and disk volumes?
2. What are label records?
3. What is a cylinder?
4. What is a VTOC?
5. What is an extent?
6. Suppose that when a particular tape drive writes fixed unblocked records it uses an interblock gap of 0.6 inch. What size would the gap be when that drive writes blocked records?
7. What is the purpose of blocking?
8. What parameters must be coded on a DD statement to create a permanent data set on a disk?
9. When you use a COBOL program to create a data set on disk, the data set has three names: the file name used in the COBOL program, the ddname, and the data set name. Which of these names, if any, must be the same when you later access that data set?
10. What are the three subparameters of the DISP parameter?
11. How do the status subparameters OLD, SHR, and MOD differ?
12. Suppose DISP is not coded. What is the default?
13. What is the advantage of using a group name when you code the UNIT parameter?
14. What is the meaning of SPACE=(300,(200,100))?
15. When will a secondary allocation be made? How many times will a secondary allocation be made?
16. How do you return unused space on a DASD to the system?

17. In what order must the keyword parameters DSN, DISP, UNIT, VOL, SPACE, and DCB be coded?

18. Write a DD statement to create a sequential data set on a disk. Use MONDAY as the ddname, BLUE as the DSN, SYSDA as the UNIT, and DISK44 as the volume serial number. The data set should be kept if the job terminates normally and deleted if it terminates abnormally. The record length is 120 bytes, and a blocking factor of 10 should be used. Request space in blocks. There will be about 10,000 records in your data set. Request a secondary allocation of 100 blocks, and release unused space.

19. What does coding DEN=4 mean?

20. Write a DD statement to create a sequential data set on tape. Use TUESDAY as the ddname, RED as the DSN, and 2400 as the UNIT. The data set should be kept no matter how the job terminates. Do not code the DCB parameter.

21. Rewrite correctly any entry that is wrong.
    a. DSN=PAYROLLFILE
    b. DISP=NEW,KEEP,KEEP
    c. DISP=OLD
    d. DISP=(OLD,OLD,OLD)
    e. VOL=SER=DISK01
    f. VOL=TAPE05
    g. SPACE=(500,500)
    h. SPACE=(TRK(10,4)RLSE)
    i. DCB=(RECFM=FB,LRECL=100,BLOCKSIZE=550)
    j. DCB=(RECFM=VB,LRECL=200,BLOCKSIZE=400)

Programming Assignment

Execute a job to use IEBGENER to create a sequential data set on a disk. Use the data given in Appendix D or data suggested by your advisor.

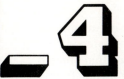

Accessing Sequential Data Sets

In this chapter you will learn

- how to add records to a data set

- how to catalog a data set

- how to code control statements for IEBGENER and IEBPTPCH

- how to code a job stream that contains more than one step

- how to read the system messages produced when a job abends

- how to use the parameters COND and TIME

Now that you have created a data set and stored it on a disk, the next thing you must learn is how to access that data set. Most job streams contain more than one step; in this chapter you will also learn how to code multistep job streams. So far you have used IEBGENER in its simplest form; you are now ready to learn how to code control statements to modify the processing that IEBGENER does. You will also learn how to use a second utility program, IEBPTPCH.

Listing a Disk Data Set

In Chapter 3 we created WYL.QB.JCL.POLYFILE. From now on, whenever there is no chance of confusion, only the last part of the data set name will be used—in this case, POLYFILE. The output produced by the job that created POLYFILE is shown in Figure 3.5. You may have noticed when you studied Figure 3.5 that there is no output showing the data records that were put on the disk. The system messages indicate that the job ran properly and there is every reason to believe that all the records in the input stream data were successfully put on the disk, but it would be nice to be sure. The way to be sure is to list POLYFILE. The system flowchart for listing POLYFILE is shown in Figure 4.1.

Listing POLYFILE should be easy, for back in Chapter 2 we listed input stream data using the job stream in Figure 2.2. All we have to do is change the SYSUT1 DD statement in Figure 2.2 so that it refers to POLYFILE instead of to input stream data. The DD statement shown in Figure 4.2 would work.

Comparing this DD statement with the SYSUT2 DD statement in Figure 3.4, which was used to create the data set, reveals several interesting things. First, the same DSN that created the data set is used to access it. Remember that it is the data set name that is the permanent name of the data set—the name stored in the disk pack's VTOC. The ddname has no permanent association with the data set; when POLYFILE was created the ddname SYSUT2 was used, and now to access it the ddname SYSUT1 is used.

The second thing to notice is the way the DISP parameter is coded. Because the data set exists, we code the status as OLD, and because we want to retain the data set when this job is over, we code the normal disposition as KEEP. The abnormal-disposition subparameter is not coded because the default value is KEEP, which is what is desired.

Figure 4.1

System Flowchart to List POLYFILE

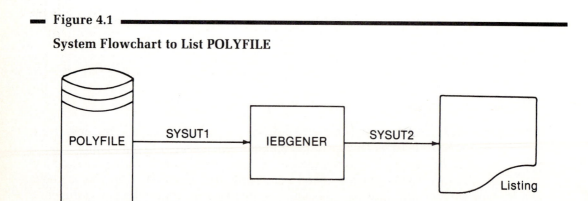

Figure 4.2

DD Statement to Access an Existing Data Set

```
//SYSUT1    DD DSN=WYL.QB.JCL.POLYFILE,
//             DISP=(OLD,KEEP),
//             UNIT=DISK,
//             VOL=SER=WYL002
```

The DISP parameter could just as well have been coded as

```
DISP=OLD
```

because for an existing data set the default value for the normal disposition is KEEP.

The third thing to notice is that the UNIT and VOL parameters are coded exactly as they were when we created the data set. Finally, notice that the SPACE and DCB parameters are not coded. The only time the SPACE parameter is needed is when you are creating a data set on a disk, in which case the system needs to know how much space is required. Once the data set has been created, the space has already been obtained.

Similar considerations apply to the DCB parameter. The only time the DCB parameter is needed is when you are creating a data set and you want to assign values to RECFM, LRECL, BLKSIZE, DEN, and other subparameters you will learn about later. (As you will learn in Chapter 11, the DCB parameter is always required with ISAM data sets.) As mentioned in Chapter 3, when the data set is created, this DCB information is stored in the header labels. Because the system can get the information by reading the header labels, the DCB parameter need not be coded to access the data set.

To repeat: If we replace the SYSUT1 DD statement in Figure 2.2 by the DD statement in Figure 4.2, we can run the job and produce a listing of POLY-FILE. But before we do that, let's discuss how to catalog a data set and how to add control statements for IEBGENER so that the output produced will be easier to read.

Cataloging a Data Set

Table 3.1 shows that the normal-disposition and abnormal-disposition subparameters can be assigned the value CATLG. Coding CATLG causes the data set to be cataloged. When a data set is **cataloged,** its DSN, UNIT, and volume serial number are recorded in the system catalog. The system catalog is a data set that the system uses to determine the UNIT and volume serial number of a data set once its DSN is known. The benefit of cataloging to the programmer is that once a data set has been cataloged, only the DSN and DISP

■ **Figure 4.3** ■

DD Statement to Access an Existing Data Set and Catalog It

```
//SYSUT1    DD DSN=WYL.QB.JCL.POLYFILE,
//              DISP=(OLD,CATLG),
//              UNIT=DISK,
//              VOL=SER=WYL002
```

parameters need be coded to access the data set — the system uses the system catalog to determine the UNIT and volume serial number. Both disk and tape data sets may be cataloged. POLYFILE could have been cataloged when it was created simply by coding the DISP parameter in Figure 3.4 as

```
DISP=(NEW,CATLG,DELETE)
```

The only reason the data set wasn't cataloged then was to prevent the discussion in Chapter 3 from getting too complicated.

To catalog WYL.QB.JCL.POLYFILE, we merely change the DD statement in Figure 4.2 to the version shown in Figure 4.3. Notice that in Figure 4.3 we must specify the UNIT and VOL parameters. At this time the data set has not yet been cataloged; after this job is run, the data set will be cataloged, and then we will be able to omit the UNIT and VOL parameters. You have to catalog a data set only once. It remains cataloged until either you delete it or you uncatalog it by coding a disposition of UNCATLG.

It should be clear that if two cataloged data sets had the same DSN, the system would have no way of knowing which of the two you wanted when you tried to access one. Thus, although you can have data sets with the same DSN on different disk packs and tape reels or cartridges, only one of them may be cataloged.

Utility Control Statements

So far we have used IEBGENER only to copy a sequential data set. Chapter 2 mentioned that IEBGENER could edit a data set as it copied it. To have IEB-GENER edit, you must include control statements in the SYSIN data set. **Control statements** are used to describe exactly what you want the utility program to do. Because this is the first example, let us keep the editing simple and just have IEBGENER insert seven spaces between fields. Even this simple formatting will make the output much easier to read. The editing to be done is shown in Figure 4.4. To have IEBGENER insert seven spaces between fields, we must use the two control statements shown in Figure 4.5.

Editing to Be Performed by IEBGENER

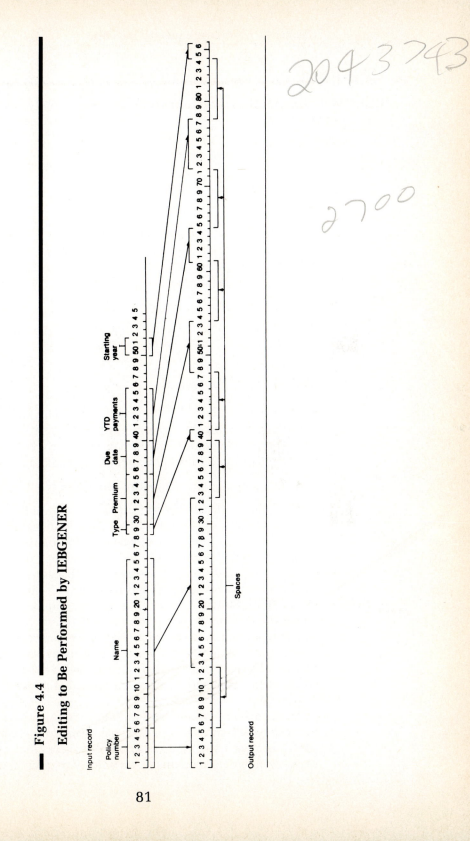

■ **Figure 4.5** ■

IEBGENER Control Statements to Insert Seven Blanks Between Fields in POLYFILE

```
    GENERATE MAXFLDS=13,                                              *
             MAXLITS=42
    RECORD FIELD=(5,1,,1),                                           *
             FIELD=(7,'        ',,6),                               *
             FIELD=(20,6,,13),                                       *
             FIELD=(7,'        ',,33),                              *
             FIELD=(1,29,,40),                                       *
             FIELD=(7,'        ',,41),                              *
             FIELD=(6,30,,48),                                       *
             FIELD=(7,'        ',,54),                              *
             FIELD=(4,36,,61),                                       *
             FIELD=(7,'        ',,65),                              *
             FIELD=(6,40,,72),                                       *
             FIELD=(7,'        ',,78),                              *
             FIELD=(2,50,,85)
```

Column 2

Column 16

Column 72

Control Statement Format

Control statements for all the utilities you will study in this book have the same format (with the exception of IEBUPDTE, which you will study in Chapter 5, and IDCAMS, which you will study in Chapter 12). The control statements contain four fields, which are coded in the following order:

```
    label operation operand comments
```

Control statements are coded in columns 1 through 71. Column 72 is used to indicate that the statement is being continued, as will be explained shortly, and columns 73 through 80 may be used for identification or sequence numbers. The four fields must be separated by at least one space, but as in the case of JCL statements, you can use as many spaces as you like.

The label field is optional, but if it is used it must begin in column 1. The label field is usually omitted, and the statements in Figure 4.5 do not have one. If the label field is omitted, column 1 must be blank.

The operation field specifies the type of control statement. In Figure 4.5, the operation field of the first statement is GENERATE and of the second is RECORD. The operation field must be preceded by at least one blank, but other than that can start anywhere you like. In Figure 4.5 the operation was arbitrarily started in column 2.

The next field is the operand field. The operand field consists of one or more keyword parameters, separated by commas. In Figure 4.5, the GENERATE statement contains two parameters, MAXFLDS and MAXLITS, and the RECORD statement contains thirteen FIELD parameters.

The operand field must be separated from the operation field by one or more blanks. By convention I usually separate them by one blank. To make the control statement easier to read, I usually code only one parameter on a line. If there is more than one parameter, as in both the GENERATE and RECORD statements in Figure 4.5, I continue the statement onto the next line.

As with JCL statements, to continue a control statement you interrupt it after the comma following a parameter. There are two additional rules for continuing control statements, however, which are stricter than the rules for continuing JCL statements. First, you must put a nonblank character in column 72 of the statement that is being continued. In Figure 4.5 an asterisk is the nonblank character. Notice that there is no asterisk in column 72 of the MAXLITS line or in the last FIELD line in Figure 4.5; although these lines are continuations of the previous lines, they themselves are not continued, so they must not have a nonblank character in column 72. Second, whereas a continued JCL statement could begin anywhere between columns 4 and 16, continued control statements must begin in column 16. (Some utilities relax these rules. IEBGENER, for example, does not require a nonblank character in column 72, and the continued statement may begin anywhere between columns 4 and 16. If you use these rules, however, you'll never be wrong.)

IEBGENER Control Statements

The three most frequently used IEBGENER control statements are the GENERATE, MEMBER, and RECORD statements. When they are used, these statements must be coded in that order. The statements are described in Table 4.1.

The GENERATE Statement. The four parameters of the GENERATE statement are MAXFLDS, MAXLITS, MAXNAME, and MAXGPS. The MAXFLDS parameter is used to specify the number of FIELD parameters that are coded on the following RECORD statements. In Figure 4.5 MAXFLDS=13 is coded, because there are thirteen FIELD parameters coded on the following RECORD statement.

The MAXLITS parameter is used to specify the number of characters of literal data that appear in the literal fields of the FIELD parameters that are coded on the following RECORD statements. In Figure 4.5 MAXLITS=42 is coded. Exactly how this number was calculated will be explained shortly when the RECORD statement is discussed.

The MAXNAME and MAXGPS parameters will be discussed in Chapter 5, for they involve libraries. *omit .*

The MEMBER Statement. Because it is used with libraries, the MEMBER statement will be discussed in Chapter 5.

The RECORD Statement. The only RECORD statement parameters we will discuss in this text are the FIELD and IDENT parameters. The FIELD parameter specifies the fields to be copied and where they are to be put in the output

Table 4.1
The IEBGENER Control Statements

Control Statement	Parameter	Meaning
GENERATE	MAXFLDS=a	a is greater than or equal to the number of FIELD parameters in the following RECORD statements.
	MAXLITS=b	b is greater than or equal to the number of characters contained in the literal fields of the FIELD parameters in the following RECORD statements.
	MAXNAME=c	c is greater than or equal to the number of names and aliases in the following MEMBER statements.
	MAXGPS=d	d is greater than or equal to the number of IDENT parameters in the following RECORD statements.
MEMBER	NAME=(name[,alias] ...)	name is the name and alias the alias of the member of a partitioned data set that is being created.
RECORD	FIELD=(length, {input-location|'literal'}, conversion, output-location)	length is the length, in bytes, of the input field or literal to be processed. Default is 80. input-location is the starting byte of the input field to be processed. Default is 1.

Cont.

Table 4.1 (Cont.)

Control Statement	Parameter	Meaning
		`'literal'` is the literal to be placed in the output location. It may not require more than 40 bytes.
		`conversion` is the type of conversion to be done to the field. `PZ` causes packed data to be unpacked, `ZP` causes unpacked data to be packed, and `HE` causes BCD data to be converted to EBCDIC. If it is omitted, no conversion is done.
		`output-location` specifies the starting location of this field in the output record. Default is 1.
	`IDENT=(length,` `'literal',` `input-location)`	`length` is the length, in bytes, of the identifying name. `length` must be less than 9.
		`'literal'` is the literal that identifies the last input record of a record group.
		`input-location` specifies the starting location of the field that contains the `'literal'` in the input records.

record. The IDENT parameter will be discussed in Chapter 5, for it involves libraries.

Let us use the description of the FIELD parameter in Table 4.1 to interpret the first FIELD parameter in Figure 4.5,

```
FIELD=(5,1,,1)
```

This parameter controls the printing of the policy number field, which, as shown in Figure 4.4, occupies the first five bytes of the policy record. The values coded indicate that the field being copied has a length of 5 bytes, starts at byte 1 in the input record, and is to be moved to byte 1 in the output record. There is no conversion, so the conversion subparameter was omitted. Because these are positional subparameters, however, a comma was coded to indicate that the conversion subparameter was omitted, just as when a positional subparameter is omitted from a JCL statement.

Because the second FIELD parameter is a little different, let's decipher it also:

```
FIELD=(7,'       ',,6)
```

This parameter moves seven blanks to the output record starting in byte 6. The 7 specifies the length of the literal, and the literal is seven blanks enclosed within apostrophes. Again no conversion was specified. The blanks are moved to byte 6 because the policy number occupies bytes 1 through 5.

You must move spaces to the output area when you use IEBGENER for the same reason that you move spaces to the output area when you write assembler, COBOL, or PL/I programs — because if you did not, the output area could contain garbage left over from the previous program that used these storage locations.

Of the thirteen FIELD parameters in Figure 4.5, six move seven blanks each to the output record. The total number of characters of literal data is therefore $6 \times 7 = 42$. That is how the 42 that is specified for MAXLITS on the GENERATE statement was calculated.

MAXFLDS and MAXLITS actually specify the maximum number of FIELD parameters and characters of literal data that may follow in RECORD statements. The job will execute properly as long as the number of FIELD parameters is not greater than the value specified for MAXFLDS and the number of characters of literal data is not greater than the value specified for MAXLITS. So if Figure 4.5 had been coded

```
MAXFLDS=100,
    MAXLITS=100
```

the job would have executed properly.

You must be careful when you code values for MAXFLDS and MAXLITS, because the error message you get if the values are too small, INVALID SPACE ALLOCATION, is confusing and likely to send you on a wild goose chase checking the SPACE parameter on a DD statement.

To convert data in a field from one form to another, you code a value for the `conversion` subparameter. When we created `POLYFILE`, we could have packed the numeric fields by using a `RECORD` statement with `ZP` coded for the `conversion` subparameter for the numeric fields. If we pack the numeric fields when the data set is created, those numeric fields have to be unpacked when they are printed. They can be unpacked by coding `PZ` for the `conversion` subparameter.

When you pack and unpack fields, you must remember that the length of the field will change. Suppose the length of an unpacked numeric field is n bytes. If n is an odd number, then when the field is packed it will occupy $(n-1)/2 + 1$ bytes. For example, if $n = 7$, the packed field will occupy 4 bytes. If n is an even number, then when the field is packed it will occupy $n/2 + 1$ bytes. For example, if $n = 8$, the packed field will occupy 5 bytes.

When you want to print a packed numeric field, you must unpack it and allow for the length increase. If the length of a packed numeric field is m bytes, then when the field is unpacked it will occupy $2m - 1$ bytes. For example, if $m = 4$, the unpacked field will occupy 7 bytes.

Besides permitting you to insert spaces between fields, the `RECORD` statement allows you to rearrange and omit fields during copying. For example, suppose we wanted to print only the name, premium, and policy number fields of `POLYFILE` in that order and we wanted 5 spaces between the first two fields and 10 spaces between the second and third fields. The following control statements could be used:

```
GENERATE MAXFLDS=5,                                          *
             MAXLITS=15
RECORD FIELD=(20,6,,1),                                      *
          FIELD=(5,'         ',,21),                         *
          FIELD=(6,30,,26),                                  *
          FIELD=(10,'              ',,32),                   *
          FIELD=(5,1,,42)
```

`MAXFLDS`, `MAXLITS`, and `MAXNAME` are keyword parameters and may be coded in any order. The `FIELD` parameters also may be coded in any order.

The Complete Job Stream

The complete job stream to list and catalog `POLYFILE` is shown in Figure 4.6.

The TIME Parameter

The `TIME` parameter is coded on the `JOB` statement. It specifies the maximum amount of CPU time that a job may use. The format of the `TIME` parameter is

```
TIME=(minutes,seconds)
```

In Figure 4.6 a time limit of 0 minutes and 5 seconds is specified.

Figure 4.6

Job Stream to List and Catalog an Existing Data Set

```
//JCLQB033 JOB ,'J.C.LEWIS',
//              REGION=40K,
//              TIME=(0,5)  ←── ( TIME parameter )
//*
//* USING IEBGENER TO LIST A DISK DATA SET
//* WITH CONTROL CARDS TO FORMAT THE OUTPUT
//*
//LIST      EXEC PGM=IEBGENER
//SYSPRINT DD SYSOUT=A
//SYSIN DD *
 GENERATE MAXFLDS=13,                                          *
              MAXLITS=42
 RECORD FIELD=(5,1,,1),                                        *
              FIELD=(7,'          ',,6),                       *
              FIELD=(20,6,,13),                                *
              FIELD=(7,'          ',,33),                      *
              FIELD=(1,29,,40),                                *
              FIELD=(7,'          ',,41),                      *
              FIELD=(6,30,,48),                                *
              FIELD=(7,'          ',,54),                      *
              FIELD=(4,36,,61),                                *
              FIELD=(7,'          ',,65),                      *
              FIELD=(6,40,,72),                                *
              FIELD=(7,'          ',,78),                      *
              FIELD=(2,50,,85)
/*
//SYSUT1    DD DSN=WYL.QB.JCL.POLYFILE,
//              DISP=(OLD,CATLG),
//              UNIT=DISK,
//              VOL=SER=WYL002
//SYSUT2    DD SYSOUT=A,DCB=(RECFM=FB,LRECL=86,BLKSIZE=860)
//
```

Do not confuse CPU time with clock time. CPU time is the time the job has exclusive control of the CPU. Because of multiprogramming, the actual elapsed clock time may be much greater.

If you want no time limit applied to your job, you can code

```
TIME=1440
```

(Notice that 1440 is the number of minutes in 24 hours.) Never code TIME=1440 unless you have a working, fully tested program and are sure that much time is required.

If you don't code a TIME parameter, the time limit is the system default, which varies from one computer center to another. The actual time a job required is printed in the system messages. If your job requires more than the default time, you must code the TIME parameter; otherwise the job will use the default amount of time and then abnormally terminate. Even if your job requires less than the default time, it's a good idea to code the TIME parameter, using as the time limit a reasonable estimate of the time the job should require. That way, if you make a mistake and your program goes into an endless loop, you'll avoid wasting a lot of CPU time. It is hard to imagine how IEBGENER could go into an endless loop, but the TIME parameter is coded in Figure 4.6 to ensure that there will be no problem.

The DD Statements

In Figure 4.6, to supply control statements to IEBGENER, we code an asterisk as the operand of the SYSIN DD statement and follow this statement with the control statements in Figure 4.5. To catalog POLYFILE we use the SYSUT1 DD statement in Figure 4.3.

To print the data set, we direct SYSUT2 to the printer by coding SYSOUT=A. In addition, however, we must code a DCB parameter. To understand why we need the DCB parameter, recall that if DCB information is not specified for SYSUT2, IEBGENER will copy the DCB information from SYSUT1. In this case that means that SYSUT2 will have a logical record length of 80 bytes. But that is impossible, as our control statements specify that the last field is to be printed in byte positions 85 and 86. Therefore we must specify the logical record length of SYSUT2 to be at least 86 bytes.

For efficiency, the JCL specifies that SYSUT2 should be blocked. It may seem contradictory to block printer output, but remember that with spooling output is first written on disk, for which blocking is useful, and then sent to the printer.

Executing the Job Stream

The job stream in Figure 4.6 was executed, and the output produced is shown in Figure 4.7. (You have had enough experience reading output that from now on uninteresting parts of the output will be omitted. Also the original page divisions will no longer be shown.) You can see in this figure that POLYFILE has been cataloged. In addition, you can see that the total CPU time required by the job was 0.07 second. The 5-second limit allowed was ample.

Notice that IEBGENER lists the control statements. Because the control statements are not printed as part of the JCL listing (after all, they are data statements, not JCL statements), this listing is the only place on the output where the control statements appear. Finally, note that POLYFILE was printed with seven spaces between fields, as requested.

Adding Records to a Data Set and Listing It

Our next problem is to add some new records to the end of POLYFILE. The records to be added are shown in Appendix C. After the records have been

Figure 4.7

Output Produced by Executing the Job Stream in Figure 4.6

```
//JCLQB033 JOB ,'J.C.LEWIS',                                                    *  *
// REGION=40K,
// TIME=(0,5)
//*
//* USING IEBGENER TO LIST A DISK DATA SET
//* WITH CONTROL CARDS TO FORMAT THE OUTPUT
//*
//LIST     EXEC PGM=IEBGENER
//SYSPRINT DD SYSOUT=A
//SYSIN DD *
//*
//SYSUT1   DD DSN=WYL.QB.JCL.POLYFILE,
//            DISP=(OLD,CATLG),
//            UNIT=DISK,
//            VOL=SER=WYL002
//SYSUT2   DD SYSOUT=A,DCB=(RECFM=FB,LRECL=86,BLKSIZE=860)
//
     1     //JCLQB033 JOB ,'J.C.LEWIS',                                          *
           // REGION=40K,                                                        *
           // TIME=(0,5)
           //***
           //*** USING IEBGENER TO LIST A DISK DATA SET
           //*** WITH CONTROL CARDS TO FORMAT THE OUTPUT
           //***
     2     //LIST     EXEC PGM=IEBGENER
     3     //SYSPRINT DD SYSOUT=A
     4     //SYSIN DD *,DCB=BLKSIZE=80
     5     //SYSUT1   DD DSN=WYL.QB.JCL.POLYFILE,
           //            DISP=(OLD,CATLG),
           //            UNIT=DISK,
           //            VOL=SER=WYL002
     6     //SYSUT2   DD SYSOUT=A,DCB=(RECFM=FB,LRECL=86,BLKSIZE=860)
           //

IEF142I JCLQB033 LIST - STEP WAS EXECUTED - COND CODE 0000
IEF285I  LIST.SYSPRINT                                     SYSOUT
IEF285I  JESI0001                                          SYSIN
IEF285I  WYL.QB.JCL.POLYFILE                               CATALOGED    ────▶   ( POLYFILE cataloged )
IEF285I  VOL SER NOS= WYL002.
IEF285I  SYSCTLG.VWYL001                                   KEPT
IEF285I  VOL SER NOS= WYL001.
IEF285I  LIST.SYSUT2                                       SYSOUT

** START - JOB=JCLQB033        DATE=12/29/81    CLOCK=11.19.02
** END   -                     DATE=12/29/81    CLOCK=11.19.09    CPU TIME =    0 MIN   0.07 SEC   **
```
(Total CPU time)

90

```
DATA SET UTILITY - GENERATE
GENERATE MAXFLDS=13,
         MAXLITS=42
RECORD FIELD=(5,1,,1),
       FIELD=(7,,,6),
       FIELD=(20,6,,13),
       FIELD=(7,,,33),
       FIELD=(1,29,,40),
       FIELD=(7,,,41),
       FIELD=(6,30,,48),
       FIELD=(7,,,54),
       FIELD=(4,36,,61),
       FIELD=(7,,,65),
       FIELD=(6,40,,72),
       FIELD=(7,,,78),
       FIELD=(2,50,,85)
```

Listing of control statements

PROCESSING ENDED AT EOD

13009	REED, TINA	A	084200	0426	072100	74
15174	HANDJANY, HAIDEH	H	022900	0220	022900	71
17337	BUTERO, MAURICE	H	050100	0434	050100	63
19499	LAFER, BRUCE	A	070600	0819	050000	52
21661	LEE, SUI	A	039017	0303	030017	76
23821	COOPER, LUCY	L	074500	0730	070000	64
25980	NELSON, LAWRENCE	L	051300	0217	051300	78
28138	KRUKIS, SONIA	A	034600	0510	034600	59
30295	CHEN, YIN	H	029500	0514	010000	81
32451	SIMPKINS, KEVIN	L	038800	0321	038806	76
34605	PORTER, MICHELE	A	062750	0128	042700	65
36759	DECICCO, RICHARD	A	025500	0619	010000	71
38912	ABREU, JUANITA	H	073200	1030	070000	80
41063	HIGH, CAROL	L	031100	0521	031100	82
43214	ENGLISH, REYNOLDS	A	044300	0228	043300	82
45363	LEE, BOHYON	A	051500	0214	050000	79
47512	THOMPSON, STANLEY	H	064075	0307	064075	66
49659	VALDEZ, FÁBIO	L	070600	0430	070600	71
51805	AMATO, ROBERT	A	046600	0417	015000	63
53950	RIZZUTO, JAMES	A	069300	0822	000000	81
56094	SCHWARTZ, MICHAEL	H	103700	0605	050000	67
58238	RUFINO, CARLOS	L	067300	0520	047300	64
60380	MORLEY, JOHN	A	078600	0514	078600	71
62521	BREVIL, JAMES	H	081200	0314	081200	55
64660	FALCONER, EDWARD	L	108000	0227	008000	74
66799	MARTIN, KATHLEEN	L	089500	0129	089500	65
68937	YEUNG, SUK	A	051700	0816	050000	49
71074	PAUL, MARINA	A	044100	0414	034100	80
73210	FRADIN, SHIRLEY	L	066800	0728	066800	56
75344	BURNS, JEFFREY	L	070600	0226	070000	57

added to POLYFILE, the whole data set should be listed. The system flow-chart for this job is shown in Figure 4.8. The vertical line shows the order in which the steps should be executed.

Neither of these tasks is difficult. Adding records to an existing data set requires a small change in the DISP parameter, and listing a disk data set is the problem we just solved. Instead of using IEBGENER to list the data set, however, we will use a different IBM utility program named IEBPTPCH.

Using IEBPTPCH

IEBPTPCH, which is usually pronounced "IEB print-punch," is an IBM utility program used to print or punch data sets. You already know how to use IEBGENER to print a data set, but IEBPTPCH was designed for this purpose and can do some things that IEBGENER cannot do.

IEBPTPCH uses the same four data sets IEBGENER does: SYSPRINT for messages, SYSIN for control statements, SYSUT1 for the input file, and SYSUT2 for the output file. SYSUT2 should always be directed to either the

Figure 4.8

System Flowchart to Add Records to POLYFILE and List It

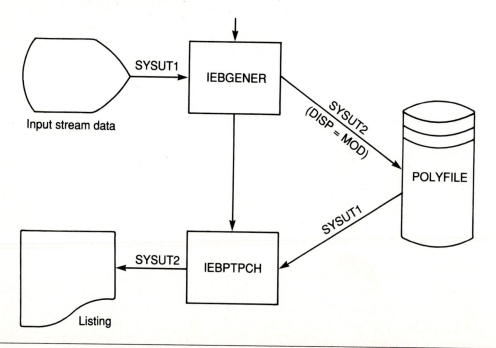

printer, which is usually `SYSOUT=A`, or the punch, which is usually `SYS-OUT=B`.

IEBPTPCH Control Statements. Remember that when `IEBGENER` is used to make an unedited copy of a data set, no control statements are required. Unfortunately, `IEBPTPCH` always requires at least one control statement.

The control statements for `IEBPTPCH` are `PRINT`, `PUNCH`, `TITLE`, `MEMBER`, and `RECORD`. The parameters for the `PRINT` and `PUNCH` statements are described in Table 4.2, and the `TITLE`, `MEMBER`, and `RECORD` statements are described in Table 4.3. `PRINT` specifies that the data are to be printed and `PUNCH` that they are to be punched. `TITLE` specifies that a title is to be printed, `MEMBER` specifies that a member of a library is to be printed or punched (we will study libraries in Chapter 5), and `RECORD` specifies the editing that is to be performed.

Every execution of `IEBPTPCH` must include either a `PRINT` or a `PUNCH` control statement, and it must be the first statement. The other statements are optional, but if they are used they must be coded in the following order: `TITLE`, `MEMBER`, `RECORD`.

The PRINT Statement. You can print a data set by coding the `PRINT` statement with no parameters:

```
PRINT
```

No other control statements are required. The format rules that you learned in the section on control statement format apply to `IEBPTPCH` control statements. Therefore `PRINT` must not begin in the first column. `IEBPTPCH` does not require a nonblank character in column 72 of a continued statement.

If you use the simple `PRINT` control statement to print a data set, the output will be printed in groups of eight characters separated by two blanks. The first fifteen records from `POLYFILE` printed in this format are shown in Figure 4.9. As you can see, the inserted blanks make the output difficult to read. To get output that is easier to read, you have to use the `RECORD` statement to edit the output. You will see how to do that later.

Notice the asterisks at the end of each line and the double asterisk at the end of the tenth line in Figure 4.9. If no editing is done, `IEBPTPCH` prints an asterisk at the end of each logical record and a double asterisk at the end of each block.

You should know about another nice feature of `IEBPTPCH`. When the input record length is greater than the length of the printer line and no editing is done, `IEBPTPCH` prints the whole record, using as many lines as necessary. `IEBGENER`, on the other hand, prints whatever will fit on one line and discards the rest of the record.

The parameters that may be coded on a `PRINT` statement are shown in

Parameters for the IEBPTPCH PRINT and PUNCH Control Statements

Parameter	Control Statement PRINT	PUNCH	Meaning
PREFORM={A|M}	Yes	Yes	Specifies that the first character of each record is a control character. A means that the control character is an ASA character, and M means that it is a machine-code character. If PREFORM is coded, all other operands and control statements are ignored.
TYPORG={PS|PO}	Yes	Yes	Specifies the organization of the input data set. PS means sequential, and PO means partitioned. Default is PS.
TOTCONV={XE|PZ}	Yes	Yes	Specifies that the data are to be converted before being printed or punched. XE means that the data are to be converted to hexadecimal, and PZ means that packed data are to be unpacked. If TOTCONV is omitted, no conversion is done.
CNTRL=a	Yes	Yes	For printing, specifies line spacing: a=1 is single spacing a=2 is double spacing a=3 is triple spacing For punching, specifies stacker, either 1 or 2. Default is 1.
STRTAFT=b	Yes	Yes	Skip b records before starting printing or punching.
STOPAFT=c	Yes	Yes	c is the number of records to be printed or punched.
SKIP=d	Yes	Yes	Print or punch every dth record.
MAXNAME=e	Yes	Yes	e is greater than or equal to the number of MEMBER statements that follow.
MAXFLDS=f	Yes	Yes	f is greater than or equal to the number of FIELD parameters in the following RECORD statements.
INITPG=g	Yes	No	g is the initial page number. Default is 1.
MAXLINE=h	Yes	No	h is the maximum number of lines printed on a page. Default is 60.

Cont.

Table 4.2 (Cont.)

Parameter	Control Statement PRINT	Control Statement PUNCH	Meaning
CDSEQ=i	No	Yes	i is the initial sequence number punched in columns 73 through 80. If CDSEQ is not coded, the cards are not numbered.
CDINCR=j	No	Yes	j is the increment used to generate sequence numbers. Default is 10.

Table 4.3
The IEBPTPCH TITLE, MEMBER, and RECORD Control Statements

Control Statement	Parameter	Meaning
TITLE	ITEM=('title', output-location)	'title' is the title to be printed on each page. 'title' may not be longer than 40 bytes.
		output-location is the byte position in the output record where the title is to start. Default is 1.
MEMBER	NAME=name	name is the name of the member of a partitioned data set that is to be printed or punched.
RECORD	FIELD=(length, input-location, conversion, output-location)	length is the length, in bytes, of the input field to be processed.
		input-location is the starting byte of the input field to be processed. Default is 1.
		conversion is the type of conversion to be done to the field. PZ causes packed data to be unpacked, and XE causes data to be converted to hexadecimal. If it is omitted, no conversion is done.
		output-location specifies the starting location of this field in the output record. Default is 1.

**The First Fifteen Records of POLYFILE Printed by IEBPTPCH
Using a PRINT Control Statement**

```
13009REE  D,TINA          A084  20004260  72100  74  *
15174HAN  DJANY,HA  IDEH  H022  90002200  22900  71  *
17337BUT  ERO,MAUR  ICE   H050  10004340  50100  63  *
19499LAF  ER,BRUCE        A070  60008190  50000  52  *
21661LEE  ,SUI            A039  01703030  30017  76  *
23821COO  PER,LUCY        L074  50007300  70000  64  *
25980NEL  SON,LAWR  ENCE  L051  30002170  51300  78  *
28138KRU  KIS,SONI  A     L034  60005100  34600  59  *
30295CHE  N,YIN           H029  50005140  10000  81  *
32451SIM  PKINS,KE  VIN   L038  80003210  38806  76  **
34605POR  TER,MICH  ELE   A062  75001280  42700  65  *
36759DEC  ICCO,RIC  HARD  A025  50006190  10000  71  *
38912ABR  EU,JUANI  TA    H073  20010300  70000  80  *
41063HIG  H,CAROL         L031  10005210  31100  82  *
43214ENG  LISH,REY  NOLDS A044  30002280  43300  82  *
```

Table 4.2. You can have the data set printed in hexadecimal by using the following control statement:

```
PRINT TOTCONV=XE
```

Figure 4.10 shows the first five records of POLYFILE printed in hexadecimal. Because it takes two hexadecimal digits to represent one byte, a record could not fit on one line. Using the EBCDIC code in Table 1.2, you could easily interpret Figure 4.10. You would print a data set in hexadecimal if it contained data that were not character data or if you didn't know what it contained. Printing a data set in hexadecimal allows you to see exactly what's there.

The RECORD Statement.   To eliminate the blanks that IEBPTPCH inserts after every eight characters, you have to edit the output, using the FIELD parameter of the RECORD statement. Fortunately, as Table 4.3 shows, the FIELD parameter for IEBPTPCH works very much like the FIELD parameter for IEBGENER, in which you are by now an expert. The only difference is that with IEBGENER you can move a literal to the output area, whereas with IEBPTPCH you are not permitted to do so.

Assuming the logical record length is 80, you can prevent IEBPTPCH from inserting blanks by using the following statement:

```
RECORD FIELD=(80,1,,1)
```

This RECORD statement instructs IEBPTPCH to treat the whole input record as one field, starting at input byte 1 for a length of 80 bytes, and to print it, starting at output byte 1, with no conversion. Alternatively, this RECORD statement could be written in the simpler form

```
RECORD FIELD=(80)
```

with default values used for the starting bytes for the input and the output. (You might think that because this FIELD parameter contains only one positional subparameter, you could code this statement without the parentheses. The rule that the parentheses may be omitted when there is only one positional subparameter applies to JCL statements, however, not utility control statements. The parentheses are required in utility control statements.)

The following control statements prevent IEBPTPCH from inserting blanks and show how the STRTAFT, SKIP, and STOPAFT parameters work:

```
PRINT MAXFLDS=1,                                          *
              STRTAFT=5,                                   *
              SKIP=2,                                      *
              STOPAFT=4
RECORD FIELD=(80)
```

Notice that the MAXFLDS parameter is coded on the PRINT statement. MAXFLDS is required because of the FIELD parameter on the RECORD state-

Figure 4.10

The First Five Records of POLYFILE Printed by IEBPTPCH in Hexadecimal

```
F1F3F0F0  F9D9C5C5  C46BE3C9  D5C14040  40404040  40404040  40404040  C1F0F8F4  F2F0F0F0  F4F2F6F0  F7F2F1F0  F0404040
40F7F440  40404040  40404040  40404040  40404040  40404040  40404040  40404040*
F1F5F1F7  F4C8C1D5  C4D1C1D5  E86BC8C1  C9C4C5C8  40404040  40404040  C8F0F2F2  F9F0F0F0  F2F2F0F0  F2F2F9F0  F0404040
40F7F140  40404040  40404040  40404040  40404040  40404040  40404040  40404040*
F1F7F3F3  F7C2E4E3  C5D9D66B  D4C1E4D9  C9C3C540  40404040  40404040  C8F0F5F0  F1F0F0F0  F4F3F4F0  F5F0F1F0  F0404040
40F6F340  40404040  40404040  40404040  40404040  40404040  40404040  40404040*
F1F9F4F9  F9D3C1C6  C5D96BC2  D9E4C3C5  40404040  40404040  40404040  C1F0F7F0  F6F0F0F0  F8F1F9F0  F5F0F0F0  F0404040
40F5F240  40404040  40404040  40404040  40404040  40404040  40404040  40404040*
F2F1F6F6  F1D3C5C5  6BE2E4C9  40404040  40404040  40404040  40404040  C1F0F3F9  F0F1F7F0  F3F0F3F0  F3F0F0F1  F7404040
40F7F640  40404040  40404040  40404040  40404040  40404040  40404040  40404040*
```

■ **Figure 4.11** ━━━━━━━━━━━━━━━━━━━━━━━━━━━━━━━

Selected, Edited Records of POLYFILE Printed by IEBPTPCH

```
25980NELSON,LAWRENCE          L0513000217051300      78
30295CHEN,YIN                 H0295000514010000      81
34605PORTER,MICHELE           A0627500128042700      65
38912ABREU,JUANITA            H0732001030070000      80
```

ment. MAXFLDS works exactly the same way for IEBPTPCH as it does for IEBGENER, specifying the number of FIELD parameters on the following RECORD statement.

The output produced when these control statements are applied to POLY-FILE is shown in Figure 4.11. The STRTAFT=5 parameter causes the first five records to be skipped; the SKIP=2 parameter causes every second record to be printed, starting with the seventh record; and the STOPAFT=4 parameter causes the printing to stop after four records have been printed. The STRTAFT, SKIP, and STOPAFT parameters are useful when you have a large data set and want to print only a sample of the records.

The control statements required to print POLYFILE with seven spaces between the fields are shown in Figure 4.12. The RECORD statement in Figure 4.12 is the same as the RECORD statement used with IEBGENER in Figure 4.6, except that the FIELD parameters that move spaces to the output record have been deleted; with IEBPTPCH you may not specify a literal as part of the FIELD parameter. Remember that when we used IEBGENER to print POLY-FILE, we had to move spaces to the unused parts of the output record. With IEBPTPCH that is not necessary, because IEBPTPCH automatically moves spaces to the unused part of the output record. As a result, in Figure 4.12 we

■ **Figure 4.12** ━━━━━━━━━━━━━━━━━━━━━━━━━━━━━━━

IEBPTPCH Control Statements to Print Titles and Insert Seven Blanks Between Fields in POLYFILE

```
PRINT MAXFLDS=7
TITLE ITEM=('LISTING OF POLYFILE WITH ADDED RECORDS',25)
TITLE ITEM=('NUMBER              NAME                TY'),        *
            ITEM=('PE      PREMIUM      DUE DATE     YTD PMTS',41),  *
            ITEM=('YEAR',84)
RECORD FIELD=(5,1,,1),                                            *
            FIELD=(20,6,,13),                                     *
            FIELD=(1,29,,40),                                     *
            FIELD=(6,30,,48),                                     *
            FIELD=(4,36,,61),                                     *
            FIELD=(6,40,,72),                                     *
            FIELD=(2,50,,85)
```

need only seven FIELD parameters, whereas in Figure 4.6 we needed thirteen.

The TITLE Statement.   Figure 4.12 also illustrates the use of the TITLE statement. The TITLE statement causes a title to be printed on each page of output. A maximum of two TITLE statements may be coded, to print a title and a subtitle. The title in each ITEM parameter may be no longer than 40 characters. As the second TITLE statement shows, longer titles may be created by using more than one ITEM parameter. The number following the title specifies the position in the print line where the title starts printing. In this example, coding 25 for this number in the first TITLE statement roughly centers the title.

The PUNCH Statement.   So far all the examples have involved printing a data set. In order to have a data set punched, only two changes are required: the SYSUT2 data set must be directed to the punch, usually by coding SYS-OUT=B, and the PRINT control statement must be replaced by the PUNCH control statement. When punching a data set, IEBPTPCH does not insert blanks, the way it does when printing. So the simple control statement

```
PUNCH
```

may be used to punch a data set.

If desired, parameters may be coded on the PUNCH statement. As Table 4.2 shows, many of the same parameters may be coded for both the PRINT and the PUNCH statement. In addition, when a data set is punched, sequence numbers can be punched in columns 73 through 80. (Of course, you would punch sequence numbers in columns 73 through 80 only if those columns didn't already contain data.) The initial sequence number is specified by coding CDSEQ=number, and the increment to be used between sequence numbers is specified by coding CDINCR=increment. So the control statement

```
PUNCH CDSEQ=1000,                                              *
            CDINCR=100
```

will cause IEBPTPCH to punch a data set with sequence number 00001000 in columns 73 through 80 on the first card, sequence number 00001100 on the second card, and so on.

The MEMBER Statement.   Because it is used with libraries, the MEMBER statement will be discussed in Chapter 5.

Comparing IEBGENER and IEBPTPCH.   Now that you know two IBM utilities that can be used to print or punch data sets, you might wonder which one you should use. The answer depends on what you want to do.

If you want a simple listing or punching of a data set and if the logical record length of the data set is not greater than the length of the output device (typically 132 bytes for the printer and 80 bytes for the punch), IEBGENER is easier to use because it does not require any control statements. If the logical record length of the data set exceeds the length of the output device, however, IEBGENER will truncate the record, whereas IEBPTPCH will use as many lines or cards as necessary to print or punch the whole record.

If you want to edit the record, IEBPTPCH is easier to use because you do not have to move spaces to unused portions of the output record. Finally, if you want to print a title, or control the number of lines printed per page, or print or punch selected records, or punch sequence numbers, or in general use any of the parameters listed in Table 4.2, you must use IEBPTPCH.

Appendix F contains a listing of commonly required functions and the utilities that may be used to perform them. As Appendix F shows, it is common for several utilities to perform similar functions.

The Complete Job Stream

Now that you understand how to use IEBPTPCH, we can get back to the original problem, which was to add records to POLYFILE and to list the whole data set. (The system flowchart for this problem was shown in Figure 4.8.) We can both add records and list the data set in one job. The job stream is shown in Figure 4.13.

This job stream contains only one JOB statement, so you know that it contains only one job. It contains two EXEC statements, however, so one job contains two job steps. The name of the first step is ADD, and the name of the second step is LIST. This is the first job stream you have seen that contains more than one job step, but in practice jobs that contain several steps are much more common than jobs that contain only one step.

Notice how the job stream is arranged. The JOB statement must always be the first statement. Following the JOB statement is the first EXEC statement, along with the DD statements that that EXEC statement requires. In Figure 4.13, the first EXEC statement causes IEBGENER to be executed, and following that EXEC statement are the familiar SYSPRINT, SYSIN, SYSUT1, and SYSUT2 DD statements.

The second step has the same arrangement: an EXEC statement followed by the DD statements that the EXEC statement requires. In Figure 4.13 the second EXEC statement causes IEBPTPCH to be executed. It is just a coincidence that the four DD statements required by IEBPTPCH have the same ddnames as the four DD statements required by IEBGENER. If the job had additional steps, they would follow the same pattern.

Now let's examine some of the interesting parts of Figure 4.13 more closely.

━━ **Figure 4.13** ━━━

Job Stream to Add Records to a Disk Data Set and List It

```
//JCLQB057 JOB ,'J.C.LEWIS',
//              REGION=40K,
//              TIME=(0,5)
//*
//* A TWO STEP JOB TO ADD RECORDS TO A DATA SET
//* AND THEN TO LIST IT
//*
//* STEP 1 USING IEBGENER TO ADD RECORDS
//ADD       EXEC PGM=IEBGENER
//SYSPRINT DD SYSOUT=A
//SYSIN     DD DUMMY
//SYSUT1    DD *
77478KATZ,HAL              A0485000406038500     64
79610WRIGHT,DONNA         H0926000901092000     75
81742CUOMO,DONNA          L0900000313090000     69
83872LOPEZ,ANNA           A0679000716010000     80
86002ALEXANDER,LISA       A0402000623030200     73
88130GOLDBERG,LORI        H0987000524095000     67    Records to be added
92057HOFMANN,PATRICA      H0737000315040000     77
92384PUGH,CLIFFORD        A0750000423075000     80
94509FERRIS,LAURA         A0135000815013500     73
96633BERGIN,MICHAEL       L1608000116100000     74
//SYSUT2    DD DSN=WYL.QB.JCL.POLYFILE,
//              DISP=(MOD,PASS)
//*
//* STEP 2 USING IEBPTPCH TO LIST THE DATA SET
//*
//LIST      EXEC PGM=IEBPTPCH,
//              COND=(4,LT)
//SYSPRINT DD SYSOUT=A
//SYSIN     DD *
 PRINT MAXFLDS=7
 TITLE ITEM=('LISTING OF POLYFILE WITH ADDED RECORDS',25)
 TITLE ITEM=('NUMBER            NAME                   TY'),        *
              ITEM=('PE     PREMIUM     DUE DATE     YTD PMTS',41), *
              ITEM=('YEAR',84)
 RECORD FIELD=(5,1,,1),                                             *
              FIELD=(20,6,,13),                                     *
              FIELD=(1,29,,40),                                     *
              FIELD=(6,30,,48),                                     *
              FIELD=(4,36,,61),                                     *
              FIELD=(6,40,,72),                                     *
              FIELD=(2,50,,85)
//SYSUT1    DD DSN=WYL.QB.JCL.POLYFILE,
//              DISP=(OLD,KEEP)
//SYSUT2    DD SYSOUT=A
//
```

Accessing a Cataloged Data Set

The ADD step is similar to the one that was used in Figure 3.4 to create POLYFILE. In this case, however, the SYSUT2 DD statement is simpler, because now POLYFILE exists and is cataloged. To access a cataloged data set, you need code only the DSN and DISP parameters. Notice that we don't have to do anything special to indicate that POLYFILE is cataloged. When the system notices that we have not coded the unit and volume information, it assumes that POLYFILE must be cataloged, so it automatically accesses the catalog to determine the unit and volume information.

Adding Records to a Data Set

[handwritten annotation: Line 12 // SYSUT2 DD DSN = WYL.AB.BWD. Andrea ,]

The DISP parameter involves coding that is new to you:

```
DISP=(MOD,PASS)
```

A value of MOD coded for the status subparameter means that the data set exists and that new records are going to be added to the end of it. If we ran this job with the status subparameter equal to OLD, the new records would be written to the beginning of the data set and the original data would be lost.

Passing a Data Set

A value of PASS coded for the normal-disposition subparameter means that at the end of the current job step, the data set will be passed to a later step. Whenever a data set will be used in a later step, it is better to code PASS rather than KEEP as the normal disposition. If a data set is passed, the system remembers the unit and volume information and that information is available when the data set is used in a later step. Therefore, when you refer to a "passed" data set, you do not have to code the UNIT or VOL parameters. On the other hand, when you refer to a "kept" data set, unless it is cataloged you do have to code UNIT and VOL parameters. Even with a cataloged data set, if the data set is used in a later step, it is better to code PASS rather than KEEP. If you code KEEP, the system has to refer to the catalog to determine the unit and volume information. By coding PASS you can avoid that extra reference to the catalog.

There is an additional advantage to coding PASS when the data set resides on tape. As mentioned in Chapter 3, if KEEP is coded, the tape reel is rewound and unloaded. When the data set is used in a later step, the operator must load the tape again. If PASS is coded, the tape is rewound but not unloaded, so it is ready to be used by a later step.

POLYFILE, which is passed by the SYSUT2 DD statement in the first step, is received by the SYSUT1 DD statement in the second step. For a passed data set that is being received, you code the DSN and DISP parameters just as you do for a cataloged data set. The status of a received data set is OLD, SHR, or MOD, all of which mean that the data set existed before the current job step began. Even if a data set is created in one job step and passed to a later step, by the time the data set is received in the later step it already exists, so in the later step the status is OLD, MOD, or SHR.

A data set may be passed through several job steps. In each step that uses the data set, you code PASS as the normal disposition. In the last step that uses the data set, you specify the final disposition of the data set, which could be DELETE, KEEP, CATLG, or UNCATLG. For POLYFILE a final disposition of KEEP is coded. As explained earlier, it is not necessary to code CATLG. POLYFILE was cataloged in a previous job; it does not need to be cataloged every time it is used. It will remain cataloged until a disposition of UNCATLG or DELETE is coded.

No abnormal disposition is coded for POLYFILE, which means that the default value is used. As discussed in Chapter 3, the default value for the abnormal disposition is the value coded for the normal disposition. If the first step were to abend, POLYFILE would be passed to the second step. If a step abends, however, the following steps usually are not executed. (The conditions under which the following steps are executed are discussed in the next section.) Therefore, if the first step abended, the second step would not be executed and POLYFILE would be a passed data set that was never received. The final disposition of a passed data set that is never received depends on its original status. If its original status is OLD, the data set is kept. That is POLYFILE's situation, so it would be kept. If its original status is NEW, the data set is deleted. If, however, any step specifies KEEP or CATLG rather than PASS for the normal disposition and the data set is subsequently passed and not received, it is kept.

You should not be surprised that in Figure 4.13 the ddname of POLYFILE is different in the two steps. In the first step POLYFILE is the output data set from IEBGENER, so its ddname is SYSUT2. In the second step POLYFILE is the input data set to IEBPTPCH, so its ddname is SYSUT1. Both these names are shown in the system flowchart in Figure 4.8. As mentioned earlier, the only name permanently associated with a data set is the data set name.

Using IEBPTPCH to List a Data Set

The IEBPTPCH control statements in Figure 4.13 were shown in Figure 4.12 and were discussed earlier. Notice that we did not have to code a DCB parameter for the SYSUT2 DD statement in the LIST step, as we did in Figure 4.6 when we used IEBGENER to produce an edited listing of POLYFILE. Unlike IEBGENER, IEBPTPCH does not copy DCB information for SYSUT2 from SYSUT1. Instead IEBPTPCH uses LRECL default values of 121 for printing and 81 for punching. If you wanted to print more than 121 characters on a line (many printers allow lines of up to 133 characters), you would code a DCB on

Table 4.4

Operators That May Be Used with the COND Parameter

Operator	Meaning	Flip Side of Operator	Opposite Operator
GT	Greater than	LT	LE
GE	Greater than or equal to	LE	LT
EQ	Equal to	EQ	NE
NE	Not equal to	NE	EQ
LT	Less than	GT	GE
LE	Less than or equal to	GE	GT

the SYSUT2 DD statement to override the default value. The LRECL you specify must be at least one greater than the length of the record you want to print, because IEBPTPCH adds one byte to the record for carriage control.

Controlling Step Execution — The COND Parameter

In Chapter 2 you learned that programs can provide a return code, and that for IBM utilities and compilers a return code of 0 means that the program ran successfully, 4 signifies that minor errors occurred, and 8, 12, and 16 indicate that progressively more serious errors occurred.

The COND parameter offers a method of testing the return codes issued by the previous steps to determine whether a step will be executed. The format of a simplified version of the COND parameter is

```
COND=(value,operator)
```

value is a number between 0 and 4095, and operator is one of the symbols in Table 4.4. The COND parameter causes the value you enter to be tested against the return codes from the previous steps, using the operator you choose. If the test condition is true, the step is skipped. If the test condition is false, the step is executed.*

For example, the EXEC statement of the LIST step has the COND parameter

```
COND=(4,LT)
```

This coding is interpreted as follows: If 4 is less than the return code from the previous step, skip this step. In other words, skip this step if the return code is 8, 12, or 16. One reason for coding a COND parameter is to avoid wasting

---

* One way to remember this rule is to think of the king pronouncing sentence: "Execute the liar."

computer time. In Figure 4.13, if the ADD step encountered serious errors, there would be no point in executing the LIST step.

Many students find the operation of the COND parameter confusing. It is often helpful to write the COND parameter as an IF statement. For example, if we let RC stand for the return code from the ADD step, the COND parameter above is equivalent to the following IF statement:

```
IF  4  LT  RC
    THEN
        skip this step
    ELSE
        execute this step.
```

Expressed this way, the statement is fairly easy to interpret: If RC is 0, 1, 2, or 3, the LIST step will be executed; otherwise it will be skipped.

Notice that when a COND parameter is expressed as an IF statement, the number precedes the return code. Because conditions are usually expressed in the reverse order, you will sometimes have to reverse, or flip, a condition to get the correct COND operator. The reverses, or flip sides, of the operators are given in Table 4.4. For example, suppose we want to skip a step if the return code is greater than or equal to 8. To determine the coding of the COND parameter, we must flip this condition. Table 4.4 shows that the flip side of GE is LE, so we flip the condition to "skip the step if 8 is less than or equal to the return code." Stated this way, the condition is easy to code correctly:

```
COND=(8,LE)
```

Another complication is that instead of knowing the conditions under which a step should be skipped, you will sometimes know only the conditions under which a step should be executed. For example, suppose we want to execute a step only if the return code is less than 12. Getting the correct COND parameter requires two steps. First, we must flip the condition, as we did in the preceding paragraph, to get the new condition "execute the step if 12 is greater than the return code." Second, we must take the opposite operator to get the conditions under which the step should be skipped. The opposite operators are given in Table 4.4, which shows that the opposite of GT is LE. So we finally express the condition as "skip this step if 12 is less than or equal to the return code," from which we easily get the correct coding:

```
COND=(12,LE)
```

If there is more than one previous step, the return code from each of the previous steps is separately tested. If any of the tests are true, the step is skipped. Thus the parameter

```
COND=(612,GE)
```

might read as "if 612 is greater than or equal to the return code from any previous steps, skip this step." Although the return codes issued by utilities and compilers are 0, 4, 8, 12, and 16, you may recall from Chapter 2 that in your programs you can set the return code to any value between 0 and 4095.

You may code more than one test, up to a maximum of eight separate tests, as in

```
COND=((2,EQ),(8,LT))
```

When more than one test is coded, all the tests must be enclosed in parentheses. If any of the tests are true, the step will be skipped. In this example, the step will be skipped if 2 is equal to the return code or if 8 is less than the return code. (This is the Boolean or.) That is, the step will be executed only if the return codes from the previous steps are 0, 1, 3, 4, 5, 6, 7, or 8. We can still rewrite the COND tests as an IF statement:

```
IF (2 EQ RC) OR (8 LT RC)
    THEN
         skip this step
    ELSE
         execute this step.
```

Determining when the condition in the IF statement is true is now more complicated, however.

In analyzing these more complicated cases, it is helpful to use the numerical values coded in the COND parameter to divide the possible return codes (0–4095) into a set of ranges. Then each range can be tested separately. For example, in the case of COND=((2,EQ),(8,LT)), we can construct the following table.

Value of RC	2 EQ RC	8 LT RC	Result
0–1	False	False	Execute step.
2	True	False	Skip step.
3–7	False	False	Execute step.
8	False	False	Execute step.
9–4095	False	True	Skip step.

You must be careful when you code more than one test, because it is easy to code incompatible tests that prevent the step from ever being executed. For example, if

```
COND=((4,LT),(8,GT))
```

is coded, the step will never be allowed to execute.

A more elaborate version of the COND parameter allows us to specify a stepname. The format is

```
COND=(value,operator,stepname)
```

Suppose you have a six-step job, in which the steps are named STEP1, STEP2, STEP3, etc. On the STEP5 EXEC statement, you might code

```
COND=((0,NE,STEP1),(4,EQ,STEP2),(8,LT))
```

This parameter means that if 0 is not equal to the return code from STEP1 or 4 is equal to the return code from STEP2 or 8 is less than the return code from any step, STEP5 is to be skipped. Notice again that if any of the tests are true, the step is skipped; all the tests must be false for the step to be executed.

Abnormal Termination — EVEN and ONLY.   Chapter 2 mentioned that some kinds of errors may cause a program to abnormally terminate, or abend. If one step of a multistep job abends, usually all the remaining steps are skipped. There may be cases, however, in which you want to execute a step even if a previous step abends. In other cases, you may want to execute a step only if a previous step abends. You can do this by coding EVEN or ONLY in the COND parameter as follows:

```
COND=EVEN
```

or

```
COND=ONLY
```

EVEN or ONLY counts as one of the eight possible tests in the COND parameter. As the names imply, EVEN causes a step to be executed even if a previous step abends, and ONLY causes a step to be executed only if a previous step abends. You may not code both EVEN and ONLY in the same COND parameter. As an illustration of when you might want to code EVEN or ONLY, consider the case where STEP1 updates a file, STEP2 removes the changes (backs out) from the file, and STEP3 lists the file. In this case, you would want STEP2 to execute only if STEP1 fails and STEP3 to execute no matter what happens. The code to accomplish this might appear as follows:

```
//          JOB
//STEP1     EXEC PGM=UPDATE
              .
              .
              .

//STEP2     EXEC PGM=BACKOUT,
//            .   COND=ONLY
              .
              .

//STEP3     EXEC PGM=LIST,
//            .   COND=EVEN
              .
              .
```

Table 4.5
Analysis of a Job Stream with Several COND Parameters

Input Stream	Analysis	Result	RC

`//TESTJOB JOB`
`//STEP1    EXEC PGM=A`
.
.
.
	No analysis; the first step is always executed.	Execute step.	8

`//STEP2    EXEC PGM=B,`
`//            COND=(4,LT)`
.
.
.
	Is 4 less than 8? Yes.	Skip step.	—

`//STEP3    EXEC PGM=C,`
`//            COND=(8,GT,STEP2)`
.
.
.
	Step 2 was skipped; test is ignored.	Execute step.	0

`//STEP4    EXEC PGM=D,`
`//            COND=(ONLY)`
.
.
.
	Did any previous step abend? No.	Skip step.	—

`//STEP5    EXEC PGM=E` . . .	No COND.	Execute step.	Abend

`//STEP6    EXEC PGM=F,`
`//            COND=((0,NE),EVEN)`
.
.
.
	Is 0 not equal to the return code from any previous step? Yes, 0 is not equal to 4, the return code from STEP1.	Skip step.	—

`//STEP7    EXEC PGM=G,` `//            COND=(8,GT)`	Is EVEN or ONLY coded? No.	Skip step.	—

Suppose STEP5 of the six-step job discussed earlier were coded

```
COND=((0,EQ,STEP4),EVEN)
```

Even when EVEN and ONLY are coded, the basic rule still applies: If any of the other tests are true, the step is skipped. With this coding, STEP5 will be skipped if STEP4 issues a return code of 0; under all other circumstances, even an abend, STEP5 will be executed.

If a step abends, causing later steps to be skipped, return codes are not issued for the skipped steps and any later tests that refer to a return code from a skipped step are ignored. For example, assume STEP1 abends, STEP2 is skipped, and STEP3 has the following COND:

```
COND=((0,EQ,STEP2),EVEN)
```

The test involving the return code from STEP2 is ignored, and the EVEN ensures that STEP3 will be executed. Neither EVEN nor ONLY may be coded with a stepname. An analysis of a job stream with several COND parameters is shown in Table 4.5.

Executing the Job Stream

The job stream in Figure 4.13 was executed and produced the output shown in Figure 4.14. You can see that each step has its own messages, showing the region used, the disposition of the data sets, the return code, etc. (Recall that the terms return code and condition code are used interchangeably.) IEBPTPCH used only 24K, and both steps issued return codes of 0000. In addition, there are START and END statements for the whole job, which show total CPU time used by the job. This job required only 0.11 second, so our time limit of 5 seconds was certainly generous. You can see that WYL.QB.JCL.POLYFILE was PASSED at the end of the ADD step and KEPT at the end of the LIST step.

The output also includes the familiar message from IEBGENER (PROCESS-ING ENDED AT EOD), the control statements for IEBPTPCH, and two messages from IEBPTPCH (EOF ON SYSIN, which means that all the control statements were read, and END OF DATA FOR SDS OR MEMBER, which corresponds to IEBGENER's PROCESSING ENDED AT EOD and means that the complete input data set was processed). **SDS** stands for sequential data set. You'll learn what MEMBER means in Chapter 5. Finally, you can see the edited listing of POLY-FILE, including the titles and the added records.

Parameters Common to the JOB and EXEC Statements

You have learned how to code the REGION and TIME parameters on the JOB statement and the COND parameters on the EXEC statement, but in fact all three parameters may be coded on either the JOB or the EXEC statements.

Figure 4.14

Output Produced by Executing the Job Stream in Figure 4.13

```
1    //JCLQB057 JOB ,'J.C.LEWIS',
     // REGION=40K,
     // TIME=(0,5)
     //***
     //*** A TWO STEP JOB TO ADD RECORDS TO A DATA SET
     //*** AND THEN TO LIST IT
     //***
     //*** STEP 1 USING IEBGENER TO ADD RECORDS
2    //ADD      EXEC PGM=IEBGENER
3    //SYSPRINT DD SYSOUT=A
4    //SYSIN    DD DUMMY
5    //SYSUT1   DD *,DCB=BLKSIZE=80
6    //SYSUT2   DD DSN=WYL.QB.JCL.POLYFILE,
     //         DISP=(MOD,PASS)
     //***
     //*** STEP 2 USING IEBPTPCH TO LIST THE DATA SET
     //***
7    //LIST     EXEC PGM=IEBPTPCH,
     //             COND=(4,LT)
8    //SYSPRINT DD SYSOUT=A
9    //SYSIN    DD *,DCB=BLKSIZE=80
10   //SYSUT1   DD DSN=WYL.QB.JCL.POLYFILE,
     //         DISP=(OLD,KEEP)
11   //SYSUT2   DD SYSOUT=A
```

```
IEF142I JCLQB057 ADD - STEP WAS EXECUTED - COND CODE 0000
IEF285I    ADD.SYSPRINT                              SYSOUT
IEF285I    JES0001                                   SYSIN
IEF285I    WYL.QB.JCL.POLYFILE                       PASSED
IEF285I    VOL SER NOS= WYL002.
IEF285I    SYSCTLG.VWYL001                           KEPT
IEF285I    VOL SER NOS= WYL001.

** START - STEP=ADD JOB=JCLQB057 DATE=12/29/81 CLOCK=14.45.05 PGM=IEBGENER REGION USED= 36K OF 40K **
** END  -              DATE=12/29/81 CLOCK=14.45.09 CPU TIME = 0 MIN 0.05 SEC     CC= 0  **
```

POLYFILE was PASSED

START and END messages for ADD step

Cont.

Figure 4.14 (Cont.)

```
IEF142I JCLQB057 LIST - STEP WAS EXECUTED - COND CODE 0000
IEF285I    LIST.SYSPRINT                              SYSOUT
IEF285I    JESI0002                                   SYSIN
IEF285I    WYL.QB.JCL.POLYFILE                        KEPT
IEF285I    VOL SER NOS= WYL002.
IEF285I    LIST.SYSUT2                                SYSOUT
```
POLYFILE was KEPT

```
** START - STEP=LIST JOB=JCLQB057 DATE=12/29/81 CLOCK=14.45.09 PGM=IEBPTPCH REGION USED= 24K OF 40K **
** END   -                       DATE=12/29/81 CLOCK=14.45.18 CPU TIME = 0 MIN 0.06 SEC       CC=0     **
```
START and END messages for LIST step

```
** START - JOB=JCLQB057      DATE=12/29/81      CLOCK=14.45.05
** END   -                   DATE=12/29/81      CLOCK=14.45.18      CPU TIME =    0 MIN    0.11 SEC   **
```
START and END messages for job

Total CPU time

```
DATA SET UTILITY - GENERATE

PROCESSING ENDED AT EOD

PRINT/PUNCH DATA SET UTILITY
PRINT MAXFLDS=7
TITLE ITEM=('LISTING OF POLYFILE WITH ADDED RECORDS',25)
TITLE ITEM=('NUMBER          NAME              DUE DATE     YTD PMTS',41),                    *
        ITEM=('PE      PREMIUM                                                    TY'),       *
        ITEM=('YEAR',84)
RECORD FIELD=(5,1,,1),
       FIELD=(20,6,,13),                                                                      *
       FIELD=(1,29,,40),                                                                      *
       FIELD=(6,30,,48),                                                                      *
       FIELD=(4,36,,61),                                                                      *
       FIELD=(6,40,,72),                                                                      *
       FIELD=(2,50,,85)

EOF ON SYSIN
END OF DATA FOR SDS OR MEMBER
```

Title   Title   PAGE 0001

LISTING OF POLYFILE WITH ADDED RECORDS

NUMBER	NAME	DUE DATE	YTD PMTS	TYPE	PREMIUM	YEAR
13009	REED,TINA	0426	072100	A	084200	74
15174	HANDJANY,HAIDEH	0220	022900	H	022900	71
17337	BUTERO,MAURICE	0434	050100	H	050100	63
19499	LAFER,BRUCE	0819	050000	A	070600	52
21661	LEE,SUI	0303	030017	A	039017	76

112

ID	Name					Grade
23821	COOPER, LUCY	L	074500	0730	070000	64
25980	NELSON, LAWRENCE	L	051300	0217	051300	78
28138	KRUKIS, SONIA	A	034600	0510	034600	59
30295	CHEN, YIN	H	029500	0514	010000	81
32451	SIMPKINS, KEVIN	L	038800	0321	038806	76
34605	PORTER, MICHELE	A	062750	0128	042700	65
36759	DECICCO, RICHARD	A	025500	0619	010000	71
38912	ABREU, JUANITA	H	073200	1030	070000	80
41063	HIGH, CAROL	L	031100	0521	031100	82
43214	ENGLISH, REYNOLDS	A	044300	0228	043300	82
45363	LEE, BOHYON	A	051500	0214	050000	79
47512	THOMPSON, STANLEY	H	064075	0307	064075	66
49659	VALDEZ, FABIO	L	070600	0430	070600	71
51805	AMATO, ROBERT	A	046600	0417	015000	63
53950	RIZZUTO, JAMES	A	069300	0822	000000	81
56094	SCHWARTZ, MICHAEL	H	103700	0605	050000	67
58238	RUFINO, CARLOS	L	067300	0520	047300	64
60380	MORLEY, JOHN	A	078600	0514	078600	71
62521	BREVIL, JAMES	H	081200	0314	081200	55
64660	FALCONER, EDWARD	L	108000	0227	008000	74
66799	MARTIN, KATHLEEN	L	089500	0129	089500	65
68937	YEUNG, SUK	A	051700	0816	050000	49
71074	PAUL, MARINA	A	044100	0414	034100	80
73210	FRADIN, SHIRLEY	L	066800	0728	066800	56
75344	BURNS, JEFFREY	L	070600	0226	070000	57
77478	KATZ, HAL	A	048500	0406	038500	64
79610	WRIGHT, DONNA	H	092600	0901	092000	75
81742	CUOMO, DONNA	L	090000	0313	090000	69
83872	LOPEZ, ANNA	A	067900	0716	010000	80
86002	ALEXANDER, LISA	A	040200	0623	030200	73
88130	GOLDBERG, LORI	H	098700	0524	095000	67
92057	HOFMANN, PATRICA	H	073700	0315	040000	77
92384	PUGH, CLIFFORD	A	075000	0423	075000	80
94509	FERRIS, LAURA	A	013500	0815	013500	73
96633	BERGIN, MICHAEL	L	160800	0116	100000	74

Added records

You learned earlier that when TIME is coded on the JOB statement, it specifies the maximum amount of time permitted for the job. When TIME is coded on an EXEC statement, it specifies the maximum amount of time permitted for that step. If TIME is coded on both the JOB and the EXEC statements, each step is limited to the amount of time specified on its EXEC statement and the whole job is limited to the amount of time specified on the JOB statement. If any step exceeds its limit or if the job as a whole exceeds its limit, the job is abnormally terminated.

When REGION is coded on an EXEC statement, it requests main storage for that step. If a job consists of several steps that require substantially different amounts of main storage, it is desirable to code REGION on the EXEC statements, so that each step gets the amount of main storage it requires. When REGION is coded on the JOB statement, the amount of main storage requested applies to the whole job. So if you code REGION on the JOB statement instead of on the EXEC statements, you must request the largest amount of space required by any of the steps. If you code REGION on both the JOB and the EXEC statements, the REGION parameters on the EXEC statements are ignored.

When COND is coded on the JOB statement, it applies to every step in the job. If the test condition specified is found to be true for any step, all the remaining steps are skipped. Suppose that you code

```
COND=(4,LE)
```

on the JOB statement for a five-step job. If the first step issues a return code of 8, all the remaining steps will be skipped.

If COND is coded on both the JOB and the EXEC statements, all tests are checked before a step is executed. If one of the test conditions coded on the JOB statement is true, the current step and all the remaining steps are skipped. If none of the test conditions coded on the JOB statement is true, the tests coded on the EXEC statement are checked. If any of these test conditions are true, the step is skipped.

Only the simple form of the COND parameter,

```
COND=(value,operator)
```

is legal on the JOB statement. You may not specify a stepname to restrict a test to the return code issued by a particular step, nor may you code EVEN or ONLY. You may, however, code up to eight tests.

Backward Reference

In Figure 4.13, when we wanted to refer to POLYFILE in the LIST step, we coded the DSN. There is another way we could have referred to POLYFILE; we could have used a technique known as **backward reference.** When you use a backward reference, you copy information from an earlier DD statement.

The `SYSUT1` DD statement in the `LIST` step could have been coded

```
//SYSUT1     DD  DSN=*.ADD.SYSUT2,
//               DISP=(OLD,KEEP)
```

This coding uses a backward reference to copy the DSN from the `SYSUT2` DD statement in the ADD step. One general form of a backward reference is

```
DSN=*.stepname.ddname
```

Notice especially the asterisk and the period.

If you make a backward reference to an earlier DD statement in the same step, you do not have to code the stepname. You can write

```
DSN=*.ddname
```

Copying DCB Information

You can also use a backward reference to copy DCB information. You could code

```
DCB=*.ddname
```

or

```
DCB=*.stepname.ddname
```

depending on whether the earlier DD statement was in the same step. When you copy DCB information using a backward reference, you may at the same time add or change DCB subparameters by coding them. For example,

```
DCB=(*.STEP1.MASTER,BLKSIZE=1600)
```

copies DCB information from the `MASTER` DD statement in `STEP1`, but changes (or adds) the `BLKSIZE` subparameter. When you code a backward reference with one or more subparameters, it is necessary to enclose all the values in parentheses.

It is important to understand that when you make a backward reference to a DD statement, the DCB information is copied from the DD statement, not from the data set's header label. Suppose you have

```
//STEP1      EXEC  PGM=PGM1
//MASTER     DD  DSN=SALEFILE,
//               DISP=(NEW,KEEP),
//               UNIT=DISK,
//               VOL=SER=DISK01,
//               SPACE=(TRK,10),
//               DCB=(RECFM=FB,LRECL=80,BLKSIZE=800)
             .
             .
             .
```

```
//STEP2      EXEC PGM=PGM2
//COPY       DD DSN=COPYFILE,
//              DISP=(NEW,PASS),
//              UNIT=DISK,
//              VOL=SER=DISK02,
//              SPACE=(TRK,10),
//              DCB=(*.STEP1.MASTER,BLKSIZE=1600)
```

This coding works fine. The system will copy the DCB for COPYFILE from the DCB on the MASTER DD statement, changing the BLKSIZE from 800 to 1600. But suppose SALEFILE is a cataloged data set. Then we might code the MASTER DD statement as follows:

```
//MASTER     DD DSN=SALEFILE,
//              DISP=OLD
```

In this case the backward reference will not work, because the MASTER DD statement does not contain a DCB parameter. The system knows SALEFILE's DCB information because it is contained in SALEFILE's header label, but the system does not examine the header label to obtain the DCB information for the backward reference; it examines only the JCL.

You can have the system copy DCB information from the header label of a cataloged data set, however. This is done by coding a reference to a data set name, rather than to a DD statement. For example, you could replace the backward reference for COPYFILE by coding

```
//              DCB=(SALEFILE,BLKSIZE=1600)
```

For a reference to a data set name to work, the referenced data set must be cataloged and must reside on a direct access volume, and the volume must be mounted before the step begins execution.

It is not necessary for the referenced data set to be used in the job stream. Even if SALEFILE were not used in an earlier step, the reference to the data set would work. This is convenient because it permits a computer center to create cataloged data sets that may be used as DCB patterns. For example, suppose programmers at a particular center frequently had to store 80-byte card images on a disk. Someone at the computer center could determine the optimal blocksize for such records. Then a data set could be cataloged that had a RECFM=FB, a LRECL=80, and a BLKSIZE equal to the optimal value. Assuming that data set were named CARDS, programmers could then copy the DCB values simply by coding in their job stream

```
//              DCB=CARDS
```

Copying Volume Information

You can also use a backward reference to specify a volume serial number. Suppose, for example, that you are creating a new data set and you want it to be placed on the same volume as an old data set. You could code

```
//OLD  DD    DSN=WYL.QB.JCL.OLD,
//              DISP=OLD,
//              VOL=SER=USR012,
//              UNIT=DISK
//NEW  DD    DSN=WYL.QB.JCL.NEW,
//              DISP=(NEW,KEEP),
//              VOL=REF=*.OLD,
//              SPACE=(TRK,10)
```

Notice that REF must be coded in a backward reference for VOL. This backward reference will cause WYL.QB.JCL.NEW to be put on disk pack USR012. When you use a backward reference to copy volume information, the system obtains unit information also, so it is not necessary to code the UNIT parameter.

If in the above example the OLD and NEW DD statements were not in the same step, the stepname would have to be included in the backward reference. So if the OLD DD statement were in a step named UPDATE, the backward reference would have to be

```
//        VOL=REF=*.UPDATE.OLD,
```

Just as for DCB information, you may also specify a volume serial number by coding a reference to a data set name. The referenced data set must be cataloged or passed. You could have a new data set put on the same volume as a cataloged data set named ACCOUNTS by coding

```
//        VOL=REF=ACCOUNTS
```

Notice that REF is required when you refer to a data set name, just as it is when you refer back to a DD statement.

Errors

Skipping a Step

In order to illustrate how the COND parameter works, the SYSIN DD statement was eliminated from the ADD step in Figure 4.13 and the job rerun. The output produced is shown in Figure 4.15. The missing SYSIN DD statement prevented IEBGENER from executing properly, and it issued a return code of 12. The COND parameter coded on the LIST EXEC statement specifies that the LIST step should be skipped if 0 is not equal to the return code issued by the previous step. Because 0 is not equal to 12, the LIST step was skipped. Notice how clear the message is:

```
STEP WAS NOT RUN BECAUSE OF CONDITION CODES
```

Output Produced by Executing a Job Stream That Contains a Syntax Error, Showing How the COND Parameter Causes a Step to Be Skipped

```
1     //JCLQB050 JOB ,'J.C.LEWIS',
      // REGION=40K,                                      *
      // TIME=(0,5)                                        *
      //***
      //*** A TWO STEP JOB TO ADD RECORDS TO A DATA SET
      //*** AND THEN TO LIST IT
      //***
      //*** STEP 1 USING IEBGENER TO ADD RECORDS
2     //ADD      EXEC PGM=IEBGENER
3     //SYSPRINT DD SYSOUT=A
4     //SYSUT1   DD *,DCB=BLKSIZE=80
5     //SYSUT2   DD DSN=WYL.QB.JCL.POLYFILE,
      //            DISP=(MOD,PASS)
      //***
      //*** STEP 2 USING IEBPTPCH TO LIST THE DATA SET
      //***
6     //LIST     EXEC PGM=IEBPTPCH,
      //            COND=(4,LT)
7     //SYSPRINT DD SYSOUT=A
8     //SYSIN    DD *,DCB=BLKSIZE=80
9     //SYSUT1   DD DSN=WYL.QB.JCL.POLYFILE,
      //            DISP=(OLD,KEEP)
10    //SYSUT2   DD SYSOUT=A
      //
```

```
IEC130I SYSIN    DD STATEMENT MISSING          ← Error message
IEF142I JCLQB050 ADD - STEP WAS EXECUTED - COND CODE 0012   ← Return code = 12
IEF285I ADD.SYSPRINT                            SYSOUT
IEF285I JESI0001                                SYSIN
IEF285I WYL.QB.JCL.POLYFILE                     PASSED   ← POLYFILE was PASSED
IEF285I VOL SER NOS= WYL002.
IEF285I SYSCTLG.VWYL001
IEF285I VOL SER NOS= WYL001.

** START - STEP=ADD JOB=JCLQB050 DATE=12/29/81 CLOCK=13.46.07 PGM=IEBGENER REGION USED= 32K OF 40K **
** END -                        DATE=12/29/81 CLOCK=13.46.11 CPU TIME = 0 MIN 0.03 SEC   CC= 12 **

IEF202I JCLQB050 LIST - STEP WAS NOT RUN BECAUSE OF CONDITION CODES  } LIST step skipped
IEF272I JCLQB050 LIST - STEP WAS NOT EXECUTED.
IEF285I WYL.QB.JCL.POLYFILE                     KEPT   ← POLYFILE was KEPT
IEF285I VOL SER NOS= WYL002.

** START - JOB=JCLQB050    DATE=12/29/81    CLOCK=13.46.07
** END -                  DATE=12/29/81    CLOCK=13.46.23 CPU TIME = 0 MIN 0.03 SEC **
```

For some reason, the system printed two almost identical messages about the LIST step's being skipped.

The system messages show that WYL.QB.JCL.POLYFILE was PASSED at the end of the ADD step. The LIST step that was supposed to receive it, however, was skipped. As you learned earlier in this chapter, in such cases data sets that existed before the job are kept. Because WYL.QB.JCL.POLY-FILE existed before the job, we would expect it to be kept, and the system messages at the end of the LIST step confirm that it was kept.

Abnormal Termination

In order to show you an abend, POLYFILE was misspelled as POLYFIEL on the SYSUT1 DD statement in Figure 4.6 and the job rerun. The output is shown in Figure 4.16. Notice that at this point POLYFILE has not yet been

■ **Figure 4.16** ■

Output Produced by Executing a Job Stream That Causes an Abend

```
IAT6140 JOB ORIGIN FROM GROUP=LOCAL    , DSP=IJP, DEVICE=INTRDR  , 000
14:57:11 IAT5200 JOB 5943 (JCLQB033) IN SETUP ON MAIN=M2
14:57:11 IAT5210 SYSUT1    USING D WYL002 ON 377   WYL.QB.JCL.POLYFIEL
14:57:11 IAT2000 JOB 5943 JCLQB033 SELECTED M2      GRP=BATCH
14:57:11
14:57:11 IATXXXX  ADJUSTED CPU TIME LIMIT FOR JOB JCLQB033 ON M2
14:57:11 IATXXXX                          IS    0 MIN 02 SEC
14:57:11
14:57:11 M2 R= JCLQB033 IEF403I JCLQB033 - STARTED
14:57:12 M2 R= JCLQB033 IEF450I JCLQB033 LIST - ABEND S213 U0000        (A)
14:57:12 M2 R= JCLQB033 IEF404I JCLQB033 - ENDED
    1    //JCLQB033 JOB ,'J.C.LEWIS',                                *
         // REGION=40K,                                             *
         // TIME=(0,5)
         ***
         *** USING IEBGENER TO LIST A DISK DATA SET
         *** WITH CONTROL CARDS TO FORMAT THE OUTPUT
         ***
    2    //LIST      EXEC PGM=IEBGENER
    3    //SYSPRINT DD SYSOUT=A
    4    //SYSIN DD *,DCB=BLKSIZE=80
    5    //SYSUT1    DD DSN=WYL.QB.JCL.POLYFIEL,  ←  (POLYFILE misspelled)
         //             DISP=(OLD,CATLG),
         //             UNIT=DISK,
         //             VOL=SER=WYL002
    6    //SYSUT2  DD SYSOUT=A,DCB=(RECFM=FB,LRECL=86,BLKSIZE=860)
         //     (B)

IEC143I 213-04,IFG0195G,JCLQB033,LIST,SYSUT1,377,WYL002,
IEC143I WYL.QB.JCL.POLYFIEL                                        (C)
IEF472I JCLQB033 LIST - COMPLETION CODE - SYSTEM=213 USER=0000
IEF285I    LIST.SYSPRINT                        SYSOUT
IEF285I    JESI0001                             SYSIN
IEF285I    WYL.QB.JCL.POLYFIEL                  CATALOGED
```

cataloged. In several places, marked Ⓐ, Ⓑ, and Ⓒ in Figure 4.16, the system prints notices of the abend.

The messages at Ⓐ, Ⓑ, and Ⓒ give essentially the same information: The LIST step abnormally terminated with a system completion code of 213. (Don't confuse a completion code, which you get only when a step abends, with the condition code, which you get every time a step executes.) The system **completion code** may be used to determine what error caused the abend. Common system completion codes and the conditions that cause them are listed on the inside back cover of this book. For a more complete listing, refer to the *System Codes* manual for your system. In this manual you will find the system completion codes listed in order, with explanations of conditions that cause the errors. The manual indicates that a system completion code of 213 is caused by an error that occurred during the execution of an OPEN instruction.

Some completion codes are accompanied by additional information that is helpful in finding the cause of the error. At point Ⓑ in Figure 4.16, you can see the message IEC143I and 213-04. The 04 is called a return code (not to be confused with *the* return code, which is a synonym for the condition code). You can look up system messages in a second set of manuals named *System Messages*. If you looked up message IEC143I with a return code of 04 in this manual, you would find the statement "Make sure that the DSN parameter is correct." Checking the DSN parameter in Figure 4.16 reveals that POLYFILE was misspelled.

The messages U0000 and USER=0000 at points Ⓐ and Ⓒ both refer to a user completion code of zero, which means that the user did not specify a completion code. It is possible for assembly language programmers to specify a user completion code by invoking the ABEND macro. Coding

```
ABEND     789
```

gives an abend with a user completion code of 789. COBOL programmers must define a working storage item with USAGE COMP:

```
01 COMP-CODE          PIC S999 USAGE COMP.
```

They may move a numerical value to that item and call module ILBOABN0, as follows:

```
MOVE 789 to COMP-CODE.
CALL 'ILBOABN0' USING COMP-CODE.
```

(The fourth character of ILBOABN0 is the letter oh; the last is the number zero.) This coding will give an abend with a user completion code of 789. For some kinds of errors, COBOL itself (not the COBOL programmer) will cause an abend with a user completion code. To find the cause of that abend, you must consult the *COBOL Programmer's Guide*.

It is not possible for PL/I or FORTRAN programmers to specify a user completion code.

Canceling a Job

Another kind of error occurs when the name of a cataloged data set is misspelled. In order to show you this kind of error, POLYFILE was misspelled as POLYFIEL in the SYSUT1 statement in the LIST step of Figure 4.13 and the job rerun. The output is shown in Figure 4.17. The message that POLYFIEL was not found is at point Ⓐ, and the message that the job was canceled is at point Ⓑ. A job that is canceled is *not* the same as a job that abends. You might think of this difference as the difference between a baseball game that was never started because of rain and a game that was stopped because it began to rain during the fourth inning.

Some Special DD Statements

Sometimes, especially when a user-written program abends, the information in the *System Codes* and *System Messages* manuals is not sufficient to allow you to correct the error. In those cases it may be necessary to examine the

■ Figure 4.17 ■

Output Produced When a Job Is Canceled Because a Cataloged Data Set's Name Is Misspelled

```
IAT6140 JOB ORIGIN FROM GROUP=LOCAL    , DSP=IJP, DEVICE=INTRDR  , 000
16:27:17 IAT4401  LOCATE FOR STEP=LIST     DD=SYSUT1   DSN=WYL.QB.JCL.POLYFIEL
                                                            Ⓐ
16:27:17 IAT4404 DATASET NOT FOUND ON MAIN PROCESSOR M1←──Ⓐ
16:27:17 IAT4801 JOB JCLQB057 (7463) EXPRESS CANCELED BY INTERPRETER DSP    *
   1     //JCLQB057 JOB ,'J.C.LEWIS',                       Ⓑ                *
         // REGION=40K,
         // TIME=(0,5)
         ***
         *** A TWO STEP JOB TO ADD RECORDS TO A DATA SET
         *** AND THEN TO LIST IT
         ***
         *** STEP 1 USING IEBGENER TO ADD RECORDS
   2     //ADD       EXEC PGM=IEBGENER
   3     //SYSPRINT DD SYSOUT=A
   4     //SYSIN     DD DUMMY
   5     //SYSUT1    DD *,DCB=BLKSIZE=80
   6     //SYSUT2    DD DSN=WYL.QB.JCL.POLYFILE,
         //             DISP=(MOD,PASS)
         ***
         *** STEP 2 USING IEBPTPCH TO LIST THE DATA SET
         ***
   7     //LIST      EXEC PGM=IEBPTPCH,
         //             COND=(4,LT)
   8     //SYSPRINT DD SYSOUT=A
   9     //SYSIN     DD *,DCB=BLKSIZE=80
  10     //SYSUT1    DD DSN=WYL.QB.JCL.POLYFILE,
         //             DISP=(OLD,KEEP)
  11     //SYSUT2    DD SYSOUT=A
```

contents of main storage at the time of the abend. A listing of the contents of main storage is called a **dump.** You can have a dump produced by including either a SYSUDUMP, SYSABEND, or, for MVS systems only, SYSMDUMP DD statement in the step that abends. SYSUDUMP and SYSABEND produce a formatted dump, so the data sets defined by these statements are usually directed to a printer:

```
//SYSUDUMP DD SYSOUT=A
```

or

```
//SYSABEND DD SYSOUT=A
```

The difference between SYSUDUMP and SYSABEND lies in how much of main storage is dumped. SYSUDUMP dumps the storage area used by the program. SYSABEND dumps the storage area used by the program plus certain system areas. The dump produced by SYSABEND is usually much larger than the dump produced by SYSUDUMP. In most cases the smaller dump provided by SYSUDUMP is all the user needs. These are the usual definitions of SYSUDUMP and SYSABEND, but computer centers may modify these definitions to suit their needs.

Because even a dump produced by SYSUDUMP can be quite large, many computer centers request that you assign dump output to a special class. For example, you might be asked to code

```
//SYSUDUMP DD SYSOUT=D
```

where D signifies that the output is to be held. You can then examine your output and determine whether you need the dump to find the error. If you need the dump, it can be printed, but if you don't, it can be purged, saving printer time and paper.

In MVS systems SYSMDUMP produces an unformatted, machine-readable dump. SYSMDUMP output must be directed to magnetic tape or DASD. The SYSMDUMP DD statement

```
//SYSMDUMP DD DSN=DUMP,
//              DISP=(NEW,KEEP),
//              UNIT=2400
```

directs the output to magnetic tape.

COBOL programmers can request that COBOL produce a formatted dump of their DATA DIVISION by coding the SYMDMP parameter, as explained in Chapter 7. The dump is written to a data set with the ddname SYSDBOUT. Similarly, PL/I programmers can obtain a dump formatted for their use by including a PLIDUMP DD statement.

Summary   In this chapter you have learned

—how to code MOD, PASS, CATLG, and UNCATLG for the DISP parameter to add records to a data set, pass a data set, and catalog and uncatalog a data set

—how to code control statements for IEBGENER and IEBPTPCH

—how to code a job stream that contains more than one job step

—how to code the COND parameter to control step execution

—how to code the TIME parameter

—how to code a backward reference to obtain DSN, DCB, and volume information

—how to read the system messages, including the completion code, produced when a job abends

—how to use the SYSUDUMP, SYSABEND, or SYSMDUMP DD statement to produce a dump when a job abends

Vocabulary   In this chapter you have been introduced to the meanings of the following terms:

backward reference
cataloged
completion code
control statement
dump
SDS

Exercises   1. True or false: The SPACE parameter is coded only when a data set is created on a DASD.

2. Usually you do not code the DCB parameter when you access an existing data set. Why?

3. Why would a programmer want to catalog a data set?

4. Although you can have data sets with the same DSN on different volumes, you can catalog only one of them. Why?

5. a. A data set named EXAMPL is stored on disk pack DISK01. You want this data set to be input to IEBGENER. Code the required DD statement.

   b. Suppose the data set EXAMPL is cataloged. Code the required DD statement.

6. Name the four fields of utility control statements. Which fields are optional?
7. True or false: If the label field is omitted, the operation field may begin in column 1.
8. What are the rules for continuing a utility control statement?
9. Explain how the value assigned to MAXFLDS is determined.
10. Explain how the value assigned to MAXLITS is determined.
11. What does the FIELD parameter FIELD=(4,26,PZ,35) do?
12. A student tried to use IEBGENER to edit a data set, but got the following output. Correct the error. (You may assume that the asterisks are in column 72 and that there are ten blanks between the apostrophes in the second FIELD parameter.)

```
DATA SET UTILITY - GENERATE
   GENERATE MAXFLDS=3                                              *
                MAXLITS=10
   RECORD FIELD=(9,5,,1),                                         *
                FIELD=(10,'          ',,10),                      *
      IEB342I INVALID SPACE ALLOCATION
                FIELD=(25,35,,20)
```

13. Code a TIME parameter to request 2.5 minutes of CPU time.
14. When you execute IEBPTPCH, you must supply at least one control statement. What is it?
15. Each line of output in Figure 4.9 ends with a single or double asterisk. What do these asterisks mean?
16. A data set has 80-byte records. Code the IEBPTPCH control statements to punch this data set and insert sequence numbers in columns 73 through 80. The first sequence number should be 100, and the increment should be 10.
17. The records in a data set contain a name in bytes 1 through 20, an address in bytes 21 through 50, and a phone number in bytes 60 through 69. You want to list this data set, with five spaces between the name and address and ten spaces between the address and the phone number.
    a. Write the IEBGENER control statements required.
    b. Write the IEBPTPCH control statements required.
18. Under what circumstances would you use IEBPTPCH instead of IEBGENER to print a data set?
19. A job stream contains five job steps. How many JOB, EXEC, DD, delimiter, and null statements does it contain?
20. In Figure 4.13, in the ADD step, MOD is coded as the status of POLYFILE. Why?
21. Use the COPY utility described in Exercise 31 in Chapter 2 to print a cataloged data set named INVENTRY.

22. Consider the following job stream skeleton:

```
//EXAMPLE  JOB  ,'MINNIE',
//               COND=(8,LE)
              .
              .
              .

//STEP1     EXEC PGM=PGM1,
//               COND=(0,EQ)
              .
              .
              .

//STEP2     EXEC PGM=PGM2
              .
              .
              .

//STEP3     EXEC PGM=PGM3,
//               COND=ONLY
              .
              .
              .

//STEP4     EXEC PGM=PGM4,
//               COND=((2,GT,STEP1),(5,EQ,STEP2))
              .
              .
              .

//STEP5     EXEC PGM=PGM5,
//               COND=EVEN
```

a. Under what circumstances will STEP1 be skipped? Comment on the COND parameter for STEP1.
b. Under what circumstances will STEP2 be skipped?
c. Under what circumstances will STEP3 be skipped?
d. Under what circumstances will STEP4 be skipped?
e. Simple Simon says that the EVEN coded for STEP5 ensures that STEP5 will be executed under all possible circumstances. Comment.

23. You have a four-step job in which the steps are named STEP1, STEP2, STEP3, and STEP4. Code the COND parameters to do the following:
a. If any step issues a return code of 8, 12, or 16, skip all the remaining steps.
b. Skip STEP2 unless STEP1 issues a return code of 0 or 4.
c. Skip STEP3 if STEP2 issues a return code of 500.
d. Skip STEP4 unless STEP3 abends.

24. Suppose that on a two-step job TIME=1 is coded three times: on the JOB statement and on both EXEC statements. What is the maximum amount of CPU time the job may use?
25. Which parameters may be copied using a backward reference?
26. When you copy volume information using a backward reference, you may refer either to an earlier DD statement or to a cataloged data set. Code examples of both kinds of backward references.
27. Consider the following job stream:

```
//EX1        JOB ,'MICKEY'
//STEP1      EXEC PGM=PGM1
//DD1        DD DSN=DATASET1,
//              DISP=OLD
//DD2        DD DSN=DATASET2,
//              DISP=(NEW,KEEP),
//              UNIT=DISK,
//              VOLUME=PACK07,
//              SPACE=(TRK,(5,2)),
//              DCB=(RECFM=VB,LRECL=150,BLKSIZE=900)
//STEP2      EXEC ?
//DD3        DD DSN=?
//              DISP=OLD
//DD4        DD DSN=DATASET4,
//              DISP=(NEW,KEEP),
//              ?
```

Complete the coding so as to satisfy the following criteria, using backward references where possible.
a. STEP2 should execute the same program as STEP1.
b. The data set referenced in the DD3 DD statement should be DATASET1.
c. DATASET4 should be on the same volume as DATASET7. (DATASET7 is a cataloged data set.)
d. DATASET4 should have the same DCB as DATASET2.
e. DATASET4 should have the same space allocation as DATASET2.
28. What condition would cause an abend with a completion code of 322?
29. What is the reason for including a SYSUDUMP DD statement in a job step?

Programming Assignments

1. Execute a job to have IEBGENER list the data set you created in Chapter 3. Use control statements to insert five spaces between each field.
2. Execute a job to add the additional records in Appendix D to the data set you created in Chapter 3. In the same job use IEBPTPCH to produce an

edited listing of the complete data set. Use the COND parameter to skip the listing step if the return code from the first step is greater than 4.

3. Misspell IEBGENER in the job stream you wrote for Programming Assignment 2 and rerun the job. What completion code do you get? What return code accompanies the completion code? What explanations do you find in the *System Codes* and *System Messages* manuals?

5

Libraries

In this chapter you will learn

- what a library is

- how a library is used

- how to create, access, and modify libraries
  with the utility programs IEFBR14, IEBGENER,
  IEBPTPCH, IEBUPDTE, IEBCOPY, IEHPROGM,
  and IEHLIST

What Is a Library?

A **library** consists of groups of sequential records and a directory. Another name for a library is a **partitioned data set (PDS)**. The terms library and PDS are synonymous. Each group of sequential records is called a **member** and may be treated as a physical sequential data set. All the members must have the same DCB characteristics. If one member consists of 80-byte records blocked 1600, all members must consist of 80-byte records blocked 1600. A library must reside on one DASD volume.

Figure 5.1 illustrates a PDS that occupies seven tracks and contains three members named A, C, and E. The **directory** occupies the beginning of the PDS. It is made up of one or more 256-byte blocks, called **directory blocks**, as shown in Figure 5.2a. The first two bytes indicate how many bytes of the block are in use. The lowest value that this field may contain is 2, which is the size of this field. The rest of the block consists of entries for members. As shown in Figure 5.2b, each entry for a member is from 12 to 74 bytes long. In Figure 5.2b, eight bytes are allocated for the member name. This means that the member name is limited to eight characters. These eight characters must be alphameric, except the first, which must be alphabetic or one of the three

Figure 5.1

Structure of a PDS Showing Directory and Members

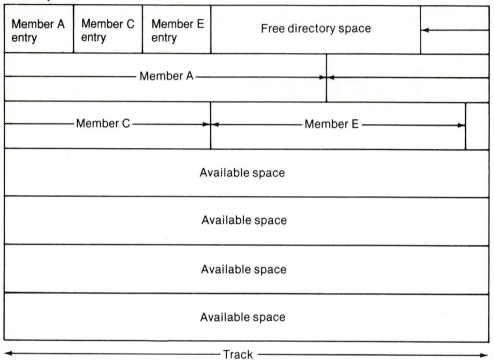

nationals (@, $, #). Basically, the rules for jobnames, stepnames, and ddnames, which you learned in Chapter 2, also govern member names. The next three bytes contain the pointer, which indicates where the member is located on the DASD. When we access the member, the pointer tells the system where the member is. We will not discuss the optional data that may be included in the directory entry for a member.

Figure 5.3 shows what happens when member B is added to the PDS shown in Figure 5.1. Although the new member itself is added to the end of the data set, the entry is inserted in the directory in sort sequence. (The EBCDIC sort sequence is shown in Table 1.2.) The directory has entries for members A, B, C, and E in that order, but the members themselves are in the order in which they were added to the library.

Figure 5.4 shows what happens when member E is replaced with a larger version. The new version is shown as being added to the end of the data set.

■ Figure 5.2 ■

(a) Contents of a PDS Directory Block

Key

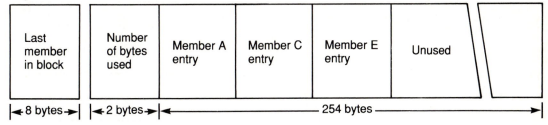

(b) Entry in a PDS Directory Block

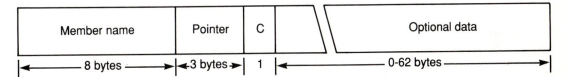

The pointer is in the form TTR, where

TT is the track number
R is the block number relative to the start of the track

C contains control information

The entry in the directory for member E is changed to point to the new member. The old version of member E is still there, but it cannot be accessed because there is no pointer to it.

Figure 5.5 shows what happens when member A is deleted from the PDS illustrated in Figure 5.4. The entry for member A is removed from the directory, and so member A is no longer accessible in the same way that the old version of member E is no longer available.

When members are replaced or deleted, the space is not recovered. Eventually the PDS becomes full and must be reorganized in order to reclaim the lost space. We will discuss how to reorganize a PDS later in this chapter.

⬒ Library Use

If each member of a library may be treated as a physical sequential data set, why bother using libraries at all? To answer this question, think back to the

Figure 5.3

PDS with a New Member

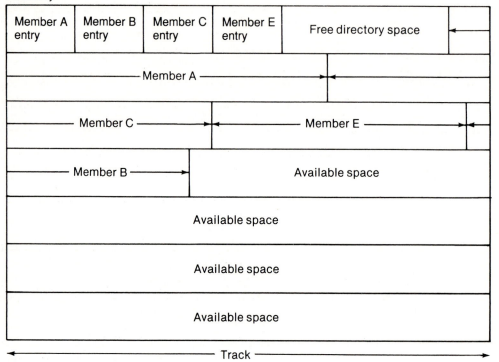

Directory

jobs run in previous chapters. The DD statements told the system where to find the input information and where to write the output data, but how did the system find the program to be executed? As standard procedure the system goes to a system library whose DSN is usually SYS1.LINKLIB. The executable forms of the utility programs are located in this library. Unless told otherwise, the system always searches the directory of SYS1.LINKLIB to find the program to be executed. (Chapter 7 will discuss how to access programs in other libraries.) If you have a group of programs in a library, only one data set need be searched to find a desired program. In most installations source code for programs is kept in one library and executable code in another. One advantage of keeping source code in a library is that when a program must be changed, you know where to find it.

Another advantage of using a library is that the DASD space is used more efficiently. If you refer back to Figure 5.1, you will see that member C starts on

■ Figure 5.4 ■

PDS with a Replaced or Changed Member

Directory

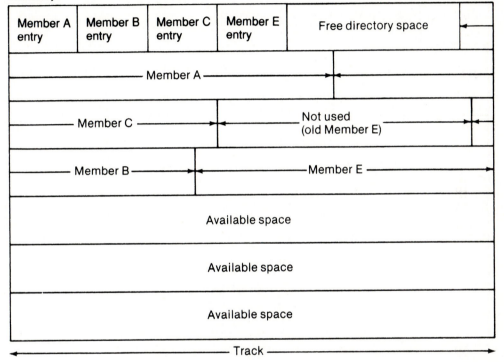

the same track as member A. If the three members in Figure 5.1 were independent physical sequential data sets, three tracks would be needed instead of two.

JCL to Create a Library

Using IEFBR14

Figure 5.6 illustrates a job that could be used to create a library named SOURCE.LIBRARY. The program used is IEFBR14. Strictly speaking, IEFBR14 is not a utility program because it does nothing. The name is derived from the fact that the entire program consists of two assembly language instructions: the first clears register 15, and the second, BR (branch) 14,

■ **Figure 5.5** ━━━━━━━━━━━━━━━━━━━━━━━━━━━━━━

PDS with a Deleted Member

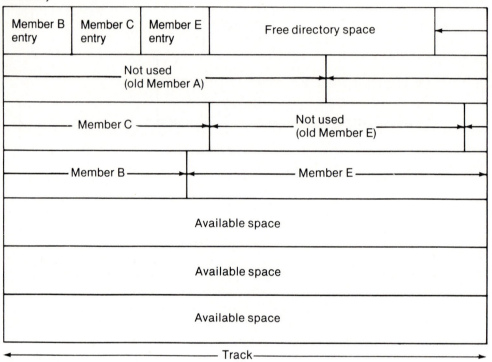

Directory

■ **Figure 5.6** ━━━━━━━━━━━━━━━━━━━━━━━━━━━━━━

Creating a Library Using IEFBR14

```
//JCLQB500 JOB ,'SLEEPY',
//           REGION=32K
//CREATE   EXEC PGM=IEFBR14
//DD1      DD DSN=WYL.QB.JCL.SOURCE.LIBRARY,
//           DISP=(,CATLG),
//           UNIT=SYSDA,
//           VOL=SER=WYL004,
//           SPACE=(TRK,(5,2,10)),
//           DCB=(RECFM=FB,LRECL=80,BLKSIZE=1680,
//           DSORG=PO)
//
```

immediately returns control to the operating system. Because IEFBR14 does not do anything itself, you might wonder why it is needed. Sometimes, as in Figure 5.6, you merely want to process one or more DD statements. You may not submit a job that consists of just a JOB and DD statements, however; every job must have at least one EXEC statement. So executing IEFBR14 permits the disposition specified in the DD statement to occur. If, for example, DISP=(OLD,DELETE) is coded, the data set is deleted. If DISP=(,KEEP) is specified, a new, empty data set is created. In Figure 5.6 DISP=(,CATLG) is specified. This means that when the job ends, a new, empty data set will have been created and cataloged.

DD Statement Parameters

Let us now look at the DD statement in Figure 5.6. The first notable difference between this statement and those you have studied in earlier chapters is in the SPACE parameter. In addition to a primary and secondary space alloca-tion, there is a third number specified. This number indicates the number of directory blocks to be allocated within the PDS. In Figure 5.6 ten directory blocks are requested.

Depending on how much optional data each entry includes, a directory block of 256 bytes can hold from 3 to 21 entries. With ten directory blocks the PDS can hold from 30 to 210 entries. Make sure that you specify enough space for the directory in the initial allocation. Although more space may be ob-tained for the data set as a whole through the secondary allocation, the number of directory blocks is fixed. The space for the directory blocks is included in the primary allocation. In the example shown in Figure 5.6, the primary allocation is five tracks. The directory will be in the beginning of the first of these five tracks. This means that slightly less than five tracks will initially be available for members.

The secondary allocation was specified as two tracks. If we had chosen not to have a secondary allocation, the SPACE parameter would have been coded as

```
//                SPACE=(TRK,(5,,10))
```

Note the double comma following the primary allocation. The second comma indicates the absence of a value for the secondary allocation.

The next notable difference in the JCL in Figure 5.6 is the subparameter DSORG=PO in the DCB parameter. DSORG stands for data set organization. DSORG=PO means that the data set organization is partitioned.

To summarize, the two special features of the JCL to create a PDS are (1) inclusion of a third number in the SPACE parameter to request directory blocks and (2) specification of PO for the data set organization. Actually, the DCB subparameter DSORG=PO is optional. If a value for the number of direc-tory blocks is coded in the SPACE parameter, a library will be created.

You may have noticed that there are no comment statements in Figure 5.6. Comment statements are important, and all the previous examples have contained them. Because these examples are part of a book, however, and are discussed in the text, comment statements are not really necessary. Therefore, from now on comment statements will be used sparingly. Your programs are not part of a book and must be understandable on their own, so you should continue to use comment statements in your programs.

Adding a Member with IEBGENER

You already know how to use IEBGENER with physical sequential data sets. In this section you will see how to use IEBGENER with libraries.

At the beginning of this chapter you were told that a member of a PDS could be treated either as a sequential data set or as a member of a PDS. Both methods are shown in Figure 5.7, in which IEBGENER is used to add the member COB1 to SOURCE.LIBRARY, which was created in Figure 5.6. The

▬ Figure 5.7 ▬

(a) Adding a PDS Member as a Sequential Data Set

```
//JCLQB502 JOB ,'BASHFULL',
//              REGION=40K
//PDSCREAT EXEC PGM=IEBGENER
//SYSPRINT DD SYSOUT=A
//SYSUT1   DD DSN=WYL.QB.JCL.TAPEIN,
//              DISP=OLD
//SYSUT2   DD DSN=WYL.QB.JCL.SOURCE.LIBRARY(COB1),
//              DISP=OLD
//SYSIN    DD DUMMY
//
```

(b) Adding a PDS Member as a PDS Member

```
//JCLQB503 JOB ,'BASHFULL',
//              REGION=40K
//PDSCREAT EXEC PGM=IEBGENER
//SYSPRINT DD SYSOUT=A
//SYSUT1   DD DSN=WYL.QB.JCL.TAPEIN,
//              DISP=OLD
//SYSUT2   DD DSN=WYL.QB.JCL.SOURCE.LIBRARY,
//              DISP=OLD
//SYSIN    DD *
 GENERATE  MAXNAME=1
 MEMBER NAME=COB1
/*
//
```

input, defined by the SYSUT1 DD statement, is a cataloged physical sequential data set on tape, named TAPEIN.

In Figure 5.7a COB1 is treated as a sequential data set, with the member name appearing in parentheses following the library name: WYL.QB.JCL.SOURCE.LIBRARY(COB1). Notice that the DISP coded on the SYSUT2 DD statement is OLD. The member we are adding to SOURCE.LI-BRARY is new, but DISP refers to the whole PDS, which in this case already exists. For the same reason, you cannot delete a member of a PDS by coding

```
//DD1       DD DSN=LIBRARY(MEMBER),
//              DISP=(OLD,DELETE)
```

This coding deletes the whole PDS named LIBRARY, not just the member named MEMBER. The way to delete members of a library is discussed later in this chapter.

None of the SYSUT DD statements in Figure 5.7 has explicit DCB information in it. The necessary information will be found by the system in the standard labels. When you add a member to a library, you must make sure that the physical sequential data set that is the input data set has the same logical record length as does the library to which the new member is being added.

No control statements are needed in Figure 5.7a, so the SYSIN DD statement is dummied. That is not the case in Figure 5.7b, in which COB1 is treated as a member of a PDS. Notice that the SYSUT2 DD statement in Figure 5.7b does not include the member name. The member name is specified in the MEMBER statement, which we will consider next.

The MEMBER Statement

Let us look at the control statements in Figure 5.7b. The GENERATE statement was discussed in Chapter 4. The MAXNAME parameter was listed in Table 4.1 but was not discussed in Chapter 4. MAXNAME is related to the MEMBER statement. How to determine the value to assign to MAXNAME will be explained later. The MEMBER statement indicates the name of the member being created. In Figure 5.7b the name of the member being created is COB1. If several members are being created, each member must have its own MEMBER statement. We will study an example of multiple MEMBER statements later.

Figure 5.7b shows the simplest version of the MEMBER statement. A member in a PDS can have more than one name. The first name is the member name; any other name is an alias. If you wished the member to have an alias, the MEMBER statement would be coded as follows:

```
MEMBER NAME=(COB1,UPDATE)
```

As a result of this MEMBER statement, a member will be created with the name COB1 and the alias UPDATE. The member may be referred to by either its name or its alias. If you wanted COB1 to have three aliases, the MEMBER statement would be coded as follows:

```
MEMBER  NAME=(COB1,UPDATE,PGM1,ASSIGN1)
```

If the idea of an alias confuses you, think of your friendly neighborhood gangster. He has a name that appears on his birth certificate; it is equivalent to COB1 in the example. He is also known to the police by other names or aliases; these are equivalent to UPDATE, PGM1, and ASSIGN1 in the example. It is obvious why your friendly neighborhood gangster might wish to use different names, but why might you want a library member to have more than one name? Generally, the reason is to facilitate identification of the member. I originally gave the name PRNTMEMB to a library member containing JCL that I use to print library members, but I frequently would get confused and refer to that member as MEMBPRNT. I solved the problem by giving member PRNTMEMB an alias of MEMBPRNT.

Let us return to the MAXNAME parameter in the GENERATE statement. The value assigned to the MAXNAME parameter must be greater than or equal to the number of names and aliases in the MEMBER statements that follow. Because there is only one name in Figure 5.7b, MAXNAME is set equal to 1. As with the MAXFLDS and MAXLITS parameters, which we discussed in Chapter 4, if you set MAXNAME equal to a higher value than is needed, the job will execute properly. If, for example, there are a total of six names and aliases, MAXNAME must be set equal to 6 or more. A value of 7 will work, but 5 will not.

The IDENT Parameter

Figure 5.8 illustrates the creation of a library named GENERLIB with four members. If the SYSUT2 DD statement referenced an existing library instead of a new one, this job would add four members to that library. The data to create the four members are contained in the cataloged data set named SEQIN.

If you examine the first control statement in Figure 5.8, the GENERATE statement, you will see a new parameter, MAXGPS. MAXGPS indicates how many IDENT parameters will appear in the RECORD statements that follow. MAXGPS must be equal to or greater than the actual number of IDENT parameters in the following RECORD statements. If we had specified 6 for MAXGPS in the example in Figure 5.8, the job would work. If, on the other hand, we had specified 2, the job would not work.

If you look at the control statements in Figure 5.8, you will see four MEMBER statements and three RECORD statements. The first MEMBER statement is followed by a RECORD statement, as are the second and third MEMBER statements. The first RECORD statement applies to the first MEMBER statement, the

Figure 5.8

Creating a Library Containing Four Members Using IEBGENER

```
//JCLQB504 JOB ,'GRUMPY',
//              REGION=40K
//CREATPDS EXEC PGM=IEBGENER
//SYSPRINT DD SYSOUT=A
//SYSUT1   DD DSN=WYL.QB.JCL.SEQIN,
//              DISP=OLD
//SYSUT2   DD DSN=WYL.QB.JCL.GENERLIB,
//              UNIT=SYSDA,
//              VOL=SER=WYL002,
//              DISP=(,CATLG),
//              SPACE=(TRK,(10,2,5),RLSE),
//              DCB=(RECFM=FB,LRECL=100,BLKSIZE=2000,DSORG=PO)
//SYSIN    DD *
 GENERATE MAXNAME=4,                                                    *
             MAXGPS=3
 MEMBER NAME=MEM1
 RECORD IDENT=(8,'11111111',1)
 MEMBER NAME=MEM2
 RECORD IDENT=(8,'22222222',1)
 MEMBER NAME=MEM3
 RECORD IDENT=(8,'33333333',1)
 MEMBER NAME=MEM4
/*
//
```

second to the second MEMBER statement, and the third to the third MEMBER statement. No RECORD statement applies to the last MEMBER statement.

The IDENT parameter in the RECORD statement is used to create multiple members from one physical sequential data set. In Figure 5.8 the IDENT parameter of the first RECORD statement specifies an eight-byte literal, 11111111, that starts in position 1 of the record. As each record is read, it is examined to determine whether it contains the characters 11111111 starting in position 1. Once this literal is found, the first member, MEM1, is completed. Then the second member, MEM2, is built, followed by the third member, MEM3. The last member, MEM4, consists of the remaining records in the input data set.

As Table 4.1 shows, the general format of the IDENT parameter is

```
IDENT=(length,'literal',input-location)
```

The IDENT parameter in the RECORD statement supplies a literal, its length (which has a maximum value of 8), and its position, to mark the end of the input for a member. Be aware that the record that includes this literal becomes part of the member.

Accessing a Library with IEBPTPCH

You have already studied how to use IEBPTPCH to print or punch a physical sequential data set. As you learned earlier, members of a PDS may be treated as physical sequential data sets. The JCL to print a member of a PDS as a sequential data set is illustrated in Figure 5.9a. If you compare this job with those shown in Chapter 4, the only significant difference you will find is in the DSN for the SYSUT1 DD statement, where the member name is coded in parentheses following the library name.

Figure 5.9b illustrates the JCL used to print MEM1, treating it as a member of the library GENERLIB. The DD statements are no different from those shown in Chapter 4. The SYSUT1 DD statement points to the library that has the members we wish to print. Note that you cannot tell that WYL.QB.JCL.GENERLIB is a library just by looking at the DD statement. The rules for DD statements are no different for accessing a partitioned data set than for ac-

Figure 5.9

(a) Printing a PDS Member as a Sequential Data Set

```
//JCLQB506 JOB ,'DOC',
//            REGION=32K
//PRNTSEQ  EXEC PGM=IEBPTPCH
//SYSPRINT DD SYSOUT=A
//SYSUT1   DD DSN=WYL.QB.JCL.GENERLIB(MEM1),
//            DISP=SHR
//SYSUT2   DD SYSOUT=A
//SYSIN    DD *
 PRINT MAXFLDS=1
 RECORD FIELD=(100)
/*
//
```

(b) Printing a PDS Member as a PDS Member

```
//JCLQB508 JOB ,'SNEEZY',
//            REGION=130K
//PRNTPDS  EXEC PGM=IEBPTPCH
//SYSPRINT DD SYSOUT=A
//SYSUT1   DD DSN=WYL.QB.JCL.GENERLIB,
//            DISP=SHR
//SYSUT2   DD SYSOUT=A
//SYSIN    DD *
 PRINT TYPORG=PO,                                          *
              MAXFLDS=1,                                   *
              MAXNAME=1
 MEMBER NAME=MEM1
 RECORD FIELD=(100)
/*
//
```

cessing a physical sequential data set that resides on DASD. If you have any doubts about the rules for accessing a physical sequential data set on DASD, refer back to Chapter 4.

The Control Statements

Let us now look at the control statements for IEBPTPCH in Figure 5.9b. In the PRINT statement you see the parameter TYPORG=PO. This means that the type of organization is partitioned organization. It is through this parameter that IEBPTPCH learns that GENERLIB is a library and not a physical sequential data set. In the example in Figure 5.9a, the PRINT statement could have been coded TYPORG=PS, which means that the type of organization is physical sequential. This coding is the default value and so was omitted.

The next new parameter is MAXNAME=1. MAXNAME has the same function here as it has on the IEBGENER GENERATE control statement.

The MEMBER statement indicates the name of the member to be printed. In Figure 5.9b there is only one MEMBER statement, so only one member, named MEM1, will be printed. If you want to print several members from a library, you must include a separate MEMBER statement for each one.

Although the MEMBER statements in Figure 5.9b, Figure 5.7b, and Figure 5.8 are similar, their meanings are quite different. When a MEMBER statement is used with IEBPTPCH, it names the member being used as input. When a MEMBER statement is used with IEBGENER, it names the member being created. As shown in Table 4.3, the general format of the MEMBER statement is

```
MEMBER  NAME=membername
```

If TYPORG=PO is coded and no MEMBER statements are included, all the members of the library will be printed or punched.

As you learned in Chapter 4, IEBPTPCH control statements must be coded in the order PRINT (or PUNCH), MEMBER, RECORD.

The IEBUPDTE Utility

The IEBUPDTE utility program can be used to create and update a library; however, the record length of the members must not be greater than 80 bytes. Because of this restriction, IEBUPDTE is used mainly for source code and JCL libraries. In many installations a library maintenance system will be used in lieu of this utility. Although this utility can deal with sequential data sets, the scope of this discussion will be limited to PDS input and output. We will discuss adding a new member to a new or existing PDS, changing an existing PDS member, replacing an existing PDS member, and copying a member from one PDS to another.

Figure 5.10 shows, in general terms, the JCL used for the IEBUPDTE utility.

■ Figure 5.10 ■

JCL Required for IEBUPDTE

```
//JCLQB510 JOB ,'HAPPY',
//              REGION=130K
//UPDTSTEP EXEC PGM=IEBUPDTE,
//              PARM={NEW|MOD}
//SYSPRINT DD SYSOUT=A
//SYSUT1   DD Input Data Set
//SYSUT2   DD Output Data Set
//SYSIN    DD *

          Control Data Set

/*
//
```

IEBUPDTE uses the four DD statements that you are now familiar with: SYS-PRINT is used for messages; SYSUT1 is the input data set; SYSUT2 is the output data set; and SYSIN is used for control statements. As you will see, you don't always need both SYSUT1 and SYSUT2.

IEBUPDTE uses two kinds of control statements: function statements and detail statements. The four function statements are ADD, which is used to add a member to a new or existing PDS; CHANGE, which is used to change an existing member; REPL, which is used to replace an existing member; and REPRO, which is used to copy (reproduce) a member from one PDS to another. The two detail statements are NUMBER, which is used to add identifying sequence numbers to records in a member, and DELETE, which is used to delete selected records from a member.

In the EXEC statement there is a PARM field, which can be set to either MOD or NEW. The PARM parameter, which is discussed in more detail in Chapter 7, offers a way of supplying data to a program. In this case the data may be the word NEW or the word MOD.* If the PARM field is not coded, the default value is MOD. If MOD is specified explicitly or by default, there must be a SYSUT1 DD statement, which means that an existing PDS will be input to this job. Exactly how it is input will be discussed later. If NEW is specified, no SYSUT1 DD statement is expected and the input is contained in the SYSIN data set. The only time you may specify NEW—and therefore omit the SYSUT1 DD statement—is when you use the ADD function statement to add a member to a new or existing PDS.

Creating a New PDS

Assume that a data processing instructor wants to create a PDS named CLASSLIB. A member will be created for each course she teaches. The

* These values have nothing to do with the similarly named DISP subparameters.

records in these members will contain the names and social security numbers of the students in the course. For her convenience, the records will be in alphabetical order by student name. To keep the example to a manageable size, assume that only a few students are registered in each class. Figure 5.11a illustrates how IEBUPDTE may be used to create such a PDS and add two members to it. In Figure 5.11a, the first member is named COBOL, and the second is named JCL.

The PARM field in the EXEC statement specifies NEW, which means that the SYSUT1 DD statement is not required. The SYSUT2 DD statement defines the new library. Notice that DSORG=PO is not coded, because coding DSORG is optional. The request for ten directory blocks in the SPACE parameter tells the system that we are creating a library.

The SYSIN DD statement defines the control data set that contains control statements and the data records that will be used to create members COBOL and JCL.

Let us now examine the control statements in Figure 5.11a. IEBUPDTE is unique in that it is the only utility whose control statements are identified by a period in column 1 and a slash in column 2. A label can follow the slash, but it is not necessary and is not recommended. If a label is not coded, column 3 must be blank. The first control statement in Figure 5.11a is an ADD function statement. The data records that follow the ADD statement will be used to create a new member. Only the NAME parameter, which gives the member its name, need be specified. The parameter LIST=ALL is included to generate a listing of the member being added. Other parameters that you might care to use can be found in Table 5.1; however, in general it is not necessary to use them, because the default values are usually acceptable.

The next control statement in Figure 5.11a is the NUMBER detail statement. As in the function statement, column 1 contains a period, column 2 a slash, and column 3 is blank (it may contain the start of a label, but again the label is not recommended). The operation is NUMBER, which specifies that sequence numbers are to be added to the statements being added. The sequence numbers start in column 73 and are 8 bytes long. This position and this length are the defaults. The parameter NEW1=10 means that the first record in the data set will have a sequence number of 00000010. The parameter INCR=10 means that the sequence numbers in the records will differ by 10. Consequently, the second record will have a sequence number of 00000020, the third 00000030, and so forth. The importance of the sequence numbers will become obvious when we discuss changing a member.

The records that follow these two control statements must not have any data in columns 73 through 80, because IEBUPDTE will insert the sequence numbers in these columns.

The only difference between the control statements used to add member JCL and those used to add member COBOL is in the NUMBER statement. The first record of JCL will have a sequence number of 00000100, the second 00000110, and so forth.

Figure 5.11

(a) JCL to Create a PDS Using IEBUPDTE

```
//JCLQB512 JOB ,'DOPEY',
//              REGION=38K
//STEPCRT  EXEC PGM=IEBUPDTE,
//              PARM=NEW
//SYSPRINT DD SYSOUT=A
//SYSUT2   DD DSN=WYL.QB.JCL.CLASSLIB,
//              DISP=(,CATLG),
//              UNIT=SYSDA,
//              VOL=SER=USR006,
//              SPACE=(TRK,(5,2,10)),
//              DCB=(RECFM=FB,LRECL=80,BLKSIZE=1600)
//SYSIN    DD *
./ ADD NAME=COBOL,LIST=ALL
./ NUMBER NEW1=10,INCR=10
BOOKMEYER,BARBARA      281090522
DONOHUE,JAMES          494122185
FRADIN,SHIRLEY         687965722
RIZZUTO,JAMES          806578420
./ ADD NAME=JCL,LIST=ALL
./ NUMBER NEW1=100,INCR=10
ABOLITZ,HANNA          015761231
BURNS,JEFFREY          825494122
FALCONER,EDWARD        205100235
FRADIN,SHIRLEY         867965722
SCHWARTZ,MICHAEL       073671186
./ ENDUP
/*
//
```

144

(b) IEBUPDTE Messages

```
                          NEW MASTER                              IEBUPDTE LOG PAGE 0001

  SYSIN
  ./ ADD NAME=COBOL,LIST=ALL
  ./ NUMBER NEW1=10,INCR=10
                          BOOKMEYER,BARBARA        281090522             00000010
                          DONOHUE,JAMES            494122185             00000020
                          FRADIN,SHIRLEY           687965722             00000030
                          RIZZUTO,JAMES            806578420             00000040
IEB817I MEMBER NAME (COBOL   ) NOT FOUND IN NM DIRECTORY.  STOWED WITH TTR.
                          NEW MASTER                              IEBUPDTE LOG PAGE 0002

  SYSIN
  ./ ADD NAME=JCL,LIST=ALL
  ./ NUMBER NEW1=100,INCR=10
                          ABOLITZ,HANNA            015761231             00000100
                          BURNS,JEFFREY            825494122             00000110
                          FALCONER,EDWARD          205100235             00000120
                          FRADIN,SHIRLEY           867965722             00000130
                          SCHWARTZ,MICHAEL         073671186             00000140

  ./ ENDUP
IEB817I MEMBER NAME (JCL     ) NOT FOUND IN NM DIRECTORY.  STOWED WITH TTR.
IEB818I HIGHEST CONDITION CODE WAS 00000000
IEB819I END OF JOB IEBUPDTE.
```

145

■ **Table 5.1**
IEBUPDTE ADD, CHANGE, REPL, and REPRO Parameters

Parameter	Definition
LIST=ALL	Specifies that the SYSPRINT data set is to contain the entire updated member.
SEQFLD=col	Gives the column in which the sequence number is to start and the length of the sequence field. The default is 738, which means that the sequence field starts in column 73 and is 8 bytes long.
NEW=PO NEW=PS	Is used only if the SYSUT1 and SYSUT2 data sets have different organizations. PO means that SYSUT2 will be partitioned and PS that it will be physical sequential.
NAME=memb	Supplies the name of the member.
COLUMN=nn	Specifies the starting column for the data. This parameter applies only to the change operation. The default is 1.
UPDATE=INPLACE	Specifies that the member is to be changed where it currently is. This means that the member size must remain the same and the SYSUT2 DD statement is not required.

The parameters used in the NUMBER detail statement are shown in Table 5.2. Note that a NUMBER statement may not follow a REPRO statement.

Skipping to the end of Figure 5.11a, you come to the ENDUP statement, which marks the end of the control data set. If this control statement were omitted, the delimiter statement by itself would mark the end of the control data set.

Figure 5.11b shows the output produced when the job stream in Figure 5.11a was executed. Because we coded LIST=ALL, the records in each member were printed. Also, sequence numbers were added to each member as a result of our coding the NUMBER statement. These sequence numbers will be useful when we update the members.

Adding a Member to a PDS

Figure 5.12 illustrates the addition of a new member named BAL to CLASS-LIB. If you compare Figure 5.11a and Figure 5.12, you will see that the only difference between them is in the SYSUT2 DD statement. In Figure 5.11a the

■ Table 5.2 ■
IEBUPDTE NUMBER and DELETE Parameters

Parameter	DELETE	NUMBER	Definition
SEQ1=cccc	Yes	Yes	Specifies the sequence number of the first record to be deleted or renumbered.
SEQ2=cccc	Yes	Yes	Specifies the sequence number of the last record to be deleted or renumbered.
SEQ1=ALL	No	Yes	Specifies that the entire member is to be renumbered. This parameter is used only following a CHANGE statement.
NEW1=cccc	No	Yes	Specifies the first number assigned to new or replacement data, or the first sequence number assigned in a renumbering operation.
INCR=cccc	No	Yes	Specifies an incremental value for the sequence numbers.

SYSUT2 DD statement defines a new PDS, whereas in Figure 5.12 it points to an existing PDS. In both examples the PARM field is set equal to NEW. Remember that specifying NEW in the PARM field does not mean that the PDS is new. It means only that there is no SYSUT1 DD statement.

Changing a Member in a Library

Assume that two new students, Alexander and Osborn, have registered for the JCL class, and records for these students are to be inserted in their proper alphabetical position. Assume also that Falconer has dropped the course, so his record is to be deleted. Finally, an error in Fradin's social security number must be corrected.

Figure 5.13a illustrates changing a member. If you examine the JCL statements in Figure 5.13a, you will notice that PARM is not coded, so the default MOD applies. Therefore we need both SYSUT1 and SYSUT2 DD statements. SYSUT1 defines the input PDS, and SYSUT2 defines the output PDS. The

Figure 5.12

Adding a Member to an Existing PDS Using IEBUPDTE

```
//JCLQB514 JOB ,'J.C.LEWIS',
//              REGION=38K
//STEPADD  EXEC PGM=IEBUPDTE,
//              PARM=NEW
//SYSPRINT DD SYSOUT=A
//SYSUT2   DD DSN=WYL.QB.JCL.CLASSLIB,
//              DISP=OLD
//SYSIN    DD *
./ ADD NAME=BAL,LIST=ALL
./ NUMBER NEW1=100,INCR=100
AMATO,ROBERT           403015422
ENKOWITZ,STEVE         557049836
HUYNH,CHAM             864524753
MORLEY,JOHN            465302116
PFLUGBEIL,MARIE        104523232
SCHWARTZ,MICHAEL       073671186
./ ENDUP
/*
//
```

member to be changed is read from the input PDS defined by SYSUT1, changed, and then written to the output PDS defined by SYSUT2. In this example both SYSUT1 and SYSUT2 refer to CLASSLIB, so the system will read a member from CLASSLIB, change it, and then write it back to CLASS-LIB. Later you will see an example in which the input and output PDSs are not the same.

Let us now examine the control statements following the SYSIN DD statement. The first one is the CHANGE statement. The NAME parameter specifies which member is to be changed. Additional parameters are defined in Table 5.1. In this case all the defaults are acceptable except for LIST=ALL; it is a good idea to see what the changed member looks like.

The next control statement is the NUMBER statement. The NUMBER statement in Figure 5.13a differs from those in Figures 5.11a and 5.12 only in the presence of the SEQ1=ALL parameter. This parameter, which can be coded only with a CHANGE operation, means that the entire member is to be renumbered after the changes are made. The NEW1 and INCR parameters will work the same way here as with the NUMBER statement used with the ADD function.

Following the NUMBER statement are the data records and the DELETE statement. The data records have sequence numbers in columns 73 through 80. IEBUPDTE uses these sequence numbers to determine where these new data records should be inserted in member JCL. Figure 5.11b shows how member JCL looked when it was created. The new record for Alexander should be inserted in its proper alphabetical position between the records for Abolitz and Burns, which have sequence numbers of 100 and 110. So in

Figure 5.13

(a) Changing a Member Using IEBUPDTE

```
//JCLQB516 JOB ,'MARLA',
//         REGION=38K
//STEPCHNG EXEC PGM=IEBUPDTE
//SYSPRINT DD SYSOUT=A
//SYSUT1   DD DSN=WYL.QB.JCL.CLASSLIB,
//         DISP=OLD
//SYSUT2   DD DSN=WYL.QB.JCL.CLASSLIB,
//         DISP=OLD
//SYSIN    DD *
./ CHANGE NAME=JCL,LIST=ALL
./ NUMBER SEQ1=ALL,NEW1=100,INCR=100
ALEXANDER,LISA    71988436                 00000105
./ DELETE SEQ1=120,SEQ2=120
FRADIN,SHIRLEY    68796572                 00000130
OSBORN,BRIAN      13646272                 00000135
./ ENDUP
/*
//
```

(b) IEBUPDTE Change Messages

```
SYSIN                                NEW MASTER              IEBUPDTE LOG PAGE 0001
./ CHANGE NAME=JCL,LIST=ALL
./ NUMBER SEQ1=ALL,NEW1=100,INCR=100
   ABOLITZ,HANNA      015761231                     00000100
   ALEXANDER,LISA     71988436                      00000200 *      INSERTED*
./ DELETE SEQ1=120,SEQ2=120
   BURNS,JEFFREY      825494122                     00000300 *      DELETED*
   FALCONER,EDWARD    205100235                     00000130 *      REPLACED*
   FRADIN,SHIRLEY     867965722                     00000400 *      REPLACEMENT*
   FRADIN,SHIRLEY     687965722                     00000500 *      INSERTED*
   OSBORN,BRIAN       136462732
./ ENDUP
   SCHWARTZ,MICHAEL   073671186                     00000600

IEB816I MEMBER NAME (JCL ) FOUND IN NM DIRECTORY. TTR IS NOW ALTERED.
IEB818I HIGHEST CONDITION CODE WAS 00000000
IEB819I END OF JOB IEBUPDTE.
```

Figure 5.13a Alexander's data record is given a sequence number of
00000105. (The leading zeros are required.)

Skipping the DELETE statement for a second, you see that the data record
for Fradin has a sequence number of 00000130. Because this new record has
the same sequence number as a record already in member JCL, it will replace
the existing record. The new record has Fradin's correct social security number, so this is exactly what we want to happen.

The data record for Osborn has a sequence number of 00000135. This
sequence number will cause Osborn's record to be inserted between Fradin's
(sequence number 130) and Schwartz's (sequence number 140), which is its
proper alphabetical position.

Let us now return to the DELETE statement. The DELETE statement may be
coded only with a CHANGE statement. The parameters for the DELETE statement are shown in Table 5.2. The DELETE statement in Figure 5.13a will
cause the record whose sequence number is 00000120 to be deleted. The
DELETE statement can also be used to delete several consecutive records. If
we coded

```
./ DELETE SEQ1=110,SEQ2=130
```

all the records with sequence numbers from 110 through and including 130
would be deleted.

The data records and DELETE statements must be coded in order by sequence number. Alexander's record is coded first because its sequence number is the lowest, 105. It is followed by the DELETE statement, because this
statement deletes the record whose sequence number is 120. The DELETE
statement is followed by the data records whose sequence numbers are 130
and 135. If we used a different order—for example, coding the DELETE
statement before Alexander's record—the job would not run. If we wanted to
delete Schwartz's record, we would include a second DELETE statement,

```
./ DELETE SEQ1=140,SEQ2=140
```

after Osborn's data record.

The output produced when the job in Figure 5.13a was executed is shown
in Figure 5.13b. You can see that the output contains a clear record of the
changes that were made. Notice that the NUMBER statement caused the entire
member to be renumbered after the changes were made. We were able to
change the numbering sequence by coding INCR=100 instead of INCR=10,
which was used when member JCL was created.

In-Place Member Change

Figure 5.14 illustrates the one and only time when the SYSUT2 DD statement
is not required. In this example we are replacing two statements in member

Figure 5.14

In-Place Member Change Using IEBUPDTE

```
//JCLQB518 JOB ,'BENITO',
//              REGION=32K
//INPLACE  EXEC PGM=IEBUPDTE
//SYSPRINT DD SYSOUT=A
//SYSUT1    DD DSN=WYL.QB.JCL.CLASSLIB,
//              DISP=OLD
//SYSIN     DD *
./ CHANGE NAME=BAL,LIST=ALL,UPDATE=INPLACE
HUYNH,CHAM          864534753                                 00000300
PFLUGBEIL,MARIA     104523232                                 00000500
./ ENDUP
/*
//
```

BAL because of an error in the social security number of record 300 and a misspelling of the name in record 500.

Because this change will leave the member exactly the same size it was, we can make the change in place. This means that the member stays in its original position in the PDS; it is not moved to the end of the library as the one in the previous example was. The only difference between the CHANGE control statement in this example and the one in Figure 5.13a is the UPDATE=INPLACE parameter.

Replacing a Member

The REPL control statement is used to replace a member in a library. The data records that follow the REPL statement are used to replace the member named by the NAME parameter. Both SYSUT1 and SYSUT2 DD statements are required and point to the same PDS.

Assume that there are so many errors in member COBOL that it is easier to completely replace the member than to correct it. Figure 5.15 illustrates the coding for replacing a PDS member. When you code REPL, the named member must exist in the library. Thus, unless COBOL is the name of a member in CLASSLIB, the job in Figure 5.15 will fail. If COBOL is not in CLASSLIB, we should use the ADD statement to add it rather than the REPL statement.

Copying Members

Members may be copied from one library to another using the REPRO control statement. Figure 5.16 illustrates copying two members, COB1 and COB2, from SOURCE.LIBRARY to PGMLIB. After this job is executed, COB1 and COB2

■ Figure 5.15 ■

Replacing a PDS Member Using IEBUPDTE

```
//JCLQB520 JOB ,'MELITA',
//              REGION=38K
//REPLACE   EXEC PGM=IEBUPDTE
//SYSPRINT DD SYSOUT=A
//SYSUT1    DD DSN=WYL.QB.JCL.CLASSLIB,
//              DISP=OLD
//SYSUT2    DD DSN=WYL.QB.JCL.CLASSLIB,
//              DISP=OLD
//SYSIN     DD *
./ REPL NAME=COBOL,LIST=ALL
./ NUMBER NEW1=100,INCR=100
BOTERO,MAURICE      526206289
CHAU,YIN            427476080
DESCOVICH,STEVEN    178050554
GOLD,STEPHEN        238340187
./ ENDUP
/*
//
```

will exist in both SOURCE.LIBRARY and PGMLIB. The parameters for the REPRO control statement are shown in Table 5.1.

Figure 5.16 also shows how the CHANGE statement may be used to change a member while it is being copied from one library to another. Member COB3 is in SOURCE.LIBRARY. It will be changed and then stored in PGMLIB. After

■ Figure 5.16 ■

Copying a Member from One PDS to Another Using IEBUPDTE

```
//JCLQB522 JOB ,'J.C.LEWIS',
//              REGION=38K
//REPRODUC EXEC PGM=IEBUPDTE
//SYSPRINT DD SYSOUT=A
//SYSUT1    DD DSN=WYL.QB.JCL.SOURCE.LIBRARY,
//              DISP=OLD
//SYSUT2    DD DSN=WYL.QB.JCL.PGMLIB,
//              DISP=OLD
//SYSIN     DD *
./ REPRO NAME=COB1,LIST=ALL
./ REPRO NAME=COB2,LIST=ALL
./ CHANGE NAME=COB3,LIST=ALL
./ NUMBER SEQ1=ALL,NEW1=100,INCR=100
./ DELETE SEQ1=200,SEQ2=500
./ ENDUP
/*
//
```

this job is executed, there will be two versions of COB3: the original version in SOURCE.LIBRARY and the changed one in PGMLIB.

Remember that when you use IEBUPDTE the maximum record size is 80 bytes.

The IEBCOPY Utility

IEBCOPY is a utility program that may be used to copy one or more members from an existing PDS to a new or existing PDS, to make a backup copy of a PDS, and to reorganize a PDS in order to reclaim the unused space, as shown in Figure 5.5.

Copying the Entire PDS

Figure 5.17 illustrates a job that copies all the members of a PDS to a new PDS. We will examine this job in detail because it demonstrates the basic function of IEBCOPY. Once you understand how this job works, you will have no difficulty with the rest of this section.

The EXEC statement invokes the program IEBCOPY, and the SYSPRINT DD statement provides the message data set.

The next two DD statements, SYSUT3 and SYSUT4, are different from those you have seen before, so let us pause a second to discuss them. First, notice

▬ Figure 5.17 ▬▬▬▬▬▬▬▬▬▬▬▬▬▬▬▬▬▬▬▬▬▬▬▬▬▬▬▬▬

Copying a Library Using IEBCOPY

```
//JCLQB524 JOB ,'JOE TINKER',
//              REGION=130K
//COPYLIB  EXEC PGM=IEBCOPY
//SYSPRINT DD SYSOUT=A
//SYSUT3   DD UNIT=VIO,
//              SPACE=(TRK,(1))
//SYSUT4   DD UNIT=VIO,
//              SPACE=(TRK,(1))
//INPUT    DD DSN=WYL.QB.JCL.GENERLIB,
//              DISP=OLD
//OUTPUT   DD DSN=WYL.QB.JCL.COPYLIB,
//              DISP=(,CATLG),
//              UNIT=SYSDA,
//              VOL=SER=WYL003,
//              SPACE=(TRK,(5,2,3)),
//              DCB=(RECFM=FB,LRECL=100,BLKSIZE=1600)
//SYSIN    DD *
 COPY INDD=INPUT,OUTDD=OUTPUT
/*
//
```

that DISP is not coded. This means that the default values, (NEW,DELETE), apply. The DD statements SYSUT3 and SYSUT4 define data sets that provide workspace to be used by IEBCOPY. These are **temporary data sets** that exist only for the duration of the job, so (NEW,DELETE) are satisfactory values for DISP. Next, notice that no DSN value is coded. Because we never have to refer to these data sets, we do not need to give them names. (For its own purposes the system will assign names, but that is no concern of ours.) Another unusual feature of these DD statements is that VOL is not coded. Usually we specify the volume when we define a DASD data set, but because these are temporary data sets we don't care which volumes are used. Thus we allow the system to select them.

The one really new feature of the DD statements SYSUT3 and SYSUT4 is the value coded for UNIT: VIO. VIO, which stands for **virtual input/output** and is available only on MVS systems, requests that a data set use the virtual paging facility of the operating system. VIO data sets are allocated space within the system's paging data sets. The advantage of VIO is that reading and writing are performed much faster than they are with the usual access methods. Certain conditions must be met, however, in order for a data set to be eligible for VIO. First, the data set must be temporary, so the disposition may be only DELETE or PASS. Second, the VOL=SER parameter must not be coded. Third, the DSN parameter may be omitted, as it is here, or it may specify a temporary data set name. A **temporary data set name** consists of two ampersands (&&) followed by an unqualified data set name. So, for example, if we had coded DSN=&&WORK1 on the SYSUT3 DD statement in Figure 5.17, the data set would still have been eligible for VIO. Finally, the UNIT parameter must specify a VIO unit name. Each computer center may define its own VIO unit names, but VIO is almost always a valid VIO name. At the CUNY computer center, a unit name of SYSDA will also assign VIO to eligible data sets. Your advisor will tell you the valid VIO names at your computer center; you should write them in the place provided on the inside front cover.

On both DD statements one track is requested. There are complex formulas that can be used to calculate the amount of space required, but these formulas are usually unnecessary because one track is generally sufficient. [If you are thinking that the SPACE parameter could be coded SPACE=(TRK,1), you are correct. The extra set of parentheses is not required. Because you will see examples of both forms in your work, however, both forms are included in this book.]

Although the SPACE parameter is coded in this example, with VIO data sets SPACE is optional. If it is not coded, SPACE=(1000,(10,5)) is used. So the simplest possible VIO data set request would be

```
//DD1      DD UNIT=VIO
```

The INPUT DD statement defines an existing PDS, and OUTPUT defines a new PDS. The ddnames for the input and output PDSs are selected by the programmer. The names INPUT and OUTPUT were selected for this example because they reflect what is being done. Let us now examine these DD statements a little more carefully. The INPUT DD statement obviously points to the cataloged data set named GENERLIB, which was created in Figure 5.8. The OUTPUT DD statement points to a new data set named COPYLIB, which is to be cataloged upon job end. We know that a library is being created because three directory blocks are specified in the SPACE parameter.

The DCB parameter is coded on the OUTPUT DD statement, although it is not required. If a DCB is not coded for the output PDS, the DCB information is copied from the input PDS. When you do code the DCB parameter for the output PDS, you must keep the logical record length the same as in the input PDS but you may change the blocksize.

The control statements in the SYSIN data set tell IEBCOPY what is to be done. The control statement in Figure 5.17 is the simplest form of the statement. The operation is COPY and its specification indicates the start of the copy operation. We invented the ddnames for the input and output PDSs, so we must tell IEBCOPY the names we invented. The parameter INDD gives the ddname of the input PDS, and OUTDD gives the ddname of the output PDS.

To summarize, when the job shown in Figure 5.17 is executed, a new PDS named COPYLIB is created which contains all the members that are in GENERLIB. The main difference between GENERLIB and COPYLIB is that all the free space is at the end of COPYLIB and, consequently, available for use.

Merging Libraries Together

Figure 5.18 illustrates a job that copies the members from two libraries into an existing library. If you compare this job with the one in Figure 5.17, you will

■ Figure 5.18 ■

Merging Two Libraries into an Existing Library Using IEBCOPY

```
//JCLQB526 JOB ,'JOHN EVERS',
//              REGION=130K
//COPYMULT EXEC PGM=IEBCOPY
//SYSPRINT DD SYSOUT=A
//SYSUT3   DD UNIT=SYSDA,
//              SPACE=(TRK,(1))
//SYSUT4   DD UNIT=SYSDA,
//              SPACE=(TRK,(1))
//IN1      DD DSN=WYL.QB.JCL.OLDLIB1,
//              DISP=OLD
//IN2      DD DSN=WYL.QB.JCL.OLDLIB2,
//              DISP=OLD
//OUT      DD DSN=WYL.QB.JCL.MIXLIB,
//              DISP=OLD
//SYSIN    DD *
 COPY OUTDD=OUT,INDD=(IN1,(IN2,R)),LIST=NO
/*
//
```

see one more DD statement and a slightly different control statement. Let us examine the control statement. As in the previous example, the operation is COPY. The OUTDD parameter points to the DD statement OUT, which in turn points to an existing PDS named MIXLIB. The INDD parameter points to two DD statements, IN1 and IN2, which point to existing PDS's, OLDLIB1 and OLDLIB2.

During this copy operation IEBCOPY finds the first member in the PDS pointed to by the DD statement IN1. If a member with the same name is *not* found in the output PDS, the member is added to the output PDS. If a member with the same name *is* found in the output PDS, the member is not added to the output PDS. This operation continues until all the members in the PDS pointed to by the IN1 DD statement have been processed. Then IEBCOPY proceeds with the PDS referenced by DD statement IN2. In the control statement IN2 is followed by R, which means replace. Thus, if there are members in the output PDS with the same names as members in the PDS pointed to by IN2, they will be replaced with those in the input PDS.

The last parameter in the control statement is LIST=NO. This means that the SYSPRINT data set will not include a list of the members copied. This parameter is not recommended but is included to illustrate the coding.

Selectively Adding Members to a Library

You are more likely to wish to copy a few members of a library into a new or existing library than to want to copy the entire library. The procedure for selectively adding members to a PDS is illustrated in Figure 5.19. The principal difference between this job and the preceding one is in the control statements. Abbreviations are used in the first control statement: C is for COPY, I is for INDD, and O is for OUTDD. If you use this utility frequently, use of the abbreviations is recommended. If, on the other hand, you do not use it often, do not abbreviate, because you will forget what the abbreviations mean.

Immediately following the COPY control statement is a SELECT control statement. The SELECT control statement applies to the COPY statement preceding it and restricts the copy operation. The COPY statement alone would cause each member in the input PDS to be copied to the output PDS unless that particular member name were already in the output PDS. The SELECT control statement indicates that we want only the members named in this statement to be copied from the input PDS to the output PDS. In this case MEMB1, MEMB2, and MEMB4 will be copied from the input PDS to the output PDS if those member names are not already in the output PDS. MEMB3 will be copied to the output PDS even if a member with that name is already there, because R is specified. This R coded on the SELECT statement has the same meaning as the R coded on the COPY statement in Figure 5.18.

Notice the extra comma coded for MEMB3:

```
(MEMB3,,R)
```

■ Figure 5.19 ■

Selectively Adding Members to a PDS Using IEBCOPY

```
//JCLQB528 JOB ,'FRANK CHANCE',
//              REGION=130K
//SELECOPY EXEC PGM=IEBCOPY
//SYSPRINT DD SYSOUT=A
//SYSUT3    DD UNIT=SYSDA,
//              SPACE=(TRK,(1))
//SYSUT4    DD UNIT=SYSDA,
//              SPACE=(TRK,(1))
//IN1       DD DSN=WYL.QB.JCL.OLDLIB1,
//              DISP=OLD
//IN2       DD DSN=WYL.QB.JCL.OLDLIB2,
//              DISP=OLD
//OUT       DD DSN=WYL.QB.JCL.MIXLIB,
//              DISP=OLD
//SYSIN     DD *
  C I=IN1,O=OUT
  SELECT MEMBER=(MEMB1,MEMB2,(MEMB3,,R),MEMB4)
  C I=IN2,O=OUT
  EXCLUDE MEMBER=(MEMB1,MEMB2,MEMB3,MEMB4)
/*
//
```

As you have probably guessed, these are positional parameters and the extra comma is coded to indicate that a positional parameter has been omitted. The positional parameter omitted is the new name that could be given to the member. This parameter will be discussed later when we study renaming members.

The SELECT in the control statement could be abbreviated as S and the parameter MEMBER as M.

This job, unlike the preceding ones, includes a second copy operation, which is also restricted. The EXCLUDE statement that follows the COPY statement prevents the copy from being a total one. Here, the entire input PDS is to be copied with the exception of the four members MEMB1, MEMB2, MEMB3, and MEMB4.

The EXCLUDE could be abbreviated as E and the parameter MEMBER as M.

A single copy operation may not have both SELECT and EXCLUDE statements applied to it. A copy operation may have more than one SELECT or EXCLUDE statement follow it, however. The subsequent statements are treated as continuation statements.

Renaming a Member

Figure 5.20 shows how to copy a member from one library to another, giving the member a new name in the process. The SELECT control statement is

Figure 5.20

Renaming a Member as It Is Copied Using IEBCOPY

```
//JCLQB530 JOB ,'J.C.LEWIS',
//              REGION=130K
//RENCOPY   EXEC PGM=IEBCOPY
//SYSPRINT DD SYSOUT=A
//SYSUT3    DD UNIT=SYSDA,
//              SPACE=(TRK,(1))
//SYSUT4    DD UNIT=SYSDA,
//              SPACE=(TRK,(1))
//IN     DD DSN=WYL.QB.JCL.OLDLIB1,

 WILL BE UNAVAILABLE ON 2/4 AT 7AM FOR 5 MINUTES DUE TO SYSTEM MAINTENANCE.

//              DISP=OLD
//OUT    DD DSN=WYL.QB.JCL.MIXLIB,
//              DISP=OLD
//SYSIN  DD *
 COPY INDD=IN,OUTDD=OUT
 SELECT MEMBER=((MEMB1,MEMBA),(MEMB2,MEMBB,R))
/*
//
```

used to accomplish this purpose. In Figure 5.19 the SELECT statement selected the members to be copied from one PDS to another. In this example, in addition to selecting members, the SELECT statement provides new names for them. The SELECT statement shows that the first member to be processed is MEMB1. The library referenced by the DD statement IN is searched for member MEMB1. If MEMB1 is not found, the SELECT statement is in error. If MEMB1 is found, the library referenced by the DD statement OUT is searched for a member named MEMBA. If MEMBA is not found in the output library, MEMB1 from the input library is copied to the output library and given the name MEMBA. If MEMBA is found in the output library, MEMB1 is not copied.

The second member to be copied from the input PDS is MEMB2. In the output PDS it will have the name MEMBB. Because R is specified, even if MEMBB already exists in the output library, MEMB2 will be copied and given the name MEMBB.

Later in this chapter we will discuss how to rename a member already in a library.

Reorganizing a Library

Periodically libraries must be reorganized to reclaim the unused space between members (see Figure 5.5). This process is known as **compressing** a library, because it involves squeezing the active members together and recovering the unused space. There are several ways to compress a library; we will look at two methods of compressing COPYLIB, which was created in Figure 5.17.

The first method is shown in the system flowchart in Figure 5.21. In the first step IEBCOPY copies COPYLIB to a sequential data set on tape, in an operation known as **unloading**. Of course, a PDS cannot be used while it is in the form of a sequential data set because, among other things, individual members cannot be accessed. The unloaded PDS, however, can later be used to re-create the PDS, in an operation known as **loading**. The main reasons for unloading a PDS are to produce a backup copy, which is what we are doing here, and to facilitate transport of the PDS to another computer center, as tape is easier to carry than DASD. In the second step the library is actually compressed.

Figure 5.21

System Flowchart to Backup a PDS and Compress It in Place Using IEBCOPY

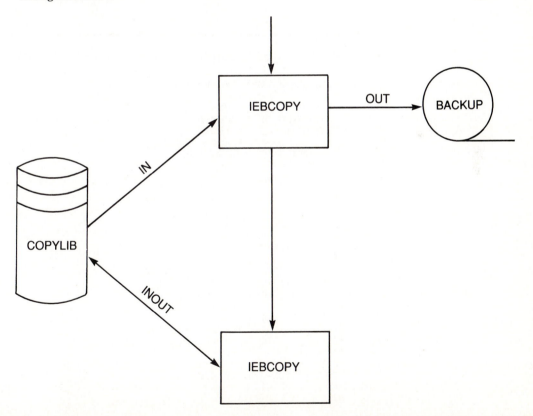

The flowchart in Figure 5.21 is implemented in Figure 5.22. The first step, which creates the backup tape, is run for safety's sake. If the system were to go down for any reason during the next step, which does the compressing, the library would probably be destroyed. If we have made a backup tape, we can re-create the library with it. In most well-run installations, even if the library does not need to be reorganized, a backup tape will be created on a regular basis in case the library is somehow destroyed.

In the output (OUT) DD statement, only the data set name, unit, and disposition have been coded. This is all that is required for a backup tape. IEBCOPY will supply the DCB information. Because volume has not been specified, the operator is free to use any available tape. When we receive the output, the deallocation message will tell us which volume was used.

Notice that there are no special control statements to tell IEBCOPY that we are unloading COPYLIB rather than just copying it. IEBCOPY will examine the output DD statement and, finding that the statement represents a sequential data set, automatically perform an unload rather than a copy operation.

The second step actually reorganizes the PDS. Because of the COND param-

■ Figure 5.22 ■

Creating a PDS Backup and Compressing in Place Using IEBCOPY

```
//JCLQB532 JOB ,'M. HART',
//              REGION=130K
//BACKUP    EXEC PGM=IEBCOPY
//SYSPRINT DD SYSOUT=A
//SYSUT3    DD UNIT=SYSDA,
//              SPACE=(TRK,(1))
//SYSUT4    DD UNIT=SYSDA,
//              SPACE=(TRK,(1))
//IN        DD DSN=WYL.QB.JCL.COPYLIB,
//              DISP=OLD
//OUT       DD DSN=WYL.QB.JCL.BACKUP,
//              DISP=(,KEEP),
//              UNIT=TAPE
//SYSIN     DD *
 COPY OUTDD=OUT,INDD=IN
/*
//COMPRESS EXEC PGM=IEBCOPY,COND=(0,NE)
//SYSPRINT DD SYSOUT=A
//SYSUT3    DD UNIT=SYSDA,
//              SPACE=(TRK,(1))
//SYSUT4    DD UNIT=SYSDA,
//              SPACE=(TRK,(1))
//INOUT     DD DSN=WYL.QB.JCL.COPYLIB,
//              DISP=OLD
//SYSIN     DD *
 COPY OUTDD=INOUT,INDD=INOUT
/*
//
```

Figure 5.23

System Flowchart to Unload and Then Load a PDS Using IEBCOPY

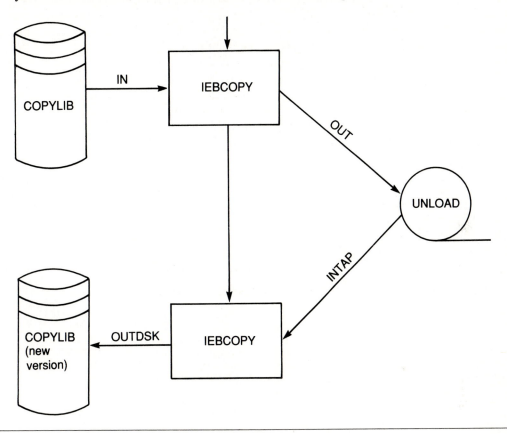

eter coded on the second EXEC statement, the second step will not execute unless the backup tape has been successfully created. The COPY control statement points to the same PDS for both input and output. When the PDS remains in the same DASD space that it was in before the operation began, the compress is called a compress in place.

The second method of compressing a library is shown in Figure 5.23. Here again we start by creating a backup copy of COPYLIB on tape, but we then use the tape to create a new version of COPYLIB. This flowchart is implemented in Figure 5.24.

The first step in Figure 5.24 performs the same function as the first step in Figure 5.22 does. The only difference is in the disposition of the PDS and the tape. In Figure 5.22 the PDS is kept. In Figure 5.24 the PDS is deleted unless

■ Figure 5.24 ■

Unloading and Then Loading a PDS Using IEBCOPY

```
//JCLQB534 JOB ,'S. RAND',
//              REGION=130K
//UNLOAD    EXEC PGM=IEBCOPY
//SYSPRINT DD SYSOUT=A
//SYSUT3    DD UNIT=SYSDA,
//              SPACE=(TRK,(1))
//SYSUT4    DD UNIT=SYSDA,
//              SPACE=(TRK,(1))
//IN        DD DSN=WYL.QB.JCL.COPYLIB,
//              DISP=(OLD,DELETE,KEEP)
//OUT       DD DSN=WYL.QB.JCL.UNLOAD,
//              DISP=(,PASS),
//              UNIT=TAPE
//SYSIN     DD *
 COPY OUTDD=OUT,INDD=IN
/*
//LOAD      EXEC PGM=IEBCOPY,
//              COND=(0,NE)
//SYSPRINT DD SYSOUT=A
//SYSUT3    DD UNIT=SYSDA,
//              SPACE=(TRK,(1))
//SYSUT4    DD UNIT=SYSDA,
//              SPACE=(TRK,(1))
//INTAP     DD DSN=WYL.QB.JCL.UNLOAD,
//              DISP=(OLD,KEEP)
//OUTDSK    DD DSN=WYL.QB.JCL.COPYLIB,
//              UNIT=SYSDA,
//              VOL=SER=WYL004,
//              DISP=(,CATLG),
//              SPACE=(TRK,(5,2,3))
//SYSIN     DD *
 COPY OUTDD=OUTDSK,INDD=INTAP
/*
//
```

the step abends, in which case it is kept. In Figure 5.22 the backup tape is kept, although it could have been cataloged. In Figure 5.24 the backup tape is passed. Because we have no way of knowing which volume will be used, we cannot possibly code the volume serial number in the second step, where this tape forms the input. By specifying PASS for the disposition, we eliminate the need to know the volume serial number.

In the LOAD step a new library is created using the unloaded tape as input. The disposition of the tape in this step is specified as KEEP. We will retain this tape for backup purposes until the next time this job is run. If, for some reason, the library is destroyed, it can be re-created using this tape. Because we did not code a DCB parameter for the new PDS, it will have the same characteristics as the original PDS.

The IEHLIST Utility — Listing Library Member Names

The utility program used to list the names of the members of a library is IEHLIST. IEHLIST can do more than just list the names of the members of a PDS, as will be discussed in Chapter 13. For now, however, let us concentrate on listing the names of members of a library.

Figure 5.25 illustrates the use of IEHLIST to list the names of the members in OLDLIB1 and OLDLIB2. The EXEC statement invokes the utility IEHLIST, and the SYSPRINT DD statement provides the message data set. Both OLD-LIB1 and OLDLIB2 reside on WYL004. The job must have a DD statement that makes WYL004 available — that is the function of the ANYNAME DD statement. The ddname ANYNAME is used in this example because you can use any legal name. Notice also that no data set name is coded, and that the DISP is OLD. This is the standard way of coding DD statements for utilities whose names begin with IEH. In general you will find that utility programs whose names begin with IEB require access to a particular data set, whereas those whose names begin with IEH require access to a DASD volume as a whole. Furthermore, for IEH utilities, the user may employ any legal ddname.

The control statement specifies the LISTPDS operation. We could have coded a label starting in column 1 of the control statement, but there would have been no point in doing so. In the control statement, unlike the DD statement, the parameter DSNAME may *not* be abbreviated.

A listing of the names of members that are in the two libraries OLDLIB1 and OLDLIB2 is requested. More than two libraries could have been named in the control statement, provided they all resided on the same DASD volume. The VOL parameter is used to indicate the unit type and DASD volume upon which the library or libraries may be found. The coding of the VOL parameter is quite different from what you would expect. It is

```
VOL=unit-type=volume-serial-number
```

Figure 5.25

Listing Members of a Library with IEHLIST

```
//JCLQB538 JOB ,'J.C.LEWIS',
//              REGION=38K
//LISTPDS   EXEC PGM=IEHLIST
//SYSPRINT DD SYSOUT=A
//ANYNAME   DD UNIT=SYSDA,
//              VOL=SER=WYL004,
//              DISP=OLD
//SYSIN     DD *
 LISTPDS DSNAME=(WYL.QB.JCL.OLDLIB1,WYL.QB.JCL.OLDLIB2),          *
              VOL=SYSDA=WYL004
/*
//
```

For unit-type you code what is usually coded in the UNIT parameter of a DD statement: DISK, SYSDA, 3380, etc. In some installations only actual unit types such as 3380 are permitted. Check with your advisor for the correct coding of this parameter, and write it in the place provided on the inside front cover. Make sure that you understand this parameter, because it is used in the same form with several other utility programs.

If OLDLIB1 and OLDLIB2 were on different volumes, then each would have to have its own LISTPDS control statement and there would have to be another DD statement making the second volume available to the job. The next example shows how to use two DD statements in one job step.

The IEHPROGM Utility

Figure 5.26 shows how the IEHPROGM utility program can be used to delete and rename members and data sets, as well as to catalog and uncatalog data

Figure 5.26

Renaming, Cataloging, Uncataloging, and Scratching Data Sets and Members of a PDS Using IEHPROGM

```
//JCLQB540 JOB ,'J.C.LEWIS',
//              REGION=36K
//LIBPROGM EXEC PGM=IEHPROGM
//SYSPRINT DD SYSOUT=A
//ANYNAME1 DD UNIT=SYSDA,
//              VOL=SER=WYL004,
//              DISP=OLD
//ANYNAME2 DD UNIT=SYSDA,
//              VOL=SER=WYL002,
//              DISP=OLD
//SYSIN    DD *
 RENAME MEMBER=MEMB1,DSNAME=WYL.QB.JCL.OLDLIB1,       *
              VOL=SYSDA=WYL004,                        *
              NEWNAME=MEMBA
 RENAME DSNAME=WYL.QB.JCL.GENERLIB,                   *
              VOL=SYSDA=WYL002,                        *
              NEWNAME=WYL.QB.JCL.IEBGENER.LIB
 UNCATLG DSNAME=WYL.QB.JCL.GENERLIB
 CATLG DSNAME=WYL.QB.JCL.IEBGENER.LIB,                *
              VOL=SYSDA=WYL004
 SCRATCH DSNAME=WYL.QB.JCL.OLDLIB2,                   *
              VOL=SYSDA=WYL004,                        *
              PURGE
 UNCATLG DSNAME=WYL.QB.JCL.OLDLIB2
 SCRATCH MEMBER=MEMB2,DSNAME=WYL.QB.JCL.OLDLIB1,      *
              VOL=SYSDA=WYL004
 /*
 //
```

sets. IEHPROGM requires JCL very similar to that required by IEHLIST, including a SYSPRINT statement for messages, SYSIN for control statements, and a DD statement with an arbitrary name to make available each volume used in the processing.

The RENAME Control Statement

The first control statement in Figure 5.26 renames member MEMB1, which resides in OLDLIB1 on volume WYL004, as MEMBA. The MEMBER parameter tells IEHPROGM that we are renaming a member of a library. The DSNAME parameter names the library; unlike the JCL parameter, it may *not* be abbreviated to DSN. The VOL parameter, which has the same unusual form as in IEHLIST, provides the unit type, SYSDA, and the serial number, WYL004, of the volume upon which the data set resides. The ANYNAME1 DD statement makes volume WYL004 available to the job. Finally, the NEWNAME parameter supplies the new name.

The next RENAME statement renames GENERLIB as IEBGENER.LIB. The only difference between this RENAME statement and the previous one is that in this statement the MEMBER parameter is not used. Omission of this parameter tells IEHPROGM that we are renaming the whole data set and not just a particular member. Because GENERLIB resides on volume WYL002, the ANYNAME2 DD statement makes that volume available to the job.

Although you are learning about IEHPROGM in the context of libraries, you should realize that IEHPROGM can operate on any non-VSAM data set. If the data set resided on several volumes (remember that a library cannot reside on more than one volume), the VOL parameter might be coded as

```
VOL=SYSDA=(WYL002,WYL003,WYL004)
```

and the DD statement as

```
//ANYNAME     DD UNIT=SYSDA,
//              VOL=SER=(WYL002,WYL003,WYL004),
//              DISP=OLD
```

The CATLG and UNCATLG Control Statements

If a cataloged data set such as GENERLIB is renamed, the old name should be uncataloged and the new name cataloged. These operations are performed by the next two control statements. The UNCATLG control statement uncatalogs GENERLIB. Notice that only the DSNAME need be coded; it is not necessary to code the VOL parameter, nor is it generally necessary to provide access to the volume on which the data set resides. Because the data set is cataloged (if it were not, why would we be bothering to uncatalog it?), the system knows where it is. In other words, to uncatalog a data set, the system needs access only to the system catalog, not to the data set itself. Uncataloging a data set means removing information about the data set from the system catalog. In fact, the volume containing the data set need not even be mounted.

The CATLG control statement catalogs the data set under its new name, IEBGENER.LIB. On the CATLG control statement, both the DSNAME and VOL parameters must be coded so that the system knows where to find the needed information about the data set.

The SCRATCH Control Statement

Now that you understand the RENAME control statement, you will find the SCRATCH statements in Figure 5.26 quite simple. Let us look at the first one. The DSNAME parameter names the data set you want scratched, and the VOL tells where to find it. The PURGE parameter says that you want the data set scratched even if its expiration date has not arrived. As you will learn, you set the expiration date with the LABEL parameter in the DD statement. As a result of the first SCRATCH statement, data set OLDLIB2 will be deleted from volume WYL004. Because OLDLIB2 is a cataloged data set, it is uncataloged when it is deleted.

The next SCRATCH statement removes a member from the library. The difference between this SCRATCH statement and the preceding one is in the MEMBER parameter. The MEMBER parameter names the member to be deleted from the library named in the DSNAME parameter.

The parameters MEMBER, DSNAME, VOL, and NEWNAME are keyword parameters and may be coded in any order. In the SCRATCH and RENAME control statements in Figure 5.26, the MEMBER parameter was coded first when the control statement referenced a library member. If you code the MEMBER parameter first, you probably will not accidentally scratch or rename the entire library.

The IEFBR14 Utility and Disposition Processing

If you want to scratch a member of a library, you must use IEHPROGM. If you want to scratch, catalog, or uncatalog a data set, however, you can use either IEHPROGM or disposition processing. Using disposition processing is easier. For example, to delete a data set you need only name it in a DD statement with the DISP parameter coded as (OLD,DELETE). In Figure 5.6 disposition processing, using IEFBR14, was used to create and catalog SOURCE.LIBRARY. Figure 5.27 shows how disposition processing, again using IEFBR14, can be used to scratch SOURCE.LIBRARY. Because we did not code unit or volume information, SOURCE.LIBRARY is also uncataloged when it is scratched.

■ Figure 5.27 ■

Scratching a PDS Using IEFBR14

```
//JCLQB541 JOB ,'J.C.LEWIS',
//              REGION=32K
//SCRATCH  EXEC PGM=IEFBR14
//DD1       DD DSN=WYL.QB.JCL.SOURCE.LIBRARY,
//              DISP=(OLD,DELETE)
//
```

Summary

In this chapter you have learned

—how a library is organized

—how to create a library

—how to use IEBGENER to add members to a library

—how to use IEBPTPCH to list members in a library

—how to use IEBUPDTE to add members to a library, change and replace members in a library, and copy members from one library to another

—how to use IEBCOPY to copy members from one library to another and to compress a library

—how to use IEHLIST to list the names of the members in a library

—how to use IEHPROGM to scratch or rename a physical sequential data set, a library, or a member of a library

—how to use IEHPROGM to catalog and uncatalog a physical sequential data set or a library

—how to use IEFBR14 to create, catalog, uncatalog, and delete a data set

Vocabulary

In this chapter you have been introduced to the meanings of the following terms:

compressing	partitioned data set (PDS)
directory	temporary data set
directory block	temporary data set name
library	unloading
loading	virtual input/output (VIO)
member	

Exercises

1. What is a library?
2. What is another name for a library?
3. What type of device may be used for a library?
4. How many volumes may be used for a library?
5. What are the rules governing member names?
6. In what order are members listed in the directory?
7. In what order are members stored in the library?
8. What happens to the space released when a member is deleted?
9. How large is a directory block?
10. What information is stored in a directory block?
11. Name two reasons to use a library instead of separate physical sequential data sets.
12. When you look at JCL, what tells you that a library is being created?
13. How do you code JCL to treat a member of a library as a sequential data set?
14. Why would you use IEBPTPCH instead of IEBGENER to print a library member?
15. Why would you use IEBGENER instead of IEBUPDTE to add a member to a library?
16. How do you assign a name to a member when IEBGENER is used to add the member to a library? How do you assign a name when IEBUPDTE is used?
17. When do you code PARM=NEW on the EXEC statement for IEBUPDTE?
18. Why do records in members processed by IEBUPDTE usually have sequence numbers in columns 73 through 80?
19. Why would you want to use VIO for a data set? What conditions must a data set satisfy in order to be eligible for VIO?
20. What ddname is used to identify the input library for IEBCOPY?
21. What does it mean to say that a library has been unloaded to tape? Why would you want to unload a library? What special control statements does IEBCOPY need in order to perform an unload operation?
22. Why would you use IEBCOPY instead of the REPRO function of IEBUPDTE to copy a member from one library to another?
23. Why would you compress a library?
24. Two methods of compressing a library were illustrated in this chapter. Code the job stream to compress a library named OLDLIB, using a third method: In the first step use IEBCOPY to copy OLDLIB to a new library named NEWLIB. At the end of the first step, delete OLDLIB. In the second step, use IEHPROGM to rename NEWLIB as OLDLIB and catalog OLDLIB. Assume that NEWLIB is created on DISK05 with a primary allocation of five tracks, a secondary allocation of 0 tracks, and ten directory blocks.
25. What is the name of the IEHLIST control statement that lists the names of the members of a library?
26. Which utility program can be used to rename a data set? Can the same utility be used to rename a member of a library?

27. Suppose IEHPROGM is to be used to change the name of an uncataloged data set from TESTDATA to DATATEST. TESTDATA occupies ten tracks on disk pack PACK11. Code the appropriate DD and control statements.
28. What are two ways to scratch a library? Can the same two ways be used to scratch a member of a library?

Programming Assignments

1. Use IEFBR14 to create and catalog a library named FIRSTLIB. Request one track and one directory block. The logical record length should be 80 and the blocksize 800.
2. Prepare the following data records:

```
CEREAL
TOAST
COFFEE
AAAAAAAA
BOLOGNA SANDWICH
MILK
ICE CREAM
BBBBBBBB
HAMBURGER
FRENCH FRIES
PIE
COFFEE
```

With these data records as input, use IEBGENER to store three members, named BKFAST, LUNCH, and DINNER, in FIRSTLIB.
3. Execute a job that will list members BKFAST and DINNER.
4. Use IEBUPDTE to copy members LUNCH and DINNER from FIRSTLIB to a new, cataloged library named SCONDLIB. You want to number the data records so they can be modified, but because a NUMBER statement may not follow a REPRO statement, you will have to use a CHANGE statement between the REPRO and NUMBER statements.
5. Use IEBUPDTE to modify member DINNER. Change FRENCH FRIES to MASHED POTATOES, and add STRING BEANS.
6. Use IEBCOPY to copy member BKFAST from FIRSTLIB to SCONDLIB.
7. Execute a job that will list the names of the members in FIRSTLIB.
8. Execute a job that will rename member DINNER as SUPPER.
9. Execute a job that will rename SCONDLIB as SECOND.LIB, uncatalog SCONDLIB, and catalog SECOND.LIB.
10. Execute a job that will scratch member LUNCH.
11. Execute a job that will scratch and uncatalog SECOND.LIB.
12. Use IEBGENER to create a library and store the source statements for a program as a member of the library. The program may be written in any language you like.

6

Generation Data Groups

In this chapter you will learn

- what a generation data group is
- how to create a generation data group
- how to use a generation data group

What Is a Generation Data Group?

A **generation data group** is a collection, or group, of cataloged data sets having the same name and related to one another chronologically. Each of these data sets is called a **generation data set** or, simply, a **generation.** Each generation contains successive versions of the same data. An example would be a cumulative year-to-date payroll, where a new generation is created every pay day.

Each generation may be a physical sequential data set, a partitioned data set, a direct data set, or, under special conditions, an indexed sequential data set. (Chapter 11 provides a full discussion of indexed sequential data sets and some discussion of direct data sets.) Each generation data set may reside on tape or DASD. Usually all the generation data sets of a generation data group will be on the same kind of device. It is possible, however, to have a generation data group in which one generation is a physical sequential data set residing on tape and another is a partitioned data set residing on DASD.

Unlike other data set names, which may be up to 44 characters long, the data set name for a generation data set is limited to 35 characters. Each generation data set is distinguished from the others by the **generation number.** The generation number may be relative or absolute. The system uses absolute numbers, but application programmers usually employ relative numbers because relative numbers are easier to use. If the data set name of the group is GEN.DATA.GROUP, then to access the current generation, you code DSN=GEN.DATA.GROUP(0). To access the previous generation, you code DSN=GEN.DATA.GROUP(-1); the generation before would be DSN=GEN.DATA.GROUP(-2). If you want to create a new generation, you code DSN=GEN.DATA.GROUP(+1). If you want to create a second version, you specify a relative number of +2.

The absolute number used by the system is in the form GxxxxVyy, where xxxx is a generation number from 0000 to 9999 and yy is a version number from 00 to 99. Thus the generation specified as DSN=GEN.DATA.GROUP(0) might appear to the system, for example, as GEN.DATA.GROUP.G0006V00. Then the data set with a relative number of (-1) would be GEN.DATA.GROUP.G0005V00, and the newly created one with a relative number of (+1) would be GEN.DATA.GROUP.G0007V00. If instead of specifying a relative number of +1 you specified +2, a data set whose name was GEN.DATA.GROUP.G0008V00 would be created. There would be no data set with an absolute generation number of 7, because one generation would be skipped.

Before a generation data set may be created, the programmer must create a generation group index and a model data set control block. How this is done will be discussed next.

Generation Group Index

The **generation group index** contains information on how many generations are to be retained and what to do when the index gets full. If four generations are specified in the index, four data sets will be retained. What is done when the fifth is created is determined by the index. One possibility is to delete all four previous data sets. Another possibility is to retain the four data sets but to remove their entries from the index. The usual approach is either to remove the index entry for the oldest data set and delete the data set or to remove the index entry for the oldest data set but retain the data set itself.

The index may be created using either the VSAM utility IDCAMS or the utility IEHPROGM. At some computer centers you must use IDCAMS, at others you must use IEHPROGM, and at still others you may use either. Your advisor will tell you which utility is used at your computer center, and you should write it in the place provided on the inside front cover.

Using IDCAMS

IDCAMS will be discussed in detail in Chapter 12; for now you merely need to know a few rules. IDCAMS requires a region of 300K, a SYSPRINT DD statement for messages, and a SYSIN DD statement for control statements. The syntax rules for `IDCAMS` control statements are very convenient. For example, the statement may start in any column after column 1, a continuation is indicated by a hyphen (-), and the continued statement also may begin in any column after column 1.

The command format is

```
DEFINE GDG (parameters)
```

where `GDG` stands for generation data group. The parameters that may be coded are defined in Table 6.1. The `DEFINE GDG` statement in Figure 6.1 creates an index named `WYL.QB.JCL.POLYGEN` in the system catalog. The entry `LIMIT(4)` requests space for four entries. When a fifth entry is created, the entry for the oldest existing data set (whose relative number is -3) is removed from the index, but the data set itself is kept. Thereafter, if you wish to access it, you must use the absolute number assigned by the system, such as `WYL.QB.JCL.POLYGEN.G0051V00`.

The `DEFINE GDG` statement in Figure 6.1 contains only the required parameters `NAME` and `LIMIT`. If we had coded `SCRATCH`,

```
DEFINE GDG (NAME(WYL.QB.JCL.POLYGEN) -
            LIMIT(4) -
            SCRATCH)
```

Table 6.1
Define GDG Parameters

Parameter	Abbr.	Meaning
NAME (entryname)		Generation data group name.
LIMIT (limit)	LIM	The number of generations permitted for this GDG. The maximum is 255.
EMPTY	EMP	If EMPTY is specified, all data sets are to be removed from the index when the limit is reached. NOEMPTY is the default.
NOEMPTY	NEMP	
OWNER (ownerid)		User identification (optional).
SCRATCH	SCR	If SCRATCH is specified, the data set is scratched when a data set is removed from the index. NOSCRATCH is the default.
NOSCRATCH	NSCR	
TO (date)		Data set retention period.
FOR (days)		

■ Figure 6.1 ■

Defining a Generation Group Index Using IDCAMS

```
//JCLQB544 JOB ,'MISS SCARLET',
//               REGION=300K
//STEPGDG EXEC PGM=IDCAMS
//SYSPRINT  DD SYSOUT=A
//SYSIN     DD *
 DEFINE    GDG (NAME(WYL.QB.JCL.POLYGEN) -
                LIMIT(4))
/*
//
```

then when the fifth entry was created, not only would the index entry for the oldest generation have been removed, but the oldest generation itself would have been scratched.

If we had coded EMPTY,

```
DEFINE GDG (NAME(WYL.QB.JCL.POLYGEN) -
            LIMIT(4) -
            EMPTY
```

then when the fifth entry was created, all four entries would have been removed from the index, but the data sets themselves would have been kept.

Finally, if we had coded both SCRATCH and EMPTY,

```
DEFINE GDG (NAME(WYL.QB.JCL.POLYGEN) -
            LIMIT(4) -
            SCRATCH -
            EMPTY
```

then when the fifth entry was created, all four entries would have been removed from the index and the data sets would have been scratched.

Using IEHPROGM

The index may also be created using the BLDG control statement of the utility program IEHPROGM. The job shown in Figure 6.2 illustrates the BLDG control statement. Execution of this control statement will result in the creation of the index in the system catalog.

The BLDG control statement builds an index named WYL.QB.JCL.POLY-GEN. ENTRIES=4 requests space for four entries. When a fifth entry is created, the entry for the oldest existing data set (whose relative number is -3) is removed from the index, but the data set itself is kept. If you wish to access it, however, you must use the absolute number—for example, WYL.QB.JCL.POLYGEN.G0051V00.

The BLDG statement in Figure 6.2 contains only the required parameters,

Figure 6.2

Building a Generation Group Index Using IEHPROGM

```
//JCLQB542 JOB ,'COL. MUSTARD',
//              REGION=36K
//STEPBLD   EXEC PGM=IEHPROGM
//SYSPRINT DD SYSOUT=A
//SYSIN     DD *
 BLDG INDEX=WYL.QB.JCL.POLYGEN,                                *
              ENTRIES=4
/*
//
```

INDEX and ENTRIES. Either one or both of two optional parameters, DELETE and EMPTY, may also be coded.

If we had coded DELETE,

```
BLDG INDEX=WYL.QB.JCL.POLYGEN,                                *
             ENTRIES=4,                                       *
             DELETE
```

then when the fifth entry was created, not only would the index entry for the oldest generation have been removed, but the oldest generation itself would have been scratched.

If we had coded EMPTY,

```
BLDG INDEX=WYL.QB.JCL.POLYGEN,                                *
             ENTRIES=4,                                       *
             EMPTY
```

then when the fifth entry was created, all four entries would have been removed from the index, but the data sets themselves would have been kept.

Finally, if we had coded both DELETE and EMPTY,

```
BLDG INDEX=WYL.QB.JCL.POLYGEN,                                *
             ENTRIES=4                                        *
             DELETE,                                          *
             EMPTY
```

then when the fifth entry was created, all four entries would have been removed from the index and the data sets would have been scratched.

Notice that EMPTY has the same meaning here as in the DEFINE GDG statement of IDCAMS. ENTRIES is equivalent to LIMIT, and DELETE is equivalent to SCRATCH.

Model Data Set Control Block

Every generation data group must have a **model data set control block (DSCB)** from which the system obtains DCB information. Figure 6.3 illustrates a job

■ Figure 6.3 ■

Creating a Model Data Set Control Block for a Generation Data Group

```
//JCLQB546 JOB ,'PROF. PLUM',
//          REGION=32K
//MODLDSCB EXEC PGM=IEFBR14
//DD1      DD DSN=WYL.QB.JCL.POLYGEN,
//            DISP=(,KEEP),
//            UNIT=SYSDA,
//            VOL=SER=WYL001,
//            SPACE=(TRK,0),
//            DCB=(RECFM=FB,LRECL=80,BLKSIZE=1600)
//
```

that could be run to create the model DSCB. Because we want just the DD statement to be processed, we execute the program IEFBR14, discussed in Chapter 5. This job will create a model DSCB named WYL.QB.JCL.POLYGEN. Notice that the model DSCB is not cataloged. Because the model DSCB has the same name as the generations, either the model DSCB or the generations can be cataloged, but not both.

The model DSCB must reside on the same volume as the system catalog. At the CUNY computer center, the serial number of the appropriate volume is WYL001. Your advisor will tell you the serial number to use at your computer center; you should write it in the place provided on the inside front cover. If no one can tell you the serial number of the volume that contains the system catalog, you can get it yourself by reading the allocation messages from a job that uses the catalog. Figure 4.7, for example, contains the messages

```
IEF285I    SYSCTLG.VWY001          KEPT
IEF285I    VOL SER NOS=WYL001.
```

These messages indicate that the system catalog is on DASD volume WYL001.

Because we are only placing information in the data set label, no space is required. Thus the SPACE parameter requests zero tracks.

Instead of running the job shown in Figure 6.3, we could have created the model DSCB by including the DD1 DD statement in either the job in Figure 6.1 or the one in Figure 6.2.

It is not necessary to code DCB information in the model DSCB. You can provide some or all of the information when the generation is created.

Creating and Accessing a Generation

Figure 6.4 illustrates a simple two-step job. In the first step IEBGENER is used to create a generation data set named POLYGEN using as input the first 30

Figure 6.4

Two-Step Job Using Generation Data Sets

```
//JCLQB548 JOB ,'MR. GREEN',
//              REGION=40K
//STEP1     EXEC PGM=IEBGENER
//SYSPRINT DD SYSOUT=A
//SYSUT1    DD *
13009REED,TINA                A0842000426072100      74
15174HANDJANY,HAIDEH          H0229000220022900      71
17337BUTERO,MAURICE           H0501000434050100      63
19499LAFER,BRUCE              A0706000819050000      52
21661LEE,SUI                  A0390170303030017      76
23821COOPER,LUCY              L0745000730070000      64
25980NELSON,LAWRENCE          L0513000217051300      78
28138KRUKIS,SONIA             A0346000510034600      59
30295CHEN,YIN                 H0295000514010000      81
32451SIMPKINS,KEVIN           L0388000321038806      76
34605PORTER,MICHELE           A0627500128042700      65
36759DECICCO,RICHARD          A0255000619010000      71
38912ABREU,JUANITA            H0732001030070000      80
41063HIGH,CAROL               L0311000521031100      82
43214ENGLISH,REYNOLDS         A0443000228043300      82
45363LEE,BOHYON               A0515000214050000      79
47512THOMPSON,STANLEY         H0640750307064075      66
49659VALDEZ,FABIO             L0706000430070600      71
51805AMATO,ROBERT             A0466000417015000      63
53950RIZZUTO,JAMES            A0693000822000000      81
56094SCHWARTZ,MICHAEL         H1037000605050000      67
58238RUFINO,CARLOS            L0673000520047300      64
60380MORLEY,JOHN              A0786000514078600      71
62521BREVIL,JAMES             H0812000314081200      55
64660FALCONER,EDWARD          L1080000227008000      74
66799MARTIN,KATHLEEN          L0895000129089500      65
68937YEUNG,SUK                A0517000816050000      49
71074PAUL,MARINA              A0441000414034100      80
73210FRADIN,SHIRLEY           L0668000728066800      56
75344BURNS,JEFFREY            L0706000226070000      57
/*
//SYSUT2    DD DSN=WYL.QB.JCL.POLYGEN(+1),
//              DISP=(,PASS),
//              UNIT=SYSDA,
//              VOL=SER=WYL005,
//              SPACE=(TRK,(2,1))
//SYSIN     DD DUMMY
//STEP2     EXEC PGM=IEBPTPCH
//SYSPRINT DD SYSOUT=A
//SYSUT1    DD DSN=WYL.QB.JCL.POLYGEN(+1),
//              DISP=(OLD,CATLG)
//SYSUT2    DD SYSOUT=A
//SYSIN     DD *
 PRINT MAXFLDS=1
 RECORD FIELD=(80)
/*
//
```

Two Jobs Using Generation Data Sets

```
//JCLQB550 JOB ,'MRS. WHITE',
//          REGION=40K
//STEP1     EXEC PGM=IEBGENER
//SYSPRINT DD SYSOUT=A
//SYSUT1    DD *
13009REED,TINA                A0842000426072100    74
15174HANDJANY,HAIDEH          H0229000220022900    71
17337BUTERO,MAURICE           H0501000434050100    63
19499LAFER,BRUCE              A0706000819050000    52
21661LEE,SUI                  A0390170303030017    76
23821COOPER,LUCY              L0745000730070000    64
25980NELSON,LAWRENCE          L0513000217051300    78
28138KRUKIS,SONIA             A0346000510034600    59
30295CHEN,YIN                 H0295000514010000    81
32451SIMPKINS,KEVIN           L0388000321038806    76
34605PORTER,MICHELE           A0627500128042700    65
36759DECICCO,RICHARD          A0255000619010000    71
38912ABREU,JUANITA            H0732001030070000    80
41063HIGH,CAROL               L0311000521031100    82
43214ENGLISH,REYNOLDS         A0443000228043300    82
45363LEE,BOHYON               A0515000214050000    79
47512THOMPSON,STANLEY         H0640750307064075    66
49659VALDEZ,FABIO             L0706000430070600    71
51805AMATO,ROBERT             A0466000417015000    63
53950RIZZUTO,JAMES            A0693000822000000    81
56094SCHWARTZ,MICHAEL         H1037000605050000    67
58238RUFINO,CARLOS            L0673000520047300    64
60380MORLEY,JOHN              A0786000514078600    71
62521BREVIL,JAMES             H0812000314081200    55
64660FALCONER,EDWARD          L1080000227008000    74
66799MARTIN,KATHLEEN          L0895000129089500    65
68937YEUNG,SUK                A0517000816050000    49
71074PAUL,MARINA              A0441000414034100    80
73210FRADIN,SHIRLEY           L0668000728066800    56
75344BURNS,JEFFREY            L0706000226070000    57
/*
//SYSUT2    DD DSN=WYL.QB.JCL.POLYGEN(+1),
//             DISP=(,CATLG),
//             UNIT=SYSDA,
//             VOL=SER=WYL005,
//             SPACE=(TRK,(2,1))
//SYSIN     DD DUMMY
//
//JCLQB552 JOB ,'J.C.LEWIS',
//             REGION=32K
//STEP1     EXEC PGM=IEBPTPCH
//SYSPRINT DD SYSOUT=A
//SYSUT1    DD DSN=WYL.QB.JCL.POLYGEN(0),
//             DISP=SHR
//SYSUT2    DD SYSOUT=A
//SYSIN     DD *
 PRINT MAXFLDS=1
 RECORD FIELD=(80)
/*
//
```

records listed in Appendix C. (These data were used in Chapter 3 to create the original version of POLYFILE.) In the second step IEBPTPCH is used to print the newly created generation. Note that in both steps the relative number is (+1).

Figure 6.5 does exactly the same thing as Figure 6.4, but using two jobs instead of one job with two steps. Note that the two figures differ with respect to the relative number used in the second step or job. This is because the system uses an index to maintain the generation number, and this index is updated after the job ends. Thus whereas in Figure 6.4 the generation number is not updated until after both steps are executed, in Figure 6.5 the generation number is updated after the first job ends. Therefore, to print the current generation in the second job, we must use a relative number of (0).

Figure 6.6 shows how one generation of POLYGEN may be modified to create a new generation. The input to IEBGENER consists of two data sets. The first data set is the current generation of POLYGEN, which is accessed using the relative number (0); the second data set consists of the last ten records in Appendix C. These two data sets are concatenated to form the input to IEB-GENER. Concatenation allows more than one data set to be read with one DD statement. Concatenation is thoroughly discussed in Chapter 7; at this point

Figure 6.6

Creating a New Generation

```
//JCLQB554 JOB ,'MRS. PEACOCK',
//              REGION=40K
//STEP1     EXEC PGM=IEBGENER
//SYSPRINT DD SYSOUT=A
//SYSUT1    DD DSN=WYL.QB.JCL.POLYGEN(0),
//              DISP=SHR
//          DD *
77478KATZ, HAL              A0485000406038500      64
79610WRIGHT,DONNA          H0926000901092000      75
81742CUOMO, DONNA          L0900000313090000      69
83872LOPEZ, ANNA           A0679000716010000      80
86002ALEXANDER, LISA       A0402000623030200      73
88130GOLDBERG, LORI        H0987000524095000      67
92057HOFMANN, PATRICA      H0737000315040000      77
92384PUGH, CLIFFORD        A0750000423075000      80
94509FERRIS, LAURA         A0135000815013500      73
96633BERGIN,MICHAEL        L1608000116100000      74
/*
//SYSUT2    DD DSN=WYL.QB.JCL.POLYGEN(+1),
//              DISP=(,CATLG),
//              UNIT=SYSDA,
//              VOL=SER=WYL002,
//              SPACE=(TRK,(2,1))
//SYSIN     DD DUMMY
//
```

■ **Figure 6.7** ━━━

Listing an Entire Generation Data Group

```
//JCLQB556 JOB ,'J.C.LEWIS',
//                REGION=32K
//STEP1    EXEC PGM=IEBPTPCH
//SYSPRINT  DD SYSOUT=A
//SYSUT1    DD DSN=WYL.QB.JCL.POLYGEN,
//                DISP=SHR
//SYSUT2    DD SYSOUT=A
//SYSIN     DD *
 PRINT MAXFLDS=1
 RECORD FIELD=(80)
/*
//
```

all you need to know is that the current generation of POLYGEN and the ten input stream records are read as one data set.

The output of Figure 6.6 consists of a new generation of POLYGEN, which is specified using the relative number (+1). Figure 6.5 may seem similar to Figure 4.13, in which the last ten records in Appendix C were added to the end of the original version of POLYFILE, but in fact the two job streams are very different. In Figure 4.13 there was only one version of POLYFILE. At the end of the job, POLYFILE contained all 40 records in Appendix C. In contrast, after the job in Figure 6.6 is run, there exist two generations of POLYGEN; the older generation contains the first 30 records from Appendix C, and the current generation contains all 40 records.

If all the generations in a generation data group have the same data control block information, the entire generation data group may be processed using one DD statement. Figure 6.7 illustrates this process with the utility program IEBPTPCH. This job will print all the generations in the generation data group. Notice that when you wish to process the entire generation data group, you code the DSN without a relative number.

Using the Model DSCB

When the data sets were created in Figures 6.4, 6.5, and 6.6, no DCB information was provided; the information was obtained from the model DSCB. You don't have to use the information in the model DSCB exactly as provided, however. Figure 6.8a illustrates the taking of all the DCB information except the block size from the model DSCB.

Figure 6.8b illustrates the creation of a generation using the model DSCB of

Figure 6.8

(a) Modifying DCB Information from Model DSCB

```
//DD1        DD DSN=WYL.QB.JCL.POLYGEN(+1),
//              DISP=(,CATLG),
//              UNIT=SYSDA,
//              VOL=SER=WYL002,
//              SPACE=(TRK,(2,1)),
//              DCB=BLKSIZE=880
```

(b) Using Model DSCB from Another Generation Data Group

```
//DD2        DD DSN=GEN.DATA.COLLECT(+1),
//              DISP=(,CATLG),
//              UNIT=SYSDA,
//              VOL=SER=WYL001,
//              SPACE=(TRK,(3,1)),
//              DCB=(GEN.DATA.GROUP)
```

(c) Using Modified Model DSCB from Another Generation Data Group

```
//DD3        DD DSN=GEN.DATA.COLECT(+1),
//              DISP=(,CATLG),
//              UNIT=SYSDA,
//              VOL=SER=WYL005,
//              SPACE=(TRK,(3,1),RLSE),
//              DCB=(GEN.DATA.GROUP,LRECL=40)
```

another generation data group. In this case a generation of GEN.DATA.COL-LECT is created using the model DSCB of GEN.DATA.GROUP.

Figure 6.8c illustrates the use of a modified model DSCB of another generation data group. In this example, the DCB information is taken from the model DSCB of GEN.DATA.GROUP, but the logical record length is set equal to 40.

Deleting a Generation Group Index

Either IDCAMS or IEHPROGM may be used to delete a generation group index. Before a generation group index may be deleted, however, all the generations must be scratched. The generations may be scratched by means of either IEHPROGM or disposition processing using IEFBR14.

Figure 6.9 shows how the IDCAMS DELETE control statement may be used to delete the generation data group index created in Figure 6.1. Figure 6.10 shows how the IEHPROGM DLTX control statement may be used to delete the generation data group index created in Figure 6.2.

Figure 6.9

Deleting a Generation Group Index Using IDCAMS

```
//JCLQB543 JOB ,'J.C.LEWIS',
//              REGION=300K
//DELETE EXEC PGM=IDCAMS
//SYSPRINT DD SYSOUT=A
//SYSIN    DD *
 DELETE  WYL.QB.JCL.POLYGEN -
         GDG
/*
//
```

Figure 6.10

Deleting a Generation Group Index Using IEHPROGM

```
//JCLQB542 JOB ,'J.C.LEWIS',
//              REGION=36K
//STEPDLTX EXEC PGM=IEHPROGM
//SYSPRINT DD SYSOUT=A
//SYSIN    DD *
 DLTX INDEX=WYL.QB.JCL.POLYGEN
/*
//
```

Pros and Cons

The main advantage of using a generation data group is that the same JCL can be reused without change. Each time the job illustrated in Figure 6.4 is run, a new data set is created. If the output of IEBGENER were not a generation, the data set would have to be scratched before the job could be rerun. Similarly, no matter how many generations are created, the second job in Figure 6.5 prints the current generation.

The main disadvantage of using a generation data group is that machine procedures must be strictly enforced. If, for example, a machine operator starts a job, cancels it, and then starts it again, the results may be disastrous because the generation numbers may be updated twice. Also, the system programmer must keep an eye on the generation number, because the results are unpredictable when the maximum value of 9999 is reached.

Summary

In this chapter you have learned

—how a generation data group is organized

—how to use IDCAMS and IEHPROGM to create and delete a generation group index

—how to create a model data set control block

—how to create and access a generation

—how to use IEBPTPCH to list all the generations in a generation data group

Vocabulary

In this chapter you have been introduced to the meanings of the following terms:

generation   generation group index
generation data group   generation number
generation data set   model data set control block (DSCB)

Exercises

1. What is a generation data group?
2. What kind of data sets may be included in a generation data group?
3. What types of devices may be used with a generation data group?
4. How long may a generation data group DSN be?
5. How is one generation distinguished from another?
6. How would an application programmer usually specify a generation?
7. How might a system programmer specify a generation?
8. When is a generation group index updated?
9. From where may the DCB information be obtained if it is not specified in the DD statement when the generation is created?
10. What two items must be created before a generation data group may be used?
11. What information is included in the index?
12. How would the index be created?

Programming Assignments

1. Use IDCAMS or IEHPROGM to create a generation group index. In the same job, create a model DSCB.
2. With the first 30 records in Appendix D as input, use IEBGENER to create a generation.
3. With the first generation and the last ten records in Appendix D as input, use IEBGENER to create a new generation.
4. Use IEBPTPCH to print both generations. In how many ways may this be done?
5. Use IEFBR14 to scratch the two generations and the model DSCB you created. Use IDCAMS or IEHPROGM to delete the generation group index.

7

Using System Procedures

In this chapter you will learn

- what a compiler is
- what a procedure is
- how to use cataloged procedures to compile a program
- what the loader is
- how to use cataloged procedures to compile and execute programs
- what the linkage editor is
- how to use cataloged procedures to compile and link edit programs
- how to use cataloged procedures to compile, link edit, and execute programs
- how to add a program to a load library
- how to execute a program from a load library

The examples in the previous chapters have all involved executing programs. In your EXEC statements you coded PGM= . If you examine JCL used by professionals, you will not usually find PGM= on their EXEC statements, because they usually use procedures. A **procedure** is precoded JCL. You probably have encountered procedures in language-coding classes, where they are commonly used to compile programs. We will start our study with these commonly used procedures. First, however, we will discuss compilers so that you will have a better understanding of what these procedures do. In your professional career you may never need many of the compiler functions you will be shown here; the compiler is being used here as a vehicle to illustrate some aspects of JCL.

Function of a Compiler

Computers can follow only instructions entered in machine language, but people usually have a great deal of difficulty working with machine language. To make computers more accessible, computer specialists developed easier methods of telling the computer what to do.

All instructions consist of an operation (what to do) and one or more operands (what to do it to). In machine language these instructions are written in binary notation (ones and zeros). The first programming simplification consisted of replacing the binary operation with a symbolic one so that, for example, a programmer could use A instead of 0 0 0 1 1 0 1 0 to mean add. Now, however, the program was no longer directly executable. It became the input to another program that replaced the symbolics with their binary values. The next step in the simplification process was to replace the binary values of the operands with symbolic names, now known as variables. This line of development led to the modern **assembler** language and the assembler program, which usually generates one machine-language instruction for each assembly-language instruction.

Assembler languages have many advantages over machine language, but they are difficult to learn and programs written in them usually take a relatively long time to code and test. As a result, assembler language does not provide sufficient simplification for most people.

Computer specialists and scientists turned the problem around and developed the requirements for a language that would meet users' needs. The languages that meet these requirements are called high-level languages. FORTRAN, whose name comes from formula translation, was developed to meet the needs of the scientific community, and COBOL, whose name comes from common business oriented language, was developed for the business community. Programs were created to translate programs written in a particular high-level language into machine language. A program that does this type of translation is called a **compiler.** Each high-level language has its own compiler.

At one time there was a distinct difference between a compiler and an assembler. A compiler generated several machine-language instructions for each high-level language instruction, whereas an assembler always generated one machine-language instruction for each assembler instruction. Now the distinction has become blurred because many assembler languages have macro instructions which generate several machine-language instructions for each instruction. For simplicity, references here to a high-level language mean assembler language as well as FORTRAN, COBOL, and PL/I.

Compiling a Program

Figure 7.1 shows a system flowchart for a standard compilation. With some minor differences, this flowchart applies to FORTRAN, COBOL, and PL/I compilations as well as to assembler. The high-level language program, called the **source code** or the **source module,** is input to the compiler using the ddname SYSIN. Figure 7.1 shows input stream data, but there is no restriction regarding medium. Although the ddnames SYSUT1, SYSUT2, SYSUT3, and SYSUT4 indicate that there are four work data sets used by the compiler for intermediate storage, only the COBOL compiler uses all four. The PL/I compiler uses only one; FORTRAN, two; and assembler, three. The DD statement SYSLIB is always used by assembler for macro definitions. In addition, precoded assembler, COBOL, and PL/I code accessible with the COPY and INCLUDE commands would be found in the data set referenced by the SYSLIB DD statement. The SYSPRINT data set holds the program listing and compiler messages in all four cases.

There are three more ddnames in Figure 7.1: SYSPUNCH, SYSGO, and SYSLIN. They are used to hold the compiler output, which is usually called an **object module.** The forked output path to these data sets indicates that at a given time you might want one or the other, but usually not both. SYSPUNCH is shown as a deck of cards and SYSLIN and SYSGO as a disk data set; these are the system defaults. SYSGO is the ddname used by assembler, and SYSLIN is used by the other high-level languages we are considering.

The compilers set return codes, which may be tested with the COND parameter in subsequent steps. In general, if the return code is 0, there are no errors in the compilation and the object module, if produced, is good. If the return code is 4, there are warning messages but the object module is probably good. If the return code is 8, there are errors but the object module may be good; the programmer should examine the error list before trying to use the object module. If the return code is 12, the errors are sufficiently serious that the object module is useless. If the return code is 16, you have a disaster. In this case, it is not unusual for the compiler itself to have failed.

Even though the object module consists of machine-language instructions, it is not executable. Before it can be executed, the object module must be processed by the linkage editor or loader. We will discuss these two programs later.

Figure 7.1

System Flowchart for Compilation

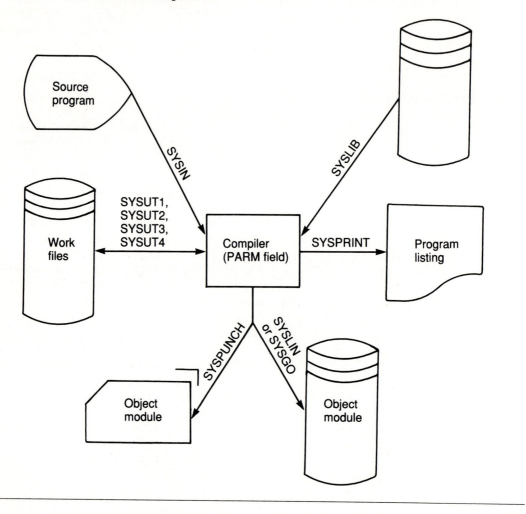

Procedures to Compile a Program

Whenever a program is written in a high-level language, it must be compiled before it can be used. Obviously, it is necessary to code JCL to compile a program. How will this JCL differ for the various PL/I programs you are working on? How will this JCL differ for your PL/I program and your colleague's? Very little — with minor modification, you can use the same JCL for all your PL/I program compilations and so can anyone else. So instead of coding the same JCL for each program you write, you use procedures, which are precoded JCL. Procedures are stored in a system library usually named SYS1.PROCLIB. If you wished to write a procedure and add it to SYS1.PROCLIB, you would use the utility program IEBUPDTE, which was discussed in Chapter 5. Procedures stored in this library are called **cataloged procedures.** A different kind of procedure, called an in-stream procedure, will be discussed in Chapter 8.

We will discuss how to write a procedure in Chapter 8. In this chapter we will discuss how to use procedures in general and how to use the procedures to compile and execute your programs in particular. Figure 7.2 contains listings of IBM procedures to compile PL/I, COBOL, FORTRAN, and assembler programs. In this section we will study the contents of these procedures and how to use them.

Names of Procedures

The name of a cataloged procedure is its member name in the system library SYS1.PROCLIB. For example, the JCL used to compile a COBOL program is stored in SYS1.PROCLIB as member COBUC.

Names are assigned to the cataloged procedures that are used to compile and execute programs in a way that makes it easy to remember which one you want to use. The first three or four letters of the name indicate the language with which the procedure is used. The COBOL procedures begin with the letters COB, the PL/I procedures with PLI, the FORTRAN procedures with FORT, and the assembler procedures with ASM.

The next letter indicates which version of the compiler is used. In the procedures discussed here, the COBOL procedures use the letter U, the PL/I and FORTRAN procedures use the letter X, and the assembler procedures use the letter F. This is the most variable part of the name. At your computer center, the FORTRAN procedures might use the letter G and the assembler procedures the letter H, or entirely different letters might be used. In fact, there may be several procedures for different versions of the same language.

The last part of the name indicates what the procedure does. Names of procedures that only compile end with the letter C. Names of procedures that compile a program and invoke the loader to execute it end with the letters CG (the G stands for GO, which is what executing is called). Names of procedures that compile and link edit end with the letters CL (the L stands for link edit). Finally, names of procedures that compile, link edit, and execute end with the letters CLG.

The COBUC Procedure

Let us examine procedure COBUC in Figure 7.2a, which is used to compile a COBOL program. There is an EXEC statement with a stepname of COB. We

Figure 7.2

(a) The COBUC Procedure

```
//COB       EXEC PGM=IKFCBL00,PARM='DECK,NOLOAD,SUPMAP',REGION=86K
//SYSPRINT DD SYSOUT=A
//SYSPUNCH DD SYSOUT=B
//SYSUT1    DD DSNAME=&&SYSUT1,UNIT=SYSDA,SPACE=(460,(700,100))
//SYSUT2    DD DSNAME=&&SYSUT2,UNIT=SYSDA,SPACE=(460,(700,100))
//SYSUT3    DD DSNAME=&&SYSUT3,UNIT=SYSDA,SPACE=(460,(700,100))
//SYSUT4    DD DSNAME=&&SYSUT4,UNIT=SYSDA,SPACE=(460,(700,100))
```

(b) The PLIXC Procedure

```
//PLIXC     PROC
//PLI       EXEC PGM=IEL0AA,PARM='OBJECT,NODECK',REGION=100K
//SYSPRINT DD SYSOUT=A
//SYSLIN    DD DSN=&&LOADSET,DISP=(MOD,PASS),UNIT=SYSSQ,
//             SPACE=(80,(250,100))
//SYSUT1    DD DSN=&&SYSUT1,UNIT=SYSDA,SPACE=(1024,(200,50),,CONTIG,ROUND),
//             DCB=BLKSIZE=1024
```

(c) The FORTXC Procedure

```
//FORTXC PROC FXPGM=IFEAAB,FXREGN=256K,FXPDECK=DECK,
//             FXPOLST=NOLIST,FXPOPT=O,FXLNSPC='3200,(25,6)'
//*
//*              PARAMETER   DEFAULT-VALUE      USAGE
//*
//*              FXPGM       IFEAAB             COMPILER NAME
//*              FXREGN      256K               FORT-STEP REGION
//*              FXPDECK     DECK               COMPILER DECK OPTION
//*              FXPOLST     NOLIST             COMPILER LIST OPTION
//*              FXPOPT      O                  COMPILER OPTIMIZATION
//*              FXLNSPC     3200,(25,6)        FORT.SYSLIN SPACE
//*
//FORT    EXEC PGM=&FXPGM,REGION=&FXREGN,COND=(4,LT),
//             PARM='&FXPDECL.&FXPOLST,OPT(&FXPOPT)'
//SYSPRINT    DD SYSOUT=A,DCB=BLKSIZE=3429
//SYSTERM     DD SYSOUT=A
//SYSUT1      DD UNIT=SYSSQ,SPACE=(3465,(3,3)),DCB=BLKSIZE=3465
//SYSUT2      DD UNIT=SYSSQ,SPACE=(2048,(10,10))
//SYSPUNCH    DD SYSOUT=B,DCB=BLKSIZE=3440
//SYSLIN      DD DSN=&&LOADSET,DISP=(MOD,PASS),UNIT=SYSSQ,
//             SPACE=(&FXLNSPC),DCB=BLKSIZE=3200
```

(d) The ASMFC Procedure

```
//ASMFC     PROC   MAC='SYS1.MACLIB',MAC1='SYS1.MACLIB'
//ASM       EXEC   PGM=IFOX00,REGION=128K
//SYSLIB    DD     DSN=&MAC1,DISP=SHR
//          DD     DSN=&MAC1,DISP=SHR
//SYSUT1    DD     DSN=&&SYSUT1,UNIT=SYSSQ,SPACE=(1700,(600,100),
//             SEP=(SYSLIB)
//SYSUT2    DD     DSN=&&SYSUT2,UNIT=SYSSQ,SPACE=(1700,(300,50)),
//             SEP=(SYSLIB,SYSUT1)
//SYSUT3    DD     DSN=&&SYSUT3,UNIT=SYSSQ,SPACE=(1700,(300,50))
//SYSPRINT DD     SYSOUT=A,DCB=BLKSIZE=1089
//SYSPUNCH DD     SYSOUT=B
```

must know the stepname, for reasons that will become clear when we use the procedure. The program that is executed is named IKFCBLOO. That is the name of the COBOL compiler.

The EXEC statement in the COBUC procedure uses the PARM keyword parameter. In Chapter 5 the PARM parameter was used to pass the word MOD or NEW to IEBUPDTE. Here it is used to pass three values, DECK, NOLOAD, and SUPMAP, to the compiler. Information is passed to the compiler to request special processing. The values that may be passed, their meanings, and the default values are described in the programmer's guide for each language. (See the Bibliography.)

The more important values that may be specified for the COBOL compiler are explained in Table 7.1. At the present time IBM supports two COBOL compilers, OS/VS COBOL and VS COBOL II; because the options are not the same for the two compilers, Table 7.1 has a separate column for each compiler. (The values shown in Figure 7.2a are for OS/VS COBOL.) IBM distributes the compilers with preset default values for the compiler options. Personnel at the computer center, however, can change the default values in two ways: they can modify the compiler itself, or they can code PARM values on the EXEC statement in the procedure that invokes the compiler, as in Figure 7.2a. Because the IBM defaults may not apply at your installation, they are not listed in Table 7.1.*

As Table 7.1 shows, the DECK and NOLOAD values cause the compiler to write the object module to the SYSPUNCH data set and not to the SYSLIN data set. Notice that the SYSLIN DD statement is not included. It is not necessary, because the SYSLIN data set is not used.

The data set names on the SYSUT1, SYSUT2, SYSUT3, and SYSUT4 DD statements start with a double ampersand. As you learned in Chapter 3, any data set whose name starts with a double ampersand is a temporary data set. It does not exist before the job starts and will not exist after the job ends. A temporary data set comes into being for the life of the job.

Because there are no DISP parameters in the SYSUT1, SYSUT2, SYSUT3, and SYSUT4 DD statements, the default value (NEW, DELETE) is used. This is exactly what you would expect for temporary data sets.

The SYSIN DD statement is not included in the procedure because the SYSIN data set points to the source code, the form of which cannot be defined in advance. The source code is frequently in the form of input stream data, but it can also be on tape or DASD, as either a sequential data set or a member of a PDS. You must code the SYSDIN DD statement when you use the procedure.

---

* You can easily determine the default values at your computer center: Just execute the COBUC procedure without coding PARM on your EXEC statement, as shown in Figure 7.3. The resulting execution will invoke the default values in effect at your computer center. The compiler options in effect are listed on a separate page following the source program listing. (See Figure 7.7.)

Table 7.1

COBOL Compiler Options That May Be Specified Using PARM

OS/VS COBOL	VS COBOL	Function
SOURCE	SOURCE	Prints the source listing (suppressed by NOSOURCE).
CLIST	CLIST	Prints a condensed listing of the Procedure Division that gives the address of each statement (suppressed by NOCLIST).
DMAP	MAP	Produces a map of the Data Division that shows the address of every field (suppressed by NODMAP or NOMAP).
PMAP	LIST	Prints an assembler-language expansion of the program (suppressed by NOPMAP or NOLIST).
SUPMAP	—	Suppresses PMAP if errors are found during compilation (suppressed by NOSUPMAP).
ADV	ADV	Indicates that the first column of printed records does not have to be reserved for carriage control (suppressed by NOADV).
VERB	—	Prints procedure names and verb names on the Procedure Division map (suppressed by NOVERB).
VBSUM	VBREF	Prints a brief summary of the verbs used in the program and a count of how often each verb appeared (suppressed by NOVBSUM or NOVBREF).
LOAD	OBJECT	Produces the object module on DASD (suppressed by NOLOAD or NOOBJECT).
DECK	DECK	Punches the object deck (suppressed by NODECK).
QUOTE	QUOTE	Specifies that quotation marks (' ') are used to enclose nonnumeric literals.
APOST	APOST	Specifies that apostrophes (') are used to enclose nonnumeric literals.
XREF	—	Prints a cross-reference listing showing all Data Division fields and the Procedure Division statements that reference those fields.
SXREF	SXREF	Prints a sorted cross-reference listing.
STATE	—	Prints the number of the statement being executed when an abend occurred (suppressed by NOSTATE).
FLOW=n	—	Prints the last n procedures executed before an abend occurred (suppressed by NOFLOW).
SYMDMP	FDUMP	Prints a formatted dump if an abend occurs (suppressed by NOSYMDMP or NOFDUMP).
LIB	LIB	Permits COPY statements to be used in the program (suppressed by NOLIB).

JCL to Execute the COBUC Procedure

The JCL in Figure 7.3 employs the procedure COBUC to compile a COBOL program. The EXEC statement is slightly different from the EXEC statements we have used before. In previous examples we coded, for example, PGM=IEBGENER. In this example COBUC is coded. When a procedure is invoked, only the procedure name need be specified on the EXEC statement. PROC=COBUC could have been coded, but PROC is the default and thus is not usually coded. The system knows that a program is invoked when PGM= is coded and that a procedure is invoked when either PROC= or just the procedure name is coded.

The ddname in the DD statement in Figure 7.3 is also different from those we have used before. The ddname is COB.SYSIN. The COB portion tells the system that this DD statement belongs to the procedure step whose stepname is COB. The SYSIN part is the ddname that the COBOL compiler, invoked by the procedure step COB, expects. The coding is similar to that of the SYSIN DD statement used with IEBGENER, except that here we must include the procedure stepname as part of the ddname, for we are executing a procedure. Because it is necessary to code the procedure stepname as part of the ddname, it is not always possible to begin DD in column 12. Procedure step is frequently abbreviated to **procstep.**

The PARM Parameter. In the PARM parameter in Figure 7.2a, the values DECK, NOLOAD, and SUPMAP are passed to the compiler. These values can be changed by coding an overriding PARM parameter on the EXEC statement. APOST, for example, is a valid COBOL compiler PARM value. If you wanted to override the PARM field, you would code

```
//COMPARM EXEC COBUC,
//              PARM.COB=APOST
```

Notice that the **procstepname** is added to the PARM parameter.

You must be careful, however: This PARM parameter completely replaces

---

■ **Figure 7.3** ■■■■■■■■■■■■■■■■■■■■■■■■■■■■■■■■■■■■■■■

Compiling a COBOL Program

```
//JCLQB610 JOB ,'J.C.LEWIS'
//COMPILEC EXEC COBUC
//COB.SYSIN DD *

        COBOL Source Code

/*
//
```

the PARM parameter coded in the procedure, so DECK, NOLOAD, and SUPMAP no longer apply. If you wanted to retain those values and just add APOST, you would code

```
//COMPARM EXEC COBUC,
//                PARM.COB='APOST,DECK,NOLOAD,SUPMAP'
```

The order in which the PARM values are coded is not significant. The PARM values must be separated by commas, and because the comma is a special character, the whole PARM field is enclosed by apostrophes. In this case parentheses could replace the apostrophes used to enclose the PARM field:

```
PARM.COB=(APOST,DECK,NOLOAD,SUPMAP)
```

If the PARM field contains a special character other than the comma, special rules apply. For example, if you wanted to code the COBOL compiler PARM value FLOW=20 in a PARM field, you could code either

```
PARM.COB=('FLOW=20',APOST,DECK,NOLOAD,SUPMAP)
```

or

```
PARM.COB='FLOW=20,APOST,DECK,NOLOAD,SUPMAP'
```

Even if FLOW=20 were the only value you wanted to code, it would have to be enclosed by apostrophes:

```
PARM.COB='FLOW=20'
```

If a PARM field is continued, it must be interrupted at a comma and the whole field must be enclosed by parentheses, as in

```
PARM.COB=('FLOW=20',APOST,DECK,NOLOAD,SUPMAP,
OPTMIZE,CLIST)
```

The number of characters that may be passed using the PARM field is limited to 100.

The PLIXC Procedure

The PROC Statement. If you examine the procedure PLIXC in Figure 7.2b, which is used to compile a PL/I program, you will find that the first statement is a JCL statement you have never seen before. It is a PROC statement. This statement, if used, must be the first statement in the procedure. A PROC statement is not required in a cataloged procedure (but, as you will learn in Chapter 8, it is required for in-stream procedures). Columns 1 and 2 have slashes. The name starts in column 3 and is from one to eight characters long. The same rules apply to this name as to jobnames, stepnames, and ddnames. PROC statements of cataloged procedures do not require a name, but PROC statements of in-stream procedures do require a name. If there is no name in

━━ **Figure 7.4** ━━

Compiling a PL/I Program

```
//JCLQB615 JOB ,'J.C.LEWIS'
//COMPILEP EXEC PLIXC
//PLI.SYSLIN DD DUMMY
//PLI.SYSIN DD *

              PL/I Source Code

/*
//
```

the `PROC` statement, column 3 must be blank. There must be at least one blank in front of the `PROC` operation.

The name of the procedure in `SYS1.PROCLIB` is usually the same as the name coded on the `PROC` statement. This is true for the procedures `PLIXC`, `FORTXC`, and `ASMFC` shown in Figure 7.2. The two names do not have to be the same, however. Remember, you use a cataloged procedure by coding the member name of the procedure as it appears in `SYS1.PROCLIB`.

Execution of `PLIXC` as it is coded in Figure 7.2b will result in the object module's being written on disk under the ddname `SYSLIN`. This is because the `PARM` field contains `OBJECT` and `NODECK`, which tells the PL/I compiler to use the `SYSLIN` DD statement and not to use the `SYSPUNCH` DD statement.

The Override Statement. Figure 7.4 illustrates use of `PLIXC` to obtain only the compilation listing and not an object module. The `EXEC` statement is very similar to the one in Figure 7.3. The DD statement following the `EXEC` statement, however, has no corresponding statement in Figure 7.3. This is an **override statement,** which is a DD statement in a job stream that is used to replace a DD statement in a procedure. As you may recall from Figure 7.1, the object module is written to the `SYSPUNCH` or `SYSLIN` data set. In `PLIXC` there is a `SYSLIN` DD statement that is to receive the object module. In order to suppress creation of the object module, we replace the `SYSLIN` DD statement in the procedure `PLIXC` with a `DUMMY` DD statement.* The override statement accomplishes this purpose.

The ddname on the override statement consists of the stepname (`PLI`), a period, and the ddname of the statement in the procedure that is being overridden (`SYSLIN`). Here we are using an override statement to completely replace one data set (`&&LOADSET`) by an entirely different data set (`DUMMY`). An override statement does not have to replace the data set in its

_____

* The creation of the object module could have been suppressed by coding `PARM=NOOBJECT`, but this method illustrates how to code override statements.

entirety, however. For example, suppose we wanted to make the SYSLIN data set in Figure 7.2b into a permanent data set on a volume whose serial number is USRO02. To change the DSN to a permanent data set name and the DISP to KEEP, we would code the override statement as

```
//PLI.SYSLIN DD DSN=WYL.QB.JCL.OBJMOD,
//              DISP=(,KEEP),
//              VOL=SER=USRO02
```

Notice that neither the SPACE nor the UNIT parameter is coded, because the SPACE and UNIT parameters in the DD statement in the cataloged procedure are satisfactory. In the override statement, only those parameters you want changed should be coded. The reason you might want to store the object module permanently will be explained later in this chapter.

If you want to create a library and store the object module in it, code

```
//PLI.SYSLIN DD DSN=WYL.QB.JCL.OBJLIB(PGM1),
//              DISP=(,KEEP),
//              VOL=SER=USRO02,
//              SPACE=(TRK,(10,4,7))
```

In this code PGM1 is the member name of the object module. Notice that you must code the SPACE parameter to request directory space for OBJLIB.

In Figure 7.4, the override DD statement for the SYSLIN was coded before the additional DD statement, SYSIN, because statements that are overriding DD statements must precede statements that are being added. If the order of SYSLIN and SYSIN had been reversed, the override statement would have been ignored. If you want to override more than one statement, your override statements must be in the same order as the statements you are overriding in the procedure. For example, if, for some reason, you chose to override the SYSUT1 DD statement in Figure 7.2b as well as the SYSLIN, you would have to insert the SYSUT1 override statement after the SYSLIN override statement. If the SYSUT1 override statement preceded the SYSLIN override statement, the SYSLIN override statement would be ignored.

The FORTXC Procedure

Symbolic Parameters. If you examine the procedure FORTXC in Figure 7.2c, which is used to compile a FORTRAN program, you will see that the first line of the procedure, which is the PROC statement, contains more information than was discussed earlier. Let us skip down to the EXEC statement in the FORTXC procedure. In the EXEC statement is the parameter PGM=&FXPGM. This does not look right. Earlier a program name was described as starting with either an alphabetic character or one of the three nationals. An ampersand does not fit this definition; therefore it must have another significance. It does: A leading ampersand indicates a **symbolic parameter.** &FXPGM is not the name of the program to be executed but rather a symbolic parameter that stands for the name of the program to be executed. At execution time the symbolic parameter will be replaced with a value. This value may be a default value, or it may be one specified by the programmer.

The default values for symbolic parameters are assigned in the PROC statement. In the FORTXC procedure default values are supplied for symbolic parameters FXPGM, FXREGN, FXPDECK, FXPOLST, FXPOPT, and FXLNSPC. In this procedure the PROC statement requires a continuation statement. The rules for continuation are the same as for any other JCL statement.

If you are going to use symbolic parameters, you have to know which ones are used in the procedure, what they stand for, and what their default values are. You get this information by reading the procedure. If the author of the procedure did a good job, this information will be given in a set of easy-to-understand comments, like the comments in the FORTXC procedure.

Figure 7.5 shows how a programmer assigns a value to a symbolic parameter. In this figure the procedure FORTXC is used to compile a FORTRAN program. The value LIST is assigned to the symbolic value FXPOLST by coding FXPOLST=LIST on the EXEC statement. When a value for a symbolic parameter is supplied, the ampersand is not coded. When you assign a value to a symbolic parameter, that value applies only to your job; the value of the symbolic parameter in the cataloged procedure does not change.

If a symbolic parameter has no value assigned to it either by default or by the procedure user, nothing is inserted in the resulting JCL statement. If, in FORTXC, no value were assigned to the symbolic parameter FXPGM, the first line of the resulting EXEC statement would appear as

```
//FORT      EXEC PGM=,REGION=256K,COND=(4,LT),
```

This statement is obviously incorrect and would result in a JCL error.

The only time a symbolic parameter does not have to have a value assigned

---

■ Figure 7.5 ■

Compiling a FORTRAN Program

```
//JCLQB620 JOB ,'J.C.LEWIS'
//COMPILEF EXEC FORTXC,FXPOLST=LIST
//FORT.SYSIN DD *

           FORTRAN Source Code

/*
//
```

to it is when the symbolic parameter stands for a data set name, as in

```
//TEMP        DD DSN=&NAME,
```

If a value is assigned to `NAME`, `&NAME` acts just like a symbolic parameter. But if a value is not assigned, `&NAME` is assumed to be a temporary data set name, equivalent to `&&NAME`.

Note the symbolic parameter `FXLNSPC` in Figure 7.2c. Unlike the values assigned to other parameters, the value assigned to it includes special characters (in this case, commas and parentheses). To set a symbolic parameter equal to a value that includes special characters, you must include the entire expression within apostrophes. The proper way to do this is illustrated in Figure 7.2c by the statement assigning a value to symbolic parameter `FXLNSPC`. If, in Figure 7.5, `FXPOLST='LIST'` had been coded, there would have been no problem. If, on the other hand, `FXLNSPC=3200,(50,6)` had been coded on the `EXEC` statement, a JCL error would have resulted.

The ASMFC Procedure

Concatenation. If you examine the procedure `ASMFC` In Figure 7.2d, you will observe that following the `SYSLIB` DD statement is a DD statement without a ddname. This type of linking together, called **concatenation,** is not restricted to procedures.* If you wrote a program to do some statistical analysis on payroll, for example, and decided that you wanted to use as input both the January and February data instead of just the January data, you would not need to either change the program or run it twice. You could concatenate the two data sets. The following is an example:

```
//INPUT       DD DSN=JAN,
//               DISP=SHR
//            DD DSN=FEB,
//               DISP=SHR
```

In this case, when end of file on the data set `JAN` is reached, processing continues with the data set `FEB`. When end of file on `FEB` is encountered, the end-of-file processing in the program takes place. Although the above example shows only 2 data sets being concatenated, up to 255 sequential data sets or 16 partitioned data sets may be concatenated.

For data sets to be concatenated, they must be the same type. You cannot concatenate a physical sequential data set and a library, although you can concatenate a physical sequential data set and a member of a library if they have the same record length.

Concatenated data sets must have the same record length, but they may have different blocksizes. Just remember to code first the data set whose

---

* Concatenation was used in Figure 6.6.

blocksize is largest. If you wished to concatenate two data sets ALEF and BET, where ALEF's blocksize is 1600 and BET's is 3200, you would code

```
//INCATDD   DD DSN=BET,
//             DISP=SHR
//          DD DSN=ALEF,
//             DISP=SHR
```

The DD statement for data set BET is coded first because BET's blocksize is larger than ALEF's.

JCL to Execute the ASMFC Procedure. Figure 7.6 illustrates use of the procedure ASMC. In the EXEC statement the symbolic parameter MAC1 is set equal to 'MT.SOURCE'. The PROC statement in procedure ASMFC in Figure 7.2d contains two symbolic parameters, MAC and MAC1. Both are set equal to 'SYS1.MACLIB', which is the system macro library. These symbolic parameters are used in the concatenated SYSLIB statements to supply the data set names. Obviously, we do not need or really want to concatenate 'SYS1.MACLIB' to itself. The second DD statement is a place holder, which makes it easy for a user to supply his or her own library. In Figure 7.6 this was done by setting MAC1 equal to 'MT.SOURCE'. Notice that MT.SOURCE is enclosed in apostrophes because it includes a special character, a period. If the assembler program does not find what it is looking for in SYS1.MACLIB, it will search MT.SOURCE.

The three DD statements that follow the EXEC statement in Figure 7.6 are used to change the SYSLIB-concatenated DD statements. The first one contains the ddname ASM.SYSLIB but no parameters, because the first SYSLIB DD statement in the procedure is satisfactory and doesn't need to be changed. The disposition of the second procedure DD statement is to be changed from SHR to OLD; thus the second DD statement in Figure 7.6 has no ddname and

━━ **Figure 7.6** ━━━━━━━━━━━━━━━━━━━━━━━━━━━━━━━━━━━━━

Assembling an Assembler Program

```
//JCLQB625 JOB ,'J.C.LEWIS'
//ASSEMBLE EXEC ASMFC,MAC1='MT.SOURCE'
//ASM.SYSLIB DD
//          DD DISP=OLD
//          DD DSN=SCF.SOURCE,DISP=SHR
//ASM.SYSPUNCH DD DUMMY
//ASM.SYSIN DD *

          Assembler Source Code


/*
//
```

Figure 7.7

Actual COBOL Compilation

```
1  //JCLQB682 JOB ,'J.C.LEWIS'
2  //COBCEX   EXEC COBUC
3  //COB.SYSIN DD *
4  /*
5  //
6   1   //JCLQB682 JOB ,'J.C.LEWIS'                                                    00000100
7   2   //COBCEX   EXEC COBUC                                                          00000200
8   3   XXCOBUC   PROC SUT1=15,SOBJ=15                                                 00000300
9   4   XXCOB     EXEC PGM=IKFCBL00                                                    00000400
10  5   XXSYSLIN  DD   DSNAME=&LOADSET,DCB=BLKSIZE=3120,DISP=(MOD,PASS),               00000500
11      XX             UNIT=3330,SPACE=(6400,(&SOBJ,10))                              00000600
12  6   XXSYSPRINT DD  SYSOUT=A,DCB=BLKSIZE=1936                                      00000700
13  7   XXSYSPUNCH DD  SYSOUT=B,DCB=BLKSIZE=2000                                      00000800
14  8   XXSYSUT1  DD   UNIT=3330,SPACE=(TRK,(&SUT1,5))                                00000900
15  9   XXSYSUT2  DD   UNIT=3330,SPACE=(TRK,(&SUT1,5))                                00001000
16  10  XXSYSUT3  DD   UNIT=3330,SPACE=(TRK,(&SUT1,5))
17  11  XXSYSUT4  DD   UNIT=3330,SPACE=(TRK,(&SUT1,5))
18  12  //COB.SYSIN DD *,DCB=BLKSIZE=80
19      //
20  STMT NO. MESSAGE
21   5   IEF653I SUBSTITUTION JCL - UNIT=3330,SPACE=(6400,(15,10))
22   8   IEF653I SUBSTITUTION JCL - UNIT=3330,SPACE=(TRK,(15,5))
23   9   IEF653I SUBSTITUTION JCL - UNIT=3330,SPACE=(TRK,(15,5))
24  10   IEF653I SUBSTITUTION JCL - UNIT=3330,SPACE=(TRK,(15,5))
25  11   IEF653I SUBSTITUTION JCL - UNIT=3330,SPACE=(TRK,(15,5))
26
```

200

```
27 PP 5734-CB2 V4 RELEASE 1.5 10NOV77          IBM OS AMERICAN NATIONAL STANDARD COBOL                    DATE FEB  5,1982
28    1
29 00001    IDENTIFICATION DIVISION.
30 00002    PROGRAM-ID.  LISTER.
31 00003    ENVIRONMENT DIVISION.
32 00004    INPUT-OUTPUT SECTION.
33 00005    FILE-CONTROL.
34 00006        SELECT INPUT-FILE
35 00007            ASSIGN TO UR-S-INPUT.
36 00008        SELECT OUTPUT-FILE
37 00009            ASSIGN TO UR-S-OUTPUT.
38 00010    DATA DIVISION.
39 00011    FILE SECTION.
40 00012    FD INPUT-FILE
41 00013        LABEL RECORDS ARE OMITTED.
42 00014    01  INPUT-REC                    PIC X(80).
43 00015    FD OUTPUT-FILE
44 00016        LABEL RECORDS ARE OMITTED.
45 00017    01  OUTPUT-REC                   PIC X(80).
46 00018    PROCEDURE DIVISION.
47 00019    PAR-1.
48 00020        OPEN INPUT INPUT-FILE
49 00021             OUTPUT OUTPUT-FILE.
50 00022        READ INPUT-FILE
51 00023            AT END
52 00024                STOP RUN.
53 00025        MOVE INPUT-REC TO OUTPUT-REC.
54 00026        WRITE OUTPUT-REC
55 00027            AFTER ADVANCING 1 LINES.
56 00028        STOP RUN.
57
58 *STATISTICS*   SOURCE RECORDS = 28   DATA DIVISION STATEMENTS =   4   PROCEDURE DIVISION STATEMENTS =   6
59 *OPTIONS IN EFFECT*   SIZE = 124000 BUF = 30000 LINECNT = 52 SPACE1, FLAGW,  SEQ,   SOURCE
60 *OPTIONS IN EFFECT*   NODMAP, NOPMAP, NOCLIST, SUPMAP, NOXREF, NOSXREF, LOAD, NODECK, APOST,  NOTRUNC, NOFLOW
61 *OPTIONS IN EFFECT*   NOTERM, NONUM, NOBATCH, NONAME, COMPILE=01, STATE, NORESIDENT, NODYNAM, NOLIB, NOSYNTAX
62 *OPTIONS IN EFFECT*   NOOPTIMIZE, NOSYMDMP, NOTEST,  VERB,  ZWB, SYST, NOENDJOB, NOADV
```

201

only the disposition is coded. The third DD statement makes available to the assembler a third library named SCF.SOURCE. Note that to add an additional data set to a concatenation in a procedure, you must code DD statements for all the existing DD statements in the procedure and then the additional DD statement. Thus, two DD statements precede the added DD statement. Coding

```
//ASM.SYSLIB DD DSN=SCF.SOURCE,
//               DISP=SHR
```

would have caused the first SYSLIB DD statement in the procedure to be overridden, and thus the assembler would not have had access to the system library SYS1.MACLIB. It would have had access only to SCF.SOURCE and MT.SOURCE.

The JCL in Figure 7.6 overrides the SYSPUNCH DD statement as well as the second SYSLIB DD statement. A lot of errors are to be expected in the initial testing, so it would be a waste of cards to produce an object module.* The important thing to note is that the override for SYSLIB is coded before the override for SYSPUNCH. The reason, as mentioned earlier, is that override statements must be coded in the same order as the DD statements in the procedure.

The last statement in Figure 7.6 is the SYSIN for the assembler source code. This statement must be last, for you must code all the override statements before you code the statements that are being added.

Executing a Compile Procedure

Figure 7.7 is an actual COBOL compilation as run on the CUNY system. Line numbers have been added on the left of the listing to make the discussion easier to follow. Lines 1 through 5 represent the JCL entered to run the compilation.

Let us look at lines 6 through 19. Lines 6, 7, 18, and 19 were actually coded. Lines 8 through 17 are from the cataloged procedure. Because COBUC is a relatively simple procedure, it is easy to distinguish the code written by the programmer from the statements supplied by the procedure. In most cases this is not true, however, so you need a mechanism to separate your JCL from that supplied by the procedure. Looking at the listing, you will note that the first two positions of the statements supplied by the programmer contain slashes, whereas those from the procedure COBUC have X's.

Let us digress for a moment. In Chapter 2 we discussed the MSGLEVEL parameter on the JOB statement, in which coding a value of 1 for the first subparameter (the statements subparameter) causes both the input JCL and

---

* Coding PARM=NODECK would have suppressed the punching of the object module, but this method shows you how to code the override statement.

the JCL from cataloged procedures to be printed. At the CUNY computer center the default value for the statements subparameter, which was used in Figure 7.7, is 1. It was this default value of 1 that caused lines 8 through 17 to be printed. If a value of 0 had been coded, only the JOB statement, line 6, would have been printed. If a value of 2 had been coded, only the input JCL, lines 6, 7, 18, and 19, would have been printed.

If you examine the statements supplied by the CUNY version of the COBUC procedure, you will notice that they are different from the IBM version shown in Figure 7.2a. You will find that at most computer centers the IBM-supplied procedures have been modified to meet local needs. For example, unlike the IBM-supplied procedure, the COBUC procedure used here has a PROC statement with default values for symbolic parameters used in the procedure. Lines 21 through 25 show the JCL as it looks after values have been substituted for the symbolic parameters.

Lines 29 through 56 contain the program listing. Those of you who are familiar with COBOL will recognize this program as a program named LISTER that reads a record and then prints it. If there had been errors in the program, error messages would have followed the program listing.

The compiler options that are in effect during this compilation are shown on lines 59 through 62. Lines 2 and 9 show the EXEC statements for the procedure and compiler. Because there are no PARM fields to set compiler options, all of the compiler options here are the installation defaults.

Similar output is produced when the other procedures illustrated in Figure 7.2 are executed.

Function of the Loader

As mentioned earlier, before the object module produced by a compiler can be executed, it must undergo additional processing. One way of doing the additional processing is to use the loader. The same loader is used irrespective of which programming language is used. The **loader** resolves external references, includes modules from the SYSLIB library, relocates address constants, and then causes the program to begin executing. **External references** are module or program names that are used in a module or program but are not in that module or program. If, for example, you write a program named TESTMAIN that calls a program named TESTSUB that you have written, the name TESTSUB is an external reference to TESTMAIN. The loader resolves these external references, which means that these modules or programs are loaded in with the main program. Thus the object module of TESTSUB is loaded in with TESTMAIN so that TESTSUB may be referenced by TESTMAIN. If the loader cannot resolve external references, it marks the program not executable. The loader is described in detail in the *Linkage Editor and Loader* manual for your system.

■ **Figure 7.8** ■

System Flowchart for the Loader

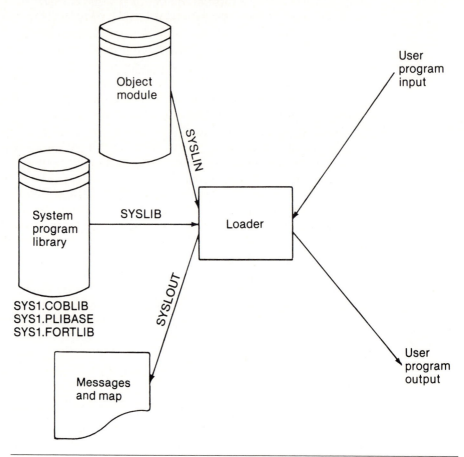

Figure 7.8 is a system flowchart that illustrates how the loader works. There are two inputs to the loader itself: the object module produced by the compiler under the ddname SYSLIN and a library under the ddname SYS-LIB. The library or libraries used depend on the programming language; assembler does not use a library. The loader searches these libraries to resolve external references. SYSLOUT is used by the loader for error and warning messages as well as the list of called modules if requested. This list of called modules is referred to as a **map.**

The loader executes the user's program, so Figure 7.8 also shows input to the user's program and output produced by the user's program.

The functions performed by the loader are also performed by the linkage editor, which will be discussed later in this chapter. The loader is used for testing purposes. When testing is complete, the linkage editor is used. As you will see when we discuss the linkage editor, there are situations in which the loader cannot be used because the system under development is too complex.

Procedures to Compile and Execute a Program

Figure 7.9 contains listings of the IBM-supplied procedures that compile a program and invoke the loader to execute the program. These are called compile and go procedures, and their names end with the letters CG. The procedures listed are for COBOL, PL/I, FORTRAN, and assembler language. In all four procedures the loader is invoked in the GO step.

In all the procedures the PARM parameter is coded on the EXEC statement to modify the loader processing and the listing produced. The values that may be coded, their meanings, and the default values are listed in Table 7.2. Usually the default values are satisfactory. As in the case of the compilers, however, you may change the PARM values by coding an overriding PARM parameters on your EXEC statement, as in

```
//CGPARM        EXEC COBUCG,
//                    PARM.GO='NOMAP,LET'
```

If you wanted to change the PARM values for both the compiler and the loader, you would code

```
//CGPARM        EXEC COBUCG,
//                    PARM.COB='APOST',
//                    PARM.GO='NOMAP,LET'
```

You must code the PARM parameters in order by stepname. Because in the COBUCG procedure the COB step precedes the GO step, the override PARM for the COB step must be coded before the override PARM for the GO step.

An interesting feature of the listing of these procedures is the use of the COND parameter on the EXEC statement for the loader. All of the procedures except FORTXCG use the format COND=(x,LT,stepname) (the FORTRAN procedure does not include a stepname). Stepname is the compilation step name, and x is 5 for COBOL, 4 for FORTRAN, 8 for assembler, and 9 for PL/I. The result of this COND parameter is that the loader will execute if the compile has a return code of 0 or 4 in all cases. If the return code is 8, the loader will execute only for PL/I and assembler.

Another interesting feature is the use of the referback or backward reference for the data set in the SYSLIN DD statement in the GO step of the COBUCG procedure. In this situation it appears to be more trouble to use the referback than to code the actual data set name. Suppose, however, you wanted to override the SYSLIN DD statement in the compile step to retain the data set. If

the SYSLIN DD statement in the GO step did not use a referback, you would
have to replace the entire SYSLIN DD statement in the GO step. With the
referback, only the disposition need be changed, from (OLD,DELETE) to
(OLD,KEEP).

Executing a Compile and Go Procedure

We will examine how the loader works by using it to execute the COBOL
program named LISTER that was compiled in Figure 7.7. This program reads
input stream data under the ddname INPUT and produces printer output
under the ddname OUTPUT. (The methods used in COBOL, FORTRAN, PL/I,
and assembler to specify the ddnames used for input and output data sets
were discussed in Chapter 2.) Sample JCL to execute the compile and go
procedure COBUCG is shown in Figure 7.10. The JCL for the other three
languages is very similar.

Notice how GO has been added to the ddnames on the INPUT and OUTPUT
DD statements. These DD statements are required during the GO step when the

■ Figure 7.9 ■

(a) The COBUCG Procedure

```
//COB       EXEC PGM=IKFCBL00,PARM='LOAD',REGION=86K
//SYSPRINT  DD SYSOUT=A
//SYSUT1    DD DSNAME=&&SYSUT1,UNIT=SYSDA,SPACE=(460,(700,100))
//SYSUT2    DD DSNAME=&&SYSUT2,UNIT=SYSDA,SPACE=(460,(700,100))
//SYSUT3    DD DSNAME=&&SYSUT3,UNIT=SYSDA,SPACE=(460,(700,100))
//SYSUT4    DD DSNAME=&&SYSUT4,UNIT=SYSDA,SPACE=(460,(700,100))
//SYSLIN    DD DSNAME=&&LOADSET,DISP=(MOD,PASS),
//             UNIT=SYSDA,SPACE=(80,(500,100))
//GO        EXEC PGM=LOADER,PARM='MAP,LET',COND=(5,LT,COB),REGION=106K
//SYSLIN    DD DSNAME=*.COB.SYSLIN,DISP=(OLD,DELETE)
//SYSLOUT   DD SYSOUT=A
//SYSLIB    DD DSNAME=SYS1.COBLIB,DISP=SHR
```

(b) The PLIXCG Procedure

```
//PLIXCG    PROC LKLBDSN='SYS1.PLIBASE'
//PLI       EXEC PGM=IEL0AA,PARM='OBJECT,NODECK',REGION=100K
//SYSPRINT  DD SYSOUT=A
//SYSLIN    DD DSN=&&LOADSET,DISP=(MOD,PASS),UNIT=SYSSQ,
//             SPACE=(80,(250,100))
//SYSUT1    DD DSN=&&SYSUT1,UNIT=SYSDA,SPACE=(1024,(200,50),,CONTIG,ROUND),
//             DCB=BLKSIZE=1024
//GO        EXEC PGM=LOADER,PARM='MAP,PRINT',REGION=100K,
//             COND=(9,LT,PLI)
//SYSLIB    DD DSN=&LKLBDSN,DISP=SHR
//          DD DSN=SYS1.PLIBASE,DISP=SHR
//SYSLIN    DD DSN=&&LOADSET,DISP=(OLD,DELETE)
//SYSLOUT   DD SYSOUT=A
//SYSPRINT  DD SYSOUT=A
```

Cont.

(c) The FORTXCG Procedure

```
//FORTXCG PROC FXPGM=IFEAAB,FXREGN=256K,FXPDECK=NODECK,
//              FXPOLST=NOLIST,FXPOPT=O,GOF5DD='DDNAME=SYSIN',
//              GOF6DD='SYSOUT=A',GOF7DD='SYSOUT=B',GOREGN=100K
//*
//*              PARAMETER    DEFAULT-VALUE       USAGE
//*
//*              GOREGN       100K                GO-STEP REGION
//*              FXPGM        IFEAAB              COMPILER NAME
//*              FXREGN       256K                FORT-STEP REGION
//*              FXPDECK      NODECK              COMPILER DECK OPTION
//*              FXPOLST      NOLIST              COMPILER LIST OPTION
//*              FXPOPT       O                   COMPILER OPTIMIZATION
//*              GOF5DD       DDNAME=SYSIN        GO.FT05F001 OPERAND
//*              GOF6DD       SYSOUT=A            GO.FTO6F001 OPERAND
//*              GOF7DD       SYSOUT=B            GO.FT07F001 OPERAND
//*
//FORT     EXEC PGM=&FXPGM,REGION=&FXREGN,COND=(4,LT),
//              PARM='&FXPDECK,&FXPOLST,OPT(&FXPOPT)'
//SYSPRINT   DD SYSOUT=A,DCB=BLKSIZE=3429
//SYSTERM    DD SYSOUT=A
//SYSUT1     DD UNIT=SYSSQ,SPACE=(3465,(3,3)),DCB=BLKSIZE=3465
//SYSUT2     DD UNIT=SYSSQ,SPACE=(2048,(10,10))
//SYSPUNCH   DD SYSOUT=B,DCB=BLKSIZE=3440
//SYSLIN     DD DSN=&&LOADSET,DISP=(MOD,PASS),UNIT=SYSSQ,
//              SPACE=(3200,(25,6)),DCB=BLKSIZE=3200
//GO       EXEC PGM=LOADER,COND=(4,LT),REGION=&GOREGN,
//              PARM='LET,NORES,EP=MAIN'
//SYSLOUT    DD SYSOUT=A
//SYSLIB     DD DSN=SYS1.FORTLIB,DISP=SHR
//SYSLIN     DD DSN=&&LOADSET,DISP=(OLD,DELETE)
//FT05F001   DD &GOF5DD
//FT06F001   DD &GOF6DD
//FT07F001   DD &GOF7DD
```

(d) The ASMFCG Procedure

```
//ASMFCG    PROC MAC='SYS1.MACLIB',MAC1='SYS1.MACLIB'
//ASM       EXEC PGM=IFOX00,PARM=OBJ,REGION=128K
//SYSLIB    DD   DSN=&MAC1,DISP=SHR
//          DD   DSN=MAC1,DISP=SHR
//SYSUT1    DD   DSN=&&SYSUT1,UNIT=SYSSQ,SPACE=(1700,(600,100),
//               SEP=(SYSLIB)
//SYSUT2    DD   DSN=&&SYSUT2,UNIT=SYSSQ,SPACE=(1700,(300,50)),
//               SEP=(SYSLIB,SYSUT1)
//SYSUT3    DD   DSN=&&SYSUT3,UNIT=SYSSQ,SPACE=(1700,(300,50))
//SYSPRINT  DD   SYSOUT=A,DCB=BLKSIZE=1089
//SYSPUNCH  DD   SYSOUT=B
//SYSGO     DD   DSN=&&OBJECT,UNIT=SYSSQ,SPACE=(80,(200,50)),
//               DISP=(MOD,PASS)
//GO        EXEC PGM=LOADER,PARM='MAP,PRINT,NOCALL,LET',
//               COND=(8,LT,ASM)
//SYSLIN    DD   DSN=&&OBJECT,DISP=(OLD,DELETE)
//SYSLOUT   DD   SYSOUT=A
```

■ **Table 7.2**
Loader Options Specified in the PARM Field

Option	Definition
MAP NOMAP	Instructs the loader to produce a list of the module names and where they will be loaded in storage. NOMAP is the default.
RES NORES	Causes the link-pack area to be searched after the SYSLIN data set but before the SYSLIB library. RES is the default.
CALL NCALL	Specifies automatic search of the SYSLIB library. CALL is the default.
LET NOLET	Permits execution even if certain types of errors occur. NOLET is the default.
SIZE=n	Specifies the amount of main storage for the loader. 100K is the default.
EP=name	Supplies the name of the entry point.
NAME=name	Supplies a name other than GO to the loaded program. The default name is **GO.
PRINT NOPRINT	Causes informational and diagnostic messages to appear in the SYSLOUT data set. PRINT is the default.
TERM NOTERM	Sends certain messages to the SYSTERM data set. NOTERM is the default.

■ **Figure 7.10**

COBOL Compile and Go

```
//JCLQB630 JOB ,'J.C.LEWIS'
//COBOLCG  EXEC COBUCG
//COB.SYSIN DD *

          COBOL Source Code

/*
//GO.INPUT DD *

          Input Data

/*
//GO.OUTPUT DD SYSOUT=A
//
```

program is executed. Using GO. as the first part of their ddnames causes them to be added to the GO step, just as adding COB. to the SYSIN ddname in Figure 7.3 caused that DD statement to be added to the COB step.

Figure 7.11 shows the output produced when the job in Figure 7.10 was executed using the program LISTER as the COBOL source code. The output produced by the compiler has been eliminated from Figure 7.11, because it is identical to the output in Figure 7.7.

Remember that the COBUCG procedure executed was modified to meet the needs of CUNY and consequently is different from the IBM procedures listed in Figure 7.9. You will probably find that these procedures have been changed in your installation as well.

Look at lines 9 through 36 in Figure 7.11. As you will recall, those statements starting with // were coded by the programmer and those starting with XX came from the procedure. Notice how line 22, the source code input DD statement, is inserted immediately prior to the GO step EXEC statement, because it is being added to the compile step COB. Lines 34 and 35 show how our two GO DD statements are inserted at the end of the GO step.

Lines 48 through 58 are output from the loader. Line 49 shows the options used by the loader. Back in line 23, the PARM field contains the options MAP and LET; the remaining options indicated in line 49 are the defaults. Lines 51 through 56 list the names of the modules used. This list is a result of the MAP option. The first name, LISTER, is the program name as indicated in line 30 of Figure 7.7. The remainder are modules that have been called in from libraries referenced by the SYSLIB statement in the GO step. Line 57 gives the length of the program in hexadecimal form, and line 58 is the entry address that corresponds to the entry address given for LISTER on line 51. The result of executing the program is line 60, which is the record that was read. (Because there is no carriage control field in the output record in the COBOL program, the first character is not printed. Therefore, the message WHEN YOU DRINK WATER FROM A WELL, REMEMBER WHO DUG IT is started in column 2 of the record.)

Passing Values to Your Programs

You have seen how to use the PARM parameter to pass values to compilers and the loader. The PARM parameter may also be used to pass values to programs. If you are using a compile and go procedure, the PARM values for your program are included in the PARM.GO field after the loader parameters. Suppose you have a program that can produce either a full report or a summary report and you can control the operation of the program by passing it either an F or an S. If you wanted to print the season, FALL, WINTER, etc., on the report, you might code the PARM parameter as follows:

```
PARM.GO='NOMAP,LET/SWINTER'
```

Actual COBOL Compile and Go Run

```
1  //JCLQB687 JOB ,'J.C.LEWIS'
2  //COBEXMPL EXEC COBUCG
3  //COB.SYSIN DD *
4  /*
5  //GO.INPUT DD *
6  /*
7  //GO.OUTPUT DD SYSOUT=A
8  //

9     1     //JCLQB687 JOB ,'J.C.LEWIS'                                                    00000100
10    2     //COBEXMPL EXEC COBUCG                                                          00000200
11    3     //COBUCG   PROC SUT1=15,SOBJ=15,ADDLIB='SYS1.ADDLIB',                           00000300
12          XX             STEPLIB=SYS1.ADDLIB'                                             00000400
13    4     //COB      EXEC PGM=IKFCBL00                                                    00000500
14    5     //SYSPRINT DD   SYSOUT=A,DCB=BLKSIZE=1936                                       00000600
15    6     //SYSUT1   DD   UNIT=3330,SPACE=(TRK,(&SUT1,5))                                 00000700
16    7     //SYSUT2   DD   UNIT=3330,SPACE=(TRK,(&SUT1,5))                                 00000800
17    8     //SYSUT3   DD   UNIT=3330,SPACE=(TRK,(&SUT1,5))                                 00000900
18    9     //SYSUT4   DD   UNIT=3330,SPACE=(TRK,(&SUT1,5))                                 00001000
19   10     //SYSUT5   DD   UNIT=3330,SPACE=(TRK,(&SUT1,5)),DISP=(,PASS)                    00001100
20   11     //SYSLIN   DD   DSNAME=&LOADSET,DCB=BLKSIZE=3120,DISP=(MOD,PASS),
21          XX             UNIT=3330,SPACE=(6400,(&SOBJ,10))
22   12     //COB.SYSIN DD  *,DCB=BLKSIZE=80                                                00001200
23   13     //GO      EXEC PGM=LOADER,PARM='MAP,LET',COND=(5,LT,COB)                        00001300
24   14     //SYSLIB   DD   DSN=&ADDLIB,DISP=SHR                                            00001400
25   15     //         DD   DSN=SYS1.COBLIB,DISP=SHR                                        00001500
26   16     //SYSLIN   DD   DSNAME=*.COB.SYSLIN,DISP=(OLD,DELETE)                           00001600
27   17     //SYSLOUT  DD   SYSOUT=A,DCB=BLKSIZE=1936                                       00001700
28   18     //STEPLIB  DD   DSNAME=SYS1.COBLIB,DISP=SHR                                     00001800
29   19     //         DD   DSN=&STEPLIB,DISP=SHR                                           00001900
30   20     //SYSUT5   DD   DSN=*.COB.SYSUT5,DISP=(OLD,DELETE)                              00002000
31   21     //SYSDBOUT DD   SYSOUT=A,DCB=BLKSIZE=1936                                       00002100
32   22     //DISPLAY  DD   SYSOUT=A,DCB=(RECFM=FA,LRECL=121,BLKSIZE=121,BUFNO=1)           00002200
33   23     //SYSOUT   DD   SYSOUT=A
34   24     //GO.INPUT DD   *,DCB=BLKSIZE=80
35   25     //GO.OUTPUT DD  SYSOUT=A
36          //
```

```
37 STMT NO.  MESSAGE
38   -
39      6      IEF653I SUBSTITUTION JCL - UNIT=3330,SPACE=(TRK,(15,5))
40      7      IEF653I SUBSTITUTION JCL - UNIT=3330,SPACE=(TRK,(15,5))
41      8      IEF653I SUBSTITUTION JCL - UNIT=3330,SPACE=(TRK,(15,5))
42      9      IEF653I SUBSTITUTION JCL - UNIT=3330,SPACE=(TRK,(15,5))
43     10      IEF653I SUBSTITUTION JCL - UNIT=3330,SPACE=(TRK,(15,5)),DISP=(,PASS)
44     11      IEF653I SUBSTITUTION JCL - UNIT=3330,SPACE=(6400,(15,10))
45     14      IEF653I SUBSTITUTION JCL - DSN=SYS1.ADDLIB,DISP=SHR
46     19      IEF653I SUBSTITUTION JCL - DSNAME=SYS1.ADDLIB,DISP=SHR
47
48                                        VS LOADER
49 OPTIONS USED - PRINT,MAP,LET,CALL,RES,NOTERM,SIZE=163840,NAME=**GO
```

NAME	TYPE	ADDR	NAME	TYPE	ADDR	NAME	TYPE	ADDR	NAME	TYPE	ADDR	NAME	TYPE	ADDR
LISTER	SD	AC010	ILBOSRV *	SD	AC688	ILBOSRV0*	LR	AC6C2	ILBOSR *	LR	AC6C2	ILBOSR3 *	LR	AC6C2
ILBOSRV1*	LR	AC6C6	ILBOSTP1*	LR	AC6C6	ILBOST *	LR	AC6CA	ILBOSTP0*	LR	AC6CA	ILBODBG *	SD	ACA08
ILBODBG0*	LR	ACA3A	ILBODBG1*	LR	ACA3E	ILBODBG2*	LR	ACA42	ILBODBG3*	LR	ACA46	ILBODBG4*	LR	ACA4A
ILBODBG5*	LR	ACA4E	ILBODBG6*	LR	ACA52	ILBODBG7*	LR	ACA56	ILBOEXT *	SD	AD780	ILBOEXT0*	LR	AD782
ILBOCOM0*	SD	AD7F8	ILBOCOM *	LR	AD7F8	ILBOCMM *	SD	AD900	ILBOCMM0*	LR	AD932	ILBOCMM1*	LR	AD936
ILBOBEG *	SD	ADCD0	ILBOBEG0*	LR	ADD02	ILBOMSG *	SD	ADDA0	ILBOMSG0*	LR	ADDD2			

```
57 TOTAL LENGTH      1E68
58 ENTRY ADDRESS     AC010
59
60 WHEN YOU DRINK WATER FROM A WELL, REMEMBER WHO DUG IT
```

The rule is that the loader options are coded first, followed by a slash, and the data to be passed to the program are coded after the slash. Even if you do not code any loader options, the slash is required.

There is one peculiar feature of using a PARM field in PL/I. The PL/I compiler adds code that allows your program to accept data from a PARM field. To distinguish between these added data and the data you want placed in the PARM field, code an extra slash, as in

```
PARM.GO='NOMAP,LET//SWINTER'
```

If you want to pass an apostrophe to a program, you must code two apostrophes:

```
PARM='PANDORA''S BOX'
```

Similarly, if you want to pass an ampersand to a program, you must code two ampersands.

Now that you know how to pass information to a program using the PARM field, let us examine how the program receives it.

Upon entry into your assembler program, register 1 points to the field that contains the address of the PARM field. The first two bytes of this field contain the length of the data passed in the PARM field. If the PARM field contains 'SWINTER', these two bytes will contain 7. Your assembler program could access the PARM field using code similar to the following:

```
L   R2,0(R1)  REGISTER 2 POINTS TO LENGTH OF PARM FIELD
LA  R3,2(R2)  REGISTER 3 POINTS TO DATA IN PARM FIELD
```

As befits a high-level language, PL/I needs only the following code to handle a PARM field:

```
PGM1: PROCEDURE (PARMFLD) OPTIONS (MAIN);
      DCL PARMFLD CHAR (100) VARYING;
```

You may use any valid PL/I variable name for the PARM field. You must declare the receiving field with the VARYING attribute and a length of 100 characters, even if you know that the data you will pass will be less than that. The PL/I string-handling functions can be used to separate the fields passed in the PARM field.

Handling a PARM field in COBOL is equally easy. A record to receive the PARM data must be defined in the LINKAGE section as follows:

```
LINKAGE SECTION.
01 PARM-FIELD.
   05 PARM-LENGTH                       PIC S9(4) COMP.
   05 REPORT-FLAG                       PIC X.
   05 SEASON-DATA                       PIC X(6).
   05 FILLER                            PIC X(93).
```

You may use any legal COBOL identifier names you like, but the first field in the record must be defined with PIC S9(4) COMP and the remaining fields must have a combined length of 100 bytes.

The PROCEDURE DIVISION header is coded as

```
PROCEDURE DIVISION USING PARM-FIELD.
```

Function of the Linkage Editor

The main function of the **linkage editor** is to create a load module, taking as input the object module produced by a compiler. A **load module** is a program module in a form suitable for loading into storage for execution. The same linkage editor is used no matter which compiler produced the object module. Like the loader, the linkage editor creates a load module by resolving external references and relocating address constants. Unlike the loader, the linkage editor does not execute the load module. Instead it writes the load module to a disk as a member of a library. This is the main difference between the linkage editor and the loader; if you want to save the load module as a member of a library, you must use the linkage editor.

Figure 7.12 is a system flowchart that shows how the linkage editor works. The name of the linkage editor is IEWL. If you compare Figure 7.12 with Figure 7.8, which illustrates the loader, you will see that they are similar. Both have a SYSLIB DD statement that points to one or more libraries used to resolve external references. In both cases the library used depends on the programming language and assembler does not use a library.

Because the library defined on the SYSLIB DD statement is automatically used by the linkage editor to resolve external references, it is known as an **automatic-call library.** Any library concatenated with SYSLIB is also an automatic-call library. Additional automatic-call libraries can be defined by the LIBRARY control statement, which we will discuss later.

For the loader, the SYSLIN DD statement identifies the input data. For the linkage editor, the SYSLIN DD statement identifies the primary input data, which consist of an object module produced by a compiler. Additional input data in the form of linkage editor control statements may be supplied using the ddname SYSIN. When we study the compile and link edit procedures in the next section, the relationship between SYSLIN and SYSIN DD statements will be explained.

The linkage editor can perform functions that the loader cannot. These additional functions, which are invoked with the linkage editor control statements, are illustrated in Table 7.3. The control statements most frequently used by application programmers will be discussed later in this chapter.

The printed linkage editor output goes to the SYSPRINT DD statement. The load module, which is the main linkage editor output, is written as a member of the library specified by the SYSLMOD DD statement.

Figure 7.12

System Flowchart for the Linkage Editor

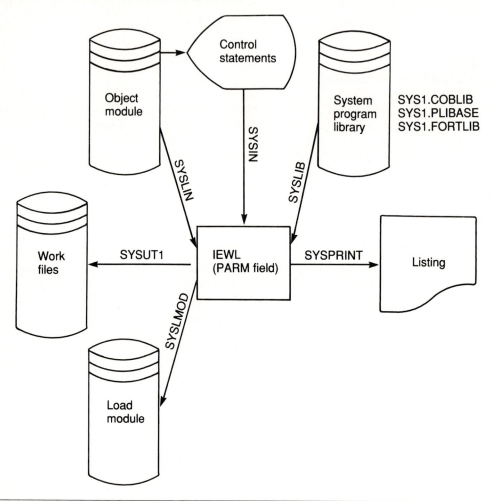

As with the loader, with the linkage editor you can modify the load module produced, invoke special processing, and change the output listings by using the PARM field in the EXEC statement. The values that may be specified in the PARM field are listed in Table 7.4. Use the default values unless you have a reason to do otherwise.

Table 7.3
Linkage Editor Control Statements

Linkage Editor Control Statement	Function
ALIAS	Supplies additional names for the load module.
CHANGE	Causes an external reference in a module to be replaced with another external reference.
ENTRY	Supplies the name of the first instruction to be executed.
EXPAND	Is used to lengthen one or more control sections.
IDENTIFY	Supplies data to be entered into the identification records for a particular control section.
INCLUDE	Identifies DD statements that supply input to the linkage editor. The input may be sequential or partitioned data sets.
INSERT	Repositions a control section to a segment in an overlay structure.
LIBRARY	Specifies additional automatic-call libraries, restricted no-call function, and never-call function.
NAME	Supplies the member name for the load module.
ORDER	Indicates the sequence in which control sections appear in the output load module.
OVERLAY	Indicates the beginning of an overlay segment or region.
PAGE	Aligns a control section on a 4K page boundary in the load module.
REPLACE	Specifies the replacement of one control section with another or the deletion of a control section or entry name.
SETCODE	Assigns the specified authorization code to the output load module.
SETSSI	Specifies hexadecimal data to be placed in the system status index of the directory entry for the output module.

■ **Table 7.4** ■
Linkage Editor Options Specified in the PARM Field

Option	Definition
AC=n	Sets an authorization code for the load module. The SETCODE control card may override this value.
ALIGN2	Sets the load module to be loaded on a 2K boundary. 4K is the default.
DCBS	Permits the SYSLMOD blocksize to be specified.
LET	Allows the load module to execute with certain errors.
LIST	Prints the linkage editor control cards.
MAP	Prints a list of the modules in the load module and their relative position.
NCAL	Prevents automatic library calls.
NE	Prevents the load module from being processed by the linkage editor again.
OVLY	Indicates that an overlay program is being processed.
REFR	Permits the load module to be refreshed.
REUS	Permits the load module to be serially reusable.
SCTR	Allows the load module to be loaded into noncontiguous main storage.
SIZE=(v1,v2)	Specifies the amount of main storage for the linkage editor (v1) and for the buffer space (v2).
XCAL	Allows valid exclusive calls.
XREF	Produces a cross-reference listing.

Procedures to Compile and Link Edit a Program

Figure 7.13 shows the listings of the IBM-supplied procedures to compile and link edit a program. The names of these procedures end with the letters CL. Most of these procedures are very similar to one another. The compile step is the same, or almost the same, as the corresponding compiler procedure in Figure 7.2. In all cases the object module is written to a temporary data set with the ddname SYSLIN (SYSGO for assembler).

In all four procedures the linkage editor steps use the stepname LKED. There are three main differences among these procedures. First, each one specifies slightly different options in the PARM field (they all specify XREF and

LIST). You can check Table 7.4 to determine the meaning of the options named.

Second, in each procedure the COND parameter in the linkage editor EXEC statement specifies a different number. The numbers are the same as in the compile and go procedures we saw earlier on the loader EXEC statement, however.

Figure 7.13

(a) The COBUCL Procedure

```
//COB        EXEC PGM=IKFCBL00,REGION=86K
//SYSPRINT DD SYSOUT=A
//SYSUT1    DD DSNAME=&&SYSUT1,UNIT=SYSDA,SPACE=(460,(700,100))
//SYSUT2    DD DSNAME=&&SYSUT2,UNIT=SYSDA,SPACE=(460,(700,100))
//SYSUT3    DD DSNAME=&&SYSUT3,UNIT=SYSDA,SPACE=(460,(700,100))
//SYSUT4    DD DSNAME=&&SYSUT4,UNIT=SYSDA,SPACE=(460,(700,100))
//SYSLIN    DD DSNAME=&&LOADSET,DISP=(MOD,PASS),UNIT=SYSDA,
//             SPACE=(80,(500,100))
//LKED       EXEC PGM=IEWL,PARM='LIST,XREF,LET',COND=(5,LT,COB),
//             REGION=96K
//SYSLIN    DD DSNAME=&&LOADSET,DISP=(OLD,DELETE)
//          DD DDNAME=SYSIN
//SYSLMOD   DD DSNAME=&&GOSET,DISP=(NEW,PASS),UNIT=SYSDA,
//             SPACE=(1024,(50,20,1))
//SYSLIB    DD DSNAME=SYS1.COBLIB,DISP=SHR
//SYSUT1    DD UNIT=(SYSDA,SEP=(SYSLIN,SYSLMOD)),
//             SPACE=(1024,(50,20))
//SYSPRINT DD SYSOUT=A
```

(b) The PLIXCL Procedure

```
//PLIXCL     PROC LKLBDSN='SYS1.PLIBASE'
//PLI        EXEC PGM=IEL0AA,PARM='OBJECT,NODECK',REGION=100K
//SYSPRINT DD SYSOUT=A
//SYSLIN    DD DSN=&&LOADSET,DISP=(MOD,PASS),UNIT=SYSSQ,
//             SPACE=(80,(250,100))
//SYSUT1    DD DSN=&&SYSUT1,UNIT=SYSDA,SPACE=(1024,(200,50),,CONTIG,ROUND),
//             DCB=BLKSIZE=1024
//LKED       EXEC PGM=IEWL,PARM='XREF,LIST',COND=(9,LT,PLI),REGION=100K
//SYSLIB    DD DSN=&LKLBDSN,DISP=SHR
//          DD DSN=SYS1.PLIBASE,DISP=SHR
//SYSLMOD   DD DSNAME=&&GOSET(GO),DISP=(NEW,PASS),UNIT=SYSDA,
//             SPACE=(1024,(50,20,1))
//SYSUT1    DD DSN=&&SYSUT1,UNIT=SYSDA,SPACE=(1024,(200,50),,CONTIG,ROUND),
//             DCB=BLKSIZE=1024
//SYSPRINT DD SYSOUT=A
//SYSLIN    DD DSN=&&LOADSET,DISP=(OLD,DELETE)
//          DD DDNAME=SYSIN
//SYSIN     DD  DUMMY
```

Cont.

(c) The FORTXCL Procedure

```
//FORTXCL PROC FXPGM=IFEAAB,FXREGN=256K,FXPDECK=NODECK,FXPOLST=NOLIST,
//              FXPNAME=MAIN,FXPOPT=O,PGMLB='&&GOSET'
//*
//*              PARAMETER  DEFAULT-VALUE       USAGE
//*
//*                FXPGM      IFEAAB            COMPILER NAME
//*                FXREGN     256K              FORT-STEP REGION
//*                FXPDECK    NODECK            COMPILER DECK OPTION
//*                FXPOLST    NOLIST            COMPILER LIST OPTION
//*                FXPNAME    MAIN              COMPILER NAME OPTION
//*                FXPOPT     O                 COMPILER OPTIMIZATION
//*                PGMLB      &&GOSET           LKED.SYSLMOD DSNAME
//*
//FORT     EXEC PGM=&FXPGM,REGION=&FXREGN,COND=(4,LT),
//              PARM='&FXPDECK,&FXPOLST,NAME(&FXPNAME),OPT(&FXPOPT)'
//SYSPRINT     DD SYSOUT=A,DCB=BLKSIZE=3429
//SYSTERM      DD SYSOUT=A
//SYSUT1       DD UNIT=SYSSQ,SPACE=(3465,(3,3)),DCB=BLKSIZE=3465
//SYSUT2       DD UNIT=SYSSQ,SPACE=(2048,(10,10))
//SYSPUNCH     DD SYSOUT=B,DCB=BLKSIZE=3440
//SYSLIN       DD DSN=&&LOADSET,DISP=(MOD,PASS),UNIT=SYSSQ,
//                SPACE=(3200,(25,6)),DCB=BLKSIZE=3200
//LKED     EXEC PGM=IEWL,REGION=96K,COND=(4,LT),
//              PARM='LET,LIST,MAP,XREF'
//SYSPRINT     DD SYSOUT=A
//SYSLIB       DD DSN=SYS1.FORTLIB,DISP=SHR
//SYSUT1       DD UNIT=SYSDA,SPACE=(1024,(200,20))
//SYSLMOD      DD DSN=&PGMLB.(&FXPNAME),UNIT=SYSDA,
//              DISP=(NEW,PASS),SPACE=(TRK,(10,10,1),RLSE)
//SYSLIN       DD DSN=&&LOADSET,DISP=(OLD,DELETE)
//             DD DDNAME=SYSIN
```

(d) The ASMFCL Procedure

```
//ASMFCL     PROC MAC='SYS1.MACLIB',MAC1='SYS1.MACLIB'
//ASM        EXEC PGM=IFOX00,PARM=OBJ,REGION=128K
//SYSLIB     DD   DSN=&MAC1,DISP=SHR
//           DD   DSN=&MAC1,DISP=SHR
//SYSUT1     DD   DSN=&&SYSUT1,UNIT=SYSSQ,SPACE=(1700,(600,100),
//                SEP=(SYSLIB)
//SYSUT2     DD   DSN=&&SYSUT2,UNIT=SYSSQ,SPACE=(1700,(300,50)),
//                SEP=(SYSLIB,SYSUT1)
//SYSUT3     DD   DSN=&&SYSUT3,UNIT=SYSSQ,SPACE=(1700,(300,50))
//SYSPRINT DD   SYSOUT=A,DCB=BLKSIZE=1089
//SYSPUNCH DD   SYSOUT=B
//SYSGO      DD   DSN=&&OBJECT,UNIT=SYSSQ,SPACE=(80,(200,50)),
//                DISP=(MOD,PASS)
//LKED       EXEC PGM=IEWL,PARM=(XREF,LET,LIST,NCAL),REGION=128K,
//                COND=(8,LT,ASM)
//SYSLIN     DD   DSN=&&OBJSET,DISP=(OLD,DELETE)
//           DD   DDNAME=SYSIN
//SYSLMOD    DD   DSN=&&GOSET(GO),UNIT=SYSDA,SPACE=(1024,(50,20,1)),
//                DISP=(MOD,PASS)
//SYSUT1     DD   DSN=&&SYSUT1,UNIT=(SYSDA,SEP=(SYSLIN,SYSLMOD),
//                SPACE=(1024,(50,20)
//SYSPRINT DD   SYSOUT=A
```

Third, the SYSLIB DD statements differ. Although assembler does not specify an automatic-call library (via the SYSLIB DD statement), each of the high-level languages uses a different automatic-call library.

In all cases the SYSLMOD data set where the load module is written is a library. Load modules must be written as members of a library because the linkage editor expects to write the load module as a library member. In addition, the operating system executes only programs that are library members. In the four procedures the SYSLMOD DD statement points to a temporary library named GOSET.

The DDNAME Parameter

If you examine the SYSLIN DD statement in each link edit step of Figure 7.13, you will see another DD statement concatenated to it. The only information coded in the DD statement is DDNAME=SYSIN. DDNAME is a new keyword parameter called a **forward reference.**

The DDNAME parameter must be used because the input to the linkage editor, which is supplied under the ddname SYSLIN, actually consists of two concatenated data sets. The first data set is &&LOADSET, which is the object module produced by the compiler, and the second data set is the linkage editor control statements to be used. The DDNAME parameter permits you to concatenate the linkage editor control statements in the job stream with &&LOADSET. In effect, the parameter says that the data set which should be defined in this DD statement so that it can be concatenated with &&LOADSET will in fact be defined later (which is why the coding is called a forward reference) with a DD statement that has the ddname SYSIN. You must therefore code your linkage editor control statements using the ddname SYSIN. Because in our example we want the control statements added to the LKED step, the name we will use is LKED.SYSIN.

Although you may use up to five forward references in a step, provided all the ddnames are different, use of more than one is rare.

Executing a Compile and Link Edit Procedure

Figure 7.14 illustrates use of the procedure COBUCL. The SYSLMOD DD statement has been overridden so that the load module will be written to the previously created personal load library named LOADLIB.

If LOADLIB did not exist, it could be created in this job by coding the following DD statement:

```
//LKED.SYSLMOD DD DSN=WYL.QB.JCL.LOADLIB,
//               DISP=(NEW,CATLG),
//               VOL=SER=WYL005,
//               SPACE=(CYL,(5,1,10))
```

■ **Figure 7.14** ■

COBOL Compile and Link Edit

```
//JCLQB635 JOB ,'J.C.LEWIS'
//COMPLKD1 EXEC COBUCL
//COB.SYSIN DD *

              COBOL Source Code

/*
//LKED.SYSLMOD DD DSN=WYL.QB.JCL.LOADLIB,
//             DISP=OLD
//LKED.SYSIN DD *
 NAME LISTER(R)
/*
//
```

Notice that the DSN, DISP, VOL, and SPACE parameters are changed, but the UNIT parameter is not. Nor is the DCB parameter coded. The values coded for UNIT and DCB in the SYSLMOD DD statement in the procedure are acceptable.

Linkage Editor Control Statements

As stated earlier, the linkage editor control statements are supplied under the ddname LKED.SYSIN. The various linkage editor control statements are described in Table 7.3. In Figure 7.14 the NAME control statement is coded. The NAME control statement supplies the member name. When you want to execute a program, it is the member name that you code on the EXEC statement. In Figure 7.14 (R) is coded following the member name in the NAME control statement. This means that if member LISTER already exists in the library named in the SYSLMOD DD statement, it is to be replaced by the version created in this job. If (R) had not been coded in the NAME control statement and the member already existed, the job step would have failed. [It is also possible to specify the member name in the DSN—for example, WYL.QB.JCL.LOADLIB(LISTER). In that case the NAME control statement would not be necessary.]

Let us digress a moment and discuss the general format of the linkage editor control statements. The operations, such as NAME, must start in or after column 2. The first operand must be separated from the operation by at least one blank. The rules for continuing linkage editor control statements are the same as the rules discussed in Chapter 4 for continuing utility control statements: The last operand on a statement ends with a comma and column 72 contains a nonblank character; the continuation statement starts in column

16; there is no limit on the number of continuation statements. Remember that a symbol cannot be split.

Figure 7.15 shows the output when the job in Figure 7.14 was executed using the program LISTER as the COBOL source code. Once again the output produced by the compiler has been eliminated. Remember that the procedures used in this example and the others in this chapter are not the IBM-supplied procedures, but rather procedures that have been modified to meet the needs of the CUNY system.

In Figure 7.15 statements 1 through 9 represent the coded JCL. Lines 10 through 36 contain the execution JCL, a mixture of the cataloged procedure and the coded JCL. The COBOL source code is input following the COB.SYSIN DD statement, which is line 22 of the execution JCL. It is a DD statement added to the compile step. As mentioned earlier, in the execution JCL you can always spot your JCL because it has // in the first two positions. The JCL from the procedure, on the other hand, has XX in the first two positions. Lines 26 and 27 contain the override information for the SYSLMOD DD statement. Lines 28 and 29 contain the original information from the cataloged procedure.

Line 28 is unusual in that it has X/ in the first two positions, which indicates a statement in the procedure that is being overridden. Whenever you override a DD statement in a procedure, provided the statement subparameter of the MSGLEVEL parameter is 1, your statement will be printed immediately before the statement you are overriding. The overridden statement will be printed with X/ in the first two positions. Notice that the resulting DD statement, which is a combination of the parameters you coded and the parameters on the original statement, is not printed anywhere. The last DD statement on line 35 is the added statement for the linkage editor control statements.

Linkage Editor Output

The linkage editor output starts on line 37, which shows the options selected for the linkage editor. If you compare them with the PARM field information in line 23, you will see that they are the same. Line 38 shows the default values for the amount of storage reserved for the linkage editor and the amount of storage reserved for the buffer space. Line 39 shows the linkage editor control statement that was entered. This line appears because the LIST option was specified.

Lines 41 through 71 appear because the XREF option was specified. The COBOL program is named LISTER. Those of you familiar with COBOL will observe that the code does not explicitly refer to any other modules. The additional modules in the cross-reference listing are called in as a result of compiler action. In lines 72 and 73 the entry address is given as 00 and the program length as 1E68. When the program is loaded, it will not actually be

Figure 7.15

Actual COBOL Compile and Link Edit Run

```
1  //JCLQB623 JOB ,'J.C.LEWIS'                                                              00000100
2  //COMPLKD1 EXEC COBUCL                                                                   00000200
3  //COB.SYSIN DD *                                                                         00000300
4  /*                                                                                       00000400
5  //LKED.SYSLMOD DD DSN=WYL.QB.JCL.LOADLIB,                                                00000500
6  //             DISP=OLD                                                                  00000600
7  //LKED.SYSIN DD *                                                                        00000700
8  /*                                                                                       00000800
9  //                                                                                       00000900
                                                                                           00001000

10     //JCLQB623 JOB ,'J.C.LEWIS'
11     //COMPLKD1 EXEC COBUCL
12  XXCOBUCL PROC SUT1=15,SOBJ=15,SLUT1=50,SLUT2=20,SLMOD1=50,SLMOD2=20,                    00001100
13  XX            ADDLIB='SYS1.ADDLIB'                                                       00001200
14  XXCOB     EXEC PGM=IKFCBL00                                                              00001300
15  XXSYSPRINT DD  SYSOUT=A,DCB=BLKSIZE=1936
16  XXSYSUT1  DD  DSN=&&SYSUT1,UNIT=3330,SPACE=(TRK,(&SUT1,5))                               00001400
17  XXSYSUT2  DD  DSN=&&SYSUT2,UNIT=3330,SPACE=(TRK,(&SUT1,5))                               00001500
18  XXSYSUT3  DD  DSN=&&SYSUT3,UNIT=3330,SPACE=(TRK,(&SUT1,5))                               00001600
19  XXSYSUT4  DD  DSN=&&SYSUT4,UNIT=3330,SPACE=(TRK,(&SUT1,5))                               00001700
20  XXSYSLIN  DD  DSN=&&LOADSET,DCB=BLKSIZE=3120,DISP=(MOD,PASS),                            00001800
21  XX            UNIT=3330,SPACE=(6400,(&SOBJ,10))                                          00001900
                                                                                           00002000
22     //COB.SYSIN DD *,DCB=BLKSIZE=80
23  XXLKED    EXEC PGM=IEWL,PARM='LIST,XREF,LET',COND=(5,LT,COB)
24  XXSYSLIN  DD  DSN=&&LOADSET,DISP=(OLD,DELETE)
25  XX            DDNAME=SYSIN
26  //LKED.SYSLMOD DD DSN=WYL.QB.JCL.LOADLIB,
27  //             DISP=OLD
28  X/SYSLMOD  DD  DSN=&&GOSET,DISP=(NEW,PASS),UNIT=3330,
29  XX            SPACE=(1024,(&SLMOD1,&SLMOD2,1))
30  XXSYSLIB  DD  DSN=&ADDLIB,DISP=SHR
31  XX        DD  DSN=SYS1.COBLIB,DISP=SHR
32  XXSYSUT1  DD  UNIT=(3330,SEP=(SYSLIN,SYSLMOD)),
33  XX            SPACE=(1024,(&SLUT1,&SLUT2))
34  XXSYSPRINT DD  SYSOUT=A,DCB=BLKSIZE=1936
35     //LKED.SYSIN DD *,DCB=BLKSIZE=80
36     //

37  F64-LEVEL LINKAGE EDITOR OPTIONS SPECIFIED LIST,XREF,LET
38     DEFAULT OPTION(S) USED - SIZE=(196608,65536)
39  IEW0000        NAME LISTER(R)
40
```

222

CROSS REFERENCE TABLE

NAME	ORIGIN	LENGTH	ENTRY NAME	LOCATION	NAME	LOCATION	NAME	LOCATION	NAME	LOCATION
CONTROL SECTION										
LISTER	00	676								
ILBOCOM0*	678	102	ILBOCOM	678						
ILBODBG *	780	D78								
			ILBODBG0	7B2	ILBODBG1	7B6	ILBODBG2	7BA	ILBODBG3	7BE
			ILBODBG4	7C2	ILBODBG5	7C6	ILBODBG6	7CA	ILBODBG7	7CE
ILBOEXT *	14F8	72	ILBOEXT0	14FA						
ILBOSRV *	1570	37C	ILBOSRV0	15AA	ILBOSR	15AA	ILBOSR3	15AA	ILBOSRV1	15AE
			ILBOSTP1	15AE	ILBOST	15B2	ILBOSTP0	15B2		
ILBOBEG *	18F0	CA	ILBOBEG0	1922						
ILBOCMM *	19C0	3C9	ILBOCMM0	19F2	ILBOCMM1	19F6				
ILBOMSG *	1D90	D8	ILBOMSG0	1DC2						

LOCATION	REFERS TO SYMBOL	IN CONTROL SECTION	LOCATION	REFERS TO SYMBOL	IN CONTROL SECTION
478	ILBOSRV0	ILBOSRV	47C	ILBODBG0	ILBODBG
480	ILBOSR	ILBOSRV	484	ILBODBG4	ILBODBG
488	ILBOEXT0	ILBOEXT	48C	ILBOSRV1	ILBOSRV
400	ILBOCOM0	ILBOCOM0	13B4	ILBOFLW0	$UNRESOLVED (W)
13B8	ILBOFLW2	$UNRESOLVED (W)	13BC	ILBOTEF3	$UNRESOLVED (W)
13C0	ILBOSTN0	$UNRESOLVED (W)	1860	ILBOCOM0	ILBOCOM
1864	ILBOCMM0	ILBOCMM	1868	ILBOBEG0	ILBOBEG
186C	ILBOMSG0	ILBOMSG			

ENTRY ADDRESS   00
TOTAL LENGTH   1E68
****LISTER   NOW ADDED TO DATA SET
AUTHORIZATION CODE IS   0.

223

loaded into address 0 0; it will be loaded wherever the system finds space for it. Line 74 indicates that the program LISTER has been added to the data set specified in the SYSLMOD DD statement. The authorization code is a security feature that has not been implemented at the CUNY computer center.

In COBOL programs the PROGRAM-ID entry supplies the internal program name (see line 30 in Figure 7.7). The linkage editor control statement NAME supplies the name of the member under which the load module is stored in the load library. In Figure 7.15 both have the name LISTER. Although using the same name is good practice, it is not necessary.

Executing a Program from a Library

When we ran Figure 7.14, we added the load module named LISTER to a library; we would now like to execute it. Executing it is relatively simple, as shown in Figure 7.16. The EXEC statement is similar to the EXEC statements we used to execute IEBGENER and the other utility programs. Looking at Figure 7.16, we cannot tell that LISTER was originally written in COBOL. Of course, we must provide the INPUT and OUTPUT DD statements, but notice that GO is not included as part of the ddnames. That is because we are executing a program and not a procedure with a GO step. The output is shown in the last line.

Figure 7.16

Execution of a COBOL Program

```
//JCLQB627 JOB ,'J.C.LEWIS'
//JOBLIB   DD DSN=WYL.QB.JCL.LOADLIB,
//            DISP=SHR
//LODEXMPL EXEC PGM=LISTER
//INPUT    DD *
/*
//OUTPUT   DD SYSOUT=A
//SYSUDUMP DD SYSOUT=A
//
     1    //JCLQB627 JOB ,'J.C.LEWIS'
     2    //JOBLIB   DD DSN=WYL.QB.JCL.LOADLIB,
          //            DISP=SHR
     3    //LODEXMPL EXEC PGM=LISTER
     4    //INPUT    DD *,DCB=BLKSIZE=80
     5    //OUTPUT   DD SYSOUT=A
     6    //SYSUDUMP DD SYSOUT=A
          //

WHEN YOU DRINK WATER FROM A WELL, REMEMBER WHO DUG IT
```

The JOBLIB DD Statement

The only new feature in Figure 7.16 is the JOBLIB DD statement. Up until now all programs we have executed have been located in a library named SYS1.LINKLIB. You did not know that, and you did not have to know it because the system automatically looks in SYS1.LINKLIB to find programs that are to be executed. LISTER, however, is not in SYS1.LINKLIB, but in WYL.QB.JCL.LOADLIB. In Figure 7.16 the JOBLIB DD statement tells the system to search WYL.QB.JCL.LOADLIB for program LISTER.

The JOBLIB DD statement is coded immediately after the JOB statement and applies to all steps in the job. If you use a JOBLIB DD statement, the system will search the specified library first. The JOBLIB DD statement may point to several libraries if they are concatenated. If the program (actually the load module) is not in the library or libraries pointed to by the JOBLIB DD statement, the SYS1.LINKLIB library is searched. If the load module is not found in SYS1.LINKLIB, the job abends with a system completion code of 806, which means the load module cannot be found. Perhaps the program name was misspelled, or perhaps the JOBLIB statement points to the wrong library.

Figure 7.17 shows the use of a JOBLIB DD statement in a multistep job. The JOBLIB DD statement points to one library, LOADLIB. The system will search this library first for the programs. PROG1 and PROG2 will be found there, but because IEBGENER is usually in SYS1.LINKLIB, it will not be found in

■ **Figure 7.17** ■

Using a JOBLIB DD Statement

```
//JCLQB675 JOB ,'J.C.LEWIS'
//JOBLIB    DD DSN=LOADLIB,
//             DISP=SHR
//STEP1     EXEC PGM=PROG1
//SYSPRINT DD SYSOUT=A
//INPUT     DD DSN=TESTDATA,
//             DISP=OLD
//OUTPUT    DD SYSOUT=A
//STEP2     EXEC PGM=PROG2
//SYSPRINT DD SYSOUT=A
//REPORT    DD SYSOUT=A
//DATA      DD DSN=DATATEST,
//             DISP=OLD
//STEP3     EXEC PGM=IEBGENER
//SYSPRINT DD SYSOUT=A
//SYSUT2    DD SYSOUT=A
//SYSUT1    DD DSN=SOURCE.LIB,
//             DISP=SHR
//SYSIN     DD DUMMY
//
```

LOADLIB. After the system determines that IEBGENER is not in LOADLIB, it will search SYS1.LINKLIB, where IEBGENER will be found.

Because we coded only the data set name and disposition on the JOBLIB DD statement in Figure 7.17, the load library named must be cataloged. Load libraries are usually cataloged, but if the one you need is not cataloged and you do not want it to be, the normal disposition must be coded as PASS. For example, you could code

```
DISP=(SHR,PASS)
```

The STEPLIB DD Statement

If your job has many steps and the program executed in each step is in a different library, concatenating all the libraries in the JOBLIB DD statement may not be the best approach, as the search time required to find a program to be executed would be quite long. The search time can be reduced by using a STEPLIB statement in each step in place of the JOBLIB statement.

The STEPLIB DD statement is coded like any other DD statement that points to an existing library. Unlike the JOBLIB DD statement, it does not have to be in any particular position within the step, although it is often coded immediately after the EXEC statement.

If the program named in the EXEC statement is not found in the library or libraries referenced by the STEPLIB DD statement, SYS1.LINKLIB is searched. If the program is not found in SYS1.LINKLIB, the job will abend with a system completion code of 806.

If all but one of the programs to be executed in a job are in the same library, a JOBLIB DD statement would be used to point to that library. A STEPLIB DD statement would then be used in the one step that uses a program from another library. When a STEPLIB DD statement is specified and the program is not found in the STEPLIB library, the system will search SYS1.LINKLIB but not the library indicated by the JOBLIB DD statement. If, for example, in Figure 7.17 we wished to prevent library LOADLIB from being searched in STEP3, we could have coded a STEPLIB DD statement naming SYS1.LINKLIB as the library to be searched.

You may use the PARM parameter to pass data to your program even when the program is stored in executable form in a load library. You simply code the PARM parameter on the EXEC statement, without, of course, including a procstepname.

There is one peculiar feature to keep in mind when you use a PARM field with a PL/I program. The PL/I compiler adds code to your program that allows it to accept data from a PARM field. To distinguish between these added data and the data you want placed in the PARM field, code a slash before your data, as in

```
PARM='/SWINTER'
```

Dynamic Linking

In some systems not all modules required by a program are linked to it when it is link edited. Some modules are linked when the program is executing, in a process called **dynamic linking.** If modules are to be linked at execution, the library in which they are stored must be made available to the job. This can be done by concatenating the appropriate library — for example, SYS1.COBLIB — to the JOBLIB or STEPLIB DD statement.

Linking Programs

If you are working on a large system in which you are writing one module and your coworker another, the two object modules must be link edited to form a single load module. Figure 7.18 shows how a main program and subprogram may be compiled and link edited. The resulting load module is stored in the library named PLILOAD. [It is not necessary to compile a main program and a subprogram separately; they may be compiled together using batch compilation. The rules for batch compilation are explained in the programmer's guide for each language (see the Bibliography). Assembler, however, does not permit batch compilation. Batch compilation is not used in Figure 7.18 because this example leads naturally to the next example, for which batch compilation may not be used.] Figure 7.18 illustrates PL/I, but the other languages are used the same way.

The important point is that in the first step you execute the compile only

Figure 7.18

Compiling and Link Editing a PL/I Program and Subprogram

```
//JCLQB640 JOB ,'GROUCHO'
//COMPLKD2 EXEC PLIXC
//PLI.SYSIN DD *

          Main Program

//STEP2    EXEC PLIXCL
//PLI.SYSIN DD *

          Subprogram

//LKED.SYSLMOD DD DSN=WYL.QB.JCL.PLILOAD,
//              DISP=SHR
//LKED.SYSIN DD *
 NAME module-name
/*
//
```

procedure. This step puts the main program's object module into the temporary data set named &&LOADSET. In the second step you execute the compile and link edit procedure. This step first puts the subprogram's object module into &&LOADSET and then link edits the two object modules to form a load module.

You might wonder why the subprogram's object module did not erase the main program's existing object module when the subprogram was added to &&LOADSET. The answer lies in the clever coding of the DISP parameter for LOADSET. As shown in Figure 7.13, in the procedures for all the languages, the status subparameter for the data set that receives the object module is coded as MOD and the VOL parameter is not coded. If a data set does not exist, as LOADSET did not exist at the start of the first step, and if a specific volume is not requested, MOD has the same effect as NEW. If the data set does exist, however, as LOADSET did at the start of the second step, then, as you learned in Chapter 4, MOD means add to the end of the data set. Because the procedures use MOD this way, you may compile as many programs as you want and have them all added to the same data set.

There is one last point to be made about Figure 7.18. Notice that the main program was compiled first, followed by the subprogram. That is because the computer will start execution with the first program in the linkage editor's input. We want to start execution with the main program, so we put the main program first. Actually, PL/I programs always start execution with the main program, so the order of the programs in Figure 7.18 was not important. For other languages, however, the order is important. Thus it is good practice to make a habit of always compiling the main program first. Sometimes you cannot put the main program first. You will see what to do in those cases a little later.

Linking a Previously Compiled Program

Now let us assume that your coworker has compiled her subprogram and stored the object module in a library. In this case the linkage editor control statement INCLUDE is used to bring your coworker's object module into the load module. Figure 7.19 illustrates this situation. A PL/I program is compiled and link edited with an object module found in a private library. This object module was produced from COBOL source code. (It is not usual for a large system to use two high-level languages; usually one language is used. If a second language is used, it is usually assembler. The example in Figure 7.19 uses two high-level languages to illustrate what happens in this slightly more complex situation. Later you will notice the simplification when both programs are written in the same language.)

The first thing to observe in Figure 7.19 is the concatenation of the COBOL library and the SYSLIB DD statement. This will give the COBOL object module access to the COBOL modules required. How do we know the data set

■ Figure 7.19 ■

Compiling a PL/I Program and Link Editing It with a COBOL Module

```
//JCLQB645 JOB ,'CHICO'
//COMPLKD2 EXEC PLIXCL
//PLI.SYSIN DD *

            PL/I Source Code

/*
//LKED.SYSLIB DD
//         DD DSN=SYS1.COBLIB,
//            DISP=SHR
//LKED.SYSLMOD DD DSN=WYL.QB.JCL.LOADLIB,
//            DISP=OLD
//LKED.PRIVATE DD DSN=WYL.QB.JCL.OBJLIB,
//            DISP=OLD
//LKED.SYSIN DD *
 INCLUDE PRIVATE(COBMOD)
 NAME LOADPLC(R)
/*
//
```

name of the COBOL library—in this case, SYS1.COBLIB? Look at the SYS-LIB DD statement in the link edit step of the COBUCL procedure.

In Figure 7.19 the SYSLMOD override statement points to an existing load library, just as it did in Figure 7.14. The next DD statement makes a private object module library named OBJLIB available to the linkage editor. The linkage editor control statements following the LKED.SYSIN DD statement will tell the linkage editor how to use this private object module library. After the input is taken from the primary input, which is the SYSLIN data set, the linkage editor control statements are read. The INCLUDE control statement points to the library member named COBMOD that is in a library defined by the DD statement whose name is PRIVATE. The INCLUDE statement must be placed before the NAME statement. (We will take a closer look at the INCLUDE statement shortly.)

The load module produced will be named LOADPLC and will replace an existing module in LOADLIB. The order of the modules in the load module will be shown in the output listing if MAP is coded in the PARM field of the link edit step. The order of modules in the load module (excluding modules called in by the compiler) will reflect the order in which the modules are input. The load module produced as a result of executing the job in Figure 7.19 would have the PL/I program first, because it came from the SYSLIN DD statement, followed by the COBOL program.

As mentioned earlier, it is common for the main program and subprogram to be written in the same language. In that case the job stream in Figure 7.19

could be simplified, as there would be no need to concatenate a library to the SYSLIB DD statement.

The INCLUDE Statement.   The object module to be included may reside in a library, or it may reside in a physical sequential data set. If the object module were in a physical sequential data set, the INCLUDE statement would be coded as

```
INCLUDE dd1
```

where dd1 is the ddname of the DD statement that points to the object module. If you wish to include more than one object module, then, instead of coding several INCLUDE statements, you code

```
INCLUDE dd1,dd2, . . .
```

where dd1,dd2, . . . are the ddnames of the DD statements that point to the various object modules.

In many computer centers there is a special library for object modules. When the object module is in a library, the INCLUDE statement is coded as illustrated in Figure 7.19. If you want several modules from the same library, you code the control statement as

```
INCLUDE dd1(mod1,mod2, . . .)
```

where dd1 is the ddname of the DD statement that points to the object module library and mod1,mod2, . . . are the particular object modules that you want included. You can use the same INCLUDE statement to point to several libraries. In fact, you can point to sequential data sets and libraries on the same control statement simply by coding the ddnames and, in the case of libraries, the module names and separating the entries by commas.

The ENTRY Statement.   In Figure 7.19 we want to begin execution with the main program. Because the PL/I program is the main program, it is appropriate to code it first. Suppose, however, that the PL/I program were the subprogram and the COBOL program were the main program. We would need some way to tell the system to begin execution with the COBOL program. We would do this with the ENTRY control statement.

The ENTRY control statement is coded as follows:

```
ENTRY entryname
```

where entryname is the name of the program with which execution is to start. The entryname in each language is different. In assembler it is the name specified in the CSECT instruction of the main program; in COBOL it is the name specified in the PROGRAM-ID instruction of the main program; in FORTRAN it is MAIN; and in PL/I it is PLISTART. The order of the ENTRY and INCLUDE statements does not matter, but they must both be placed before the NAME statement.

Creating Multiple Load Modules

Figure 7.20 illustrates how the linkage editor can be used to create several load modules in one job. The load modules created are stored as members of a library created in this job. SYSLMOD is overridden to create the load library. Notice that no DCB information is provided; none is required unless you specify DCBS in the linkage editor PARM field. Do not do this unless you must.

The object library named FORTOBJ is made available to the linkage editor with the additional DD statement whose name is PRIVATE. This library contains previously created object modules. The first linkage editor control statement supplies the module name for the object code found in the primary input, the SYSLIN data set. The next two linkage editor control statements belong together. The INCLUDE statement takes the object module named MOD2 from the library pointed to by the DD statement PRIVATE. The linkage editor will process this object module and create a second load module. The NAME statement assigns the name MOD2 to this load module. Notice that the object module and load module members have the same name. If the source code were a member of a source library, the same name would be used for the source code member. The advantage of this approach is that there is only one name to remember for the three states of the program — that is, source, object, and load modules.

The last two control statements will result in the creation of a third load module named MOD3. The INCLUDE statement takes three object modules —

■ **Figure 7.20** ■■■■■■■■■■■■■■■■■■■■■■■■■■■■■■■

Creating Several Load Modules in One Job

```
//JCLQB650 JOB ,'HARPO'
//COMPLKD3 EXEC FORTXCL
//FORT.SYSIN DD *

           FORTRAN Source Code

/*
//LKED.SYSLMOD DD DSN=WYL.QB.JCL.FORTLOAD,
//              DISP=(,KEEP),
//              VOL=SER=SCR002,
//              SPACE=(CYL,(10,1,10))
//LKED.PRIVATE DD DSN=WYL.QB.JCL.FORTOBJ,
//              DISP=SHR
//LKED.SYSIN DD *
 NAME MOD1
 INCLUDE PRIVATE(MOD2)
 NAME MOD2
 INCLUDE PRIVATE(MODA,MODB,MODC)
 NAME MOD3
/*
//
```

MODA, MODB, and MODC — from the library pointed to by the PRIVATE DD statement.

You should understand that there are three separate linkage editor tasks accomplished by the job in Figure 7.20 — the creation of load modules MOD1, MOD2, and MOD3 — and that these three tasks are independent of one another. The primary function of the job in Figure 7.20 is to compile a FOR-TRAN program and to link edit the object module produced to create the load module MOD1. It was convenient to create MOD2 and MOD3 at the same time because the job invoked the linkage editor and made available the FORTOBJ library, which is required to create MOD2 and MOD3. (Also, it provided an opportunity to show you how to create several load modules in one job.)

In this example we assumed that all the object modules were originally written in the same language. If different languages were used, additional libraries would have to be made available, as shown in Figure 7.19.

The LIBRARY Statement

The job coded in Figure 7.21 illustrates the use of the LIBRARY linkage editor control statement. In this example assembler modules are assumed. The extra modules will be found in libraries ASMOBJ1 and ASMOBJ2, which are concatenated under the ddname PRIVATE. Let us examine the first LIBRARY control statement in Figure 7.21. LIBRARY is the operation, and PRIVATE(MODA,MODB) is the operand. PRIVATE is the ddname of the DD state-

---

■ **Figure 7.21** ━━━━━━━━━━━━━━━━━━━━━━━━━━━━━━━━━━━━━━

Assembling a Program and Link Editing It into a Load Library

```
//JCLQB655 JOB ,'GUMMO'
//COMPLKD4 EXEC ASMFCL
//ASM.SYSIN DD *

              Assembler Source Code

/*
//LKED.SYSLMOD DD DSN=WYL.QB.JCL.MODLIB,
//              DISP=OLD
//LKED.PRIVATE DD DSN=WYL.QB.JCL.ASMOBJ1,
//              DISP=SHR
//           DD DSN=WYL.QB.JCL.ASMOBJ2,
//              DISP=SHR
//LKED.SYSIN DD *
 LIBRARY PRIVATE(MODA,MODB)
 LIBRARY (CITYTAX)
 NAME PAY(R)
/*
//
```

ment pointing to the library in which object modules MODA and MODB will be found.

The general form of the LIBRARY control statement is

```
LIBRARY dd1(mod1,mod2, . . . )
```

It is possible that these object modules, MODA and MODB, also exist in a standard library and that new versions are being tested. The LIBRARY control statement tells the linkage editor to take the object modules from the library or libraries pointed to by the specified DD statement instead of from the SYSLIB library or libraries.

The LIBRARY and INCLUDE statements are similar, but not the same. Any module specified with an INCLUDE statement is immediately incorporated into the load module. On the other hand, a module named in a LIBRARY statement is not called until it is required to resolve an external reference. In fact, if no reference is made to a module named in a LIBRARY statement, it will not be incorporated into the load module.

The second LIBRARY control statement in Figure 7.21 is used to exclude a module from a load module. Any reference to CITYTAX in the load module to be named PAY will remain unresolved when the automatic-call library is searched. Why would you want to exclude an object module from a load module? To create a smaller load module. If no one in the installation lives in the city, for example, there is no point in including the CITYTAX module in a payroll program. The general format of the LIBRARY statement to exclude a module is

```
LIBRARY (mod1,mod2, . . . )
```

Overlay*

In all the cases we have examined so far, the load module created is loaded into storage and remains there until execution ceases. The **overlay structure** creates a load module that will be loaded into storage in pieces. Each of these pieces is called a **segment.** When a new piece, or segment, is needed, it is brought into storage for execution. Figure 7.22 shows a sample hierarchical organization and the related linkage editor control statements. The INSERT statement causes the linkage editor to take a module that it will find in the SYSLIN data set. If the modules were in one or more different libraries, INCLUDE statements would be used in place of the INSERT statement. The OVERLAY statement identifies the point at which the overlay is made. In Figure 7.22 these places are labeled ONE, TWO, THREE, and FOUR.

---

*This section may be skipped without loss of continuity.

Figure 7.22

Hierarchical Organization and Linkage Editor Control Statements

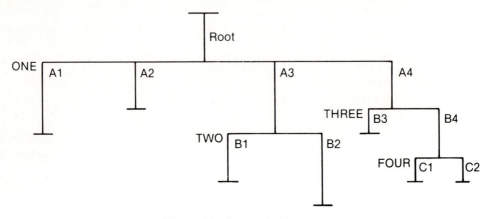

Hierarchical organization

```
ENTRY BEGIN
INSERT ROOT
OVERLAY ONE
INSERT A1
OVERLAY ONE
INSERT A2
OVERLAY ONE
INSERT A3
OVERLAY TWO
INSERT B1
OVERLAY TWO
INSERT B2
OVERLAY ONE
INSERT A4
OVERLAY THREE
INSERT B3
OVERLAY THREE
INSERT B4
OVERLAY FOUR
INSERT C1
OVERLAY FOUR
INSERT C2
```

When the linkage editor is invoked for overlay structure, OVLY must be specified in the PARM field.

Let us discuss what will happen if the modules shown in Figure 7.22 are executed. Initially the segment labeled ROOT will be loaded into storage. This segment will remain in storage for the life of the execution. When called by the ROOT segment, segment A1 will be loaded and executed. After execution of A1 ends, control will be returned to the ROOT segment. Notice that the INSERT statements for A1, A2, and A3 are preceded by the statement OVER-LAY ONE. This OVERLAY statement means that if segment A2 is called, it will be placed in the same starting location as A1. Similarly, if segment A3 is called, it will be loaded in the same starting storage location as A1 and A2. The INSERT B1 and B2 statements are preceded by a different OVERLAY statement, OVERLAY TWO. Segment A3 can, while remaining in storage, call segments B1 and B2, which would be loaded and executed in storage following segment A3. When control is returned to the ROOT segment, if segment A4 is called, it will be loaded in the same location as A3. If B4 is called, it will be loaded following segment A4. If B4 were to call either C1 or C2, either one would be loaded following segment B4.

Overlay structure was formerly an important technique for making the most of limited main storage. It has fallen into disuse because of the decrease in the cost of main storage and because of the development of virtual storage, which gives the illusion of much more storage than is actually available. With the growth of small personal computers, however, knowledge of this concept may prove helpful.

Procedures to Compile, Link Edit, and Execute a Program

Figure 7.23 shows listings of IBM-supplied procedures to compile, link edit, and execute. The names of these procedures end with the letters CLG.

The principal difference between the procedures in Figure 7.23 and the compile and link edit procedures in Figure 7.13 is the addition in the former of a third step, which executes the program just compiled and link edited. The third step's name is GO.

If you compare the SYSLMOD statement in the COBUCL procedure with that in COBUCLG, you will see a difference in the data set name. In the COBUCLG procedure the member name GO is included in the data set name. In the COBUCL procedure the user must supply the member name in some fashion, such as with the NAME linkage editor control statement.

The third step in these procedures, which causes the program to execute, uses a new form of the EXEC statement. Instead of naming the program to be executed, it uses a backward reference. The same rules that apply to a data set backward reference apply here. The asterisk tells the system that this is a backward reference. The next element in the field names the step in which

Figure 7.23

(a) The COBUCLG Procedure

```
//COB       EXEC PGM=IKFCBL00,PARM=SUPMAP,REGION=86K
//SYSPRINT DD SYSOUT=A
//SYSUT1    DD DSNAME=&&SYSUT1,UNIT=SYSDA,SPACE=(460,(700,100))
//SYSUT2    DD DSNAME=&&SYSUT2,UNIT=SYSDA,SPACE=(460,(700,100))
//SYSUT3    DD DSNAME=&&SYSUT3,UNIT=SYSDA,SPACE=(460,(700,100))
//SYSUT4    DD DSNAME=&&SYSUT4,UNIT=SYSDA,SPACE=(460,(700,100))
//SYSLIN    DD DSNAME=&&LOADSET,DISP=(MOD,PASS),UNIT=SYSDA,
//             SPACE=(80,(500,100))
//LKED      EXEC PGM=IEWL,PARM='LIST,XREF,LET',COND=(5,LT,COB),
//             REGION=96K
//SYSLIN    DD DSNAME=&&LOADSET,DISP=(OLD,DELETE)
//          DD DDNAME=SYSIN
//SYSLMOD   DD DSNAME=&&GOSET(GO),DISP=(NEW,PASS),UNIT=SYSDA,
//             SPACE=(1024,(50,20,1))
//SYSLIB    DD DSNAME=SYS1.COBLIB,DISP=SHR
//SYSUT1    DD UNIT=(SYSDA,SEP=(SYSLIN,SYSLMOD)),
//             SPACE=(1024,(50,20))
//SYSPRINT DD SYSOUT=A
//GO        EXEC PGM=*.LKED.SYSLMOD,COND=(5,LT,COB),(5,LT,LKED))
```

(b) The PLIXCLG Procedure

```
//PLIXCLG  PROC LKLBDSN='SYS1.PLIBASE'
//PLI       EXEC PGM=IEL0AA,PARM='OBJECT,NODECK',REGION=100K
//SYSPRINT DD SYSOUT=A
//SYSLIN    DD DSN=&&LOADSET,DISP=(MOD,PASS),UNIT=SYSSQ,
//             SPACE=(80,(250,100))
//SYSUT1    DD DSN=&&SYSUT1,UNIT=SYSDA,SPACE=(1024,(200,50),,CONTIG,ROUND),
//             DCB=BLKSIZE=1024
//LKED      EXEC PGM=IEWL,PARM='XREF,LIST',COND=(9,LT,PLI),REGION=100K
//SYSLIB    DD DSN=&LKLBDSN,DISP=SHR
//          DD DSN=SYS1.PLIBASE,DISP=SHR
//SYSLMOD   DD DSNAME=&&GOSET(GO),DISP=(MOD,PASS),UNIT=SYSDA,
//             SPACE=(1024,(50,20,1))
//SYSUT1    DD DSN=&&SYSUT1,UNIT=SYSDA,SPACE=(1024,(200,50)),
//             DCB=BLKSIZE=1024
//SYSPRINT DD SYSOUT=A
//SYSLIN    DD DSN=&&LOADSET,DISP=(OLD,DELETE)
//          DD DDNAME=SYSIN
//SYSIN     DD  DUMMY
//GO        EXEC PGM=*.LKED.SYSLMOD,COND=(9,LT,PLI),(9,LT,LKED)),
//             REGION=100K
//SYSPRINT DD SYSOUT=A
```

(c) The FORTXCLG Procedure

```
//FORTXCLG PROC FXPGM=IFEAAB,FXREGN=256K,FXPDECK=NODECK,
//             FXPOLST=NOLIST,FXPOPT=O,GOREGN=100K,
//             GOF5DD='DDNAME=SYSIN',GOF6DD='SYSOUT=A',
//             GOF7DD='SYSOUT=B'
//*
//*             PARAMETER   DEFAULT-VALUE     USAGE
//*
```

Cont.

```
//*                FXPGM     IFEAAB          COMPILER NAME
//*                FXREGN    256K            FORT-STEP REGION
//*                FXPDECK   NODECK          COMPILER DECK OPTION
//*                FXPOLST   NOLIST          COMPILER LIST OPTION
//*                FXPOPT    O               COMPILER OPTIMIZATION
//*                GOREGN    100K            GO-STEP REGION
//*                GOF5DD    DDNAME=SYSIN    GO.FT05F001 OPERAND
//*                GOF6DD    SYSOUT=A        GO.FTO6F001 OPERAND
//*                GOF7DD    SYSOUT=B        GO.FT07F001 OPERAND
//*
//FORT   EXEC PGM=&FXPGM,REGION=&FXREGN,COND=(4,LT),
//             PARM='&FXPDECK,&FXPOLST,OPT(&FXPOPT)'
//SYSPRINT      DD SYSOUT=A,DCB=BLKSIZE=3429
//SYSTERM       DD SYSOUT=A
//SYSUT1        DD UNIT=SYSSQ,SPACE=(3465,(3,3)),DCB=BLKSIZE=3465
//SYSUT2        DD UNIT=SYSSQ,SPACE=(5048,(10,10))
//SYSPUNCH      DD SYSOUT=B,DCB=BLKSIZE=3440
//SYSLIN        DD DSN=&&LOADSET,DISP=(MOD,PASS),UNIT=SYSSQ,
//                 SPACE=(3200,(25,6)),DCB=BLKSIZE=3200
//LKED   EXEC PGM=IEWL,REGION=96K,COND=(4,LT),
//             PARM='LET,LIST,MAP,XREF'
//SYSPRINT      DD SYSOUT=A
//SYSLIB        DD DSN=SYS1.FORTLIB,DISP=SHR
//SYSUT1        DD UNIT=SYSDA,SPACE=(1024,(200,20))
//SYSLMOD       DD DSN=&&GOSET(MAIN),DISP=(,PASS),UNIT=SYSDA,
//                 SPACE=(TRK,(10,10,1),RLSE)
//SYSLIN        DD DSN=&&LOADSET,DISP=(OLD,DELETE)
//              DD DDNAME=SYSIN
//GO     EXEC PGM=*.LKED.SYSLMOD,REGION=&GOREGN,COND=(4,LT)
//FT05F001      DD &GOF5DD
//FT06F001      DD &GOF6DD
//FT07F001      DD &GOF7DD
```

(d) The ASMFCLG Procedure

```
//ASMFCLG  PROC MAC='SYS1.MACLIB',MAC1='SYS1.MACLIB'
//ASM      EXEC PGM=IFOX00,PARM=OBJ,REGION=128K
//SYSLIB   DD   DSN=&MAC1,DISP=SHR
//         DD   DSN=&MAC1,DISP=SHR
//SYSUT1   DD   DSN=&&SYSUT1,UNIT=SYSSQ,SPACE=(1700,(600,100),
//              SEP=(SYSLIB)
//SYSUT2   DD   DSN=&&SYSUT2,UNIT=SYSSQ,SPACE=(1700,(300,50)),
//              SEP=(SYSLIB,SYSUT1)
//SYSUT3   DD   DSN=&&SYSUT3,UNIT=SYSSQ,SPACE=(1700,(300,50))
//SYSPRINT DD   SYSOUT=A,DCB=BLKSIZE=1089
//SYSPUNCH DD   SYSOUT=B
//SYSGO    DD   DSN=&&OBJECT,UNIT=SYSSQ,SPACE=(80,(200,50)),
//              DISP=(MOD,PASS)
//LKED     EXEC PGM=IEWL,PARM=(XREF,LET,LIST,NCAL),REGION=128K,
//              COND=(8,LT,ASM)
//SYSLIN   DD   DSN=&&OBJSET,DISP=(OLD,DELETE)
//         DD   DDNAME=SYSIN
//SYSLMOD  DD   DSN=&&GOSET(GO),UNIT=SYSDA,SPACE=(1024,(50,20,1),
//              DISP=(MOD,PASS)
//SYSUT1   DD   DSN=&&SYSUT1,UNIT=(SYSDA,SEP=(SYSLIN,SYSLMOD),
//              SPACE=(1024,(50,20)
//SYSPRINT DD   SYSOUT=A
//GO       EXEC PGM=*.LKED.SYSLMOD,COND=((8,LT,ASM),(4,LT,LKED)
```

■ **Figure 7.24** ■

Compiling, Link Editing, and Executing a COBOL Program

```
//JCLQB660 JOB ,'J.C.LEWIS'
//COMPLG1  EXEC COBUCLG
//COB.SYSIN DD *

              COBOL Source Code

/*
//GO.INPUT DD *

          Input Data

/*
//GO.OUTPUT DD SYSOUT=A
//
```

the DD statement will be found, and the last one names the DD statement itself. Thus the backward reference in COBUCLG is pointing to the load library member to be executed. Outside of these procedures, backward references are rarely used to identify the program to be executed.

Executing a Compile, Link Edit, and Go Procedure

Figures 7.24 and 7.25 illustrate the JCL used to invoke COBUCLG and PLIXCLG. Notice how similar the JCL is in both jobs. Also, except for the procedure name, the JCL in Figure 7.24 is identical to the JCL used in Figure 7.10 to invoke COBUCG. In both cases the COBOL source code follows the

■ **Figure 7.25** ■

Compiling, Link Editing, and Executing a PL/I Program

```
//JCLQB665 JOB ,'J.C.LEWIS'
//COMPLG2  EXEC PLIXCLG
//PLI.SYSIN DD *

            PL/I Source Code

/*
//GO.CARDIN DD *

          Input Data

/*
//GO.PRINTER DD SYSOUT=A
//
```

9. In the procedure name COBUCLG, what do the letters CLG stand for?
10. Which keyword parameter is used to pass information to the compiler to request special processing?
11. If you wanted to invoke the procedure COBUC, how would you code the EXEC statement?
12. How would you code the DD statement to input the COBOL source code?
13. What is a PROC statement?
14. Where in a procedure must the PROC statement be located?
15. For which type of procedure is the PROC statement required?
16. In a cataloged procedure, what information is coded on a PROC statement?
17. If you needed to change information in a DD statement of a procedure for one run, what would you do?
18. If you are coding both an overriding DD statement and an added DD statement, in what order should they be coded?
19. In the COBUC procedure in Figure 7.2a, if you wished to change the UNIT of SYSUT2 and SYSUT3 to SYSQ, what would you code?
20. What is a symbolic parameter? How do you assign a value to a symbolic parameter? When must you use apostrophes in assigning a value to a symbolic parameter?
21. What is concatenation? When would you use it?
22. If you wished to add a third library to the SYSLIB DD statement when using ASMFC, what would you code?
23. What does the loader do?
24. When would you use the loader?
25. How do you modify the execution of the loader?
26. What functions are performed by the compile and go procedures?
27. When you add a DD statement to a multistep procedure, how do you indicate the step to which the DD statement should be added?
28. On an output listing, how can you distinguish your JCL statements from JCL statements added to your job stream by a cataloged procedure?
29. What function performed by the loader is not performed by the linkage editor?
30. What function do both the linkage editor and the loader perform?
31. What is the primary input to the linkage editor? Under what ddname is it supplied?
32. What function does the linkage editor perform that the loader cannot?
33. What is the output of the linkage editor? Under what ddnames is it produced?
34. How would you invoke the additional functions of the linkage editor?
35. How would you modify the execution of the linkage editor?
36. How do you code a forward reference?
37. Figure 7.28 shows the execution of a job that attempts to add a load module named COBPGM1 to a load library named WYL.QB.JCL.LINK-

Actual Execution

```
//JCLQB633 JOB ,'J.C.LEWIS'
//COBLOAD  EXEC COBUCL
//COB.SYSIN DD *
/*
//LKED.SYSIN DD *
/*
//LKED.SYSLMOD DD DSN=WYL.QB.JCL.LINKLIB,
//              DISP=(NEW,CATLG),
//              UNIT=DISK,
//              VOL=SER=WYL004,
//              SPACE=(1024,(50,10,1),RLSE)
```

```
 1  //JCLQB633 JOB ,'J.C.LEWIS'                                                     00000100
 2  //COBLOAD  EXEC COBUCL                                                          00000200
 3  XXCOBUCL  PROC SUT1=15,SOBJ=15,SLUT1=50,SLUT2=20,SLMOD1=50,SLMOD2=20,           00000300
    XX             ADDLIB='SYS1.ADDLIB'                                             00000400
 4  XXCOB     EXEC PGM=IKFCBL00                                                     00000500
 5  XXSYSPRINT DD SYSOUT=A,DCB=BLKSIZE=1936                                         00000600
 6  XXSYSUT1  DD DSN=&&SYSUT1,UNIT=3330,SPACE=(TRK,(&SUT1,5))                       00000700
 7  XXSYSUT2  DD DSN=&&SYSUT2,UNIT=3330,SPACE=(TRK,(&SUT1,5))                       00000800
 8  XXSYSUT3  DD DSN=&&SYSUT3,UNIT=3330,SPACE=(TRK,(&SUT1,5))                       00000900
 9  XXSYSUT4  DD DSN=&&SYSUT4,UNIT=3330,SPACE=(TRK,(&SUT1,5))                       00001000
10  XXSYSLIN  DD DSN=&&LOADSET,DCB=BLKSIZE=3120,DISP=(MOD,PASS),
    XX           UNIT=3330,SPACE=(6400,(&SOBJ,10))
11  //COB.SYSIN DD *,DCB=BLKSIZE=80
12  XXLKED    EXEC PGM=IEWL,PARM='LIST,XREF,LET',COND=(5,LT,COB)                    00001100
13  XXSYSLIN  DD DSN=&&LOADSET,DISP=(OLD,DELETE)                                    00001200
14  XX        DD DDNAME=SYSIN                                                       00001300
15  XXSYSLMOD DD DSN=&&GOSET,DISP=(NEW,PASS),UNIT=3330,                             00001400
    XX           SPACE=(1024,(&SLMOD1,&SLMOD2,1))                                   00001500
```

```
16    XXSYSLIB    DD    DSN=&ADDLIB,DISP=SHR                        00001600
17    XX          DD    DSN=SYS1.COBLIB,DISP=SHR                    00001700
18    XXSYSUT1    DD    UNIT=(3330,SEP=(SYSLIN,SYSLMOD)),           00001800
      XX                SPACE=(1024,(&SLUT1,&SLUT2))                00001900
19    XXSYSPRINT DD     SYSOUT=A,DCB=BLKSIZE=1936                   00002000
20    //LKED.SYSIN DD *,DCB=BLKSIZE=80
21    //LKED.SYSLMOD DD DSN=WYL.QB.JCL.LINKLIB,
      //                DISP=(NEW,CATLG),
      //                UNIT=DISK,
      //                VOL=SER=WYL004,
      //                SPACE=(1024,(50,10,1),RLSE)

F64-LEVEL LINKAGE EDITOR OPTIONS SPECIFIED LIST,XREF,LET
      DEFAULT OPTION(S) USED - SIZE=(196608,65536)
IEW0000
      NAME COBPGM1
```

LOCATION	REFERS TO SYMBOL	IN CONTROL SECTION	LOCATION	REFERS TO SYMBOL	IN CONTROL SECTION
478	ILBOSRV0	ILBOSRV	47C	ILBODBG0	ILBODBG
480	ILBOSR	ILBOSRV	484	ILBODBG4	ILBODBG
488	ILBOEXT0	ILBOEXT	48C	ILBOSRV1	ILBOSRV
400	ILBOCOM0	ILBOCOM0	13B4	ILBOFLW0	$UNRESOLVED(W)
13B8	ILBOFLW2	$UNRESOLVED(W	13BC	ILBOTEF3	$UNRESOLVED(W)
13C0	ILBOSTN0	$UNRESOLVED(W	1860	ILBOCOM	ILBOCOM0
1864	ILBOCMM0	ILBOCMM	1868	ILBOBEG0	ILBOBEG
186C	ILBOMSG0	ILBOMSG			

```
ENTRY ADDRESS        00
TOTAL LENGTH         1E68
***COBPGM1  NOW ADDED TO DATA SET
AUTHORIZATION CODE IS       0.
```

LIB. The output seems to indicate that the job ran perfectly, but when a programmer later tried to execute COBPGM1, using a JOBLIB statement that pointed to WYL.QB.JCL.LINKLIB, the job abended with a completion code of 806. Why?

38. What is the difference between the linkage editor control statements NAME MOD and NAME MOD(R)?

39. How do you add a load module to a permanent library?

40. Using the linkage editor, how would you give a name to the load module?

41. When you want to execute a load module that is stored in a private library, how do you tell the system where to find it?

42. Which linkage editor control statement is used to obtain an object module from a source other than the primary input?

43. How would you change the JCL in Figure 7.19 if the program called for a FORTRAN module?

44. Which linkage editor control statement is used to exclude a module from a load module?

45. Why would overlay structure be used?

46. In the compile, link edit, and go procedures, how is the program named in the execute, or GO, step?

Programming Assignments

1. Using the COBOL program LISTER or any other simple program in either COBOL, PL/I, FORTRAN, or assembler language, execute each of the four procedures we have discussed. Make the program available to the procedure either as input stream data or as a member of the library you created as your solution to Programming Assignment 12 in Chapter 5. Modify the compile and link edit procedures' execution so that the load module is stored in either a new or an existing load library. After the module has been stored in a load library, execute the program from the load library using a JOBLIB DD statement.

2. In any language you like, write a main program and a subprogram. Compile the subprogram, and store the object module as a sequential data set. Using the compile, link edit, and execute procedure, compile the main program, link edit it with the subprogram, and execute the resulting load module.

8

User-Written Procedures

In this chapter you will learn

- how to write, test, and use user-written procedures
- how to code in-stream procedures
- how to use symbolic parameters in user-written procedures
- how to include JCL statements in input stream data

In Chapter 7 you learned how to use system procedures. In this chapter you will learn how to create, test, and use your own procedures.

Creating an In-Stream Procedure

As our first example, let us write a procedure that uses the program IEFBR14 to create a library. The coding we need is shown in Figure 8.1. When the coding in Figure 8.1 is executed, it will catalog a library named MYLIB on disk pack WYL003. The library will occupy five tracks and contain seven directory blocks; the record size will be 80 bytes; the blocksize will be 1600 bytes.

To convert the coding in Figure 8.1 into a cataloged procedure, we have to add it to the procedure library. It is a good idea to execute it first, however, to

■ **Figure 8.1** ━━

JCL to Create a PDS Using IEFBR14

```
//LIBMAKE    EXEC PGM=IEFBR14,
//              REGION=32K
//LIBDD     DD DSN=WYL.QB.JCL.MYLIB,
//             DISP=(,CATLG),
//             UNIT=DISK,
//             VOL=SER=WYL003,
//             SPACE=(TRK,(5,,7)),
//             DCB=(RECFM=FB,LRECL=80,BLKSIZE=1600)
```

make sure there are no errors. The way to do that is to convert it into an in-stream procedure.

Figure 8.2 shows how the coding in Figure 8.1 is converted into an in-stream procedure. (Notice the name: A procedure in the input stream is called an in-stream procedure. Data in the input stream are called input stream data.)

As you can see, the conversion is very easy. All we do is add a PROC statement at the start of the procedure and a PEND statement at the end. You studied the PROC statement in Chapter 7. There you learned that in cataloged procedures the PROC statement is optional. For in-stream procedures the PROC statement is required and must have a name coded in the name field. In Figure 8.2 the name is CREATE, which is used when the in-stream procedure is executed.

The PEND statement is used only to mark the end of an in-stream procedure. The rules for coding the PEND statement are the same as for all the other JCL statements: Slashes must appear in columns 1 and 2; a name field is optional; and there must be at least one space before and after the operation PEND. It is not customary to code a name on the PEND statement, and in Figure 8.2 none is coded.

■ **Figure 8.2** ━━

An In-Stream Procedure to Create a PDS Using IEFBR14

```
//CREATE     PROC
//LIBMAKE    EXEC PGM=IEFBR14,
//              REGION=32K
//LIBDD     DD DSN=WYL.QB.JCL.MYLIB,
//             DISP=(,CATLG),
//             UNIT=DISK,
//             VOL=SER=WYL003,
//             SPACE=(TRK,(5,,7)),
//             DCB=(RECFM=FB,LRECL=80,BLKSIZE=1600)
//           PEND
```

■ **Figure 8.3** ■

Executing the In-Stream Procedure in Figure 8.2

```
//JCLQB710 JOB ,'J.C.LEWIS'
//CREATE   PROC
//LIBMAKE  EXEC PGM=IEFBR14,
//              REGION=32K
//LIBDD    DD DSN=WYL.QB.JCL.MYLIB,
//              DISP=(,CATLG),
//              UNIT=DISK,
//              VOL=SER=WYL003,
//              SPACE=(TRK,(5,,7)),
//              DCB=(RECFM=FB,LRECL=80,BLKSIZE=1600)
//         PEND
//CREATLIB EXEC CREATE
//
```

There are some general rules about procedures—both cataloged and in-stream—that you should know. A procedure may not contain a JOB statement, a delimiter statement (/ *), or a null statement (//). It may not contain a JOBLIB DD statement, input stream data, or a DD statement for input stream data (such as DD *). Finally, an EXEC statement in a procedure may execute only programs and not procedures.

Now that we have created an in-stream procedure, we must execute it to make sure that it is correct. Figure 8.3 shows how the in-stream procedure in Figure 8.2 is executed. The important point to note in Figure 8.3 is that the EXEC statement that executes the procedure must follow the procedure. The procedure name coded on the EXEC statement is the name on the PROC statement—CREATE.

When an in-stream procedure is executed, the source of the JCL statements in the effective job stream is identified on the output listing (provided you code 1 for the statements subparameter in the MSGLEVEL parameter). The identification method used is similar to the one used to identify the source of JCL statements when a cataloged procedure is executed, which was discussed in Chapter 7. In-stream procedure statements that you did not override are identified by ++ in columns 1 and 2. In-stream procedure statements that you did override are identified by +/ in columns 1 and 2. Comment statements are identified by *** in columns 1, 2, and 3.

▬ Adding a Procedure to the Procedure Library

After proper execution has proven that an in-stream procedure does not contain any errors, the procedure may be added to the procedure library. IEBUPDTE is usually used to do this.

You should remember how to use IEBUPDTE from the discussion in Chapter 5, so we will discuss only points of special interest. The name of the procedure library is usually SYS1.PROCLIB. In most computer centers only systems programmers are authorized to add procedures to the procedure library. If you wanted a procedure added to the procedure library, you would create a job stream like the one shown in Figure 8.4 and give it to a systems programmer to execute.

On the ADD control statement, the NAME operand is used to assign the name CREATE to the procedure. Notice that the name of the procedure is the same as the name on the PROC statement. Although making the names the same is good practice, it is not necessary. In fact, cataloged procedure CREATE does not even require a PROC statement. (The conditions under which a cataloged procedure requires a PROC statement are discussed later in this chapter. As mentioned earlier, in-stream procedures always require a PROC statement.)

The statements that will be used to create cataloged procedure CREATE include all the statements from in-stream procedure CREATE except for the PEND statement. PEND statements are used only to mark the end of an in-stream procedure; it is illegal to have a PEND statement in a cataloged procedure.

■ **Figure 8.4** ■

Adding a Procedure to the Procedure Library

```
//JCLQB715 JOB ,'J.C.LEWIS',
//              REGION=38K
//ADDPROC  EXEC PGM=IEBUPDTE,
//              PARM=NEW
//SYSPRINT DD  SYSOUT=A
//SYSUT2   DD  DSN=SYS1.PROCLIB,
//              DISP=OLD
//SYSIN    DD  DATA
./ ADD NAME=CREATE,LIST=ALL
./ NUMBER NEW1=100,INCR=100
//CREATE   PROC
//LIBMAKE  EXEC PGM=IEFBR14,
//              REGION=32K
//LIBDD    DD  DSN=WYL.QB.JCL.MYLIB,
//              DISP=(,CATLG),
//              UNIT=DISK,
//              VOL=SER=WYL003,
//              SPACE=(TRK,(5,,7)),
//              DCB=(RECFM=FB,LRECL=80,BLKSIZE=1600)
/*
//
```

The DATA Parameter

There is one more interesting feature in Figure 8.4. Notice that on the SYSIN DD statement the parameter DATA is coded, rather than an asterisk. DATA is a positional parameter that is used when input stream data contain JCL statements.

You may recall from Chapter 2 that the delimiter statement in Figure 2.2 was not required because input stream data are terminated by any JCL statement. This raises the question of what to do if you want to include JCL statements in input stream data. As Figure 8.4 shows, the answer is to use the DATA parameter instead of the asterisk parameter. If an asterisk had been coded on the SYSIN statement, the statement

```
//CREATE      PROC
```

would have terminated the input stream data and the job would not have executed properly.

Input stream data that follow a DD DATA statement are terminated only by a delimiter statement. If the delimiter statement had been omitted in Figure 8.4, the null statement would have been made part of the procedure. Because a cataloged procedure may not contain a null statement, the procedure would not be usable. A procedure may not contain a DD DATA statement.

Executing a Cataloged Procedure

After CREATE has been added to the procedure library, it may be executed by the job stream shown in Figure 8.5, which will create a library named MYLIB. That is very nice, you may think, but how many times will you want to create MYLIB? It seems that this procedure is not very useful. Actually, procedures rarely do exactly what you want them to do. You must learn to change a procedure to match your needs. One way of doing that, as you learned in Chapter 7, is by coding DD statements that will override DD statements in the procedure.

■ **Figure 8.5** ■

Executing the CREATE Procedure

```
//JCLQB720 JOB ,'J.C.LEWIS'
//CREATLIB EXEC CREATE
//
```

■ Figure 8.6 ■■■

Executing the CREATE Procedure Using an Overriding DD Statement

```
//JCLQB725 JOB ,'J.C.LEWIS'
//CREATLIB EXEC CREATE
//LIBMAKE.LIBDD DD DSN=WYL.QB.JCL.SAVELIB,
//               VOL=SER=WYL005,
//               SPACE=(TRK,(3,,7)),
//               DCB=BLKSIZE=800
//
```

Overriding DD Statements

Suppose you want to create a library named SAVELIB. You want it to be on WYL005 and to have three tracks, seven directory blocks, and a blocksize of 800 bytes. You can use procedure CREATE to create SAVELIB provided you code an overriding DD statement to change some of the parameters, as shown in Figure 8.6. Notice that the ddname coded in the overriding DD statement consists of the procedure stepname (LIBMAKE), followed by a period, followed by the ddname of the DD statement in the procedure you are overriding (LIBDD). (The format corresponds exactly to that of the LKED.SYSLMOD DD statements coded in Chapter 7.) Only those parameters you want to change should be coded on the DD statement. In Figure 8.6 DSN, VOL, SPACE, and DCB needed to be altered, so those parameters were coded with the desired values. The original coding of DISP and UNIT was acceptable, so those parameters were not coded.

Notice that the complete SPACE parameter had to be coded, even though only the number of tracks, and not the number of directory blocks, needed to be changed. On the other hand, for the DCB parameter only the BLKSIZE subparameter was coded. The other two parameters, RECFM and LRECL, retain their original values. The DCB parameter is the only one for which you may override individual keyword subparameters.

As you examine Figure 8.6, you may once more come to the conclusion that procedure CREATE is not especially useful. It seems to be as much work to code the overriding DD statement as it would have been to use IEFBR14 directly, and after all, the main purpose of procedures is to save programmers the trouble of coding a lot of repetitive JCL. It is true that use of CREATE does not save a lot of coding, as it consists of only two statements. Because of its small size, however, CREATE serves effectively as a simple example that is easy to follow. Later in this chapter we will study more useful procedures.

Using Symbolic Parameters

In Chapter 7 you learned that symbolic parameters offer a convenient way of changing a procedure to fit your requirements. Figure 8.7 shows the CREATE procedure, renamed CREATE2, rewritten to include symbolic parameters. The choice of which values to code as symbolic parameters is up to the programmer. Generally symbolic parameters are used for values that are likely to change frequently. In Figure 8.7 the data set name, the serial number of the disk pack, the number of tracks, and the number of directory blocks have been made into symbolic parameters. Symbolic parameters could also have been defined for the values of DISP, UNIT, and DCB. Because the purpose of symbolic parameters is to make using the procedure more convenient, the documentation in Figure 8.7 is very helpful.

Symbolic parameter names may consist of from one to seven alphameric or national characters preceded by an ampersand. The first character must be alphabetic or national. EXEC statement keyword parameters may not be used as names of symbolic parameters. For example, it is illegal to use &REGION as a symbolic parameter because REGION is an EXEC statement keyword parameter. This restriction does not extend to DD statement keyword parameters. Notice that in Figure 8.7 &DSN is used as a symbolic parameter.

The names you invent for symbolic parameters should be meaningful, so that they will be easy to remember. In Figure 8.7 &DSN is used for the data set name, &PACK for the volume serial number of the disk pack, &TRACKS for the number of tracks, and &BLOCKS for the number of directory blocks.

The CREATE2 procedure could be added to the procedure library using a

■ Figure 8.7 ■

Adding Symbolic Parameters to the CREATE Procedure

```
//CREATE2   PROC
//*
//*              PARAMETER    MEANING
//*              DSN          DATA SET NAME
//*              PACK         SERIAL NUMBER OF DISK PACK
//*              TRACKS       NUMBER OF TRACKS IN DATA SET
//*              BLOCKS       NUMBER OF DIRECTORY BLOCKS
//*
//LIBMAKE   EXEC PGM=IEFBR14,
//               REGION=32K
//LIBDD     DD DSN=&DSN,
//               DISP=(,CATLG),
//               UNIT=DISK,
//               VOL=SER=&PACK,
//               SPACE=(TRK,(&TRACKS,,&BLOCKS)),
//               DCB=(RECFM=FB,LRECL=80,BLKSIZE=1600)
```

■ **Figure 8.8** ━━━━━━━━━━━━━━━━━━━━━━━━━━━━━━━━━━━━

Executing the CREATE2 Procedure Using Symbolic Parameters and an Overriding DD Statement

```
//JCLQB730 JOB ,'J.C.LEWIS'
//CREATLIB EXEC CREATE2,
//              DSN='WYL.QB.JCL.SAVELIB',
//              PACK=WYL005,
//              TRACKS=3,
//              BLOCKS=7
//LIBMAKE.LIBDD DD DCB=BLKSIZE=800
//
```

job like the one shown in Figure 8.4, which was used to add CREATE to the procedure library. Figure 8.8 shows how CREATE2 may be used to create SAVELIB. SAVELIB was previously created using CREATE in Figure 8.6. Figures 8.8 and 8.6 perform exactly the same function.

In Figure 8.8 values are assigned to the symbolic parameters by coding the symbolic parameters and their values on the EXEC statement. As you learned in Chapter 7, if the value contains special characters, as WYL.QB.JCL. SAVELIB does, it must be enclosed in apostrophes.

You may recall that one of the specifications for SAVELIB was that it was to have a blocksize of 800 bytes. Because BLKSIZE has not been made into a symbolic parameter, it can be changed only by coding an overriding DD statement.

When the procedure is executed, the values coded for the symbolic parameters are substituted for the symbolic parameters wherever they appear in the procedure. As mentioned in the discussion of Figure 7.4, when the system substitutes a value for a symbolic parameter, it informs you by printing the message SUBSTITUTION JCL, together with the JCL statement as it appears after the substitution has been made. Of course, only the currently executing version of the procedure is altered by these substitutions; the original version of the procedure, which is stored in the procedure library, remains unaltered.

After the values in Figure 8.8 have been substituted for the symbolic parameters in Figure 8.7 and after the blocksize has been changed by the overriding DD statement, the job stream actually submitted for execution looks like this:

```
//JCLQB730 JOB ,'J.C.LEWIS'
//LIBMAKE   EXEC PGM=IEFBR14,
//              REGION=32K
//LIBDD    DD DSN=WYL.QB.JCL.SAVELIB,
//              DISP=(,CATLG),
//              UNIT=DISK,
```

```
//                        VOL=SER=WYL005,
//                        SPACE=(TRK,(3,,7)),
//                        DCB=(RECFM=FB,LRECL=80,BLKSIZE=800)
```

Assigning Default Values to Symbolic Parameters

Suppose that most applications of CREATE2 call for the library created to reside on WYL005 and to have five tracks and seven directory blocks. This means that most of the time the programmer will code

```
//                        PACK=WYL005,
//                        TRACKS=5,
//                        BLOCKS=7
```

This repetitive coding can be eliminated by making WYL005, 5, and 7 default values. In procedure CREATE3, illustrated in Figure 8.9, the symbolic parameters &PACK, &TRACKS, and &BLOCKS are assigned default values. As you learned in Chapter 7, default values are assigned to symbolic parameters on the PROC statement. The only time a cataloged procedure requires a PROC statement is when you want to assign default values to symbolic parameters, which you do exactly the same way as on an EXEC statement: You code the symbolic parameter without the ampersand and set it equal to a value.

Let us create SAVELIB one more time, this time using CREATE3. Figure 8.10 shows how it is done. The only difference between Figure 8.10 and Figure 8.8 is that in Figure 8.10 we do not have to assign values to PACK and BLOCKS because the default values assigned within the procedure are accept-

■ Figure 8.9 ■

Assigning Default Values to Symbolic Parameters

```
//CREATE3   PROC PACK=WYL005,
//               TRACKS=5,
//               BLOCKS=7
//*
//*             PARAMETER   MEANING                          DEFAULT VALUE
//*             DSN         DATA SET NAME
//*             PACK        SERIAL NUMBER OF DISK PACK        WYL005
//*             TRACKS      NUMBER OF TRACKS IN DATA SET      5
//*             BLOCKS      NUMBER OF DIRECTORY BLOCKS        7
//*
//LIBMAKE   EXEC PGM=IEFBR14,
//               REGION=32K
//LIBDD     DD DSN=&DSN,
//               DISP=(,CATLG),
//               UNIT=DISK,
//               VOL=SER=&PACK,
//               SPACE=(TRK,(&TRACKS,,&BLOCKS)),
//               DCB=(RECFM=FB,LRECL=80,BLKSIZE=1600)
```

■ **Figure 8.10** ■

Executing the CREATE3 Procedure Using Symbolic Parameters and an Overriding DD Statement

```
//JCLQB735 JOB ,'J.C.LEWIS'
//CREATLIB EXEC CREATE3,
//              DSN='WYL.QB.JCL.SAVELIB',
//              TRACKS=3
//LIBMAKE.LIBDD DD DCB=BLKSIZE=800
//
```

able. Notice that to override the default value assigned to TRACKS, we simply assign TRACKS the value we want on the EXEC statement.

In general, all the symbolic parameters used in a procedure must be assigned a value either in the PROC statement within the procedure or on the EXEC statement that calls the procedure. The one exception, as you learned in Chapter 7, is a symbolic parameter assigned to the DSN parameter. In this case, if a value is not assigned, the symbolic parameter is treated as a temporary data set name. For example, if no value is assigned to &DSN when CREATE3 is used, &DSN is assumed to be a temporary data set name.

Symbolic parameters are very convenient. You can use them to make a procedure flexible; you can assign them default values so that the programmer need code only the symbolic parameters whose values must be changed.

Nullifying Symbolic Parameters

Sometimes instead of assigning a value to a symbolic parameter, you want to eliminate it from the procedure. For example, suppose you wanted to allocate and name space for a physical sequential data set. You could use the CREATE3 procedure if you could eliminate the &BLOCKS symbolic parameter. You do not want to set &BLOCKS equal to 0; you want to completely eliminate it.

Eliminating a symbolic parameter is called nullifying it. To **nullify** a symbolic parameter, you code the symbolic parameter without the ampersand, followed by an equals sign. No value is coded after the equals sign. To nullify &BLOCKS you would code

```
BLOCKS=
```

Suppose you want to use CREATE3 to create a physical sequential data set; you are willing to accept the DCB parameters and the numbers of tracks as they are coded in the procedure, but you want to make a nonspecific volume request. To make a nonspecific volume request, you have to nullify PACK. Figure 8.11 shows a job to do this.

■ Figure 8.11 ■

Nullifying Symbolic Parameters

```
//JCLQB740 JOB ,'J.C.LEWIS'
//CREATSEQ EXEC CREATE3,
//              DSN='WYL.QB.JCL.SEQFILE',
//              PACK=,
//              BLOCKS=
//
```

Special Considerations for Symbolic Parameters

There are some circumstances in which coding symbolic parameters requires special care. For example, suppose you want to write a procedure that contains a DD statement with the ddname REPORT. Suppose, further, that this DD statement refers to a report that you sometimes want to print and sometimes want to suppress. The way to suppress a report is to DUMMY its DD statement. You might think that the following coding solves the problem:

```
//RUNPROC PROC DUM=DUMMY
    .
    .
    .
//REPORT   DD &DUM,SYSOUT=A
```

If you execute the procedure simply by calling it,

```
//STEP1    EXEC RUNPROC
```

&DUM will be assigned the default value DUMMY and the REPORT DD statement will become

```
//REPORT   DD DUMMY,SYSOUT=A
```

This will cause the report to be suppressed, which is what you want.

The trouble comes in when you nullify &DUM in order to print the report. In that case the EXEC statement will be

```
//STEP 1   EXEC RUNPROC,
//              DUM=
```

When &DUM is nullified, the REPORT DD statement will look like

```
//REPORT   DD ,SYSOUT=A
```

The leading comma in this statement constitutes a syntax error, and the job will not run.

The way to solve this problem is to use a period as the separator between

`&DUM` and `SYSOUT=A`. The correct way to write this procedure is

```
//RUNPROC PROC DUM='DUMMY,'
     .
     .
     .
//REPORT   DD &DUM.SYSOUT=A
```

Notice that it is necessary to include the comma in the default value for `DUM`. Because the comma is a special character, the whole value must be enclosed in apostrophes.

If you execute the procedure without nullifying `&DUM`, the `REPORT` `DD` statement will look like

```
//REPORT   DD DUMMY,SYSOUT=A
```

Notice that the period, which is only a separator, is removed when the value of the symbolic parameter is substituted. On the other hand, if you execute the procedure and nullify `&DUM`, the `REPORT` statement will look like

```
//REPORT   DD SYSOUT=A
```

The leading comma, which caused a syntax error before, has been eliminated.

The rule is

If a symbolic parameter stands for a positional parameter and if it is followed by another parameter, you should use a period as the separator between them.

Another rule is

If a symbolic parameter is followed by an alphameric character, a national character, or a period, you should use a period as the separator between them.

For example, suppose we want to create a series of data sets named `JANTAX`, `FEBTAX`, etc., using `&MONTH` as a symbolic parameter. The correct coding is

```
DSN=&MONTH.TAX
```

When we assign, for instance, `JAN` to `&MONTH`, the period that we used as a separator will be eliminated and `DSN` will be assigned the correct value, `JANTAX`.

The fact that the period used as a separator is eliminated when a value is substituted for a symbolic parameter means that if you *want* a period to appear you must code two of them. For example, suppose you were writing a procedure named ALLOCATE, to be used by any programmer at Queensborough Community College to create a data set named LIB. As explained in Chapter 3, at the CUNY computer center, data set names start with WYL., followed by two letters that identify the programmer's school (QB stands for Queensborough Community College), followed by three letters that identify the programmer. In the procedure the DSN could be coded as follows:

```
DSN=WYL.QB.&INIT..LIB
```

If a student with the initials XYZ used this procedure, he or she would code

```
//STEP1        EXEC ALLOCATE,
//                  INIT=XYZ
```

When &INIT is replaced by its value, one of the periods will be eliminated and the resulting DSN will be

```
DSN=WYL.QB.XYZ.LIB
```

which is correct.

You do not have to be concerned about commas that remain when a symbolic parameter that stands for the value of a keyword parameter is nullified. For example, suppose in a procedure you have the following coding:

```
//DD1       DD DSN=&NAME,
//             DISP=&DISP,
//             UNIT=TAPE,
//             VOL=SER=&NO
```

If you nullify NAME, &DISP, and &NO when you execute the procedure that contains this DD statement, the statement will become

```
//DD1       DD DSN=,
//             DISP=,
//             UNIT=TAPE,
//             VOL=SER=
```

This statement is perfectly legal.

Creating a More Complicated Procedure

The various versions of the CREATE procedure have illustrated a number of points about user-written procedures, but in fact the CREATE procedures are too simple to be very useful. User-written procedures really show their value when they include all the JCL needed to execute a complicated system.

A system flowchart for a more complicated system is shown in Figure 8.12. This system updates a master file. The transactions are edited and sorted and then are used to update a master file. In the last step a report is printed. This system involves a generation data set, which you studied in Chapter 6, and a

Figure 8.12

System Flowchart for an Inventory Update System

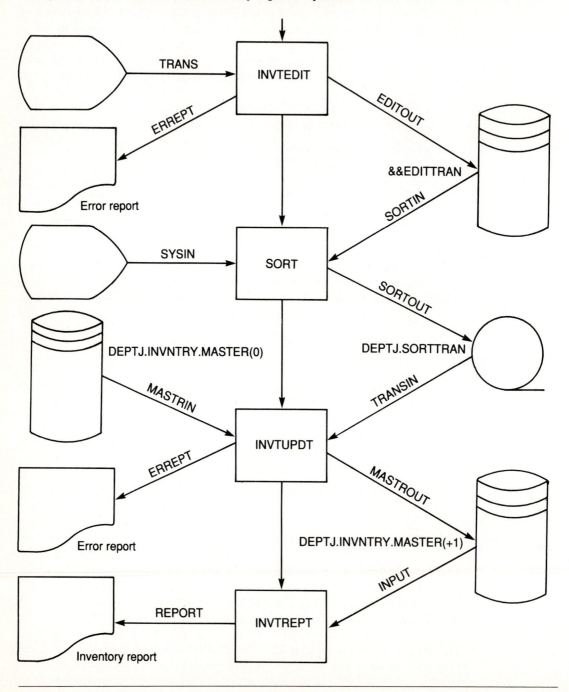

sort, which you will study in Chapter 9. Even though at this point you may not know anything about sorting, you can still use the procedure, just as you were able to use the compile and link edit procedures in Chapter 7 without being an expert on compilers or the linkage editor.

The procedure to carry out the processing in Figure 8.12 is shown in Figure 8.13. There are a number of important points to note about Figure 8.13. First, the SORT program obtains SORT program modules and prints messages using data sets that are not shown in Figure 8.12, because Figure 8.12 shows the flow of data through the system and not incidental data sets. (You may recall that in Figure 3.3 we did not show the SYSIN and SYSPRINT data sets used by IEBGENER.) Second, three STEPLIB DD statements are coded. The fact that programs INVTEDIT, INVTUPDT, and INVTREPT reside in DEPTJ.UPDTLIB might lead you to think that one JOBLIB statement could have been coded instead. Remember, however, that a procedure may not contain a JOBLIB statement. Third, every EXEC statement, except the first, has a COND parameter coded on it to control the execution of the step. Finally, all the data sets required by the system are included in the procedure, except the TRANS input to the INVTEDIT program and the SYSIN input to the SORT program. TRANS supplies the transactions to the EDIT program. SYSIN supplies the control statements to the SORT program in much the same way as SYSIN supplies the control statements to the utilities we have studied. Both TRANS and SYSIN will be coded as input stream data, and a procedure may not contain input stream data. The TRANS and SYSIN DD statements will be coded as part of the JCL when the procedure is executed.

Executing the INVTUPDT Procedure

A job that executes the INVTUPDT procedure is shown in Figure 8.14. This is the simplest possible job that can be written using this procedure, as only the two required DD statements have been coded. The two DD statements must be in the order shown in Figure 8.14, for that is the order of the two steps in Figure 8.13.

Because the same SORT control statements will be used every time this procedure is executed, obtaining the SORT control statements from a library would be more convenient than supplying them as input stream data. Exercise 16 explores this idea.

Overriding and Adding Parameters on an EXEC Statement

Suppose we want to execute INVTUPDT with several changes. In the EDIT-STEP we want to add a TIME parameter to limit the step to 3.5 minutes and increase the REGION to 120K. In the SORTSTEP we want to change the value

Figure 8.13

The INVTUPDT Procedure for the Inventory Update System

```
//INVTUPDT PROC PRI=5,
//              SEC=1
//*
//*      THIS PROCEDURE IMPLEMENTS DEPT J'S
//*      INVENTORY UPDATE SYSTEM
//*
//*      SYMBOLIC      MEANING                   DEFAULT
//*      PRI           PRIMARY ALLOCATION           5
//*                    (IN CYLINDERS) OF EDITED
//*                    AND OF SORTED TRANSACTIONS
//*                    DATA SETS
//*
//*      SEC           SECONDARY ALLOCATION         1
//*                    AS ABOVE
//*
//*      EDITSTEP READS THE RAW TRANSACTIONS
//*      AND PRODUCES A TEMPORARY DATA SET OF
//*      EDITED TRANSACTIONS AND AN ERROR REPORT
//*
//EDITSTEP EXEC PGM=INVTEDIT,
//              REGION=80K
//STEPLIB  DD DSN=DEPTJ.UPDTLIB,
//              DISP=SHR
//ERREPT   DD SYSOUT=A
//EDITOUT  DD DSN=&&EDITTRAN,
//              DISP=(,PASS),
//              UNIT=DISK,
//              SPACE=(CYL,(&PRI,&SEC))
//*
//*      SORTSTEP SORTS THE EDITED TRANSACTIONS ON
//*      INVENTORY NUMBER AND DATE AND CREATES SORTTRAN
//*
//SORTSTEP EXEC PGM=SORT,
//              PARM='SIZE=MAX',
//              COND=(4,LT,EDITSTEP),
//              REGION=192K
//SORTLIB  DD DSN=SYS1.SORTLIB,
//              DISP=SHR
//SORTWK01 DD UNIT=SYSDA,
//              SPACE=(CYL,5,,CONTIG)
//SORTWK02 DD UNIT=SYSDA,
//              SPACE=(CYL,5,,CONTIG)
//SORTWK03 DD UNIT=SYSDA,
//              SPACE=(CYL,5,,CONTIG)
//SYSOUT   DD SYSOUT=A
//SORTIN   DD DSN=*.EDITSTEP.EDITOUT,
//              DISP=(OLD,DELETE)
//SORTOUT  DD DSN=DEPTJ.SORTTRAN,
//              DISP=(,PASS),
//              UNIT=TAPE
//*
```

Cont.

```
//*      UPDTSTEP UPDATES AND CREATES A
//*      NEW GENERATION OF THE INVENTORY
//*      MASTER DATA SET
//*
//UPDTSTEP EXEC PGM=INVTUPDT,
//              COND=((4,LT,EDITSTEP),(0,NE,SORTSTEP)),
//              REGION=132K
//STEPLIB  DD DSN=DEPTJ.UPDTLIB,
//              DISP=SHR
//TRANSIN  DD DSN=*.SORTSTEP.SORTOUT,
//              DISP=(OLD,KEEP)
//MASTRIN  DD DSN=DEPTJ.INVNTRY.MASTER(0),
//              DISP=OLD
//MASTROUT  DD DSN=DEPTJ.INVNTRY.MASTER(+1),
//              DISP=(,PASS),
//              UNIT=DISK,
//              VOL=SER=DISK01,
//              SPACE=(CYL,(10,5))
//ERREPT   DD SYSOUT=A
//*
//*      REPTSTEP PRODUCES A REPORT BASED
//*      ON THE NEW MASTER FILE
//*
//REPTSTEP EXEC PGM=INVTREPT,
//              COND=((4,LT,EDITSTEP),(0,NE,SORTSTEP),(4,LE,UPDTSTEP)),
//              REGION=64K
//STEPLIB  DD DSN=DEPTJ.UPDTLIB,
//              DISP=SHR
//INPUT    DD DSN=*.UPDTSTEP.MASTOUT,
//              DISP=(OLD,CATLG)
//REPORT   DD SYSOUT=A
```

■ Figure 8.14 ■

Executing the INVTUPDT Procedure

```
//JCLQB745 JOB ,'J.C.LEWIS'
//UPDATE1  EXEC INVTUPDT
//EDITSTEP.TRANS DD *

         Transaction Records

/*
//SORTSTEP.SYSIN DD *

         Sort Control Statements

/*
//
```

in the COND parameter to 8 and decrease the REGION to 164K. We want to set the symbolic parameter PRI to 10 and SEC to 2. We want to use a new version of the INVTEDIT program, which is stored in a library named DEPTJ.TEST-LIB. We want to add a SORTWK04 DD statement to the SORTSTEP. And finally, in the REPTSTEP, we want to direct the REPORT to output class C. All of these changes are made in Figure 8.15.

As Figure 8.15 shows, any parameters you want to add or override on any of the EXEC statements in a procedure are coded on the EXEC statement that invokes the procedure. To add or override a parameter on an EXEC statement in a procedure, you code

```
parameter.procstepname=value
```

So to add a TIME parameter on the EDITSTEP EXEC statement we coded

```
TIME.EDITSTEP=(3,30)
```

and to override the REGION parameter on the EDITSTEP EXEC statement we coded

```
REGION.EDITSTEP=120K
```

Exactly the same technique was used in Chapter 7 with the PARM parameter; you can now see that the same rule applies to all the EXEC statement

---

■ Figure 8.15 ■

Executing the INVTUPDT Procedure with Changes

```
//JCLQB750 JOB ,'J.C.LEWIS'
//UPDATE2  EXEC INVTUPDT,
//              TIME.EDITSTEP=(3,30),
//              REGION.EDITSTEP=120K,
//              REGION.SORTSTEP=164K,
//              COND.SORTSTEP=(8,LT,EDITSTEP),
//              PRI=10,
//              SEC=2
//EDITSTEP.STEPLIB DD DSN=DEPTJ.TESTLIB
//EDITSTEP.TRANS   DD *

        Transaction Records

/*
//SORTSTEP.SORTWK04 DD UNIT=SYSDA,
//              SPACE=(CYL,5,,CONTIG)
//SORTSTEP.SYSIN DD *

        Sort Control Statements

/*
//REPTSTEP.REPORT DD SYSOUT=C
//
```

---

parameters. Parameters are coded in the same way whether they are to be added or overridden. If you code a parameter that does not exist on the EXEC statement, the parameter will be added. That is what will happen to the TIME parameter shown in Figure 8.15. If, on the other hand, you code a parameter that does exist on the EXEC statement, the value you code will replace the original value coded. That is what will happen to the two REGION parameters and the COND parameter shown in Figure 8.15. You may recall that this is exactly the way parameters coded on overriding DD statements are processed.

You must code all the parameters for one step before you code the parameters for a later step. In Figure 8.15 both EDITSTEP parameters are coded before the SORTSTEP parameters. The order in which you code the parameters for a particular step is not significant. In Figure 8.15, for the EDITSTEP, the TIME parameter is coded first, followed by REGION, but REGION could just as well have been coded first. The symbolic parameters are coded last in Figure 8.15, but they could be coded in any position.

Omitting the Stepname. You do not have to code the procedure stepname when coding a parameter. What happens when you omit the procedure stepname depends on which parameter you are coding. If you omit the procedure stepname on the TIME parameter, the value you code applies to the whole procedure. If Figure 8.15 had been coded

```
TIME=(3,30)
```

the 3.5-minute limitation would apply to the whole procedure, not to any particular step.

If you omit the procedure stepname on the PARM parameter, the value you code applies only to the first procedure step. PARM parameters coded on any other EXEC statements in the procedure are nullified. It is hard to imagine under what circumstances you would want to do that, so in most cases the PARM parameter should be coded with a procedure stepname.

If you omit the procedure stepname on any parameter other than TIME or PARM, the parameter you code applies to all the steps in the procedure. So, for example, coding

```
REGION=212K
```

has the effect of making REGION 212K on every step in the procedure.

If you omit the procedure stepname on any parameter, that parameter must be coded before any parameters that do have procedure stepnames.

Using COND Parameters with Procedures

When COND parameters in a procedure refer to steps within that procedure, they are coded in the same way as COND parameters in a job that refer to steps within that job. When the COND parameters in a procedure refer to steps outside that procedure, however, or when COND parameters outside a procedure refer to steps within a procedure, special considerations apply.

Suppose we have a three-step job with steps STEP1, STEP2, and STEP3. STEP1 executes a program; STEP2 executes the COBUCG procedure, which, you may recall from Chapter 7, contains a COB step and a GO step; and STEP3 executes a program. We want to skip STEP3 if either step in the procedure referenced by STEP2 returns a condition code greater than 4. You might think that you could code

```
//STEP3    EXEC PGM=PGM3,
//              COND=(4,LE,STEP2)
```

but that coding is *wrong*. The rule is

> The stepname coded on a COND parameter must not be the name of a step that executes a procedure.

The proper way to code the COND parameter in this situation is to add the procedure stepname to the stepname, as in

```
//STEP3    EXEC PGM=PGM3,
//              COND=((4,LE,STEP2.COB),(4,LE,STEP2.GO))
```

As another example, suppose we want to skip STEP2 if STEP1 returns a condition code greater than 8, and within STEP2 we want to skip the GO step if the COB step returns a condition code greater than 4. We achieve this goal by coding

```
//STEP2    EXEC COBUCG,
//              COND.COB=(8,LE,STEP1),
//              COND.GO=((8,LE,STEP1),(4,LE,COB))
```

In the second test in the second COND parameter, we don't have to code STEP2.COB because the COB step and the GO step are within the same procedure.

Overriding and Adding DD Statements

The DD statements in Figure 8.15 require careful study. Recall that the DD statements must be coded in the order in which the steps they refer to are coded in the procedure. So in Figure 8.15 the DD statements for the EDITSTEP are coded before the DD statements for the SORTSTEP, which in turn are coded before the DD statement for the REPTSTEP. Within a step, the overriding DD statements must be coded in the order in which they occur and before the additional DD statements. In the EDITSTEP, the STEPLIB DD statement, which is an overriding DD statement, must be coded before the TRANS DD statement, which is an additional DD statement. In the SORTSTEP, both DD statements are additional statements, so their order does not matter.

The STEPLIB DD statement applies only to the EDITSTEP. The programs INVTUPDT and INVTREPT in Figure 8.13 will still be taken from DEPTJ.UPDTLIB. Taking INVTREPT, for example, from DEPTJ.TESTLIB would require a REPTSTEP.STEPLIB DD statement pointing to DEPTJ.TESTLIB.

Summary

In this chapter you have learned

— how to write, test, and use user-written procedures

— how to code in-stream procedures

— when and how to use the PROC and PEND statements

— when and how to use the DATA parameter

— how to code symbolic parameters in procedures

— how to assign default values to symbolic parameters

— how to override and add parameters to EXEC statements when a procedure is executed

Vocabulary

In this chapter you have been introduced to the meaning of the following term:

nullify

Exercises

1. What is the function of the PEND statement?
2. Which JCL statements may not be used in a procedure?
3. Under what circumstances do in-stream procedures require a PROC statement?
4. Under what circumstances do cataloged procedures require a PROC statement?
5. Should the EXEC statement for an in-stream procedure be placed before or after the procedure?
6. On the output listing, how can you recognize JCL statements that were added to your job stream as a result of calling an in-stream procedure?
7. Which DD statement parameter is used in place of the asterisk when you want to include JCL statements in input stream data? Why is it necessary?
8. In Figure 8.6, could the DD parameters have been coded in a different order?
9. What are the rules for naming symbolic parameters?

10. Why are symbolic parameters assigned default values?
11. How are symbolic parameters assigned default values?
12. How are symbolic parameters assigned values when a procedure is executed?
13. Modify the CREATE3 procedure in Figure 8.9 to make the values of RECFM, LRECL, and BLKSIZE symbolic parameters. Assign default values of FB to RECFM, 150 to LRECL, and 1500 to BLKSIZE. Show how you would use this procedure to create a library named BKUPLIB, which resides on disk pack DISK43 and has ten tracks, five directory blocks, a logical record length of 100, and a blocksize of 500.
14. How is a symbolic parameter nullified?
15. When should you use a period instead of a comma as a separator between a symbolic parameter and the coding that follows it?
16. The same sort control statements will be used every time the INVTUPDT procedure in Figure 8.13 is executed. Therefore, obtaining the control statements from a control statement library would be more convenient than coding them as input stream data. Modify the INVTUPDT procedure to obtain the sort control statement from member UPDATE of a library named SORT.CNTLLIB.
17. How do you override parameters on EXEC statements in a procedure?
18. Below is a cataloged procedure named SUMMARY.

```
//SUMMARY  PROC
//EDIT      EXEC PGM=EDIT
//OUTPUT   DD DSN=&&OUTPUT,
//              DISP=(NEW,PASS),
//              UNIT=SYSDA,
//              SPACE=(TRK,10)
//RUN       EXEC PGM=SALES
//INPUT    DD DNS=&&OUTPUT,
//              DISP=(OLD,DELETE)
//REPORT        DD SYSOUT=A
```

Code the JCL required to execute this procedure with the following modifications:
   a. Program EDIT should have a REGION of 80K.
   b. Program SALES should not be executed if program EDIT returns a condition code equal to 100.
   c. Program EDIT requires input stream data supplied under the ddname TRANFILE.
   d. Data set &&OUTPUT requires 20 tracks.
19. Below is a cataloged procedure named ABCXYZ.

```
//ABCXYZ    PROC TRACKS=10,
//              DISP=DELETE
//ABC       EXEC PGM=ABC,
//              REGION=80K
```

```
//ABCOUT     DD  DSN=&NAME,
//               UNIT=3330,
//               DISP=(NEW,PASS),
//               SPACE=(TRK,(&TRACKS)),
//               VOL=SER=PACK07
//XYZ        EXEC PGM=XYZ
//XYZIN      DD  DSN=*.ABC.ABCOUT,
//               DISP=(OLD,&DISP)
//XYZOUT     DD  SYSOUT=A
```

Code the JCL required to execute this procedure with the following modifications:

a. Program ABC should have a REGION of 100K.

b. Program XYZ should not be run if program ABC returns a condition code of 12 or higher.

c. The disk data set's name should be ABC.DATAFILE, and its final disposition should be KEEP.

d. Program ABC requires input stream data supplied under the ddname INSTREAM.

20. Consider a three-step job with steps STEP1, STEP2, and STEP3. STEP1 executes PGM1; STEP2 executes a procedure named PROC2, which contains STEPA and STEPB; and STEP3 executes PGM3. We want to skip STEP2 and STEP3 if STEP1 returns a condition code of 13, and we want to skip STEPB (of STEP2) and STEP3 if STEPA (of STEP2) returns a condition code greater than 4. Code the EXEC statements for STEP2 and STEP3.

21. A system flowchart for a payroll system is shown in Figure 8.16. Write a procedure to implement this system. Additional information is given below.

General information: All tape units are TAPE, and all disk units are DISK. Any names required but not given may be invented.

Program information:

Step	Program Name	Library	Region	Time	Conditions
1	DATADISK	LIB1	50K	20 sec	—
2	PAYEDIT	PAYLIB	130K	4 min	Do not run unless the condition code from step 1 is 0.
3	PAYUPDT	PAYLIB	100K	10 min	Do not run unless the condition code from step 1 is 0 and from step 2 is less than 8.

Figure 8.16

System Flowchart for a Payroll System

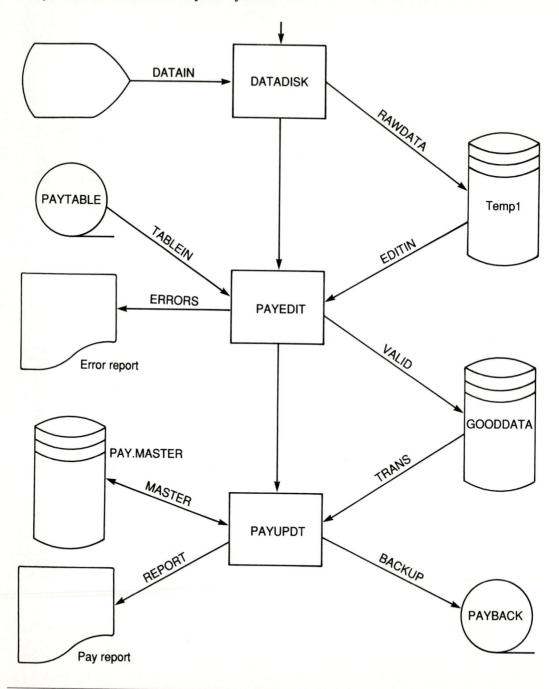

Data set information: All data sets that exist before a job is run should be retained at the end of the job.

Data Set	Volume	Space	Comments
`Temp1`	nonspecific	In 800-byte blocks. Primary 5000, secondary 500. Release unused space.	Invent a legal temporary DSN. Use a backward reference to this data set in step 2.
`GOODDATA`	`PACK46`	In cylinders. Primary 20, secondary 5.	Delete if job runs, keep if job abends.
`PAYTABLE`	cataloged	—	—
`PAY.MASTER`	cataloged	—	Do not allow any other programs to access this data set while it is being updated.
`PAYBACK`	nonspecific	—	—

After you have written the procedure, write the JCL to execute it, supplying the required input stream data DD statement.

Programming Assignments

1. Write a procedure named `LISTER` that uses `IEBGENER` to list any cataloged data set. Make the name of the data set to be listed a symbolic parameter. Execute the procedure as an in-stream procedure, listing the data set you created in Chapter 3.
2. Write a procedure named `COMPRESS` that uses `IEBCOPY` to compress a library. Make the name of the library to be compressed a symbolic parameter. Execute the procedure as an in-stream procedure, compressing `FIRSTLIB`, which you created in Chapter 5.
3. Write a two-step procedure named `COPYMEMB`. In the first step use `IEBCOPY` to copy a member from one library into another. In the second step use `IEBPTPCH` to list the member just copied. The second step should not be executed if the condition code from the first step is greater than 4. The names of the two libraries should be symbolic parameters. Execute the procedure as an in-stream procedure to copy to `FIRSTLIB`, which you created in Chapter 5, a member from either a fellow student's library or a library your advisor suggests.

Sorting and Merging

In this chapter you will learn

■ how to use the sort/merge program

Sorting is an important computer task; it means putting records in a data set into a specified order. Merging is closely related to sorting; it means combining records from two or more sorted data sets into one data set that is in the same order. IBM provides a sort/merge program, which is described in this chapter. In addition, many software companies sell their own sort/merge programs, but the JCL and control statements these programs use are frequently identical to those used by the IBM program.

Sort/merge programs may be invoked from user-written programs in assembler, COBOL, or PL/I. In this chapter you will learn how to perform a sort or merge directly by coding JCL statements and sort/merge control statements.

Sorting

When you perform a sort, you have to give the sort program* three pieces of information: where to find the input data, which fields in the records to do the sorting on, and where to put the sorted output data set. The sort program expects its input to be supplied under the ddname SORTIN. The input data may be input stream data or a tape or disk data set, but with all your experi-

---

* In this text, the discussions about sorting will refer to the sort program, and the discussions about merging will refer to the merge program. You should keep in mind, however, that sorting and merging are done by the same program.

■ **Figure 9.1** ■

Data Used for Sorting Illustrations

```
WEST        NF
NUTLEY      YF
KOREN       NM
STANLEY     NF
BRYCE       YF
EVANS       YM
ROONEY      YM
```

ence coding DD statements you should have no trouble coding the SORTIN DD statement, no matter where the data are coming from. Similarly, the sort program writes its output under the ddname SORTOUT. You might want to make the output a tape or disk data set or direct it to a printer; but again, you should have no trouble writing the SORTOUT DD statement, no matter where the output is going.

So you see that the only new thing you have to learn in order to use the sort program is how to specify the fields on which you want the sort done. This information is provided by the sort control statements, so a large part of this chapter will be devoted to learning how to code sort control statements.

Major and Minor Control Fields

Before we begin discussing the details of how to code sort control statements, let us look a little more carefully at what is meant by specifying the fields in the records on which you want the sorting done. Let us sort the seven records shown in Figure 9.1. These records contain three fields. The first field contains the person's name; the second, the person's marital status (Y = married, N = not married); and the third, the person's sex (F = female, M = male).

Initially we will sort on only one field. The selected field is called the **control field** or the **key field**. We must specify whether we want the sort to be

■ **Figure 9.2** ■

Data in 9.1 Sorted in Ascending Order by Name

```
BRYCE       YF
EVANS       YM
KOREN       NM
NUTLEY      YF
ROONEY      YM
STANLEY     NF
WEST        NF
```

■ Figure 9.3 ■

■ Figure 9.3 ■

Data in 9.1 Sorted in Ascending Order by Marital Status and Name

```
KOREN       NM
STANLEY     NF
WEST        NF
BRYCE       YF
EVANS       YM
NUTLEY      YF
ROONEY      YM
```

done in ascending order from A to Z or descending order from Z to A. If we sort this data set in ascending order using the name as the control field, we get the results shown in Figure 9.2. If we had sorted in descending order, the results would have been reversed, with West being the first record and Bryce being the last. Notice that when you sort records, the complete record is rearranged, not just the control field you specify.

More interesting situations result when more than one control field is specified. The first field specified is called the **major control field** or **major key**, and the other fields are called the **minor control fields** or **minor keys**. If we sort the records in Figure 9.1 in ascending order using marital status as the major control field and name as the minor control field, we get the results shown in Figure 9.3. The sort program first sorts on the major control field. Then those records *that have the same value in the major control field* are sorted on the minor control field. In this case the records are first sorted by marital status. Then the records that have a marital status of N are sorted by name, and the records that have a marital status of Y are sorted by name separately.

If we wanted the married people listed first, we would specify that we wanted the sort done in descending order by marital status and ascending order by name. In that case we would get the results shown in Figure 9.4.

■ Figure 9.4 ■

Data in 9.1 Sorted in Descending Order by Marital Status and Ascending Order by Name

```
BRYCE       YF
EVANS       YM
NUTLEY      YF
ROONEY      YM
KOREN       NM
STANLEY     NF
WEST        NF
```

Notice that these results are *not* simply the results in Figure 9.3 in reverse order.

It is important to understand that the sort on the minor control field is done only for records that have the same value in the major control field. If we sort in ascending order using name as the major control field and marital status as the minor control field, we get the same result as we got when we sorted by name only. This is because no two records have the same value for the name field.

You can specify more than one minor control field. Suppose we want to sort the records in Figure 9.1 in ascending order using marital status as the major control field and sex and name, in that order, as the minor control fields. When several control fields are specified, they are frequently simply listed; it is understood that the major control field is listed first and the minor control fields follow in order of importance. So the problem can be restated as sorting the records in Figure 9.1 in ascending order by marital status, sex, and name. The results are shown in Figure 9.5.

Sometimes programmers refer to the major control field as the primary sort field, the first minor as the secondary, and the second minor as the tertiary. In this example marital status is the primary field, sex is the secondary, and name is the tertiary.

The sort program sorts first on the major, or primary, control field and then on the minor control fields in the order named. In this case the records are sorted first by marital status. Then the records that have a marital status of N and those that have a marital status of Y are sorted separately by sex. Finally, the records that have the same value for marital status and sex — Stanley and West, Bryce and Nutley, and Evans and Rooney — are sorted by name.

Equal Control Fields

What happens if two or more records have the same value in the control fields? Suppose in the previous example the name was omitted as a control field and the sorting was done only by marital status and sex. When the

━ **Figure 9.5** ━━━━━━━━━━━━━━━━━━━━━━━━━━━━━━━━━━━━━

Data in 9.1 Sorted in Ascending Order by Marital Status, Sex, and Name

```
STANLEY     NF
WEST        NF
KOREN       NM
BRYCE       YF
NUTLEY      YF
EVANS       YM
ROONEY      YM
```

sorting was finished, there would be three pairs of records — Stanley and West, Bryce and Nutley, and Evans and Rooney — with the same value for marital status and sex. What would their order be in the output?

Sometimes the final order is not important; Stanley followed by West and West followed by Stanley might be equally acceptable. But sometimes you would like records with the same value in the control fields to have the same order in the output as they have in the input. In that case the pairs would be West followed by Stanley, Bryce followed by Nutley, and Evans followed by Rooney (see the original order in Figure 9.1). You will learn later how to tell the sort program to retain the original order for records that have the same value in the control fields.

Collating Sequence

In the previous examples of sorting on alphabetic fields, the meanings of ascending order (A to Z) and descending order (Z to A) were easily understood. When sorting is done on numeric fields, what is meant by ascending and descending order is equally obvious. (Remember that negative numbers are considered to be less than positive numbers.) But in sorting on alphanumeric fields, things get a little more complicated. Suppose you were sorting on an address field and you ran across the addresses 123 Elm Street and 123 59th Avenue. The control fields on these two records are equal until you get the E on the first record and the 5 on the second record. To put these two records in order you have to know whether E is greater or less than 5, which means that you must know the collating sequence used by the computer. The **collating sequence** is simply the sequence used by the computer to sort data stored in character form. IBM computers use the EBCDIC collating sequence, which is shown in Table 1.2. In the EBCDIC collating sequence, E is less than 5, so 123 Elm Street would be less than 123 59th Avenue.

If you want an IBM computer to use something other than the EBCDIC collating sequence, you can specify that you want a sort performed using a modified collating sequence. How to specify the modifications will be discussed later.

JCL to Invoke the Sort Program

Every computer center has a cataloged procedure to invoke the sort program. This procedure is usually named SORTD and is tailored to meet local requirements. A typical SORTD procedure is shown in Figure 9.6.

The PROC statement assigns default values to the symbolic parameters, and the EXEC statement executes the sort program and assigns a default value to the PARM field. The values that may be coded in the PARM field will be explained a little later. The SORTLIB DD statement points to the library that

■ **Figure 9.6** ■

The SORTD Cataloged Procedure

```
//SORTD     PROC SIZE=MAX,SPACE=3
//SORT     EXEC PGM=SORT,PARM='SIZE=&SIZE'
//SORTLIB   DD DSN=SYS1.SORTLIB,DISP=SHR
//SORTWK01  DD UNIT=SYSDA,SPACE=(CYL,&SPACE)
//SORTWK02  DD UNIT=SYSDA,SPACE=(CYL,&SPACE)
//SORTWK03  DD UNIT=SYSDA,SPACE=(CYL,&SPACE)
//SORTWK04  DD UNIT=SYSDA,SPACE=(CYL,&SPACE)
//SORTWK05  DD UNIT=SYSDA,SPACE=(CYL,&SPACE)
//SORTWK06  DD UNIT=SYSDA,SPACE=(CYL,&SPACE)
//SYSOUT    DD SYSOUT=A
```

contains the sort/merge program modules. The DD statements SORTWK01 through SORTWK06 provide work areas for the sort program. The number of work areas you need depends on which versions of the operating system and sort you are using; in some cases you do not need any SORTWK DD statements. You do not have to be concerned about how many SORTWK DD statements to code, because the SORTD procedure at your computer center will have been designed to work with your system. In general, the more work areas you provide, the faster the sort is done. The six work areas provided in this procedure will probably be enough for even the largest sorts. Unlike most utilities, which use a SYSPRINT DD statement for messages, the sort program uses the SYSOUT DD statement for messages.

When you use the SORTD procedure, you have to provide three additional DD statements. The SORTIN DD statement defines the input data set, the SORTOUT DD statement defines the output data set, and the SYSIN DD statement defines the control statement data set. If the records in Figure 9.1 were input stream data and we wanted to direct the output to the printer, we would use the job stream shown in Figure 9.7.

Ddnames in One-Step Procedures

When the ddnames on the three DD statements in Figure 9.7 were coded, the rules in Chapters 7 and 8 for creating ddnames were followed: The procedure stepname (SORT) was combined with the required ddname (SORTIN, SORTOUT, or SYSIN). This coding is correct, but unnecessarily complicated. When you have a one-step procedure such as SORTD, the DD statements can be added only to that one step, so it is not necessary to include a procedure stepname as part of the ddname. In future examples in this chapter, SORT will be omitted from the ddnames.

You may omit the procedure stepname from the ddname even when you have a multistep procedure. In that case the system assumes that the DD

━━ **Figure 9.7** ━━━━━━━━━━━━━━━━━━━━━━━━━━━━

Job Stream to Sort the Data in 9.1

```
//JCLQB755 JOB ,'J.C.LEWIS'
//SORTEXPL EXEC SORTD
//SORT.SORTIN DD *
WEST       NF
NUTLEY     YF
KOREN      NM
STANLEY    NF
BRYCE      YF
EVANS      YM
ROONEY     YM
/*
//SORT.SORTOUT DD SYSOUT=A
//SORT.SYSIN DD *

              Sort Control Statements

/*
//
```

statements apply to the first step. Thus, in Figure 8.15 EDITSTEP could have been omitted from the ddnames. But because omitting the procedure step-name in a multistep procedure makes the coding less clear, it is not recommended. You may, however, see such coding, and you should understand it.

▬ Sort Control Statements

All that needs to be done to execute the job stream in Figure 9.7 is to code the sort control statements. The most commonly used sort control statements are the SORT and MERGE statements. The parameters used with these two statements are identical; they are described in Table 9.1.

The FIELDS Parameter*

Let us assume that in the records in Figure 9.7, the name field is in the first ten positions of the record, the marital status is in the eleventh position, and the sex is in the twelfth position. Then, to sort these records in ascending order on the name field, we would code the following SORT statement:

```
SORT FIELDS=(1,10,CH,A)
```

* Notice that the SORT parameter is FIELDS, whereas the IEBGENER and IEBPTPCH parameter is FIELD.

Table 9.1

Parameters for SORT and MERGE Statements

Parameter	Meaning
`FIELDS=(position,length,` `format,sequence...)`	`position` is the starting byte of the control field in the record.
or	`length` is the length in bytes of the control field.

`FIELDS=(position,length,`
        `sequence...),`
        `FORMAT=format`
	`format` is the format of the data in the control field. Commonly used values are `ZD` for zoned decimal, `PD` for packed decimal, `BI` for binary, `AC` for ASCII character, `CH` for EBCDIC character, `AQ` for EBCDIC character using alternative collating sequence. `sequence` is either `A` for ascending or `D` for descending.

`FILSZ=x`	`x` is the number of records to be sorted. If `x` is an estimate, precede it with `E` (e.g., `FILSZ=E1000`). Optional.
`SKIPREC=z`	Skip `z` records before sorting. Optional. Not permitted for a merge.
`EQUALS`	`EQUALS` means that records with the same value in the control fields should retain the order they had in the input.
`NOEQUALS`	`NOEQUALS` means that the order need not be retained. Optional.
	The default is set when the sort program is installed. Not permitted for a merge.
`CKPT`	Checkpoints should be taken.

We can use the description of the FIELDS parameter in Table 9.1 to interpret this statement. The 1 means that the control field begins at the first byte in the record. The 10 means that the control field is 10 bytes long. (Notice that the order of the position and length subparameters in the SORT FIELDS parameter is the opposite of their order in the IEBGENER and IEBPTPCH FIELD parameters. That is to make it easy—to get mixed up.) The CH means that the data in the control field are in EBCDIC character form. The name field starts at the first byte, is 10 bytes long, and is in EBCDIC character form, so these three values specify the name as the control field. The A means that the sort should be in ascending order. If this control statement were used in Figure 9.7, the records would be sorted as shown in Figure 9.2. (Table 9.1 shows two formats for the FIELDS parameter. When to use each one will be explained a little later.)

The coding rules for the sort control statements are similar to those for the other utility control statements you have studied. Unless the statement contains a label, which it usually does not, column 1 must be blank. The operand SORT may start anywhere; it usually starts in column 2. SORT must be separated from the parameters by one or more blanks; one blank is common. There must not be any embedded blanks within the parameters. The parameters may be coded in any order, although the order shown in Table 9.1 is used most often. Control statements may not extend beyond column 71. If a control statement must be continued, it should be interrupted at a comma and continued on the following line between columns 2 and 16. It is not necessary to have a nonblank character in column 72.

A control statement that could be used to sort the records in ascending order by marital status and name is

```
SORT FIELDS=(11,1,CH,A,1,10,CH,A)
```

In this statement two control fields are defined. The first four values (11,1,CH,A) define the major control field, and the last four values (1,10,CH,A) define the minor control field. The major control field starts at the eleventh byte in the record, is 1 byte long, and is in EBCDIC character form. These values correspond to the marital status field, which is therefore the major control field. As before, the A means that the sort should be done in ascending order. The coding for the minor control field is identical to that in the previous example, as it should be, for both cases describe the name field. If this control statement were used in Figure 9.7, the records would be sorted as shown in Figure 9.3.

This sort control statement can be simplified slightly. When all the control fields have the same format, as they do in this case, the second form of the FIELDS parameter shown in Table 9.1 may be used. Using the second form, we have the control statement

```
SORT FIELDS=(11,1,A,1,10,A),FORMAT=CH
```

The point of this form of the FIELDS parameter is that the format need be specified only once if all the control fields have the same format.

If we want to sort in descending order by marital status and ascending order by name, we have only to change the first A to a D:

```
SORT FIELDS=(11,1,D,1,10,A),FORMAT=CH
```

Used in Figure 9.7, this control statement would produce the output in Figure 9.4.

A control statement that could be used to sort the records in ascending order by marital status, sex, and name is

```
SORT FIELDS=(11,1,A,12,1,A,1,10,A),FORMAT=CH
```

Used in Figure 9.7, this control statement would produce the output in Figure 9.5.

Other SORT Statement Parameters

Four additional SORT statement parameters are described in Table 9.1. All four are optional.

The purpose of the FILSZ parameter is to improve the efficiency of the sort by giving the sort program either the exact number or an estimate of the number of records to be sorted. If the SORTIN data set contains exactly 15,357 records, you can code

```
FILSZ=15357
```

If the actual number of records is not 15,357, the sort will terminate.

Frequently you do not know the exact number of SORTIN records. In that case you can specify an estimate of the number of records. The estimate should be at least as great as the number of records. So, for example, if you have approximately 15,357 records, you can code

```
FILSZ=E16000
```

The E indicates that 16,000 is an estimate.

Although it is optional, FILSZ should be coded because it improves the efficiency of the sort.

SKIPREC causes records in SORTIN to be skipped before the sort begins. To skip the first 250 records, you would code

```
SKIPREC=250
```

EQUALS means that you want records that have equal values in the control fields to retain the order they had in the input. NOEQUALS means that the order does not have to be retained. When the sort program is installed, the computer center can decide whether to make EQUALS or NOEQUALS the default. EQUALS may slow down the sort, so most computer centers make NOEQUALS the default.

CKPT causes checkpoints to be taken. Checkpoints are discussed fully in the next chapter.

As an example of how all the parameters could be used, consider the sorting of a data set that contains approximately 20,000 records. The major control field begins at byte 5, is 4 bytes long, and contains packed decimal data. The minor control field begins at byte 96, is 20 bytes long, and contains character data. The sort should be in ascending order on both fields. Records that have the same value in the control fields should retain the same order in the output as they have in the input. The first 500 records should be skipped. Checkpoints should be taken. The control statement that could be used for this problem is

```
SORT FIELDS=(5,4,PD,A,96,20,CH,A),
     FILSZ=E20000,
     SKIPREC=500,
     EQUALS,
     CKPT
```

As is usual with control statements, there may not be embedded blanks in the parameter list.

Specifying a Modified Collating Sequence

As mentioned earlier, it is possible to specify that you want the sort done using a modified collating sequence. Suppose, for example, you are sorting by account number and the first byte of the account number contains a code consisting of a blank, an asterisk, or an A. For this particular sort, you want the records that contain an asterisk to be listed first. If you sort in ascending order, the records that contain a blank will be first. If you sort in descending order, the records that contain an A will be first. In order to make the records that contain an asterisk first, you have to change the position of the asterisk in the collating sequence.

You must do two things to modify a collating sequence. First, you must specify that you want the field sorted using a modified collating sequence. You do this by coding AQ for the format of that field. If the account number begins at byte 1 and is 8 bytes long and the sort is to be in ascending order, the SORT statement is

```
SORT FIELDS=(1,8,AQ,A)
```

The AQ coded for the format tells the sort that this field should be sorted using a modified collating sequence.

The ALTSEQ Statement.   The second thing you have to do is specify the modified collating sequence. This is done by using the ALTSEQ statement. Because you are sorting in ascending order, to cause the records that have an asterisk to be listed before those that have a blank, you must move the asterisk from its normal position in the collating sequence to a position before the blank. The following statement does this:

```
ALTSEQ CODE=(5C00)
```

In the ALTSEQ statement you must use the hexadecimal representation in the EBCDIC code (given in Table 1.2) of the characters whose positions you are changing. The hexadecimal representation of an asterisk is 5C. This ALTSEQ statement moves the asterisk from its normal position to the position whose hexadecimal representation is 00. Because 00 is the lowest hexadecimal value, this change puts the asterisk before the blank.

The format of the ALTSEQ statement is

```
ALTSEQ CODE=(fftt,fftt,...,fftt)
```

where ff is the hexadecimal representation of the character whose position is to be changed and tt is the hexadecimal representation of the position to which it is to be moved. The ellipses (. . .) indicate that you may code as many sets of fftt as you want. Suppose you wanted to move the digits 0 through 9 from their normal position following the upper-case letters to a position between the lower-case letters and the upper-case letters. The following statement could be used:

```
ALTSEQ CODE
   =(F0B0,F1B1,F2B2,F3B3,F4B4,F5B5,F6B6,F7B7,F8B8,F9B9)
```

Table 1.2 shows that F0 through F9 represent the digits 0 through 9 and that the hexadecimal values B0 through B9 fall between the lower-case and upper-case letters. Notice that the sets of four hexadecimal digits are separated by commas.

Additional Sort Control Statements

The newest versions of the sort program provide control statements that allow the programmer to select records to be passed to the sort and to reformat the records both before and after the sort.

The Include and Omit Statements.   The INCLUDE and OMIT statements are used to select the records to be included in the sort. By selecting records for the sort, you can decrease the amount of time the sort requires. The amount of time a sort requires depends on the number of records sorted and the length of the records. (A way to reduce the length of sorted records is discussed later.) Only one INCLUDE or OMIT statement is permitted in a sort.

INCLUDE and OMIT statements are discussed together because their coding is identical:

```
INCLUDE COND=(test)
OMIT COND=(test)
```

The only difference between INCLUDE and OMIT is in the result. If test coded with INCLUDE is true for a particular record, that record is *included* in the sort; whereas if test coded with OMIT is true, that record is *omitted* from the sort. Whether you choose to code INCLUDE or OMIT will depend on whether it is easier to specify the records to be included or the records to be omitted. In either case test is coded as

```
test=(position,length,format,operator,value)
```

[handwritten: logical operator]

The position, length, and format subparameters specify a field in the record, just as they do with the SORT FIELDS parameter. The operator subparameter may have the same values as it may have when coded with the COND parameter: GT, GE, EQ, NE, LT, and LE. The last subparameter, value, may be either a field in the record — specified by its own position, length, and format — or a constant. Numeric constants are coded as simple values, such as 46 or -15. Character constants are enclosed in apostrophes and preceded by a C, as in C'DEC'. Hexadecimal constants are enclosed in apostrophes and preceded by an X, as in X'F1F2C3'.

If more than one test is coded, the tests are joined by the Boolean operator AND or OR.

Suppose we wanted to select from POLYFILE only life insurance policies. Appendix C shows that life insurance records contain an L in column 29. We could select those records by coding

```
INCLUDE COND=(29,1,CH,EQ,C'L')
```

In this case we could just as easily specify the records to be omitted by coding

```
OMIT COND=(29,1,CH,NE,C'L')
```

The INREC and OUTREC Statements.   The INREC and OUTREC statements are used to reformat the records. The INREC statement is used before the sort to shorten the records by eliminating unwanted fields. As mentioned earlier, the amount of time a sort requires depends on the length of the records as well as on the number of records, so using INREC to shorten the records results in faster sorting. The OUTREC statement is used after the sort to improve readability.

INREC and OUTREC have identical formats:

```
INREC  FIELDS=(nX,position,length,align,...)
OUTREC FIELDS=(nX,position,length,align,...)
```

The first subparameter, nX, is optional; it specifies the number of spaces to be inserted in the reformatted record. It is rarely used with INREC. The next two subparameters, position and length, specify the field in the input record. The third subparameter, align, is optional; the possible values H, F, and D specify alignment on a half-word, full-word, and double-word boundary, respectively. Notice that there is no way to specify the position of the field in the reformatted record. That is because each field is placed adjacent to the previous field. An example will make that clear.

Suppose we want to sort POLYFILE, but we want to include only the policy number (columns 1 through 5), the name (columns 6 through 25), and the year the policy started (columns 50 and 51). The INREC statement that selects those fields includes just the position and length subparameters:

```
INREC FIELDS=(1,5,6,20,50,2)
```

In the reformatted record the policy number occupies columns 1 through 5; the name, columns 6 through 25; and the year the policy started, columns 26 and 27.

The reformatting specified by INREC occurs before the sort, so the SORT FIELDS parameter must refer to the control fields as they are in the reformatted record. For example, if we want to sort these records on the year field, we must refer to columns 26 and 27, which contain the year field in the reformatted records. The correct SORT statement is

```
SORT FIELDS=(26,2,CH,A)
```

Now suppose we want to reformat the records after the sort so that each reformatted record contains ten blanks, the name, five blanks, the policy number, five blanks, and the year. The OUTREC statement that performs this reformatting is

```
OUTREC FIELDS=(10X,6,20,5X,1,5,5X,26,2)
```

Coding Parameters for the Sort Program

You may code a PARM field on the EXEC statement to pass parameter values to the sort program. These parameters specify the sorting technique that should be used and whether diagnostic messages and sort control statements should be printed. In most cases default values for these parameters are satisfactory.

You may also specify how much main storage the sort program is allowed to use. The amount of main storage is specified using the SIZE parameter, as in

```
SIZE=130000
```

or

```
SIZE=MAX
```

In the first example 130,000 bytes of storage are allocated to the sort program. In the second example the sort is instructed to use all the available main storage. MAX is recommended because it makes the sort more efficient. The procedure in Figure 9.6 uses a symbolic parameter named &SIZE to assign a value to the SIZE parameter. The default value of &SIZE is MAX. In most computer centers the default value assigned to the SIZE parameter is MAX; because MAX is the recommended value, most of the time users do not have to code any PARM values.

Merging

Merging is closely related to sorting. When you merge, you start with two or more sorted data sets and create a new data set that is in the same sorted order. The JCL and control statements used for merging are very similar to those used for sorting.

The only difference between the JCL used for sorting and merging is that in the latter you must specify more than one input data set. These data sets have the ddnames SORTINnn, where nn may range from 01 to 16. This means that up to 16 data sets may be merged in one operation. The DD statements must be coded in order: SORTIN01, followed by SORTIN02, and so on. The input data sets may have different blocksizes, but the data set with the largest blocksize must be defined by the SORTIN01 DD statement. The input data sets may not be concatenated.

The major difference between the control statements used for sorting and merging is that in the latter the operation specified is MERGE instead of SORT. An example will clarify how a merge is coded. Suppose we have four data sets named FRESHMEN, SOPHS, JUNIORS, and SENIORS. The record formats in all the data sets are identical. Among other data, each record contains the student's major as character data in bytes 56 and 57 and his or her grade point average as packed decimal data in bytes 43 and 44. The data sets have previously been sorted with each student's major as the major control field and grade point average as the minor control field. We now want to merge all four data sets to produce a new data set named STUDENTS. STUDENTS will also be in order, with major as the major control field and grade point average as the minor control field. A job stream that does this processing is shown in Figure 9.8.

Notice that even though we are merging, we execute the SORTD procedure. The fact that we want to perform a merge is indicated by the word MERGE coded in the control statement. The rest of the control statement is identical to the statement we would code if we were sorting these data sets by major and grade point average rather than merging them. As required, each input data set is named by its own DD statement, SORTIN01 through SORTIN04. Also as required, the SORTINnn statements are coded in numerical order. As mentioned earlier, it is not necessary to include the procedure stepname SORT as part of the ddname, so in Figure 9.8 it is omitted.

There are several minor differences between MERGE and SORT statements. SKIPREC and EQUALS/NOEQUALS options are not used on the MERGE state-

■ **Figure 9.8** ━━━━━━━━━━━━━━━━━━━━━━━━━━━━━━━━━━━━

Job Stream to Merge Four Data Sets

```
//JCLQB760 JOB ,'J.C.LEWIS'
//MERGE    EXEC SORTD
//SORTIN01 DD DSN=FRESHMEN,
//            DISP=OLD
//SORTIN02 DD DSN=SOPHS,
//            DISP=OLD
//SORTIN03 DD DSN=JUNIORS,
//            DISP=OLD
//SORTIN04 DD DSN=SENIORS,
//            DISP=OLD
//SORTOUT  DD DSN=STUDENTS,
//            DISP=(,CATLG),
//            UNIT=DISK,
//            VOL=SER=DISK89,
//            SPACE=(TRK,(3,1),RLSE)
//SYSIN    DD *
 MERGE FIELDS=(56,2,CH,A,43,2,PD,A)
/*
//
```

ment. For merging, the value specified for FILSZ should be the total number of records in all the input data sets.

Summary

In this chapter you have learned

— how to sort using major and minor control fields

— how to use the SORTD procedure to perform a sort

— how to code the SORT and MERGE statements

— how to modify the collating sequence used in a sort or merge

— how to use the parameters FILSZ, SKIPREC, and EQUALS/NOEQUALS

— how to use the INCLUDE and OMIT statements to select records to be sorted

— how to use the INREC and OUTREC statements to reformat records before and after they are sorted

Vocabulary

In this chapter you have been introduced to the meanings of the following terms:

collating sequence
control field, major and minor
key field, major and minor

Exercises

1. What ddnames are used to supply the sort program with its input, its output, and its control statements?
2. What is a major control field? What is a minor control field?
3. Show what the result would be if the records in Figure 9.1 were sorted in ascending order by sex, marital status, and name.
4. In the following records, the brand is in positions 1 through 10, the type in positions 11 through 19, and the price in positions 20 through 22.

Brand	Type	Price
Taylor	Burgundy	279
Taylor	Burgundy	500
Taylor	Chablis	419
Gallo	Rhine	288
Gallo	Chablis	300
Gallo	Burgundy	295
Gallo	Rhine	165
Masson	Chablis	345
Masson	Rhine	318

Show what the results would be if these records were sorted in ascending order by

a. price
b. brand and price
c. price and brand
d. type, brand, and price
e. brand, type, and price

5. Which collating sequence is used by IBM computers?
6. In the collating sequence used by IBM computers, which is highest—a, A, or 1? Which is lowest?
7. What is the name of the cataloged procedure that is used to execute the sort/merge program?
8. In the SORT statement

```
SORT FIELDS=(a,b,c,d)
```

what are the meanings of a, b, c, and d?

9. Code the sort control statements required to perform the sorting indicated in Exercise 4, parts a through e.
10. True or false: If a sort is performed in ascending order on the major control field, it must also be performed in ascending order on the minor control fields.

11. How do you indicate that records that have equal values in the control fields should retain in the output the order they had in the input?
12. What is the purpose of the FILSZ parameter?
13. How do you indicate that you want a field sorted using a modified collating sequence?
14. Code the ALTSEQ statement that will cause a blank to collate higher than a 9.
15. Code the INCLUDE or OMIT statement to select from the records described in Exercise 4 those for which the type is *not* Burgundy.
16. Code the INREC statement to reformat the records selected in Exercise 15 so that the type occupies columns 1 through 9 and the price, columns 10 through 12. (The brand does not appear in the reformatted records.) Code the SORT FIELDS statement to sort these reformatted records in ascending order by price.
17. Code the OUTREC statement to reformat the records sorted by Exercise 16 so that the output record contains 20 blanks, the price, 10 blanks, and the type.
18. What does coding the parameter SIZE=MAX do?
19. What ddname is used for the input data sets in a MERGE operation? How many input data sets may be merged in one operation?
20. Figure 9.8 shows how to merge the four sorted data sets FRESHMEN, SOPHS, JUNIORS, and SENIORS to produce the STUDENTS data set. You could instead concatenate them and use the concatenation as the input to a sort. What would be the advantage, if any, of merging over sorting in this case?
21. The data in the following three sets start in column 1.

Set 1	Set 2	Set 3
627A	318B	136C
714A	712B	419C
863A	713B	984C

You will notice that the data in each set have been sorted using the first three columns as the key. Show what the results would be if these three data sets were merged, using the first three columns as the key. Could these three data sets be merged using the first four columns as the key? If they could be, show what the results would be.

Programming Assignments

1. Enter the data listed in Exercise 4, and then sort them as requested in Exercise 4, parts a through e. Direct the output to the printer.
2. Enter the data listed in Exercise 21, and then merge them as requested in Exercise 21.
3. Sort the data in Appendix D. Select only those records for which the major is *not* DP. Reformat the records to include only the name, major, and grade point average fields. Sort these records on major and, within major, on grade point average. Finally, reformat the sorted records to insert five blanks before the first field and between consecutive fields. Direct the output to the printer.
4. As mentioned before, when the sort/merge program is installed, the computer center chooses to make either EQUALS or NOEQUALS the default. Design and execute an experiment that will indicate whether EQUALS or NOEQUALS is the default at your computer center.

10

Advanced JCL Features

In this chapter you will learn

- additional parameters that may be coded on the JOB, EXEC, and DD statements

- how to code the OUTPUT statement

- how to use the checkpoint/restart feature

JOB Statement Parameters

The MSGCLASS Parameter

The MSGCLASS parameter may be used to direct system messages and JCL statements to a particular output class. MSGCLASS is coded as

```
MSGCLASS=output-class
```

MSGCLASS is very similar to SYSOUT, which also directs output to a particular output class, but SYSOUT applies only to the DD statement on which it is coded, whereas MSGCLASS applies to all system messages and JCL statements. If MSGCLASS is not coded, a default value is invoked, which usually directs the output to the same device as does SYSOUT=A. Like those for the SYSOUT parameter, the values that may be coded for output-class are defined by the computer center.

The MPROFILE Parameter

In VS1 systems only, the MPROFILE parameter may be used in place of the MSGCLASS parameter to assign an output class to a job's messages.

The format of the MPROFILE parameter is

```
MPROFILE='message-profile-string'
```

The message-profile-string describes the job's requirements. The format is established at each computer center. For example, you might code

```
MPROFILE='FORM=CARBON'
```

This message-profile-string specifies that the job's messages should be printed on carbon paper. The system will use this specification to assign an output class to the job's messages. This message-profile-string is valid, however, only if the values FORM and CARBON have been given meanings at your computer center.

The NOTIFY Parameter

In MVS systems only, the NOTIFY parameter is used to request that a message be sent to a time-sharing terminal when processing of a job submitted from that terminal has been completed.

The format of the NOTIFY parameter is

```
NOTIFY=user-id
```

The PROFILE Parameter

In VS1 systems only, the PROFILE parameter may be used to assign a job class and a priority to each job. (PROFILE may also be coded on a DD statement, as explained later in this chapter.) You describe the job's requirements, and the system translates these requirements into a job class and a priority.

The format of the PROFILE parameter is

```
PROFILE='profile-string'
```

The profile-string describes the job's requirements. The format of the profile-string is established at each computer center. For example, you might code

```
PROFILE=('RUN=PROD','LANG=COBOL','TIME=5')
```

This profile-string describes this job as a production job, written in COBOL, requiring five minutes. The system uses these specifications to assign a job class and priority to the job. Of course, this profile-string is valid only if the values RUN, PROD, LANG, and so on have been assigned meanings at your computer center.

The PRTY Parameter

The PRTY parameter specifies a job's priority for execution within its job class. PRTY is coded as

    PRTY=n

where n is a number representing the job's priority. The lowest priority is 0. The highest priority is 13 (JES3) or 15 (JES2). If two jobs with the same job class are waiting in the input work queue, the job with the higher priority will be selected first. If PRTY is not coded, an installation-defined default applies. Usually there is an extra charge for a job run at a high priority.

The TYPRUN Parameter

The two main functions of the TYPRUN parameter are to hold a job for later processing and to have a job's JCL checked for syntax errors. To have your job held, you code

    TYPRUN=HOLD

If a job uses a data set that is created by a different job, you can use TYPRUN to hold the job until the data set has been created. You must then tell the operator when the held job should be released.

You can have your job's JCL checked by coding

    TYPRUN=SCAN

This statement causes the job's JCL to be checked for syntax errors and prevents the job from executing. Suppose a job you have just written uses a data set that has not yet been created. The job obviously cannot be executed, but you might want to check the JCL syntax. This is the kind of situation in which TYPRUN=SCAN is useful.*

JOB and EXEC Statement Parameters

The two parameters ADDRSPC and PERFORM may be coded on either the JOB statement or an EXEC statement.

The ADDRSPC Parameter

The ADDRSPC parameter is used to permit or prevent paging of a job or a step between real and virtual storage. When ADDRSPC is coded on the JOB state-

---

* TYPRUN=SCAN is also useful if you are writing a JCL textbook and want to be sure that the examples do not contain syntax errors.

ment it applies to the whole job, and when it is coded on an EXEC statement it applies only to that step.

```
ADDRSPC=REAL
```

means that the job or step must occupy real storage, and therefore paging is prevented.

```
ADDRSPC=VIRT
```

means that the job or step may occupy virtual storage, and therefore paging is permitted. If ADDRSPC is not coded, paging is permitted. Most programs may be paged and preventing paging degrades the system's performance, so generally you will either code VIRT or omit the ADDRSPC parameter altogether. In fact, at some computer centers you are not allowed to code ADDRSPC=REAL unless you get special permission.

The PERFORM Parameter

In MVS systems only, the PERFORM parameter is used to associate a job with a performance group. A **performance group,** which is defined by the computer center, specifies the workload-dependent processing rate at which a job or jobstep should execute. When the workload is light all performance groups are given good processing rates, but when the workload becomes heavier some performance groups will be given lower processing rates than others.

The PERFORM parameter is coded as

```
PERFORM=n
```

where n, which is the number of the performance group, must be between 1 and 999.

When PERFORM is coded on the JOB statement it applies to the whole job, and when it is coded on the EXEC statement it applies only to that step.

EXEC Statement Parameter — The DPRTY Parameter

In MVS systems only, the DPRTY parameter is used to assign a dispatching priority to a jobstep. The dispatching priority determines the order in which jobsteps that are executing but are in a wait state are given control of the CPU. The DPRTY parameter is different from the JOB statement PRTY parameter, which sets the priority controlling the order in which jobs in the input work queue are selected for execution.

The format of DPRTY parameter is

```
DPRTY=(value1,value2)
```

where value1 and value2 are numbers from 0 through 15. These values are used in an equation to calculate the dispatching priority.

If the DPRTY parameter is not coded, the system assigns a default priority.

DD Statement Parameters

This section will discuss additional features of the UNIT, VOL, SPACE, SYS-OUT, and DCB parameters; additional parameters that are coded with SYSOUT; and some new parameters.

The UNIT Parameter

In Chapter 3 you learned how to use the UNIT parameter to specify the kind of unit required. The complete format for the UNIT parameter is

$$
\text{UNIT}=\left(\left[\begin{array}{l}\texttt{address}\\ \texttt{device-type}\\ \texttt{group-name}\end{array}\right]\left[\begin{array}{l},\texttt{unit-count}\\ ,\texttt{P}\end{array}\right][\,,\texttt{DEFER}\,][\,,\texttt{SEP=ddname}\,]\right)
$$

You know how to code address, device-type, and group-name. The unit-count subparameter is used with data sets that extend over more than one volume. Suppose you have a data set that occupies three tape volumes. By coding a 3 for the unit-count, you can request that all three tape volumes be mounted at the start of the job. For example,

```
UNIT=(TAPE,3)
```

requests that three tape drives be allocated to this data set. Notice the required parentheses.

Instead of coding a number for the unit-count, you can code the letter P, which stands for parallel mounting. P means that the number of units to be allocated to this data set is to be obtained from information given in the VOL parameter. (How the VOL parameter is coded for multivolume data sets is the next topic.) If you do not code a unit-count value or the letter P, one unit is allocated to the data set, in which case the job stops executing when each volume is finished and the system informs the operator that the current volume must be demounted and the next volume be mounted.

Requesting multiple units for a multivolume data set improves operating efficiency, as the jobstep does not have to be interrupted to allow the operator to demount and mount volumes. On the other hand, if you request many units, your job may have to wait a long time for all the units to be available before execution can begin. Furthermore, while your job is using the units, they are not available to other jobs.

Code DEFER when you want to defer mounting a volume — for example, when there is a data set that might not be used during an execution of your program. If you code DEFER, the system does not ask the operator to mount the volume until your program opens the data set. If your program never opens the data set, the volume will not be mounted. When DEFER is coded for a new data set on a direct access device, it is ignored.

Except for SEP, the UNIT subparameters are positional, so if you omit one and want to code a later one, you must code a comma to indicate the missing parameter. Suppose you have a cataloged data set for which you do not need to code the device type but you do want to request five units. You code

```
UNIT=(,5)
```

As another example, suppose you have a cataloged data set that requires only one unit, but for which you want to specify deferred mounting. You code

```
UNIT=(,,DEFER)
```

Sometimes getting the right number of commas can be tricky. One way of making sure that you have the right number of commas is to code all the parameters, with their commas, and then to erase the parameters you want to omit, leaving the commas.

The SEP subparameter is available only on VS1 systems and applies only to DASD. The ddname must be the name of an earlier DD statement in the same jobstep. SEP means that you want this data set and the earlier data set to be on separate units. If two data sets are heavily used, you might want them on separate units to reduce access arm movement. Most computer centers that use VS1 have installed a program that does I/O load balancing, however, so unit separation is done automatically. Therefore you generally do not have to code the SEP subparameter.

The AFF Subparameter.   The UNIT parameter has a second format that is sometimes used. It is

```
UNIT=AFF=ddname
```

AFF stands for affinity, and ddname is the name of an earlier DD statement in the same jobstep. AFF is the opposite of SEP. You code this form of the UNIT parameter when you want two data sets to have **unit affinity** — that is, to use the same unit.

Consider the following coding:

```
//STEP1        EXEC PGM=STATS
//DD1          DD DSN=SALETBLE,
//                 DISP=SHR,
//                 UNIT=TAPE,
//                 VOL=SER=111111
```

```
//DD2         DD DSN=SALESTAT,
//               DISP=(NEW,KEEP),
//               UNIT=AFF=DD1,
//               VOL=SER=222222
```

When this step begins execution, volume 111111 will be mounted. When SALESTAT is opened by the program, the system will tell the operator to mount volume 222222 on the same tape drive.

Coding AFF reduces the number of units used by a jobstep, but it can only be used in certain circumstances. In the example above, for AFF to work properly the program must be finished with SALETBLE before it starts writing SALESTAT.

AFF and SEP Parameters

In VS1 systems, the AFF and SEP parameters may be used to request channel separation. A **channel** is a device over which data are transmitted between main storage and I/O devices. Processing time may be shortened if the data sets that are used in a jobstep are transmitted over separate channels.

The format of the SEP parameter is

```
SEP=(ddname,...)
```

As an illustration of how the SEP parameter is used, consider the following example:

```
//DDA         DD DSN=ALPHA,
//               DISP=OLD
//DDB         DD DSN=BETA,
//               DISP=(NEW,KEEP),
//               UNIT=TAPE
//DDC         DD DSN=GAMMA,
//               DISP=OLD,
//               SEP=(DDA,DDB)
//DDD         DD DSN=DELTA,
//               DISP=(NEW,PASS),
//               UNIT=2400,
//               SEP=(DDA,DDB)
```

The system will attempt to assign the data sets named GAMMA and DELTA to a channel or channels other than those assigned to ALPHA and BETA. (ALPHA and BETA may or may not be assigned to the same channel.)

The AFF parameter offers an alternative way of requesting channel separation. The format of the AFF parameter is

```
AFF=ddname
```

where ddname is the name of an earlier DD statement that contains the SEP parameter. The AFF parameter copies the separation specified on the earlier

DD statement. Thus the last DD statement in the previous example could have been coded as

```
//DDD          DD DSN=DELTA,
//                DISP=(NEW,PASS),
//                UNIT=2400,
//                AFF=DDC
```

This coding means that DELTA is to have the same channel separation as is specified in the DD statement whose name is DDC. This is exactly the same channel separation as was requested above by coding SEP=(DDA,DDB).

The VOL Parameter

In Chapter 3 you learned how to use the VOL parameter to specify a serial number, and in Chapter 4 you learned how to code a backward reference. The complete format of the VOL parameter is

$$VOL=\left([PRIVATE][,RETAIN][,vol-seq-no][,vol-count]\begin{bmatrix}SER=(ser-no,\dots)\\REF=reference\end{bmatrix}\right)$$

SER and REF are keyword parameters; the other parameters are positional.

The PRIVATE Subparameter.   PRIVATE means that no other output data set is to be allocated in this volume unless a specific volume request is made. Suppose you are using a disk volume that has been assigned to your use. There should not be any other jobs that specifically request that volume. But the system might assign that volume to satisfy a nonspecific volume request. You can ensure that your job has exclusive use of the volume by coding PRIVATE. Tape volumes for which you make a specific volume request are automatically made private, as are tape volumes used for permanent data sets. In these cases you do not have to code PRIVATE.

If you specify or imply PRIVATE, the system will request that the operator demount the volume after its last use in the jobstep, unless the data set is passed or you code RETAIN.

The RETAIN Subparameter.   RETAIN has meaning only for tape volumes. For private tape volumes, RETAIN specifies that the volume should not be demounted at the end of a jobstep. If a volume will be used in more than one step, coding RETAIN saves the operator the trouble of demounting and mounting the volume.

The Volume Sequence Number Subparameter.   If you do not want to start processing multivolume data sets with the first volume, you code vol-seq-no, which is an abbreviation for volume sequence number. For example, suppose a data set in sequence by name occupies four volumes. Names beginning with

A to E are on the first volume, F to L are on the second volume, M to R are on the third volume, and S to Z are on the fourth volume. If you want to begin processing with names starting with M, you code

```
//INPUT      DD DSN=NAMEFILE,
//              DISP=OLD,
//              VOL=(,,3)
```

NAMEFILE is a cataloged data set. The UNIT information and volume serial numbers are recorded in the catalog, and therefore you do not have to code them. Notice that you may specify that processing should begin with the third volume without explicitly coding the volume serial numbers. The two commas in the coding for the VOL parameter indicate that the positional subparameters PRIVATE and RETAIN have been omitted.

The SER Subparameter.   The ellipses (. . .) in the description of the SER subparameter mean that more than one serial number may be coded. Suppose you are creating on tape a data set that requires three reels of tape. You could code

```
//DD1        DD DSN=BIGFILE,
//              DISP=(NEW,KEEP),
//              UNIT=(2400,2),
//              VOL=SER=(TAPE06,TAPE18,TAPE42)
```

Notice the parentheses that are required when more than one serial number is coded. This coding means that BIGFILE will be written to TAPE06, TAPE18, and TAPE42, in that order. As mentioned earlier in the discussion of the UNIT parameter, the 2 specified for the unit-count indicates that two tape drives should be allocated to this data set. When the step begins, the system will request that the operator mount TAPE06 and TAPE18. When TAPE06 is full, the system will start writing to TAPE18 while the operator demounts TAPE06 and mounts TAPE42 on the same tape drive.

The Volume Count Subparameter.   vol-count, which is an abbreviation for volume count, is used only for output data sets: either a new data set or an existing data set that is being extended. For example,

```
//OUTPUT     DD DSN=NEWFILE,
//              DISP=(NEW,CATLG),
//              UNIT=(TAPE,P),
//              VOL=(,,,5,SER=(TAPE46,TAPE47))
```

defines a data set that is being created. You expect that two tape volumes, TAPE46 and TAPE47, will be enough to hold the data set, but by coding a volume count of 5 you are telling the system that, if required, up to three more volumes may be allocated. The need for additional volumes will be treated as a nonspecific volume request. Notice that a P is coded in the UNIT parameter.

This P indicates that the number of units allocated to this data set should be either the number specified for the volume count subparameter or the number of serial numbers coded, whichever is higher. In this case five tape units will be allocated. Tying up five tape drives when only two are needed is wasteful. To reduce such waste, many computer centers limit the number of drives that may be requested.

Notice that in this example SER is preceded by a comma, whereas in the previous example SER was not preceded by a comma. The rule is that when SER is coded with one or more other subparameters it must be preceded by a comma, but when it is the only subparameter it is not preceded by a comma.

The SPACE Parameter

In Chapter 3 you learned how to request and release primary and secondary space allocations, and in Chapter 5 you learned how to request directory blocks when creating a library. The complete format of the SPACE parameter is

$$
\text{SPACE} = \left(\left\{ \begin{array}{l} \text{TRK} \\ \text{CYL} \\ \text{blocksize} \end{array} \right\}, \left(\text{primary}[\,,\text{secondary}] \right) \left[\begin{array}{l} ,\text{directory} \\ ,\text{index} \end{array} \right] \right)
$$

$$
[\,,\text{RLSE}] \left[\begin{array}{l} ,\text{CONTIG} \\ ,\text{MXIG} \\ ,\text{ALX} \end{array} \right] [\,,\text{ROUND}] \,)
$$

(index will be discussed in Chapter 11). All the SPACE subparameters are positional.

The CONTIG, MXIG, and ALX Subparameters.   You may recall that an extent is a group of contiguous tracks, all of which either are being used by a data set or are available. Chapter 3 explained that the system always tries to satisfy the primary request using one extent. If the specified volume does not contain an available extent large enough to satisfy the primary request, up to five extents will be used. The subparameters CONTIG, MXIG, and ALX offer three different ways to ensure that the whole primary allocation is made in contiguous space.

When you code CONTIG, you specify that the primary allocation must be contiguous. If the specified volume does not contain enough contiguous space to satisfy the primary allocation, the job will fail. MXIG specifies that the space allocated to the data set must be the largest area of contiguous space on the volume. If this space is not equal to or greater than the primary request, the job will fail. ALX specifies that up to five extents should be allocated to the data set and that each extent must be at least as large as the primary request. The system will allocate as many extents as it can find on the volume that are as least as large as the primary request, up to a maximum of five extents. If it cannot find at least one extent as large as the primary request, the job will fail.

The ROUND Subparameter. Coding ROUND offers a way of getting cylinders when space is requested by blocksize. When you request space by blocksize, the request is normally converted into the equivalent whole number of tracks and the allocation is made in tracks. When you code ROUND, however, the system calculates the smallest number of cylinders needed to satisfy the request and the allocation is made in cylinders. For example, you might code

```
//BLKS       DD  DSN=BLOCKS,
//               DISP=(NEW,CATLG),
//               UNIT=3330,
//               VOL=SER=WYL002,
//               SPACE=(600,(1000,200),,,ROUND)
```

The SPACE parameter requests a primary allocation of 1000 600-byte records. If ROUND had not been coded, Table E.1 in Appendix E shows that 56 tracks would have been allocated. ROUND will cause this allocation to be made in cylinders—the 56 tracks will be rounded up to three cylinders. The secondary allocation of 200 600-byte records will also be made in cylinders. The three commas indicate that two positional parameters have been omitted.

Multivolume Data Sets. When space is requested for a multivolume data set, the primary request must be satisfied on the first volume specified or the job will fail. Secondary requests may be satisfied on either the first volume or subsequent volumes. Suppose you code

```
//CREATE     DD  DSN=LARGESET,
//               DISP=(NEW,KEEP),
//               UNIT=DISK,
//               VOL=SER=(WYL004,WYL006),
//               SPACE=(TRK,(100,20))
```

If disk pack WYL004 does not contain at least 100 tracks in 5 or fewer extents, the job will fail. If secondary space is required, the system will allocate 20 tracks at a time, taking them from WYL004. This process will continue either until there is not enough space on WYL004 to allocate 20 tracks or until a total of 16 extents have been allocated on WYL004 to the data set. At that point the system will begin allocating 20 tracks at a time from WYL006. Each disk pack may contain a total of 16 extents.

Requesting Specific Tracks. There is another form of the SPACE parameter in which you specify the tracks you want to be used for the data set:

$$\text{SPACE}=\left(\text{ABSTR},\left(\text{primary},\text{address}\left[\begin{array}{c},\text{directory}\\,\text{index}\end{array}\right]\right)\right)$$

In this form, `primary` specifies the number of tracks, `address` specifies the relative track number, and `directory` specifies the number of directory blocks.

For example,

```
SPACE=(ABSTR,(100,500))
```

requests 100 tracks, starting at relative track number 500. If any of the requested tracks are being used, the job will fail.

This form of the `SPACE` parameter is used only when there is a special reason for wanting a data set to be on particular tracks. For example, because the data on tracks serviced by the fixed heads of direct access devices can be read and written much faster than the data on tracks serviced by the movable heads, it might be desirable to have a critical data set located on the track serviced by the fixed heads.

The SPLIT Parameter

In VS1 systems, the `SPLIT` parameter is used to allocate space to two or more data sets in such a way that the data sets share tracks in a cylinder. This is useful when data sets have corresponding records. For example, one data set may contain customers' names and addresses, and a second data set may contain their financial data. If these data sets share tracks in a cylinder, access arm motion will be reduced.

The `SPLIT` parameter allows space to be requested in cylinders or blocks. When cylinders are used, the format is

```
SPLIT=(n,CYL,(primary[,secondary]))
```

and

```
SPLIT=n
```

Here n is the number of tracks per cylinder you want allocated, and the other subparameters have their usual meanings. Suppose you want to allocate 13 cylinders on a 3330 for three data sets named RED, ORANGE, and YELLOW. On a 3330, each cylinder contains 19 tracks. You want RED to occupy 11 tracks per cylinder; ORANGE, 5 tracks per cylinder; and YELLOW, the remaining 3 tracks per cylinder. You code

```
//DD1        DD DSN=RED,
//              DISP=(,KEEP),
//              UNIT=3330,
//              VOL=SER=123456
//              SPLIT=(11,CYL,13)
//DD2        DD DSN=ORANGE,
//              DISP=(,KEEP),
//              SPLIT=5
```

```
//DD3       DD DSN=YELLOW,
//             DISP=(,KEEP),
//             SPLIT=3
```

Notice that volume and unit information are coded for RED, but not for ORANGE and YELLOW. ORANGE and YELLOW are using space allocated to RED, so they must have the same volume and unit as RED. Notice also that when you code SPLIT you do not code SPACE; SPLIT allocates the space.

The format to use when you want to allocate space in blocks is

```
SPACE=(percent,blocksize,(primary[,secondary]))
```

and

```
SPLIT=percent
```

Here percent is the percent of each cylinder you want to allocate. Suppose the average blocksize is 2000 bytes, and you need space for 1500 blocks for two data sets named GREEN and BLUE. You want GREEN to occupy 70 percent of the tracks per cylinder and BLUE 30 percent of the tracks per cylinder. You code

```
//DDA       DD DSN=GREEN,
//             DISP=(,KEEP),
//             UNIT=DISK,
//             VOL=SER=ABC123,
//             SPLIT=(70,2000,1500)
//DDB       DD DSN=BLUE,
//             DISP=(,KEEP),
//             SPLIT=30
```

The percentage you request is converted into tracks and rounded down. Therefore the percent you request must equal at least one track.

The SUBALLOC Parameter

In VS1 systems, the SUBALLOC parameter offers another way to allocate space to a data set. You first create a master data set that contains a lot of space, and then you suballocate that space to other data sets.

The format of the SUBALLOC parameter is

$$
\text{SUBALLOC}=\left(\left\{ \begin{array}{l} \text{TRK} \\ \text{CYL} \\ \text{blocksize} \end{array} \right\},(\text{primary}[,\text{secondary}][,\text{directory}]),\text{ddname}\right)
$$

As you can see, the format is similar to that of the SPACE parameter, except for the ddname subparameter. The ddname is the name of the DD statement defining the master data set that contains the space being suballocated.

Let us clarify these ideas by examining the following coding:

```
//ONE        DD  DSN=APPLES,
//               DISP=(NEW,CATLG),
//               UNIT=DISK,
//               VOL=SER=DISK07,
//               SPACE=(CYL,20,,CONTIG)
//TWO        DD  DSN=PEACHES,
//               DISP=(NEW,CATLG),
//               SUBALLOC=(CYL,5,ONE)
//THREE      DD  DSN=CHERRIES,
//               DISP=(NEW,KEEP),
//               SUBALLOC=(TRK,(20,5),ONE)
```

The master data set is named APPLES and is defined on the DD statement named ONE. APPLES is allocated 20 contiguous cylinders. (When space is to be suballocated, it must be contiguous. Five cylinders of the space allocated to APPLES is requested for the data set named PEACHES. Notice that unit and volume information are not coded for PEACHES. PEACHES is suballocating space allocated to APPLES, so it must have the same volume and unit as APPLES. Twenty tracks of the space allocated to APPLES is requested for the data set named CHERRIES, as well as a secondary allocation of five tracks.

You may suballocate space from an existing data set, but your job must include a DD statement defining the master data set. This DD statement need not be in the same jobstep as the DD statement for the data set that is suballocating space. If the DD statement defining the master data set is in an earlier jobstep, you replace the ddname subparameter by stepname.ddname. Similarly, if the DD statement defining the master data set is in a procedure step that is called by an earlier jobstep, you replace ddname by stepname.procstepname.ddname. This is the usual technique for backward references to earlier steps.

The SYSOUT Parameter

So far you have used only the simple form of the SYSOUT parameter,

```
SYSOUT=class
```

where class has usually been A for the printer and B for the punch. The complete format for the SYSOUT parameter is

$$\text{SYSOUT}=\left(\text{class[,program-name]}\left[\begin{array}{c}\text{,form-name}\\\text{,code-name}\end{array}\right]\right)$$

If you code an asterisk for class, the output is directed to the output class you specified in the MSGCLASS parameter on the JOB statement.

If you want to have the output data set written by a program in the system library rather than by the job entry system, you use program-name to specify the name of the program. This subparameter is rarely used.

`form-name` is the name of the form on which you want the output printed. The `form-name` is assigned by the computer center. A `form-name` of `UNLN` might mean unlined paper, `TWO` might mean two-part paper, and so on.

```
SYSOUT=(C,,TWO)
```

directs the output to output class `C` and indicates that you want this output printed on the form identified by `TWO`.

`code-name` refers to an earlier JES2 `/*OUTPUT` statement that applies to this data set. The JES2 `/*OUTPUT` statement is described in Chapter 15.

The PROFILE Subparameter. In VS1 systems only, the following form of the `SYSOUT` parameter may be used to assign an output class:

```
SYSOUT=PROFILE='sysout-profile-string'
```

You use the `sysout-profile-string` to describe the data set's printing requirements, and the system assigns an output class. The format of the `sysout-profile-string` is established at each computer center. For example, if `FORM` and `CHECKS` have been assigned meanings at your computer center, you could code

```
//PAYOUT    DD SYSOUT=PROFILE='FORM=CHECKS'
```

to specify that this data set should be printed on check forms. The system uses this specification to assign an output class to this data set.

Parameters Used with SYSOUT

Several parameters may be used with `SYSOUT` to exert more control over printing or punching.

The COPIES Parameter. The `COPIES` parameter specifies the number of copies of the data set to be printed. The statement

```
//REPORT    DD SYSOUT=A,
//              COPIES=24
```

will cause 24 copies of the data set to be printed. A maximum of 255 copies may be requested, except in JES3, where the limit is 254 copies. `COPIES` has an additional feature used only with the IBM 3800 printer; it will be discussed later.

The DEST Parameter. Normally output is routed to the workstation from which the job was submitted. The `DEST` parameter can be used to route the output to a different location. Suppose a job stream contains the following two

DD statements:

```
//ABC        DD  SYSOUT=A
//XYZ        DD  SYSOUT=A,
//               DEST=RMT1
```

The workstation from which the job was submitted will receive the output defined by the ABC DD statement, and the workstation named RMT1 will receive the output defined by the XYZ DD statement. The names of the workstations are assigned by the computer center, except for LOCAL and ANYLO-CAL, which mean an output device attached to the central CPU.

The HOLD Parameter.   The HOLD parameter is used to prevent a data set from being printed or punched until it is released. For example, you might code

```
//BIGONE    DD  SYSOUT=A,
//              COPIES=200,
//              HOLD=YES
```

Because 200 copies of this data set are requested, printing will take a long time. Therefore the coding specifies that the data set should be held and a message left with the operator to release it for printing on a late shift, when the printer is not very busy.

The OUTLIM Parameter.   The OUTLIM parameter is used to limit the number of lines printed or cards punched. It is particularly useful during debugging, when a program may go into a loop and print thousands of lines of garbage. It is coded as follows:

```
//OUTPUT    DD  SYSOUT=A,
//              OUTLIM=2000
```

If the program tries to write more than 2000 lines to this data set, the job will abend. If OUTLIM is omitted, in JES2 there is no default for the number of output records. In JES3 there is a default limit defined by the computer center.

The UCS Parameter.   The UCS parameter is used to request that a particular character set be used to print the data set. This parameter has meaning only if output is directed to a printer with the universal character feature — that is, a 1403, 3203-5, or 3211 printer. The parameter is used as follows:

```
//TEXT      DD  SYSOUT=A,
//              UCS=TN
```

This code requests that the data set be printed using the TN print chain. The character sets that may be requested are defined by IBM. You can use only those IBM character sets for which print chains are available at your computer center. User-defined character sets are also permitted.

The OUTPUT Parameter.   The OUTPUT parameter is used to associate a sysout data set with an earlier OUTPUT statement. The OUTPUT statement, which will be discussed shortly, is used to specify processing options for the sysout data set. The OUTPUT parameter is coded as follows:

```
//EX1        DD SYSOUT=A,
//              OUTPUT=*.OUT1
```

This OUTPUT parameter specifies that the data set is to be printed using the options coded on an earlier OUTPUT statement named OUT1. Notice that the usual form for a backward reference, an asterisk followed by a period, is used to specify the OUTPUT statement.

This example assumes either that the OUTPUT statement is in the same step as EX1 or that it is coded at the job level (that is, before the first EXEC statement). If the OUTPUT statement is in a different step, the stepname must be included, just as in the usual backward reference. For example, if the OUT1 OUTPUT statement is in STEP1, the correct coding is

```
//EX2        DD SYSOUT=A,
//              OUTPUT=*.STEP1.OUT1
```

It is possible to refer to more than one OUTPUT statement, but in that case the names must be enclosed in parentheses:

```
//EX3        DD SYSOUT=A,
//              OUTPUT=(*.OUT1,*.OUT2)
```

Why you would want to do that will be explained when the OUTPUT statement is discussed.

Parameters Used with the 3800 Printing Subsystem.   IBM's laser printer is called the 3800 Printing Subsystem. Special features offered by this printer are invoked by coding keyword parameters on the DD statement that defines a data set routed to a 3800 printer. The printer is described in *IBM 3800 Printing Subsystem Programmer's Guide.*

The COPIES Parameter.   When the COPIES parameter is used with a 3800 printer, you can specify how you want multiple copies to be printed by coding group values. For example, in

```
//REPORT     DD SYSOUT=A,
//              COPIES=(0,(1,4,2))
```

the 1, 4, and 2 are the group values. This coding causes 7 copies of the data to be printed in three groups. The first group contains 1 copy of each page in the data set, the second group contains 4 copies of each page, and the third group contains 2 copies of each page. Notice that when group values are coded, the value specified for the number of copies (in this example, 0) is ignored. Up to 8 group values may be coded.

The BURST Parameter.   Before we consider the other features of this printer, let us examine in general how the 3800 Printing Subsystem works. Figure 10.1 shows the path of the paper through the system. The paper starts at the input station and is brought into contact with the photoconductor drum at the transfer station, where the data are transferred to the paper. The data are fused on the paper at the fuser. From there the paper goes either to the continuous forms stacker or to an optional burster and trimmer, which bursts it into separate sheets. The burster and trimmer is very useful for producing letters for a mass mailing.

To use the 3800 burster and trimmer, you code the DD statement as follows:

```
//REPORT     DD SYSOUT=A,
//                BURST=Y
```

If you do not want to use it, you code

```
//REPORT     DD SYSOUT=A,
//                BURST=N
```

The FLASH Parameter.   Let us look at what happens around the photoconductor drum in Figure 10.1. First the cleaner removes whatever is currently on the drum. Then the charge corona prepares the surface to receive the image. The next station is one of the special features of the 3800, the forms overlay. With standard printers special forms are required for certain jobs. The 3800 Printing Subsystem, however, eliminates the need for different types of forms. Plain paper is used with the forms overlay, a device that, when

---

■ Figure 10.1 ■■■

Overview of the IBM 3800 Printing Subsystem

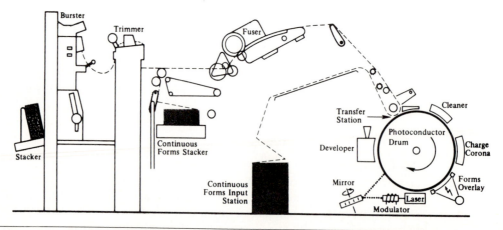

Reprinted by permission from *IBM 3800 Printing Subsystem Programmer's Guide* (GC26-3846-3). © 1975 by International Business Machines Corporation.

inserted in the 3800, causes the desired form to be printed on plain paper. Once a particular form is no longer required, the forms overlay is disposed of, without the loss of a large supply of now unneeded forms. When you want a particular forms overlay inserted in the system, you code the FLASH parameter on the DD statement, as in

```
//REPORT     DD SYSOUT=A,
//               FLASH=SCRN
```

On the operator's terminal a message will appear informing the operator that the forms overlay named SCRN is to be inserted in the system. The name of the forms overlay may be from one to four characters in length. There may be occasions when you want one copy of a report printed on a form and a second copy printed on plain paper. In that case the DD statement is coded as

```
//REPORT     DD SYSOUT=A,
//               COPIES=2,
//               FLASH=(SCRN,1)
```

Specifying 1 with the FLASH parameter prevents the forms overlay from being used to produce the form on both copies of the output.

The CHARS Parameter. The 3800 Printing Subsystem also offers the user a variety of type styles. IBM provides a number of type styles, including DUMP, which is used with SYSUDUMP and SYSABEND DD statements to print dumps with 204 characters per line. Users can create additional type styles using the utility program IEBIMAGE, which will be discussed in Chapter 13. In one installation the old Germanic script shown in Figure 10.2 was implemented for fun. It is invoked with the DD statement

```
//REPORT     DD SYSOUT=A,
//               CHARS=GRMN
```

The CHARS parameter specifies that the type style named GRMN is to be used when this data set is printed. The name used to invoke the type style with the CHARS parameter may be from one to four characters in length.

The MODIFY Parameter. Frequently, printed documents must include a legal disclaimer of some sort. This legal disclaimer may have to appear on

---

Figure 10.2

Sample of Germanic Script

Thif if a fample of the old germanic fcript created at one inftallation. It waf created for fun and not for ufe fince even in Germann it if not commonly ufed. The fentence, "The quicf brown fox jumped over the lasn dogf", illuftratef the ufe of the entire alfabet. The fentence when written in capital letterf appearf af "THE QUICF BROWN FOX JUMPED OVER THE LASD DOGF".

several documents and may change periodically based on current legal activity. In the past, this disclaimer had to be included in the program for each document, and the programs had to be changed every time the disclaimer changed. With the 3800 Printing Subsystem, this is no longer necessary. By means of the utility program IEBIMAGE, a copy modification module is stored in a system library named SYS1.IMAGELIB. This module is invoked with the DD statement

```
//REPORT    DD SYSOUT=A,
//              MODIFY=MODI
```

The MODIFY parameter specifies that the copy modification module named MODI is to be used when this data set is printed. The name of the module used with the MODIFY parameter may be from one to four characters in length.

The copy modification module also offers the user the ability to print information on one copy but not on another. For example, in a manufacturing environment it might be desirable to include the unit cost on the manufacturer's copy of the invoice but not on the customer's copy.

The FCB Parameter.   On the old impact printers, vertical spacing was handled with a carriage control tape made of paper. The carriage control tape had 12 columns on it. These columns were referred to as channels. By tradition, channel 1 had a hole punched in it to indicate the start of a new page. When a form or specially sized paper was used, the operator had to physically change the carriage control tape. Being made of paper, carriage control tapes were fragile and had to be replaced frequently. Modern impact printers, such as the 3211, use a forms control buffer (FCB) to supply the information previously provided by the carriage control tape. For the 3800 Printing Subsystem, the FCB is a module stored in library SYS1.IMAGELIB by the utility program IEBIMAGE. To invoke a particular FCB module, you code the DD statement as

```
//REPORT    DD SYSOUT=A,
//              FCB=CCT1
```

The FCB parameter specifies that the module named CCT1 is to be used when the data set is printed. In JES3 systems only, the module named STD3 may be used to print dumps with eight lines per inch. The FCB module name may be one to four characters in length.

The LABEL Parameter

The format of the LABEL parameter is

$$\text{LABEL}=\left(\text{[seq-no][,label-type]}\begin{bmatrix},\text{PASSWORD}\\,\text{NOPWREAD}\end{bmatrix}\begin{bmatrix},\text{IN}\\,\text{OUT}\end{bmatrix}\begin{bmatrix}\text{RETPD=nnnn}\\\text{EXPDT=yyddd}\end{bmatrix}\right)$$

All the subparameters are positional except RETPD and EXPDT.

The Data Set Sequence Number Subparameter. `seq-no`, which is an abbreviation for data set sequence number, applies only to tape. A tape volume may contain more than one data set. The data set sequence number specifies the number of the data set with which processing is to begin. If you wanted to read or write the third data set on a tape volume, you would code

    LABEL=3

If a data set sequence number is not specified, the system assumes that the data set is the first one on the volume, unless the data set is passed or cataloged. If the data set is passed, the system obtains the data set sequence number from the passing step. If the data set is cataloged, the system obtains the data set sequence number from the catalog.

Although a tape volume may contain more than one data set, if you write over a particular data set, the following data sets are no longer accessible. For example, if a tape volume contains five data sets and you write over the second data set, the third, fourth, and fifth are no longer usable.

The Label-Type Subparameter. `label-type` specifies the kind of labels the data set has. The values that may be coded and their meanings are shown in Table 10.1. Data sets on direct access devices must have either IBM standard labels (`SL`) or IBM standard and user labels (`SUL`). If `label-type` is not coded, IBM standard labels are assumed. `label-type` is not stored in the catalog or passed with passed data sets, so if a data set has labels other than IBM standard labels you must code the `LABEL` parameter whenever you access the data set.

In previous chapters discussions concerning data sets on tape always assumed that the data set accessed was the first one on the tape volume and that it had standard labels. Because these are the default values, it was not necessary to code the `LABEL` parameter.

■ Table 10.1
Label Types and Their Meanings

Label Type	Meaning
SL	IBM standard labels
SUL	IBM standard and user labels
AL	American National standard labels
AUL	American National standard and user labels
NSL	Nonstandard labels
NL	No labels
BLP	System should bypass label processing
LTM	A leading tapemark may be present

Data Set Protection. PASSWORD and NOPWREAD are used to protect a data set against unauthorized access. Coding PASSWORD causes a protection byte in the label to be turned on. When the protection byte is on, the system asks the operator to enter the data set's password whenever a job attempts to read, write to, or delete the data set. NOPWREAD works the same way, except that jobs may read the data set without a password. In order for a job to write to or delete the data set, however, the operator must enter the data set's password. If the operator enters the incorrect password twice, the job is terminated. (To err is human, but to err twice causes an abend.) Passwords are assigned by using the system utility IEHPROGM to enter a data set's name and password into a data set named PASSWORD. Because PASSWORD itself is password protected, the assignment of passwords may be done only by authorized personnel. If neither PASSWORD nor NOPWREAD is coded, the data set is not password protected. This feature is not widely used today; the IBM program product Resource Access Control Facility (RACF) is more common.

Restricting Data Set Usage. The next subparameter, which may be coded as either IN or OUT, is used to restrict the way a data set is used. IN means that the data set can be used only for input, and OUT means that the data set can be used only for output. If the program attempts to violate these restrictions, the job will abend.

Specifying a Retention Period. The final subparameter offers two ways to specify a time period during which a data set may not be deleted or written over. One method is to specify a retention period; the number of days specified must be a one- to four-digit number. To specify a retention period of 60 days, for example, you code

```
RETPD=60
```

The other method is to specify a date before which the data set may not be deleted or written over. The date is specified by giving a two-digit year number and a three-digit day number in the form yyddd. This form of the data is frequently called the **Julian date**.* For example, January 1, 1989 is 89001, and February 1, 1989 is 89032. The coding

```
EXPDT=89365
```

sets the expiration date as the 365th day of 1989 (December 31, 1989).

To delete a data set before its retention period or expiration date has passed, you can use the system utility IEHPROGM, described in Chapter 13.

---

* In some JCL parameters the Julian date is specified in the form dddyy. You must be careful to use the form that is required.

Label Parameter Examples.   As mentioned earlier, the default value for `seq-no` is 1 and for `label-type` is IBM standard labels. If these are the values you want, you may accept the default values and not code the `LABEL` parameter. If the other subparameters are not coded, however, they do not apply. Therefore, if you want password protection, or if you want to specify that the data set should be used only for input or only for output, or if you want to assign a retention period, you must code the `LABEL` parameter.

The parameter

```
LABEL=(5,,PASSWORD,RETPD=90)
```

indicates that the data set is the fifth on the tape volume, that it has standard labels, that it is to be password protected, and that it is to be protected against accidental erasure for 90 days.

The `LABEL` parameter

```
LABEL=EXPDT=90365
```

sets the expiration date as December 31, 1990.

Notice that in this example `EXPDT` is not preceded by a comma, whereas in the previous example `RETPD` was preceded by a comma. The rule is that when `EXPDT` or `RETPD` is the only subparameter coded it is not preceded by a comma, but if any other subparameter is coded `EXPDT` and `RETPD` must be preceded by a comma.

The following example uses all the appropriate subparameters:

```
LABEL=(2,AL,NOPWREAD,OUT,RETPD=10)
```

This parameter specifies that the data set is the second on the volume, that it has American National standard labels, and that it is to be password protected, used only for output, and protected against accidental erasure for 10 days.

Additional DCB Subparameters

In Chapter 3 you learned the most frequently used `DCB` subparameters, `RECFM`, `LRECL`, `BLKSIZE`, and `DEN`. In Chapter 11 you will learn some additional subparameters that are used with ISAM data sets. Here we will discuss several other subparameters that you may have occasion to use. Be aware, however, that there are more than 30 `DCB` subparameters. Many of them are used only under very special circumstances and thus will not be discussed in this text.

`BUFNO` is used to specify the number of buffers to be used with the data set. When data are read or written, they are temporarily held in an area of main storage called a **buffer**. Usually two buffers are used, so that the data in one can be processed while the other is being filled. To request six buffers you would code

```
BUFNO=6
```

The DISPLAY DD statement in Figure 7.11 requests one buffer. If BUFNO is not coded, a default number of buffers, which depends on the operating system and access method being used, is assigned.

PRTSP is used to control the line spacing used with an on-line printer. For example,

```
PRTSP=2
```

specifies double spacing. You may code values from 0 (no spacing) to 3 (triple spacing). If PRTSP is not coded, single spacing is used. This parameter is not valid if RECFM specifies either machine (RECFM=M) or ANSI (RECFM=A) control characters.

STACK is used to select the stacker bin into which cards are placed after they are punched. For example,

```
STACK=2
```

directs the cards to stacker 2. You may select either stacker 1 or stacker 2. If STACK is not coded, stacker 1 is used.

TRTCH is used to read or write seven-track tape. Usually nine-track tape is used. If seven-track tape is to be used, you must code TRTCH. You may specify whether or not you want data conversion, whether or not you want BCD to EBCDIC translation, and whether you want odd or even parity. The format is

$$
\text{TRTCH} = \begin{Bmatrix} C \\ E \\ T \\ ET \end{Bmatrix}
$$

C means that you want data conversion, which makes it possible to write eight binary bits of data on seven tracks. E means that you want even parity; if E is not coded, odd parity is used. T means that you want BCD to EBCDIC translation for reading and EBCDIC to BCD translation for writing. BCD is a coding scheme that was used on early computers to represent data in storage and is used on seven-track tape. BCD is similar to EBCDIC, but it uses six bits for each character instead of eight. If TRTCH is not coded, odd parity is used with no data conversion and no translation.

Coding DSN=NULLFILE

You already know how and why to code DUMMY on a DD statement. Coding

```
DSN=NULLFILE
```

has the same effect as coding DUMMY. The reason there are two ways to accomplish the same goal is that it is sometimes convenient to define a dummy data set by coding a complete DD statement, using NULLFILE as the DSN. When you want to use a real data set, you need change only the DSN.

The DLM Parameter

In Chapter 2 you learned that input stream data introduced by a DD * statement terminate when the system encounters a delimiter statement (/* in columns 1 and 2) or any JCL statement (// in columns 1 and 2). In Chapter 8 you learned that if you want to include JCL statements in your input stream data, you must use the DD DATA statement instead of the DD * statement to introduce the input stream data. But what do you do if you want to include delimiter statements in your input stream data? You use the DLM parameter to change the delimiter. For example,

```
//EVRYTHNG DD DATA,DLM=ZZ
   .
   .
   .
(input stream data containing /* and //
 in columns 1 and 2)
   .
   .
   .
ZZ
```

changes the delimiter, for this input stream data set only, from /* to ZZ. The record that contains ZZ in columns 1 and 2 marks the end of this input stream data set.

You may choose any two characters as the delimiter. You must be careful to include a record containing your delimiter in columns 1 and 2 at the end of the input stream data. If you forget the record containing the delimiter, the rest of your job stream and any other job streams submitted with your job will be included as part of your input stream data. That is not the way to make yourself popular.

The FREE Parameter

In MVS systems only, the FREE parameter allows you to specify whether you want a data set deallocated at the end of a jobstep or when the data set is closed. The advantage of deallocating a data set when it is closed is that the resources used, a device or a volume, are made available to other users sooner. The format of the FREE parameter is

$$FREE=\begin{Bmatrix} END \\ CLOSE \end{Bmatrix}$$

Coding END causes the data set to be deallocated at the end of the jobstep, and coding CLOSE causes the data set to be deallocated when the data set is closed. If FREE is not coded, the data set is deallocated at the end of the jobstep.

The TERM Parameter

The TERM parameter is used with time-sharing systems to indicate that the data set is coming from or going to a time-sharing system. (In VS1 systems the TERM parameter is used differently.) The format of the TERM parameter is

```
TERM=TS
```

The only parameters that may be coded with the TERM parameter are SYSOUT and DCB. The following DD statement illustrates the use of the TERM parameter:

```
//RESULTS    DD TERM=TS
```

The OUTPUT Statement

The OUTPUT statement is a new addition to MVS and is available in only the most recent versions. The OUTPUT statement is used to specify processing options for sysout data sets. The syntax is the usual JCL syntax: slashes in columns 1 and 2; an optional name field; the operation, OUTPUT; the operand field, which consists of optional keyword parameters; and, finally, an optional comments field.

Twenty-nine parameters are listed in the JCL manual, but we will discuss only the more commonly used ones, which are shown in Table 10.2. The parameters BURST, CHARS, COPIES, DEST, FCB, FLASH, MODIFY, and UCS are equivalent to the DD statement parameters with the same names. The CLASS and FORMS parameters are equivalent to the class and form-name subparameters of the SYSOUT parameter. The CONTROL, DEFAULT, JESDS, LINECT, and PRTY parameters have no corresponding DD statement parameters.

In addition to learning how to code the parameters, you must learn how to

Table 10.2
Parameters That May Be Coded with an OUTPUT Statement

Parameter	Meaning
BURST= $\begin{Bmatrix} YES \\ Y \\ NO \\ N \end{Bmatrix}$	Specifies whether or not the 3800 printer burster and trimmer should be used.
CHARS=name	Names the character set to be used with the 3800 printer.
CLASS=class	Specifies the output class to be used.

Cont.

Table 10.2 (Cont.)

Parameter	Meaning
CONTROL={ PROGRAM / SINGLE / DOUBLE / TRIPLE }	Specifies the spacing to be used to print the data set: PROGRAM indicates that the records contain carriage control codes, SINGLE specifies single spacing, DOUBLE specifies double spacing, and TRIPLE specifies triple spacing.
COPIES={ nnn / (,(group-value,...)) }	Specifies the number of copies printed. Works exactly like the DD statement COPIES parameter.
DEFAULT={ YES / Y / NO / N }	Specifies whether or not this is a default OUTPUT statement.
DEST=destination	Names the destination where this data set should be printed.
FCB=name	Names the forms control buffer to be used to print this data set.
FLASH=name	Names the forms overlay to be used by the 3800 Printing Subsystem to print this data set.
FORMS=name	Names the form on which this data set should be printed.
JESDS={ ALL / JCL / LOG / MSG }	Specifies the JES data sets to which this statement applies: ALL means all, JCL means the JCL statements, LOG means the job's log, and MSG means the job's system messages. Must be coded on a job-level OUTPUT statement.
LINECT=nnn	Specifies the maximum number of lines to be printed on a page (JES2 only).
MODIFY=name	Names the copy modification module to be used to print this data set.
PRTY=nnn	Specifies the priority to be assigned to printing this data set. nnn is a number between 0 (lowest priority) and 255 (highest priority).
UCS=name	Names the character set to be used to print this data set.

associate a particular OUTPUT statement with a particular sysout data set. The simplest approach is to name the OUTPUT statement in an OUTPUT parameter:

```
//OUT1       OUTPUT COPIES=5
//DD1        DD SYSOUT=A,
//              OUTPUT=*.OUT1
```

When the DD1 data set is printed, the OUTPUT statement will cause five copies to be printed. You might wonder what the point of coding the OUTPUT statement is, as we could simply have coded the COPY parameter on the DD statement. One reason for coding an OUTPUT statement is that you can code all the processing options once on the OUTPUT statement and then have several SYSOUT DD statements refer to that OUTPUT statement.

The most convenient way to have several SYSOUT DD statements refer to an OUTPUT statement is to make that OUTPUT statement a default statement by coding the DEFAULT parameter:

```
//OUT2       OUTPUT DEFAULT=Y,
//              DEST=RMT1
```

An OUTPUT statement that contains a DEFAULT=Y (or YES) parameter is called a default OUTPUT statement. The effect of a default OUTPUT statement depends on where it is placed. If it is placed before the first EXEC statement, it is called a job-level default OUTPUT statement; if it is placed within a step, it is called a step-level default OUTPUT statement. A job-level default OUTPUT statement applies to all the SYSOUT DD statements in the job that (1) are not in a step that has a step-level default OUTPUT statement and (2) do not explicitly name an OUTPUT statement with an OUTPUT parameter.

Consider the following example:

```
//EXPLJOB    JOB
//JOBOUT1    OUTPUT DEFAULT=Y,
//              BURST=Y,
//              COPIES=2,
//              FORMS=PYRL
//JOBOUT2    OUTPUT LINECT=45
//STEP1      EXEC ...
//DD1        DD SYSOUT=A
//DD2        DD SYSOUT=A,
//              OUTPUT=*.JOBOUT2,
//              COPIES=5
//STEP2      EXEC ...
//STEPOUT1   OUTPUT DEFAULT=Y
//              CONTROL=DOUBLE
//DD3        DD SYSOUT=A
//STEP3      EXEC ...
//DD4        DD SYSOUT=A,
//              COPIES=3
```

The JOBOUT1 OUTPUT statement is a job-level default OUTPUT statement. It applies to the DD1 and DD4 statements; it does not apply to the DD2 statement, because that statement contains an OUTPUT parameter that explicitly names the JOBOUT2 OUTPUT statement. It does not apply to the DD3 statement, because that statement is in a step that contains STEPOUT1, which is a step-level default OUTPUT statement.

When the data set is printed, JES combines the parameters from the DD statement and any OUTPUT statement that applies to it. So, for example, when the DD2 data set is printed, the parameters that apply are LINECT=45 (from the JOBOUT2 OUTPUT statement) and COPIES=5 (from the DD2 statement). Notice that the DD4 data set has two contradictory specifications for the number of copies: COPIES=2 from the JOBOUT1 OUTPUT statement and COPIES=3 from the DD4 statement. The rule is

---

When parameters are coded on both an OUTPUT statement and a DD statement, the DD statement values override the OUTPUT statement values.

Therefore three copies of DD4 will be printed.

The fact that DD parameters override OUTPUT parameters means that special coding must be used when you want to specify CLASS on an OUTPUT statement. For example, in

```
//OUT3        OUTPUT CLASS=H
//DD5         DD SYSOUT=(,),
//                OUTPUT=*.OUT3
```

the special coding SYSOUT=(,) assigns DD5 a null class, so that the CLASS parameter from the OUTPUT statement applies.

By referencing more than one OUTPUT statement, it is possible to process a sysout data set more than one way. For example, the coding

```
//OUT4        OUTPUT CONTROL=TRIPLE,
//                DEST=RMT2
//OUT5        OUTPUT COPIES=3
//DD6         DD SYSOUT=A,
//                OUTPUT=(*.OUT4,*.OUT5)
```

will cause a triple-spaced copy of DD6 to be printed at destination RMT2 and three copies to be printed locally.

The Checkpoint/Restart Feature

When a job is interrupted because of a system error or a program error, it may be desirable to save computer time by restarting the job from where the interruption occurred, rather than from the beginning of the job. This capability is provided by the checkpoint/restart feature. The job may be restarted either from the beginning of the step in which the interrupt occurred, through a process called step restart, or from within the step in which the interrupt occurred, through a process called checkpoint restart. The restart may be either automatic, which means that the job will be rerun immediately, or deferred, which means that the job will be rerun when the programmer resubmits it.

Deferred restarts from the beginning of a step are the easiest to understand and code, so we will begin with these.

Deferred Step Restart

Suppose you run a job that has eight steps named STEP1 through STEP8, and the job fails during STEP6. If a system error caused the failure, you may be able simply to resubmit the job starting at STEP6. If a program error caused the failure, you may be able to examine the output, correct the error, and resubmit the job starting at STEP6.

You can resubmit the job starting at STEP6 by coding the RESTART parameter on the JOB statement as follows:

```
RESTART=STEP6
```

Rerunning a job may sound simple, and indeed coding the RESTART parameter is simple, but many other factors must be considered. For example, STEP4 may create a temporary data set and pass it to STEP6. In that case it is necessary to restart the job from STEP4. Or suppose STEP6 creates a disk data set. Depending on how the DISP parameter is coded, that data set may not have been deleted when the job failed. When you rerun the job and STEP6 tries to create the data set again, you will get the message DUPLICATE NAME ON DIRECT ACCESS VOLUME. In this case you have to delete the data set or change the disposition from NEW to OLD.

If STEP6 updates a data set, those records that were updated before the failure occurred will be updated a second time if STEP6 is rerun. To prevent records from being updated twice, it may be necessary to include, for example, a last-date-updated field in each record. When the step is rerun, that field may be tested to determine whether the record was updated on the run that failed. Even that strategy will not work if records may legally be updated more than once during a run.

You should also be aware that COND parameters that refer to a step preceding the restarted step will be ignored.

You can restart a job from a step within a procedure by coding the step-name and procstepname. For example,

```
RESTART=(STEP6.GO)
```

means that the job should be restarted at the GO step within the procedure invoked on the STEP6 EXEC statement.

Checkpoint Restart

With checkpoint restart, execution starts within a step. To use checkpoint restart you must establish checkpoints in your program. At each **checkpoint** the status of your job and of the system is written to a checkpoint data set. Writing this status information is called taking a checkpoint. This status information may be used to restart the job at the checkpoint within a step.

To establish checkpoints you must code the appropriate instruction in your program. Assembler programs use the CHKPT macro, COBOL programs use the RERUN clause, and PL/I programs use the CALL PLICKPT instruction. FORTRAN does not permit checkpointing. To specify that you want checkpoints taken during a sort or merge, you code the CKPT parameter on the SORT or MERGE control statement.

For multivolume data sets you can request that a checkpoint be taken when the end of a volume is encountered by coding the CHKPT parameter on the DD statement for that data set. For example, coding

```
//DD1      DD DSN=LARGE,
//              DISP=OLD,
//              UNIT=TAPE,
//              VOL=SER=(TAPE01,TAPE02,TAPE03),
//              CHKPT=EOV
```

will cause checkpoints to be taken at the end of TAPE01 and TAPE02. CHKPT may be coded only for sequential data sets.

You must also provide either a sequential or partitioned data set to which the checkpoint records are written. Assembler, COBOL, and PL/I programmers specify the ddname of the checkpoint data set in their programs. The ddname of the data set used for sort checkpoints is SORTCKPT. The ddname of the data set used for checkpoints generated by the CHKPT parameter is SYSCKEOV.

In order for all the checkpoints written to be saved, the disposition of this data set must be MOD. If the disposition is NEW, each checkpoint will overwrite the previous one. A DD statement that could be used is

```
//CHEK       DD DSN=CHECKPNT,
//              DISP=(MOD,CATLG),
//              UNIT=TAPE
```

Each time a checkpoint is taken, the system prints a message that includes the checkpoint identification, a seven-digit number preceded by the letter C. The first checkpoint is C0000001, the second is C0000002, and so on. As you will see later, these identifications may be used to perform a delayed checkpoint restart.

If your program takes checkpoints, it is assumed that you want automatic checkpoint restart. Therefore, if a program that has taken one or more checkpoints is interrupted because of failure or because of an abend that returned one of the eligible completion codes, the system will send a message to the operator asking whether the job should be restarted. If the operator gives permission, the job will be restarted automatically from the latest checkpoint. The eligible completion codes are established by IBM but may be changed by the computer center. If you want automatic checkpoint restart, you do not have to do anything. If you do not want automatic checkpoint restart, you can tell the operator not to give permission. It is, however, more convenient to control automatic restart using the RD parameter.

The RD Parameter

The RD parameter is used to request automatic step restart or to suppress automatic checkpoint restart. It is also used to prevent checkpoints from being taken. The RD parameter may be coded on either the JOB or EXEC statements. If it is coded on the JOB statement, it overrides any RD parameters coded on EXEC statements.

The RD parameter is coded as follows:

```
RD=request
```

The values that may be coded for request and their meanings are shown in Table 10.3.

If you code R you will get automatic step restart, provided the interrupt was due to a system failure or to an abend that returned one of the eligible completion codes. If, however, the program contains instructions to take checkpoints and one or more checkpoints were taken before failure, you will get automatic checkpoint restart instead of automatic step restart. In this case you must code RNC to get automatic step restart. Coding RNC prevents check-

■ **Table 10.3** ■
Values That May Be Coded for the RD Parameter

Value	Meaning
R	Requests automatic step restart. Has no effect on checkpoint instructions.
NR	Does not request automatic step restart. Allows checkpoints to be taken, but suppresses automatic checkpoint restart.
RNC	Requests automatic step restart. Suppresses all checkpoint instructions.
NC	Does not request automatic step restart. Suppresses all checkpoint instructions.

points from being taken, even if the program contains instructions to take checkpoints. Only by coding R or RNC can you get automatic step restart.

You would code NC if your program contained instructions to take checkpoints and you wanted to suppress those instructions. Coding NC allows a program containing checkpoint instructions to be used when the checkpoint function is not wanted.

You would code NR if your program contained instructions to take checkpoints and you wanted the checkpoints taken but did not want automatic checkpoint restart. The checkpoints could be used to perform a delayed checkpoint restart. To perform a delayed checkpoint restart, you must code the RESTART parameter and you must include the checkpoint data sets in the job stream.

In coding the RESTART parameter, you must identify the checkpoint at which you want to restart, as well as the stepname. For example,

```
RESTART=(STEP6,C0000004)
```

specifies that the job is to be restarted within STEP6 at the checkpoint named C0000004.

The checkpoint data set must have the ddname SYSCHK, and the SYSCHK DD statement must be placed immediately before the first EXEC statement in the job. For the checkpoints written using the DD statement given earlier, the SYSCHK statement could be

```
//SYSCHK    DD DSN=CHECKPNT,
//              DISP=OLD
```

Summary

In this chapter you have learned

—how to code the JOB statement parameters MPROFILE, NOTIFY, PROFILE, PRTY, and TYPRUN

—how to code the JOB and EXEC statement parameters ADDRSPC and PERFORM

—how to code the EXEC statement parameter DPRTY

—how to code the full form of the UNIT, VOLUME, SPACE, and LABEL parameters

—how to code the DD statement parameters AFF, SEP, SPLIT, SUBALLOC, FREE, and TERM

—how to code the following parameters used with SYSOUT: COPIES, DEST, HOLD, OUTLIM, PROFILE, UCS, and OUTPUT

—how to request special features of the 3800 Printing Subsystem by using the parameters COPIES, BURST, FLASH, CHARS, MODIFY, and FCB

—how to code the DCB subparameters BUFNO, PRTSP, STACK, and TRTCH

—how to code the OUTPUT statement

—how to use the checkpoint/restart feature

Vocabulary

In this chapter you have been introduced to the meanings of the following terms:

buffer
channel
checkpoint

Julian date
performance group
unit affinity

Exercises

1. What is the function of the PRTY parameter?
2. What are the functions of the TYPRUN parameter?
3. What is the function of the ADDRSPC parameter?
4. What is the function of the PERFORM parameter?
5. Code a UNIT parameter that requests five model 2400 tape drives. Specify deferred mounting.
6. What is parallel mounting and how do you get it?
7. What is unit affinity and how do you get it?
8. What is a private volume and how do you get one?
9. Code a VOL parameter that will cause processing to start at the second volume of a cataloged data set.
10. Code a VOL parameter that could be used to create a four-volume data set on tape. The serial numbers of the four volumes are A, B, C, and D. Code the associated UNIT parameter, requesting two model 3420 tape drives.
11. What are the functions of the CONTIG, MXIG, and ALX subparameters?
12. What is wrong with the following coding?

```
SPACE=(TRK,10,RLSE,,ROUND)
```

13. Code a SPACE parameter that requests a primary allocation of 100 cylinders and a secondary allocation of 20 cylinders. The space should be contiguous. Release unused space.
14. Code a SYSOUT parameter that directs output to class G and uses a form named LBLS, with labels.
15. Code a DD statement that directs a sysout data set to class F, requests 15 copies, directs the output to WKS7, and limits the output to 5000 lines.
16. Which print chains are available at your computer center? How do you request them?

17. If the output were directed to a 3800 printer, how many copies would the parameter

    ```
    COPIES=(5,(1,2,3,4))
    ```

    cause to be printed?
18. What is the function of the BURST parameter?
19. What is the function of the FLASH parameter?
20. What is the function of the CHARS parameter?
21. What is the function of the MODIFY parameter?
22. What is the function of the FCB parameter?
23. GRADES is the fifth data set on a tape. It is accessed using the following statement:

    ```
    //INPUT     DD DSN=GRADES,
    //              DISP=SHR
    ```

    Why isn't the LABEL parameter coded to specify the data set sequence number? What kind of labels does this data set have?
24. What is the difference between PASSWORD and NOPWREAD?
25. What does coding the LABEL subparameters IN and OUT do?
26. What is the difference between RETPD and EXPDT?
27. Code a LABEL parameter to protect a data set. Allow the data set to be read without a password.
28. Code a LABEL parameter that will set a retention period of 100 days.
29. Code a LABEL parameter for a data set that is the third on a tape volume, that has IBM standard and user labels, that may be used only for output, and that has an expiration date of December 31, 1999.
30. What is the function of the DLM parameter?
31. Code a DLM parameter on a DD DATA statement to change the delimiter to !!. What record must you put at the end of the input stream data?
32. Code an OUTPUT statement that causes output to be double spaced, requests the form named CHKS, and assigns the highest priority to printing. Code a SYSOUT DD statement that explicitly references this OUTPUT statement.
33. Code a job-level default OUTPUT statement that prints a data set at the remote workstation named HDQT. Where in the job stream must this statement be placed?
34. Code an OUTPUT statement that assigns a sysout data set to class W, and then code a SYSOUT DD statement that explicitly references this OUTPUT statement.
35. Simple Simon says that a job-level default OUTPUT statement applies to all sysout data sets in a job. Explain why he is wrong.
36. Why would you want a SYSOUT DD statement to reference more than one OUTPUT statement?
37. What is the purpose of the checkpoint/restart feature?

38. What is the difference between an automatic restart and a deferred restart? How is each requested?
39. What is the difference between step restart and checkpoint restart? How is each requested?
40. What is the function of the CHKPT parameter?
41. Code the RESTART parameter to restart a job at the seventh checkpoint taken in STEP3.
42. When is the ddname SYSCHK used?

ISAM Data Sets

In this chapter you will learn

- what ISAM is
- how to code JCL to create an ISAM data set
- how to code JCL to access an ISAM data set
- how to use the utility programs IEBISAM and IEBDG

Processing Data Sets

Up to this point we have discussed data sets that are processed sequentially. In sequential processing, records can be directly added only to the end of the data set — provided, of course, that a disposition of MOD has been specified. If you want to add a record in the middle of the data set, you must completely re-create the data set. Figure 11.1 illustrates one sequence of operations to add a record to a sequential data set. As you can see, three separate steps have to be executed every time a record is to be added to the data set, unless a decision is made to group the update records together and run the job, say, once a day. Such grouping is called batch processing. One disadvantage of batch processing is that the data set is accurate only once a day, immediately after the batch run.

Similarly, if you wish to read a particular record that is somewhere in the middle of a sequential data set, you must start with the first record and read each record until you find the one you want. If you are in a situation where you are responding to inquiries that do not come in any special order, you will not be able to answer the questions very quickly because of the massive I/O required.

System Flowchart to Add a Record to a Sequential Data Set

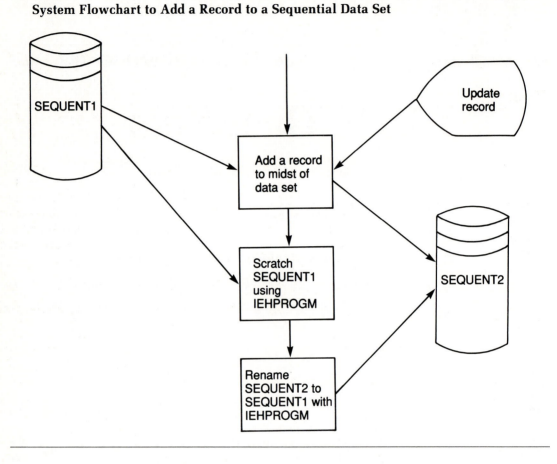

What is needed is the ability to read the desired record directly and change a particular record or add a new record in the middle of the data set without re-creating the entire data set. This ability is called **random access**. Random access requires that the records be identified by keys. A **key** is a field within the record used to uniquely identify the record. All keyed data sets must reside on DASD.

The Basic Direct Access Method

The first access method to accomplish this goal was called the **basic direct access method** or **BDAM**. In BDAM the key of the record is used in some fashion to point to the record's location on DASD. The data set may be created by specifying each record's location on DASD either as a relative address or as an absolute address. If you use an absolute address, the data usually cannot be moved. The absolute address is given in the form MBBCCHHR, where M is a one-byte value that gives the relative location of an entry in a data extent block, BB is a two-byte number for bin or cell, CC is the two-byte number that identifies the cylinder, HH is the two-byte number that names the reading head or track address, and R is a one-byte number that identifies which block contains the data sought.

A relative address may be a relative block address or a relative track address. The relative block address is a three-byte number that tells the location of the block in the data set. The relative block address of the first block is 0. If a relative block address is used, the records must be fixed length and unblocked, because the system uses the relative block address to calculate the absolute address of the record. The relative track address, which may be used with blocked or unblocked records of fixed or variable length, is a total of three bytes in length. The first two bytes are the actual relative track address, and the third byte is the record number on the track. The relative track address of the first block is 0.

The main problem with BDAM was that the key always had to be a number. If you wanted to create a data set that contained information about nuts, you could not use the name of the nut as the key because the name was alphabetic. Many techniques were developed to resolve this problem. For example, algorithms were developed to convert the actual key, such as 'ACORN', to a relative or absolute address. These algorithms were frequently very difficult to develop and did not always work well for long. If, for example, an algorithm was developed for a tool manufacturer's inventory, when a new line of tools was made with very different names it was necessary to develop a new algorithm and re-create the inventory file. This process was time consuming and expensive. There had to be a better way, and it was called the **indexed sequential access method** or **ISAM**.

As we go on to discuss ISAM, please be aware that there are times when BDAM may still be the best choice. If the keys can be used as the addresses without any complex manipulation, your access time will be much better with BDAM than with ISAM. BDAM data sets do not usually need reorganization, which will be discussed in detail later. For the present, it is enough to know that reorganization is a time-consuming operation that generally must be performed at regular intervals with ISAM data sets.

What Is ISAM?

What made ISAM unique when it was developed was its index. The index keeps track of the DASD addresses of the records in the data sets. The index is created by the system, so with ISAM, unlike BDAM, the programmer need not be concerned with developing DASD addresses. With ISAM, however, the minimum number of read operations required to retrieve a record is two, whereas with BDAM it is one. With BDAM the system can normally read a particular record in one read operation, with the programmer supplying the DASD address. With ISAM the index is read first, and from it the system learns the DASD address, which is then used to read the desired record.

ISAM Organization

An ISAM data set may consist of up to three parts: the prime area, the index area, and the independent overflow area. Space for an ISAM data set is allo-

Figure 11.2

A Cylinder in the Prime Area

Track																
0	147	Trk 1 Rec 1	147	Trk 1 Rec 1	175	Trk 2 Rec 1	175	Trk 2 Rec 1	230	Trk 3 Rec 1	230	Trk 3 Rec 1	274	Trk 4 Rec 1	274	Trk 4 Rec 1

Track index

Track						
1	106	124	131	139	147
2	152	159	168	171	175
3	186	195	208	222	230
4	238	246	253	261	274
5					

Prime area

Cylinder overflow

cated in cylinders. If you specify tracks, the system will round up to the nearest cylinder.

Prime Area

Unlike the index and independent overflow areas, the **prime area** is always required. In addition to data, each cylinder of the prime area must contain a track index and may contain an overflow area. Figure 11.2 illustrates a prime area cylinder with the required track index and the optional overflow area called the **cylinder overflow**. For convenience, the cylinder shown in Figure 11.2 contains only six tracks, numbered from 0 to 5. The prime area shows only the keys of the records, because for this discussion the rest of the record is unimportant.

Notice that all the records are in sort sequence. The records in the prime area are always in sort sequence. The records used to initially load an ISAM data set must be sorted on the key. In Figure 11.2 the overflow area is shown as empty. When an ISAM data set is created, the overflow area is always empty.

There is an entry in the track index for each prime data track in the cylinder. This entry contains the highest key on the track and the address of the first record on that track. The apparent doubling of the data in the track index in Figure 11.2 is explained by Figure 11.3, which shows that each entry in the track index actually consists of two parts: a normal entry and an overflow entry. You will see why when we discuss adding records to an ISAM data set.

Index Area

If the ISAM data set occupies more than one cylinder, the system will automatically create a **cylinder index**. In addition, you can request that the sys-

Figure 11.3

Entry in a Track Index

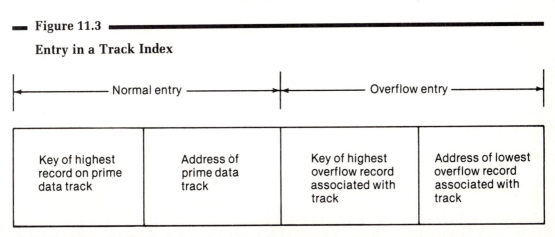

← Normal entry →		← Overflow entry →	
Key of highest record on prime data track	Address of prime data track	Key of highest overflow record associated with track	Address of lowest overflow record associated with track

tem create a **master index**. These indexes may be stored on the first cylinder of the prime area, but if the data set is even moderately large, it is recommended that a separate **index area** be created. (How a separate index area is created will be discussed later in this chapter.)

There is one entry in the cylinder index for each cylinder in the prime area. This entry contains the highest key on the cylinder and the address of the track index of that cylinder.

Figure 11.4 shows the cylinder index that would be created if the ISAM data set we started in Figure 11.2 expanded to the three cylinders 42, 43, and 44 shown in Figure 11.4. The cylinder index is on cylinder 178.

The purpose of a cylinder index is to speed up access to a particular record. Without a cylinder index, the track index of each cylinder would have to be read to locate the desired record. In Figure 11.4 a maximum of three track indexes would have to be read, but if there were, say, twenty cylinders in the data set, an average of ten track indexes would have to be read to locate a specific record, with the disk read/write head moving each time.

With a cylinder index, locating a record requires reading only two tracks: the track in the cylinder index, which sends the system to the correct cylinder, and the track index of that cylinder. The disk read/write head moves only twice, because it is in position to read the data once it is positioned to read the track index.

If the data set is very large, however, the cylinder index can expand to several tracks, slowing down record retrieval. Creating a master index eliminates this problem. As shown in Figure 11.5, one entry is made in the master index for each track in the cylinder index.

Overflow Area

There are two kinds of **overflow areas**. One is the cylinder overflow, which is part of the prime area and is shown in Figures 11.2 and 11.4. If there is no room for a record in the track where it belongs and there is space in a cylinder overflow, the record may be written in the cylinder overflow and the access arm of the DASD need not be moved. If either there is no more space available in the cylinder overflow or there is no cylinder overflow, the record is written in the independent overflow area, if one exists. The independent overflow area is not required, but it is recommended, particularly if there are likely to be many additions to the data set.

Adding Records to an ISAM Data Set

Figures 11.6 through 11.9 illustrate what happens in the prime area when records are added to an ISAM data set. If you compare the information in Figure 11.3, which defines the fields in the track index entry, with the infor-

Figure 11.4

Three Cylinders of an ISAM Data Set with Their Cylinder Index

Cylinder index

Cylinder 178	274	Cyl 42 Trk 0	362	Cyl 43 Trk 0	451	Cyl 44 Trk 0

Separate index area

Track index

Prime area

Cylinder 42	147	T1 R1	147	T1 R1	175	T2 R2	175	T2 R2	230	T3 R1	230	T3 R1	274	T4 R1	274	T4 R1

106	124	131	139	147
152	159	168	171	175
186	195	208	222	230
238	246	253	261	274

Cont.

Cylinder 43

269	T1 R1	269	T1 R1	311	T2 R1	311	T2 R1	337	T3 R1	337	T3 R1	362	T4 R1	362	T4 R1

278	281	287	294	296
299	301	305	307	311
314	318	326	334	337
341	342	356	359	362

Track indexes

Cylinder 44

384	T1 R1	384	T1 R1	399	T2 R1	399	T2 R1	413	T3 R1	413	T3 R1	451	T4 R1	451	T4 R1

368	372	373	379	384
387	388	392	397	399
400	406	409	411	413
426	432	437	446	451

Figure 11.5

Index Area Showing Master and Cylinder Indexes

Master index

451	Cyl 178 Trk 1	695	Cyl 178 Trk 2	919	Cyl 178 Trk 3

Cylinder index   Cylinder 178

Track

Track						
1	274	Cyl 42 Trk 0	362	Cyl 43 Trk 0	451	Cyl 44 Trk 0
2	537	Cyl 45 Trk 0	603	Cyl 46 Trk 0	695	Cyl 47 Trk 0
3	737	Cyl 48 Trk 0	808	Cyl 49 Trk 0	919	Cyl 50 Trk 0

mation in the original track index entry at the top of Figure 11.2, you will notice that those fields that are supposed to contain overflow information actually contain the same information as the normal entry. Notice also that before any additions are made to the data set, the cylinder overflow in Figure 11.2 is empty.

Figure 11.6 shows what happens if we add a record whose key is 137 to the data set. The first thing the system does is locate the track on which the record belongs. The system compares the key of the record to be added with the highest key on each track. The first key that is higher than the key to be added indicates the track on which the record belongs. The highest key on the first track is 147; therefore the record we are adding belongs on the first track. (If the highest key on track 1 had been 50, for example, the highest key of the second track would have been examined.)

There is no room on the first track for another record, however, so we must use an overflow area. Because the cylinder overflow is not full (in fact, at this point it is empty), the system uses it instead of the independent overflow area. The new record is inserted in its proper place in the prime area. Because there is no room left for the record whose key is 147, it is then placed in the cylinder overflow area with a pointer back to track 1. The track index entry must be changed. The highest record on the prime data track is now 139, but the prime data track address remains the same (track 1). The field that contains the highest overflow record associated with track 1 remains 147, but the field that

■ **Figure 11.6** ━━━━━━━━━━━━━━━━━━━━━━━━━━━━

Cylinder After the Record with Key 137 Is Added

Track

0	139	Trk 1 Rec 1	147	Trk 5 Rec 1	175	Trk 2 Rec 1	175	Trk 2 Rec 1	230	Trk 3 Rec 1	230	Trk 3 Rec 1	274	Trk 4 Rec 1	274	Trk 4 Rec 1

1	106	124	131	137	139
2	152	159	168	171	175
3	186	195	208	222	230
4	238	246	253	261	274
5	147	Trk 1			

has the address of the lowest overflow record associated with the track is changed to track 5, record 1.

Now let us add a second record to this data set, as shown in Figure 11.7. Because the record we are adding has a key of 112, it also belongs on track 1, which means that the record whose key is 139 falls off and must be added to the cylinder overflow. A pointer is added to that record to point to the next record in the data set that belongs to track 1. This record, whose key is 147, is the first record in the track of the cylinder overflow. Two fields in the track index entry must be changed: The key of the highest record on the prime data track goes from 139 to 137, and the field that contains the address of the lowest overflow record changes from track 5, record 1 to track 5, record 2.

Figure 11.8 illustrates the addition of two more records. The first record added has a key of 165. It is inserted in its proper position on track 2, and

Figure 11.7

Cylinder After the Record with Key 112 Is Added

Track

0	137	Trk 1 Rec 1	147	Trk 5 Rec 2	175	Trk 2 Rec 1	175	Trk 2 Rec 1	230	Trk 3 Rec 1	230	Trk 3 Rec 1	274	Trk 4 Rec 1	274	Trk 4 Rec 1

1	106	112	124	131	137
2	152	159	168	171	175
3	186	195	208	222	230
4	238	246	253	261	274

5	147	Trk 1	139	Trk 5 Rec 1			

record 175 is placed in the overflow area. The track index entry for track 2 is modified to reflect these changes.

The next record added has a key of 143. It belongs on track 1, whose highest key is 147. At the present time, however, the highest key on track 1 is 137. Thus the new record is added directly to the cylinder overflow. This addition does not require any changes in the track index. The record whose key is 143 is added to the overflow, with a pointer to the record whose key is 147. The pointer of the record whose key is 139 is changed so that it no longer points to the record whose key is 147 but instead points to the new record.

Let us see what happens when we try to read the record whose key is 147. The overflow entry in the track index for track 1 sends us to record 2 on track 5. We read the key of that record and discover that it is not the record we want. The pointer of that record directs us to record 4 on track 5. We read the

Figure 11.8

Cylinder After Records with Keys 165 and 143 Are Added

Track

0	137	Trk 1 Rec 1	147	Trk 5 Rec 2	171	Trk 2 Rec 1	175	Trk 5 Rec 3	230	Trk 3 Rec 1	230	Trk 3 Rec 1	274	Trk 4 Rec 1	274	Trk 4 Rec 1

Track					
1	106	112	124	131	137
2	152	159	165	168	171
3	186	195	208	222	230
4	238	246	253	261	274
5	147	Trk 1	139	Trk 5 Rec 4	175	Trk 2	143	Trk 5 Rec 1	

key of that record and again find that it is not the record we want. This time the pointer directs us to record 1 on track 5, and when we read the key of that record we finally find that it is the record we are looking for. Reading all these records takes time, which is why it is desirable to reorganize an ISAM data set after a number of records have been added to it. When an ISAM data set is reorganized, all the records in the overflow area are inserted in their proper sequential position in the prime area. How an ISAM data set is reorganized will be explained later in this chapter.

Notice the logical similarity between the normal and overflow index entries. In Figure 11.8 the normal entry for track 1 indicates that a sequence of records starts at the beginning of track 1, the last record having a key of 137. The overflow entry indicates that a sequence of records starts with the second record of track 5, the last record having a key of 147.

Deleting Records

Figure 11.9 illustrates the deletion of the record whose key is 230. What actually happens is that the **delete byte**, which is the first byte in a fixed length record or the fifth byte in a variable length record, is set to hexadecimal FF. Under certain conditions, this record can still be read. If, however, a record whose key is, say, 214 is added, the record whose key is 230 will be deleted. The system would normally place the record whose key is 230 in the cylinder overflow, but before doing so it checks the delete byte. Because there is a hexadecimal FF in the delete byte, the record is discarded.

Figure 11.9

Cylinder After the Record with Key 230 Is Deleted and the Record with Key 214 Is Added

Track

0	137	Trk 1 Rec 1	147	Trk 5 Rec 2	171	Trk 2 Rec 1	175	Trk 5 Rec 3	222	Trk 3 Rec 1	222	Trk 3 Rec 1	274	Trk 4 Rec 1	274	Trk 4 Rec 1

1	106	112	124	131	137
2	152	159	168	171	175
3	186	195	208	214	222
4	238	246	253	261	274

5	147	Trk 1	139	Trk 5 Rec 4	175	Trk 2	143	Trk 5 Rec 1

JCL to Create an ISAM Data Set

When an ISAM data set is created, there are four possible forms it may assume. The ISAM data set may consist of index, prime, and overflow; index and prime; prime and overflow; or prime only. Creating the data set may require one, two, or three DD statements, depending on which form you want.

Using One DD Statement

Figure 11.10 illustrates a DD statement that could be used to create an ISAM data set using one DD statement. Most of the information in the DD statement should be familiar to you. The principal differences between this DD statement and those you studied earlier are in the SPACE parameter and the DCB parameter. Let us examine the SPACE parameter first. The space allocation is in cylinders as opposed to tracks, because cylinders are required for ISAM. If you code tracks, the system will round up to the nearest cylinder.

If you specify ABSTR instead of CYL in the SPACE parameter, the primary quantity, which must be tracks when ABSTR is specified, must be equal to a whole number of cylinders. The second parameter, which gives the secondary allocation when CYL or TRK is specified, gives the address of a particular track when ABSTR is specified and in this case must be the first track in a cylinder. The use of ABSTR is definitely not recommended.

In the SPACE parameter in Figure 11.10, a primary allocation of five cylinders is requested. There is no secondary space allocation because for ISAM it is forbidden. The 1 represents the space to be reserved for the index. How does the system know that the request is for one cylinder for an index and not for one 256-byte directory block for a library, as discussed in Chapter 5? In the DCB parameter, the subparameter DSORG is set equal to IS, which identifies this data set as an ISAM data set. DSORG=IS *must always be included when an ISAM data set is created or accessed.* We will not discuss the DCB subparameters LRECL, BLKSIZE, and RECFM, as there is no difference between their use here and in earlier discussions.

The DCB subparameter KEYLEN tells how long the record key is. In the

---

Figure 11.10

Creating an ISAM Data Set Using One DD Statement

```
//ISAMDD1   DD DSN=WYL.QB.JCL.ISAM1,
//             DISP=(,KEEP),
//             UNIT=SYSDA,
//             VOL=SER=WYL004,
//             SPACE=(CYL,(5,,1)),
//             DCB=(DSORG=IS,RECFM=FB,LRECL=80,BLKSIZE=1680,
//             KEYLEN=5,RKP=1,CYLOFL=2,NTM=4,OPTCD=LMRUWY)
```

example in Figure 11.10, it is five bytes. RKP stands for **relative key position**. If the record is variable in length, RKP must be greater than or equal to 4, because the first four bytes are reserved for system use, as discussed in Appendix E. If you specify RKP=0 for fixed length or RKP=4 for variable length records, the key will start in the first data byte of the record; it will then be impossible to delete the records in the data set because the delete byte will be part of the key. In Figure 11.10 RKP is equal to 1, meaning that the key starts in the second byte of the record and the first byte is available for use as a delete byte.

The subparameter OPTCD may be set equal to I, L, M, R, U, W, and/or Y. I means that an independent overflow area is desired. Actually creating the independent overflow area requires a special DD statement which we will discuss later. Y means that cylinder overflow is desired. If you code Y, you must also code CYLOFL to specify the number of tracks in each prime area cylinder that should be reserved for cylinder overflow. In Figures 11.2, 11.6, 11.7, 11.8, and 11.9, one track in the prime area is labeled as cylinder overflow. In Figure 11.10 CYLOFL=2 reserves two tracks of each cylinder for overflow.

L indicates that the first byte of the record is to be used as the delete byte; RKP must be set equal to a value that leaves the first byte available for use as the delete byte. M requests that the system create and maintain a master index after the cylinder index in the index area (see Figures 11.4 and 11.5) occupies a certain number of tracks. The exact number is specified in the DCB subparameter NTM. In this example NTM is set equal to 4, which means that after there are four tracks in the cylinder index, a master index will be created. R causes reorganization data to be placed in the data control block. U, which can be used only with fixed length records, causes the system to accumulate the data for the track index and write them as a group. W requests a validity check for each write operation. Validity checking involves reading each record immediately after it is written and comparing what is read with what was supposed to have been written. This process obviously decreases the speed of the operation, but it increases its accuracy.

In COBOL programs the key length and position are specified in the RECORD KEY clause, so COBOL programmers usually do not code KEYLEN or RKP subparameters on the DD statement. The other ISAM DCB subparameters, CYLOFL, NTM, and OPTCD, must be coded on the DD statement. In PL/I programs the key length and position may be specified either in the ENV entry for the file or on the DD statement. As in the case of COBOL, the other ISAM subparameters must be coded on the DD statement. In assembler programs all the subparameters may be coded either within the program in the DCB macro or on the DD statement. Generally, when a parameter may be coded either in the program or on the DD statement, it is better to code it on the DD statement, because that makes the program more flexible.

You will notice that the disposition specifies that the data set is to be kept at job end. CATLG could have been specified in this case, because there is only one DD statement. If two or three DD statements are used, CATLG may not be specified in the DISP parameter.

If you choose not to code the index value in the SPACE parameter, the system will create an index at the end of the prime area anyway. Therefore, in Figure 11.10 the SPACE parameter could have been coded as

```
SPACE=(CYL,(6))
```

If you want to specify the size of the index area, you must code the index value in the SPACE parameter, but if you are willing to let the system determine the size, you can omit the index value. Omitting the index value is a good idea when you are creating a small ISAM data set of one or two cylinders, because if you specify an index value in the SPACE parameter, the index alone must be at least one cylinder.

Using Two DD Statements

Figure 11.11 illustrates the JCL used to create an ISAM data set with index and prime DD statements, and Figure 11.12 shows the JCL needed to create an ISAM data set with prime and independent overflow DD statements. When more than one DD statement is used to define an ISAM data set, you indicate which part of the data set the DD statement is defining by including INDEX, PRIME, or OVFLOW in parentheses following the data set name. The DD statements must be concatenated and must be coded in the following order: INDEX, PRIME, OVFLOW. You will notice that the SPACE parameter for the prime DD statement in Figure 11.11 does not have an index value, whereas the one in Figure 11.12 does. The reason is that the index is explicitly defined in Figure 11.11. None of the additional subparameters of the SPACE parameter have been coded; all but CONTIG are forbidden for ISAM.

■ **Figure 11.11** ━━

Creating an ISAM Data Set with Index and Prime Areas

```
//DD2ISAMA DD DSN=WYL.QB.JCL.ISAM2(INDEX),
//              DISP=(,KEEP),
//              UNIT=SYSDA,
//              VOL=SER=WYL004,
//              SPACE=(CYL,(1)),
//              DCB=(DSORG=IS,RECFM=FB,LRECL=80,BLKSIZE=1680,
//              KEYLEN=5,RKP=1,CYLOFL=2,NTM=4,OPTCD=LMRUWY)
//           DD DSN=WYL.QB.JCL.ISAM2(PRIME),
//              DISP=(,KEEP),
//              UNIT=SYSDA,
//              VOL=SER=WYL004,
//              SPACE=(CYL,(5)),
//              DCB=*.DD2ISAMA
```

■ Figure 11.12 ■

Creating an ISAM Data Set with Prime and Independent Overflow Areas

```
//DD2ISAMB DD DSN=WYL.QB.JCL.ISAM3(PRIME),
//              DISP=(,KEEP),
//              UNIT=SYSDA,
//              VOL=SER=WYL004,
//              SPACE=(CYL,(10,,1)),
//              DCB=(DSORG=IS,RECFM=FB,LRECL=80,BLKSIZE=1680,
//              KEYLEN=5,RKP=1,CYLOFL=2,NTM=4,OPTCD=ILMRUWY)
//          DD DSN=WYL.QB.JCL.ISAM3(OVFLOW),
//              DISP=(,KEEP),
//              UNIT=SYSDA,
//              VOL=SER=WYL005,
//              SPACE=(CYL,(5)),
//              DCB=*.DD2ISAMB
```

The DCB information in the DD statements must be the same in all of the statements; the backward reference in the second DD statement in both Figure 11.11 and Figure 11.12 ensures agreement.

The disposition for the data sets is KEEP. In these two cases CATALG cannot be specified. If you wish to catalog an ISAM data set defined with two or three DD statements, the utility IEHPROGM may be used. IEHPROGM may be used to catalog an ISAM data set as long as all the parts of the data set reside on the same type of device. For example, in Figure 11.12 the prime and index areas of ISAM3 are on disk pack WYL004, and the overflow area is on WYL005. Both these disk packs are 3380s, so IEHPROGM may be used to catalog ISAM3. If the volumes were different types (for example, if WYL004 were a 3380, but WYL005 were a 3350), the data set could not be cataloged.

Figure 11.13 shows how IEHPROGM may be used to catalog ISAM3. Notice

■ Figure 11.13 ■

Cataloging an ISAM Data Set

```
//JCLQB810 JOB ,'J.C.LEWIS',
//              REGION=48K
//CATALOG   EXEC PGM=IEHPROGM
//SYSPRINT DD SYSOUT=A
//DD2       DD UNIT=SYSDA,
//              VOL=SER=(WYL004,WYL005),
//              DISP=OLD
//SYSIN     DD *
 CATLG DSNAME=WYL.QB.JCL.ISAM3,                              *
              VOL=SYSDA=(WYL004,WYL005)
/*
//
```

that all the volumes on which the data set resides must be named in both the DD statement and the control statement. The use of IEHPROGM is discussed more fully in Chapter 13.

Using Three DD Statements

Figure 11.14 illustrates the JCL used to create an ISAM data set with all three DD statements. All three parts of the ISAM data set are on the same volume. If speed of operation were important, however, it would be wise to place the index area and the prime on different volumes, thus eliminating the need for the access arm to move with each read.

Multivolume Data Sets

If you are dealing with a very large ISAM data set, you want to use more than one volume. Figure 11.15 illustrates the coding in this case. Notice that INDEX consists of 10 cylinders on volume WYL001, OVFLOW consists of 50 cylinders on volume WYL005, and PRIME consists of 300 cylinders (100 cylinders each on volumes WYL002, WYL003, and WYL004).

You might not have expected that 100 cylinders would be taken from each of the three volumes, because you learned in Chapter 10 that, for sequential data sets, the primary request is taken from the first-named volume and the other volumes are used only to satisfy the secondary requests. But the space allocation works differently for ISAM data sets. When the DD statement that

■ Figure 11.14 ■

Creating an ISAM Data Set Using Three DD Statements

```
//ISAMDD3   DD DSN=WYL.QB.JCL.ISAM4(INDEX),
//             DISP=(,KEEP),
//             UNIT=SYSDA,
//             VOL=SER=WYL004,
//             SPACE=(CYL,(1)),
//             DCB=(DSORG=IS,RECFM=FB,LRECL=80,BLKSIZE=1680,
//             KEYLEN=5,RKP=1,CYLOFL=2,NTM=4,OPTCD=ILMRUWY)
//           DD DSN=WYL.QB.JCL.ISAM4(PRIME),
//             DISP=(,KEEP),
//             UNIT=SYSDA,
//             VOL=REF=*.ISAMDD3,
//             SPACE=(CYL,(10)),
//             DCB=*.ISAMDD3
//           DD DSN=WYL.QB.JCL.ISAM4(OVFLOW),
//             DISP=(,KEEP),
//             UNIT=SYSDA,
//             VOL=REF=*.ISAMDD3,
//             SPACE=(CYL,(5)),
//             DCB=*.ISAMDD3
```

Figure 11.15

Creating an ISAM Data Set on Multiple Volumes

```
//ISAMDD4   DD DSN=WYL.QB.JCL.ISAM5(INDEX),
//             DISP=(,KEEP),
//             UNIT=SYSDA,
//             VOL=SER=WYL001,
//             SPACE=(CYL,(10)),
//             DCB=(DSORG=IS,RECFM=FB,LRECL=80,BLKSIZE=1680,
//             KEYLEN=5,RKP=1,CYLOFL=2,NTM=4,OPTCD=ILMRUWY)
//          DD DSN=WYL.QB.JCL.ISAM5(PRIME),
//             DISP=(,KEEP),
//             UNIT=(SYSDA,3),
//             VOL=SER=(WYL002,WYL003,WYL004),
//             SPACE=(CYL,(100)),
//             DCB=*.ISAMDD4
//          DD DSN=WYL.QB.JCL.ISAM5(OVFLOW),
//             DISP=(,KEEP),
//             UNIT=SYSDA,
//             VOL=SER=WYL005,
//             SPACE=(CYL,(50)),
//             DCB=*.ISAMDD4
```

defines the prime area names more than one volume, the number of cylinders requested is taken from each of the volumes.

JCL to Access an ISAM Data Set

When an ISAM data set is created, from one to three DD statements are used, as illustrated in Figures 11.10, 11.11, 11.12, 11.14, and 11.15. Accessing any of these data sets, however, requires only one DD statement. Figure 11.16 shows how ISAM4, which was created in Figure 11.14 using three DD statements, may be accessed using only one DD statement. Notice that to access an ISAM data set you do not have to include the qualifiers INDEX, PRIME, or OVFLOW, even though they may have been used when the data set was created. When you update a data set, code a disposition of OLD, as shown in Figure 11.16. This

Figure 11.16

Accessing an ISAM Data Set

```
//ISAMREAD DD DSN=WYL.QB.JCL.ISAM4,
//            DISP=OLD,
//            UNIT=SYSDA,
//            VOL=SER=WYL004,
//            DCB=DSORG=IS
```

prevents another program from reading the data set while this program is in the process of changing it. When you read a data set, you do not need exclusive control; there is no problem with having other programs read the data set at the same time. Consequently you code a disposition of SHR, which permits multiple use of the data set.

In Figure 11.16 the one required DCB subparameter, DSORG=IS, is coded. The other DCB information is not necessary; it can be found in the data set control block. DSORG=IS tells the system that this data set is an ISAM data set, something the system must know before it reads the data set control block (DSCB). There are a few conditions under which it is not necessary to code DCB=DSORG=IS, but they are rather complex, so why bother remembering them when it is always correct to code DCB=DSORG=IS?

Figure 11.17 shows JCL to access ISAM data sets on multiple volumes. The first example shows how to access ISAM5, which was created in Figure 11.15 using three DD statements and which resides on five volumes. The unit parameter indicates five devices, and five serial numbers are specified in the volume parameter. Even though the data set was created with multiple DD statements, because all the volumes are the same type only one DD statement is required to access it. The second example in Figure 11.17 illustrates a situation in which multiple DD statements are required. The first DD statement indicates a 3330 disk drive, and the second shows a 2314. It is the difference in device type that creates the need for multiple DD statements. When multiple DD statements are used to access an ISAM data set, they must be concatenated and coded in the order in which they were coded when the data set was created.

■ **Figure 11.17** ■

Accessing Multivolume ISAM Data Sets

```
//ISAMUPD1 DD  DSN=WYL.QB.JCL.ISAM5,
//             DISP=SHR,
//             UNIT=(SYSDA,5),
//             VOL=SER=(WYL001,WYL002,WYL003,WYL004,WYL005),
//             DCB=DSORG=IS


//ISAMUDD2 DD  DSN=WYL.QB.JCL.ISAM6,
//             DISP=SHR,
//             UNIT=3330,
//             VOL=SER=WYL003,
//             DCB=DSORG=IS
//          DD DSN=WYL.QB.JCL.ISAM6,
//             DISP=SHR,
//             UNIT=(2314,2),
//             VOL=SER=(DISK01,DISK02),
//             DCB=DSORG=IS
```

If the ISAM data set is cataloged, as ISAM3 was cataloged in Figure 11.13, it can, like any other cataloged data set, be accessed through coding of only DSN and DISP; UNIT and VOL can be omitted. For ISAM data sets, however, you must always code DCB=DSORG=IS to be safe.

ISAM and Generation Data Groups

ISAM data sets do not naturally form generation data groups; they have to be forced into the mold. After the ISAM data set is created, perhaps using JCL similar to that shown in Figure 11.14, a job similar to that shown in Figure 11.18 is run. The first command for the utility program IEHPROGM renames the ISAM data set to give it the next generation number and any version number you wish. In the example in Figure 11.18, the generation number is 36 and the version is 00. After the data set is renamed, it is cataloged and becomes part of the generation data group.

Figure 11.18

Creating a Generation Data Group from an ISAM Data Set

```
//JCLQB820  JOB ,'RICK',
//               REGION=48K
//ISAMGDG   EXEC PGM=IEHPROGM
//SYSPRINT DD SYSOUT=A
//DD1       DD UNIT=SYSDA,
//               VOL=SER=WYL004,
//               DISP=OLD
//SYSIN     DD *
 RENAME DSNAME=WYL.QB.JCL.ISAM4,VOL=SYSDA=WYL004,               *
              NEWNAME=WYL.QB.JCL.ISAM4.G0036V00
 CATLG DSNAME=WYL.QB.JCL.ISAM4.G0036V00,VOL=SYSDA=WYL004
/*
//
```

Loading an ISAM Data Set

Loading an ISAM data set usually requires a program written in assembler, COBOL, or PL/I. Writing a creation program that is used once and then discarded is wasteful of programming effort. (Remember that you, the programmer, are the most expensive part of a data processing installation.) There must be a better way, and its name is IEBDG.

IEBDG

IEBDG is a utility program designed to produce test data, but it may also be used to create an ISAM data set. Let us first consider the simple case of creating an ISAM file named POLYISAM, using POLYFILE as input. The job stream is shown in Figure 11.19.

When an ISAM data set is created, the data must be presented in sort sequence. Each time a record is written, the system checks the key to make sure that it is greater than the key of the previously written record. For that reason it is usual to sort the input data set before using it to create the ISAM data set. By inspecting the listing of POLYFILE in Chapter 4, we can see that it is already in sort sequence. Consequently, we do not have to sort it. You should keep in mind, however, the general requirement that data sets used to create ISAM data sets must be in sort sequence.

Look at the control statements in Figure 11.19. The first control statement is the DSD statement, which must be first and which is used to supply the ddnames of the data sets to be used. Notice that the ddnames must be enclosed in parentheses.

The next two statements are FD (field definition) statements. These statements define the fields that are used to create the output record. The first FD statement creates data to be used for the delete byte. It names and describes a field that starts in the first byte of the output record and is 1 byte long. The name supplied is BYTE0. You know that it is the first byte because START-

■ **Figure 11.19** ■

Creating an ISAM Data Set Using IEBDG

```
//JCLQB830 JOB ,'ILSA LUND',
//               REGION=32K
//CREATE EXEC PGM=IEBDG
//SYSPRINT DD SYSOUT=A
//SEQIN     DD DSN=WYL.QB.JCL.POLYFILE,
//             DISP=SHR
//ISAM      DD DSN=WYL.QB.JCL.POLYISAM,
//             DISP=(NEW,CATLG),
//             UNIT=DISK,
//             VOL=SER=SCR001,
//             SPACE=(CYL,1),
//             DCB=(DSORG=IS,RKP=1,KEYLEN=5,OPTCD=YL,CYLOFL=2,
//             RECFM=FB,LRECL=81,BLKSIZE=810)
//SYSIN DD *
 DSD OUTPUT=(ISAM),INPUT=(SEQIN)
 FD NAME=BYTE0,LENGTH=1,STARTLOC=1,FILL=X'00'
 FD NAME=FLD1,LENGTH=80,STARTLOC=2,FROMLOC=1,INPUT=SEQIN
 CREATE NAME=(BYTE0,FLD1),INPUT=SEQIN
 END
/*
//
```

LOC=1 is coded, and you know that its length is 1 byte because LENGTH=1 is coded. The FILL parameter specifies that this field will contain hexadecimal zeros, which is exactly what is desired for the delete byte.

The second FD statement copies data from the input data set. FLD1 is 80 bytes long and starts in the second byte of the output record. The data for this field will be copied from the input data set identified by the ddname SEQIN. Eighty bytes will be copied, starting in the first byte (FROMLOC=1) of each input record.

The next control statement is the CREATE statement, which is used to specify the data to be included in the output record. In this case the output record will consist of the two fields named BYTE0 and FLD1. INPUT=SEQIN is also coded to specify the ddname of the data set that will provide the input data. Notice that the ddname of the input data set is specified on both the FD and the CREATE statements.

The last control statement in the job is the END statement. It marks the end of the group of control statements that apply to the creation of the data set named in the previous DSD control statement. Another group of control statements starting with a DSD statement could follow this END statement. In this case no other control statements are coded, so the END statement could have been omitted.

Notice that because POLYISAM was created using only one DD statement, a disposition of CATLG could legally be coded.

The result of executing this job will be the creation of a cataloged ISAM data set named POLYISAM, containing the same data as are in POLYFILE.

The control statements in Figure 11.19 are complicated because the delete byte had to be added to the data record in POLYFILE. The control statements could be simplified if the records in POLYISAM were made exactly the same as the records in POLYFILE. In that case the DSD statement would remain the same, but the two FD statements would be eliminated and the CREATE statement would be simplified to

```
CREATE INPUT=SEQIN
```

There are situations in which the information used for an ISAM record is computed from multiple sources. In such cases you cannot create the data set by copying information from a sequential data set. You do not, however, want to invest time developing another program whose purpose would be to create the ISAM data set with dummy records. Figure 11.20 illustrates a job that copies the input information without requiring a separate create program.

Note that there is no input parameter in the DSD control statement. Because there is no input data set in this example, the input parameter is not required. The data to be written in the output records are generated in the two FD control statements. The first sets the delete byte in the output record to hexadecimal FF. The only difference between this FD control statement and the first one in Figure 11.19 is the value coded for the FILL parameter.

■ **Figure 11.20** ■

Creating an ISAM Data Set with Dummy Records Using IEBDG

```
//JCLQB840 JOB ,'VICTOR LASZLO',
//               REGION=32K
//ISAMDUM EXEC PGM=IEBDG
//SYSPRINT DD SYSOUT=A
//ISAMOUT  DD DSN=WYL.QB.JCL.ISAM8,
//               DISP=(,CATLG),
//               UNIT=SYSDA,
//               VOL=SER=SCR001,
//               SPACE=(CYL,1),
//               DCB=(DSORG=IS,RECFM=FB,LRECL=75,BLKSIZE=1500,
//               KEYLEN=10,RKP=1,CYLOFL=2,OPTCD=LY)
//SYSIN      DD *
 DSD OUTPUT=(ISAMOUT)
 FD NAME=BYTE0,LENGTH=1,STARTLOC=1,FILL=X'FF'
 FD NAME=KEYFD,LENGTH=10,STARTLOC=2,FORMAT=PD,INDEX=10
 CREATE NAME=(BYTE0,KEYFD),QUANTITY=100,FILL=X'40'
 /*
 //
```

In this example the FILL parameter is used to set the field equal to hexadecimal FF.

The next FD control statement sets the value of the key field. Note that the LENGTH agrees with the KEYLEN subparameter of the DCB parameter, and the STARTLOC agrees with the RKP subparameter. The FORMAT=PD parameter indicates that the field should contain packed decimal data. Zoned decimal (ZD), binary (BI), alphameric (AN), or alphabetic (AL) could have been specified instead of PD. For numeric fields the first value generated is +1. For packed and binary numbers, SIGN=- can be coded to generate -1.

INDEX=10 means that 10 will be added to this packed decimal field each time it is used. Consequently, the first record will have a packed decimal field containing a 1; the second, an 11; and so on. The value coded for INDEX must be positive.

The CREATE statement defines the output record as consisting of the two fields defined with the FD statements. The record length in the DCB parameter of the DD statement is 75. The combined length of the two defined fields is 11, leaving 64 bytes to be defined. The FILL parameter in the CREATE statement supplies the data for these 64 bytes. The record created as a result of this operation will have a hexadecimal FF in the first, or delete, byte; a packed decimal number in the second through eleventh bytes; and blanks (hexadecimal 40) in the rest of the record. The QUANTITY parameter indicates that 100 records are to be created.

Study the example in Figure 11.20 carefully, because you are likely to need this coding. You do not often have the data prepared as a sequential data set, as illustrated in Figure 11.19. Usually you must write a program that creates the data from multiple sources. If you understand the example in Figure 11.20, you can avoid writing a creation program. You can use IEBDG to create the data set with dummy records and then use your update program to actually store information in the ISAM data set.

You will find more information about IEBDG in Chapter 13.

Using IEBISAM

IEBISAM is the utility program used to process ISAM data sets. It offers four functions: load, unload, copy, and print. IEBISAM is different from most utility programs in that there are no control statements. The PARM field is used to tell IEBISAM what should be done.

IEBISAM Print

The basic print function is the easiest to understand. Figure 11.21 illustrates the JCL required to print a data set in character format. The job consists of a JOB statement, an EXEC statement, and three DD statements whose ddnames are SYSPRINT, SYSUT1, and SYSUT2.

The three DD statements have the same functions for IEBISAM as they do for IEBGENER and IEBPTPCH: SYSPRINT is for messages, SYSUT1 is for the input data set, and SYSUT2 is for the output data set. IEBISAM does not use control statements, so a SYSIN DD statement is not required.

For the print operation, SYSUT1 is the ISAM data set to be printed, and SYSUT2 directs the output to the printer. Coding PARM='PRINTL,N' in the EXEC statement causes the ISAM data set to be printed in character form. The apostrophes are necessary because of the comma in the PARM field. If PARM=PRINTL is coded, the ISAM data set is printed in hexadecimal form.

■ Figure 11.21 ■

Printing an ISAM Data Set Using IEBISAM

```
//JCLQB850 JOB ,'LOUIS RENAULT',
//               REGION=32K
//LIST   EXEC   PGM=IEBISAM,PARM='PRINTL,N'
//SYSPRINT DD SYSOUT=A
//SYSUT1    DD DSN=WYL.QB.JCL.POLYISAM,
//              DISP=SHR,
//              DCB=DSORG=IS
//SYSUT2    DD SYSOUT=A
//
```

IEBISAM Copy

Figure 11.22 illustrates the copy operation. IEBISAM knows that a copy operation is to be performed because PARM=COPY is coded in the EXEC statement. SYSUT1 points to the ISAM data set to be copied. SYSUT2 defines the new ISAM data set named COPYISAM. For the DCB parameter only the required DSORG=IS is coded. The other DCB parameters will be copied from POLY-ISAM. Because L was specified for the DCB subparameter OPTCD when POLYISAM was created, records marked for deletion will not be copied to COPYISAM. Any records that are in the cylinder overflow area will be inserted in their proper places in the prime area of COPYISAM. If POLYISAM had an independent overflow area, records from it would also be inserted in their proper places in the prime area.

IEBISAM Unload

The unload operation creates a physical sequential data set from the ISAM data set. The physical sequential data set produced by IEBISAM consists of 80-byte records regardless of the record length of the ISAM data set. In Figure 11.23, which illustrates the JCL for the unload operation, the output is blocked, but you may choose not to block the output or to block at a different value. The ISAM data set is unloaded to a volume of tape. Depending on your needs, you might choose to unload a disk pack. Why bother to unload at all? One reason, indicated by the data set name selected, is to create a back-up copy. If for some reason the ISAM data set on disk were destroyed, it could in part be re-created from the back-up copy. If the changes made to the ISAM data set since the back-up copy was created were retained, the ISAM data set could be completely re-created. Another reason to unload an ISAM data set would be to move the ISAM data set to another system.

■ **Figure 11.22** ■

Copying an ISAM Data Set Using IEBISAM

```
//JCLQB860  JOB ,'STRASSER',
//              REGION=32K
//COPYISM   EXEC PGM=IEBISAM,PARM=COPY
//SYSPRINT DD SYSOUT=A
//SYSUT1    DD DSN=WYL.QB.JCL.POLYISAM,
//              DISP=SHR,
//              DCB=DSORG=IS
//SYSUT2    DD DSN=WYL.QB.JCL.COPYISAM,
//              DISP=(,CATLG),
//              UNIT=SYSDA,
//              VOL=SER=SCR001,
//              SPACE=(CYL,(1),),
//              DCB=DSORG=IS
//
```

Figure 11.23

Unloading an ISAM Data Set Using IEBISAM

```
//JCLQB870 JOB ,'FERRARI',
//              REGION=32K
//UNLOAD   EXEC PGM=IEBISAM,PARM=UNLOAD
//SYSPRINT DD SYSOUT=A
//SYSUT1   DD DSN=WYL.QB.JCL.POLYISAM,
//              DISP=SHR,
//              DCB=DSORG=IS
//SYSUT2   DD DSN=WYL.QB.JCL.BACKUP,
//              DISP=(,CATLG),
//              UNIT=TAPE,
//              DCB=(RECFM=FB,LRECL=80,BLKSIZE=1600)
//
```

You will notice that no VOL parameter is coded. This permits the operator to mount any available tape volume for output. The volume serial number can be learned from the deallocation message.

IEBISAM Load

The load function uses as input the physical sequential data set created by an IEBISAM unload operation. The output is an ISAM data set. Figure 11.24 shows how BACKUP may be used to create NEWISAM. The key length and relative key position must be the same as in the original ISAM data set. If the records are of fixed length, the record length cannot be changed in the new ISAM data set. If the records are of variable length, the record length may be increased. In either case the blocking may be changed.

The only DCB subparameter coded is the required DSORG=IS, so the other DCB subparameters of NEWISAM will be copied from the ISAM data set used to

Figure 11.24

Loading an ISAM Data Set Using IEBISAM

```
//JCLQB880 JOB ,'UGARTE',
//              REGION=32K
//LOADISM  EXEC PGM=IEBISAM,PARM=LOAD
//SYSPRINT DD SYSOUT=A
//SYSUT1   DD DSN=WYL.QB.JCL.BACKUP,
//              DISP=OLD
//SYSUT2   DD DSN=WYL.QB.JCL.NEWISAM,
//              DISP=(,CATLG),
//              UNIT=SYSDA,
//              VOL=SER=SCR001,
//              SPACE=(CYL,(1)),
//              DCB=DSORG=IS
//
```

■ **Figure 11.25** ■■■■■■■■■■■■■■■■■■■■■■■■■■■■■■■■■■■■

Using an IEBISAM Exit

```
//JCLQB890 JOB ,'SAM',
//          REGION=32K
//LIST     EXEC  PGM=IEBISAM,PARM='PRINTL,N,EXIT=ISAMUPLO'
//STEPLIB  DD DSN=WYL.QB.JCL.LOADLIB,
//            DISP=SHR
//SYSPRINT DD SYSOUT=A
//SYSUT1   DD DSN=WYL.QB.JCL.ISAMLOW,
//            DISP=OLD
//SYSUT2   DD SYSOUT=A
//
```

create BACKUP, which was POLYISAM. Because L was included in the OPTCD subparameter of POLYISAM, records marked for deletion will not appear in the new data set. Records that were in the cylinder overflow area will be merged into the prime area of NEWISAM. If POLYISAM had an independent overflow area, records from it would also be inserted in their proper places in the prime area.

IEBISAM Exit*

It is sometimes desirable to have IEBISAM pass control to a user-written program before it processes each record, so that the user-written program can modify the record. This process is called linking to an exit routine. As an example of when you might want to use an exit routine, consider the following situation. IEBISAM is to print an ISAM data set, but the data set contains both upper- and lower-case letters and the printer available has only upper-case letters. An assembler language program is written to convert lower-case letters to upper case and leave all other characters unchanged. The program is compiled and link edited and stored in the load library named LOADLIB under the name ISAMUPLO.

Figure 11.25 shows how coding EXIT=ISAMUPLO in the PARM field causes IEBISAM to pass control to ISAMUPLO. A STEPLIB statement is also included to make LOADLIB available.

Every time it reads a record from the SYSUT1 data set, IEBISAM invokes the exit program with the instruction

```
BALR     14,15
```

The exit routine ISAMUPLO can expect to find the address of an input record buffer in register 1 and the address of the record heading buffer in register 0.

---

* Those unfamiliar with assembly language might prefer to skip this section.

ISAMUPLO must save registers 2 through 14 so that when ISAMUPLO ends the registers may be restored before control is returned to IEBISAM. Register 14 will contain the address inside IEBISAM to which control is to be passed when ISAMUPLO completes its function. The instruction to return control to IEBISAM is

```
BR          14
```

Before control is returned to IEBISAM, a value of either 0, 4, 8, or 12 must be stored in register 15. A 0 means that the content of the input buffer is to be printed; a 4 means that the content of the input buffer is to be printed and the operation is to be terminated; an 8 means that processing is to continue but nothing is to be printed; a 12 indicates that nothing is to be printed and the operation is to be terminated.

The assembler language program that converts lower-case letters to upper case is shown in Figure 11.26. Notice the technique used to access the record. Recall that IEBISAM puts the address of the input record buffer in register 1. As the comment in the program indicates, IEBGENER and IEBPTPCH also provide for user-written exit routines, but they use a different addressing scheme, and the L (load) instruction, which is shown in the program as a comment, must be included.

Figure 11.26

Sample Program Used as an IEBISAM Exit

```
ISAMUPLO CSECT
         STM  R14,R12,12(R13)      SAVE REGISTERS
         BALR R12,0                LOAD ADDRESS INTO R12
         USING *,R12               ESTABLISH R12 AS BASE REG
         LA   R2,SAVEAREA          HOUSEKEEPING
         ST   R2,8(R13)
         ST   R13,4(R2)
         LR   R13,R2
* IEBGENER AND IEBPTPCH WORK SLIGHTLY DIFFERENTLY.
* WHEN THIS PROGRAM IS USED WITH IEBGENER OR IEBPTPCH
* THE FOLLOWING STATEMENT (WHICH IS HERE A COMMENT) MUST BE INCLUDED
*        L    R1,0(R1)             GET PARM ADDRESS
*
         TR   0(80,R1),TRTABLE     TRANSLATE LOWER CASE CHARS
         L    R13,4(R13)           GET SAVE AREA
         SR   R15,R15              CLEAR RC
         ST   R15,16(R13)          SAVE RC
         LM   R14,R12,12(R13)      RESTORE REGS
         BR   R14                  RETURN TO IEBISAM
*
*
SAVEAREA DS   18F                  SAVE AREA OS
TRTABLE  DC   CL256' '
         ORG  TRTABLE
```

Cont.

```
        ORG    TRTABLE+X'81'
        DC     C'ABCDEFGHI'
        ORG    TRTABLE+X'91'
        DC     C'JKLMNOPQR'
        ORG    TRTABLE+X'A2'
        DC     C'STUVWXYZ'
        ORG    TRTABLE+C'A'
        DC     C'ABCDEFGHI'
        ORG    TRTABLE+C'J'
        DC     C'JKLMNOPQR'
        ORG    TRTABLE+C'S'
        DC     C'STUVWXYZ'
        ORG    TRTABLE+C'0'
        DC     C'0123456789'
        ORG    TRTABLE+X'4A'
        DC     X'4A4B4C4D4E4F50'
        ORG    TRTABLE+X'5A'
        DC     X'5A5B5C5D5E5F606162'
        ORG    TRTABLE+X'6A'
        DC     X'6A6B6C6D6E6F'
        ORG    TRTABLE+X'79'
        DC     X'797A7B7C7D7E7F80'
        ORG    TRTABLE+X'8B'
        DC     X'8B8C8D8E8F'
        ORG    TRTABLE+X'9B'
        DC     X'9B9C9D9E9FA0A1'
R0      EQU    0
R1      EQU    1
R2      EQU    2
R3      EQU    3
R4      EQU    4
R5      EQU    5
R6      EQU    6
R7      EQU    7
R8      EQU    8
R9      EQU    9
R10     EQU    10
R11     EQU    11
R12     EQU    12
R13     EQU    13
R14     EQU    14
R15     EQU    15
        END
```

Reorganization

As mentioned earlier, records in the overflow areas take longer to access than do records in the prime area. Therefore, after a number of records have been added to an ISAM data set, performance deteriorates. Also, records marked for deletion are not actually deleted and continue to take up space. For these two reasons, ISAM data sets are periodically reorganized. When a **reorganiza-**

tion of an ISAM data set is carried out, a new ISAM data set is created, which differs from the original data set in two ways: (1) records marked for deletion are not included in the new data set, and (2) records written in the cylinder overflow and independent overflow area are integrated into the prime area. Consequently, when you reorganize an ISAM data set, you recover lost space from the deleted records. You also get faster access time, because all the records are in the prime area and only one data access is required.

There are two principal ways to reorganize an ISAM data set. Both methods, each involving two steps, are illustrated in Figure 11.27. In the first case IEBISAM is executed twice. In the first execution the ISAM data set is unloaded to tape, and in the second execution the data set on tape is loaded back to disk. The unloaded data set is shown as residing on tape; disk could have been specified instead. The advantage of tape is that it may be retained for use as a back-up. This approach accomplishes two maintenance tasks with one job: It reorganizes the ISAM data set and provides a back-up.

The advantage to the second approach shown in Figure 11.27 is that it is faster. The system processes the ISAM data set only once. In the first step IEBISAM is used to copy the ISAM data set to another DASD location, which may be on the same disk pack if there is enough space. In the second step the utility program IEHPROGM is used first to scratch the original ISAM data set and then to change the name of (rename) the new ISAM data set from the current value to the original name.

ISAM and Higher-Level Languages

The purpose of this section is not to teach you how to access ISAM data sets from your COBOL and PL/I programs, but rather to give you sufficient background so that you can tie together your newly acquired JCL knowledge and your COBOL and PL/I knowledge.

ISAM and COBOL*

Creating an ISAM Data Set. Your COBOL program must have a SELECT statement for the ISAM data set. For example, you could code

```
SELECT ISAM-DATA-FILE
    ASSIGN TO DA-I-ISAMDD
    RECORD KEY IS KEY-VAL
    ACCESS IS SEQUENTIAL.
```

---

* Those who are not familiar with COBOL should skip this section.

**(a) System Flowchart to Reorganize an ISAM Data Set Using
IEBISAM**

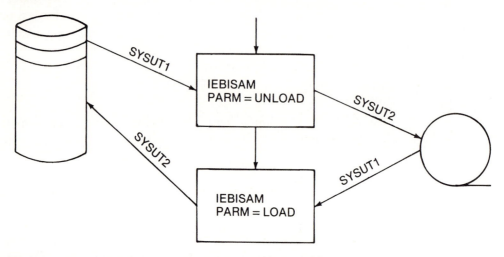

**(b) System Flowchart to Reorganize an ISAM Data Set Using
IEBISAM and IEHPROGM**

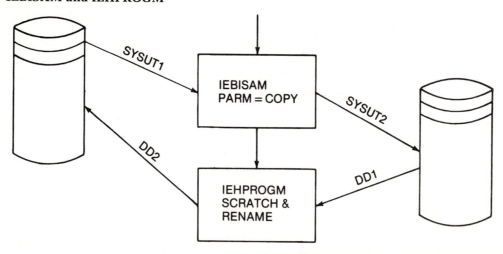

ACCESS IS SEQUENTIAL is the default, so that clause is optional. The ddname on the DD statement referencing the ISAM data set is ISAMDD. The record key KEY-VAL must be part of the ISAM data set's record. You might have coded

```
FD  ISAM-DATA-FILE
    RECORD CONTAINS...
    BLOCK CONTAINS...
    LABEL RECORDS ARE STANDARD.
01  ISAM-RECORD.
    05 DELETE-BYTE          PIC X.
    05 KEY-VAL              PIC ...
    05 ...
```

In creating an ISAM data set, you must access it sequentially and open it as OUTPUT. For example, you could code

```
OPEN OUTPUT ISAM-DATA-FILE.
```

The data set is created using a WRITE statement with an INVALID KEY clause, such as

```
WRITE ISAM-RECORD
      INVALID KEY PERFORM BAD-WRITE-RTN.
```

The INVALID KEY clause is executed if the record key of the current record is less than or equal to the record key of the previously written record.

Randomly Updating an ISAM Data Set. The SELECT sentence to randomly access an ISAM data set could be

```
SELECT ISAM-DATA-FILE
    ASSIGN TO DA-I-ISAMDD
    RECORD KEY IS KEY-VAL
    NOMINAL KEY IS KEY-VAL-WS
    ACCESS IS RANDOM.
```

The NOMINAL KEY field must be defined in WORKING-STORAGE and must have the same PICTURE and USAGE as the RECORD KEY field.

To update an ISAM data set, you must open it as I-O. For example, you could code

```
OPEN I-O ISAM-DATA-FILE.
```

To randomly update an ISAM data set, you must move the key of the record that is to be updated into the NOMINAL KEY field, as, for example, by coding

```
MOVE KEY-IN TO KEY-VALUE-WS.
```

A READ statement retrieves the record:

```
READ ISAM-DATA-FILE
      INVALID KEY PERFORM BAD-READ-RTN.
```

The INVALID KEY clause is executed if the file does not contain a record whose key is equal to the value in the NOMINAL KEY field.

After the record has been updated, it is placed back in the data set using a REWRITE statement:

```
REWRITE ISAM-RECORD
      INVALID KEY PERFORM BAD-REWRITE-RTN.
```

The INVALID KEY clause will be executed if the NOMINAL KEY and RECORD KEY fields do not contain the same value. It is hard to see how that could happen, but imaginative students have been known to find a way.

Deleting records is a variation on updating. The first byte must be changed to hexadecimal FF, as, for example, through the statement

```
MOVE HIGH-VALUES TO DELETE-BYTE.
```

Then the record is rewritten. Records may be deleted only if L was specified as a value for the DCB subparameter OPTCD.

To add a record, you use the WRITE statement. First the key value is moved to the NOMINAL KEY field, and then a WRITE statement is executed:

```
WRITE ISAM-RECORD
      INVALID KEY PERFORM BAD-ADD-RTN.
```

The INVALID KEY clause is executed if the data set already contains a record with a key equal to the value in the NOMINAL KEY field.

ISAM and PL/I*

Your PL/I program must have a DECLARE statement for the ISAM data set. If the data set is to be accessed sequentially,

```
DCL ISAMFLE FILE RECORD INPUT ENV (INDEXED);
```

is valid. If the data set is to be accessed randomly, the DECLARE statement must include the parameter KEYED, as in

```
DCL ISAMFLE FILE RECORD INPUT KEYED ENV (INDEXED);
```

In any case, ISAMFLE would be the ddname in the DD statement referencing the ISAM data set.

If you are reading the records sequentially, either

```
READ FILE (ISAMFLE) INTO (REC);
```

or

```
READ FILE (ISAMFLE) SET (PTR);
```

---

* Those who are not familiar with PL/I should skip this section.

will work. If you wish to read a particular record, the READ statement becomes

```
READ FILE (ISAMFLE) INTO (REC) KEY (KEY_VAL);
```

or

```
READ FILE (ISAMFLE) SET (PTR) KEY (KEY_VAL);
```

The variable KEY_VAL would be the length of the key and would be set equal to the key of the record being sought.

If you wish to add a record to an ISAM data set, the file declaration must specify OUTPUT instead of INPUT and the WRITE statement should be in the form

```
WRITE FILE (ISAMFLE) FROM (REC) KEYFROM (KEY_VAL);
```

The KEYFROM parameter indicates where the record key may be found. The key field is usually indicated in the record to be written.

If you wish to change a record, the file declaration must specify UPDATE. For example, you could code

```
DCL ISAMFLE FILE RECORD KEYED UPDATE ENV (INDEXED);
```

The rewrite may be coded as

```
REWRITE FILE (ISAMFLE);
```

in which case the record will be written as it appears in the input buffer. Or it may be coded as

```
REWRITE FILE (ISAMFLE) FROM (REC);
```

in which case the record to be written will be found in the variable REC.

Records may be deleted either by using the DELETE statement, as in

```
DELETE FILE (ISAMFLE) KEY (KEY_VAL);
```

or by rewriting the record after setting the delete byte (byte 0) equal to hexadecimal FF.

Your program should include the ONKEY condition in which the ONCODE value is tested. Within the ONKEY condition, an ONCODE value of 51 indicates that the record is not in the file, 52 indicates an attempt to add a duplicate record, 53 indicates an attempt to load a record out of sequence, and 57 means that there is no more space left for the record.

Summary

In this chapter you have learned

—how ISAM data sets are organized

—how to write DD statements to create and access ISAM data sets

—how to use IEBDG to create an ISAM data set

—how to use IEBISAM to print, copy, load, and unload an ISAM data set

—how to reorganize an ISAM data set and why ISAM data sets must be reorganized

—how to code an exit from IEBISAM (if you are an assembler programmer)

—how to use ISAM data sets in your COBOL and PL/I programs

Vocabulary

In this chapter you have been introduced to the meanings of the following terms:

basic direct access method (BDAM)	key
cylinder index	master index
cylinder overflow	overflow area
delete byte	prime area
index area	random access
indexed sequential access method (ISAM)	relative key position (RKP)
	reorganization

Exercises

1. Can an ISAM or BDAM file be written on tape?
2. What is a key?
3. How does the system locate a record in a BDAM data set?
4. How many parts may an ISAM data set contain? What are they?
5. How many different types of indexes are there in an ISAM data set? What are they? Where are they found?
6. What has to be done to data before they are loaded into an ISAM data set?
7. Would an allocation of seven tracks for the prime area be enough?
8. When you examine a DD statement, what tells you that it represents an ISAM data set?
9. What are the functions that may be performed by the utility program IEBISAM?
10. Why would you reorganize an ISAM data set?

Programming Assignments

1. Execute a job that uses IEBDG to create an ISAM data set. As input use the sequential data set you created for the Programming Assignment in Chapter 3.
2. Execute a job to have IEBISAM print the data set you created in Programming Assignment 1.
3. Execute a job to reorganize the data set you created in Programming Assignment 1.

12

VSAM Data Sets

In this chapter you will learn

- types and organization of VSAM data sets
- the JCL used to access VSAM data sets
- how to use access method services to

    delete a VSAM data set

    print a VSAM data set

    load a VSAM data set

    create a VSAM data set

    create a VSAM user catalog

    correct a cluster

Types of VSAM Data Sets

VSAM data sets come in three flavors. There are key sequence data sets, entry sequence data sets, and relative record data sets.

A **key sequence data set (KSDS)** has in the records identifying keys that may be used to read a particular record. A KSDS is the VSAM equivalent of an ISAM data set, and like an ISAM data set it has an index portion and a data portion. In VSAM these two pieces form a **cluster**, and usually it is the cluster name that is given as the data set name in the DD statement. Unlike ISAM, VSAM has no overflow area. When a KSDS is created, unused space may be scattered throughout the data set; when records are added later, they are inserted in this unused space, or **freespace**.

The records of a VSAM KSDS may have more than one key field. One of the record keys, called the **prime key**, is the primary identifier of the record. Together, the index of prime keys and the data portion of the data set are called the **base cluster**. Each additional record key is known as an **alternate key**. A separate **alternate index** is built for each such key.

In an **entry sequence data set (ESDS)**, records are stored in the order in which they are entered, as you might guess from the name entry sequence. An ESDS is the VSAM equivalent of a physical sequential data set. New records may be added only to the end of an ESDS. Unlike a KSDS, an ESDS consists of only one piece, the data portion. Each record in an ESDS is located by its **relative byte address (RBA)**, which is the number of bytes from the beginning of the data set to the first byte of the record. An alternate index, however, can be set up for an ESDS. Here is the apparently crazy case of a data set in its base form being equivalent to a physical sequential data set but capable of being accessed by a key. As with a KSDS, there may be more than one alternate index.

A **relative record data set (RRDS)** is halfway between a KSDS and an ESDS. An RRDS is the VSAM equivalent of a direct data set. Like an ESDS, an RRDS has only a data portion. On the other hand, records can be inserted randomly in a manner reminiscent of a KSDS. In an RRDS each record is uniquely identified by its position in the data set — that is, its record number, 1, 2, 3, etc. All RRDSs must consist of fixed length records. Unlike KSDSs and ESDSs, RRDSs may not have a secondary key.

Control Intervals and Control Areas

All VSAM data set records are stored in control intervals, which are fixed-size units. When information is transferred from a DASD (all VSAM data sets must reside on a DASD) to virtual storage, a **control interval (CI)** is the unit of information moved. A control interval is between .5K and 32K in size. Several control intervals are grouped together to form a **control area (CA)**, and one or more control areas form the VSAM data set. A control area is between one track and one cylinder in size.

Let us look at the format of the control interval in a little more detail. Figure 12.1 illustrates a control interval. Although the control interval is fixed in size, the records may be variable in length. Data records are stored starting on the left. Control information is stored starting on the right. The first piece of information on the right is the **control interval definition field (CIDF)**, which contains information about the control interval, including the amount and location of freespace. When you want to add a record to a KSDS, the system determines which control interval it belongs in and checks the CIDF to see whether there is sufficient space in that control interval. If there is sufficient

A Control Interval

space, the record is added to that control interval. Later in this chapter we will discuss what happens if there is not enough space for the record.

The next field shown on the right is the **record definition field (RDF)**. As shown in Figure 12.2, the RDF is a three-byte field that contains a one-byte control field and a two-byte number. For a KSDS, this number gives the length of the record described by this RDF; for an RRDS, it gives the record number. In a KSDS, if each record in the control interval is a different length, there will be one RDF for each record. If all the records are the same length, there will be two RDFs in the CI: one defining the record length and one indicating how many contiguous records are of this length.

An RDF

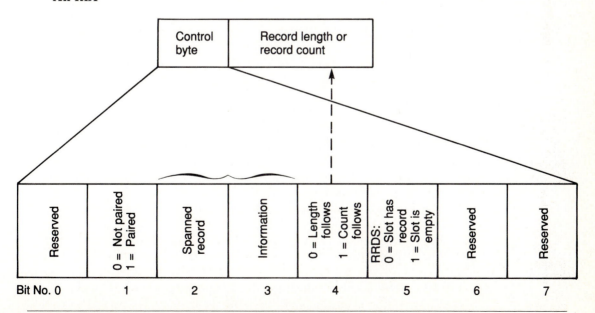

Table 12.1

Comparison of Entry Sequence, Relative Record, and Key Sequence Data Sets

Characteristic	ESDS	RRDS	KSDS
Record sequence	In the order in which they are entered	In relative record number order	In collating sequence by key field
Access method	Sequential	By relative record number, which is treated like a key	Sequentially or directly by key through an index
Record format	Fixed or variable	Fixed	Fixed or variable
Records added	Only at the end of the data set	In empty slots throughout the data set	In freespace distributed throughout the data set
Records deleted	No	Yes, and an empty slot can be reused	Yes, and space given up by deleted records is reclaimed
Records replaced	Yes, if the new record is the same length as the replaced record	Yes	Yes
Alternate index	May have one or more	Not allowed	May have one or more

In an RRDS, there is one RDF for each record in the control interval, even though all the records are the same length. The purpose of the RDF in an RRDS is to indicate whether the slot represented by this RDF contains a record. As Figure 12.2 shows, if bit five of the control byte is 1, the slot contains a record; if it is 0, the slot does not contain a record.

An ESDS CI may have some freespace between the data records and the RDFs. As in a KSDS, the records in an ESDS may be of variable length, although the CI is fixed in size.

The three kinds of data sets are compared in Table 12.1.

Adding and Deleting Records

Let us look more closely at how records may be added to and deleted from an RRDS. As mentioned earlier, an RRDS consists of numbered record positions.

Deleting a record means setting a flag in the RDF indicating that the record position is empty; the record position still exists. Inserting a record means placing information in an empty record position. Replacing a record means exchanging the information in the record position for new information. With an RRDS, deleting a record does not recover space and inserting a record does not expand the size of the data set.

With a KSDS, adding a record may expand the data set and deleting a record will recover space. When a KSDS record is deleted, the CI is rewritten without the new record and the size of the freespace is increased. When a KSDS record is added, the CI is rewritten with the new record added and the freespace is decreased. Insertion of the record whose key is 23 is illustrated in Figure 12.3. Notice the decrease in the size of the freespace and the addition of an RDF. If the three records were fixed length, or variable length and all the same size, the additional RDF would not be required.

Another record whose key is 18 and whose length is greater than the available freespace in the CI obviously will not fit into this CI. Adding it to the KSDS will cause a **control interval split**, which is illustrated in Figure 12.4. The new record plus the CI becomes two CIs.

Just as the CI may have freespace for additional records, the CA may have one or more unused CIs. If so, one of these unused CIs will be employed as the second CI in the split. If there is no unused CI in the CA, a **control area split** will occur. Such a split requires more DASD space for the data set. If none is available or if all the secondary extents have already been used, the record cannot be added to the data set. The program attempting this insertion will either abend or perform an error routine, if one was provided in the program.

Figure 12.3

Adding a Record to a KSDS

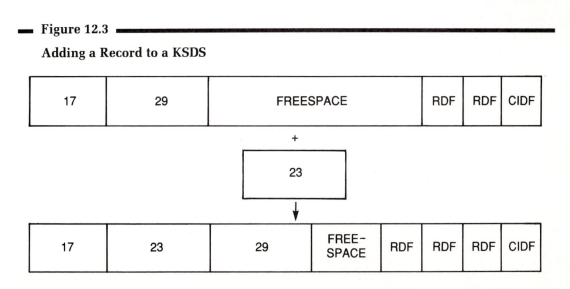

Figure 12.4

A Control Interval Split

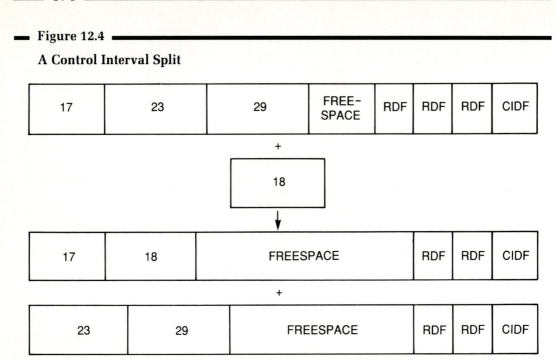

Locating Records

Both Figure 12.3 and Figure 12.4 show how records are added to the data portion of a KSDS. What these figures do not show is how the system knows that the record should be inserted in this particular CI. This information is obtained from the index portion of the KSDS. Figure 12.5 illustrates the index CIs that apply to the before-split data CIs shown in Figures 12.3 and 12.4. Each entry in the index CI contains the highest key in that data CI as well as location information for that data CI. Before the split there is only one data CI, so the index CI contains only the single entry 29. Figure 12.6 shows the index CI after the split. The first entry points to the first CI and the second to the

Figure 12.5

An Index Control Interval (Reference Figure 12.3)

Freespace pointer	29	

Figure 12.6

An Index Control Interval (Reference Figure 12.4)

Freespace pointer	18	29

second, but what is in the entry labeled freespace pointer? In the CI split discussion, we said that the system had to find an empty CI in the CA, but no mention was made of how this is done. It is done by means of the freespace pointer, which points to the available CIs.

Let us now look at what happens when we wish to read the record whose key is 23 (refer to Figures 12.4 and 12.6). First the index CI is read, and the key of the desired record is compared with those in the index. Because 23 is greater than 18, the record cannot be in the first data CI; 23 is then compared with 29. Because 23 is less than 29, the record is in the CI pointed to by the second index entry.

VSAM stores all the index information for one data CA in one index CI. The set of index CIs pointing to each data CI is called the **sequence set**. If a data set occupies 100 CAs, its sequence set will occupy 100 index CIs. On the average, 50 index CIs will have to be searched to find a particular record, which could take an unacceptably long time. To reduce the time required to search a sequence set that occupies more than one CI, the system builds an index to the index, as shown in Figure 12.7. This higher-level index is called the **index**

Figure 12.7

Index Structure

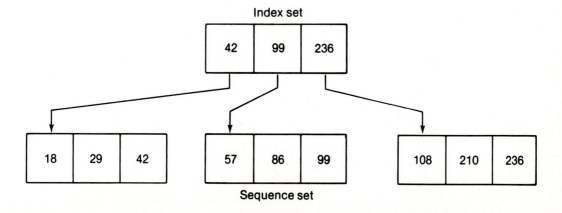

set. When the system searches for a particular data record, it reads the index set first, which directs it to the proper CI in the sequence set. As a result, 2 CIs are read instead of 50.

With very large data sets the index set may have several layers. We as application programmers need not be concerned, however, as the system handles the building of the indexes.

Catalogs

Catalogs are more important with VSAM data sets than with non-VSAM data sets. One reason is that all VSAM data sets *must* be cataloged. Another reason is that catalogs for VSAM data sets contain all the information that for non-VSAM data sets is stored in both the catalog and the DASD volume's VTOC.

When IBM introduced VSAM, it also introduced a new type of catalog known as the VSAM catalog. More recently IBM has introduced an improved catalog called the **integrated catalog facility (ICF)**, which can be used for both VSAM and non-VSAM data sets. You should know which catalog is used at your computer center, because some commands that will be discussed later in this chapter are not valid with ICF. Your advisor will be able to tell you which type of catalog is used at your computer center; you should write this information in the place provided on the inside front cover.

There is one master catalog, which is usually created by the systems programmer. In an MVS system this catalog is created at system generation time. In VS1 systems it may be created later. In addition to the master catalog, there may be user catalogs. User catalogs are not required, but computer centers that have many VSAM data sets generally group them by area (such as payroll) in user catalogs to reduce search time and accelerate the execution of jobs.

You might wonder how to specify which catalog you want to use if there are several catalogs. As you will see later in this chapter, it is possible to name the catalog explicitly, but it is also possible to have the data set name select the catalog implicitly. If no catalog is explicitly named and if the highest-level qualifier of a data set's name is the same as the name or alias of a catalog, that catalog is used.* For example, at the CUNY computer center, there is one user catalog named USERCAT, whose alias is VSAM, and users are required to use VSAM as the highest-order qualifier for their VSAM data sets. So when student JCL uses data sets named VSAM.QB.JCL., USERCAT is automatically used. Your computer center may or may not have rules for naming VSAM data sets. If rules have been established, you should write them in the place provided on the inside front cover.

---

*Aliases are assigned using the access method services command DEFINE ALIAS, which is beyond the scope of this book.

JCL to Access VSAM Data Sets

Because all VSAM data sets must be cataloged, the DD statement to access a VSAM data set is quite simple. All you need specify is the data set name (actually the cluster name) and the disposition, which should be SHR if you are only reading and OLD if you are writing and/or changing the data set.

```
//VSAMFLE DD DSN=VSAMCLST,
//               DISP=SHR
```

and

```
//FLEVSAM DD DSN=CLSTVSAM,
//               DISP=OLD
```

are valid DD statements for VSAM data sets. The same DD statement form is used for a KSDS, ESDS, and RRDS.

How does the system know which type of VSAM data set is to be used? The information is in a catalog. In the JCL in Figure 12.8, a VSAM cluster named DEPT46.VSAMFLE is accessed using the ddname VSAMIN. The system will look in the user catalog whose name (or alias) matches the highest-order qualifier of the data set name — in this case, DEPT46. If no such catalog exists or if the data set is not found in that catalog, the system will next look in the master catalog.

If you want a particular user catalog to be searched, you can include either a JOBCAT or a STEPCAT DD statement. Catalogs identified on JOBCAT or STEPCAT DD statements are searched before the catalog that matches the highest-order qualifier and the master catalog. The JOBCAT DD statement is coded after the JOB statement and after the JOBLIB statement, if there is one, but before the first EXEC statement, as in

```
//JOBNAME1 JOB ,MSGCLASS=A
//JOBLIB    DD DSN=MYLIB,
//               DISP=SHR
//JOBCAT    DD DSN=UCAT01,
//               DISP=SHR
//STEP1     EXEC PGM=MYPROG
```

The user catalog (or catalogs, if you concatenate) applies to the entire job when you code the JOBCAT DD statement. The STEPCAT DD statement is coded after the EXEC statement and applies only to that step:

```
//JOBNAME2 JOB ,MSGCLASS=A
//STEP1     EXEC PGM=MYPROG
//STEPCAT   DD DSN=UCAT02,
//               DISP=SHR
```

If both JOBCAT and STEPCAT are coded, the STEPCAT applies to that step and the JOBCAT applies to the rest of the job. For example, consider the

Figure 12.8

JCL to Access a VSAM Data Set

```
//JCLQB100 JOB ,'J. C. LEWIS'
//STEP1    EXEC PGM=MYPROG
//STEPLIB  DD DSN=MYLIB,
//            DISP=SHR
//SYSPRINT DD SYSOUT=A
//SYSUDUMP DD SYSOUT=A
//VSAMIN   DD DSN=DEPT46.VSAMFLE,
//            DISP=SHR
//REPORT   DD SYSOUT=A
//
```

following coding:

```
//JOBNAME3 JOB ,MSGLEVEL=1
//JOBCAT   DD DSN=UCAT,
//            DISP=SHR
//STEP1    EXEC PGM=MYPROG1
              .
              .
              .

//STEP2    EXEC PGM=MYPROG2
//STEPCAT  DD DSN=UCAT01,
//            DISP=SHR
              .
              .
              .

//STEP3    EXEC PGM=MYPROG3
              .
              .
              .
```

The user catalog UCAT01, named in the STEPCAT statement, is used in STEP2; UCAT, named in the JOBCAT statement, is used in STEP1 and STEP3. Coding a disposition of SHR for all STEPCAT and JOBCAT statements ensures that the catalogs may be shared among jobs.

Access Method Services

Access method services (AMS) is the VSAM utility program. Its program name is IDCAMS. This single utility program provides for VSAM data sets services for which many different utility programs are required for non-VSAM data sets. For example, to print a non-VSAM physical sequential data set you would use IEBPTPCH, and to delete it you would use IEHPROGM. A VSAM data set, however, can be both printed and deleted using IDCAMS.

AMS Basic JCL

Figure 12.9 shows the basic JCL required for any invocation of AMS; to perform most operations, additional DD statements must be added. Let us examine this basic JCL. The JOB statement is required for all jobs. IDCAMS requires about 300K of storage and the default at the CUNY computer center is 192K, so the REGION parameter is used to request 300K. The EXEC statement names the AMS utility program IDCAMS. The SYSPRINT DD statement provides a location for the messages that IDCAMS will write. The SYSIN DD statement provides a location for the AMS commands that tell the program IDCAMS what you want done.

AMS Command Format

The AMS command statement usually consists of the command, the parameters, and the terminator. Here we will deal with a limited subset of the commands available — namely, DELETE, PRINT, REPRO, VERIFY, and part of DEFINE.

A command statement may begin in column 2 or later and may extend to column 72. The commands and parameters must be separated by one or more blanks. To make the command statements easy to read, code only one parameter on a line; if the command has more than one parameter, continue the statement onto the next line. A statement may be continued by coding a hyphen as the last character. A blank or parenthesis must separate the parameter from the hyphen. The continuation statement may begin anywhere between columns 2 and 72. Again, to make the statements easy to read, line up the parameters. For example, instead of coding

```
DELETE VSAMCLS CLUSTER
```

write

```
DELETE VSAMCLS -
       CLUSTER
```

━━ **Figure 12.9** ━━━━━━━━━━━━━━━━━━━━━━━━━━━━━━━━━━━━

Access Method Services Basic JCL

```
//JCLQB110 JOB ,'J. C. LEWIS',
//              REGION=300K
//STEP     EXEC PGM=IDCAMS
//SYSPRINT DD SYSOUT=A
//SYSIN    DD *

   AMS Commands

/*
//
```

Another way to show continuation is with a plus sign, which works somewhat differently from the hyphen; for example,

```
DELETE VSAMCLS -
       CLUSTER -
       ERA+
       SE
```

is the same as

```
DELETE VSAMCLS -
       CLUSTER -
       ERASE
```

When you use the plus sign for continuation, the system looks for the first
nonblank character on the next line and concatenates it to the character that
preceded the plus sign. Use of the plus sign to signal continuation is not
recommended, because it makes your coding hard to read.

In the above examples the parameters are separated with blanks. Commas
may be used instead; the choice is yours. Each statement is ended by not
continuing it. A semicolon may be used instead to terminate a statement, as in

```
DELETE VSAMCLS -
       CLUSTER,ER+
       ASE;
```

A parameter may have a subparameter; for example, in

```
DELETE VSAMCLS -
       CLUSTER -
       FILE (DD1)
```

the parameter FILE has a subparameter, DD1, which is coded within parentheses. The blank between the E of FILE and the opening parenthesis is
optional, but it makes reading easier.

Creating VSAM Data Sets

Before we look at how a VSAM data set is created, let us review how a
non-VSAM data set is created. Normally you just run a program that has been
either specially written or bought, and the data set is created on the fly. The
SPACE parameter tells the system how much DASD space to reserve, the
DISP parameter indicates that the data set is new and what you want done
with it when the jobstep ends, and the DCB parameter supplies descriptive
information. Of course the DCB information may be given in the program
instead of with the DCB parameter on the DD statement. Any of several utility
programs could also be used to accomplish many of these functions. Running

IEFBR14 would reserve the space on a DASD and supply the DCB information, as in

```
//JOBC1     JOB
//STEP      EXEC PGM=IEFBR14
//DD1       DD DSN=NONVSAM,
//              DISP=(NEW,KEEP),
//              UNIT=DISK,
//              VOL=SER=DISK01,
//              DCB=(RECFM=FB,LRECL=80,BLKSIZE=800)
```

Executing IEHPROGM would catalog the data set, as in

```
//JOBC2     JOB
//STEP      EXEC PGM=IEHPROGM
//SYSPRINT DD SYSOUT=A
//DD1       DD UNIT=DISK,
//              VOL=SER=DISK01,
//              DISP=OLD
//SYSIN     DD *
  CATLG DSNAME=NONVSAM,
                VOL=DISK=DISK01
  /*
```

IEBGENER could be used to load input stream data for the data set, as in

```
//JOBC3     JOB
//STEP      EXEC PGM=IEBGENER
//SYSPRINT DD SYSOUT=A
//SYSIN     DD DUMMY
//SYSUT1    DD *
  (Input stream data to be loaded)
  /*
//SYSUT2    DD DSN=NONVSAM,
//              DISP=(MOD,KEEP)
//
```

After loading, you would want to see what you had, so you might use IEBPTPCH to print the data set, as in

```
//JOBC4     JOB
//STEP      EXEC PGM=IEBPTPCH
//SYSPRINT DD SYSOUT=A
//SYSIN     DD *
  PRINT MAXFLDS=1
  RECORD FIELD=(80)
  /*
//SYSUT1    DD DSN=NONVSAM,
//              DISP=SHR
//SYSUT2    DD SYSOUT=A
```

To summarize, let us review the steps that are taken to create a non-VSAM data set:

1. Allocate space on a DASD.
2. Supply a description of the data set (DCB information).
3. Set the data set's disposition (CATLG or KEEP).
4. Load the data set.
5. Make sure that the correct data are in the data set.

Obviously these or similar functions have to be performed for a VSAM data set, but they are not done in the same way. For VSAM data sets, unlike non-VSAM data sets, a utility program must be used to perform these functions (with the exception of loading the data set, for which either a user-written COBOL, PL/I, or assembler program or a utility program can be used). The utility program that performs all of these functions is IDCAMS.

The first thing to do is to decide where to catalog the VSAM data set. Do you want to use the master catalog or a user catalog? If you choose to use the master catalog, you can go on to the next step. If you choose to use a user catalog, you must define it if it does not already exist. Defining a user catalog may be done by the systems programmer or by the lead programmer on a team. How to define a user catalog is explained later in this chapter.

The next step is to decide which DASD space to use for the data set. If you decide that this data set is to occupy space by itself, you can go on to the next step. If you decide to group several VSAM data sets in the same space, however, the space must be obtained for use with VSAM by executing IDCAMS using a DEFINE SPACE command. (DEFINE SPACE has no meaning under ICF.) Again, this task is usually performed not by the application programmer but by a systems programmer or lead programmer. In some computer centers there is a group responsible for controlling the use of DASDs. If your computer center has such a group, a member of the group would execute the DEFINE SPACE function.

The next step is to use the DEFINE CLUSTER command, with which all the descriptive information about the VSAM data set is supplied. This command is the most complex one that we will discuss and also the most important.

The REPRO command may be used to load data into a VSAM data set. The input may come from a physical sequential, ISAM, or even VSAM data set. REPRO is also used to back up and to reorganize a VSAM data set. REPRO does not have to be used to load the data set initially. As mentioned earlier, the loading may be done with a user-written program.

Finally, the PRINT command is used to obtain a listing of a VSAM data set. It is best to print your data set immediately after loading, so that you are sure that what you have is what you want.

PRINT Command

We will discuss five commands involved in creating a VSAM data set. Because it is the easiest of the five, we will begin with the PRINT command. The parameters used with the PRINT command are shown in Table 12.2. The job stream in Figure 12.10a prints all of the VSAM data set VSAM.QB.JCL.PLYKSDS1. Because of the STEPCAT statement, the system will search the user catalog USERCAT to obtain information about VSAM.QB.JCL.PLYKSDS1. As mentioned earlier, at the CUNY computer center, that catalog would have been searched even if the STEPCAT statement had not been coded, for USERCAT has the alias VSAM and the highest-level qualifier of the data set name is VSAM. Most of the examples in this book will include either a STEPCAT or a JOBCAT statement, however, because in the CUNY system they do no harm and in other systems they may be required.

Notice that the INFILE parameter names the DD statement DD1, which describes the VSAM data set to be printed. Because the OUTFILE parameter is not coded, the output is automatically directed to the output class specified in the SYSPRINT DD statement, which is the printer.

The desired format for the listing is not specified, so we get DUMP, which is the default. DUMP means that the data set will be printed in both character and hexadecimal representations. The output produced by this job stream is shown in Figure 12.10b.

In MVS systems only, the same output is produced by using the INDATASET parameter instead of the INFILE parameter. To use INDATASET, we replace the control statement in Figure 12.10a with

```
PRINT INDATASET (VSAM.QB.JCL.PLYKSDS1)
```

and eliminate the DD1 DD statement. Without the DD1 DD statement, the system will not be able to determine the name of the data set being processed when it scans the JCL. It will find out the name of the data set only when the job goes into execution and the control statements are interpreted. At that time the data set will be allocated. Allocating a data set after execution of a job has begun is called **dynamic allocation**. For dynamic allocation of a data set to be successful, it is necessary that the volume on which the data set resides be mounted before execution of the job begins. VS1 cannot perform dynamic allocation.

Because INFILE is correct for both VS1 and MVS systems whereas INDATASET is correct only for MVS systems, all examples here will use INFILE. Even though INDATASET is easier to code, one reason for using INFILE in MVS systems is that the implied disposition of the data set named by INDATASET is OLD. If there is a possibility that more than one job will access a data set at the same time, it is better to code INFILE and code SHR for the disposition on the DD statement.

■ Table 12.2 ■
PRINT Command Parameters

Parameter	Abbreviation	Definition
INFILE (ddname/password)	IFILE	Names the DD statement of the VSAM data set to be printed.
INDATASET (entryname/ password)*	IDS	Names the VSAM data set.
OUTFILE (ddname)	OFILE	Points to the DD statement that names the output data set. If this parameter is not supplied, the class coded in the SYSPRINT DD statement is used.
CHARACTER	CHAR	Means that each byte will be printed in character format.
HEX		Means that each byte will be printed in hexadecimal format.
DUMP		Means that both character and hexadecimal will be printed. DUMP is the default.
FROMKEY (key)	FKEY	Names the key of the first record to be printed; used with a KSDS.
FROMADDRESS (address)	FADDR	Names the relative byte address (RBA) of the first record to be printed; may be used with all three types of data sets.
FROMNUMBER (number)	FNUM	Gives the relative record number of the first record to be printed; used with an RRDS.
SKIP (count)		Indicates the number of records to be bypassed.
TOKEY (key)		Indicates the last record to be printed.
TOADDRESS (address)	TADDR	
TONUMBER (number)	TNUM	
COUNT (count)		Tells the number of records to be printed.

* For MVS systems only.

Figure 12.10

(a) Printing a VSAM Data Set

```
//JCLQB140 JOB ,'ARIES',
//         REGION=300K
//PRNT1    EXEC PGM=IDCAMS
//STEPCAT  DD DSN=USERCAT,
//         DISP=SHR
//SYSPRINT DD SYSOUT=A
//DD1      DD DSN=VSAM.QB.JCL.PLYKSDS1,
//         DISP=SHR
//SYSIN    DD *
PRINT INFILE (DD1)
/*
//
```

(b) Sample Output of the Print Operation

```
LISTING OF DATA SET -VSAM.QB.JCL.PLYKSDS1
KEY OF RECORD - F1F3F0F0F9
000000 F1F3F0F0 F9D9C5C5 C46BE3C9 D5C14040   40404040 40404040 C1F0F8F4    *13009REED,TINA         A084*
000020 F2F0F0F0 F4F2F6F0 F7F2F1F0 F0404040   40F7F440 40404040 40404040    *2000426072100        74   *
000040 40404040 40404040 40404040                                          *                          *

KEY OF RECORD - F1F5F1F7F4
000000 F1F5F1F7 F4C8C1D5 C4D1C1D5 E86BC8C1   C9C4C5C8 40404040 C8F0F2F2    *15174HANDJANY,HAIDEH   H022*
000020 F9F0F0F0 F2F2F0F0 F2F2F9F0 F0404040   40F7F140 40404040 40404040    *9000220022900        71   *
000040 40404040 40404040 40404040                                          *                          *

KEY OF RECORD - F1F7F3F3F7
000000 F1F7F3F3 F7C2E4E3 C5D9D66B D4C1E4D9   C9C3C540 40404040 C8F0F5F0    *17337BUTERO,MAURICE    H050*
000020 F1F0F0F0 F3F4F0F5 F0F1F0F0 F0404040   40F6F340 40404040 40404040    *100034050100         63   *
000040 40404040 40404040 40404040                                          *                          *

KEY OF RECORD - F1F9F4F9F9
000000 F1F9F4F9 F9D3C1C6 C5D96BC2 D9E4C3C5   40404040 40404040 C1F0F7F0    *19499LAFER,BRUCE       A070*
000020 F6F0F0F0 F8F1F9F0 F5F0F0F0 F0404040   40F5F240 40404040 40404040    *600081905000         52   *
000040 40404040 40404040 40404040                                          *                          *

KEY OF RECORD - F2F1F6F6F1
000000 F2F1F6F6 F1D3C5C5 6BE2E4C9 40404040   40404040 40404040 C1F0F3F9    *21661LEE,SUI           A039*
000020 F0F1F7F0 F3F0F3F0 F3F0F0F1 F7404040   40F7F640 40404040 40404040    *017030303017         76   *
000040 40404040 40404040 40404040                                          *                          *
```

If the PRINT command were

```
PRINT INFILE (DD1) -
      CHARACTER -
      SKIP (20) -
      COUNT (20)
```

the twenty-first through the fortieth records would be printed in character format.

```
PRINT INFILE (DD1) -
      HEX -
      FROMKEY (19499) -
      TOKEY (43214)
```

implies that the VSAM data set is a KSDS. In fact, if the data set VSAM.QB.JCL.PLYKSDS1 is not a KSDS, this command will fail. Printing will start with the record whose key is 19499 and proceed to the record whose key is 43214. The listing will be in hexadecimal format. If the key specified in either FROMKEY or TOKEY contains any special characters, it must be enclosed in single quotes—for example, TOKEY('A=B'). The key may be given in hexadecimal format as well—for example, FROMKEY(X'3CFF').

The job in Figure 12.11 shows the use of the OUTFILE parameter to name the DD2 DD statement that directs the output to output class C. POLYRRDS is an RRDS, and the command will print from record number 6 to record number 20.

■ **Figure 12.11** ■

Printing Selected Records of an RRDS

```
//JCLQB150 JOB ,'TAURUS',
//              REGION=300K
//JOBCAT    DD DSN=USERCAT,
//              DISP=SHR
//PRNT2     EXEC PGM=IDCAMS
//SYSPRINT DD SYSOUT=A
//DD1       DD DSN=VSAM.QB.JCL.POLYRRDS,
//              DISP=SHR
//DD2       DD SYSOUT=C
//SYSIN     DD *
  PRINT INFILE (DD1) -
        OUTFILE (DD2) -
        FROMNUMBER (6) -
        TONUMBER (20)
  /*
  //
```

REPRO Command

The REPRO command is quite useful. It can be used to load a VSAM data set, to convert an ISAM data set to VSAM, to reorganize a VSAM KSDS, to merge two VSAM data sets, or to create a back-up copy.

Table 12.3 shows the parameters of the REPRO command. The examples will not use FROMKEY, FROMADDRESS, FROMNUMBER, SKIP, TOKEY, TOAD-DRESS, TONUMBER, and COUNT, for these parameters are used in the same way here as in the PRINT command. Because OUTFILE is correct for both VS1 and MVS systems whereas OUTDATASET is correct for only MVS systems, all examples here will use OUTFILE.

The job shown in Figure 12.12 uses the REPRO command to load data from the sequential data set POLYFILE into the previously created VSAM cluster PLYKSDS1. (In Figure 12.18 PLYKSDS1 is defined as a KSDS.) This job, there-fore, uses as input a sequential data set and creates a KSDS. The job shown in Figure 12.13 uses the REPRO command to load data from the ISAM data set POLYISAM into the previously created cluster PLYKSDS2. PLYKSDS2 was previously defined as a KSDS, so this job uses as input an ISAM data set and creates a KSDS. Because ENVIRONMENT (DUMMY) is specified, dummy records and records marked for deletion (those records that contain a hexa-decimal value of FF in the first byte) will be copied to PLYKSDS2.

The REPRO command can accomplish several functions depending on what types of data sets the input and output data sets are and whether the output data set contains data or is empty. Let us assume that you have a job like those shown in Figure 12.12 and Figure 12.13, but that the DSN of the input data set is INPUT and of the output data set is OUTPUT.

Table 12.3
REPRO Command Parameters

Parameter	Abbreviation	Definition
INFILE (ddname/password ENVIRONMENT (DUMMY))	IFILE ENV (DUM)	Points to the DD statement that names the input data set. ENVIRONMENT (DUMMY) means that dummy ISAM records are to be copied.
INDATASET (entryname/ password ENVIRONMENT (DUMMY))*	IDS	Gives the name of the entry to be copied.
OUTFILE (ddname/ password)	OFILE	Points to the DD statement that names the output data set.

Cont.

Table 12.3 (Cont.)

Parameter	Abbreviation	Definition
OUTDATASET (entryname/ password)*	ODS	Gives the name of the output data set.
REPLACE	REP	In copying a KSDS into an existing KSDS, means to take the input record for equal keys. In copying an RRDS into an existing RRDS, means to take the input record for equal relative record numbers.
NOREPLACE	NREP	Means to keep the old record. NOREPLACE is the default.
REUSE	RUS	Means that the output data set is to be rebuilt every time the REPRO function is used.
NOREUSE	NRUS	The default.
FROMKEY (key)	FKEY	Gives the key of the first record in a KSDS to be copied.
FROMADDRESS (address)	FADDR	Gives the RBA of the first record to be copied.
FROMNUMBER (number)	FNUM	Gives the relative record number of the first record to be copied.
SKIP (count)		Tells how many records are to be bypassed before copying begins.
TOKEY (key)		Gives the key of the last record to be copied.
TOADDRESS (address)	TADDR	Gives the RBA of the last record to be copied.
TONUMBER (number)	TNUM	Gives the relative record number of the last record to be copied.
COUNT (count)		Tells how many records are to be copied.

* For MVS systems only.

Figure 12.12

Loading a VSAM KSDS with Data from an SDS

```
//JCLQB160 JOB ,'GEMINI',
//              REGION=300K
//REPRO1   EXEC PGM=IDCAMS
//STEPCAT  DD DSN=USERCAT,
//              DISP=SHR
//SYSPRINT DD SYSOUT=A
//DD1      DD DSN=WYL.QB.JCL.POLYFILE,
//              DISP=SHR
//DD2      DD DSN=VSAM.QB.JCL.PLYKSDS1,
//              DISP=OLD
//SYSIN    DD *
 REPRO INFILE (DD1) -
       OUTFILE (DD2)
/*
//
```

If OUTPUT is empty, the REPRO command will load it with data from INPUT, no matter what kind of data set INPUT or OUTPUT is.

If OUTPUT contains data, what will happen will depend on what kind of VSAM data set OUTPUT is, as well as what INPUT is. If OUTPUT is an ESDS, all the records in INPUT will be added to the end of OUTPUT, no matter what kind of data set INPUT is. If OUTPUT is a KSDS, the records in INPUT will be merged into OUTPUT based on the value of the key, no matter what kind of data set

Figure 12.13

Loading a VSAM KSDS with Data from an ISAM Data Set

```
//JCLQB170 JOB ,'CANCER',
//              REGION=300K
//JOBCAT   DD DSN=USERCAT,
//              DISP=SHR
//REPRO2   EXEC PGM=IDCAMS
//SYSPRINT DD SYSOUT=A
//DD1      DD DSN=WYL.QB.JCL.POLYISAM,
//              DISP=SHR,
//              DCB=DSORG=IS
//DD2      DD DSN=VSAM.QB.JCL.PLYKSDS2,
//              DISP=OLD
//SYSIN    DD *
 REPRO INFILE (DD1 ENVIRONMENT (DUMMY)) -
       OUTFILE (DD2) -
       REPLACE
/*
//
```

INPUT is. In the case of duplicate keys, the record in OUTPUT will be kept and the record in INPUT will not be used. If, however, the command were

```
REPRO INFILE (DD1) -
      OUTFILE (DD2) -
      REPLACE
```

the record in INPUT would replace the record in OUTPUT with the same key.

The job will fail if OUTPUT is an RRDS with data, unless INPUT is also an RRDS. If both are RRDSs, the records will be merged by relative record number. In the case of duplicate relative record numbers, the record in OUTPUT will be retained unless REPLACE is specified.

Figure 12.14 shows a job stream to create a back-up copy of a VSAM file on tape. The job stream assumes that the records are 80 bytes in length. The records will be blocked on tape. Note that REPLACE is not coded because it has meaning only when the output data set is old. Part of the VSAM file could be backed up by using a FROM value together with a TO value.

Reorganizing a KSDS

After a number of CI and/or CA splits have occurred, the physical sequence of the KSDS will be different from the logical sequence. This condition is illustrated in Figure 12.15. The index shows the logical sequence and the data the physical sequence. At this point reorganizing the KSDS to make the physical and logical sequence the same would result in faster read time, particularly in sequential access.

■ **Figure 12.14** ────────────────────────────────

Creating a Tape Backup of a VSAM Data Set

```
//JCLQB180 JOB ,'LEO',
//             REGION=300K
//JOBCAT   DD DSN=USERCAT,
//             DISP=SHR
//REPRO3   EXEC PGM=IDCAMS
//SYSPRINT DD SYSOUT=A
//DD1      DD DSN=VSAM.QB.JCL.PLYKSDS1,
//             DISP=SHR
//DD2      DD DSN=WYL.QB.JCL.BACKUP,
//             DISP=(,KEEP),
//             UNIT=TAPE,
//             DCB=(RECFM=FB,LRECL=80,BLKSIZE=1600)
//SYSIN    DD *
 REPRO INFILE (DD1) -
       OUTFILE (DD2)
 /*
 //
```

Figure 12.15

Differing Physical and Logical Sequences in a KSDS

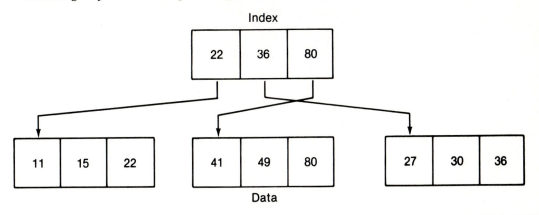

A VSAM KSDS cannot be reorganized in one step. The job stream in Figure 12.16 illustrates one sequence of steps that can be used to carry out a reorganization. In Figure 12.16 a JOBCAT DD statement is used, because both data sets are cataloged in one user catalog. A STEPCAT statement could have been used in each step; if the master catalog had been used, neither a JOBCAT nor a STEPCAT would be needed. The first step is to define the temporary cluster TEMP1. The coding of this step will be discussed in the next section. The second step is to copy the data from the original VSAM KSDS to the temporary one. Notice that COND=(0,NE) is coded on the EXEC statements of all but the first step. Each step depends on the successful execution of the preceding steps; by checking the return code, we make sure that each execution was successful. The third step deletes the original VSAM KSDS. You can see that we would be in serious trouble if we deleted the data set without having a copy of it. The last step uses the ALTER command to rename the temporary VSAM KSDS and make it *the* VSAM KSDS.

This job contains one complication which must be explained. Notice that in the second step the UNIT and VOL parameters are coded for TEMP1. Because TEMP1 is cataloged, you might wonder why the UNIT and VOL parameters are coded. Recall that before execution of a job starts, the reader-interpreter searches the catalog to obtain information about all the cataloged data sets used in the job. But before execution of this job starts, TEMP1 does not exist; if the reader-interpreter searched the catalog, it would not find an entry for TEMP1 and the job would fail. TEMP1 is defined and cataloged in the first step, but it is defined and cataloged using control statements, not JCL statements, and the reader-interpreter does not read control statements.

Briefly, then, UNIT and VOL are coded for TEMP1 to prevent the reader-

■ Figure 12.16 ■

Reorganizing a VSAM Cluster

```
//JCLQB190 JOB ,'VIRGO',
//              REGION=300K
//JOBCAT   DD DSN=USERCAT,
//            DISP=SHR
//REPRO4A  EXEC PGM=IDCAMS
//SYSPRINT DD SYSOUT=A
//SYSIN    DD *
  DEFINE CLUSTER (NAME (VSAM.QB.JCL.TEMP1) -
                  RECORDS (1000 200) -
                  FREESPACE (20 20) -
                  INDEXED -
                  KEYS (5 0) -
                  RECORDSIZE (80 80) -
                  UNIQUE -
                  VOLUMES (SCR001) )
/*
//REPRO4B  EXEC PGM=IDCAMS,
//              COND=(0,NE)
//SYSPRINT DD SYSOUT=A
//DD1      DD DSN=VSAM.QB.JCL.PLYKSDS1,
//            DISP=SHR
//DD2      DD DSN=VSAM.QB.JCL.TEMP1,
//            DISP=OLD,
//            UNIT=SYSDA,
//            VOL=SER=SCR001,
//            AMP=AMORG
//SYSIN    DD *
  REPRO INFILE (DD1) -
        OUTFILE (DD2)
/*
//REPRO4C  EXEC PGM=IDCAMS,
//              COND=(0,NE)
//SYSPRINT DD SYSOUT=A
//DD1      DD UNIT=SYSDA,
//            DISP=OLD,
//            VOL=SER=SCR001
//SYSIN    DD *
  DELETE VSAM.QB.JCL.PLYKSDS1 -
         CLUSTER -
         FILE (DD1)
/*
//REPRO4D  EXEC PGM=IDCAMS,
//              COND=(0,NE)
//SYSPRINT DD SYSOUT=A
//SYSIN    DD *
  ALTER VSAM.QB.JCL.TEMP1 NEWNAME (VSAM.QB.JCL.PLYKSDS1)
/*
//
```

interpreter from searching the catalog to obtain information about TEMP1. But that raises another problem: If the catalog is not read for TEMP1, the system will not learn that TEMP1 is a VSAM data set. To tell the system that TEMP1 is a VSAM data set requires a parameter that is new to you,

```
AMP=AMORG
```

which follows the first VOL parameter in Figure 12.16.

DEFINE CLUSTER Command

The DEFINE CLUSTER command is used to create catalog entries that hold information about a VSAM data set and its components. The entries may be inserted into a specified user catalog or into the master catalog. For VSAM data sets managed by an ICF catalog, this command also allocates space for the data set. For VSAM data sets managed by a VSAM catalog, space is allocated only if the UNIQUE parameter is coded as part of the command. If UNIQUE is not coded, space for the data set is obtained from a pool of space previously established for the catalog. Such space is defined by a DEFINE SPACE command, which is discussed later. The general form of the DEFINE CLUSTER command is

```
DEFINE CLUSTER (parameters) -
       DATA (parameters) -
       INDEX (parameters) -
       CATALOG (catname/password)
```

DEFINE may be abbreviated as DEF, CLUSTER as CL, INDEX as IDX, and CATALOG as CAT. INDEX information is given only for a KSDS. catname supplies the name of the user catalog in which the information should be stored. The CATALOG parameter is optional, but if it is coded, it takes precedence over any catalog named in a JOBCAT or STEPCAT statement or implied by the highest-level qualifier of the data set name.

The parameters following the keyword CLUSTER apply to the cluster as a whole, whereas the parameters following the keywords DATA and INDEX apply to just those components. It is easiest to code parameters at the CLUSTER level; if you code parameters at the DATA or INDEX level, you have to be sure that they do not conflict. In general, it is best to code only the NAME parameter at the DATA and INDEX levels. If you do not code the NAME, the system will supply a cryptic name that will have no meaning to you. Because your catalog will have entries that you do not recognize, it will be significantly more difficult to manage your DASD space. Under special circumstances it is desirable to code parameters besides NAME at the DATA and INDEX levels. For example, Figure 12.19 shows how the VOLUME parameter may be used to assign the data and index components to different volumes.

The parameters that you may code are defined in Table 12.4. In the col-

Table 12.4
DEFINE CLUSTER Command Parameters

Parameter	Abbreviation	CL	DATA	INDEX	Definition
BUFFERSPACE (size)	BUFSP	O	O	O	Gives the minimum space for buffers.
CONTROLINTERVALSIZE (size)	CISZ	O	O	O	Gives the size of the control interval.
CYLINDER (prim sec) RECORDS (prim sec) TRACKS (prim sec)	CYL REC TRK	R	O	O	Gives the amount of DASD space for the data set. If specified in DATA and INDEX, it must equal CLUSTER as a whole.
DESTAGEWAIT NODESTAGEWAIT	DSTGW NDSTGW	O	O	O	Applies to mass storage device data sets.
ERASE	ERAS	O	O	N/A	Specifies that binary zeros are to be written over the data set when it is deleted.
NOERASE	NERAS				The default.
EXCEPTIONEXIT (entry point)	EEXT	O	O	O	Names a user-written routine that takes control when an I/O error occurs.
FILE (ddname)		R/O	O	O	Identifies the device and volume to be used for space allocation. If UNIQUE is specified, this parameter is required for VS1 systems.

Parameter	Abbr.				Description
FREESPACE (CI% CA%)	FSPC	O	O	N/A	Specifies the percentage of the CI and the percentage of the CA to be left free when the KSDS is loaded. The default is 0.
IMBED	IMBD	O	N/A	O	Specifies that the sequence set is to be placed with the data; applies to a KSDS. The default.
NOIMBED	NIMBD	O	N/A		
INDEXED	IXD	O	N/A	N/A	Means that the data set is KSDS. INDEXED is the default.
NONINDEXED	NIXD	O	N/A	N/A	Means that the data set is ESDS.
NUMBERED	NUMD				Means that the data set is RRDS.
KEYRANGES ((lowkey highkey) (lowkey highkey)...)	KRNG	O	O	N/A	For a multivolume KSDS, identifies key ranges for each volume.
KEYS (length offset)		O	O	N/A	Specifies key length and position in record. The first byte is position 0. The default is 64 and 0. Applies to KSDS.
MODEL (entryname/password) (catname/password)		O	O	O	Names an existing entry to be used as a model for this entry.
NAME (entryname)		R	P	P	Supplies the name.
ORDERED	ORD	O	O	O	Specifies that the volumes are to be used in the order in which they were listed in the VOLUMES parameter. The default.
UNORDERED	UORD				
OWNER (owner-id)		O	O	O	Names the cluster's owner.

Cont.

Table 12.4 (Cont.)

Parameter	Abbreviation	CL	DATA	INDEX	Definition
RECORDSIZE (average maximum)	RECSZ	R/O	R/O	N/A	Gives the average and maximum record size. This value must be supplied with either CLUSTER or DATA.
REPLICATE	REPL	O	N/A	O	Specifies that each index record is to be written on a track as many times as it will fit, to save rotational delay time.
NOREPLICATE	NREPL				The default.
REUSE		O	O	O	Specifies that the cluster can be opened frequently as a temporary data set.
NOREUSE					The default.
SHAREOPTIONS (crossregion crosssystem)	SHR	O	O	O	Specifies how a component or cluster can be shared among various users.
SPANNED	SPND	O	O	N/A	Indicates that a record can be bigger than the control interval.
NOSPANNED	NSPND				The default.
RECOVERY	RCVY	O	O	N/A	Means that the data area is preformatted, and the file can be recovered if the load fails. RECOVERY is the default.

Parameter	Abbrev.				Description
SPEED					Does not preformat and is faster.
STAGE		O	O	O	Used with mass storage.
BIND					
CYLINDERFAULT	CYLF				
TO (date) FOR (days)		O	N/A	N/A	Gives the retention period. A Julian date may be given; 90264 is September 21, 1990. Alternatively, a number of days may be specified.
UNIQUE	UNQ	O	O	O	Means that the data set has its own space.
SUBALLOCATION	SUBAL				Means that the data set shares space with other data sets. SUBALLOCATION is the default. This parameter has no meaning in an ICF system.
VOLUMES (volser...)	VOL	R/O	R/O	R/O	Names the volumes on which the entry is located. This parameter must be given either for the cluster as a whole or for the data and index, which permits the data to be on one volume and the index on another.
WRITECHECK	WCK	O	O	O	Causes the hardware to check that the data were written correctly.
NOWRITECHECK	NWCK				The default.

umns labeled CL, DATA, and INDEX, R means that the parameter is required, O means that it is optional or there is a default value, P means that it is optional but its use is recommended; N/A means not applicable, and R/O means that the information is required but the user can choose where to supply it. Those parameters that apply explicitly to security are not included in Table 12.4; they are listed in Table 12.5 without definition.

When you code DEFINE CLUSTER, let the system select the sizes for buffer space and for the CI. The system will choose a buffer size large enough to contain two data CIs and, if the data set is a KSDS, one index CI. As a rule, these choices strike a good balance between speed and DASD space usage. The system will use the information you supply with RECORDSIZE to choose a CI size that makes the best use of space on the DASD track.

Let us start with defining a KSDS, because a KSDS requires more parameters than any other type of VSAM data set.

The job shown in Figure 12.17 defines a KSDS cluster named VSAM.QB.JCL.KSDS. The parameter INDEXED indicates that this cluster is a KSDS. Space sufficient for 1000 records will be allocated, as specified in the RECORDS (1000 100) parameter. The 100 is for the secondary allocation, should it be necessary. In a VSAM catalog system, the space will be obtained from previously defined space. In an ICF system, the command will allocate the space. The space will be on disk pack SCR001, as specified in the VOL-UMES (SCR001) parameter. The RECORDSIZE (100 320) parameter indicates that logical record length averages 100 bytes and has a maximum of 320 bytes. (The system uses the average record length with the primary allocation in the RECORDS parameter to calculate the space required.) The KEYS (10 5) parameter tells the system that the key is 10 bytes long and starts in the sixth byte of the record. (Remember that the first byte is position 0.)

The FREESPACE (20 30) parameter specifies that when the data are loaded into this data set, 20 percent of each of the CIs and 30 percent of each of

■ **Table 12.5**
Security Parameters

Parameter	Abbreviation	CL	DATA	INDEX
ATTEMPTS (number)	ATT	O	O	O
AUTHORIZATION (entrypoint string)	AUTH	O	O	O
CODE (code)		O	O	O
CONTROLPW (password)	CTLPW	O	O	O
MASTERPW (password)	MRPW	O	O	O
READPW (password)	RDPW	O	O	O
UPDATEPW (password)	UPDPW	O	O	O

■ **Figure 12.17** ■

Defining a KSDS Cluster

```
//JCLQB200 JOB ,'LIBRA',
//              REGION=300K
//DEFCLK1  EXEC PGM=IDCAMS
//STEPCAT  DD DSN=USERCAT,
//              DISP=SHR
//SYSPRINT DD SYSOUT=A
//SYSIN    DD *
 DEFINE CLUSTER (NAME (VSAM.QB.JCL.KSDS) -
                 RECORDS (1000 100) -
                 FREESPACE (20 30) -
                 INDEXED -
                 KEYS (10 5) -
                 RECORDSIZE (100 320) -
                 IMBED -
                 SPEED -
                 VOLUMES (SCR001) ) -
          DATA (NAME (VSAM.QB.JCL.KSDSDAT) ) -
          INDEX (NAME (VSAM.QB.JCL.KSDSIND) )
 /*
 //
```

the CAs should be left free for expansion. The default for FREESPACE is no freespace, so if you expect to add records to the data set you should code FREESPACE. Be aware, however, that if you request space in terms of RECORDS, the amount of freespace will not be taken into account when the system calculates the allocation. You should therefore increase the number of records by the percentage of freespace requested. Selecting the best values for FREESPACE is not easy. There is one pitfall you should be careful to avoid: specifying less CI freespace than is needed to accommodate at least one record. For example, suppose the record size is 500 and the CI size is 4095. (You can specify the CI size, or you can let the system select it and then determine the value selected by executing a LISTCAT command, as explained later in this chapter.) If you specify a CI freespace of 10 percent, about 400 bytes will be left free in each CI. Because 400 bytes is not enough to hold one record, that space is completely wasted.

The IMBED parameter causes the sequence set index record for each CA to be stored on the first track in that CA, rather than with the other index records. This option speeds processing by reducing access arm motion. Further, because the sequence set index record does not fill a track, it is repeated (as many times as possible) on the track, which has the additional advantage of reducing rotational delay. The price you pay for this increase in processing speed, however, is that the data set requires more DASD space.

The SPEED parameter is coded to override the default RECOVERY. RECOVERY causes the CAs to be preformatted when data are initially loaded into the data set. If the load operation fails, the preformatting can be used to restart the load at the point where it failed. SPEED eliminates this preformatting, allowing the data set to be loaded more quickly.

Because the CATALOG entry is not included as part of the command, the system defaults to the catalog named in the STEPCAT statement, USERCAT. The catalog could also have been named in a JOBCAT statement. As explained earlier, the highest-level qualifier of the data set name, VSAM, is an alias of USERCAT, so USERCAT would have been used even if the STEPCAT statement had not been included.

You'll notice that there is no way to specify explicitly the size of the CA. The system selects the CA size based on your space request. If the primary and secondary requests both require one or more cylinders, the CA size is set equal to one cylinder, which gives the most efficient index structure. If either the primary or the secondary request is less than one cylinder, the CA size is set equal to the smaller value.

The job in Figure 12.18 defines a KSDS cluster named PLYKSDS1 in a user catalog. This job shows how to use the UNIQUE parameter. In a VSAM catalog system, the UNIQUE entry, which can be abbreviated as UNQ, specifies that the space requested for this data set not be drawn from a pool shared by other data sets. In an ICF system, UNIQUE has no effect. The VOLUMES (SCR001) parameter supplies the name of the volume on which the data set will reside.

■ **Figure 12.18** ■

Defining a Unique KSDS Cluster

```
//JCLQB210 JOB ,'SCORPIO',
//              REGION=300K
//JOBCAT    DD DSN=USERCAT,
//              DISP=SHR
//DEFCLU2   EXEC PGM=IDCAMS
//SYSPRINT DD SYSOUT=A
//DD1       DD UNIT=SYSDA,
//              DISP=OLD,
//              VOL=SER=SCR001
//SYSIN     DD *
 DEFINE CLUSTER (NAME (VSAM.QB.JCL.PLYKSDS1) -
                RECORDS (1000 200) -
                FILE (DD1) -
                FREESPACE (20 20) -
                INDEXED -
                KEYS (5 0) -
                RECORDSIZE (80 80) -
                UNIQUE -
                VOLUMES (SCR001) ) -
        DATA (NAME (VSAM.QB.JCL.KSDS1DAT) ) -
        INDEX (NAME (VSAM.QB.JCL.KSDS1IND) )
    /*
    //
```

Information from this parameter goes into the user catalog, but it does not enable the system to access that disk pack. Access to disk pack SCR001 is obtained via the FILE (DD1) parameter, which points to the DD statement that names the actual disk pack. If the requested space is not available on SCR001, the job will fail. The FREESPACE allocation requests that 20 percent of each of the CIs and 20 percent of each of the CAs be left free for expansion. As mentioned earlier, in MVS systems the FILE parameter is not required, because the required volume is dynamically allocated.

The records in this KSDS are fixed in length, because the average and maximum lengths are the same (RECORDSIZE (80 80)). The key is five bytes long and starts in the first position in the record (KEYS (5 0)). The RECORDSIZE and KEYS parameters are coded to be consistent with POLYFILE. PLYKSDS1 was loaded with data from POLYFILE in Figure 12.12.

The job to define PLYKSDS2, the cluster that was loaded with data from POLYISAM in Figure 12.13, is not shown. The job would be similar to the one in Figure 12.18, except that RECORDSIZE (81 81) and KEYS (5 1) would be coded to be consistent with POLYISAM.

The job in Figure 12.19 shows how the index and data components of a KSDS can be placed on different volumes. Placing these components on different volumes can increase processing speed, because access arm motion is reduced.

The jobs shown in Figures 12.17, 12.18, and 12.19 all define KSDS clusters. The system knows that KSDSs are wanted because the parameter INDEXED is specified. The parameters KEYS and FREESPACE are specified only for KSDSs.

Figure 12.19

Defining a KSDS Cluster with Data and Index Portions on Separate Volumes

```
//JCLQB220 JOB ,'SAGITTARIUS',
//              REGION=300K
//DEFCLU3  EXEC PGM=IDCAMS
//SYSPRINT DD SYSOUT=A
//SYSIN    DD *
 DEFINE CLUSTER (NAME (VSAM.QB.JCL.KSDS3) -
                 RECORDS (1000 100) -
                 FREESPACE (20 10) -
                 INDEXED -
                 KEYS (10 90) -
                 RECORDSIZE (100 100) ) -
          DATA (NAME (VSAM.QB.JCL.KSDS3DAT) -
                VOLUMES (SCR001) ) -
          INDEX (NAME (VSAM.QB.JCL.KSDS3IND) -
                 VOLUMES (SCR002) )
 /*
 //
```

■ **Figure 12.20** ■

Defining an ESDS Cluster

```
//JCLQB230 JOB ,'CAPRICORN',
//           REGION=300K
//DEFCLE1  EXEC PGM=IDCAMS
//SYSPRINT DD SYSOUT=A
//SYSIN    DD *
 DEFINE CLUSTER (NAME (VSAM.QB.JCL.ESDS1) -
                RECORDS (1000 100) -
                NONINDEXED -
                RECORDSIZE (320 670) -
                VOLUMES (SCR001) ) -
        DATA (NAME (VSAM.QB.JCL.ESDS1DAT) ) -
        CATALOG (UCAT02)
 /*
 //
```

The job in Figure 12.20 defines the cluster for an ESDS. The parameter NONINDEXED tells the system that an ESDS is being defined. The variable length records average 320 bytes and have a maximum size of 670. Space for 1000 records is reserved on volume SCR001. Notice that the CATALOG entry in the command names UCAT02 as the catalog to be used.

The job in Figure 12.21 defines an ESDS cluster to be used as a workfile. REUSE is specified, so the data set will be reloaded every time it is opened for output. Coding REUSE is the VSAM equivalent of using temporary files. Space for 1000 records will be reserved on volume SCR001. If an attempt is made to write more than 1000 records, however, the job will fail because no secondary allocation is specified.

■ **Figure 12.21** ■

Defining a Work ESDS Cluster

```
//JCLQB240 JOB ,'AQUARIUS',
//            REGION=300K
//JOBCAT    DD DSN=USERCAT,
//             DISP=SHR
//DEFCLE2   EXEC PGM=IDCAMS
//SYSPRINT DD SYSOUT=A
//SYSIN    DD *
 DEFINE CLUSTER (NAME (VSAM.QB.JCL.ESDS2) -
                RECORDS (1000) -
                NONINDEXED -
                RECORDSIZE (80 320) -
                REUSE -
                VOLUMES (SCR001) )
 /*
 //
```

◼ Figure 12.22 ▬▬▬▬▬▬▬▬▬▬▬▬▬▬▬▬▬▬▬▬▬▬▬▬▬▬▬▬▬▬▬

Defining an RRDS Cluster

```
//JCLQB250 JOB ,'PISCES',
//              REGION=300K
//DEFCLR1  EXEC PGM=IDCAMS
//STEPCAT  DD DSN=USERCAT,
//              DISP=SHR
//SYSPRINT DD SYSOUT=A
//DD1      DD UNIT=SYSDA,
//              DISP=OLD,
//              VOL=SER=SCR001
//SYSIN    DD *
 DEFINE CLUSTER (NAME (VSAM.QB.JCL.POLYRRDS) -
                RECORDS (1000 100) -
                FILE (DD1) -
                NUMBERED -
                RECORDSIZE (80 80) -
                UNIQUE -
                VOLUMES (SCR001) ) -
          DATA (NAME (VSAM.QB.JCL.PLYRRDAT) )
/*
//
```

The job in Figure 12.22 must define an RRDS because the parameter NUMBERED appears in the command. Notice that the records are of fixed length (average equals maximum), a requirement for RRDSs.

Space for a VSAM data set can be requested in units of cylinders or tracks as well as of record count, but specifying the space allocation in units of record count is easier. You generally know about how many records are to go into a data set, and this coding lets the system do the arithmetic required to determine how many tracks and/or cylinders are required.

DEFINE SPACE Command

The DEFINE SPACE command, which has meaning only in VSAM catalog systems, reserves space on a DASD volume and records the reservation in a VSAM catalog. Space obtained in this way may hold more than one VSAM data set. As you recall, if you specify UNIQUE with the DEFINE CLUSTER command, space is obtained for only that data set.

Once a data space is defined on a volume, all future data spaces defined on that volume must be defined in the same VSAM catalog. If, as illustrated in Figure 12.23, we define a data space of 10 cylinders on volume SCR001 in VSAM user catalog USERCAT, when we wish to define another data space on volume SCR001, we must again specify VSAM user catalog USERCAT. The largest possible data space would be the entire volume. A data space cannot

■■ **Figure 12.23** ■■■■■■■■■■■■■■■■■■■■■■■■■■■■■■■■■■■■■■■

Defining Space

```
//JCLQB260 JOB ,'J. C. LEWIS',
//                REGION=300K
//DEFSPC1  EXEC PGM=IDCAMS
//SYSPRINT DD SYSOUT=A
//DD1      DD UNIT=SYSDA,
//            DISP=OLD,
//            VOL=SER=SCR001
//SYSIN    DD *
 DEFINE SPACE (CYL (10) -
               VOLUMES (SCR001) -
               FILE (DD1) ) -
            CATALOG (USERCAT)
/*
//
```

exist on multiple volumes. If you look at the command parameters shown in Table 12.6, however, you will see that more than one volume can be named, so you can define data spaces on several volumes with one command. The job in Figure 12.24 illustrates the coding. Notice that the two volumes are named in one DD statement; you may not use concatenated DD statements to describe more than one volume. Also, the space requirement is given in record count and record size; computation of the number of tracks and/or cylinders is left to the system. As a result of this job, data space on volumes SCR001 and SCR002 will be defined in VSAM user catalog USERCAT.

We will not discuss the CANDIDATE parameter, which reserves entire volumes for VSAM, because this task is one that an application programmer would not normally handle.

DEFINE USERCATALOG Command

Although defining of a user catalog is usually done by a systems programmer, it may also be done by the lead programmer on a team and upon occasion by an application programmer, which is why it is included here. The following discussion does not go into great depth, but it provides enough information to permit you to do the job.

Using separate user catalogs for each application is a good idea. It makes controlling the data sets easier, and because the catalogs are smaller, it results in faster execution times.

The general form of the command is

```
DEFINE USERCATALOG (parameters) -
       DATA (parameters) -
       INDEX (parameters) -
       CATALOG (mastercatname/password)
```

Table 12.6
DEFINE SPACE Command Parameters

Parameter	Abbreviation	Definition
CANDIDATE	CAN	Means that the entire volume or volumes named are reserved for VSAM.
CYLINDERS (prim sec) TRACKS (prim sec)	CYL TRK	Reserves the named quantity on the volume named.
RECORDS (prim sec) and RECORDSIZE (aver max)	REC RECSZ	Reserves space for the given number of records of the named size.
VOLUMES (volser...)	VOL	Names the volume or volumes on which the data space is to be defined.
FILE (ddname)		Points to the DD statement for the volume on which the data space is to be defined.
CATALOG (catname/password)	CAT	Names the VSAM catalog in which the data space is to be defined.

Figure 12.24

Defining Multivolume Space

```
//JCLQB270 JOB ,'J. C. LEWIS',
//              REGION=300K
//DEFSPC2  EXEC PGM=IDCAMS
//STEPCAT  DD DSN=USERCAT,
//            DISP=SHR
//SYSPRINT DD SYSOUT=A
//DDX      DD UNIT=SYSDA,
//            DISP=OLD,
//            VOL=SER=(SCR001,SCR002)
//SYSIN    DD *
 DEFINE SPACE (RECORDS (2000 200) -
               RECORDSIZE (100 300) -
               VOLUMES (SCR001 SCR002) -
               FILE (DDX) ) -
             CATALOG (USERCAT)
/*
//
```

Table 12.7
DEFINE USERCATALOG Command Parameters

Parameter	Abbreviation	UCAT	DATA	INDEX	Definition
BUFFERSPACE (size)	BUFSP	O	O	N/A	Gives the minimum space for buffers.
CYLINDERS (prim sec) RECORDS (prim sec) TRACKS (prim sec)	CYL REC TRK	R	O	O	Gives the amount of space to be reserved on the volume.
DESTAGEWAIT NODESTAGEWAIT	DSTGW NDSTGW	O	O	O	Applies to mass storage.
FILE (ddname)		R/O	N/A	N/A	Points to the DD statement that identifies the volume on which the user catalog is being defined.
MODEL (entryname/password catname/password)		O	N/A	N/A	Names an existing VSAM user catalog that is to be used as a sample.
OWNER (owner-id)		O	N/A	N/A	Identifies the catalog owner.
RECOVERABLE	RVBL	O	O	O	Creates a catalog recovery space on each volume owned by catalog.
NOTRECOVERABLE	NRVBL				The default. This parameter has no meaning in an ICF system.
NAME (entryname)		R	N/A	N/A	Names the catalog.
TO (date) FOR (days)		O	N/A	N/A	Specifies expiration date.
WRITECHECK	WCK	O	O	O	Causes the hardware to check that the data were written correctly.
NOWRITECHECK	NWCK				The default.
VOLUME (volser)	VOL	R	N/A	N/A	Names the volume on which the user catalog is to be defined.

■ Figure 12.25 ■

Defining a User Catalog

```
//JCLQB280 JOB ,'J. C. LEWIS',
//              REGION=300K
//DEFUCAT  EXEC PGM=IDCAMS
//SYSPRINT DD SYSOUT=A
//DD1      DD UNIT=SYSDA,
//            DISP=OLD,
//            VOL=SER=SCR001
//SYSIN    DD *
 DEFINE USERCATALOG (NAME (NEWUCAT) -
                     FILE (DD1) -
                     CYL (4 1) -
                     VOLUMES (SCR001) )
 /*
 //
```

The parameters, excluding those that apply to security, are defined in Table 12.7. Those that apply to security, which are the same as for the DEFINE CLUSTER command, are shown in Table 12.5. The CATALOG entry shows that the user catalog is cataloged in the master catalog. You need specify this parameter only if a password is required.

A user catalog, like a KSDS, consists of a data and an index component. If you examine Table 12.7, you will notice that none of the parameters are required for DATA or INDEX. Unless you have a reason to code them, they should not be coded.

The job shown in Figure 12.25 will result in the creation of a user catalog on volume SCR001. The catalog will be given a primary allocation of four cylinders.

Secondary Keys

Unlike ISAM, VSAM permits more than one field in a record to be treated as a key. Why would you want to have more than one key? As an example, let us examine a typical school problem. Although it is desirable to maximize the use of classrooms, no more than one class may use a room at any one time. In addition, the administration usually wants to know how many courses a particular instructor is teaching. A typical master course record might contain a unique course number, a course name, the days and time of meeting, the room number, the instructor's name, and the number of students registered.

The course number would be used as the prime key. The administration, however, might want to access the data set by room number to determine which courses use a particular room. To permit such access, the programmer would make the room number an alternate key. The administration might also want to access the data set by the instructor's name to determine which courses each instructor is teaching. To permit such access, the programmer would make the instructor's name an additional alternate key.

Maintaining secondary keys is expensive in both CPU time and DASD space. Consequently, you must weigh the maintenance costs against the cost of obtaining the data in another way.

In order to create an alternate index for either a KSDS or an ESDS, the following steps must be performed:

1. The base cluster must be defined and loaded.
2. The IDCAMS DEFINE ALTERNATEINDEX command must be executed to create a catalog entry for the new index.
3. An IDCAMS BLDINDEX command must be executed to load the alternate index with data.
4. An IDCAMS DEFINE PATH command must be executed to create a catalog entry connecting the alternate index with the base cluster.

(The order of steps 3 and 4 may be reversed.)

DEFINE ALTERNATEINDEX Command

Once you have defined your base cluster, you may issue the command to define the alternate index. The form of this command is

```
DEFINE ALTERNATEINDEX (parameters) -
       DATA (parameters) -
       INDEX (parameters) -
       CATALOG (parameters)
```

If you refer back to the DEFINE CLUSTER command, you will notice that the only difference between the DEFINE CLUSTER and ALTERNATEINDEX commands is that the latter uses the word ALTERNATEINDEX in place of the word CLUSTER. With minor exceptions, the parameters shown in Tables 12.4 and 12.5 also apply to this command.

Figure 12.26 shows how to create an alternate index using the instructor's name as a secondary key. The NAME, KEYS, and VOLUMES parameters have the same meanings as they have in the DEFINE CLUSTER command. In this example, coding of the KEYS parameter is based on the assumption that the instructor's name starts at byte 38 and is 15 bytes long.

Three new parameters that apply to the alternate index are shown in Figure 12.26. The RELATE parameter is required; the base cluster to which this alternate index applies is named in it. In Figure 12.26 NAMEINDX is related to a previously defined base cluster named CLASMSTR. The specifica-

■ **Figure 12.26** ■

Defining an Alternate Index

```
//JCLQB290 JOB ,'J. C. LEWIS',
//              REGION=300K
//STEPAIX    EXEC PGM=IDCAMS
//STEPCAT   DD DSN=USERCAT,
//              DISP=SHR
//SYSPRINT DD SYSOUT=A
//SYSIN    DD *
 DEFINE ALTERNATEINDEX (NAME (VSAM.QB.JCL.NAMEINDX) -
                        RELATE (VSAM.QB.JCL.CLASMSTR) -
                        RECORDS (1000 100) -
                        KEYS (15 37) -
                        RECORDSIZE (27 87) -
                        VOLUMES (SCR001) -
                        FREESPACE (20 10) -
                        NONUNIQUEKEY -
                        UNIQUE -
                        UPGRADE ) -
        DATA (NAME (VSAM.QB.JCL.NAMEINDX.DATA) ) -
        INDEX (NAME (VSAM.QB.JCL.NAMEINDX.INDEX) )
 /*
 //
```

tion of UNIQUEKEY or NONUNIQUEKEY indicates whether or not more than one record may have the same alternate key. You may recall that for a KSDS the prime key must be unique, whereas for an ESDS there is no prime key. The default value is NONUNIQUEKEY. In Figure 12.26 NONUNIQUEKEY is coded because each instructor usually teaches several courses. If an alternate index based on room number were created, NONUNIQUEKEY would again be specified because several classes use the same room. On the other hand, if room number were combined with day and time of meeting for use as an alternate key, UNIQUEKEY would be coded because only one class may use a classroom at a particular time. The third parameter, UPGRADE or NOUPGRADE, specifies whether or not the alternate index is to be updated whenever a record is added to, changed in, or deleted from the base cluster. The default value is UPGRADE. You might think that you would always want to code UPGRADE in order to keep the alternate index and base cluster synchronized, but that is not so. Upgrading an alternate index takes time, and when the base cluster is used in an on-line application, it may be preferable to code NOUPGRADE and then periodically rebuild the alternate index (using the BLDINDEX command, discussed in the next section) in a batch job when the on-line application is not running.

The RECORDSIZE for a KSDS may be calculated using the equation

$$RECORDSIZE = 5 + A + (n \times B)$$

where A is the length of the alternate key, B is the length of the base cluster key, and n is the number of data records in the base cluster that contain the same alternate key value. If the alternate key is unique, then n is 1, the equation is simple to apply, and the average and maximum record sizes are the same. If the alternate key is not unique, figuring out a proper value for n can be very difficult.

There are really two problems here: determining the correct value for the average record size and determining the correct value for the maximum record size. To determine the correct value for the average record size, we can reason as follows. The system uses the average record size together with the number of records specified in the RECORDS parameter to calculate the space required for the data set. Therefore, if we request for the alternate index the same number of records as are in the base cluster, we can calculate the average record size by using the equation with n equal to 1. If we are wrong and the average value for n should be, for example, 2, the records will be twice as long, but there will be half as many of them so the space calculation will still be correct. (Actually, the equation shows that the record size with $n = 2$ is less than twice what it is with $n = 1$, so we are requesting slightly more space than we need, but erring on the side of safety is fine.)

Determining the correct value for the maximum record size can be more difficult. The guiding principle here is that if we specify a value that is too large, no great harm is done. Following that principle, some programmers code the highest possible value, 32600. Sometimes we can make a good estimate of the highest possible value of n in the equation. For example, if we can be sure that no instructor will teach more than five courses, we can use $n = 5$ to calculate the maximum record size. (The values for RECORDSIZE in Figure 12.26 were calculated using $A = 7$, $B = 15$, and $n = 5$.)

In some instances, the safest thing to do is to modify a nonunique key to make it unique. For example, suppose we want to use employee name as an alternate key in an employee record in which social security number is the prime key. We cannot predict how many Smiths will be employed, so we cannot safely estimate an upper value for n. In these cases, many programmers prefer to concatenate the prime key and the alternate key to make a new, unique alternate key. If the employee name starts in byte 1 and is 15 bytes long and the social security number starts in byte 16 and is 9 bytes long, we can define a unique alternate key that starts in byte 1 and is 24 bytes long. We can still retrieve records based on name, because the system allows us to retrieve records based on part of the key (starting from the left end).

As in defining clusters, do not — except in the case of NAME — supply parameters separately for the data and index components. Again, supply only required information, and allow the system to use default values whenever possible. In Figure 12.26 NONUNIQUEKEY and UPGRADE need not have been coded, because these are the default values. They were coded for illustrative purposes only.

BLDINDEX Command

The BLDINDEX command, which may be abbreviated BIX, loads the data into the alternate index. It cannot be executed until there is at least one record in the base cluster.

The parameters of the BLDINDEX command are shown in Table 12.8. The table may seem a little confusing at first glance. Let us pause a minute to talk about the form of the alternate index. Earlier we said that the alternate index, like a KSDS, consists of an index and a data part. The index part is obviously like the index part of a KSDS, as illustrated in Figure 12.7, but what information is in the data part? That depends on whether the base cluster is a KSDS or an ESDS. If it is an ESDS, the data part contains the secondary key and the RBA of the record in the base cluster that contains that secondary key. If it is a KSDS, the data part contains the secondary key and the prime key of the record in the base cluster that contains that secondary key. Thus accessing a record using a secondary key requires accessing the alternate index first. The record in the alternate index supplies the RBA for an ESDS or the prime key for a KSDS, which is then used to access the base cluster.

If the secondary key is nonunique and the base cluster is an ESDS, the data part of the alternate index contains the secondary key and the RBAs of all the records in the base cluster that contain that secondary key. If the base cluster is a KSDS, the data part of the alternate index contains the secondary key and the prime keys of all the records in the base cluster that contain that secondary key.

Now that you understand what is in an alternate index, let us consider how one is built. The base cluster is read, and alternate index records containing the secondary key and either the prime key or the RBA are created. In these alternate index records, the secondary keys usually will not be in sequence. As a result, the alternate index records must be sorted into the proper order. This sort may be performed internally if there is sufficient virtual storage, or externally if there is not. You may specifically request that an external sort be done, although an internal sort is faster.

Figure 12.27 illustrates a job used to build the alternate index that was defined in Figure 12.26. The first DD statement refers to the alternate index. For simplicity the ddname of AIX is used, but any valid name may be used. The second DD statement refers to the base cluster. The third and fourth DD statements are the workfiles that IDCAMS will use if there is insufficient virtual storage for an internal sort. The WORKFILES parameter is not coded in the BLDINDEX command, so the ddnames IDCUT1 and IDCUT2 had to be used. Had the WORKFILES parameter been coded, the ddnames specified by that parameter could have been used. The parameters for the workfiles' DD statements must be coded as shown. Although the DISP specified for these workfiles is OLD, they are defined by BLDINDEX while the job is executing and deleted when the sort is finished. If neither EXTERNALSORT nor

Table 12.8
BLDINDEX Command Parameters

Parameter	Abbreviation	Definition
INFILE (ddname/password)	IFILE	Names the DD statement that points to the base cluster.
INDATASET (entryname/password)*	IDS	Names the base cluster; may be used instead of INFILE.
OUTFILE (ddname/password)	OFILE	Names the DD statement that points to the alternate index or path.
OUTDATASET (entryname/password)*	ODS	Actually names the alternate index or path.
CATALOG (catname/password)	CAT	Names the catalog in which the workfiles used in building the index are defined.
EXTERNALSORT INTERNALSORT	ESORT ISORT	Determines whether the sort needed in building the index is internal or external. INTERNALSORT is the default. If EXTERNALSORT is specified, workfiles are required.
WORKFILES (ddname ddname)	WFILE	Specifies the ddnames used by the external sort. IDCUT1 and IDCUT2 are the default names; if they are used, this parameter is not required.

* For MVS systems only.

■ **Figure 12.27** ■■

Building an Alternate Index

```
//JCLQB300 JOB ,'J. C. LEWIS',
//            REGION=300K
//STEPBLD  EXEC PGM=IDCAMS
//AIX       DD DSN=VSAM.QB.JCL.NAMEINDX,
//             DISP=OLD
//BASE      DD DSN=VSAM.QB.JCL.CLASMSTR,
//             DISP=OLD
//IDCUT1    DD DSN=VSAM.QB.JCL.WORKONE,
//             DISP=OLD,
//             UNIT=SYSDA,
//             VOL=SER=SCR001,
//             AMP=AMORG
//IDCUT2    DD DSN=VSAM.QB.JCL.WORKTWO,
//             DISP=OLD,
//             UNIT=SYSDA,
//             VOL=SER=SCR001,
//             AMP=AMORG
//SYSPRINT DD SYSOUT=A
//SYSIN    DD *
 BLDINDEX INFILE (BASE) -
          OUTFILE (AIX) -
          EXTERNALSORT -
          CATALOG (USERCAT)
 /*
 //
```

INTERNALSORT had been specified in the command, the default value of INTERNALSORT would be used.

Once the BLDINDEX command has been successfully executed, the secondary index exists. One more step must be performed, however, before the secondary index can be used.

DEFINE PATH Command

The AIX DD statement in Figure 12.27 does not access the base cluster named CLASMSTR via the alternate index, but rather accesses the alternate index itself as if it were a VSAM KSDS. Accessing the base cluster via an alternate index requires defining a path from the alternate index to the base cluster. The form of the DEFINE PATH command is

```
DEFINE PATH (parameters) -
       CATALOG (catname/password)
```

The parameters used in the command are defined in Table 12.9; the parameters related to security are defined in Table 12.5.

An example of a job defining a path is shown in Figure 12.28. The JCL is

Table 12.9
DEFINE PATH Command Parameters

Parameter	Abbreviation	Definition
`NAME (entryname)`		Supplies the path name. This name appears on the DD statement when the alternate index is used.
`PATHENTRY (entryname/password)`	`PENT`	Supplies the alternate index name. Under special conditions, a cluster name may be given.
`FILE (ddname)`		Supplies the ddname of the DD statement that points to the volume used for recovery purposes. This parameter has no meaning in an ICF system.
`MODEL (entryname/password` `      catname/password)`		Supplies the name of an existing path to be used as a model.
`OWNER (owner-id)`		Identifies the owner of the path.
`TO (date)` `FOR (days)`		Specifies the expiration date.
`UPDATE` `NOUPDATE`	`UPD` `NUPD`	Indicates that the other alternate indexes will be updated when this path is processed. UPDATE is the default.

virtually the same as that shown in Figure 12.26, where the alternate index was defined. In the DEFINE PATH statement the two required parameters are NAME and PATHENTRY. The NAME parameter supplies the name for the path. The PATHENTRY parameter names the alternate index to which this path refers. Notice that the name of the base cluster does not have to be supplied.

In the example in Figure 12.28, NOUPDATE is coded; otherwise the default of UPDATE would be used. This parameter overrides the UPGRADE parameter in the definition of any other alternate index. Thus if the base cluster

━━ **Figure 12.28** ━━━━━━━━━━━━━━━━━━━━━━━━━━━━━━━

Defining a Path

```
//JCLQB310 JOB ,'J. C. LEWIS',
//          REGION=300K
//STEPATH   EXEC PGM=IDCAMS
//STEPCAT   DD DSN=USERCAT,
//          DISP=SHR
//SYSPRINT DD SYSOUT=A
//SYSIN    DD *
 DEFINE PATH (NAME (VSAM.QB.JCL.NAMEPATH) -
              PATHENTRY (VSAM.QB.JCL.NAMEINDX) -
              NOUPDATE )
/*
//
```

CLASMSTR has other alternate indexes in addition to NAMEINDX, those other alternate indexes will not be updated when a change is made using the path NAMEPATH. A record added via path NAMEPATH will not be found if the data set is accessed via a different path. Why would anyone be willing to let this happen? Usually you do not want your indexes to be out of synchronization, but there are times when lack of synchronization may be acceptable. If UP-DATE is specified for a path, all alternate indexes with UPGRADE specified must be opened and available when that path is opened. If your program is only reading the data set, why waste resources by having all the alternate indexes available? A second path for which UPDATE is specified could be defined, to be used when the data set will actually be changed.

If you want to access a base cluster via an alternate index, you code the path's data set name on the DD statement. This may surprise you, so let us look at an illustration. Suppose we want to print the base cluster CLASMASTR in alphabetical order by instructor's name. This goal can be accomplished by accessing CLASMSTR via the alternate index NAMEINDX. In Figure 12.29 the data set name of the path NAMEPATH is coded on the PRINT DD statement.

The definition in Table 12.9 indicates that the PATHENTRY parameter may name a base cluster instead of an alternate index. Thus use of PATHENTRY is one way to supply an alias for a VSAM data set. In addition, the security specified for the path may differ from that for the base cluster. Thus a path known to an entire group could permit read-only access, whereas the base cluster known to only a few would permit update access as well.

━━ **DELETE Command**

Once you no longer need a particular cluster, user catalog, alternate index, or other VSAM entity, you may wish to get rid of it. This goal is accomplished with the DELETE command.

Figure 12.29

Printing Using a Path

```
//JCLQB320 JOB ,'J. C. LEWIS',
//              REGION=300K
//PRINT3   EXEC PGM=IDCAMS
//STEPCAT  DD DSN=USERCAT,
//              DISP=SHR
//SYSPRINT DD SYSOUT=A
//PRINT    DD DSN=VSAM.QB.JCL.NAMEPATH,
//              DISP=OLD
//SYSIN    DD *
 PRINT INFILE (PRINT)
/*
//
```

Table 12.10
DELETE Command Parameters

Parameter	Abbreviation	Definition
(entryname/password...) What is		See Table 12.11.
ERASE	ERAS	Means that binary zeros will be written over deleted data.
NOERASE	NERAS	The default.
FILE (ddname)		Points to the DD statement that names either what is being deleted or the volume that contains what is being deleted.
FORCE	FRC	Enables, for example, the deletion of a VSAM user catalog that is not empty.
NOFORCE	NFRC	The default.
PURGE	PRG	Allows an entry to be deleted even if the retention period has not expired.
NOPURGE	NPRG	The default.
CATALOG (catname/password)	CAT	Names the catalog that contains the entries to be deleted.

Table 12.11
What May Be Deleted

"What is"	Abbreviation
ALIAS	
ALTERNATE INDEX*	AIX
CLUSTER*	CL
GENERATIONDATAGROUP	GDG
NONVSAM	NVSAM
PAGESPACE	PGSPC
PATH*	
SPACE*	SPC
USERCATALOG*	UCAT

* Discussed in this chapter.

The parameters used with this command are shown in Table 12.10. Table 12.11 is referenced by the "what is" line in Table 12.10. "What is" tells what type of entry is to be deleted with the DELETE command. The items in Table 12.11 marked with an asterisk are the ones we will discuss in this chapter. You already know what a cluster and a user catalog are, and we will discuss the others later.

The first parameter, entryname/password, is a positional parameter and must be named first. entryname supplies the name of what you want deleted. More than one entry may be deleted at a time; for example, you could code

```
DELETE (VSAMCL1 VSAMCL2) ...
```

Notice that when there is more than one entry, the entries must be enclosed in parentheses. Although a password is not used here, one may be required if the entry is password protected. We do not have the space to give the subject of security the attention it deserves; however, where passwords may be used is indicated in Table 12.10.

The job stream in Figure 12.30 deletes a VSAM data set; let us look at it in detail. The DD1 DD statement points to the entry to be deleted. In the DELETE command VSAM.QB.JCL.DATASET is again named as the entry to be deleted. CLUSTER indicates that VSAM.QB.JCL.DATASET is a cluster, as are all VSAM data sets. ERASE means that binary zeros are to be written over the data so that if the disk pack is dumped, the data will not be there. With large files ERASE may take a long time, so it should be used only with sensitive data. FILE (DD1) points to the DD statement DD1. PURGE means that VSAM.QB.JCL.DATASET is to be deleted even if the expiration date has not arrived. CATALOG (UCAT02) says that the entry for DATASET is in the user

■ **Figure 12.30** ■

Deleting a VSAM Cluster

```
//JCLQB120 JOB ,'J. C. LEWIS',
//              REGION=300K
//DELETE1  EXEC PGM=IDCAMS
//SYSPRINT DD SYSOUT=A
//DD1       DD DSN=VSAM.QB.JCL.DATASET,
//              DISP=OLD
//SYSIN    DD *
 DELETE VSAM.QB.JCL.DATASET -
        CLUSTER -
        ERASE -
        FILE (DD1) -
        PURGE -
        CATALOG (UCAT02)
/*
//
```

catalog UCAT02, and only that catalog is to be searched. When a cluster is deleted, related alternate indexes and paths are also deleted.

The DD1 DD statement is somewhat special. Because ERASE is coded as part of the DELETE command in Figure 12.30, this DD statement points to DATASET, which is the entry to be deleted and erased. If ERASE had not been coded, the DD1 DD statement would point to the volume that DATASET is on, as in

```
//DD1       DD UNIT=SYSDA,
//              VOL=SER=SCR001,
//              DISP=OLD
```

■ **Figure 12.31** ■

Deleting a User Catalog

```
//JCLQB130 JOB ,'J. C. LEWIS',
//              REGION=300K
//DELETE2  EXEC PGM=IDCAMS
//*
//*          DELETE USER CATALOG
//*
//SYSPRINT DD SYSOUT=A
//SYSIN    DD *
 DELETE UCAT02 -
        USERCATALOG -
        FORCE -
        PURGE
/*
//
```

In MVS systems the FILE parameter and its associated DD statement are not required.

The job in Figure 12.31 deletes a VSAM user catalog named UCAT02 even if the expiration date has not arrived and even if the catalog is not empty.

VERIFY Command

When a job abends or is canceled or the system fails, the VSAM data sets are not properly closed — that is, the end-of-data marker in the data set does not agree with what the catalog says is the end-of-data. A VSAM data set in this condition cannot be used. The VERIFY command is used to correct this problem.

Table 12.12 illustrates the two parameters that may be used with the VERIFY command; you code one or the other.

Because FILE is correct for both VS1 and MVS systems whereas DATASET is correct only for MVS systems, FILE is used in the example shown in Figure 12.32. Note that OLD, rather than SHR, is used for the disposition on the DD statement of the data set to be corrected, to ensure that no one else attempts to use it while it is being corrected.

Table 12.12
VERIFY Command Parameters

Parameter	Abbreviation	Definition
FILE (ddname/password)		Points to the DD statement that names the object to be corrected.
DATASET (entryname/password)*	DS	Names the object to be corrected.

*For MVS systems only.

LISTCAT Command

From time to time you may want to know what is in a master or user catalog. For instance, after you run a job defining some entity such as a cluster or an alternate index, you might want to see whether the entity is listed in the catalog. Or you might need to look back to see what name you gave to some entity when you defined it. To see what is in a catalog, you can use the LISTCAT command.

As you will learn in Chapter 13, non-VSAM catalogs may be listed using the LISTCTLG command of the utility program IEHLIST. By changing parameters in the LISTCTLG command, you can modify the listing. By changing

■ Figure 12.32 ■

Verifying a Data Set

```
//JCLQB350 JOB ,'J. C. LEWIS',
//           REGION=300K
//VERIFY    EXEC PGM=IDCAMS
//STEPCAT   DD DSN=USERCAT,
//              DISP=SHR
//SYSPRINT DD SYSOUT=A
//DD1       DD DSN=VSAM.QB.JCL.PLYKSDS1,
//              DISP=OLD
//SYSIN     DD *
 VERIFY FILE (DD1)
/*
//
```

parameters in the LISTCAT command of IDCAMS, you can make more exten-
sive modifications to the listing than are permitted with the IEHLIST utility
program. The LISTCAT parameters appear in Table 12.13. We will discuss
only those that you as an application programmer are likely to need.

Figure 12.33 illustrates a LISTCAT job. Note that the LISTCAT command is
abbreviated LISTC and that no parameters are specified. Because no catalog
is named in the job, the master catalog will be listed. The listing will include
only the names of the entities in the master catalog. If more information about
the entities had been required, any of the following could have been coded:

LISTC ALLOC

or

LISTC HISTORY

or

LISTC VOLUME

If all possible information had been desired,

LISTC ALL

could have been coded, but be warned: ALL gives you a lot of output.

In Figure 12.33 the LISTCAT job is run as a separate job rather than as a step
in a larger job. The reason for this is that in some situations the catalog may
not be updated until a job ends. If you define an entity in one step and then
execute a LISTCAT in a later step in the same job, you cannot be sure the
output you get represents the true state of the catalog.

If you want information about a catalog other than the master catalog,
there are three alternatives. A JOBCAT DD statement can be coded naming the
desired catalog. Or a STEPCAT DD statement can be coded. Finally, the desired

Table 12.13
LISTCAT Command Parameters

Parameter	Abbreviation	Description
CATALOG (catname/ password)	CAT	Specifies which catalog is to have its contents listed.
ALIAS		Any or all of these parameters may be specified to limit the scope of the LISTCAT command. If none of these parameters are specified, the listing includes everything in the catalog.
ALTERNATE INDEX	AIX	
CLUSTER	CL	
GENERATIONDATAGROUP	GDG	
DATA		
INDEX	IX	
NONVSAM	NVSAM	
PAGESPACE	PGSPC	
PATH		
SPACE	SPC	
USERCATALOG	UCAT	
ALL		These parameters, which are mutually exclusive, indicate the information to be provided for each entry. The default is NAME.
HISTORY	HIST	
ALLOCATION	ALLOC	
NAME		
VOLUME	VOL	
CREATION (days)	CREAT	Indicates that the listing is to include only those entries created the specified number of days ago or earlier.
ENTRIES (entryname/ password...)	ENT	Names the entries to be included in the listing.
LEVEL (level)	LVL	Is similar to the NODE parameter of the LISTCTLG command of IEHLIST. An asterisk can be used in the middle, as in LEVEL (SYS1.*.OUT).
EXPIRATION (days)	EXPIR	Specifies that the listing is to include only those entries due to expire the specified number of days from now or earlier.
NOTUSABLE	NUS	Indicates that the listing is to include only those entries marked not usable.
OUTFILE (ddname)	OFILE	Specifies a data set other than the SYSPRINT data set for output.

━━ **Figure 12.33** ━━━

Listing a Catalog

```
//JCLQB330 JOB ,'J. C. LEWIS',
//               REGION=300K
//STEPLCAT EXEC PGM=IDCAMS
//SYSPRINT DD SYSOUT=A
//SYSIN    DD *
 LISTC
/*
//
```

catalog can be named in the `LISTCAT` command as follows:

```
LISTC CATALOG (UCAT)
```

If you are interested in only the clusters in the user catalog `UCAT`, the `LIST-CAT` command is coded as

```
LISTC CATALOG (UCAT) -
      CLUSTER
```

The `LEVEL` parameter is useful if a group of people share a common user catalog and you are interested in only your clusters. As you may recall, the convention at the CUNY computer center requires that all of J. C. Lewis's VSAM data sets start with the qualifiers `VSAM.QB.JCL`. Consequently, to list his clusters in the common user catalog `USERCAT`, he would code

```
LISTC CATALOG (USERCAT) -
      CLUSTER -
      LEVEL (VSAM.QB.JCL)
```

If all the students in a particular class at Queensborough Community College were given an assignment that involved creating a VSAM data set whose last qualifier was `TRANS`, the `LISTCAT` command to determine which data sets were created would be coded as follows:

```
LISTC CATALOG (USERCAT) -
      CLUSTER -
      LEVEL (VSAM.QB.*.TRANS)
```

Notice that an asterisk is coded in place of the user's initials required by the convention.

⬛ Command Execution Control

Frequently you will want to execute a series of `IDCAMS` commands in such a way that the second command is not executed unless the first was successful and the third is not executed unless the second was successful. IDCAMS provides a convenient way to control execution of a series of commands.

Condition Codes

After each IDCAMS command is executed, a condition code is set that is similar to the condition code set by the other utilities we have studied. A condition code of 0 means the command was successfully executed; a 4 means that a problem was encountered, but that it is probably safe to continue; an 8 means that the command was completed, but not with the desired results; a 12 indicates that the command could not be executed at all, but that processing will resume with the next command in the input stream; a 16 signifies that there occurred an error of such severity that this invocation of IDCAMS must terminate.

These condition codes may be tested with the COND parameter in the JOB or EXEC statement to determine whether or not processing should continue. IDCAMS, however, allows you to check the condition code of each command as it is performed within a step. Therefore several IDCAMS commands may be executed in one jobstep, instead of in several jobsteps, eliminating the overhead involved in initializing each step.

IF-THEN-ELSE Command

Those of you who are familiar with the IF statement found in most programming languages will find the rest of this section trivial. The rest of you will find it quite simple.

Figure 12.34 contains a simple but realistic example of command execution control. First space is defined just as it was in Figure 12.23. Then the command

```
IF LASTCC = 0 -
```

tests the return code resulting from the execution of the DEFINE SPACE command. If the return code is 0, the DEFINE CLUSTER command will be executed just as it was in Figure 12.17. If the return code is any other value, the DEFINE CLUSTER command will not be executed. Notice that the IF and THEN lines contain hyphens to indicate continuation.

Coding could have specified a command to be executed if the DEFINE SPACE does not have a zero return code. For example,

```
DEFINE SPACE ...
IF LASTCC = 0 -
    THEN -
        DEFINE CLUSTER...
    ELSE -
        DELETE SPACE...
```

■ **Figure 12.34** ■

Testing Condition Codes

```
//JCLQB340 JOB ,'J. C. LEWIS',
//              REGION=300K
//STEPDEF   EXEC PGM=IDCAMS
//STEPCAT   DD DSN=USERCAT,
//              DISP=SHR
//DD1       DD UNIT=SYSDA,
//              DISP=OLD,
//              VOL=SER=SCR001
//SYSPRINT DD SYSOUT=A
//SYSIN     DD *
            DEFINE SPACE (CYL (10) -
                    VOLUMES (SCR001) -
                       FILE (DD1) ) -
                  CATALOG (USERCAT)
    IF LASTCC = 0 -
       THEN -
            DEFINE CLUSTER (NAME (VSAM.QB.JCL.KSDS) -
                    RECORDS (1000 100) -
                    FREESPACE (20 30) -
                    INDEXED -
                    KEYS (10 5) -
                    RECORDSIZE (100 320) -
                    VOLUMES (SCR001) ) -
                DATA (NAME (VSAM.QB.JCL.KSDSDAT) ) -
                INDEX (NAME (VSAM.QB.JCL.KSDSIND) )
    /*
    //
```

specifies that if the return code of the DEFINE SPACE is 0, the cluster is defined; if not (ELSE), the space is deleted. (There are conditions under which the space would be defined and a nonzero return code produced.)

If instead of defining a single cluster you wish to define several, you code

```
DEFINE SPACE...
IF LASTCC = 0 -
   THEN DO
        DEFINE CLUSTER...
        DEFINE CLUSTER...
          .
          .
          .
        END
   ELSE -
        DELETE SPACE...
```

THEN DO indicates the start of the group of commands to be executed, and END marks the stopping point. Notice that the THEN DO line does not have a hyphen indicating continuation.

If you wish to define a user catalog, space, and several clusters, you might code the commands as

```
DEFINE USERCATALOG...
DEFINE SPACE...
IF MAXCC = 0 -
    THEN DO
            DEFINE CLUSTER...
            DEFINE CLUSTER...
            .
            .
            .
        END
```

In this example it is not the last return code that is tested, but the maximum return code, MAXCC. MAXCC refers to the maximum return code that has been established by any previous command. If the return code for DEFINE SPACE or DEFINE USERCATALOG is greater than 0, the DEFINE CLUSTER commands will not be executed. To undo the previous commands, you might code

```
DEFINE USERCATALOG...
DEFINE SPACE...
IF MAXCC = 0 -
    THEN DO
            DEFINE CLUSTER...
            DEFINE CLUSTER...
            .
            .
            .
        END
    ELSE DO
            DELETE USERCATALOG...
            DELETE SPACE...
        END
```

The IF-THEN-ELSE command sequence can be summarized as follows:

```
IF {LASTCC}  comparand number -
   {MAXCC }
    THEN DO
            commands
        END
    ELSE DO
            commands
        END
```

Legal comparands and their meanings are listed in Table 12.14. These comparands are the same as the operators that may be coded with the COND parameter (see Table 4.4), except that for these comparands you may code

■ Table 12.14
IF-THEN-ELSE Comparands

Comparand	Meaning
= or EQ	Equal to
¬= NE	Not equal to
> or GT	Greater than
< or LT	Less than
>= or GE	Greater than or equal to
<= or LE	Less than or equal to

either the symbol or the two-letter abbreviation. number may be any value between 0 and 16.

Although the general form of the command permits complex comparisons, you will find that most of the time you will test for 0, as in the examples given earlier in this section.

SET Command

It is also possible to use the SET command to assign a value to LASTCC or MAXCC. The syntax is

$$SET \begin{Bmatrix} LASTCC \\ MAXCC \end{Bmatrix} = value$$

where value can be any number between 0 and 16. The value assigned to MAXCC is reported as the return code from the step, and it can be used to control execution outside of the IDCAMS step.

Consider the following example. A COBOL program that updates a VSAM data set is being debugged. Every time the program is run, you want to start with the original data set, so the COBOL step is preceded by an IDCAMS step that tells the system to DEFINE, REPRO, and PRINT the cluster. If the cluster exists, however, the DEFINE command will fail, so the DEFINE command is preceded by a DELETE command. The DELETE command also will sometimes fail. For instance, it will fail the first time the job is run and whenever the old files comprising the cluster are automatically scratched by the system. But failure of the DELETE command has no significance. So the situation is as follows: You want the COB step skipped if the DEFINE or REPRO command fails, but you want it executed if only the DELETE command fails.

Following is a skeleton of a job that will accomplish this goal:

```
//COBUPDT JOB...
//VSAM     EXEC PGM=IDCAMS
//SYSIN    DD *
 DELETE ...
 DEFINE CLUSTER ...
              .
              .
              .
 IF LASTCC = 0 -
 THEN -
     REPRO ...
              .
              .
              .
 IF LASTCC = 0 -
 THEN -
     PRINT ...
 ELSE -
     SET MAXCC = 13
//UPDATE   EXEC COBUCG COND.COB=(13,EQ,VSAM),
//               COND.GO=((13,EQ,VSAM),(5,LT,COB))
//COB.SYSIN DD *
```

The logic here is to test only the return codes from the DEFINE and REPRO operations. If either return code is not equal to 0, MAXCC is set to 13. Then, in the UPDATE step, a COND is coded to skip the COB and GO steps if the condition code from the VSAM step is 13 (if the DELETE operation failed, the condition code will be 8). The COND parameter coded on the EXEC statement overrides the COND on all the steps in the procedure, so the COND parameter for the GO step must include a test of the return code from the COB step.

VSAM and Higher-Level Languages

The purpose of this section is to give you sufficient background so that you can tie together your newly acquired JCL knowledge with your COBOL and PL/I knowledge.

VSAM and COBOL

We will discuss only KSDS, which is the type of VSAM data set most commonly processed by COBOL programs. Your COBOL program must have a SELECT statement for the VSAM data set. For example, you could code

```
SELECT VSAM-DATA-FILE
    ASSIGN TO VSAMDD
    ORGANIZATION IS INDEXED
```

```
ACCESS IS SEQUENTIAL
RECORD KEY IS KEY-VALUE
FILE STATUS IS VSAM-STATUS.
```

ACCESS IS SEQUENTIAL is the default, so that clause is not required. The ddname on the DD statement that references this data set is VSAMDD. The record key, KEY-VALUE, must be defined as part of the VSAM data set's record. You might code

```
FD   VSAM-DATA-FILE
       .
       .
       .
01   VSAM-RECORD.
     05 KEY-VALUE            PIC...
```

The FILE STATUS field must be defined in WORKING-STORAGE, and its PICTURE should be XX. After every I/O operation on the data set, the system will place in the FILE STATUS field a value that indicates the results of the operation. A value of 00 means that the operation was successful. A value of 02 can occur only when the data set is accessed via an alternate index, which we will discuss later. Other values indicate that the operation was unsuccessful. The values that may occur and their meanings are described in the COBOL manual.

To create a VSAM data set, use IDCAMS first to create the cluster. Then the records may be loaded into the data set by a COBOL program. The data set must be accessed sequentially and opened as OUTPUT, as in

```
OPEN OUTPUT VSAM-DATA-FILE.
IF VSAM-STATUS NOT = '00'
    PERFORM BAD-OPEN-RTN.
```

After every I/O operation the FILE STATUS field should be tested to ensure that the operation was successful.

The data set is created using a WRITE statement, as in

```
WRITE VSAM-RECORD.
IF VSAM-STATUS NOT = '00'
    PERFORM BAD-WRITE-RTN.
```

Records must be written so that their keys are in sequential order. If you try to write a record whose key is not greater than the key of the previously written record, the record will not be written and the FILE STATUS field will be set equal to 21.

To sequentially read a VSAM data set, you open it as INPUT and use the standard READ statement, as in

```
READ VSAM-DATA-FILE
    AT END ...
```

To randomly access a VSAM data set, you can use the SELECT statement on pages 423–424 if the ACCESS clause is changed to ACCESS IS RANDOM.

To randomly read a particular record, you must move the key of the desired record into the RECORD KEY field. For example, you might code

```
MOVE KEY-IN to KEY-VALUE.
```

A READ statement such as

```
READ VSAM-DATA-FILE.
IF VSAM-STATUS NOT = '00'
    PERFORM BAD-READ-RTN.
```

retrieves the record. If the record is not found, the FILE STATUS field will be set equal to 23.

VSAM data sets may be accessed dynamically if ACCESS IS DYNAMIC is coded in the SELECT statement. When a data set is accessed dynamically, both sequential and random access are permitted. A typical sequence would be to randomly read a particular record and then sequentially read the following records. The random read is done as shown above. The sequential read is done using the NEXT option in the READ statement, as in

```
READ VSAM-DATA-FILE NEXT
    AT END ...
```

VSAM data sets are usually updated randomly. The data set is opened as I-O. For example, you would code

```
OPEN I-O VSAM-DATA-FILE.
```

The records are read as discussed above.

After the record has been updated, it is placed back in the data set using a REWRITE statement such as

```
REWRITE VSAM-RECORD.
```

Records are deleted using a DELETE statement such as

```
DELETE VSAM-DATA-FILE.
```

The record deleted is the record whose key matches the value in the RECORD KEY field. If no record with that key value exists, the FILE STATUS field will be set equal to 23.

The WRITE statement is used to add a record. First the key of the record is moved to the RECORD KEY field, and then a WRITE statement is executed, as in

```
WRITE VSAM-DATA-FILE.
IF VSAM-STATUS NOT = '00'
    PERFORM BAD-WRITE-RTN.
```

If the data set already contains a record with a key equal to the value in the

RECORD KEY field, the record is not added and the FILE STATUS field is set equal to 22.

Alternate Keys. COBOL programs can access a VSAM data set via an alternate index. COBOL is not used to create the alternate index, however. In fact, the COBOL program that loads the base cluster should not refer to the alternate index. After the base cluster has been loaded, IDCAMS is used to define the alternate index, build it, and define the path.

The clause

```
ALTERNATE RECORD KEY IS ALT-KEY
WITH DUPLICATES
```

must be added to the SELECT statement. The WITH DUPLICATES option means that there may be more than one record with the same alternate key value and is used only if that is the case. (The primary key must, as always, be unique.) ALT-KEY must be defined as part of the VSAM data set's record.

The SELECT statement provides only one ddname, yet you must have two DD statements: one for the base cluster and one for the path. The second ddname is constructed by concatenating the digit 1 and the first seven characters of the base cluster's ddname. For the ddname VSAMDD given in the above SELECT statement, the two DD statements would be

```
//GO.VSAMDD   DD DSN=VSAM.BASE.CLUSTER,
//                DISP=OLD
//GO.VSAMDD1 DD DSN=VSAM.ALTINDX.PATH,
//                DISP=OLD
```

Suppose you want to read a data set sequentially, based on the alternate key. Before you execute the READ statement, you must inform COBOL that you want the reading based on the alternate key. One way to do this is to use the START statement. For example, you could code

```
MOVE ALT-KEY-IN TO ALT-KEY.
START VSAM-DATA-FILE KEY IS = ALT-KEY.
IF VSAM-STATUS NOT = '00'
    PERFORM BAD-START.
```

If the START is successful, the first READ will retrieve the record whose alternate key is equal to ALT-KEY-IN, and subsequent READs will retrieve succeeding records in alternate key order.

The following statements could be used to read the whole data set sequentially in alternate key order:

```
MOVE LOW-VALUES TO ALT-KEY.
START VSAM-DATA-FILE
    KEY IS NOT < ALT-KEY.
```

To randomly read a record based on its alternate key, you move the key of the desired record to the ALTERNATE KEY field. For example, you could code

```
MOVE ALT-KEY-IN TO ALT-KEY.
```

The READ statement must use the KEY option, as in

```
READ VSAM-DATA-FILE
     KEY IS ALT-KEY.
```

If the record is not found, the FILE STATUS field will be set equal to 23. If the record is found, the FILE STATUS field will be set equal to either 00 or 02. Both values mean that the record was found, but 02 means that there is at least one more record in the data set whose alternate key is the same as the alternate key of the record just read. These additional records cannot be retrieved using a random read; they must be retrieved using a sequential read, such as

```
READ VSAM-DATA-FILE NEXT.
```

Both random and sequential access are being used, so ACCESS IS DYNAMIC must have been specified for the data set.

VSAM and PL/I

The DECLARE statement for a VSAM data set must include VSAM in the ENVIRONMENT parameter—that is,

```
DCL RECFLE FILE RECORD ENV (VSAM)...
```

There is no point in specifying any other information normally specified with the DCB parameter, because by definition all VSAM data sets are cataloged. If you do specify this information, it will be compared with data found in the VSAM catalog. If the data you supply are correct, there is no problem. If, however, your information disagrees with the data found in the VSAM catalog, at best it will be ignored and at worst your program will abend. Consequently, no information beyond that required should be specified.

The performance or usage of the VSAM data set is affected by a few options you might wish to specify in the ENVIRONMENT parameter. These are BKWD, REUSE, GENKEY, SKIP, SIS, BUFSP(n), BUFNI(n), and BUFND(n). Refer either to your PL/I textbook or to the manual for information on these options.

The difference between a normal KSDS and an alternate index is in where the DD statement points. For a normal KSDS, the data set named by the DSN parameter is the KSDS. For an alternate index, the DSN refers to the path. Except with respect to loading, whatever is said about a KSDS in the following discussion also applies to an alternative index. A data set must be loaded via the base cluster.

When you are loading a VSAM data set, OUTPUT must be specified in the

DECLARE statement, as in

```
DCL RECFLE FILE RECORD OUTPUT ENV (VSAM);
```

or named in the OPEN statement. If the data set is a KSDS, KEYED must also be coded. To write the record, you would code

```
WRITE FILE (RECFLE) FROM (OUTAREA);
```

for either an ESDS or an RRDS. If you choose to code the KEYTO option, the RBA of the record will be returned in the field named in the KEYTO option. Remember that if you use this option when creating an RRDS, you must specify the KEYED parameter in the DECLARE statement.

When you are loading a KSDS, the KEYFROM option must be included in the WRITE statement, as in

```
WRITE FILE (RECFLE) FROM (OUTAREA) KEYFROM (KEYFLD);
```

The records must be written in sequential order. The KEYFROM option may also be used in loading an RRDS, but if it is, the KEYED parameter must be specified in the DECLARE statement.

The job stream that loads the VSAM data set would include a DD statement such as

```
//RECFLE    DD DSN=VSAM.DATA,
//                DISP=OLD
```

Note that the ddname RECFLE ties back to the DECLARE statement in your PL/I program, and the DSN, VSAM.DATA, is the name you used in the DEFINE CLUSTER command. The same DD statement is used for an ESDS, KSDS, or RRDS.

Reading VSAM data sets requires that INPUT be included in either the DECLARE or the OPEN statement. The DECLARE would be of the form

```
DCL RECFLE FILE RECORD INPUT ENV (VSAM);
```

To read the data set sequentially, starting with the first record in the data set, you can use either

```
READ FILE (RECFLE) INTO (INAREA);
```

or

```
READ FILE (RECFLE) SET (PTR);
```

depending on whether you are using the move mode or the locate mode. (The move mode actually moves the data into the area in your program named in the READ statement. The locate mode returns the address of the record, which remains in the input buffer.) You may specify the KEYTO option in either form of the statement. For an ESDS, the RBA will be returned in the field named. For a KSDS, the named field will contain the key of the record just read.

If you want to read a particular record — in a KSDS or in an ESDS — that is accessible with a key via an alternate index, KEYED must be included in the DECLARE statement, as in

```
DCL RECFLE FILE RECORD INPUT KEYED ENV (VSAM);
```

The READ statement must include the KEY option. Thus the READ statement could be coded as

```
READ FILE (RECFLE) INTO (INAREA) KEY (KEY_AREA);
```

or

```
READ FILE (RECFLE) SET (PTR) KEY (KEY_AREA);
```

In either case, the field KEY_AREA must be set equal to the value of the key of the desired record. This type of access is called random access.

You can read a particular record by specifying the value of the alternate key. If you do, you must include a DECLARE statement for the alternate index. The DECLARE statement could be similar to the one used for the base cluster — for example,

```
DCL ALTINDX FILE RECORD INPUT KEYED ENV (VSAM);
```

You must remember, however, that the corresponding DD statement must reference the path, as in

```
//ALTINDX  DD DSN=VSAM.PATH,
//              DISP=SHR
```

Recall that alternate keys need not be unique. After reading a record using an alternate key, you can determine whether there are additional records with the same key by testing the SAMEKEY built-in function. If the read was successful and there is an additional record with the same key, SAMEKEY (ALTINDX) will be true; otherwise it will be false.

If a VSAM data set accessible by a key is to be read sequentially, starting with a particular record, the file declaration and first READ statement will be the same as for random access. Subsequent READ statements need not include the KEY option.

The DD statement used in reading differs from the one used in loading only in that you may specify a disposition of SHR. There is no reason not to permit multiple access of the data set during reading.

If you wish to update a VSAM data set, the file declaration must include the UPDATE option and, for a KSDS and an RRDS, the KEYED option. A typical DECLARE statement would be

```
DCL RECFLE FILE RECORD UPDATE KEYED ENV (VSAM);
```

Obviously, for an ESDS the KEYED option need not be present.

Records may be changed by using the REWRITE statement. The principal restriction to keep in mind is that when you rewrite an ESDS record, its length must remain the same. You may code this statement in three ways:

```
REWRITE FILE (RECFLE);
```

or

```
REWRITE FILE (RECFLE) FROM (OUTAREA);
```

or

```
REWRITE FILE (RECFLE) FROM (OUTAREA) KEY (KEYAREA);
```

The first two examples presuppose that the record being changed was just read. In the first example, the new record is taken from the input buffer. This statement presupposes that you read the record using locate mode and made the changes to the record in the input buffer. The second example replaces the record read with the record to be found in the area named by the FROM option. In the above examples, this area is OUTAREA. The third example differs from the first two in that the record to be changed need not have been read. The KEY option names the field that holds the key for a KSDS, the RBA for an ESDS, or the record number for an RRDS.

Records may be added randomly to a KSDS, but only to the end of an ESDS or an RRDS. The DECLARE statement used here is the same as the one used in record changing, and the WRITE statement is the same as the one used in loading the data set. The DD statement should specify DISP=OLD to ensure that no one else tries to read the data set while you are in the process of changing it.

When you update or add records to a data set with alternate indexes, it is critical that unique keys remain unique. If, for example, you update a KSDS via an alternate path, you must not change the base cluster key so that it is no longer unique.

There are certain error conditions that occur only with VSAM data sets. Your program should include ON-CONDITIONS for TRANSMIT and for KEY and, if you are processing the data set sequentially, for ENDFILE. The ONCODE built-in function will return a number that will indicate the nature of the problem. Refer to your PL/I textbook or the IBM manual for detailed information.

Summary

In this chapter you have learned

— the three types of VSAM data sets: KSDS, ESDS, and RRDS

— how VSAM data sets are organized into control intervals and control areas

—how to use the utility program IDCAMS to

create a VSAM cluster, an alternate index, a path, and a user catalog

allocate VSAM space using the DEFINE command

load a VSAM data set with data using the REPRO command

build an alternate index using the BLDINDEX command

print a VSAM data set using the PRINT command

list the entries in a catalog using the LISTCAT command

fix an improperly closed VSAM data set using the VERIFY command

delete a VSAM cluster, an alternate index, a path, a user catalog, and VSAM space using the DELETE command

Vocabulary

In this chapter you have been introduced to the meanings of the following terms:

access method services (AMS)	dynamic allocation
alternate index	entry sequence data set (ESDS)
alternate key	freespace
base cluster	index set
cluster	integrated catalog facility (ICF)
control area (CA)	key sequence data set (KSDS)
control area split	prime key
control interval (CI)	record definition field
control interval definition field (CIDF)	relative byte address (RBA)
control interval split	relative record data set (RRDS)
	sequence set

Exercises

1. Name the three types of VSAM data sets.
2. What are the components of each of the three VSAM data sets?
3. When the components are put together, what are they called?
4. What is the unit of information brought into storage from a DASD as a result of an I/O operation?
5. How does the system learn the length of a record in a VSAM data set?
6. With a keyed data set, how does the system know whether there is sufficient space in a CI for a record to be added?
7. What happens if there is not enough space in the CI for the record?
8. With an ISAM data set, when a user deletes a record, it is merely marked for deletion and remains in the data set until the data set is reorganized. What happens with a VSAM data set?

9. What are the two parts of an index? Are there always two parts?
10. What information does each "record" of the index contain?
11. How does the system know that a DD statement refers to a VSAM data set?
12. Which of the following data sets definitely refer to a VSAM data set, which might refer to a VSAM data set, and which do not refer to a VSAM data set?

```
//DD1      DD DSN=DATASET1,
//               DISP=SHR,
//               DCB=DSORG=IS
//DD2      DD DSN=DATASET2,
//               DISP=OLD
//               UNIT=SYSDA,
//               VOL=SER=DISK01,
//               AMP=AMORG
//DD3      DD DSN=DATASET3,
//               DISP=OLD
//DD4      DD DSN=DATASET4,
//               DISP=SHR,
//               UNIT=SYSDA,
//               VOL=SER=VOL001
```

13. Write the command to print, in character form, a data set named MYKSDS.
14. Write the command to load data from a sequential data set named MYSEQ into a VSAM data set named MYKSDS.
15. Code the command to define a KSDS cluster. The data to go into the data set comprise an assembler language program of approximately 1000 lines. Use the number field in columns 73 through 80 as the key. Name the cluster ASMPGM.
16. Write the command to reserve 10 cylinders on disk pack SCR001 in user catalog UCAT.
17. Write the commands to create a secondary index for ASMPGM, defined in Exercise 15. Use the operand in the assembler language program as the key. Assume that the operand is in positions 10 through 15 in the record. Name the alternate index ALTINDX and the path MYPATH.
18. Write the command to delete the user catalog UCAT and everything that belongs to it.
19. Write the command to list the contents of the user catalog MYCAT.

Programming Assignments

1. If you are allowed to create a user catalog, execute a job that will create a user catalog.
2. If you are allowed to allocate space, execute a job that will allocate space on a volume.
3. Execute a job that will define a KSDS cluster. The cluster should use the space you allocated in Programming Assignment 2. If you are not allowed to allocate space, define the cluster as unique. (If your system uses an ICF,

you don't have to define space or make the cluster unique.) The cluster should be cataloged in the user catalog you created in Programming Assignment 1. If you are not allowed to create a user catalog, catalog the cluster in the catalog your advisor tells you to use. The record size and key length and location should be compatible with those of the sequential data set you created for the Programming Assignment in Chapter 3.

4. Execute a job that will load the KSDS you created in Programming Assignment 3 with data contained in the sequential data set you created for the Programming Assignment in Chapter 3. In the same job print the data set.

5. Execute a job that will define an alternate index for the KSDS cluster you created in Programming Assignment 3. Choose any field you want as the ALTERNATE KEY field. (If you used the data in Appendix D to load the base cluster, you can use the student major field, bytes 40 and 41, as the ALTERNATE KEY field.) Execute a second job that will build the alternate index and define a path. Finally, execute a job that will print the base cluster in alternate key order.

6. Execute a job that will list the names of the clusters and spaces in the user catalog you used.

7. After you have completed Programming Assignments 1 through 5, execute a job that will delete the cluster, the alternate index, the path, the data space, and the user catalog.

13

Utilities

In this chapter you will learn

- what each of the utility programs does
- how to use each of the utility programs

You have already learned to use some of the utility programs in preceding chapters. Nevertheless, they are briefly discussed in this chapter with a reference back to where they were discussed in detail. Thus, when you need any information about a utility program, you should look in this chapter first. You will find either the information you need or a reference to an earlier chapter in which that information may be found. Discussions of utility programs are presented in alphabetical order.

The functions of most utility programs are described in this chapter. Detailed usage information, however, is provided only for those functions that an application programmer needs to know. For example, when you have finished this chapter you will know that the utility program IEHDASDR is used to initialize a DASD or an MSS, but you will not know how to use it. On the other hand, you will know when and how to use IEHLIST. For some utility programs, you will know how to use some but not all functions.

The large number of utilities available may make choosing the correct utility for a particular function somewhat confusing. Appendix F contains a guide to help you choose the correct utility depending on which function you want to perform.

Earlier in this book utility programs were used to illustrate JCL coding. They provided ready examples for developing emerging skills. Here we are looking at these programs for their own sake. Properly used they can save you a considerable amount of time. Many years ago I wrote a program that read in a sequential file containing 81-byte records and wrote out 80-byte records, dropping the last byte in each record. I could have accomplished the same purpose by using IEBGENER, but I was not familiar with it then. I spent two or three days writing a program that really was unnecessary. Certainly my boss would have preferred that I spend half a day writing JCL to use IEBGENER. And a happy boss usually means a fatter paycheck.

Executing Utilities

Utilities are divided into four groups: independent utilities, the VSAM utility, data set utilities, and system utilities. Independent utilities are used to prepare I/O devices when the operating system is not available. They are used principally by operators and systems programmers. The VSAM utility, which is named IDCAMS, was discussed in Chapter 12. Data set utilities are used to manipulate data at the data set or record level. Their names start with IEB, and they are used principally by application programmers. IEBGENER is a typical example. System utilities are used to manipulate data sets and are used principally by systems programmers. Their names start with IEH or IEF. IEHLIST, which was discussed in Chapter 5, is a typical example.

A typical job to execute one of the data set or system utilities would look like the following:

```
//          JOB
//UTIL      EXEC PGM=name
//SYSPRINT DD    SYSOUT=A

(additional DD statements)

//SYSIN     DD *

(utility control statements)

/*
//
```

The JOB statement is standard, and the EXEC statement names the utility. The SYSPRINT DD statement provides the location for utility messages. It does not have to direct the messages to the printer, but that is what it most often does. The SYSIN DD statement defines the data set that contains the utility control statements. It does not have to be input stream data, but most often it is.

The additional DD statements are somewhat variable. For data set utilities, SYSUT1 is often used to define the input data set and SYSUT2 to define the output data set, but there are exceptions. These additional DD statements will be explained when each utility is discussed.

Many utilities issue a return code (which, you recall, is also called a condition code) indicating the results of the utility execution. In general, a return code of 0 means that the utility program successfully completed its function. A return code of 4 usually means that something is wrong, but the operation was probably successful. A return code of 8 means that the error is more serious. A 12 usually indicates a disaster, and a 16 signals a catastrophe. The return code, together with an explanation, is written to the message data set.

Independent Utilities

There are three independent utility programs that perform system functions. "Independent" means that the utility program does not run under the operating system. These independent utilities are used to prepare I/O devices for use when the operating system is not available. The same functions are also performed by utility programs that run under the operating system.

An application programmer is not likely to use independent utilities. This discussion will therefore be limited to a general overview of what they do and a look at some sample control statements; there will be no explanation of how to use them.

The independent utility programs do not use the JCL you have studied. The executable program is loaded into main storage, usually from a card reader. A request will generally appear on the console asking for the input device that will be used to supply the control statements required by the utility. This device can usually be either tape or card.

IBCDASDI

Before a direct access storage device volume can be used, it must be initialized. **Direct access storage device initialization** is usually referred to as **DASDI.** Many systems programmers use this acronym as if it were a verb; the original meaning has virtually been forgotten.

The independent utility program IBCDASDI may be used to perform this initialization. With this utility, DASDI may be performed in either of two ways. If the quick method is chosen, IBCDASDI will write **initial program load (IPL)*** records on records 1 and 2 of track 0, write volume labels on record 3 of track 0, and build and write the volume table of contents (VTOC). If control statements so request, IBCDASDI will write an IPL program on track 0, check for tracks previously marked bad, and write a track description record on each track, erasing existing contents.

If the slower method of DASDI is requested, all operations done with the

---

* Like DASDI, IPL has entered the data processing jargon to the point where most programmers use the acronym as a verb.

■ **Figure 13.1** ■

IBCDASDI Sample Control Statements

```
JOB  'INITIALIZE 3344'
MSG  TODEV=1403,TOADDR=00E
DADEF  TODEV=3340,TOADDR=259,VOLID=SCRATC,
       PASSES=1,BYPASS=NO
VLD  NEWVOLID=TEST01
END
```

quick method will be performed and, in addition, all alternate tracks will be unassigned, the home address will be rewritten on all tracks, defective tracks will be tested and recovered if possible, and defective tracks not recoverable will be assigned to alternates.

The object code for IBCDASDI is loaded into main storage from cards or card images on tape. The control statements are usually loaded in from a card reader. Figure 13.1 shows a sample set of control statements.

IBCDMPRS

The independent utility program IBCDMPRS is used to dump and restore DASD volumes. The receiving volume for the dump and the sending volume for the restore may be either DASD or tape volumes. The volumes used must be initialized using IBCDASDI, IEHDASDR, IEHINITT, or any other program that will initialize the volume to meet system specifications.

IBCDMPRS is loaded as either a card deck or card images on tape. The user supplies the address and the device used to input the control statements. Figure 13.2a contains sample sets of control statements that could be used to dump a disk pack to a reel of tape; Figure 13.2b shows control statements to restore a disk pack from a reel of tape.

ICAPRTBL

ICAPRTBL is an independent utility program used to load the universal character set (UCS) buffer and the forms control buffer (FCB) on an IBM 3211 printer. This utility is used only under a special set of circumstances. If your system uses an IBM 3211 printer for console output, these buffers must be loaded before the operating system can be loaded. If the console has a printer keyboard, the buffers will be loaded as part of the loading of the operating system and this utility is not needed.

Unlike the other two independent utility programs, ICAPRTBL must be loaded in card form with the control cards following it.

If this program is used, it is used by the machine operators in the process of bringing up the operating system.

Figure 13.2

(a) IBCDMPRS Sample Dump Control Statements

```
JOB 'DUMP DISK TO TAPE'
 MSG TODEV=1403,TOADDR=00E
DUMP FROMDEV=3340,FROMADDR=150,
     TODEV=2400,TOADDR=280
 END
```

(b) IBCDMPRS Sample Restore Control Statements

```
    JOB 'RESTORE DISK FROM TAPE'
    MSG TODEV=1403,TOADDR=00E
RESTORE FROMDEV=2400,FROMADDR=280,
        TODEV=3340,TOADDR=150
    END
```

The VSAM Utility IDCAMS

IDCAMS is the name of the access method services utility program that per-forms functions vital to the virtual storage access method (VSAM). It was described in detail in Chapter 12. In addition, IDCAMS also performs some of the same functions as IEHPROGM. For example, if you refer back to the discussion on generation data groups in Chapter 6, you will see that the index can be built and deleted with either IEHPROGM or IDCAMS.

Data Set Utilities

IEBCOMPR

IEBCOMPR provides you with the ability to check your copy of a data set and make sure that it matches the original. You can compare physical sequential data sets or libraries. It is always wise to verify that a copy is accurate, and using this utility program is a very simple way to do so. Figure 13.3 contains an example of the code used to execute this utility program.

The SYSUT1 and SYSUT2 statements define the data sets to be compared. These data sets may be either physical sequential or partitioned, but both must be the same. From the coding of these two DD statements, it is impossible to tell the form of the data sets. The information about the form of the data sets is supplied by the control statements. In Figure 13.3 only the COMPARE control statement is coded. Its purpose is to tell IEBCOMPR whether the data set

Figure 13.3

Sample IEBCOMPR Job

```
//JCLQB905 JOB ,'AGAMEMNON'
//COMPARE  EXEC PGM=IEBCOMPR
//SYSPRINT DD SYSOUT=A
//SYSUT1    DD DSN=DATASET1,
//             DISP=SHR
//SYSUT2    DD DSN=DATASET2,
//             DISP=OLD
//SYSIN     DD *
 COMPARE TYPORG=PS
/*
//
```

organization is physical sequential or partitioned. PS means physical sequential, and PO means partitioned. The default is physical sequential, which means that the control statement coded in Figure 13.3 is unnecessary. This job would work equally well if a dummy data set had been coded for SYSIN, as in

```
//SYSIN DD DUMMY
```

There are two conditions under which the COMPARE control statement must be coded. If the data set organization is partitioned, the COMPARE control statement is required. If you wish to use any of the other control statements, they must be preceded by the COMPARE control statement even if the data set organization is physical sequential. But before we discuss these other control statements, let us examine the process of comparing libraries.

If you want to compare libraries, PO obviously must be specified in the COMPARE control statement. For an equal comparison, it is not necessary that all the members in both libraries be identical. If the SYSUT2 library contains all the members in the SYSUT1 library plus some additional members and if the members that are in both libraries are identical, IEBCOMPR will indicate an equal condition. For example, suppose COBUC, COBUCL, and COBUCG from SYS1.PROCLIB were to be copied to a new library named COB.PROCLIB. If the two libraries were compared and if SYSUT1 pointed to COB.PROCLIB and SYSUT2 pointed to SYS1.PROCLIB, IEBCOMPR would indicate an equal condition if COBUC, COBUCL, and COBUCG were identical in both libraries. You could compare each member as a physical sequential data set, but that would require a step for each member you wanted to compare.

Let us now examine the other control statements that may be used with IEBCOMPR. The LABEL control statement applies only to tape, because only tape has user labels. Remember that the LABEL control statement applies only to user labels and not to standard labels. This control statement tells

IEBCOMPR whether user labels are to be treated as data. If the LABEL statement is coded as

```
LABEL DATA=YES
```

the user labels will be treated as data after they have been processed by the user's label processing routine. If NO is coded in place of the default value of YES, the user labels will not be treated as data. This means that no comparison of the user label data will occur. If ONLY is coded in place of YES, the system will compare only the user labels, not the data. The other alternative is to code ALL, which is only used when there is more than one user label (there can be up to 16 of them after the standard label but before the data). ALL means that even if an error is found in a user label, the remaining user labels are still to be compared.

The EXITS control statement is used to supply the names of the user exit routines to be used. In the following example all four possible exits are coded:

```
EXITS  INHDR=IN1,INTLR=IN2,ERROR=IN3,PRECOMP=IN4
```

When you use this control statement, obviously you code only those exits you need. INHDR supplies the name of the routine to process the user header labels, and INTLR the name of the routine to process user trailer labels. In the example above these routines are IN1 and IN2, respectively. ERROR supplies the name of the routine that receives control when an unequal comparison occurs. If no routine is supplied, after ten unequal comparisons the comparison ends—except when members of a library are being compared, in which case IEBCOMPR goes to the next member. PRECOMP specifies a routine that is to process the data before IEBCOMPR sees them.

If the comparison is successful, a return code of 0 is set. If the comparison fails, a return code of 8 is set. A 12 indicates that an unrecoverable error occurred; and a 16 signals that a routine specified in the EXITS statement failed.

You will find IEBCOMPR to be very easy to use and under certain circumstances very useful.

IEBCOPY

IEBCOPY is a utility program used in dealing with libraries. It may be employed to copy one or more members from an existing PDS to a new or existing PDS. IEBCOPY is also used to reorganize a library and to make back-up copies (also called an unloaded version). Refer back to Chapter 5 for a detailed discussion of these functions.

Remember that when you create an unloaded version of a PDS using IEBCOPY, you may select the members you want. Later you will learn that when you use IEHMOVE to create an unloaded version of a PDS, you must unload the entire PDS.

IEBDG

IEBDG is not often used, which is a pity. Programmers waste time writing programs to produce test data when in many cases this utility could accomplish the same goal in a fraction of the time. Chapter 11 discussed using IEBDG to create an ISAM data set. Either a physical sequential data set or a library member could have been specified as the output instead of ISAM in Figure 11.19 and Figure 11.20. The only type of data set that may not be created using IEBDG is BDAM. Sequential data sets are the only type that may be input to IEBDG.

   IEBDG may create more than one data set in a run. Information for each data set is defined by a group of control statements, the first of which is the DSD statement and the last of which is the END statement.

DSD Control Statement.   The format of the DSD statement is

```
DSD OUTPUT=(ddname),INPUT=(ddname,...)
```

The OUTPUT parameter is required; it names the DD statement that points to the data set being created. The INPUT parameter is required if input comes from one or more data sets, but not if the data are completely generated internally. Figure 11.19 illustrates the simple situation in which there is one input data set and one output data set. Figure 11.20 illustrates the case in which there is no input data set. Figure 13.4 illustrates the case in which there are two input data sets. There is no stated limit on the number of input data sets. If you have a complex situation in which there are so many ddnames that they will not fit on one statement, remember that the normal control statement continuation rules apply.

FD Control Statement.   The FD (field definition) statement defines fields that are put together in some fashion by CREATE statements, which will be discussed next. Each FD statement defines one field. If your record consists of ten different fields, you need ten FD statements. FD statements fall into two categories. There are those that take data from the input data set and those that generate data. The third and fourth FD statements in Figure 13.4 are examples of the former. The format of this type of FD statement is

```
FD NAME=fld,LENGTH=xx,STARTLOC=qq,FROMLOC=zz,INPUT=ddname
```

The NAME parameter supplies a name to the field, and the LENGTH parameter indicates the number of bytes in the field; these two fields are always required. The STARTLOC parameter indicates where in the output record you wish this field placed. If you do not supply this value, the field's position in the output record will be determined by the CREATE control statement. The INPUT parameter names the DD statement that points to the data set that

━━ **Figure 13.4** ━━━━━━━━━━━━━━━━━━━━━━━━━━━━━━

Sample IEBDG Job

```
//JCLQB910 JOB ,'ACHILLES'
//SEQMULT  EXEC PGM=IEBDG
//SYSPRINT DD SYSOUT=A
//SEQIN1   DD DSN=DATASET1,
//            DISP=SHR
//SEQIN2   DD DSN=DATASET2,
//            DISP=SHR
//SEQOUT   DD DSN=SEQOUT,
//            DISP=(,CATLG),
//            UNIT=SYSDA,
//            VOL=SER=WYL003,
//            SPACE=(CYL,(1,1)),
//            DCB=(RECFM=FB,LRECL=50,BLKSIZE=1000)
//SYSIN    DD *
 DSD OUTPUT=(SEQOUT),INPUT=(SEQIN1,SEQIN2)
 FD NAME=BYTE0,LENGTH=1,STARTLOC=1
 FD NAME=KEYFLD,LENGTH=4,STARTLOC=2,FORMAT=ZD,INDEX=1
 FD NAME=FLD1,LENGTH=45,STARTLOC=6,FROMLOC=1,INPUT=SEQIN1
 FD NAME=FLD2,LENGTH=45,STARTLOC=6,FROMLOC=1,INPUT=SEQIN2
 CREATE NAME=(BYTE0,KEYFLD,FLD1),INPUT=SEQIN1
 CREATE NAME=(BYTE0,KEYFLD,FLD2),INPUT=SEQIN2
 END
/*
//
```

supplies the data. FROMLOC indicates the starting location in the input data set from which the data are to be extracted.

The other type of FD statement generates data to be placed in an output record. Let us first examine the situation in which a constant value is to be placed in a field. The format of this type of FD statement is

```
FD NAME=fld,LENGTH=xx,STARTLOC=yy,FILL=x
```

or

```
FD NAME=fld,LENGTH=xx,STARTLOC=yy,PICTURE=1,p
```

The first three parameters are the same as in the previous FD statement. The FILL parameter is used to supply the value to be inserted into the field. The first FD statement in Figure 11.19 and Figure 11.20 illustrates supplying a hexadecimal value. If FILL='2' were coded, the character 2 would be propagated through the field. In general, when you use the FILL parameter, you supply a single character, which may be expressed in character or hexadecimal form, that is propagated through the field. Thus if the field length is 10 and the fill character is specified as 2, the resulting field will contain ten 2s. If no FILL or PICTURE is specified, a FILL character or hexadecimal zero is assumed. Because it specifies the default value, the FILL parameter in Figure

11.19 is not necessary. The default value is used in the first FD statement in Figure 13.4.

The use of PICTURE allows the insertion of multicharacter constants into the output record. The PICTURE parameter differs from the other parameters in that two pieces of information must be supplied — the data length and the data to be inserted into the field. If you code PICTURE=3, 'ABC', the resulting field will contain ABC. If you want a numeric value, you might code PICTURE=2,P'20' or PICTURE=2,B'20'. The former will give a packed decimal field set to 20, and the latter a binary field set to 20. The data length, 2 in these last two examples, must equal the number of characters within the apostrophes. If the field length, specified by the LENGTH parameter, is greater than the value generated, numeric values will be right justified and padded with 0s, whereas character values will be left justified and padded with blanks.

We can also generate changes to these fields. The format of an FD statement to change numeric fields is

```
FD NAME=fld,LENGTH=xx,STARTLOC=yy,FORMAT=zz,INDEX=i
```

or

```
FD NAME=fld,LENGTH=xx,STARTLOC=yy,PICTURE=1,p,INDEX=i
```

The only difference between these two forms is that the parameter FORMAT is used in the first and the parameter PICTURE in the second. The first form is shown in the second FD statement in Figure 11.20. In Chapter 11 we discussed the FORMAT parameter in detail. The INDEX parameter indicates how much is to be added to the field for each new record. The value coded for INDEX must be a positive number. If, as in Figure 11.20, INDEX=10 is coded, the first record will have the field set to 1, the second to 11, and so forth.

The format of an FD statement to change alphameric fields from one record to the next is

```
FD NAME=fld,LENGTH=xx,STARTLOC=yy,FORMAT=zz,ACTION=ww
```

or

```
FD NAME=fld,LENGTH=xx,STARTLOC=yy,PICTURE=1,p,ACTION=ww
```

The only new parameter in these forms is the ACTION parameter. This parameter tells IEBDG what to do to the data defined by the PICTURE parameter or implied by the FORMAT pattern AL or AN. The values that may be used for the ACTION parameter are shown in Table 13.1.

Not all of the parameters available for use on the FD statement have been discussed. Certain parameters have been omitted because they are not particularly useful. For the same reason, not all the parameters of the CREATE control statement will be discussed.

Table 13.1
ACTION Parameter Values

Parameter	Definition
SL	Shift the pattern left one position in the output field.
SR	Shift the pattern right one position in the output field.
TL	Truncate one position of the pattern on the left.
TR	Truncate one position of the pattern on the right.
RO	The field is to be rolled.
WV	The field is to be waved.
FX	The field is to be fixed. (This is the default value.)
RP	The field is to be rippled.

CREATE Control Statement. The CREATE control statement specifies what information goes into a record. The information may be from the input data set, or it may be the result of an FD control statement. The simplest form of the CREATE statement is

```
CREATE INPUT=ddname
```

With this form, the input records become the output, which is really only useful if the input is a physical sequential data set and the output is an ISAM data set. Otherwise the same purpose could have been accomplished by using IEBGENER with no control statement.

The CREATE control statements in Figures 11.19 and 11.20 build the output record from fields created with FD control statements. If an input data set is named, the number of records created is equal to the number of records in the input data set. In Figure 11.19 POLYISAM will contain the same number of records as POLYFILE. In the CREATE control statement in Figure 11.20, there is no input data set named, so IEBDG must be told explicitly how many records are to be created. This is the purpose of the QUANTITY parameter. The CREATE control statement in Figure 11.20 uses the FILL parameter to supply blanks for the specified portion of the output record.

When the job in Figure 13.4 is executed, the first CREATE statement will take records from the SEQIN1 data set, modify them as specified by the BYTE0 and KEYFLD fields, and write them to the SEQOUT data set. The number of records created will be equal to the number of records in SEQIN1. The second CREATE statement will perform a similar operation, with the records being taken from SEQIN2. The number of records created will be equal to the number of records in SEQIN2.

REPEAT Control Statement. The format of the REPEAT control statement is

```
REPEAT QUANTITY=x,CREATE=y
```

This control statement references one or more CREATE statements. The CREATE parameter in the REPEAT statement indicates the number of CREATE statements to which the REPEAT statement applies. The QUANTITY parameter indicates how many times the CREATE statement is to be executed. Consider the following code:

```
DSD OUTPUT=(NEWFILE),INPUT=(SEQIN1,SEQIN2)
FD NAME=FLD1,LENGTH=6,STARTLOC=10,PICTURE=6,'UVWXYZ'
FD NAME=FLD2,LENGTH=100,FILL='*'
REPEAT QUANTITY=6,CREATE=2
CREATE NAME=FLD1,INPUT=SEQIN1,QUANTITY=10
CREATE INPUT=SEQIN2,QUANTITY=5
CREATE NAME=FLD2
```

The first CREATE statement takes records from the SEQIN1 data set and modifies them as specified by the NAME parameter. The NAME parameter causes FLD1, which is defined in the first FD statement as a 6-byte field containing UVWXYZ, to overwrite the original data in the SEQIN1 record, starting at byte 10. The second CREATE statement does not contain a NAME parameter, so records from SEQIN2 are written to the output data set without modification.

The first two CREATE statements will cause 10 records to be taken from the SEQIN1 data set and then 5 from the SEQIN2 data. These two CREATE statements will be executed 6 times. The output to this point will contain 90 records, 60 from the SEQIN1 data set and 30 from the SEQIN2 data set. The last record will come from the data specified in the FD statement with the name FLD2. Note that the third CREATE control statement is not repeated because the CREATE parameter in the REPEAT control statement specifies 2 and not 3.

The last and easiest control statement is the END statement, which terminates a group of control statements. It is illustrated in Figure 13.4.

Now that you have an understanding of how IEBDG works, you will find it very useful.

IEBEDIT

The purpose of IEBEDIT is to create a data set containing JCL selected from an input data set in accordance with instructions supplied by the control statement or statements. You probably will not find much use for this utility program, but you should be aware of its existence and what it does.

Figure 13.5 illustrates the use of IEBEDIT. The SYSUT1 DD statement points to the input data set. In the example the input data set is on tape; it could have been on disk or in the form of input stream data. If it had been input stream data, SYSUT1 would have been coded as

```
//SYSUT1    DD DATA
```

■ **Figure 13.5** ■

Sample IEBEDIT Job

```
//JCLQB915 JOB ,'MENELAOS'
//STEPSLCT EXEC PGM=IEBEDIT
//SYSPRINT DD SYSOUT=A
//SYSUT1   DD DSN=TAPEJCL,
//            DISP=OLD
//SYSUT2   DD SYSOUT=B,
//            DCB=(RECFM=F,LRECL=80,BLKSIZE=80)
//SYSIN    DD *
 EDIT START=JOBTEST,TYPE=POSITION,STEPNAME=STEP3,NOPRINT
/*
//
```

because the input is JCL. The input cannot contain a /* statement because it would be interpreted as signaling the end of the input data stream. If you want a /* statement, code two periods and an asterisk in columns 1, 2, and 3. When IEBEDIT finds this configuration, it produces a /* statement in the output.

The SYSUT2 DD statement defines the output data set. In the example in Figure 13.5, cards are used. The control statements are defined by the SYSIN DD statement.

IEBEDIT has only one control statement. All possible parameters are illustrated in Figure 13.5. The START parameter indicates the jobname, which is necessary if there is more than one job in the input data set. If there is only one job, this parameter is not required. The TYPE and STEPNAME parameters work together. When TYPE=POSITION is coded, as in the example, the STEPNAME parameter identifies the first step to be selected from the named job in the SYSUT1 data set. The SYSUT2 data set will start with the step whose name is STEP3 in the job whose name is JOBTEST; any steps preceding STEP3 will be bypassed. STEP3 will be the first step in the output, and all the succeeding steps in job JOBTEST will be included in the output.

TYPE=POSITION is the default, so it was not necessary to explicitly code it. If TYPE=INCLUDE had been coded instead, the output would have contained only STEP3. Had TYPE=EXCLUDE been coded, all the steps in job JOBTEST except STEP3 would have been in the output.

You can include or exclude more than one step. If you coded the STEPNAME parameter as

```
TYPE=EXCLUDE,STEPNAME=(STEP2,STEP6-STEP8,STEP10)
```

STEP2 and STEP10 would be explicitly excluded, as would all the steps starting with STEP6 and ending with STEP8. If TYPE=INCLUDE had been coded, only STEP2, STEP10, and the steps starting with STEP6 and ending with STEP8 would have been included.

`NOPRINT` suppresses the listing of the output data set. Had it been omitted, the output would have been listed.

If the input data set contains a `DD DATA` statement, `IEBEDIT` will treat the JCL statements that follow it as data, not JCL. That might seem surprising, but after all that is what a `DD DATA` statement is supposed to do.

IEBGENER

`IEBGENER` deals with physical sequential data sets and libraries. `IEBGENER` may be used to make a back-up copy of a sequential data set or library member or to load a sequential data set as a library member. It may be used to change the blocking factor of a sequential data set or to expand a library. We have discussed `IEBGENER` so thoroughly in Chapters 2 through 5 that by now you should be an expert on it.

IEBIMAGE

Stop! Before you read about `IEBIMAGE`, review the section in Chapter 10 about the 3800 Printing Subsystem. In that section we discussed the six parameters (`COPIES`, `BURST`, `FLASH`, `CHARS`, `MODIFY`, and `FCB`) that apply to the 3800 Printing Subsystem. Three of these parameters (`CHARS`, `MODIFY`, and `FCB`) require entries in a library named `SYS1.IMAGELIB`. `IEBIMAGE` is the utility program that is used to create these entries.

Figure 13.6 illustrates a sample job that would be used to create a forms control buffer module. The `SYSUT1` DD statement names the library in which the modules used by the 3800 Printing Subsystem are stored. If the modules are named in the DD statement, as illustrated in Chapter 10, they must be

---

Figure 13.6

Creating an FCB Using IEBIMAGE

```
//JCLQB920 JOB ,'PARIS'
//STEPFCB  EXEC PGM=IEBIMAGE
//SYSPRINT DD SYSOUT=A
//SYSUT1   DD DSN=SYS1.IMAGELIB,
//            DISP=OLD
//SYSIN    DD *
 FCB CH1=1,CH9=(7,13,20),                                          *
              LPI=((6,1),(8,32),(12)),                             *
              SIZE=110
 NAME FCB1
/*
//
```

stored in the library named SYS1.IMAGELIB. If the modules are invoked in the program, other libraries may be used. Using other libraries, however, is outside the scope of this book.

Every module created with IEBIMAGE is named using the NAME control statement. The rules for this statement are almost the same as for the link edit control statement. The name supplied here must be one to four characters in length, and the first character need not be alphabetic — it may be a number. The reason is that IEBIMAGE will prefix the name you supply with a four-character value. What these four characters will be will depend on what kind of module you are creating. In Figure 13.6 an FCB module is being created. For an FCB the prefix is FCB3. The name supplied in the example is FCB1. As a result, the module created by IEBIMAGE and stored in SYS1.IMAGELIB will have the name FCB3FCB1. The first four characters are generated by IEBIMAGE, and the next four are supplied by the user.

FCB Control Statement.   There is always only one FCB statement used to create an FCB module. The first parameter is CH1=1, which means that there is to be a channel 1 code for line 1. The CH indicates that a channel code is being specified; the number that follows the CH indicates which channel code. Numbers from 1 through 12 are valid channel codes. The 1 on the other side of the equals sign is the line with which the channel 1 code is associated. When the programmer says that the printer should advance to channel 1, the printer will go to line 1. The second parameter coded in Figure 13.6 is CH9=(7,13,20). This means that lines 7, 13, and 20 have channel 9 coded. When the programmer says that the printer should advance to channel 9, the printer will go to line 7, 13, or 20, depending on which line is next. If the printer is currently at line 16, the printer will go to line 20. On the other hand, if it is currently at line 26, the printer will go to line 7 on the next page.

In this example, only codes 1 and 9 are specified. Remember that there are ten more channel codes that may be used.

The LPI parameter specifies the line spacing in lines per inch and specifies how many lines are to be printed at that line spacing. This is a feature unique to the 3800 Printing Subsystem. Other printers permit changing the line spacing, but only the 3800 permits changing it within a document. In the example in Figure 13.6, the first line is to be printed at 6 lines per inch; that is, it will occupy one-sixth of an inch. The next 32 lines will be printed at 8 lines per inch, which means that the next 32 lines will require four inches. The rest of the page will be printed at 12 lines per inch. The only permitted line spacings are 6, 8, and 12 lines per inch. If the LPI parameter is omitted, a default of LPI=6 is used.

The last parameter in the FCB statement is the SIZE parameter. The value coded for the SIZE parameter is equal to the number of inches in the page multiplied by 10. If, for example, you are using seven-inch paper, SIZE will be equal to 70. If no SIZE is specified, the default is 110.

To use the FCB created with the job shown in Figure 13.6, you would code the DD statement as

```
//REPORT     DD SYSOUT=A,FCB=FCB1
```

COPYMOD Control Statement.   Figure 13.7 illustrates the JCL required to create a copy modification module. The EXEC and DD statements are the same as those in Figure 13.6. The NAME specified in the NAME statement is SALE. This means that a module named MOD1SALE will be stored in the SYS1.IMAGE-LIB by IEBIMAGE. The DD statement to invoke this module would be coded

```
//REPORT     DD SYSOUT=A,COPIES=4,MODIFY=SALE
```

In the COPYMOD statement in Figure 13.7, the first parameter is the COPIES parameter. The first number is the number of the first copy to which the statement applies, and the second indicates how many copies the statement applies to. In the first COPYMOD statement, we are dealing with the first copy only. In the second, we are starting with the second copy and dealing with two copies. Thus the second COPYMOD statement applies to the second and third copies. The third COPYMOD statement applies to the fourth copy. The COPIES parameter in this statement is different from the other two. There is a number indicating which copy, but no number showing how many. When the second number is left out, it defaults to 1. Consequently, the second value could have been omitted in the first COPYMOD statement, but not in the second.

Figure 13.7

Creating a Copy Modification Module

```
//JCLQB925 JOB ,'AJAX'
//STEPMOD   EXEC PGM=IEBIMAGE
//SYSPRINT DD SYSOUT=A
//SYSUT1    DD DSN=SYS1.IMAGELIB,
//             DISP=OLD
//SYSIN     DD *
 COPYMOD COPIES=(1,1),                             *
            LINES=(1,1),                           *
            POS=10,                                *
            TEXT=(C,'CUSTOMER COPY')
 COPYMOD COPIES=(2,2),                             *
            LINES=1,                               *
            POS=10,                                *
            TEXT=(C,'FILE COPY')
 COPYMOD COPIES=4,                                 *
            LINES=1,                               *
            POS=10,                                *
            TEXT=(C,'SALESMAN''S COPY')
 NAME SALE
/*
//
```

The next parameter used in the COPYMOD statement tells the system which lines are being modified by this copy modification module. The coding of the LINES parameter is very similar to that of the COPIES parameter. The first number indicates the starting line, and the second number tells how many lines. In the second and third COPYMOD statements, only one number is specified with the LINES parameter. As with the COPIES parameter, when the second value is not coded, the parameter defaults to 1.

The third parameter in the COPYMOD statement indicates where in the line the text is to start printing. In all three statements, 10 is coded. As a result, the text to be inserted in the document will be inserted starting at position 10 of line 1.

The last parameter in the COPYMOD statement, the TEXT parameter, indicates what information is to be inserted in the document. Notice that the letter C precedes the data, which are surrounded by apostrophes. The letter C indicates that the supplied data are in character form. If the supplied data were in hexadecimal form, the letter X would have been coded. Why might you supply hexadecimal instead of character representation when you wished the data printed? One reason is that you might be coding your statements on a device that does not have the full character set to be found on the 3800. If, for example, the input device did not have an asterisk (*), you might code

```
TEXT=(X'5C5C5C')
```

to insert three asterisks in the output.

Look at the TEXT parameter in the last COPYMOD statement. SALESMAN'S COPY is to appear in the output. If it had been coded as it is written, however, an error would have resulted. When you want an apostrophe included in your text, it must be doubled, as shown in Figure 13.7.

Let us summarize the results of using this copy modification module. On line 1 starting in position 10, additional information will be printed. The first copy will have CUSTOMER COPY; the second and third, FILE COPY; and the fourth, SALESMAN'S COPY. This information will be printed on every page of these copies.

IEBIMAGE is also used to create modules that contain different character sets. These modules are invoked with the CHARS parameter in the DD statement. We will not discuss how to do so here, because an application programmer would rarely perform this function.

More information about IEBIMAGE may be found in *IBM 3800 Printing Subsystem*.

IEBISAM

IEBISAM deals exclusively with ISAM data sets. It can be used to copy an ISAM data set and to unload and load, as well as to print in either character or hexadecimal format. IEBISAM is discussed in detail in Chapter 11.

IEBPTPCH

IEBPTPCH is used to print or punch sequential data sets or members of partitioned data sets. The programmer may use control statements to print or punch parts of each record in an order different from the one in which the information appears in the original record. This utility program is discussed in detail in Chapters 4 and 5.

IEBTCRIN

IEBTCRIN is a utility program used to create a physical sequential data set from data produced on an IBM 2495 tape cartridge reader. The data may have been placed on the tape cartridge with an IBM magnetic tape Selectric type-writer or with an IBM 50 magnetic data inscriber. This utility program is not often used because it is rarely necessary to create physical sequential data sets from information on a tape cartridge. Consequently, we will not discuss how to use this utility.

IEBUPDAT

IEBUPDAT is a utility program that is no longer supported or distributed. It performed about the same function as IEBUPDTE, but it was much more difficult to use. You may come across it, however, as some installations never discard JCL.

IEBUPDTE

IEBUPDTE is used primarily to add source programs to a library or to change a source program in a library. IEBUPDTE may also be used to copy a member from one library to another. Remember that IEBUPDTE can only be used to handle library members whose record length is 80 bytes or less. IEBUPDTE is discussed in detail in Chapter 5.

IEFBR14

IEFBR14 is not, strictly speaking, a utility program. It does nothing but permit the associated DD statements to be processed. Refer to Chapter 5 for more detailed information.

System Utilities

IEHATLAS

When a program using a DASD executes, a defective track on the disk pack may cause a read or write error to occur. In this situation, your systems programmer may choose to use the utility program IEHATLAS, which will find an alternate track to replace the bad track and transfer the usable data from the defective track. Replacement data for the error record may be supplied at the same time. (Remember that disk packs contain extra cylinders that supply alternates when a track currently in use becomes defective.)

Normally IEHATLAS is used by the systems programmer, so an application programmer does not have to know exactly how to use this utility program. However, because you as application programmer probably know what information should be in the bad record that needs replacement, it is helpful if you have some knowledge of how this utility program works.

Figure 13.8 illustrates using IEHATLAS to assign an alternate track to replace a defective one and to replace the bad record. The SYSUT1 DD statement points to the data set that includes the defective track. Note that a disposition of OLD is specified. This disposition is required; it ensures that no other program will use the data set while it is being repaired. In the example in Figure 13.8, the defective track is in a data set, as opposed to unused space. The first control statement points to the defective track as well as the defective record. If the bad track were in the VTOC, VTOC would have been coded instead of TRACK. The exact details of the remainder of this statement are the responsibility of the systems programmer. The next control statement contains the replacement data in hexadecimal format. It starts in column 1 and may extend to column 80. You may use as many 80-byte records as required. When all the replacement data have been coded, you stop and leave the rest of the statement blank.

IEHDASDR

Working under the operating system, IEHDASDR does what IBCDASDI and IBCDMPRS do as independent utility programs. In fact, a disk pack dump

■ **Figure 13.8** ■

Sample IEHATLAS Job

```
//JCLQB930 JOB ,'HEKTOR'
//STEPATL   EXEC PGM=IEHATLAS
//SYSPRINT DD SYSOUT=A
//SYSUT1    DD DSN=ERRDATA,
//               UNIT=SYSDA,
//               VOL=SER=WYL003,
//               DISP=OLD
//SYSIN     DD *
 TRACK=00000002000C00010008
F1F2F3F4F5F6F7F8F9C1C2C3
/*
//
```

Figure 13.9

Sample IEHDASDR Job

```
//JCLQB935 JOB ,'ODYSSEUS'
//STEPDASD EXEC PGM=IEHDASDR
//SYSPRINT DD SYSOUT=A
//DISKPACK DD UNIT=SYSDA,
//         DISP=OLD,
//         VOL=(PRIVATE,SER=111111)
//SYSIN    DD *
 FORMAT TODD=DISKPACK,
              VTOC=6,                             *
              EXTENT=5,                           *
              NEWVOLID=SCRATC,                    *
              PURGE=YES                           *
 /*
 //
```

created using IBCDMPRS may be restored by IEHDASDR. Figure 13.9 illustrates a DASDI operation using IEHDASDR; the function performed is almost the same as the one illustrated in the IBCDASDI example in Figure 13.1. Figure 13.10 illustrates an IEHDASDR dump and restore operation that corresponds to the IBCDMPRS example in Figure 13.2.

We will not go into detail on the use of this utility because the application programmer rarely uses it.

Figure 13.10

Sample Dump and Restore Using IEHDASDR

```
//JCLQB940 JOB ,'NESTOR'
//DUMPREST EXEC PGM=IEHDASDR
//SYSPRINT DD SYSOUT=A
//DISKDUMP DD UNIT=SYSDA,
//            VOL=SER=111111,
//            DISP=OLD
//TAPEOUT  DD UNIT=TAPE9,
//            DSNAME=NEWTAPE
//DISKREST DD UNIT=SYSDA,
//            VOL=SER=DISK01,
//            DISP=OLD
//TAPEIN   DD DSNAME=OLDTAPE,
//            DISP=OLD,
//            UNIT=TAPE9,
//            VOL=SER=T12345
//SYSIN    DD *
 DUMP FROMDD=DISKDUMP,TODD=TAPEOUT
 RESTORE TODD=DISKREST,FROMDD=TAPEIN,PURGE=YES
 /*
 //
```

IEHINITT

The utility program IEHINITT is used by operations personnel or systems programmers to write the volume label on a tape reel. Because this utility program will write a label on a tape regardless of security protection or expiration date, IEHINITT is often removed from SYS1.LINKLIB to prevent its unauthorized use. When a scratch tape is mounted to be used as a standard labeled tape, the operator is requested to supply the volume serial number if one is not already written on the tape. Given that the operator can supply the volume serial number when the tape reel is being used, why bother having a separate utility program to perform this function? One reason is efficiency. When a supply of new tapes arrives, IEHINITT may be used to write the volume label on the tapes as a group so that later jobs using these tape reels are not held up waiting for the operator's response.

Figure 13.11 illustrates the layout of a normal standard labeled tape. The records that make up the labels are 80 bytes in length. The volume label contains the serial number that would be specified in the VOL parameter of the DD statement — for example,

```
//              VOL=SER=000106,
```

The HDR1 label contains system-type information, such as the expiration date, which you set with the DD statement LABEL parameter. The HDR2 label contains information that you specify with the DCB parameter when you create the data set. Not all installations have user labels, and they will be different in each installation. The trailer labels EOF1 and EOF2 contain virtually the same information as the header labels.

Obviously IEHINITT cannot supply all of this information. IEHINITT writes the volume label, containing the serial number supplied by a control statement, which we will discuss next, and a dummy HDR1 record followed by a tape mark.

Figure 13.12 illustrates the JCL to use IEHINITT. The ANYNAME DD statement may actually have any valid ddname you want. The purpose of this statement is to supply one or more tape drives to be used. Only two parameters are coded, DCB and UNIT. In the DCB parameter, the subparameter DEN=3 means that the tape volume label is to be written at a density of 1600 BPI (bytes per inch). The values that may be coded for DEN and their meanings were discussed in Chapter 3. The UNIT parameter points to the physical device to be used. The coding TAPE9 usually means that this job can use any tape drive that can read and write nine-track tape. It is possible to specify more than one tape drive. Because (as we shall see when we discuss the control statements) three tapes are being initialized in this job, it would have been more efficient to do so. The DEFER subparameter included in the UNIT parameter permits execution of the program to begin before the tape reels are mounted.

IEHINITT has only one control statement, INITT. The only required pa-

Standard Label Tape Organization

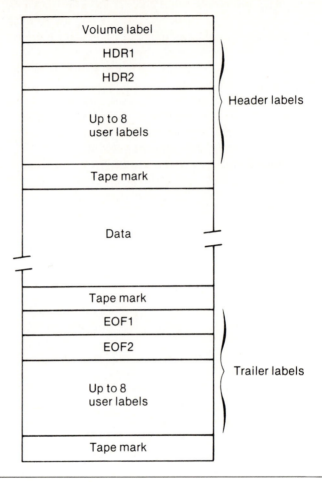

■ **Figure 13.12** ■■■■■■■■■■■■■■■■■■■■■■■■■■■■

Sample IEHINITT Job

```
//JCLQB945 JOB ,'J.C.LEWIS'
//STEPLABL EXEC PGM=IEHINITT
//SYSPRINT DD SYSOUT=A
//ANYNAME  DD DCB=DEN=3,
//            UNIT=(TAPE9,,DEFER)
//SYSIN    DD *
ANYNAME INITT DISP=REWIND,SER=000106,NUMTAPE=3
/*
//
```

rameter on this statement is the serial number supplied with the SER parameter, as illustrated in Figure 13.12. Unlike other utility control statements, INITT requires the label. It must be the same as the ddname that points to the tape drive or drives to be used. DISP=REWIND means that the tape is to be rewound after the label has been written. Alternatively, the DISP parameter could have specified UNLOAD (the default), which means that the tape is to be rewound and unloaded after the label has been written. NUMTAPE=3 means that three tapes will be initialized. How is this possible when only one serial number is given? What will happen here is that the first tape will have a serial number of 000106, the second 000107, and the third 000108. If you wish to initialize more than one reel of tape with one control statement, the serial number specified in the INITT control statement must be numeric. If, on the other hand, you do not want sequential serial numbers or you want an alphameric serial number, you must use a separate control statement for each volume. The NUMTAPE parameter would be omitted, and the default value of 1 would be taken.

If your installation uses ASCII, you should specify LABTYPE=AL on the control statement. Without this parameter the label is written in EBCDIC.

IEHLIST

IEHLIST lists non-VSAM catalog, VTOC, and PDS directory entries.* In Chapter 5 we discussed using the utility to list the names of the members in a PDS. It would be a good idea to go back to Chapter 5 now and review that material, paying particular attention to Figure 5.25.

The programmer invented for this book, J. C. Lewis, must begin all his non-VSAM data set names with the qualifiers WYL.QB.JCL, where QB stands for Queensborough Community College and JCL are Lewis's initials. Figure 13.13 shows a job that uses the LISTCTLG control statement to list the names of all cataloged data sets that belong to him.

Coding

```
NODE=WYL.QB.JCL
```

on the control statement limits the output to data set names that begin with WYL.QB.JCL. If

```
NODE=WYL.QB
```

were coded, all cataloged Queensborough data sets would be listed. If NODE were omitted, the whole catalog would be listed.

On the control statement, the VOL parameter must name the disk pack that contains the catalog. In the CUNY system the catalog is on WYL001. Notice that the ANYNAME DD statement also points to this volume. As mentioned in

* Entries in VSAM catalogs are listed using IDCAMS, as explained in Chapter 12.

■ Figure 13.13 ■

Using IEHLIST to List Part of a Catalog

```
//JCLQB948 JOB ,'J.C.LEWIS'
//LISTCTLG EXEC PGM=IEHLIST
//SYSPRINT DD SYSOUT=A
//ANYNAME   DD UNIT=SYSDA,
//             VOL=SER=WYL001,
//             DISP=OLD
//SYSIN    DD *
 LISTCTLG VOL=SYSDA=WYL001,                              *
            NODE=WYL.QB.JCL
/*
//
```

Chapter 5, you can determine the serial number of the volume that contains the system catalog by reading the allocation messages from a job that uses the catalog. In Figure 4.7, for example, the messages

```
IEF285I    SYSCTLG.VWYL001              KEPT
IEF285I    VOL SER NOS= WYL001.
```

indicate that the system catalog is on DASD volume WYL001.

In order to learn which data sets are stored on a volume, you can use the LISTVTOC control statement of IEHLIST. There are two parameters that may be used to specify the format of the output: DUMP and FORMAT. DUMP means that the listing is to be unedited and hexadecimal. FORMAT means that the listing is to be edited for easier reading. If you want to know which data sets are on disk pack WYL004, you code

```
LISTVTOC VOL=SYSDA=WYL004
```

Neither DUMP nor FORMAT is coded, so a short edited form is produced.

If you code FORMAT, part of the output is labeled FORMAT 5 DSCB. This DSCB describes the freespace that is available on the volume.

If you want to know which data sets will expire before a specified date — say, May 25, 1990, which corresponds to Julian date 14590 — you code

```
LISTVTOC VOL=SYSDA=WYL004,DATE=14590
```

In the listing, all data sets with expiration dates before May 25, 1990, will be marked with an asterisk. This parameter cannot be used if you code either DUMP or FORMAT. It is important to note that, unlike the yyddd format used with the RETPD subparameter discussed in Chapter 10, the format of the Julian date used here is dddyy.

If you are only interested in verifying that certain data sets are on a particular volume, you use the DSNAME parameter to limit the listing. To check whether data set `WYL.QB.JCL.POLYFILE` is on `WYL004` requires the following coding:

```
LISTVTOC VOL=SYSDA=WYL004,DSNAME=WYL.QB.JCL.POLYFILE
```

To check on data sets `TEST1` and `TEST2` requires the coding

```
LISTVTOC VOL=SYSDA=WYL004,DSNAME=(TEST1,TEST2)
```

As a rule, `LISTVTOC` and `LISTCTLG` control statements are of more use to systems programmers than to application programmers. Nevertheless, there are times when an application programmer needs to find out what is on a disk pack.

IEHMOVE

`IEHMOVE` can be used to move or copy data sets, groups of data sets, catalogs, and entire volumes. `IEHMOVE` cannot handle either ISAM or VSAM data sets. We will not discuss using `IEHMOVE` to move or copy catalogs or volumes because these functions are normally performed by the systems programmer. We will, however, discuss using `IEHMOVE` to move and copy data sets and groups of data sets. The `IEHMOVE` control statements and operands are summarized in Table 13.2.

It is critical that you understand the difference between the copy operation and the move operation. With the copy operation the original version still exists, but with the move operation the original version is destroyed. Using the copy operation is like using the copier. When you are done, you have the original that you started with and a copy. Using the move operation is like having movers come in; the original is destroyed and only the new version exists.

Figure 13.14 is a sample `IEHMOVE` job. Unlike most of the other utility programs that we have discussed, `IEHMOVE` requires DASD work space. `IEHMOVE` obtains this work space on the disk pack that you have made available with the `SYSUT1` DD statement.

In the job shown in Figure 13.14, three disk packs, `WYL003`, `WYL004`, and `WYL005`, are made available to `IEHMOVE` with the DD statements `DD1`, `DD2`, and `DD3`. If additional DD statements had been provided, `IEHMOVE` would have had access to more disk packs. If, say, `DD2` had been omitted, `IEHMOVE` would have had access only to `WYL003` and `WYL005`. Any valid ddname (other than restricted names such as `SYSABEND`) could have been used in Figure 13.14.

DSGROUP Parameter. The first control statement uses the `DSGROUP` parameter. What is a DSGROUP? A DSGROUP is a group of data sets whose names are partially qualified by one or more identical names. We have discussed `SYS1.PROCLIB`, which contains procedures, and `SYS1.LINKLIB`, which

Table 13.2
Operands Used with IEHMOVE Control Statements

Operand	DSGROUP Move	DSGROUP Copy	DSNAME Move	DSNAME Copy	PDS Move	PDS Copy	Remarks
`TO=device=volser`	R*	R	R	R	R	R	Specifies the device type and volume serial number of the receiving volume.
`FROM=device=volser`	N*	N	O*	O	O	O	Specifies the device type and volume serial number of the source volume. Used only for uncataloged data sets.
`UNCATLG`	O	O	O	O	O	O	For a copy operation the source data set is uncataloged. For a move operation the output data set is not cataloged.
`CATLG`	N	O	N	O	N	O	The output data set should be cataloged. If the source data set is cataloged, it will be uncataloged, unless `RENAME` is coded.
`RENAME=newname`	N	N	O	O	O	O	Specifies that the output data set should be renamed and gives the new name.
`FROMDD=ddname`	N	N	O	O	O	O	Specifies the name of the DD statement from which DCB and LABEL information can be obtained for input data sets on tape.
`TODD=ddname`	O	O	O	O	O	O	Specifies the name of the DD statement from which DCB and LABEL information can be obtained for output data sets on tape.
`UNLOAD`	O	O	O	O	O	O	The data set is to be unloaded to the receiving volume.
`EXPAND=nn`	N	N	N	N	O	O	Specifies the number of directory blocks to be added to the PDS.

* R means required, O means optional, N means not applicable.

■ Figure 13.14 ■■■■■■■■■■■■■■■■■■■■■■■■■■■■■■■■■■■■■

Sample IEHMOVE Job

```
//JCLQB950 JOB ,'J.C.LEWIS'
//STEPMOVE EXEC PGM=IEHMOVE
//SYSPRINT DD SYSOUT=A
//SYSUT1    DD UNIT=SYSDA,VOL=SER=SCR001,DISP=OLD
//DD1       DD UNIT=SYSDA,VOL=SER=WYL003,DISP=OLD
//DD2       DD UNIT=SYSDA,VOL=SER=WYL004,DISP=OLD
//DD3       DD UNIT=SYSDA,VOL=SER=WYL005,DISP=OLD
//SYSIN     DD *
 MOVE DSGROUP=A.B.C,TO=SYSDA=WYL005
 COPY DSGROUP=X.Y.Z,TO=SYSDA=WYL004,UNLOAD
 MOVE DSNAME=SAMPLE1,FROM=SYSDA=WYL005,TO=SYSDA=WYL004
 COPY DSNAME=SAMPL2,TO=SYSDA=WYL004,RENAME=SAMP2
 MOVE PDS=LIBRARY,FROM=SYSDA=WYL004,TO=SYSDA=WYL005,
              RENAME=NEWLIB,EXPAND=6                          *
 COPY PDS=OLDLIB,FROM=SYSDA=WYL004,TO=SYSDA=WYL005
 COPY PDS=MYLIB,FROM=SYSDA=WYL004,TO=SYSDA=WYL005
  INCLUDE DSNAME=NEWLIB,MEMBER=ADDIT,FROM=SYSDA=WYL005
  EXCLUDE MEMBER=OMITIT
  REPLACE DSNAME=NEWLIB,MEMBER=REPIT,FROM=SYSDA=WYL005
 COPY PDS=STDLIB,RENAME=YOURLB,TO=SYSDA=WYL004
  SELECT MEMBER=(S1,(X2,S2),S3)
/*
//
```

contains executable code; they are part of a DSGROUP. The data sets belonging to user JCL form a DSGROUP because their names start with WYL.QB.JCL.

In Figure 13.14 the first control statement moves all cataloged sequential data sets and PDSs whose names start with A.B.C from WYL003 and WYL004 to WYL005. Remember that the data sets to be moved must be cataloged or they will not be found; the control statement tells IEHMOVE where the data sets are to be placed, but not where they are to be found. With the move operation, after the data sets are written on WYL005, they are scratched from their source volume. The new versions of the data sets are cataloged to reflect their new location.

The second control statement in Figure 13.14 copies all cataloged data sets whose names begin with X.Y.Z from WYL003 and WYL005 to WYL004, where they will be written in unload format. Normally unload format is used to produce a back-up tape, but there is no technical reason why a disk pack cannot be used. When a data set is unloaded, it is converted to 80-byte blocked records. If you later move or copy an unloaded data set back to disk, IEHMOVE will automatically reconstruct its original organization. As you recall, the copy operation does not cause the source data set to be scratched. If UNLOAD had not been coded, we would have two identical versions of these data sets. One group would be the original cataloged group; the other group, written on WYL004, would not be cataloged.

With a move operation, if the source data sets are cataloged, the new data sets are automatically cataloged. To prevent the new data sets from being cataloged, UNCATLG may be coded. When used with a copy operation, however, UNCATLG has a different meaning. In this case it means that the source data sets should be uncataloged.

With a simple copy operation the new data sets are not cataloged. CATLG may be coded with a copy operation to catalog the new data sets. Data set names of cataloged data sets must be unique, so cataloging the new data sets requires that the source data sets be uncataloged, unless the new data sets are given a new name through the coding of RENAME. CATLG is the one parameter that applies only to the copy operation.

If

```
MOVE DSGROUP=P.Q.R,TO=SYSDA=WYL005,UNCATLG
```

is coded, the new data sets written on WYL005 will not be cataloged. If the operation had been COPY instead of MOVE, neither the original nor the new version would be cataloged.

If

```
COPY DSGROUP=P.Q.R,TO=SYSDA=WYL005,CATLG
```

is coded, the new data sets written on WYL005 will be cataloged but the original data sets will be uncataloged.

Remember that you can have more than one data set with the same name in your system provided that only one is cataloged and that each data set is located on a different volume.

With tape output instead of DASD, the TODD parameter can be added, as in TODD=TAPEOUT. In this case, IEHMOVE will use the DCB information provided in the TAPEOUT DD statement. Do not confuse the TO parameter, which tells IEHMOVE where to write the new version of the data set, with the TODD parameter, which tells IEHMOVE where DCB information may be found. If the output is nine-track tape with standard labels and default density, TODD may be omitted.

If

```
MOVE DSGROUP=P.Q.R,TO=TAPE9=SCRATH,UNLOAD,TODD=TAPEOUT
```

is coded, a tape is created that may be used to transport the data sets to another system. Because the move operation is specified, the data sets will be scratched upon successful completion of the move. If COPY had been coded instead of MOVE, the tape created would have been a back-up tape. When partitioned or direct data sets are moved or copied to tape, they are automatically unloaded, because tape cannot support partitioned or direct organization. Thus this example did not require UNLOAD just to unload partitioned or direct data sets. Coding UNLOAD caused all the data sets to be unloaded, including physical sequential data sets. The TODD parameter indicates where the IEHMOVE utility program will find DCB information for the unload operation. When a group of data sets are moved or copied to tape, they are written as successive data sets. That is, the first data set moved or copied is written as the first data set on the tape, the second data set as the second data set, and so on.

There are three additional parameters that may be coded with a move or copy operation for a DSGROUP. Two parameters, PASSWORD and COPYAUTH, relate to security, which is outside the scope of this book, and the third deals with the case of multiple catalogs, which is a situation that a systems programmer deals with.

Please review in your own mind the parameters CATLG, UNCATLG, UN-LOAD, and TODD. If you do not understand them, review this section again. These parameters will be used in remaining move/copy operations that we will discuss.

DSNAME Parameter.   The third control statement in Figure 13.14 illustrates using the DSNAME parameter to move a single data set. DSNAME may not be abbreviated as in the DD statement. This control statement differs from the MOVE DSGROUP control statement in that there is a FROM parameter which identifies the unit (SYSDA) and the disk pack (WYL005) where data set SAMPLE1 is to be found. The FROM parameter is used only for data sets that are not cataloged. The result of executing this command will be that data set SAMPLE1 will be written on WYL004 and scratched from WYL005.

The fourth control statement illustrates copying a cataloged data set onto WYL004 and giving the new version a new name. The original or source data set, SAMPL2, must be cataloged because no FROM parameter is coded. The new version of the data set is renamed SAMP2 through the use of the RENAME parameter. After this command is executed, there will be a cataloged data set named SAMPL2 and an uncataloged data set named SAMP2 located on WYL004. If

```
MOVE DSNAME=LOADIT,TO=SYSDA=WYL004,FROM=TAPE9=000104,  *
          FROMDD=TAPEDD
```

is coded, a data set from tape will be loaded back onto DASD. You are familiar with all the parameters in this control statement except FROMDD. FROMDD is related to the parameter TODD. When the unload tape is created, TODD points to a DD statement that contains the DCB information used in unloading the data set. FROMDD points to a DD statement that contains the DCB information used in loading the data set. FROMDD is not required if the tape that contains the unloaded data set is a standard label tape. The FROMDD parameter is needed only for unlabeled tapes.

The UNCATLG, TODD, and UNLOAD parameters are used with MOVE/COPY DSNAME in the same way as with MOVE/COPY DSGROUP. There is one difference between the way the CATLG parameter is used with COPY DSNAME and the way it is used with COPY DSGROUP. Usually if CATLG is included on a COPY control statement, the new data set is cataloged and the old data set is uncataloged. If, however, the data set is renamed, as in the previous example, coding CATLG causes the new data set to be cataloged, but the old data set is not uncataloged.

PDS Parameter.   The MOVE/COPY PDS control statement is used with libraries or partitioned data sets. In its simple form it differs little from the MOVE/COPY DSNAME, which we studied earlier. The fifth control statement in Figure 13.14 illustrates a simple move operation including the one new parameter EX-PAND. This parameter is used only when a new library is being created as a result of the control statement. It tells how many more directory blocks are to be created with the new library. If the original library in the example had 10 directory blocks, the new library would have 16. EXPAND refers only to the number of directory blocks to be added to the directory; the number of tracks in the new library will be the same as in the original library.

To summarize, as a result of the fifth control statement in Figure 13.14, a new library named NEWLIB (see the RENAME parameter) will be created on WYL005 using a PDS named LIBRARY as input. After NEWLIB has been successfully created, LIBRARY will be scratched.

The MOVE/COPY PDS may also be used to merge members from other libraries into an existing library if the libraries have the same names. The sixth control statement in Figure 13.14 assumes that there are two versions of a PDS named OLDLIB, one on WYL004 and the other on WYL005. In this case all the members that have different names will be copied from PDS OLDLIB on WYL004 and written to PDS OLDLIB on WYL005. If a member with the same name exists in both PDSs, it is not copied. For example, if OLDLIB on WYL004 has members A, B, and C and initially OLDLIB on WYL005 has members C, D, and E, after this command is executed OLDLIB on WYL005 will have members A, B, C, D, and E. Member C, which existed in both libraries, will be the member that was originally on WYL005.

The next control statement looks like an ordinary COPY PDS, but its function is modified by the following INCLUDE, EXCLUDE, and REPLACE statements. Only one INCLUDE statement is coded, but there could be more. The INCLUDE statement permits a member from another library to be included in the copy or move operation. The DSNAME parameter names the library, and the MEMBER parameter names the member to be included in the new version of MYLIB. The FROM parameter is coded if the library named by the DSNAME parameter is not cataloged. The COPY and INCLUDE statements cause members in MYLIB on WYL004 to be copied to MYLIB on WYL005, and member ADDIT from library NEWLIB to be written to MYLIB on WYL005.

The next control statement is an EXCLUDE statement, which names a member (OMITIT) in the version of MYLIB on WYL004 that is not to be moved or copied. Only one EXCLUDE statement is coded in Figure 13.14, but you may code as many as there are members that you do not want copied or moved. The REPLACE control statement causes the specified member to be taken from a different library. In the example in Figure 13.14, member REPIT is being taken from library NEWLIB on WYL005 instead of MYLIB on WYL004. So all members from MYLIB on WYL004 except members OMITIT and REPIT are copied to MYLIB on WYL005. In addition, ADDIT and REPIT from NEWLIB on WYL005 are copied to MYLIB on WYL005.

The last two control statements in Figure 13.14 illustrate how the SELECT control statement is used to modify the action of a COPY statement. The COPY control statement contains nothing new. A cataloged PDS named STDLIB is to be copied to WYL004 and then given the name YOURLIB. This straightforward operation is modified by the SELECT control statement. The SELECT control statement tells IEHMOVE that only the members named in the SELECT control statement are to be copied or moved. Only members S1, X2, and S3 are to be copied from STDLIB to the new PDS named YOURLIB. Furthermore, member X2 is to be renamed S2. The result of executing these two control statements will be the creation of a PDS named YOURLIB on WYL004. YOURLIB will contain three members, S1, S2, and S3. Remember that S2 is the same as member X2 in PDS STDLIB.

There are four control statements that may be used to modify the operation of a MOVE/COPY PDS: INCLUDE, EXCLUDE, REPLACE, and SELECT. The INCLUDE, EXCLUDE, and REPLACE control statements may be used together in any order and virtually any number. Only the INCLUDE statement may be used together with the SELECT control statement. None of these control statements may be used when data are loaded or unloaded.

You may have noticed that IEHMOVE performs many of the same operations as IEBGENER does for sequential data sets and IEBCOPY does for PDS. Nevertheless, each offers certain special features not found in the others. For example, when a tape version of a PDS is created using IEHMOVE, it is necessary to include all the members of the PDS. When a tape version of a PDS is created using IEBCOPY, however, it is possible to copy selected members. On the other hand, IEHMOVE permits copying DSGROUPs, an operation that is not possible with IEBGENER or IEBCOPY. Another advantage of IEHMOVE is that the space for the new data set does not have to be allocated in your JCL; IEHMOVE will allocate the space it needs.

IEHPROGM

IEHPROGM is a utility program that systems programmers find extremely useful. Application programmers find a few of the functions of IEHPROGM helpful. We discussed SCRATCH, CATLG, UNCATLG, and RENAME in Chapter 5 when we studied libraries. The control statements BLDG and DLTX were discussed in Chapter 6 when we studied generation data groups. Although

`IEHPROGM` can perform other functions, we will not discuss the remaining control statements, for application programmers rarely, if ever, use them.

IFHSTATR

With a system called SMF, the operating system gathers statistical information about jobs run and physical devices and media used. SMF can gather massive amounts of information about a system. In fact, the real problem is that SMF produces more information than can generally be used. When a systems programmer generates an operating system, he or she usually reduces the amount of information that SMF will produce to a level that suits the needs of the environment. SMF creates different types of records, each type monitoring the performance of a different part of the computer system. For example, type 21 records monitor the performance of tape volumes. A type 21 record is written after a tape volume is used and indicates, among other information, how many I/O errors occurred during the time the tape was used.

   `IFHSTATR` is a utility program that operations personnel use to evaluate how good the tape reels are. The input is the data created by SMF. `IFHSTATR` selects and prints type 21 records.

   Figure 13.15 illustrates the JCL needed to run `IFHSTATR`. The `SYSUT1 DD` statement points to the SMF data and `SYSUT2` to the output listing.

■ **Figure 13.15**

IFHSTATR Example

```
//JCLQB960 JOB ,'J.C.LEWIS'
//STEPTAPE EXEC PGM=IFHSTATR
//SYSUT1   DD DSNAME=SYS1.MAN,
//            UNIT=TAPE9,
//            VOL=SER=SMF021,
//            DISP=OLD
//SYSUT2   DD SYSOUT=A
/*
//
```

Summary   Virtually every utility program that may be used with the operating system has been at least mentioned in this chapter. You should know what functions each utility program can perform. In addition, you should know how to use those utility programs that an application programmer is likely to use.

Vocabulary

In this chapter you have been introduced to the meanings of the following terms:

direct access storage device
   initialization (DASDI)
initial program load (IPL)

Exercises

1. What is an independent utility?
2. What function does the independent utility program IBCDASDI perform?
3. What function does the independent utility program IBCDMPRS perform?
4. What is the utility program IEBCOMPR used for?
5. What kind of data sets may be processed by IEBCOMPR?
6. Write a job stream to use IEBCOMPR to compare two cataloged data sets named SET1 and SET2.
7. What kind of data sets may be input to IEBCOPY?
8. What are the three control statements used by IEBCOPY?
9. What functions does IEBCOPY perform?
10. What function does IEBDG perform?
11. What type of data sets may be input to or output from IEBDG?
12. What would IEBEDIT be used for?
13. Write a job stream to use IEBEDIT to print selected JCL statements in a cataloged data set named JCLSET. Print only the JCL in the step named COMPARE in the job named NEWJOB.
14. What may IEBGENER be used for?
15. What is unique about IEBIMAGE?
16. What does IEBIMAGE do?
17. What does IEBISAM do?
18. What would you use IEBPTPCH for?
19. What function does IEBTCRIN provide?
20. What would you use IEBUPDTE for?
21. What restriction limits the usefulness of IEBUPDTE?
22. Why would IEHATLAS be used?
23. Which utility program could be used instead of IBCDASDI and IBCDMPRS?
24. Why should IEHINITT be used?
25. Write a job stream to use IEHINITT to write volume serial numbers ABC on one tape and XYZ on another.
26. If you wished to learn the volume on which a cataloged data set resides, which utility program would you use? Which control statement?
27. Name the utility program and control statement used to determine which data sets are on a disk pack.
28. Write a job stream to use IEHLIST to list the VTOC on volume DISK45 and to determine whether a data set named MAYBE is on volume DISK63.

29. What is the difference between the move and copy operations of IEH-MOVE?

30. What are the control statements that may be used to modify the IEHMOVE MOVE/COPY PDS control statement?

31. A computer center has five disk packs named DISK01 through DISK05. Write a job stream to use IEHMOVE to
    a. Move all the cataloged data sets whose names start with ACCTRECV to tape TAP100.
    b. Copy members A1 and A2 from a cataloged library named ALIB to a new library named BLIB on DISK04. The members should be renamed B1 and B2.

32. For what functions would you as an application programmer use IEH-PROGM?

33. There are two versions of a data set named TWO. One version is on DISK90, and the other is on DISK10. The version on DISK90 is cataloged. Write a job stream to use IEHPROGM to uncatalog the version on DISK90 and catalog the version on DISK10.

34. Who would probably use IFHSTATR?

Programming Assignments

1. Use IEHMOVE to copy the data set you created for the Programming Assignment in Chapter 3. The new data set should be renamed and cataloged.

2. Use IEBCOMPR to compare the data set you created in Programming Assignment 1 with the original data set from which it was copied.

3. Perform an experiment to discover what the actions listed in Table 13.1 do. *Hints:* Define eight 5-byte fields, each containing a PICTURE defining a 5-byte pattern and each specifying a different action. When you wave (WV) or roll (RO), the results are more interesting if the fields have one or more blanks at the beginning and/or end. Create 20 records, and direct the output to the printer. You will have to add a DCB parameter to the output DD statement to make the record length of the output data set equal to the record length implied in your CREATE statement.

4. Using IEBIMAGE, create an FCB for a six-inch page, where the first two inches are printed at 6 lines per inch, the next two inches at 8 lines per inch, and the remaining two inches at 12 lines per inch. You need a channel 1 punch at line 1 and channel 7 punches where the line density changes. (Check with your advisor before running this job to learn whether you are permitted to add members to SYS1.IMAGELIB. If you are not, direct your output to FIRSTLIB. Remember that this only applies to the 3800 printer.)

5. If you use a systematic naming convention at your computer center, use IEHMOVE to copy all your cataloged data sets to a back-up tape.

6. For this assignment you need a library containing at least three members, although the data in the three members is not significant. You may use the FIRSTLIB you created for Programming Assignment 1 in Chapter 5. Or your advisor may suggest a library. Or you may use IEBDG to create the library and members. In this case the members should be named MEMA, MEMB, and MEMC and should consist of ten 50-byte records containing all As, Bs, or Cs. If you are clever, you can create all three members in one jobstep, using three sets of DSD-FD-CREATE-END control statements. Next, use IEHMOVE to make a copy of the library. The new library should contain any two members from the original library. Finally, use IEBCOMPR to compare the two libraries.

7. Use IEHPROGM to uncatalog any one of your data sets. Then use IEH-PROGM to recatalog it.

8. The utilities manual's discussion of IEBPTPCH says that if PZ is specified as the conversion in a FIELD parameter, a field of length L bytes will occupy $2 \times L$ characters in the printed output record. This is surprising, because a packed field of length L bytes contains $2 \times L - 1$ digits. To discover what the extra character is used for, create a data set that contains at least one packed field. You may create the data set any way you like, but perhaps the easiest way is to use IEBDG. Use IEBPTPCH to print this field, specifying a conversion of PZ.

9. The utilities manual's discussion of IEBPTPCH says that when STRTAFT=n is coded, n must not exceed 32767. If you code a value greater than 32767, however, you do not get a syntax error. To determine what happens when a value greater than 32767 is coded, create a data set containing 33,100 records. Each record should contain a field that contains the record's sequence number, with numbers running from 00001 through 33100. Add 10 more bytes containing arbitrary data so that the record length is 15 bytes. Block the records so that the BLKSIZE is 1500 bytes. An easy way to create this data set is to use IEBDG. Employ IEBPTPCH to list this data set, using STRTAFT=33000 and STOPAFT=20. What happens?

Mass Storage

In this chapter you will learn

- why a mass storage system is needed

- what a mass storage system is

- how to create a data set on a mass storage volume

- how to access a data set on a mass storage volume

- how to use the parameter MSVGP

Data Storage — MSS and MSV

As the volume of data retained in data processing installations has grown, data processing management has been confronted with the problem of where to store the data. The choice in the past has been between tape and DASD.

Tape is relatively inexpensive, quickly and relatively easily mounted, easy to transport from one installation to another, and easy to store. Tape does have its disadvantages, however. Only physical sequential data sets may be stored on tape volumes. Libraries, for example, may be stored on tape only in unloaded form, which is not directly usable. In most installations, an entire volume is used for each data set, even if the data set only requires, say, 300 feet out of the 2400 feet of tape. This results in each installation's storing a large number of tape volumes in its library. When a particular tape volume is needed for a job, the operator must first obtain the tape from the library before he or she can mount it and run the job. Although the mounting of the tape reel on the tape unit may go quickly, the entire process (including retrieving the tape from the library and returning it after the job ends) can require a significant amount of time, depending on the library procedures. In addition, the wrong volume is sometimes mounted. The operator then generally has to go to the library again for the correct tape volume. In some such cases, the job must be canceled and rerun.

Although DASD avoids these problems, magnetic disk tends to be more expensive than tape. Whereas a reel of tape costs about $20, a DASD volume costs about $500. In addition, to mount and unmount a DASD volume takes a considerable amount of time. And DASD volumes tend to be more delicate than tape reels. If you drop a tape reel, it probably will not be damaged. DASD volumes, on the other hand, are likely to be damaged, and because of their awkward size and weight they are more likely to be dropped. DASD is, however, more desirable than tape in that all types of data sets may reside on it.

What data processing management wants is a device that provides the usability of DASD at the cost of tape. The 3850 **Mass Storage System (MSS)** approaches this ideal. An MSS provides the equivalent of up to 4720 3336 Disk Packs.

In an MSS, data are stored on a **data cartridge**, often simply called a **cartridge**. Two of these cartridges can hold the same amount of information as a 3336-disk volume, and the two cartridges together are referred to as a **mass storage volume (MSV)**. Each cartridge in an MSV is stored in a hexagonal (six-sided) cell. When data from a particular cartridge are wanted, an accessor removes the cartridge from its cell. The data are then transferred to a 3336 Disk Pack where they may be accessed by the application program. This process of taking data from the MSV and writing them on a 3336 Disk Pack is called **staging**. A data set that is to reside on an MSS is actually created on a 3330-disk drive using a 3336-disk volume. After the data set is closed, it is copied from the 3336-disk volume to an MSV. This process is called **destaging**.

The important thing to remember is that from the application programmer's point of view a 3336 Disk Pack is being used. There is no difference in the way the programmer writes a program, and there are only some very minor differences in the JCL, which we will discuss later.

Using an MSS does create more work for the systems programmer, however. Because the MSS can have the equivalent of up to 4720 3336 Disk Packs, it is desirable to form groups of cartridges that are related in some way. For example, you would probably want one group for payroll and another for inventory. You would initially establish a certain number of groups, and later, as the system was fine tuned, create more. Groups are created using the CREATEG command of the utility program IDCAMS. Once a group has been established, volumes are created using the CREATEV command of IDCAMS. This creation process gives two cartridges a volume serial number so that they become an MSV. At the same time, the MSV may be assigned to a group. When the group is created, it has a default space allocation. This means that if you create a data set and name a group instead of a volume, the SPACE parameter is not needed; the system can obtain the default space from the group.

MSS JCL Parameters

Setting the UNIT parameter to 3330V indicates that the unit referenced is an MSS. In every other way, the UNIT parameter is coded as it is for any DASD.

The one new parameter is MSVGP, which is coded on the DD statement. This parameter is used only when a data set is being created. When this parameter is used, the serial subparameter in the VOL parameter is not coded. The system assigns an MSV from the group named by the MSVGP parameter.

Creating a Data Set on an MSS

Figure 14.1 illustrates examples of the DD statements required to create data sets on an MSS. You can tell that all of these examples apply to an MSS because UNIT=3330V is coded.

Let us start with a sequential data set created on any MSV belonging to a particular group; Figure 14.1a illustrates this case. It is particularly interesting to look at what is not coded. There is no VOL parameter. The system will go

---

■ Figure 14.1 ■

(a) Creating a Sequential Data Set on an MSS Using MSV Group

```
//SEQDATA   DD DSN=SEQDAT,
//             DISP=(,CATLG),
//             UNIT=3330V,
//             MSVGP=PAYROL,
//             DCB=(LRECL=80,BLKSIZE=1680,RECFM=FB)
```

(b) Creating a Library on an MSS Using MV Group

```
//PDSDATA   DD DSN=PDSLIB,
//             DISP=(,CATLG),
//             UNIT=3330V,
//             MSVGP=PAYROL,
//             SPACE=(CYL,(10,2,5)),
//             DCB=(LRECL=80,BLKSIZE=1680,RECFM=FB)
```

(c) Creating a Sequential Data Set on a Specified Volume

```
//SEQDATA   DD DSN=SEQDATA,
//             DISP=(,CATLG),
//             UNIT=3330V,
//             VOL=SER=MSS010,
//             SPACE=(CYL,(100,10),RLSE),
//             DCB=(LRECL=80,BLKSIZE=1680,RECFM=FB)
```

to group PAYROL and use any available MSV in the group. In addition, the SPACE parameter is not coded. Because an MSV group is named, the system will use the default space allocation that is part of the MSV group. The disposition is coded so that at job end the data set will be cataloged. The specific MSV is not named, so the MSV would have to be learned from the deallocation messages if the data set were not cataloged. By cataloging the data set, we eliminate the need to know which MSV is selected for use by the system. All the other parameters are ones you are familiar with.

Figure 14.1b shows a DD statement that may be used to create a PDS on an MSS. In this example, unlike the previous one, the SPACE parameter is coded. When the group indicated by the MSVGP parameter was created, directory blocks were not specified. As a result, the space default of the group can never be used when a PDS is being created; the only way the system knows that a PDS is being created is by the specification of the directory blocks in the SPACE parameter. Again, a disposition of CATLG is specified for the PDS so that we do not need to check the deallocation messages to learn which MSV was used.

The last example specifies in the VOL parameter the MSV that is to be used for the data set. Figure 14.1c illustrates the creation of a sequential data set on the MSV named MSS010. Because the MSVGP parameter is not specified, the SPACE parameter must be coded. A disposition of CATLG was chosen, although in this case KEEP could have been coded because we know the volume serial number.

Accessing a Data Set on an MSS

Accessing a data set on an MSS is virtually the same as accessing a data set on a DASD. Figure 14.2a illustrates accessing a cataloged data set. Whether the data set is a physical sequential or partitioned data set does not affect the coding of this DD statement. The fact that this data set resided on an MSS likewise makes no difference to the DD statement coding.

Figure 14.2b illustrates a DD statement that accesses an uncataloged data set. UNIT=3330V is coded, so we know that the data set resides on an MSS. There is, however, no way of knowing whether this data set is physical sequential or partitioned.

If you use the DD statement in either Figure 14.2a or Figure 14.2b to access a physical sequential data set, the data set will be staged when the open instruction is issued by the program. This means that the first time the program tries to access the data set, it is moved from the MSV to a 3336 Disk Pack where it is actually processed.

If, on the other hand, the DD statement in either Figure 14.2a or Figure 14.2b is used to access a PDS, only the directory is staged when the PDS is opened. Each member is staged as it is needed. If for some reason you want the

━━ **Figure 14.2** ━━━━━━━━━━━━━━

(a) Accessing a Cataloged Data Set on an MSS

```
//ANYDSN    DD DSN=SEQDAT,
//             DISP=OLD
```

(b) Accessing a Data Set on an MSS

```
//ANYDSN    DD DSN=SEQDAT,
//             DISP=OLD,
//             UNIT=3330V,
//             VOL=SER=MSS010
```

(c) Accessing a Library on an MSS

```
//PDSLIB    DD DSN=PDSLIB,
//             DISP=OLD,
//             DCB=OPTCD=H
```

entire PDS staged when the PDS is opened, set the OPTCD subparameter in the DCB parameter equal to H. This process is illustrated in Figure 14.2c.

MSS usage, in general, puts no additional burden on the application programmer. The systems programmer using the utility IDCAMS must create the groups and MSVs and give the group name or the volume serial number to the application programmer.

Summary

In this chapter you have learned

— why a mass storage system is needed

— what a mass storage system is

— how to create a data set on a mass storage volume

— how to access a data set on a mass storage volume

Vocabulary

In this chapter you have been introduced to the meanings of the following terms

data cartridge, or cartridge   mass storage volume (MSV)
destaging   staging
mass storage system (MSS)

Exercises

1. How many cartridges are in an MSV?
2. Where are the data when your program accesses them?
3. Define staging.
4. Define destaging.
5. What is the unique parameter that applies only to an MSS? On which JCL statement is this parameter coded?
6. When creating a data set, how do you tell the system that it is to reside on an MSV?
7. What utility program is used to create an MSV? Which command is used?
8. When creating a physical sequential data set, why don't you need to specify the SPACE parameter? What must be specified?
9. Why must the SPACE parameter always be specified for a library?
10. What does it mean when the subparameter OPTCD=H is coded for a PDS?

Programming Assignments

The following programming assignments can be done only if your computer center has an MSS.

1. Repeat the Programming Assignment in Chapter 3, storing the data set on an MSS.
2. Execute a job to have IEBGENER list the data set you created in Programming Assignment 1, above.
3. Execute a job to add the additional records in Appendix D to the data set you created in Programming Assignment 1, above. In the same job, use IEBPTPCH to produce a listing of the complete data set.

15

JES

In this chapter you will learn

- how to use JES statements that

    replace JOB statement parameters

    control printed output

    direct that a job be executed on a different CPU

    perform various functions unique to JES

- the differences between functions provided by JES2 and those provided by JES3

JES, which stands for job entry subsystem, is the part of MVS that performs job and unit record I/O scheduling.

With the increase in computer use has come a demand for systems so large that they are either prohibitively expensive or beyond the capability of current technology. One way around this problem is to bring together several computers and have each machine perform only certain facets of the overall task. JES offers simple facilities for directing each job to the machine selected to perform that particular function.

This chapter discusses the two versions of JES currently available — JES2 and JES3 — from a functional point of view. For example, we will look at how to provide accounting information using only the functions available in JES2 or only those available in JES3.

As you read this chapter, keep in mind that JES2 and JES3 are even more installation dependent than normal JCL. In most situations you will have to check with your advisor about coding details.

Syntax

JES2

All JES2 statements start with /* in columns 1 and 2. The operation starts in column 3. Following the operation there must be at least one blank, after which, with one exception, the parameters begin. The single exception is the /*OUTPUT statement, which requires a code between the operation and the parameters. The parameters, separated by commas, may extend to column 72.

If one statement cannot contain all the parameters, the statement may be repeated, as in the following example:

```
/*COMMAND ABCDEFGHIJKLMNOPQRSTUVWXYZ
/*COMMAND 1234567890
```

Instead of repeating the /*OUTPUT statement, you may continue it. The appropriate coding will be discussed later in the chapter when we talk about the /*OUTPUT statement.

JES3

All JES3 statements have //* in columns 1 through 3. The operation starts in column 4. There must be at least one blank between the end of the operation and the start of the parameters. The parameters, separated by commas, may extend to column 72.

In general (exceptions will be pointed out in the discussions of the particular JES3 statements), a statement is continued by coding a comma as the last character. The next statement must have //* in columns 1 through 3; the JES3 statement resumes in column 4. An example is

```
//*COMMAND ABCDEFGHIJKLMNOPQRSTUVWXYZ,
//*1234567890
```

Where to Execute

When several computers are connected, you can opt for **remote job entry (RJE)**, in which a job is executed by a system that is separated geographically from the device used to enter the job. As an application programmer, you do not have to concern yourself with exactly how the nodes are connected; you merely specify which system you want to execute your job. In general, if no information is provided, the job will be executed by the system on which it was submitted.

Let us consider a relatively simple network of computers, as illustrated in Figure 15.1. Suppose that this figure depicts the network belonging to the XYZ Corporation, a company that operates nationwide. In order to provide efficient service, XYZ has three regional offices. The Northern office, as well as corporate headquarters, is in Boston; the Western office is in Denver; and the Southern office is in Houston. Formerly, if the company president in Boston wanted information about what was happening in the Southern region, the job would have to be run in that location. With JES, a job can be executed at a location other than the one in which it is submitted.

JES2

JES2 offers two ways to direct that a job be executed at another installation.

The /*ROUTE XEQ Statement.   Let us look at the /*ROUTE XEQ statement first. When used to specify that a job be executed at another installation, the statement contains /*ROUTE XEQ in columns 1 through 11. If the job is to execute on another MVS, the node is usually identified with a **node number**, which consists of the letter N followed by a one- to four-digit number. Each node in Figure 15.1 would be identified by a single-digit number. If, for

■ Figure 15.1 ■

Network Configuration

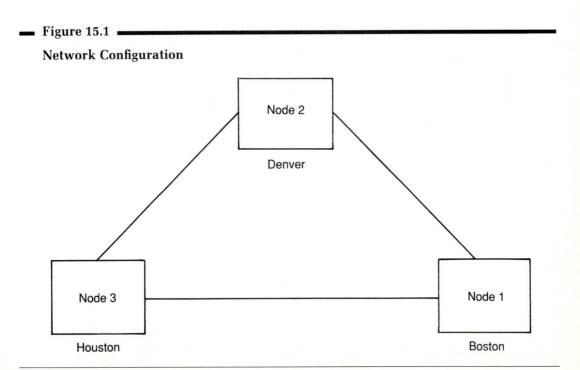

example, you wished the job to execute in Houston, you would code the
/*ROUTE statement as

    /*ROUTE XEQ N3

When you refer to a nodename in a VM system, different rules apply.* The
nodename is the name the systems programmers give to a particular installation. In Figure 15.1, the name of the city in which the installation is located
was selected as the nodename. If we had more than one system in Denver, we
might have chosen to name them DENVER1, DENVER2, and so forth. The
nodename may be from one to eight alphameric characters in length.

Suppose the Houston installation ran a VM system with two guest MVSs,
one for production and one for testing. If you wished to have your job executed in the Houston installation on that part of the system used for production, you would need to know the nodename and the user ID associated with
the production portion of the system. In this example the nodename is
HOUSTON, and let us assume the systems programmer told you that the appropriate user ID was PROD. You could then code the /*ROUTE statement as

    /*ROUTE XEQ HOUSTON.PROD

In the coding of the /*ROUTE XEQ statement, JES2 syntax allows the use of a
period (as above), colon (:), or slash (/) between the nodename and the user ID
or parentheses around the user ID, as in

    /*ROUTE XEQ HOUSTON(PROD)

The /*ROUTE XEQ statement must follow the JOB statement and must
precede any in-stream data in your job stream. Thus, if you have any DD * or
DD DATA statements in your job, they must be coded after the /*ROUTE XEQ
statement. Only one /*ROUTE XEQ statement may be coded on each job. If
you code more than one /*ROUTE XEQ statement on a job, the last one coded is
the one that will be used.

The /*XEQ Statement.   The other JES2 statement used to direct that a job be
executed at another installation is the /*XEQ statement, which always has
/*XEQ in columns 1 through 5. To cause your job to be executed on another
MVS, you would use the node number, as in

    /*XEQ N1

If the job were to be executed on a system running under VM, you would
use the nodename and the user ID, as in

    /*XEQ HOUSTON.PROD

_____

* VM is an operating system that permits a computer to function as if it were multiple
operating systems. Don't worry if you do not completely understand this concept, as this book
discusses OS and not VM.

Unlike the /*ROUTE XEQ statement, the /*XEQ statement may have only a period as a separator between nodename and user ID.

Rules for placing the /*XEQ statement in the job stream are the same as those for the /*ROUTE XEQ statement. Again, if you code more than one /*XEQ statement on a job, only the last one is used.

The /*JOBPARM Statement with the SYSAFF Parameter. When several CPUs are connected, the /*JOBPARM statement with the SYSAFF parameter may be used to specify that a job be executed by a particular CPU or by one of several designated CPUs. The code

```
/*JOBPARM SYSAFF=*
```

specifies that only the system that actually read the job is allowed to execute that job.

If you wished to have a job executed on a particular CPU other than the one on which it was submitted, you would code the four-character alphameric system ID that identifies the system, as in

```
/*JOBPARM SYSAFF=DEN1
```

You may name several systems. The code

```
/*JOBPARM SYSAFF=(DEN1,DEN3,DEN5)
```

means that the job may execute on any of the three named systems. You may code up to seven system IDs with the SYSAFF keyword parameter. If you name more than one system, however, the names must be enclosed in parentheses.

If you code

```
/*JOBPARM SYSAFF=ANY
```

any CPU within the configuration may execute the job. Because ANY is the default, it is not necessary to code this statement.

The IND Subparameter. Within the SYSAFF keyword parameter on the /*JOBPARM statement, you may include the positional parameter IND, as in

```
/*JOBPARM SYSAFF=(DEN1,DEN3,DEN5,IND)
```

If used, IND must be coded as the last subparameter of SYSAFF. IND specifies that all processing for a job must be performed on the same CPU.

JES3

JES3 provides only one statement, //*ROUTE XEQ, for directing that a job be executed at a different installation, and on this statement a node must be identified by a nodename (not a node number). If you wished a job to execute at XYZ's MVS installation in Denver, you would code

```
//*ROUTE XEQ DENVER
```

If you wanted it to execute on the production part of the VM system in Houston, you would code

```
//*ROUTE XEQ HOUSTON.PROD
```

Unlike JES2, JES3 requires that two job statements be coded in conjunction with the `//*ROUTE XEQ` statement. The first job statement applies to the sending system, and the second applies to the receiving system, on which the job is to be executed. The `//*ROUTE XEQ` statement is nestled between the two job statements. You might code

```
//JOB1  JOB . . . .
//*ROUTE XEQ DENVER
//JOB2  JOB . . . .
```

If you make a mistake on the `//*ROUTE XEQ` statement, your job will execute on the local node (in our example, in Boston). Obviously it pays to be very careful when coding these statements. To minimize the damage caused by such a mistake, you might code

```
//JOB1  JOB . . . .
//*ROUTE XEQ DENVER
//JOB2  NJB . . . .
```

If there is no error in the `//*ROUTE XEQ` statement, JES3 processing will change `NJB` to `JOB` before the job is transmitted to the system on which it is to be executed. If there is an error in the `//*ROUTE XEQ` statement, the `NJB` statement will be treated as an error and the job will not execute, which is what you would want.

JES3 Coupling.   A single JES3 system is not necessarily limited to one CPU. From two to eight CPUs may be grouped, or coupled, together. One of the CPUs is designated as the global, and it controls which jobs are executed on which CPUs. Figure 15.2 illustrates the relatively simple case of the coupling of two CPUs. The one designated as global is given a **processor ID** of 1 and a name of A, and the one designated as local is given a processor ID of 2 and a name of B. There is a single spool data set. All jobs to be executed are placed on this spool data set. The global CPU reads the job and directs it to the CPU on which it is to be executed. Normally a job is executed on the CPU on which it was submitted. If for any reason you want to have a job executed on a different CPU, one way to do this is by using the `SYSTEM` parameter on the `//*MAIN` statement.

Figure 15.2

JES3 Coupling

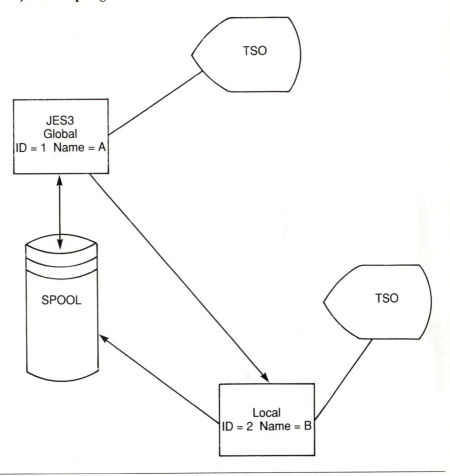

The //*MAIN Statement with the SYSTEM Parameter. In some cases only one CPU may be able to access the devices needed to run a particular job. For example, if your job needed an old seven-track tape and the only tape drive in the complex capable of processing seven-track tape was attached to the local named B, you would code the //*MAIN statement as

```
//*MAIN SYSTEM=B
```

This statement tells the global CPU that the job must execute on the CPU whose name is B.

The parameter SYSTEM=JLOCAL indicates that the job may run on any local CPU but not on the global CPU. If, on the other hand, you wanted the job to execute on the global, you would code SYSTEM=JGLOBAL. This statement means that the job *must* run on the global CPU.

If you do not care where the job executes, you might code SYSTEM=ANY, although there is no reason to do so because ANY is the default.

If you do not want your job to run on a particular CPU because, for example, there are problems on that CPU, you might code

```
//*MAIN SYSTEM=/B
```

This statement indicates that the job may run on any CPU except the one named B. Notice that JES3 syntax requires that / be coded before the CPU name in this situation.

Operator Instruction

You can code a job so that, when it is run, a message is displayed on the system log, providing the computer operator with any information he or she should have regarding the job. Be aware, however, that the operator's console is usually quite busy with system messages, and the operator may miss the message unless he or she knows that it is coming. Many installations do not even have operators during certain times. It is not unusual for there to be no operator on the premises on weekends, although the systems are being used. A job that may be run in an unattended environment should never include operator messages.

JES2

The /*MESSAGE Statement.   To permit communication with the operator with respect to a specific job, JES2 provides the /*MESSAGE statement. It contains /*MESSAGE in columns 1 through 9. Column 10 must be blank, and your message may appear in columns 11 through 71. Any information in columns 72 through 80 is ignored. If your message needs more than the 61 columns available, you may use more than one /*MESSAGE statement. A /*MESSAGE statement may not be continued.

The /*MESSAGE statement must be placed within the job (that is, after the JOB statement) so that the number the system applies to your job can be added to the message when it is printed on the operator's console. If you place the /*MESSAGE statement before the JOB statement, the system does not know to which job it belongs and merely displays an unidentified message.

The placement of the /*ROUTE XEQ statement within the job stream will determine where the message is printed. If you want the message directed only to the operator at the installation where the job will execute, you code the /*ROUTE XEQ statement first, with the /*MESSAGE statement following it. For example, coding

```
//JOB1   JOB . . . .
/*ROUTE XEQ HOUSTON
/*MESSAGE CALL BOSTON IF JOB ABENDS
```

would cause the message CALL BOSTON IF JOB ABENDS to appear only on the Houston operator's console. On the other hand, coding

```
//JOB1   JOB . . . .
/*MESSAGE CALL PROGRAMMER IF JOB ABENDS
/*ROUTE XEQ HOUSTON
```

would cause both the console in Boston and the console in Houston to receive the message CALL PROGRAMMER IF JOB ABENDS.

The SETUP Statement. JES2 also has the /*SETUP statement, which is used to ask the operator to mount one or more particular volumes. The /*SETUP statement must be coded before the first EXEC statement in the job stream. The statement

```
/*SETUP 123456,789789,ABCDEF
```

instructs the system to mount volumes 123456, 789789, and ABCDEF. Like most JES2 statements, the /*SETUP statement may not be continued; you can, however, code more than one statement in order to include all necessary volumes.

If the job is to execute on another system, remember to code the /*SETUP statement after the /*ROUTE XEQ or /*XEQ statement but before the first EXEC statement, as in

```
//JOB1   JOB . . . .
/*ROUTE XEQ HOUSTON
/*SETUP 123456,789789,ABCDEF
//STEP1 EXEC PGM=. . .
```

JES3

The OPERATOR Statement. To send a message to the operator on a system that uses JES3, the //*OPERATOR statement is used. The message to appear on the operator's console is coded in columns 13 to 80. This statement may appear anywhere after the JOB statement. An example would be

```
//*OPERATOR CALL EXT. 123 IF THE JOB ABENDS
```

Setup Information on the //*MAIN Statement. There are three parameters on the JES3 //*MAIN statement that communicate setup request information to the operator. They are SETUP, FETCH, and MSS. Let us discuss SETUP first, because the way you code FETCH depends to some degree on the way you code SETUP.

The SETUP Parameter.   Coding

```
//*MAIN SETUP=JOB
```

instructs the system to allocate all of the JES3-controlled devices required for this job before execution of the job starts. Under certain conditions this coding can cause serious problems. Suppose your installation has only two tape drives and your job needs four different tapes, two in each of two different job steps. Your job will never start if it has to wait for all four tapes to be mounted at the same time. Consequently you must exercise caution in coding SETUP=JOB.

Coding

```
//*MAIN SETUP=HWS
```

tells the system that you want "high-watermark setup"; the minimum number of devices required to run the job is to be allocated before execution of the job starts. Each step will be examined to see how many tape and/or disk drives are required. The step that needs the most of each type sets the high watermark. If STEP 1 needs two tape drives and three disk drives and STEP 2 needs one tape drive and four disk drives, two tape drives and four disk drives will have to be allocated to the job before it can start. Coding SETUP=HWS is much safer than coding SETUP=JOB. If the devices needed to start a job cannot be obtained, the job itself needs to be recorded, because it requires more devices of a type than exist on the system.

Coding

```
//*MAIN SETUP=THWS
```

means that you want high-watermark setup for your tapes, but all the disks that the job will require are to be allocated before the job begins. On the other hand, coding

```
//*MAIN SETUP=DHWS
```

means that you want high-watermark setup for your disks, but all the tape drives that the job will require are to be allocated before the job starts. The way the people in your computer center work, as well as the number of tape and disk drives available in your computer room, will influence your choice between these two values. If you cannot accept the installation default but are not quite sure whether THWS or DHWS is the correct choice, I would recommend THWS. Mounting a tape on a tape drive is relatively fast and easy, whereas mounting a volume on a disk drive usually takes a long time.

You may choose to ask explicitly that the volumes for a particular DD statement be mounted before the job starts. If you use this form of the SETUP keyword parameter, make sure that the UNIT keyword parameter on the DD statement requests a drive for each volume. If, for example, the tape data set resides on two reels of tape, be sure that the UNIT parameter on the DD statement requests two tape drives. If you ask for only one tape drive when two are needed, JES3 will cancel the job. The code

```
//*MAIN SETUP=STEP1.TAPE
```

specifies that before the job starts the system is to mount the volumes named by the DD statement that has the ddname TAPE and is part of the step whose name is STEP1. If the step is part of a procedure, you would code the procedure stepname as well, as in

```
//*MAIN SETUP=STEP1.PROCSTEP.TAPEOUT
```

If you want the devices for more than one data set premounted, separate the ddnames with commas and enclose the list in parentheses, as in

```
//*MAIN SETUP=(STEP1.TAPE,STEP2.TAPE)
```

If the ddnames will not all fit on one JES3 statement, you must repeat the keyword parameter SETUP, as in

```
//*MAIN SETUP=(STEP1.TAPE,STEP2.TAPE,STEP3.TAPE),
//*SETUP=(STEP4.TAPE,STEP5.TAPE)
```

To request that particular volumes not be mounted before the job starts, you code a slash before the stepname-ddname combination. Typical coding might be

```
//*MAIN SETUP=/STEP1.TAPE
```

You might wish to specify that certain volumes be premounted and others not be premounted. Your coding in that case would be something like

```
//*MAIN SETUP=(/STEP1.TAPE,STEP2.TAPE)
```

Omitting the SETUP keyword parameter will invoke the installation default. If you expect to need to use this keyword parameter, it would be wise to learn what the installation default is at your computer center. Your advisor should be able to tell you.

The FETCH Parameter.   Now that you understand the SETUP keyword parameter of the JES3 //*MAIN statement, let us go on to the FETCH keyword parameter. Coding

```
//*MAIN FETCH=SETUP
```

tells the system that you want a message sent to the operator requesting that the volumes you have named in the SETUP keyword parameter be mounted.

If you did not code the SETUP keyword parameter, you might as well have coded

```
//*MAIN FETCH=ALL
```

which means that you want messages sent to the operator for all volumes that need to be mounted.

If for some reason you do not want messages sent to the operator requesting the mounting of volumes, you can code the parameter as FETCH=NONE.

To have a message sent about a particular volume, you code the ddname, as in FETCH=TAPE. If more than one DD statement is involved, separate the ddnames by commas and enclose the list in parentheses, as in

```
//*MAIN FETCH=(TAPE1,TAPE2,TAPE3)
```

If all the ddnames will not fit on one JES3 //*MAIN statement, the keyword parameter FETCH must be repeated:

```
//*MAIN FETCH=(TAPE1,TAPE2,TAPE3),
//*FETCH=TAPE4
```

You can explicitly request that a FETCH message for a particular volume not appear by preceding the ddname with a slash, as in

```
//*MAIN FETCH=/TAPE1
```

You might choose to request messages for some volumes and not for others. In this situation your coding might look like

```
//*MAIN FETCH=(/TAPE1,TAPE2,/TAPE3)
```

The difference between the SETUP and FETCH keyword parameters is significant. The SETUP keyword parameter tells the system which volumes *must* be mounted before execution of the job can start. The FETCH keyword parameter merely indicates volumes for which the operator will receive FETCH messages.

The MSS Parameter.   The MSS keyword parameter tells JES3 how to handle mass storage. Unlike the SETUP keyword parameter, the MSS keyword parameter may take on only two values: JOB and HWS. You may code either

```
//*MAIN MSS=JOB
```

or

```
//*MAIN MSS=HWS
```

MSS=JOB means that each mass storage request will be assigned a separate virtual unit; MSS=HWS means that virtual units will be reused in succeeding steps. Coding HWS minimizes the number of units required for the job. Thus, unless you have a definite reason to code JOB, HWS is recommended. The system default is selected by the systems programmer; your advisor should be able to tell you what the default is at your installation.

The values you select for the SETUP keyword parameter do not have any bearing on your choice of values for the MSS keyword parameter.

Identifying the Listing

In the early days of computing, operations personnel would place the output listings on a table and the programmers would shuffle through the mass of paper, trying with varying degrees of success to find their output. Eventually the practice of printing the jobname on the first page of the listing, which came to be referred to as the separator page, made listings easier to identify. Nevertheless, programmers were still shuffling through a mass of paper, trying to find their listings. One problem was that the programmer often did not remember the jobname used for a particular job. This shuffle-through approach may have been acceptable in informal environments. It is still used during laboratory periods in data processing courses at CUNY; it definitely was not acceptable, however, in situations where even normal business security needed to be maintained. It became important that each output listing be directed only to the individual who was to handle it. A way had to be found to identify the output listing as belonging to a particular programmer or, for production runs, the application analyst responsible for the job.

JES2

JES2 offers a parameter on the /*JOBPARM statement that may be used to associate a listing with a particular user. This parameter is ROOM, which may be abbreviated to R. ROOM might be coded as

```
/*JOBPARM ROOM=B923
```

The value coded for the ROOM parameter, consisting of one to four alphameric characters, will appear on the first page of the listing. The value coded may represent the room to which the listing is to be delivered, or it may represent the number of a box from which the listing may be picked up by the programmer or application control analyst.

The /*JOBPARM statement follows the JOB statement. If the job is to be executed at a location different from the one at which it was submitted, the placement of the /*JOBPARM statement may be important. If you coded the /*JOBPARM statement after either a /*ROUTE XEQ or a /*XEQ statement, as in

```
//JOBNAME JOB . . .
/*ROUTE XEQ DENVER
/*JOBPARM R=B923
```

only the receiving location would process the information in the /*JOBPARM statement. On the other hand, if you coded the /*JOBPARM statement before the /*ROUTE XEQ statement, the sending location would check the statement for validity before sending it to the receiving location, where the /*JOBPARM statement would be checked again.

Which alternative should you choose? Do you want the /*JOBPARM statement to be checked at the receiving location only or at both sending and receiving locations? If a serious error is not located until a job reaches the receiving node, unnecessary transmission costs will be incurred. On the other hand, if a good job is checked at both sites, unnecessary computational costs will be incurred. Initially it is a good idea to have the JES statement checked at both sending and receiving sites. Once you are confident that your JES statements are correct, preferably after you have had a few good runs, you may want to move the JES statement so that it is checked only at the receiving site.

Various other parameters that may be coded in the /*JOBPARM statement will be discussed later in this chapter. The order of the parameters does not matter, but each parameter must be separated from the previous one by a comma.

JES3

JES3 does not provide a statement or parameter for identifying a listing as belonging to a particular individual. The systems programmer may choose to use an exit within JES3 to provide a function similar to that provided by JES2. In this situation you must discuss with your advisor how listings will be identified.

JOB Statement Parameter Replacements

Many of the parameters on a JOB statement may be replaced with information provided by JES statements. In some cases JES will provide more detailed information than can be provided on the JOB statement, whose original design dates back to the early days of the System/360. In this section we will discuss the parameters on the job card that can be replaced and the advantages of the JES statement that may be used to replace each one.

Accounting

The first positional parameter on the JOB statement is used for accounting information. JES offers alternative ways of providing accounting information that are potentially more restrictive but significantly easier to implement than the JOB statement parameter.

JES2. JES2 offers the /*NETACCT statement. On this statement is coded a one-to eight-character alphameric value called the network account number. The network account number may appear anywhere between columns 11 and 72. An example would be

```
/*NETACCT   ACCTFELD
```

The /*NETACCT statement must follow the JOB statement. If more than one /*NETACCT statement is coded, all but the last one are ignored. Although the /*NETACCT statement is processed only at the input node, the network account number is passed with the job stream to the receiving node. If, for example, you coded

```
//JOBNAME JOB . . .
/*JOBPARM R=B923
/*ROUTE XEQ DENVER
/*NETACCT   ACCTFELD
```

the job whose name is JOBNAME would be executed at the Denver installation (see Figure 15.1), and when it arrived in Denver it would carry the network account number ACCTFELD. Additionally, when this job was printed, the characters B923 would appear on the separator, or first, page. Each installation has its own way of handling and using the network account number.

JES3. The JES3 //*NETACCT statement offers a more structured approach to providing accounting information than does the JES2 statement. If the job is transmitted to another location, the information in the //*NETACCT statement is transmitted with the job. The //*NETACCT statement or statements, however, must be placed before the //*ROUTE XEQ statement, if present. You would code, for example,

```
//JOBNAME JOB . . .
//*NETACCT . . . .
//*ROUTE XEQ DENVER
```

The JES3 syntax rules discussed earlier apply here.

As we examine the various parameters in the following paragraphs, we will build on a single example, thus forming a string of parameters. Please remember that it is not necessary to use all of the parameters that are shown. You can use as many or as few as you wish. Each installation will provide default values for those that you omit. An installation, however, may require that you use certain parameters; consequently, before you code this statement, make sure that you check with your advisor to learn what must be included. When all the necessary information will not fit on one //*NETACCT statement, the statement may be continued. If you elect to use a special character in a parameter value, remember to place apostrophes around the whole parameter value. All of the values coded for the

`//*NETACCT` parameters, with one exception, may be from one to eight characters in length.

Let us start with `PNAME`, which is the one exception to the eight-character length limitation. For `PNAME`, which is intended to identify the programmer, 1 to 20 characters are allowed. You might code the `PNAME` parameter as

```
//*NETACCT   PNAME=LEWIS
```

`ACCT` is used to supply a network account number, which is handled like the network account number in JES2. Remember that `ACCT` can be only one to eight characters in length. It might be added as follows:

```
//*NETACCT   PNAME='J. C. LEWIS',ACCT=ACCTFLD
```

`BLDG` may be used to identify the building address at large sites where there are several buildings. The `BLDG` parameter might be added as follows:

```
//*NETACCT   PNAME='LEWIS',ACCT=ACCTFLD,BLDG=QBCCBLD2
```

The `ROOM` parameter is used to identify the room in which the programmer is located. Essentially it provides a refinement of the information supplied by the `BLDG` parameter. It differs from the JES2 parameter coded on the `/*JOBPARM` statement in that the information does not appear on the separator page. The `ROOM` parameter of the `//*NETACCT` statement might be added as follows:

```
//*NETACCT   PNAME=LEWIS,ACCT=ACCTFLD,BLDG=QBCCBLD2,ROOM=FL2C78
```

The keyword parameter `DEPT` may be used to identify the department that is to be billed for the job. Again, from one to eight characters may be coded. If the `DEPT` parameter were added to the parameters already coded, it would go beyond column 72. To include the additional information, a continuation statement must be coded:

```
//*NETACCT   PNAME=LEWIS,ACCT=ACCTFLD,BLDG=QBCCBLD2,ROOM=FL2C78,
//*DEPT=DEPT67D
```

Note that the only indication that a continuation statement follows is the final comma.

You could code two `//*NETACCT` statements instead of continuing the first. In that case a different JES3 statement could be coded between the two `//*NETACCT` statements. For example, you could code

```
//*NETACCT   PNAME=LEWIS,ACCT=ACCTFLD,BLDG=QBCCBLD2,ROOM=FL2C78
//*OPERATOR  CALL PROGRAMMER IF ABEND
//*NETACCT   DEPT=DEPT67D
```

It is not a good idea to code this way, however, because although the system will not be confused, people who have to maintain the JCL may be.

Use of the keyword parameter USERID may be required at your installation. A registered user ID uniquely identifies you in a way that the name you code with the PNAME parameter may not. For example, on different days John Charles Lewis might code PNAME as JOHN CHARLES LEWIS, JOHN C. LEWIS, J. CHARLES LEWIS, J. C. LEWIS, or J C LEWIS. Following is an example of a USERID parameter:

```
//*NETACCT   PNAME=LEWIS,ACCT=ACCTFLD,BLDG=QBCCBLD2,ROOM=FL2C78,
//*DEPT=DEPT67D,USERID=JUANCARL
```

Completion Notification

When you submit a job to be run in batch mode, you need to know when the job ends in order to view your output. Depending on installation standards and how you have coded your JCL, you may be able to look at the output at your terminal or you may have to go to a centralized location to collect your listing.

In Chapter 10 the NOTIFY parameter on the JOB statement was discussed. The user named by the NOTIFY parameter does not have to be the user who submitted the job for execution. If, for example, you were running a job for one of your coworkers, you might specify the coworker's user ID in the NOTIFY parameter so that he or she, rather than you, would be informed when the job was completed. This scheme works well as long as you are dealing with one system. You start to run into problems, however, when you submit a job on one system for execution on another system but want notification of completion either on the submitting system or on a third system.

JES2. To facilitate completion notification, JES2 provides the /*NOTIFY statement. The /*NOTIFY statement must follow the JOB statement but must precede the first EXEC statement. The advantage of this statement over the NOTIFY parameter on the JOB statement is that a node may be specified. Let us assume that John Charles Lewis uses JCLEWIS as his user ID on the Boston installation, which is part of the network illustrated in Figure 15.1. If he submits a job that is to run on the Boston installation, he can code either

```
//JOBNAME  JOB (ACCTNG),NAME,NOTIFY=JCLEWIS
```

or

```
//JOBNAME  JOB (ACCTNG),NAME, . . .
/*NOTIFY JCLEWIS
```

In this situation, coding the JES2 /*NOTIFY statement has the same effect as coding the NOTIFY parameter on the JOB statement.

If Lewis submits a job to be run on the system in Denver, however, the

`NOTIFY` parameter on the `JOB` statement is not sufficient, because it provides no way to tell the system that the user ID `JCLEWIS` refers to a user in Boston. In this case the JES2 `/*NOTIFY` statement must be used. It could be coded as

```
/*NOTIFY BOSTON.JCLEWIS
```

The nodename — in this case, `BOSTON` — is coded first and the user ID second. As mentioned earlier, the separator between the nodename and the user ID can be a period, colon, or slash, or parentheses can be placed around the user ID.

Let us consider the situation in which John C. Lewis's coworker, Jane Carol Lavender, has asked John to run a particular job for her. Jane works at the Houston installation. John knows Jane's user ID is `LAVENDR`, so he merely codes the following `/*NOTIFY` statement in the job, which causes Jane to be notified when the job ends:

```
/*NOTIFY HOUSTON(LAVENDR)
```

The `JOB` statement, JES2 statements, and `EXEC` statement might appear as

```
//JOBNAME  JOB (ACCTNG),LEWIS, . . .
/*XEQ DENVER
/*NOTIFY HOUSTON/LAVENDR
//STEP1    EXEC PGM=. . .
```

This coding would cause the job, submitted in Boston, to be executed in Denver and notification of the job's completion to be sent to the programmer in Houston.

If you code both the `NOTIFY` parameter on the `JOB` statement and the JES2 `/*NOTIFY` statement, the system will ignore the `NOTIFY` parameter on the `JOB` statement and use the information provided by the JES2 statement.

JES3. JES3 does not have a statement that fulfills the function of the JES2 `/*NOTIFY` statement. The only mechanism JES3 offers for notifying a coworker at a remote site that a job has completed is printing the output listing at the remote site. We will discuss how this is done later in this chapter.

As discussed earlier, a JES3 system can have from one to eight CPUs working together, and each CPU can have its own **TSO (time sharing option),** with its own set of users conversing from remote stations. Intrasystem completion notification is needed whenever a user submits on his or her CPU a job designed to be executed on a different CPU, or whenever a user wants a coworker to be informed when a job ends. To handle these types of situations, JES3 provides the `ACMAIN` parameter of the `//*MAIN` statement, used in conjunction with the `NOTIFY` parameter on the `JOB` statement.

Referring back to Figure 15.2, suppose that John C. Lewis is a TSO user on the global, but he wants his job run on the local. Coding

```
//JOBNAME  JOB (ACCTNG),NAME,NOTIFY=JCLEWIS
//*MAIN SYSTEM=JLOCAL
```

would cause the job to run on the local but would not cause John C. Lewis, at the global, to be notified of job completion. To handle completion notification, another parameter must be added to the JES3 //*MAIN statement: the ACMAIN parameter. The ACMAIN parameter names the CPU to which the JOB statement's NOTIFY parameter applies. The coding would be

```
//JOBNAME  JOB (ACCTNG),NAME,NOTIFY=JCLEWIS
//*MAIN ACMAIN=1,SYSTEM=JLOCAL
```

In this case ACMAIN names the CPU to which the NOTIFY parameter on the JOB statement applies.

If John's coworker, Jane C. Lavender, worked at the same installation as John but had her TSO ID on the local, coding the JOB statement as

```
//JOBNAME  JOB (ACCTNG),NAME,NOTIFY=LAVENDR
//*MAIN SYSTEM=JLOCAL
```

or

```
//JOBNAME  JOB (ACCTNG),NAME,NOTIFY=LAVENDR
//*MAIN SYSTEM=JLOCAL,ACMAIN=2
```

would cause Jane to be notified when the job ended. The job would still execute on the local.

The area of job completion notification is one in which JES2 is superior to JES3—JES2 provides more function and is easier to understand. As we continue our discussion, you will find that each JES offers certain features that the other does not. The decision as to which JES to use is based on the needs of a particular installation. Remember that not all functions offered by either JES2 or JES3 are within the scope of this book.

RESTART

After it has been interrupted, a job may be restarted by submitting it again, using the RESTART parameter coded on the JOB statement. This parameter was discussed in Chapter 10. Before continuing with this section, you might wish to review the material in Chapter 10 to be sure that you remember it.

JES2. On the /*JOBPARM statement you may code RESTART=Y or RESTART=N, where Y means yes, restart the job, and N means no, do not restart the job. This parameter covers a relatively narrow area. If the job is executing when the system goes down and if operations is able to perform a warm start, the job will be resubmitted for execution if you have coded RESTART=Y. The default for this parameter is RESTART=N, although each individual installation has the ability to set the default to RESTART=Y. It would be wise to find out what the default is at your installation.

JES3. The JES //*MAIN statement provides the FAILURE parameter, which performs a function similar to that performed by the RESTART parameter of the JES2 `/*JOBPARM` statement. This parameter tells the system what to do if the system fails while the job is executing, assuming operations is able to perform a warm start of the system. Remember that a journal is required for restart to work in a JES3 system. Either you must code

```
//*MAIN JOURNAL=YES
```

or it must be the system default.

Coding

```
//*MAIN FAILURE=RESTART
```

is equivalent to coding `RESTART=Y` on the JES2 `/*JOBPARM` statement. JES3, however, offers other alternatives not available in JES2. Coding `FAILURE=HOLD` causes the job to be placed in the hold queue, from which it must be explicitly released in order to be reexecuted. This option gives operations personnel the opportunity to determine whether execution should be resumed.

Better than coding `FAILURE=HOLD` is to code `FAILURE=PRINT`, which causes the job to be printed and then placed in the hold queue. The advantage of this approach is that it produces a listing upon which the decision as to whether to restart the job can be based. The last alternative, `FAILURE=CANCEL`, causes the job's printed output to be canceled.

Which alternative is best? It is difficult to say without looking at a particular job. The best alternative is generally to go with the installation default unless you have a reason to use another value. Your advisor will tell you what the default is at your installation.

User Identification

On a job card you may code a one- to seven-character alphameric user ID, normally associated with TSO. JES3 gives you the option of having this information on the `//*MAIN` statement. You might code, for example,

```
//*MAIN USER=USERID1
```

The `USER` keyword parameter is used mainly for security purposes. If your system has RACF or some other security package installed or if password protection is used, you will probably have to code this parameter on either the `JOB` statement or the JES3 `//*MAIN` statement to access protected data sets.

Time

As was discussed in Chapter 4, the `TIME` keyword parameter may be specified on either the `JOB` or the `EXEC` statement. When coded, it indicates the maximum amount of CPU time that may be used. Neither JES2 nor JES3 provides exactly this function. Each provides something unique.

JES2. The JES2 `/*JOBPARM` statement has a parameter for specifying an estimate of how long the job will run in real, or wall-clock, time. In general, CPU time is a fraction of real time. If the CPU time specified on the `JOB` or `EXEC` statement or set by the systems programmer as the installation default is exceeded, the job will abend. If the real time specified on the `/*JOBPARM` statement is exceeded, the operator will receive a message on the console indicating that the time has been exceeded, but the job will not automatically abend.

The `TIME` parameter, which can be abbreviated as `T` on the `/*JOBPARM` statement, may be coded as a one- to four-digit number. It represents the number of minutes you estimate the job will require. The statement

```
/*JOBPARM TIME=30
```

means that the job should run for half an hour.

JES3. JES3 offers a different timing function on the `//*MAIN` statement: the `DEADLINE` parameter. Instead of specifying how long the job is to run, it specifies *when* the job is to run. The statement

```
//*MAIN DEADLINE=10M
```

means that you want the job to start 10 minutes after it is submitted. If you choose to code minutes, you may code a one- to four-digit number with a value from `0` to `1440`.

The statement `DEADLINE=2H` means that you want the job to start 2 hours after it is submitted. If you choose to code hours, you may code a one- or two-digit number with a value from `0` to `24`.

If you wanted a job to start at a particular time, you would use military time. For example, `DEADLINE=1427` means that you want the job to start executing at 14:27, or 2:27 P.M.

The fact that you code a time when the job is supposed to run does not mean that the job will run at that time, however. If there are too many jobs executing then, your job will be delayed. At each installation the systems programmer establishes algorithms that determine how a job's priority may be changed. Each algorithm is identified by a single letter or number chosen by the systems programmer. Suppose that you code

```
//*MAIN DEADLINE=(413,A)
```

If the job does not start at 4:13 A.M., the job's priority will be changed in accordance with the algorithm represented by `A`. If you code a time that is earlier than the time at which the job was submitted, the system will use the algorithm named to revise the job's priority — the system will act as if the job had been submitted earlier and the system was unable to start the job at the correct time.

There are several ways to specify the date on which you want a job to run. In the above examples no date was given, in which case the current date is assumed. If you wanted your job to run on a particular date, you could code, for example,

```
//*MAIN DEADLINE=(1115,A,092391)
```

which would cause execution of your job to start on September 23, 1991 at 11:15 A.M. The algorithm indicated by A would be used to change the job's priority if for some reason the job could not start at that time. Note that the date is given in the form mmddyy.

For a job that is to be run on a regular basis, you could code rel,cycle in place of the date. rel stands for relative date, and cycle may be either WEEKLY, MONTHLY, or YEARLY. If, for example, you wanted a job to run every Saturday at noon, you might code

```
//*MAIN DEADLINE=(1200,A,7,WEEKLY)
```

The 7 means the seventh day of the week, or Saturday. Coding 3 in place of the 7 would cause the job to be executed on the third day of the week, or Tuesday. If you accidentally code a number greater than 7, the system will reset it to 7.

If you wanted a job to run on a regular monthly basis, you might code

```
//*MAIN DEADLINE=(1200,A,15,MONTHLY)
```

which means that the job is to start at noon on the fifteenth of every month. When the cycle is MONTHLY, the rel value must be a number between 1 and 31. If you code a number greater than 31, the system will treat it as 31.

If you wanted a job to run once a year, you might code

```
//*MAIN DEADLINE=(1200,A,1,YEARLY)
```

This statement will cause execution of the job to start at noon on New Year's Day. The rel value must be between 1 and 365 (or 366 if it is a leap year).

The DEADLINE parameter is quite useful, but if your installation engages in automated, or lights-out, operation, there are program products that provide more functions.*

Priority

Job priority, which may be set by the keyword parameter PRTY on the JOB statement, was discussed in Chapter 10. Many installations do not permit the coding of a priority on a JOB statement; a default value is used.

---

* Automated, or lights-out, operation means that the systems are left running without operators present. This practice is not unusual during weekends, when there are few people using the systems.

JES2 offers its own priority statement, which might be coded as

```
/*PRIORITY 7
```

If you use the JES2 statement, it will take precedence over the PRTY parameter on the JOB statement.

JES3 does not offer a unique way to code priority. It accepts the value supplied with the keyword parameter PRTY on the JOB statement.

Job Hold

On the JOB statement, the TYPRUN keyword parameter (see Chapter 10) may be coded to indicate that a job is to be held. JES2 does not offer an alternative to coding TYPRUN=HOLD on the JOB statement. In JES3, however, the same results may be obtained by coding the HOLD parameter on the //*MAIN statement as follows:

```
//*MAIN HOLD=YES
```

Other programmers' jobs may be held by coding the UPDATE keyword parameter on the //*MAIN statement. The purpose of this parameter is to allow a procedure library to be safely updated. Coding

```
//*MAIN UPDATE=USER.PROCLIB
```

will cause any job using USER.PROCLIB to be held until the update has been completed. If, as an application programmer, you are responsible for adding procedures to the procedure libraries, you will find this function useful. On the other hand, if the systems programmers do the additions to the libraries, you will not need this keyword parameter.

JES3 also offers an alternative to coding TYPRUN=SCAN. On the EXEC statement, you may simply replace the actual program name with either JCLTEST or JSTTEST. For testing, however, I prefer TYPRUN=SCAN because it can be added at the end of the JOB statement and then can easily be removed once testing is complete. Replacing the program name just introduces one more place where an error can be made.

Region Size

JES2 does not offer any mechanism for specifying region size; you simply code the REGION parameter on your JOB statement.

JES3 offers the LREGION parameter on the //*MAIN statement, which complements rather than replaces the REGION and ADDRSPC keyword parameters on the JOB statement. LREGION is used to indicate the maximum amount of real storage that a job will need. Correctly coded, this parameter helps speed the execution of a job. Coding too small a value for LREGION, however, will slow execution of the job, and coding too large a value will slow execution of the other jobs that are running at the same time. In some cases execution of other jobs may be held up until your job ends. So when you use this parameter, be careful. The LREGION parameter might be coded as follows:

```
//*MAIN LREGION=32K
```

You may specify from 1K to 9999K of real storage.

If you do not specify a value for LREGION and the information is not supplied by other parameters discussed later, the system will use the default value.

Class

If your installation uses JES2, the only way to specify the job class is via the CLASS keyword parameter on the JOB statement, which was described in Chapter 2.

JES3 provides an alternative means to specify the job class in the form of the CLASS keyword parameter on the //*MAIN statement. In JES3 the class name is not limited to a single character but may be from one to eight characters in length. By giving greater scope to class naming, JES3 permits the use of more meaningful classes than may be specified on the JOB statement. For example, suppose systems programming has set up a special class for maintenance jobs with the name MAINT. In that case you might code

```
//JOBNAME JOB . . .
//*MAIN CLASS=MAINT
```

If, when the job is submitted, there is no initiator that will accept jobs from class MAINT, execution of the job cannot begin until operations starts an initiator or modifies an executing one. What does this accomplish? Suppose you want this maintenance job to execute when the teleprocessing system that executes most of the day is brought down. Of course, you could instruct operations to start the maintenance job when the teleprocessing system comes down, but it may be simpler, especially if there are several maintenance jobs, to instruct operations to start a special initiator that will process the class MAINT.

When systems programming sets up classes in JES3, a default value for the LREGION parameter may be specified for each class. In addition, there may be established default values based on whether the job has a low, medium, or high rate of I/O. If, for some reason, you wish to use a particular CLASS but do not want to use the default I/O rate, you can code the keyword parameter IORATE on the //*MAIN statement. You would code

```
//*MAIN CLASS=FASTER,IORATE=LOW
```

or

```
//*MAIN CLASS=SPEEDY,IORATE=MED
```

or

```
//*MAIN CLASS=SLOWPOKE,IORATE=HIGH
```

based on your best guess as to what the actual I/O rate will be.

Job Log

The printing of job information is usually controlled by the MSGLEVEL keyword parameter on the JOB statement, which was described in Chapter 2. JES2 offers, on the /*JOBPARM statement, the option of suppressing the printing of the job log. Coding

```
/*JOBPARM NOLOG
```

is equivalent to coding MSGLEVEL=(0,0) on the job card. If NOLOG is coded on the /*JOBPARM statement, operator messages, allocation and deallocation messages, execution and completion and job step messages, and data set disposition messages will not be printed.

I do not recommend using the NOLOG parameter until you are absolutely certain that nothing can go wrong with the job. It is a good idea to have the job log to check in case of error.

Printing

Programmers need printed reports to understand what is happening with their system. Although it does not offer as many functions as the JCL OUTPUT statement described earlier, the JES2 /*OUTPUT statement is still used by many programmers and thus will be discussed in detail here.

Directing Printed Output

When the IBM Operating System was first developed, a unique printer could be specified by naming an address with the UNIT keyword parameter of the DD statement. This is still the case for local processing; however, remote processing requires more information.

JES2. JES2 offers two mechanisms for directing output to the desired printer: the /*ROUTE PRINT statement and the /*OUTPUT statement.

*The /*ROUTE PRINT Statement.* Let us examine the /*ROUTE PRINT statement first, because it is similar to the /*ROUTE XEQ statement, which we have already discussed. When you use this JES2 statement, all of the SYSOUT data will be sent to the printer you specify. You code

```
/*ROUTE PRINT dest
```

where `dest` indicates where you want the output to go. Coding `LOCAL` as the `dest` specifies that the output is to be printed on any local printer. If there is more than one local printer, the system will select the first available local printer. If your system does not have any remote printers associated with it, coding of this statement is unnecessary.

If you want your output printed on a remote printer, you have to code a different value for `dest`. (Remember that printers in the same building as your computer are considered remote if they are outside the computer room. In that case they are usually called workstations.) You might code

```
/*ROUTE PRINT R26
```

where `R` indicates a remote printer and `26` identifies the particular workstation that is to be used. Alternative ways of referring to a remote printer include `RM` and `RMT`. Coding `R0` is equivalent to coding `LOCAL`.

To direct your printed output to a remote printer at another location, you must code a node number or a nodename. For the network in Figure 15.1, you might code

```
/*ROUTE PRINT N2
```

or

```
/*ROUTE PRINT DENVER
```

In both these examples only the location is specified, not the particular printer. Once the output reaches the location, system defaults at that location take over.

Suppose, however, that the Denver location has remote printers such as the 6670 attached to it and you wish to have the output printed on that type of printer as opposed to the printer in the computer room. In that situation you would use the following slightly different form of the `/*ROUTE PRINT` statement:

```
/*ROUTE PRINT N2R10
```

This coding tells the system that you want the output printed on the printer associated with the computer in Denver (`N2`) whose remote ID is `10`. Please remember that `dest` must be eight characters or less—including, in this example, the required `N` and `R`.

You also can direct printed output to a user on a VM system. As you may recall, the Houston location in Figure 15.1 is a VM system. If you wanted the output to be directed to a user whose user ID was `JOHNCARL`, you would code the statement as

```
/*ROUTE PRINT HOUSTON.JOHNCARL
```

This coding is almost the same as the coding we used for the `/*ROUTE XEQ` statement to cause a job to execute on the guest MVS running on the VM system. The main difference is that there we gave the user ID of the guest system, here you give the user ID of a particular user.

The coding of the /*ROUTE PRINT statement is very dependent on how your systems programmers set up the system. There are many coding possibilities, so it is important to ask your advisor what the coding requirements are at your installation.

The /*OUTPUT Statement with the DEST Parameter. The JES2 /*OUTPUT statement offers the DEST keyword parameter, which may be used to indicate where output is to be printed. One advantage of the /*OUTPUT statement over the /*ROUTE PRINT statement is that not all SYSOUT data will go to the location named in the /*OUTPUT statement. Included on the statement is a code consisting of from one to four alphameric characters. In the following example, the code is REPT:

```
/*OUTPUT REPT DEST=....
```

This code is also included as the third subparameter of the SYSOUT keyword parameter on the DD statement:

```
//SYSPRINT DD SYSOUT=(A,,REPT)
```

As a result, anything written to SYSPRINT will be class A and will be directed to the destination named in the JES2 /*OUTPUT statement that contains the code REPT. Make sure that you understand this concept, because you will need to remember it when we discuss other keyword parameters on the /*OUTPUT statement.

Values that may be coded for the DEST keyword parameter are the same as those that may be coded for the /*ROUTE PRINT statement—for example, LOCAL, R0, R26, RM26, RMT26, N2, N2R10, DENVER, or HOUSTON.JOHNCARL.

Another advantage of using the JES2 /*OUTPUT statement is that you can name up to four destinations. Thus the output may be sent simultaneously to four different users on VM systems, four different printers, or a combination of VM users and printers. If you coded

```
/*OUTPUT GONE DEST=(HOUSTON.JOHNCARL,LOCAL,R10,N2R15)
```

one copy of that output identified by the code GONE in the SYSOUT parameter on the DD statement would go to VM user JOHNCARL in Houston. In addition, copies would be printed on the printer in the computer room, on the workstation identified as 10, and on the Denver workstation identified as 15.

JES3. JES3 offers two methods for directing printed output to other locations or to workstations attached either to your system or to systems at other locations.

The //*MAIN Statement with the ORG Parameter.   Using the keyword parameter ORG on the JES3 //*MAIN statement will cause *all* your SYSOUT data sets to be directed to a group or node. In this respect //*MAIN ORG is similar to the JES2 /*ROUTE PRINT statement. The statement

```
//*MAIN ORG=GROUP
```

would direct all SYSOUT data sets to the origin group indicated by the group name GROUP. **Origin groups** are classifications of printers defined by the systems programmer. When you name a particular group, you are requesting any printer within that group.

The output may, alternatively, be directed to a different location, known as a network node. The coding looks very much like the coding for a group name. An example would be

```
//*MAIN ORG=DENVER
```

If the nodename DENVER represents an MVS system, the statement

```
//*MAIN ORG=DENVER.REMOTE
```

directs the SYSOUT data sets to the workstation identified by the name RE-MOTE. If DENVER represents a VM system, the statement directs the SYSOUT data sets to the user whose VM user ID is REMOTE.

The //*FORMAT PR Statement.   The JES3 //*FORMAT PR statement, used in conjunction with the DEST parameter (to be discussed shortly), is designed to direct the printing of individual SYSOUT data sets. The particular SYSOUT data set is indicated by coding the DDNAME keyword parameter, as in

```
//*FORMAT PR DDNAME=STEPX.PRINTER
```

where PRINTER is the name of a DD statement included in the job stream as part of STEPX. If the SYSOUT data set involved is part of a procedure, the procstepname is also coded, as in

```
//*FORMAT PR DDNAME=STEPX.PROCNAME.PRINTER
```

When you code a null value for the DDNAME, as in

```
//*FORMAT PR DDNAME=,  . . .
```

the information in the statement pertains to all the SYSOUT data sets in the job that are not explicitly named in a //*FORMAT PR statement.

You also have the option of directing system output with the statement

```
//*FORMAT PR DDNAME=SYSMSG
```

which causes the system message SYSOUT data set to be formatted in accordance with the information supplied in the statement. Coding DDNAME=JESJCL causes the information found in the statement to be applied to the JCL statements and associated messages, and coding DDNAME=JESMSG does the same for the JES3 statements and operator messages.

Let us now examine in detail the coding of the keyword parameter DEST. The statement

```
//*FORMAT PR DDNAME=STEPX.PRINTER,DEST=ANYLOCAL
```

instructs the system to print the output on any local printer within the SYSOUT CLASS coded on the DD statement. This is the default value, so you really do not have to code this form of the statement unless, of course, the job is being submitted from a workstation.

A particular local device can be requested by name. The statement

```
//*FORMAT PR DDNAME=STEPX.PRINTER,DEST=DEVNAME
```

instructs the system to print the output on a device that was given the symbolic name DEVNAME by the systems programmer. A device name may be from one to eight alphameric characters in length.

A particular local device can also be requested by device number. Device number is another term for address, which you could code on the DD statement as part of the UNIT keyword parameter. A common address for a local printer is 00E; if you wanted your system messages to go to this printer, you might code

```
//*FORMAT PR DDNAME=SYSMSG,DEST=00E
```

Remember that a device number or address is three characters in length. The first character usually refers to the channel and the second and third to the particular device on the channel.

Another value that may be coded for DEST is the group name, which we discussed earlier as a possible value of the keyword parameter ORG on the JES3 //*MAIN statement. The coding would look like

```
//*FORMAT PR DDNAME=SYSMSG,DEST=GROUP
```

This statement directs the system messages to any printer within the origin group given the name GROUP by the systems programmer. Ask your advisor for the names of the groups in your installation.

DEST may also be used to specify a nodename or a combination nodename and user ID (for VM) or nodename and remote workstation name (for MVS). If you wished the JCL to print at another node, you might code

```
//*FORMAT PR DDNAME=JESJCL,DEST=DENVER
```

where DENVER is the node to which the JCL is to be directed. The statement

```
//*FORMAT PR DDNAME=JESJCL,DEST=DENVER.REMOTE
```

also directs the JCL listing to the node whose name is DENVER. If DENVER represents a VM system, the output will go to the user whose user ID is

REMOTE; if it represents an MVS system, the output will print at the workstation identified by REMOTE.

type, which is a device classification assigned by the systems programmer, can be named as the destination. If, for example, your systems programmer had assigned 3800 printers the classification 3800PRT, you could code

```
//*FORMAT PR DDNAME=JESJCL,DEST=(3800PRT)
```

to instruct the system to use any available 3800 printer. If you wished to restrict your selection to a particular group, you could code

```
//*FORMAT PR DDNAME=JESJCL,DEST=(3800PRT,GROUP)
```

where GROUP represents the group from which you want the 3800 printer selected. You can also very specifically request a particular 3800 printer, either by coding its device name, as in

```
//*FORMAT PR DDNAME=JESJCL,DEST=(3800PRT,DEVNAME)
```

or by coding its device number or address, as in

```
//*FORMAT PR DDNAME=JESJCL,DEST=(3800PRT,00E)
```

Note that in all cases you must place parentheses around the type, including within the parentheses any restrictions on the type.

As you can see, JES3 provides many useful methods of directing printed output to the desired location. When you wish the same output to go to several different locations, you may code as many JES3 //*FORMAT PR statements as are required to accomplish your goal. For example,

```
//*FORMAT PR DDNAME=JESMSG,DEST=(3800PRT,DEVNAME)
//*FORMAT PR DDNAME=JESMSG,DEST=NODENAME.REMOTE
//*FORMAT PR DDNAME=JESMSG,DEST=GROUP
```

would direct the JES3 messages to a 3800 printer whose name is DEVNAME, to either a VM user whose user ID is REMOTE or an MVS workstation identified by REMOTE, and to any printer within the group named GROUP. JES2, on the other hand, limits you to only four destinations.

In the event that you do not specify a destination printer using the DEST keyword parameter, the output will go to the first available local printer if the job was submitted locally or to the first available printer associated with the workstation if it was submitted through a workstation.

Limiting the Size of Printed Output

As you learned in Chapter 10, you can use the OUTLIM keyword parameter with the SYSOUT keyword parameter on the DD statement to limit the size of printed output. JES2 and JES3 offer different methods of specifying a limit; these methods may be more useful in certain environments.

JES2. The JES2 `/*JOBPARM` statement includes three keyword parameters that may be used to limit the size of printed output. You must ask your advisor what action is taken at your installation if the named value is exceeded.

How exactly can output be limited? One way is to limit the number of kilobytes of output that may be printed. For example, coding

```
/*JOBPARM BYTES=2000
```

limits the output to 2000 kilobytes, or roughly 2,000,000 bytes. The value specified with the keyword parameter BYTES must be a one- to six-digit number, which means that 999999 is the maximum value that you can code. Remember that although the parameter is BYTES, the value you code will be read as kilobytes.

It is unlikely that you would know the size of the output in terms of bytes or kilobytes, but you might know the maximum number of lines that you want printed. In this case you might code

```
/*JOBPARM LINES=2000
```

which tells the system that you want to limit the output to 2000 kilolines, or 2,000,000 lines. Unlike the value coded for the BYTES keyword parameter, which can be up to six digits in length, the value coded for the LINES keyword parameter can be a maximum of only four digits, which limits the output to 9,999,000 lines. Again, remember that the value you code refers to units of one thousand—in this case, thousands of lines.

The last way to limit your output is by specifying the maximum number of pages to be printed via the PAGES keyword parameter. The limit here is a five-digit number, and it refers to the actual number of pages to be printed—not thousands of pages. If you coded

```
/*JOBPARM PAGES=2000
```

the user exit coded by your systems programmer would take control after 2000 pages had been printed.

JES3. The same three keyword parameters as may be coded on the JES2 `/*JOBPARM` statement may be coded on the JES3 `//*MAIN` statement. There is, however, one significant difference. An additional subparameter coded on the `//*MAIN` statement indicates what action is to be taken if the given value is exceeded. For example, if we wished to limit the output to 2,000,000 bytes, we could code the `//*MAIN` statement in three different ways:

```
//*MAIN BYTES=(2000,WARNING)
```

or

```
//*MAIN BYTES=(2000,CANCEL)
```

or

```
//*MAIN BYTES=(2000,DUMP)
```

If WARNING is coded, a warning message will appear on the operator's console as well as on the JES3 output when the limit is exceeded, but the job will continue to execute. WARNING can also be coded as W.

If CANCEL is coded as the second subparameter, JES3 will cancel the job when the limit is exceeded. You can code C in place of CANCEL.

Coding DUMP as the second subparameter instructs JES3 to cancel the job and request a storage dump if the limit is exceeded. A storage dump can be very useful in debugging an infinite loop that produces output. You can code D in place of DUMP.

Using the JES3 //*MAIN statement, you also can limit your output in terms of thousands of lines (specifying a number of up to four digits) or in terms of pages (specifying a number of up to eight digits). For example, you might code

```
//*MAIN LINES =(2000,WARNING)
```

or

```
//*MAIN PAGES=(2000000,CANCEL)
```

Controlling Printed Output

Many different parameters may be coded on the DD statement with the SYSOUT keyword parameter to control printed output. A number of these parameters may also be coded on JES statements in similar or different form. As mentioned earlier, these parameters are very installation dependent, so check with your advisor about the correct form.

JES2. Either the /*JOBPARM or the /*OUTPUT statement may be used in a JES2 system to convey printer information. Remember that any information coded on the /*JOBPARM statement applies to all SYSOUT data sets, whereas the data coded on the /*OUTPUT statement apply only to the DD statement whose SYSOUT parameter explicitly names the code indicated in the /*OUTPUT statement. The following three parameters may be coded on either statement:

1. COPIES. This parameter indicates how many copies of the output you wish printed. If you do not supply a value, only one copy is produced.
2. FORMS. This parameter tells the operator which forms you want mounted on the printer for the printing of the output. If no value is given, the installation default set by the systems programmer is used.
3. LINECT. This parameter tells the system the maximum number of lines

to print on each page of output. If no value is coded, the value set by the systems programmer is used.

You might code these parameters as

```
/*JOBPARM COPIES=5,FORMS=STD,LINECT=60
```

or

```
/*OUTPUT CODE COPIES=5,FORMS=STD,LINECT=60
```

In either case 5 copies of the output will be produced. The paper used will be the form that the systems programmer has set as the installation standard. (Plain fanfold paper is considered by the system to be a form, although many people would not think of it as one.) Each page of output will contain a maximum of 60 lines.

If you want to use a particular character set for your output, you must code the UCS (Universal Character Set) keyword parameter on the JES2 /*OUTPUT statement. For example, if you wished to use the special character set identified as TN, you would code

```
/*OUTPUT CODE UCS=TN
```

Check with your advisor to determine appropriate values to code for FORMS and UCS at your installation.

Checkpoint Parameters. Particularly when you are dealing with large data sets, you do not want the entire data set to start printing again if printing is interrupted after a sizable amount of data has been printed. The solution is to have the system record printing status at certain checkpoints, so that printing may be resumed from some intermediate point if it is interrupted.* The frequency of checkpointing can be specified by means of two parameters, CKPTLNS and CKPTPGS, both of which may be coded on the JES2 /*OUTPUT statement. CKPTLNS defines the number of lines that form a logical page, the unit used by the system to measure distance between checkpoints. Logical pages need not be the same length as pages of printed output; the value coded for CKPTLNS may be any number from 0 to 32767. CKPTPGS indicates the number of logical pages to be printed between checkpoints. The coding

```
/*OUTPUT CODE CKPTLNS=500,CKPTPGS=100
```

tells the system to define a logical page as 500 lines and to take a checkpoint after 100 logical pages have been printed.

Unless you really understand how to determine checkpoints and how your system works, it would be wise to accept the installation defaults set by your

---

* Checkpoint as discussed in Chapter 10 refers to job execution. The checkpointing discussed here refers only to printing.

systems programmer. If you encounter a situation where, for some reason, the installation defaults are not suitable, discuss the situation with your systems programmer before you do any special coding.

JES3. In JES3 only the `//*FORMAT PR` statement may be used to supply information about printing. Remember that in this statement you must name the DD statement to which the information applies.

Quantity. The COPIES parameter indicates how many copies of the output are desired. The coding of this parameter is essentially the same as the coding of the DD statement. For example, coding

```
//*FORMAT PR DDNAME=SYSMSG,COPIES=3
```

will cause three copies of the system messages to be produced.

Spacing. The following three `//*FORMAT PR` parameters influence the spacing of information on a listing:

1. CARRIAGE. This parameter specifies the carriage tape that the operator is to mount on the printer. Coding 6 causes the installation default determined by the systems programmer to be selected. Otherwise the carriage tape may have a name from one to eight characters in length.
2. FCB. This parameter specifies the forms control buffer image to be used to control the printing of the data set. Coding this parameter presupposes that the printer can use the information supplied in an FCB. If you code the FCB keyword parameter, you cannot code the CARRIAGE keyword parameter, as a printer that uses a carriage control tape cannot use an FCB as well. Coding 6 results in the application of the installation default for FCB. The FCB name may be from one to four characters in length.
3. CONTROL. This parameter is used to specify the type of line spacing desired: SINGLE, DOUBLE, TRIPLE, or PROGRAM. SINGLE means single spacing; DOUBLE, double spacing; and TRIPLE, triple spacing. PROGRAM, which is the default, means that each logical record contains a carriage control character as the first byte of the record.

If you code

```
//*FORMAT PR DDNAME=SYSMSG,FCB=ABC,CONTROL=DOUBLE
```

your output will be double spaced and any carriage control characters in the logical record will be ignored. The FCB loaded will be member FCBxABC, where x depends on the type of printer actually used for the printing. On the other hand, if you code

```
//*FORMAT PR DDNAME=JESJCL,CARRIAGE=CAR1,CONTROL=SINGLE
```

the carriage tape named CAR1 will be used instead of an FCB.

Paper. For telling the operator which type of paper to load into the printer, JES3 provides the FORMS keyword parameter on the //*FORMAT PR statement. The value coded for FORMS is the form-name of the form you want used. The form-name can be from one to eight alphameric characters in length. The statement

```
//*FORMAT PR DDNAME=,FORMS=PLN
```

indicates that the operator is to load the form named PLN. Coding FORMS=STANDARD means that you want the form specified as the standard by your systems programmer when JES3 was initialized.

In addition to the FORMS keyword parameter, JES3 offers the OVFL parameter. The purpose of this parameter is to indicate whether the printer program is to test for forms overflow. Coding

```
//*FORMAT PR DDNAME=,FORMS=PLN,OVFL=ON
```

means that you want the system to test for forms overflow, in which case a new page is started when end of form is detected. This setting of OVFL, however, is the default. Coding OVFL=OFF tells the system not to test for overflow and to continue printing despite end of form, which can lead to very sloppy output!

Character Set. If you want to use a particular character set for your output, you must code the TRAIN keyword parameter on the //*FORMAT PR statement. Suppose you wanted all of your output printed using the print train named TN. You might code

```
//*FORMAT PR DDNAME=,TRAIN=TN
```

Before coding this keyword parameter, ask your advisor what the valid train names are at your installation.

Output Writer. The output writer to be used to control the printing of the spooled output may be named as the second subparameter of the SYSOUT keyword parameter on the DD statement. JES3 offers the alternative of specifying the output writer with the keyword parameter EXTWTR on the //*FORMAT PR statement. The writer name on the EXTWTR parameter may be from one to eight alphameric characters in length. Coding

```
//*FORMAT PR DDNAME=,EXTWTR=SPECIAL
```

indicates that printing is to be under the control of the output writer named SPECIAL.

Unique JES3 Parameters. The JES3 //*FORMAT PR statement offers the PRTY keyword parameter, which is used to determine the position of the data set in the output queue. PRTY may be set to any value from 0 to 255; 255 is the highest priority, and 0 is the lowest. Coding might look like

```
//*FORMAT PR DDNAME=,PRTY=37
```

THRESHLD is another keyword parameter unique to JES3. It sets a maximum on the size of an output data set. When the size of the data set exceeds this value, another unit of work is created. Thus there can arise the unusual situation in which several printers are printing different pieces of the same output. The maximum value that can be coded for THRESHLD is 99999999, which is also the default value. Coding

```
//*FORMAT PR DDNAME=,THRESHLD=500
```

tells the system that once 500 records have been written, another unit of work is to be created. Suppose that the job in which this statement appears involves printing a data set containing 1050 records. Suppose, further, that you specified on the DD statement that you want 2 copies. This means that 2100 records are to be printed. Because the THRESHLD value you coded specifies that a unit of work can consist of only 500 records, five units of work will be created—four with 500 records each and one with 100 records. If there are five printers available, all five printers will start to print parts of the output from this one job.

3800 Subsystem Parameters

In Chapter 10 you learned about the 3800 Printing Subsystem and how to code BURST, CHARS, COPIES, FCB, FLASH, and MODIFY on the DD statement. In place of coding these parameters on the DD statement, you can supply this information via JES.

JES2. To use JES2 to supply the special parameters applicable to the 3800 Printing Subsystem, you must use the /*OUTPUT statement. You can code the parameters exactly as you would on the DD statement—for example,

```
/*OUTPUT YELL BURST=Y,CHARS=GRMN,COPIES=(3,(2,1)),FCB=FCB1
/*OUTPUT * MODIFY=MODI
```

There is not enough space in one statement to code all six parameters on one statement, however. To continue a JES2 /*OUTPUT statement, as you can see in the above example, you must replace the code value (here, YELL) by an asterisk and then code the remaining parameters. Remember that /*OUTPUT is the only JES2 statement that may be continued.

Although all of the 3800 Subsystem information necessary can be supplied by coding the six standard parameters on the /*OUTPUT statement, JES2 provides three additional keyword parameters that may be used in conjunction with these parameters.

Let us first examine the keyword parameter MODTRC. As you know from the discussion in Chapter 10 of the MODIFY keyword parameter, coding

```
/*OUTPUT CODE CHARS=(GRMN,GS10),MODIFY=(MODI,1)
```

will cause the second character arrangement table named with the CHARS keyword parameter to be used in printing the information printed as a result of the copy modification module named MODI. The JES2 /*OUTPUT statement offers a slightly different way of producing the same result:

```
/*OUTPUT CODE CHARS=(GRMN,GS10),MODIFY=MODI,MODTRC=1
```

The FLASHC keyword parameter can replace the count subparameter of the FLASH keyword parameter. Instead of coding

```
/*OUTPUT CODE COPIES=4,FLASH=(OVER,3)
```

you have the option of coding

```
/*OUTPUT CODE COPIES=4,FLASH=OVER,FLASHC=3
```

The last of the additional 3800 Subsystem keyword parameters that may be coded on the JES2 /*OUTPUT statement is COPYG, which can replace the group-values that may be coded with the COPIES keyword parameter. For example, coding

```
/*OUTPUT CODE COPIES=(10,(3,2,4))
```

will produce the same result as coding

```
/*OUTPUT CODE COPIES=10,COPYG=(3,2,4)
```

If you wish *all* your printed output to be burst, you can code the BURST keyword parameter on the JES2 /*JOBPARM statement instead of on the /*OUTPUT statement, as in

```
/*JOBPARM BURST=Y
```

JES3. In JES3 the //*FORMAT PR statement is used to supply the 3800 Printing Subsystem parameters. The principal difference between JES2 and JES3 with respect to these parameters is that the BURST keyword parameter does not exist in JES3. In its place is a new keyword parameter, STACKER. If you want your output to be burst by the 3800 Subsystem, you code STACKER=S, which will cause the output to be burst into separate sheets. If you code STACKER=C, the output will be run as continuous forms. The remaining five keyword parameters are effectively the same as those coded in JES2 or on the DD statement. A statement for all printed output might look like

```
//*FORMAT PR  DDNAME=,FCB=FCB1,CHARS=(GS10,GU10),FLASH=NEW1,
//*COPIES=(5,(3,2,2)),MODIFY=(MOD2,0),STACKER=C
```

In JES3 coding STANDARD as the value for FLASH, STACKER, and/or CHARS will invoke the installation standards selected by your systems programmer.

 XMIT

XMIT is used to transmit records from an MVS system to another MVS system or to a DOS or VM system. If the in-stream data following the XMIT statement consists of JCL that is valid at the destination, the JCL will be executed. JCL, however, is not the only kind of information you might want to transmit; you might want to transmit data of some sort to a TSO or VM user. In that case the destination node must be prepared to process the data. Information directed to a TSO or VM user may be received as a data set that can be examined with an editor of some kind.

There are two XMIT statements: the normal JCL XMIT statement, which applies only to a system that uses JES3, and the JES2 /*XMIT statement. Both statements perform the same function, but they are coded in slightly different fashions.

JES2

The /*XMIT statement may be used to direct in-stream data to a node identified by a node number or a nodename. For example, for the network in Figure 15.1, you might code

```
/*XMIT N2
```

or

```
/*XMIT DENVER
```

If you wish to direct in-stream data to a particular TSO user or to a VM guest system, there are three possible ways to code the /*XMIT statement.* You might code

```
/*XMIT HOUSTON.PROD
```

where PROD is either the TSO user's user ID or the VM guest's user ID. Or you might use a colon or a slash in place of the period.

If you cannot use the /* to indicate end of data, you may code the keyword parameter DLM to indicate which two characters will signify end of data. Remember that the destination parameter is a positional parameter and must be coded first. You might choose to use the DLM keyword parameter if you

---

* A VM guest system was defined earlier in this chapter in the discussion of the JES2 /*ROUTE statement.

Vocabulary

In this chapter you have been introduced to the meanings of the following terms:

dependent job control (DJC) network

nodename

node number

origin group

processor ID

remote job entry (RJE)

TSO (time sharing option)

Exercises

The following exercises pertain to JES in general.

1. What does JES stand for, and what does it do?
2. What created the need for JES?
3. What IBM Operating System function was a precursor of JES?
4. In a multi-CPU system, how do you identify the system you wish to use?
5. Why should you be careful about sending messages to the operator?
6. Why is the NOTIFY keyword parameter on the JOB statement no longer sufficient?
7. What are the special parameters used with the 3800 Printing Subsystem?
8. What does the XMIT statement do?
9. What will happen to the data processed by the XMIT statement?

The following exercises pertain to JES2.

1. In JES2 how is a continuation coded for most statements?
2. Code a JES2 statement to cause your job to be executed on a remote MVS system whose nodename is TESTSYS.
3. What is the other JES2 statement that directs where the job is to execute?
4. When several CPUs have been connected, how do you indicate which CPU is to be used?
5. Which JES2 statement may be used to send a message to the operator? Where in your job stream must this statement be placed if the operator is to know to what job it belongs?
6. If your job is to be executed on a system other than yours and you want both operators to see a message, where in the job stream must you place the message statement?
7. Which JES2 statement would you use to identify your listings? Which parameter would you use, and how would it be coded?
8. Which JES2 statement provides accounting information? What is the format of this statement?
9. Using JES2 facilities, what statement would you code to cause a user to be notified of job completion? How is this statement coded?
10. How would you code the notification destination if it was another system?
11. Code the statement you would use if a job submitted on one system were to be executed on a second system and a user on a third system were to be

notified of job completion. Where in the job stream should this statement be placed?

12. Which statement is used for restart? Which keyword parameter is used?
13. Under what conditions will restart actually be invoked?
14. Which statement offers the TIME keyword parameter?
15. How does this time estimate differ from the time estimate supplied on a JOB or EXEC statement?
16. What happens when time is exceeded?
17. How is the TIME parameter coded on the JES2 statement?
18. How would you assign priority for a job?
19. How could the information that is in the JOB statement parameter MSGLEVEL=(0,0) be supplied by JES2?
20. Which two JES2 statements may be used to direct output to a particular printer? How would you code these statements?
21. What is the advantage of the /*OUTPUT statement over the /*ROUTE PRINT statement?
22. Which keyword parameters on the /*JOBPARM statement may be used to limit the size of the listing?
23. What happens if the size is exceeded?
24. Can all print control parameters be used at all installations?
25. What is the difference between providing information on the /*JOBPARM statement and on the /*OUTPUT statement?
26. Which print control parameter is unique to the /*OUTPUT statement, and what is its function?
27. Which parameters on which statement control the checkpointing of printed output?
28. What is a logical page?
29. Provide an example of coding for checkpointing, and explain your example.
30. Which JES2 statement would you use to supply the special 3800 Printing Subsystem parameters?
31. How would you continue an /*OUTPUT statement?
32. What function does the MODTRC keyword parameter on the /*OUTPUT statement perform?
33. What is the function of the FLASHC keyword parameter on the /*OUTPUT statement?
34. What is the function of the COPYG parameter?
35. What coding would cause all output printed on a 3800 Printing Subsystem to be burst?
36. How may the /*XMIT statement be coded?
37. What keyword parameter would you include on your /*XMIT statement if the data to be transmitted included /* in columns 1 and 2?
38. Code a sample job stream that makes use of a /*XMIT statement with the DLM keyword parameter.

The following exercises pertain to JES3.

1. In JES3, how is a continuation coded?
2. What JES3 statement directs that a job be executed on an MVS system?
3. What happens if there is an error in the //*ROUTE XEQ statement? How can you prevent an erroneous //*ROUTE XEQ statement from causing your job to be executed on the local node?
4. How many spool data sets would a JES3 system have?
5. How many CPUs may be coupled to form a JES3 system?
6. What do you call the master CPU that directs the others in a coupled JES3 system? What do you call the other CPUs?
7. Which statement is used to send messages to the operator? Where in the job stream would this statement be placed?
8. Which statement would be used to supply setup information to the operator?
9. In JES3, how can listings be identified?
10. Which JES3 statement is used to provide accounting information? What is the maximum length of the PNAME keyword parameter? What is the maximum length of all other keyword parameters on this statement?
11. If the job is to be executed on a system other than the one on which it was submitted, where in the job stream should the statement containing accounting information be placed?
12. What expanded notification does JES3 provide? Which JES3 statement and parameter would be used to provide this notification?
13. Which JES3 statement and parameter would be used to provide restart capability? What are the coding alternatives, and what do they mean? Which other parameter must be either coded or set by default?
14. What JES3 statement offers a timing function, and what exactly is the nature of this function?
15. Code the JES3 statement that instructs the system to start a job 20 minutes after it is submitted. Code the statement that tells the system to start a job at 5:32 P.M. Will the job run at the specified time? If not, why not? Code the statement that will cause a job to be run on a monthly basis.
16. Which statement is used to replace the TYPRUN keyword parameter?
17. What alternative does JES3 offer to coding TYPRUN=SCAN on the JOB statement?
18. If you wanted a job held, what coding would you use?
19. What parameter offered by JES3 influences region size? If this parameter is not coded, where does the system obtain the needed information?
20. Which JES3 statement is used to specify CLASS?
21. What is an important difference between coding CLASS on the JOB statement and on the JES3 statement? What is the advantage of the latter?
22. Which JES3 statements may be used to direct printed output to a specific destination?

23. What is an origin group?
24. What is the principal difference between directing printed output via the `//*MAIN` statement and via the `//*FORMAT PR` statement?
25. How do you specify the data set to which you want the `//*FORMAT PR` statement to apply?
26. How would you code the `DEST` keyword parameter on the `//*FORMAT PR` statement?
27. What three keyword parameters may be used on the `//*MAIN` statement to limit listing size? What happens if the specified value is exceeded?
28. How would you indicate the number of copies of a particular listing desired?
29. What is the function of the keyword parameter `OVFL` on the `//*FORMAT PR` statement?
30. Code a request for a character set named `GR`.
31. What function is performed by the `THRESHLD` keyword parameter on the `//*FORMAT PR` statement?
32. If `THRESHLD` is set to `500` and 3000 lines are to be printed, in theory how many printers could be used?
33. Which 3800 Printing Subsystem parameter does not exist on the JES3 statement? Which parameter is used in its place, and what are the coding choices for this parameter?
34. Code a sample JES3 statement using all of the keyword parameters that apply to the 3800.
35. Does JES3 provide an `XMIT` statement?
36. Code a job stream containing the JCL `XMIT` statement and all of its possible parameters.
37. What is the significance of the following code?

    `//*MAIN EXPDTCHK=YES`

    What other coding can be provided with `EXPDTCHK`, and what does it mean?
38. What does coding the keyword parameter `RINGCHK` on the `//*MAIN` statement mean? What are the choices in coding this parameter, and what do they mean?
39. What function does the `//*NET` statement provide?
40. What happens when the system encounters a particular `NETID` for the first time?
41. Code the statement(s) required to have `JOB1` execute, followed by `JOB2`.
42. What is the effect of the `NHOLD` keyword parameter on the `//*NET` statement?
43. How can you cause the entire DJC network to be purged if a job within the network abends? How can you cause the entire DJC network to be kept if a job within the network abends?

44. How can you cause a job's execution to depend on the preceding job's successful execution? How can you cause a job's execution to depend on the preceding job's abending?

45. How would you code the //*NET statement so that a second job would run if the first job executed successfully but would not run if the first job abended?

46. How can you express the dependency of a job in one network on a job in another network?

47. In which network is the NETREL keyword parameter coded: the network containing the job that must complete first or the network containing the dependent job?

48. What is the function of the keyword parameter RELSCHCT on the //*NET statement?

49. What is the function of the keyword parameter DEVPOOL? Which job in a DJC network should have the DEVPOOL parameter on its //*NET statement? How would you indicate that mass storage is to be used?

50. What is the purpose of the NRCMP keyword parameter on the //*NET statement? What are the coding choices, and what do they mean?

51. To which JOB statement parameter is OPHOLD similar?

Flowchart Symbols

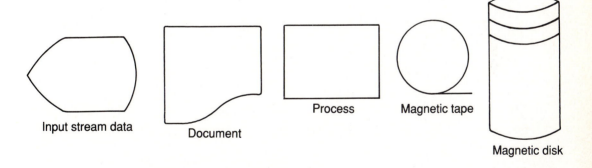

Input stream data

Document

Process

Magnetic tape

Magnetic disk

Flowlines connect data set symbols with process symbols. Data set names are written within the data set symbols, and ddnames are written on the flowlines.

Program names or functions are written within process symbols. When a job contains more than one step, flowlines connect the process symbols to show the order in which they are executed.

Format of JCL Statements

This appendix gives the format of all the parameters of the JOB, EXEC, and DD statements. The first section is for VS1 systems; the second section is for MVS systems.

VS1 Systems

The JOB Statement

//Name	Operation	Operand	P/K	Comments
//jobname	JOB	([account number][,additional accounting information,...])	P	Can be made mandatory
		[programmer's name]	P	Can be made mandatory
		$\left[ADDRSPC = \begin{Bmatrix} VIRT \\ REAL \end{Bmatrix} \right]$	K	Requests storage type
		[CLASS=jobclass]	K	Assigns A–Z, 0–9
		[COND=((code, operator),...)]	K	Specifies a maximum of 8 tests
		[MPROFILE='profile string']	K	For ISSP only
		[MSGCLASS=output class]	K	Assigns A–Z, 0–9
		$\left[MSGLEVEL = \left(\begin{bmatrix} 0 \\ 1 \\ 2 \end{bmatrix} \begin{bmatrix} ,0 \\ ,1 \end{bmatrix} \right) \right]$	K	
		[PROFILE='profile string']	K	For ISSP only
		[PRTY=priority]	K	Assigns 0–13
		$RD = \begin{Bmatrix} R \\ RNC \\ NC \\ NR \end{Bmatrix}$	K	Restart definition
		[REGION=valueK]	K	Specifies amount of storage space
		$\left[RESTART = \left(\begin{Bmatrix} * \\ stepname \\ stepname.procstepname \end{Bmatrix} [,checkid] \right) \right]$	K	For deferred restart
		$\left[TIME = \begin{Bmatrix} ([minutes][,seconds]) \\ 1440 \end{Bmatrix} \right]$	K	Assigns job CPU time limit
		$\left[TYPRUN = \begin{Bmatrix} HOLD \\ SCAN \end{Bmatrix} \right]$	K	Holds a job in job queue, or scans JCL for syntax errors

Legend:
P   Positional parameter.
K   Keyword parameter.
{}   Choose one.
[ ] Optional; if more than one line is enclosed, choose one or none.

The EXEC Statement

//Name	Operation	Operand	P/K	Comments
//[stepname]	EXEC	PGM= { program name / *.stepname.ddname / *.stepname.procstepname.ddname } [PROC=]procedure name	P	Identifies program or cataloged procedure
		[ACCT=(accounting information, ...) ACCT.procstepname=(accounting information, ...)]	K	Accounting information for step
		[ADDRSPC= { VIRT / REAL }]	K	Requests storage type
		COND=([(code,operator) / (code,operator,stepname) / (code,operator,stepname.procstepname)] [, ...][, [EVEN / ONLY]) COND.procstepname=([(code,operator) / (code,operator,stepname) / (code,operator,stepname.procstepname)] [, ...][, [EVEN / ONLY])	K	Specifies a maximum of 8 tests, or 7 tests if EVEN or ONLY is coded
		[PARM=value PARM.procstepname=value]	K	Parentheses or apostrophes enclosing value may be required
		[RD= { R / RNC / NC / NR } RD.procstepname= { R / RNC / NC / NR }]	K	Restart definition
		[REGION=valueK]	K	Specifies amount of storage space
		[TIME= { ([minutes][,seconds]) / 1440 } TIME.procstepname= { (minutes,seconds) / 1440 }]	K	Assigns step CPU time limit

Legend:
P   Positional parameter.
K   Keyword parameter.
{ }   Choose one.
[ ]   Optional; if more than one line is enclosed, choose one or none.

The DD Statement

//Name	Operation	Operand	P/K	Comments
//⎡ddname procstepname ddname⎤	DD	* DATA[,DLM=xx]	P	Defines data set in the input stream.
		[DUMMY]	P	Bypasses I/O operations on a data set (BSAM and QSAM).
		[AFF=ddname]	K	Requests channel separation.
		AMP=[,'AMORG'] [,'BUFND=number'] [,'BUFNI=number'] [,'BUFSP=number'] [,'CROPS= { NCK' NRC' NRE' RCK' }] [,'OPTCD= { I' L' IL' }] [,'RECFM= { F' FB' V' VB' }] [,'STRNO=number'] [,'SYNAD=modulename'] [,'TRACE']	K	Modifies the program processing VSAM clusters or components.
		[BURST= { Y N }][1]	K	Describes printed output.
		[CHARS= (table name, . . .)][1]	K	Describes character arrangements used in printing.
		[CHKPT=EOV]	K	For checkpoint at EOV
		[COMPACT= { NO compact table id }]	K	Identifies Compaction Table for RES output.
		[COPIES= (nnn [,(group value, . . .)])]	K	For use with the SYSOUT and UNIT parameter.
		DCB=(list of attributes) DCB=({ dsname *.ddname *.stepname.ddname *.stepname.procstepname.ddname } [,list of attributes])	K	Completes the data control block.
		[DDNAME=ddname]	K	Postpones the definition of a data set.
		[DEST=userid]	K	Specifies remote destination for SYSOUT data set.
		DISP=([NEW OLD SHR MOD] [,DELETE ,KEEP ,PASS ,CATLG ,UNCATLG] [,DELETE ,KEEP ,CATLG ,UNCATLG])	K	Assigns a status, disposition, and conditional disposition to the data set. CATLG, NEW, and UNCATLG are invalid for VSAM components and clusters.
		[DLM=delimiter]	K	Assigns delimiter other than /*.
		[DSID=(id[,V])]	K	Indicates that there is associated data for this DD statement.
		{ DSNAME DSN } = { dsname dsname(member name) dsname(generation number) dsname(area name) &&dsname &&dsname(member name) &&dsname(area name) *.ddname *.stepname.ddname *.stepname.procstepname.ddname }	K	Assigns a name to a new data set or to identify an existing data set. An un-qualified name is 1–8 characters, beginning with an alphabetic or national character. Area generation, member, and temporary names are invalid or VSAM clusters and components.
		FCB=(image-id [,ALIGN ,VERIFY])	K	Specifies forms control information. The FCB parameter is ignored if the data set is not written to a 3211 printer.
		[FLASH= (overlay name [,count])][1]	K	Specifies forms overlay option and copies to be flashed.
		[HOLD= { YES NO }]	K	Specifies whether JES writer processing of a SYSOUT data set is to be deferred or processed normally.
		LABEL=([data set seq #] [,SL ,SUL ,AL ,AUL ,NSL ,NL ,BLP ,LTM] [,PASSWORD ,NOPWREAD] [,IN ,OUT] [,EXPDT=yyddd ,RETPD=nnnn])	K	Supplies label information.

Legend:
P — Positional parameter.
K — Keyword parameter.
1 — Valid for 3800 only.

The DD Statement (con't)

//Name	Operation	Operand	P/K	Comments
// ddname procstepname. ddname	DD	[MODIFY = (module name [,table reference character])] [1]	K	Identifies copy modification patterns and table reference character.
		[MSVGP=(id[,ddname])]	K	Identifies group of mass storage volumes.
		[OUTLIM=number]	K	Limits the number of logical records you want included in the output data set.
		[QNAME=process name]	K	Specifies the name of a TPROCESS macro which defines a destination queue for messages received by means of TCAM.
		[SEP=(ddname,...)]	K	Requests channel separation.
		$SPACE=\left\{ {TRK \atop CYL \atop blocklength} \right\} \left(primary \left[,secondary \atop ,index \right] \left[,directory \right] \right) \left[,RLSE \right] \left[,{CONTIG \atop MXIG \atop ALX} \right] \left[,ROUND \right]$	K	Assigns space on a direct access volume for a new data set.
		$SPACE=(ABSTR,(primary quantity,address \left[,directory \atop ,index \right]))$	K	Assigns specific tracks on a direct access volume for a new data set.
		[2] $SPLIT= \left\{ {n \atop percent} \right\} (n,CYL,(primary quantity[,secondary quantity])) \atop percent,(percent,blocklength,(primary quantity[,secondary quantity]))$	K	Assigns space on a direct access volume for a new data set. Data sets share cylinders.
		[2] $SUBALLOC= \left\{ {TRK \atop CYL \atop blocklength} \right\} \left(primary \left[,secondary \right] \left[,directory \right] \right) \left\{ {ddname \atop stepname.ddname \atop ,stepname.procstepname.ddname} \right\}$	K	Requests part of the space on a direct access volume assigned earlier in the job.
		[SUBSYS=(name[,parm]...)]	K	Defines generalized subsystem data set.
		$SYSOUT= \left\{ {classname \atop (classname \left[,program name \right] \left[,form number \right] [,PROFILE = 'sysout profile string']) \atop PROFILE = 'sysout profile string'} \right\}$	K	Routes a data set through the output stream. For classname, assign A - Z or 0-9.
		[TERM=RT]	K	Indicates that an RTAM device is in use.
		[2] UCS=(character set code [,FOLD] [,VERIFY])	K	Requests a special character set for a 1403 printer.
		$UNIT= \left(\left\{ {unit address \atop device type \atop group name} \right\} \left[,{unit count \atop ,P} \right] [,DEFER] [,SEP=(ddname,...)] \right)$	K	Provides the system with unit information.
		UNIT=AFF=ddname		
		$\left\{ {VOLUME \atop VOL} \right\} = ([PRIVATE] [,RETAIN] [,volume seq #] [,volume count] \left[, \left\{ {SER=(serial number,...) \atop REF=dsname \atop REF=*.ddname \atop REF=*.stepname.ddname \atop REF=*.stepname.procstepname.ddname} \right\} \right])$	K	Provides the system with volume information. REF=dsname, *.stepname.ddname, and *.stepname.procstepname.ddname are invalid for VSAM components and clusters.

Legend:

P Positional parameter.
K Keyword parameter.
{ } Choose one.
[ ] Enclosing subparameter, indicates that subparameter is optional, if more than one line is enclosed, choose one or more.
[ ] Enclosing entire parameter, indicates that parameter may be optional, depending on what type of data set you are defining.
1 Valid for 3800 only.
2 Invalid for VSAM components and clusters.

Reprinted by permission from *OS/VS1 JCL Reference* (GC24-5099). © 1973 by International Business Machines Corporation.

The JOB Statement

//Name	Operation	Operand	P/K	Comments
//jobname	JOB	([account number] [,additional accounting information,...])	P	Identifies accounting information. Can be made mandatory.
		$\left[ADDRSPC = \left\{ \begin{matrix} VIRT \\ REAL \end{matrix} \right\}\right]$	K	Requests storage type.
		[CLASS=jobclass]	K	Assigns a job class to each job.
		[COND=((code,operator),...)]	K	Specifies test for a return code.
		[GROUP=group name]	K	Specifies a group associated with a RACF-defined user.
		[MSGCLASS=output class]	K	Assigns an output class for the job.
		$\left[MSGLEVEL=\left(\begin{Bmatrix} 0 \\ 1 \\ 2 \end{Bmatrix}\begin{bmatrix} ,0 \\ ,1 \end{bmatrix}\right)\right]$	K	Specifies what job output is to be written.
		[NOTIFY=user identification]	K	Requests a message be sent to a time-sharing terminal.
		[PASSWORD=(password [,new password])]	K	Specifies a password for a RACF-defined user.
		[PERFORM=n]	K	Specifies the performance group a job belongs to.
		[programmer's name]	P	Identifies programmer. Can be made mandatory.
		[PRTY=priority]	K	Specifies a job's priority.
		$\left[RD=\begin{Bmatrix} R \\ RNC \\ NC \\ NR \end{Bmatrix}\right]$	K	Specifies restart facilities to be used.
		[REGION=valueK]	K	Specifies amount of storage space.
		$\left[RESTART=\left(\begin{Bmatrix} * \\ stepname \\ stepname.procstepname \end{Bmatrix}[,checkid]\right)\right]$	K	Specifies restart facilities for deferred restart.
		$\left[TIME=\begin{Bmatrix} ([minutes] [,seconds]) \\ 1440 \end{Bmatrix}\right]$	K	Assigns a job a CPU time limit.
		$\left[TYPRUN=\begin{Bmatrix} HOLD \\ JCLHOLD \\ SCAN \\ COPY \end{Bmatrix}\right]$	K	Holds a job in job queue, scans JCL for syntax errors, or copies the input deck to SYSOUT.
		[USER=userid]	K	Identifies a RACF-defined user.

Legend:
P   Positional parameter. (Positional parameters must precede keyword parameters)
K   Keyword parameter.
{ } Choose one.
[ ] Optional; if more than one line is enclosed, choose one or none.

Reprinted by permission from *MVS JCL* (GC28-1300). © 1982 by International Business Machines Corporation.

The EXEC Statement				
//Name	Operation	Operand	P/K	Comments
// [stepname]	EXEC	[ACCT [.procstepname] = (accounting information, . . .)]	K	Accounting information for step.
		[ADDRSPC [.procstepname] = $\begin{Bmatrix} VIRT \\ REAL \end{Bmatrix}$]	K	Requests storage type.
		[COND [.procstepname] = ($\begin{Bmatrix} (code, operator) \\ (code, operator, stepname) \\ (code, operator, stepname.procstepname) \end{Bmatrix}$, . . . $\begin{bmatrix} ,EVEN \\ ,ONLY \end{bmatrix}$)]	K	Specifies a test for a return code.
		[DPRTY [.procstepname]=([value1] [,value2])]	K	Specifies dispatching priority for a job step.
		[DYNAMNBR [.procstepname] =n]	K	Specifies dynamic allocation.
		[PARM [.procstepname] =value]	K	Passes variable information to a program at execution time.
		[PERFORM [.procstepname] =n]	K	Specifies a performance group for a job.
		[PGM= $\begin{Bmatrix} program\ name \\ *.stepname.ddname \\ *.stepname.procstepname.ddname \end{Bmatrix}$]	P	Identifies program.
		[[PROC=] procedure name]	P	Identifies a cataloged or instream procedure.
		[RD [.procstepname] = $\begin{Bmatrix} R \\ RNC \\ NC \\ NR \end{Bmatrix}$]	K	Specifies restart facilities to be used.
		[REGION [.procstepname] =valueK]	K	Specifies amount of storage space.
		[TIME [.procstepname] = $\begin{Bmatrix} ([minutes] [,seconds]) \\ 1440 \end{Bmatrix}$]	K	Assigns step CPU time limit.

Legend:

K   Keyword parameter.
P   Positional parameter. (Positional parameters must precede keyword parameters)
{}   Choose one.
[]   Optional; if more than one line is enclosed, choose one or none.

The DD Statement				
//Name	Oper-ation	Operand	P/K	Comments
// [ddname / procstepname. / ddname]	DD	[*]	P	Defines data set in the input stream.
		AMP={ AMORG / ,'BUFND=number' / ,'BUFNI=number' / ,'BUFSP=number' / ,'CROPS=(RCK'/NCK'/NRE'/NRC') / ,'OPTCD=(I'/L'/IL') / ,'RECFM=(F'/FB'/V'/VB') / ,'STRNO=number' / ,'SYNAD=modulename' / ,TRACE }	K	Completes the access method control block (ACB) for VSAM data sets.
		[BURST={Y/N}]	K	Specifies whether or not paper output is to go to the Burster-Trimmer-Stacker of the 3800.
		[CHARS=(table name [,table name . . .])]	K	Specifies character arrangement table(s) to be used when printing on the 3800.
		[CHKPT=EOV]	K	For checkpoint at end of volume.
		[COPIES=(nnn [,(group value,group value . . .)])]	K	Requests multiple copies (and grouping, for the 3800 only) of the output data set.
		[DATA]	P	Defines data set in the input stream.
		[DCB=(list of attributes) / DCB=({ dsname / *.ddname / *.stepname.ddname / *.stepname.procstepname.ddname } [,list of attributes])]	K	Completes the data control block (used for all data sets except VSAM).
		[DDNAME=ddname]	K	Postpones the definition of a data set.
		DEST= { JES2: Nnn/NnnRmmm/Rnnn/RMnnn/RMTnnn/Unnn/LOCAL/name } { JES3: ANYLOCAL/device-name/device-address/group-name }	K	Specifies a destination for the output data set.

The DD Statement (con't)

//Name	Oper- ation	Operand	P/K	Comments

// ⎡ddname
  procstepname.
    ddname⎤
	DD	DISP=(⎡NEW
		 OLD
		 SHR
		 MOD
		 ,⎤ ⎡,DELETE
		 ,KEEP
		 ,PASS
		 ,CATLG
		 ,UNCATLG
		 ,⎤ ⎡,DELETE
		 ,KEEP
		 ,CATLG
		 ,UNCATLG⎤)
			K	Assigns a status, disposition, and conditional disposition to the data set.

		[DLM=delimiter]	K	Assigns delimiter other than /*.
		[DSID=(1d[,V])]	K	Indicates to a diskette reader that data is to be merged into the JCL stream at this point or specifies the name to be given to a SYSOUT data set written on a diskette.
		⎡{DSNAME} {DSN}⎤ = { dsname dsname(member name) dsname(generation number) dsname(area name) &&dsname &&dsname(member name) &&dsname(area name) *.ddname *.stepname.ddname *.stepname.procstepname.ddname }	K	Assigns a name to a new data set or to identify an existing data set.
		[DUMMY]	P	Bypasses I/O operations on a data set (BSAM and QSAM).
		[DYNAM]	P	Specifies dynamic allocation.
		⎡FCB=(image-id ⎡,ALIGN ,VERIFY⎤)⎤	K	Specifies forms control information. The FCB parameter is ignored if the data set is not written to a 3211 or 1403 printer.
		[FLASH=(overlay name[,count])]	K	Identifies the forms overlay to be used on the 3800.
		⎡FREE= {END} {CLOSE}⎤	K	Specifies dynamic deallocation.
		⎡HOLD= {YES} {NO}⎤	K	Specifies whether output processing is to be deferred or processed normally.
		LABEL=(⎡data set seq #⎤ ⎡,SL ,SUL ,AL ,AUL ,NSL ,NL ,BLP ,LTM ,⎤ ⎡,PASSWORD ,NOPWREAD⎤ ⎡,IN ,OUT⎤ ⎡,EXPDT=yyddd ,RETPD=nnnn⎤)	K	Supplies label information.
		[MODIFY=(module name[,trc])]	K	Specifies a copy modification module that is to be loaded into the 3800.

The DD Statement

//Name	Oper-ation	Operand	P/K	Comments
// [ddname procstepname. ddname]	DD	[MSVGP=(id[,ddname])]	K	Identifies a mass storage group for a mass storage system (MSS) device.
		[OUTLIM=number]	K	Limits the number of logical records you want included in the output data set.
		OUTPUT= { *.name[,*.name] ... / *.stepname.name[,*.stepname.name] ... / *.stepname.procstepname.name[,*.stepname.procstepname.name] ... }	K	Identifies which OUTPUT JCL statement the user wishes to use for output processing for this data set.
		[PROTECT=YES]	K	Requests RACF protection for tape volumes or for direct access data sets.
		[QNAME=process name]	K	Specifies the name of a TPROCESS macro which defines a destination queue for messages received by means of TCAM.
		SPACE=({TRK / CYL / blocklength} ,(primary quantity [,secondary quantity] [,directory / ,index]) [,RLSE] [,CONTIG / ,MXIG / ,ALX] [,ROUND])	K	Assigns space on a direct access volume for a new data set.
		SPACE= (ABSTR,(primary quantity ,address [,directory / ,index]))	K	Assigns specific tracks on a direct access volume for a new data set.
		SUBSYS=(subsystem name [,parm1 [,parm2] ... [,parm254]])	K	Specifies the subsystem that will process both the data set and the specified parameters.
		SYSOUT=(class name [,program name] [,form name / ,code name])	K	Assigns an output class to an output data set.
		[TERM=TS]	K	Identifies a time-sharing user.
		UCS=(character set code [,FOLD] [,VERIFY])	K	Requests a special character set for a 3211 or a 1403 printer.
		UNIT=({unit address / device type / user-assigned group name} [,unit count / ,P] [,DEFER]) / UNIT=AFF=ddname	K	Provides the system with unit information.
		{VOLUME / VOL} =([PRIVATE] [,RETAIN] [,volume seq number] [,volume count] [,] SER=(serial number, ...) REF=dsname REF=*.ddname REF=*.stepname.ddname REF=*.stepname.procstepname.ddname)	K	Provides the system with volume information.

Legend:

P   Positional parameter. (Positional parameters must precede keyword parameters)
K   Keyword parameter.
{ } Choose one.

[ ] Enclosing subparameter, indicates that subparameter is optional; if more than one line is enclosed, choose one or more

Reprinted by permission from *MVS JCL* (GC28-1300). © 1982 by International Business Machines Corporation.

The OUTPUT Statement				
//Name	Operation	Operand	P/K	Comments
//name	OUTPUT	BURST= { YES / Y / NO / N }	K	Specifies the default burst characteristic of all output data sets.
		[CHARS=(table-name[,table-name] ...)]	K	Specifies a character arrangement table for a 3800 printer.
		[CHKPTLINE=nnnnn]	K	Maximum number of lines contained on a logical page.
		[CHKPTPAGE=nnnnn]	K	Number of logical pages to be printed or transmitted before the next checkpoint.
		[CHKPTSEC=nnnnn]	K	Number of seconds that may elapse between checkpoints.
		CLASS= { * / output-class }	K	Specifies the output processing class.
		[COMPACT=compaction-table-name]	K	Specifies the symbolic name of the compaction table for SYSOUT data sets to an SNA remote terminal.
		CONTROL= { PROGRAM / SINGLE / DOUBLE / TRIPLE }	K	Specifies the type of forms control used.
		[COPIES=(nnn[,group-value[group-value]...])]	K	Specifies the number of copies to be printed.
		DEFAULT= { YES / Y / NO / N }	K	Specifies whether or not this output statement is implicitly associated with DD statements within the job or job step that do not have the output parameter specified.
		DEST= { Rnnnn / RMnnnn / RMTnnnn / Unnn / LOCAL / name / Nnnnn / NnnRmmmm / NnnnRmmm / NnnnnRmm / nodename.userid }	K	Specifies the destination of the data set.
		[FCB=fcb-name]	K	Identifies the forms control buffer or image used for printing.

The OUTPUT Statement (cont'd)				
//Name	Operation	Operand	P/K	Comments
//name	OUTPUT	[FLASH=(overlay-name,count)]	K	Identifies the forms overlay to be used on the 3800 printer.
		FORMS= { forms-name / STD }	K	Specifies the print forms used for output processing.
		[GROUPID=output-group-name]	K	Identifies which of a job's output data sets are to form a group.
		[INDEX=nn]	K	Indicates the data set indexing print position offset for the 3211 printer.
		JESDS= { ALL / LOG / JCL / MSG }	K	Specifies the processing options for this output that are to be applied to the system data sets output processing.
		[LINDEX=nn]	K	Indicates the data set indexing print position for the 3211 printer.
		[LINECT=nnn]	K	Maximum number of lines to be printed on each output page.
		[MODIFY=(module-name[,trc])]	K	Specifies the name of a copy modification module loaded into the 3880 printer.
		[PRMODE=process-mode]	K	Specifies the scheduling to be performed for this output data set.
		[PRTY=nnn]	K	Specifies an initial selection priority for this output data set.
		[UCS=ucs-name]	K	Specifies the universal character set to be used.
		[WRITER=name]	K	Specifies the name of an installation-written program that is to write the output data set.

Legend:

P   Positional parameter. (Positional parameters must precede keyword parameters)
K   Keyword parameter.

{ }   Choose one.
[ ]   Enclosing subparameter indicates that subparameter is optional; if more than one line is enclosed, choose one or more.

Reprinted by permission from *MVS JCL* (GC28-1300). © 1982 by International Business Machines Corporation.

Data Used in Examples

The following data are used in examples throughout the text. The first thirty records are printed in Chapter 2 and used to create POLYFILE in Chapter 3. The last ten records are added to POLYFILE in Chapter 4.

The data represent records of an insurance policy data set. The fields, their positions, and their lengths are as shown in the table.

Field	Columns	Length
Policy number-key	1–5	5
Name	6–25	20
Type of policy, A (auto) / H (home) / L (life)	29	1
Premium	30–35	6
Due date, MMDD	36–39	4
Year-to-date payments	40–45	6
Year policy started, YY	50–51	2

```
----+----1----+----2----+----3----+----4----+----5----+----6
13009REED, TINA               A0842000426072100     74
15174HANDJANY, HAIDEH         H0229000220022900     71
17337BUTERO, MAURICE          H0501000434050100     63
19499LAFER, BRUCE             A0706000819050000     52
21661LEE, SUI                 A0390170303030017     76
23821COOPER, LUCY             L0745000730070000     64
25980NELSON, LAWRENCE         L0513000217051300     78
28138KRUKIS, SONIA            A0346000510034600     59
30295CHEN, YIN                H0295000514010000     81
32451SIMPKINS, KEVIN          L0388000321038806     76
34605PORTER, MICHELE          A0627500128042700     65
36759DECICCO, RICHARD         A0255000619010000     71
38912ABREU, JUANITA           H0732001030070000     80
41063HIGH, CAROL              L0311000521031100     82
43214ENGLISH, REYNOLDS        A0443000228043300     82
45363LEE, BOHYON              A0515000214050000     79
47512THOMPSON, STANLEY        H0640750307064075     66
49659VALDEZ, FABIO            L0706000430070600     71
51805AMATO, ROBERT            A0466000417015000     63
53950RIZZUTO, JAMES           A0693000822000000     81
56094SCHWARTZ, MICHAEL        H1037000605050000     67
58238RUFINO, CARLOS           L0673000520047300     64
60380MORLEY, JOHN             A0786000514078600     71
62521BREVIL, JAMES            H0812000314081200     55
64660FALCONER, EDWARD         L1080000227008000     74
66799MARTIN, KATHLEEN         L0895000129089500     65
68937YEUNG, SUK               A0517000816050000     49
71074PAUL, MARINA             A0441000414034100     80
73210FRADIN, SHIRLEY          L0668000728066800     56
75344BURNS, JEFFREY           L0706000226070000     57

77478KATZ, HAL                A0485000406038500     64
79610WRIGHT, DONNA            H0926000901092000     75
81742CUOMO, DONNA             L0900000313090000     69
83872LOPEZ, ANNA              A0679000716010000     80
86002ALEXANDER, LISA          A0402000623030200     73
88130GOLDBERG, LORI           H0987000524095000     67
92057HOFMANN, PATRICA         H0737000315040000     77
92384PUGH, CLIFFORD           A0750000423075000     80
94509FERRIS, LAURA            A0135000815013500     73
96633BERGIN, MICHAEL          L1608000116100000     74
----+----1----+----2----+----3----+----4----+----5----+----6
```

Data for Programming Assignments

The following data may be used for the programming assignments. The data represent records of a student transcript data set. The fields, their positions, and their lengths are as shown in the table.

Field	Columns	Length
Student number-key	1–5	5
Name	6–25	20
Sex, M/F	30	1
Year of birth, YY	31–32	2
Date of first admission, YYMM	33–36	4
Major	40–41	2
Credits attempted	45–47	3
Credits completed	48–50	3
Grade point average	51–53	3

```
----+----1----+----2----+----3----+----4----+----5----+----6
13472ANDERSON,MARY          F638102     LA   064064342
18596BAKMAN,MICHAEL         M628102     DP   056034218
19623CARR,MICHELE           F607909     MT   076062254
20485CORNEJO,FRANK          M628209     LA   034032271
21849GORDON,BARBARA         F588202     LA   024024216
22468PERNA,JUDY             F478109     DP   048048400
28591KAPLAN,ANN             F638109     BT   064060341
34163LEHEY,JANETTE          F587702     LA   116042191
35926MARICIC,JAMES          M628109     DP   072060246
37482ROSENBERG,SCOTT        M598102     AT   036036301
38597SAGINARIO,LOUIE        M617909     CE   097097286
39432SCHNEYMAN,PAUL         M607809     DP   112112382
39582SCOTT,JOAN             F597702     DP   124120352
40613SIRACUSANO,COSMO       M638109     ME   086084275
41563YEE,MARY               F608202     LA   046036200
42691WRIGHT,JAMAL           M527709     LA   054054256
43719VAZQUEZ,JAMES          M618109     DP   046030192
44827ROSENBERG,STEVE        M638202     AC   038034257
45927RICHARDS,RANDY         F618009     ET   077070284
46218KISAREWSKI,MICHAEL     M638302     DP   026026341
47526YEUNG,SUE              F628309     LA   029020284
49627VOLIKAS,PAUL           M648302     LA   034034261
49747RUBIO,EDGAR            M638009     DP   042032217
49982REEKSTIN,ROBIN         F628002     DP   076076381
50621NOBLESALA,FERNANDO     M547209     ET   137042201
51276MURRY,RITA             F648202     LA   027025284
51384MOLINA,ANGELA          F588102     AC   047045252
51486SALERNO,ROBERT         M608209     LA   038030147
52924LYNCH,PATRICIA         F558302     DP   032032352
54621LEW,SUK YI             F628009     MT   047040259

55609BERGAMASCO,MARGARET    F457909     DP   062062384
57842CAVE,REBECCA           F638009     AT   037030199
59027FRANKLIN,CARL          M658209     DP   042042259
61347GOYA,WINSTON           M638102     MT   036026204
62427JEREZ,PATRICIA         F607909     LA   044029218
64983MANOZA,SILVIA          F627902     DP   046044337
66717FISHER,STEVEN          M648006     ET   026026261
67849GREENE,DAVID           M627909     LA   046040289
70316HARRISON,MARIE         F648109     ET   026020214
74926POWELL,JOHN            M618002     DP   060060259
----+----1----+----2----+----3----+----4----+----5----+----6
```

Magnetic Tape and Disk-Advanced Concepts

Record Formats

In Chapter 3 you learned that data may be stored on magnetic tape and disk as fixed length records and as fixed length blocked records. These two record formats are shown in Figure 3.2. There are several other record formats that are used with sequential data sets and entirely different record formats that are used with ISAM data sets. These record formats are discussed in this appendix.

Sequential Data Sets

Variable Length Records.   In Chapter 3 we assumed that all records were the same length. This does not have to be the case; records may have variable lengths. Suppose, for example, that a dentist keeps a data set containing patient information. Each record might contain identifying information about the patient and information about each visit. Patients with few visits would have short records, whereas patients with many visits would have long records.

Figure E.1a shows unblocked variable length records. When unblocked variable length records are written, the system adds four bytes, called the record descriptor word (RDW), to the beginning of each record. The system stores the logical record length in the record descriptor word. The system also adds an additional four bytes, called the block descriptor word (BDW), to the beginning of each block. The system stores the blocksize in the block descrip-

Figure E.1

Record Formats Used with Sequential Data Sets

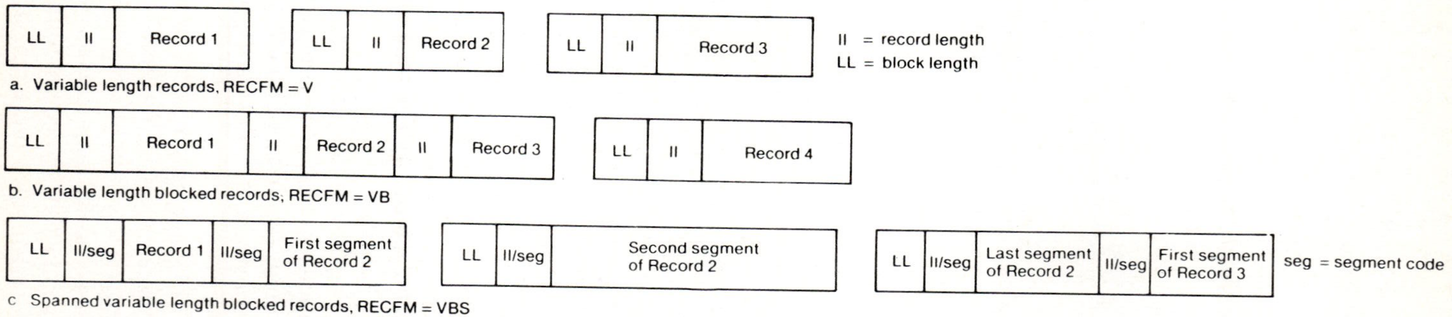
LL
ll
Record 1
LL
ll
Record 2
LL
ll
Record 3
ll = record length
LL = block length
a. Variable length records, RECFM = V
LL
ll
Record 1
ll
Record 2
ll
Record 3
LL
ll
Record 4
b. Variable length blocked records, RECFM = VB
LL
ll/seg
Record 1
ll/seg
First segment of Record 2
LL
ll/seg
Second segment of Record 2
LL
ll/seg
Last segment of Record 2
ll/seg
First segment of Record 3
seg = segment code
c Spanned variable length blocked records, RECFM = VBS

tor word. The block descriptor word is not really necessary, since for un-blocked records the blocksize is equal to the record length; nevertheless, the system adds it to each record.

Like fixed length records, variable length records are frequently blocked. As shown in Figure E.1b, when blocked variable length records are written, the system automatically adds a record descriptor word to each record and a block descriptor word to each block.

When blocked variable length records are written, the system puts into a block as many records as it can without causing the block to exceed the specified blocksize. If a record cannot fit in a block, a new block is started.

For variable length records, LRECL must be equal to the length of the largest record plus 4. So if the largest record has a length of 150 bytes, LRECL will be set equal to 154. For variable length records, the BLKSIZE must be equal to at least LRECL plus 4. So for this example, BLKSIZE could be as small as 158, but larger values would be valid, too.

Spanned Records.   Variable length records may also be spanned. With spanned records, the record length may be larger than the blocksize. As Figure E.1c shows, if the record length is larger than the blocksize, a record may occupy more than one block. In other words, the record may span more than one block, which is where the name spanned records comes from.

The system adds four bytes, called the segment descriptor word (SDW), to the start of each segment. The segment descriptor word contains the length of the segment and a code that indicates whether the segment is a complete record, the first segment, an intermediate segment, or the last segment of a record.

When spanned records are blocked, the system fills each block. If adding a record to a block would cause the block to exceed the specified blocksize, the record is split into two segments. The first segment is put into the incomplete block to bring it up to size, and the second segment is put into the next block. If the second segment is too large to fit into the next block, it is split into two segments. This splitting is repeated as many times as necessary to fit the segments into blocks.

Undefined Format Records.   Records may also have an undefined format. With undefined format records, each block is treated as a record. The blocks may have a variable size. An undefined record format is specified by coding RECFM=U.

ISAM Data Sets

The various record formats that may be used with an ISAM data set are illustrated in Figure E.2. The first difference between these formats and the other record formats we have studied is that the key field is outside the

▬ Figure E.2

Record Formats Used with ISAM Data Sets

a. Fixed length unblocked records with key in record

b. Fixed length unblocked records with key outside record

c. Fixed length blocked records

d. Variable length unblocked records

e. Variable length blocked records

ll = record length
LL = block length
Del = delete byte

550

record. Because the key is available outside the record, it is not necessary to examine the record itself to learn whether it is the one being sought.

Figure E.2a shows the layout of the fixed length unblocked record. The first field in the record is labeled "Del" for delete byte. The delete byte is in position 0 of the record. (The first byte of the record is position 0, the second is position 1, and so forth.) When the delete byte contains the hexadecimal value FF, this record is a dummy record or is marked for deletion. A dummy record is written to a data set to reserve space for future record additions. A record marked for deletion is deleted when the data set is reorganized. Notice that the key itself resides somewhere in the middle of the record. In general, if the key occupies the first byte of the record (position 0), the record cannot be deleted because there is no way to mark it for deletion.

Figure E.2b shows a fixed length unblocked record in which the key is in position 0. In this case, the key is stored only outside the record and is not repeated within the record.

Figure E.2c shows a fixed length blocked record; the key field contains the highest key in the block.

Figures E.2d and e show the record layout of variable length records. In this case, the first four bytes are reserved for system use. If you want to be able to delete records, you must save the fifth byte for use as the delete byte. The key in this situation can start in the sixth byte, or position 5.

Magnetic Disk

Over the years IBM has introduced new models of DASDs. Generally the new models have faster access times and greater capacity. The characteristics of some of these units are shown in Table E.1.

Table E.1
Characteristics of Some IBM DASD

Characteristic	3330	3340	3350	3375	3380
Maximum bytes per track	13,030	8368	19,069	35,616	47,476
Tracks per cylinder	19	12	30	12	15
Cylinders per volume	404 or 808	696	555	959	885 or 1770
Megabytes per volume	100 or 200	70	317.5	819.7	630 or 1260
Average seek time (ms)	30	25	25	19	16
Average rotational delay	8.3	10.1	8.3	10.1	8.3
Data transfer rate (megabytes per second)	0.806	0.885	1.198	1.859	3.0

Where a particular device comes in two models that have different characteristics, two numbers are given in Table E.1.

Table E.1 gives the maximum capacity of the DASD, but the actual capacity depends on the blocksize of the data set and whether or not the data set has keys. Methods of calculating the actual capacity are given in the next section.

Space Requirements

When a job requests that a data set be created on a particular disk pack, the system checks to see that there is sufficient free space on the pack to store the data set. If there is not sufficient space available, the job will not run.

To know beforehand whether your data set will fit on a disk pack, you have to know how much free space there is on the pack and how much space your data set requires. In Chapter 13, you learned how to use the utility IEHLIST to find out how much free space there is on a disk pack. To find out how much space your data set requires, you can use a table such as Table E.2.

Table E.2 refers to a 3336 Disk Pack; IBM publishes similar tables for other

Table E.2
Track Capacity of 3336 Disk Pack

Bytes per Block Without Keys		Bytes per Block with Keys		Blocks per Track	Bytes per Block Without Keys		Bytes per Block with Keys		Blocks per Track
Min	Max	Min	Max		Min	Max	Min	Max	
6448	13030	6392	12974	1	558	596	502	540	18
4254	6447	4198	6391	2	524	557	468	501	19
3157	4253	3101	4197	3	492	523	436	467	20
2499	3156	2443	3100	4	464	491	408	435	21
2060	2498	2004	2442	5	438	463	382	407	22
1746	2059	1690	2003	6	414	437	358	381	23
1611	1745	1455	1689	7	392	413	336	357	24
1328	1510	1272	1454	8	372	391	316	335	25
1182	1327	1126	1271	9	353	371	297	315	26
1062	1181	1006	1125	10	336	352	280	296	27
963	1061	907	1005	11	319	335	263	279	28
878	962	822	906	12	304	318	248	262	29
806	877	750	821	13	290	303	234	247	30
743	805	687	749	14	277	289	221	233	31
688	742	632	686	15	264	276	208	220	32
640	687	584	631	16	253	263	197	207	33
597	639	541	583	17	242	252	186	196	34

Cont.

■ Table E.2 (Cont.) ■

Bytes per Block Without Keys		Bytes per Block with Keys		Blocks per Track	Bytes per Block Without Keys		Bytes per Block with Keys		Blocks per Track
Min	Max	Min	Max		Min	Max	Min	Max	
231	241	175	185	35	56	58	2	2	68
221	230	165	174	36	54	55			69
212	220	156	164	37	51	53			70
203	211	147	155	38	48	50			71
195	202	139	146	39	46	47			72
187	194	131	138	40	43	45			73
179	186	123	130	41	41	42			74
172	178	116	122	42	39	40			75
165	171	109	115	43	36	38			76
158	164	102	108	44	34	35			77
152	157	96	101	45	32	33			78
146	151	90	95	46	30	31			79
140	145	84	89	47	28	29			80
134	139	78	83	48	26	27			81
129	133	73	77	49	24	25			82
124	128	68	72	50	22	23			83
119	123	63	67	51	20	21			84
114	118	58	62	52	19	19			85
109	113	53	57	53	17	18			86
105	108	49	52	54	15	16			87
101	104	45	48	55	13	14			88
96	100	40	44	56	12	12			89
92	95	36	39	57	10	11			90
89	91	33	35	58	9	9			91
85	88	29	32	59	7	8			92
81	84	25	28	60	6	6			93
78	80	22	24	61	4	5			94
74	77	18	21	62	3	3			95
71	73	15	17	63	1	2			96
68	70	12	14	64					
65	67	9	11	65					
62	64	6	8	66					
59	61	3	5	67					

Reprinted by permission from *IBM 3330 Series Disk Storage* (GX20-1920-1), November 1973, by International Business Machines Corporation.

disk packs. Table E.2 shows how the capacity of a disk pack depends on the size of the record and whether the data set contains keys.

For records without keys Table E.2 shows that the largest block that can fit on a track is 13,030 bytes. Because a block must fit on one track, 13,030 is the largest blocksize that may be used with a 3336 Disk Pack. For records with keys Table E.2 shows that the largest blocksize is 12,974 bytes.

To see how Table E.2 is used, suppose you have a sequential data set that contains 100,000 records and whose record length is 300 bytes. Sequential data sets do not contain keys, so you will use the columns headed "Without Keys." If you wanted to perform similar calculations for indexed or direct data sets, you would use the columns headed "With Keys."

Let us first assume that the records are unblocked, in which case each block contains one record and the blocksize is 300 bytes. The columns for records without keys in Table E.2 show that if the blocksize is between 290 bytes and 303 bytes, 30 blocks will fit on a track. Each block contains one record, so 30 records will fit on a track. The whole data set requires 100,000 records divided by 30 records per track, or 3333.33 tracks. Because space is allocated in full tracks, this figure is rounded up to 3334 tracks.

Let us next assume that the records are blocked using a blocking factor of 10, in which case the blocksize will be 3000 bytes. Table E.2 shows that four such blocks will fit on a track. Because each block contains 10 records, this is equivalent to 40 records on a track. The 100,000 records will require only $100,000/40 = 2500$ tracks. In this case, blocking the records reduces the space requirements by 834 tracks, a 25 percent reduction.

Larger blocking factors do not always reduce the space requirements, however. For example, with a blocking factor of 15, the blocksize for these records would be 4500 bytes. Table E.2 shows that only two such blocks will fit on a track. Because each block contains 15 records, this is equivalent to 30 records on a track, which is exactly what the track held when the records were not blocked.

To calculate the largest blocking factor that could be used with these records, simply divide the maximum blocksize, 13,030 bytes, by the logical record length, 300 bytes. The answer is 43.43, but because the blocking factor must be an integer, you discard the fractional part of the answer and conclude that the maximum blocking factor is 43.

For data sets on disk, it is common to choose blocking factors such that two or four blocks fit on a track. This type of blocking is called half-track or quarter-track blocking.

Exercises

Suppose a data set that you want to store on a 3336 Disk Pack contains 60,000 records, and that each record has a length of 400 bytes. Use Table E.2 to answer the following questions.

1. If the data set is unblocked, how many records will fit on a track and how many tracks will be required to store the data set?
2. If a blocking factor of 10 is used, how many records will fit on a track and how many tracks will be required to store the data set?
3. What is the maximum blocking factor that could be used with these records?

Guide to Utility Program Functions

The left column lists, in alphabetical order, tasks that you might want to perform. The middle column more·specifically defines the tasks. The right column shows the utility programs that can be used for each task. Notice that in some cases more than one program may be available to perform the same task.

Task		Utility Programs
Add	a password	`IEHPROGM`
Analyze	tracks on direct access	`IEHDASDR, IBCDASDI`
Assign alternate tracks	to a direct access volume	`IEHDASDR, IBCDASDI`
	to a direct access volume and recover usable data	`IEHATLAS`
Build	a generation index	`IEHPROGM`
	a generation	`IEHPROGM`
	an index	`IEHPROGM`
Catalog	a data set	`IEHPROGM`
	a generation data set	`IEHPROGM`
Change	data set organization	`IEBUPDTE`
	logical record length	`IEBGENER`
	volume serial number of direct access volume	`IEHDASDR`
Clean	an IBM 1403 or 3203-4 print train	`IEBPTPCH (IEBPTRCP)`

Task		Utility Programs
Compare	a partitioned data set	IEBCOMPR
	sequential data sets	IEBCOMPR
Compress-in-place	a partitioned data set	IEBCOPY
Connect	volumes	IEHPROGM
Construct	records from MTST and MTDI input	IEBTCRIN
Convert to partitioned	a sequential data set created as a result of an unload	IEBCOPY
	sequential data sets	IEBUPDTE, IEBGENER
Convert to sequential	a partitioned data set	IEBUPDTE, IEBCOPY
	an indexed sequential data set	IEBISAM, IEBDG
Copy	a catalog	IEHMOVE
	a direct access volume	IEHDASDR, IBCDMPRS, IEHMOVE
	a partitioned data set	IEBCOPY, IEHMOVE
	a volume of data sets	IEHMOVE
	an indexed sequential data set	IEBISAM
	cataloged data sets	IEHMOVE
	dumped data from tape to direct access	IEHDASDR, IBCDMPRS
	job steps	IEBEDIT
	members	IEBGENER, IEBUPDTE, IEBDG
	selected members	IEBCOPY, IEHMOVE
	sequential data sets to tape	IEBGENER, IEHMOVE, IEBUPDTE, IBCDMPRS
Create	a library of partitioned members	IEBUPDTE
	a member	IEBDG
	a sequential output data set	IEBDG
	an index	IEHPROGM
	an indexed sequential data set	IEBDG
	an output job stream	IEBEDIT
Delete	a password	IEHPROGM
	an index structure	IEHPROGM
	records in a partitioned data set	IEBUPDTE

Task		Utility Programs
Dump	a direct access volume	IEHDASDR, IBCDMPRS
Edit	MTDI input	IEBTCRIN
Edit and convert to partitioned	a sequential data set	IEBGENER, IEBUPDTE
Edit and copy	a job stream	IEBEDIT
	a sequential data set	IEBGENER, IEBUPDTE
Edit and list	error statistics by volume (ESV) records	IFHSTATR
Edit and print	a sequential data set	IEBPTPCH
Edit and punch	a sequential data set	IEBPTPCH
Enter	a procedure into a procedure library	IEBUPDTE
Exclude	a partitioned data set member from a copy operation	IEBCOPY, IEHMOVE
Expand	a partitioned data set	IEBCOPY
	a sequential data set	IEBGENER
Format	DASD volumes	IEHDASDR, IBCDASDI
Generate	test data	IEBDG
Get alternate tracks	on a direct access volume	IEHDASDR, IBCDASDI, IEHATLAS
Include	changes to members or sequential data sets	IEBUPDTE
Initialize	a direct access volume	IEHDASDR, IBCDASDI
Insert records	into a partitioned data set	IEBUPDTE
Label	magnetic tape volumes	IEHINITT
List	a password entry	IEHPROGM
	a catalog	IEHLIST
	a volume table of contents	IEHLIST
	contents of direct access volume on system output device	IEHDASDR
	number of unused directory blocks and tracks	IEBCOPY
	partitioned directories	IEHLIST
	the contents of the catalog (SYSCTLG data set)	IEHLIST

Task		Utility Programs
Load	a previously unloaded partitioned data set	IEBCOPY
	an indexed sequential data set	IEBISAM
	an unloaded data set	IEHMOVE
	UCS and FCB buffers of a 3211 or a 3203	ICAPRTBL
Merge	partitioned data sets	IEHMOVE, IEBCOPY
Modify	a partitioned or sequential data set	IEBUPDTE
Move	a catalog	IEHMOVE
	a volume of data sets	IEHMOVE
	cataloged data sets	IEHMOVE
	partitioned data sets	IEHMOVE
	sequential data sets	IEHMOVE
Number records	in a new member	IEBUPDTE
	in a partitioned data set	IEBUPDTE
Password protect	add a password	IEHPROGM
	delete a password	IEHPROGM
	list passwords	IEHPROGM
	replace a password	IEHPROGM
Print	a sequential data set	IEBGENER, IEBUPDTE, IEBPTPCH
	partitioned data sets	IEBPTPCH
	selected records	IEBPTPCH
Punch	a partitioned data set member	IEBPTPCH
	a sequential data set	IEBPTPCH
	selected records	IEBPTPCH
Read	tape cartridge reader input	IEBTCRIN
Reblock	a partitioned data set	IEBCOPY
	a sequential data set	IEBGENER, IEBUPDTE
Recover	data from defective tracks on direct access volumes	IEHATLAS
	tracks flagged as defective on some DASDs	IEHDASDR, IBCDASDI
Release	a connected volume	IEHPROGM

Task		Utility Programs
Rename	a partitioned data set member	IEBCOPY, IEHPROGM
	a sequential or partitioned data set	IEHPROGM
	moved or copied members	IEHMOVE
Renumber	logical records	IEBUPDTE
Replace	a password	IEHPROGM
	data on an alternate track	IEHATLAS
	identically named members	IEBCOPY
	logical records	IEBUPDTE
	members	IEBUPDTE
	records in a member	IEBUPDTE
	records in a partitioned data set	IEBUPDTE, IEBCOPY
	selected members	IEBCOPY
	selected members in a move or copy operation	IEBCOPY, IEHMOVE
Restore	a dumped direct access volume from tape	IBCDMPRS, IEHDASDR
Scratch	a volume table of contents	IEHPROGM
	data sets	IEHPROGM
Uncatalog	data sets	IEHPROGM
Unload	a partitioned data set	IEHMOVE, IEBCOPY
	a sequential data set	IEHMOVE
	an indexed sequential data set	IEBISAM
Update	a partitioned data set in place	IEBUPDTE
	TTR entries in the supervisor call library	IEHIOSUP
Write	IPL records and a program on a direct access volume	IBCDASDI, IEHDASDR

Access Method Services Commands

This appendix gives a capsule definition of each of the current access method services commands.

Command	Definition
ALTER	Change one or more attributes of an existing entry.
BLDINDEX	Build an alternate index.
CHKLIST	List checkpoint data sets.
CNVTCAT	Convert OS catalog entries to VSAM entries.
DEF ALIAS*	Supply another name for a user catalog or a non-VSAM data set.
DEF ALTERNATEINDEX*	Supply an alternate index.
DEF CLUSTER*	Supply a basic definition of a VSAM data set.
DEF GENERATIONDATAGROUP*	Supply information for a generation data group.
DEF NONVSAM*	Supply information for data sets that are physical sequential, ISAM, partitioned, etc., but not VSAM.
DEF PAGESPACE*	Supply information for a system data set that contains pages of virtual storage.
DEF PATH*	Supply information to show the relationship between an alternate index and its base cluster.
DEF SPACE*	Supply information for VSAM data space or reserve volumes for future VSAM use.

Command	Definition
DEF USERCATALOG*	Supply information to a master VSAM catalog and create a user catalog.
DEF MASTERCATALOG*	Create a master VSAM catalog.
DELETE	Remove information about an entity from the appropriate catalog.
EXPORT	Disconnect a user catalog or VSAM data set so that it can be transported to another system or make a back-up copy of a VSAM data set.
IMPORT	Read a VSAM data set created using EXPORT or connect a VSAM user catalog or data set to a system. This command undoes what EXPORT does.
LISTCAT	List entries in catalog.
PRINT	Print a VSAM, ISAM, or SAM data set.
REPRO	Copy data sets, convert SAM and ISAM data sets to VSAM, convert ISAM and VSAM data sets to SAM, back up a VSAM catalog, read a back-up copy of a VSAM catalog, or copy a VSAM catalog.
EXPORTRA†	Retrieve VSAM data sets and catalog entries no longer accessible from a VSAM catalog.
IMPORTRA†	Restore VSAM data sets and catalog entries to an accessible condition.
LISTCRA†	Diagnose suspected VSAM catalog errors.
RESETCAT†	Synchronize a catalog to the level of its owned volumes.
VERIFY†	Cause a catalog to correctly reflect the end of the data set when the data set was previously not properly closed.

* The DEF commands generally place information in a catalog.
† Involves recovery.

Glossary

The number in parentheses is the number of the chapter in which the term was introduced.

Abend means to abnormally terminate. (2)

Access method is a program that transfers data between main storage and I/O devices. (1)

Access method services (AMS) is a VSAM utility program that provides services for which many different programs are required for non-VSAM data sets. (12)

Affinity — see **Unit affinity.** (10)

Allocation requests space on direct access storage devices. The primary allocation is the amount of space originally requested. The secondary allocation specifies the amount of space to be requested if the primary allocation is insufficient. (3)

Alphameric characters are the twenty-six letters of the alphabet and the digits 0 through 9. (2)

Alternate index is the index in which is stored information about secondary keys for VSAM data sets. (12)

Alternate key is the secondary key for a KSDS; there may be several secondary keys. (12)

AMS — see **Access method services.** (12)

Assembler is a computer program used to translate a program written in a language that usually generates one machine-language instruction for each instruction coded. (7)

Automatic-call library is used by the linkage editor to resolve external references. It is pointed to by the SYSLIB DD statement. (7)

Auxiliary storage is used to store programs and data. It may be magnetic tape, disk, drum, or mass storage. (1)

Backward reference is used to copy information from an earlier DD statement in a job. (4)

Base cluster consists of the original index and data portion for a KSDS and the data portion for an ESDS, over which an alternate index is built. (12)

Basic direct access method (BDAM) uses the record key to point to the record's location on DASD. (11)

Batch processing involves submitting programs and their data as a unit. (1)

BDAM — see **Basic direct access method.** (11)

Bit is the smallest unit in main storage; it may be on or off, 1 or 0. (1)

Block is the area occupied by data on a volume. (3)

Blocking factor is the number of records in a block. (3)

Blocksize is the number of bytes of data in a block. (3)

Buffer is an area of main storage that is temporarily reserved for I/O operations. (1)

Byte is a group of eight bits. (1)

CA — see **Control area.** (12)

Cartridge is the basic unit on a mass storage device, equivalent to a disk pack on a disk drive. (14)

Catalog means to store information about a data set in the system catalog, which is a data set used by the system to obtain this information if it is not coded in the DD statement. (4)

Cataloged procedure is precoded JCL stored in a catalog library. (7)

Central processing unit (CPU) is that part of the computer in which instructions are actually executed. (1)

Channel is a path used to transmit data between main storage and I/O devices. (10)

Checkpoint is a point up to which information about the status of a job is retained, so that if the job subsequently fails it may be restarted from that point. (10)

CI—see **Control interval.** (12)

CIDF—see **Control interval definition field.** (12)

Cluster is the named entity used to access the VSAM data set. (12)

Collating sequence is the sequence used by the computer to sort data stored in character form. (9)

Comments field follows the operand field and is separated from it by at least one blank. This field is optional and is rarely used. It has no effect other than that the comments coded in it appear in the output. (2)

Compiler is a program that decodes instructions written in a high-level language and produces a machine-language program. (7)

Completion code is a number used to identify the error that caused an abend. (4)

Compress means to reorganize a PDS to recover unused space. (5)

Concatenation refers to the way in which several data sets of the same type are treated by the processing programs as one data set. (7)

Condition code provides a mechanism for a program to inform the operating system about the results of an execution; it may have a value from 0 to 4096. (2)

Contiguous refers to tracks that are in the same cylinder and cylinders that are next to each other. (3)

Control area (CA) consists of several control intervals. It is used with VSAM data sets. (12)

Control area split occurs when there are no more free control intervals left in a control area to which data are being added. (12)

Control field names the field in the record on which a sort is to be done. The first field is **major,** and subsequent fields are **minor.** (9)

Control interval (CI) is the unit of information moved from DASD to virtual storage when VSAM data sets are accessed; it is of fixed size. (12)

Control interval definition field (CIDF) contains information about the control interval, including the amount and location of the freespace in the control interval. (12)

Control interval split occurs when an attempt is made to add a record to a control interval that does not have sufficient freespace. The result will be that two control intervals will contain the data that used to be in one. (12)

Control statement is used to provide detailed information to a utility program about the function the utility program is to perform. (4)

CPU—see **Central processing unit.** (1)

Cylinder consists of all the tracks of a disk pack that can be accessed without moving the read/write heads of the disk drive. (3)

Cylinder index is an index within the index for an ISAM data set. It has one entry for each cylinder in the prime area of the data set. (11)

Cylinder overflow refers to tracks reserved in each cylinder of the prime area of an ISAM data set for those records that do not fit on the proper track. (11)

DASD—see **Direct access storage device.** (1)

DASDI stands for direct access storage device initialization. (13)

Data cartridge—see **Cartridge.** (14)

Data set is a collection of related records. (1)

Data set name is the name of a data set that is stored in a VTOC or label record. Simple or unqualified names have one to eight alphameric or national (#, @, $) characters, the first of which must be alphabetic or national. Qualified names may be up to forty-four characters in length and consist of several simple or unqualified names separated by periods—for example, JULY.SALES. (3)

ddname is the name field on a DD statement. (2)

Default values are those values automatically assigned to a parameter when a value is not explicitly assigned. (2)

Delete byte can be the first byte in a record of an ISAM data set. A hexadecimal FF in this field means that the record is a dummy record or is marked for deletion. (11)

Dependent job control network is a group of jobs each of which has a JES3 //*NET statement containing the same value for the NETID, or ID, parameter. (15)

Destaging copies data from a 3336 Disk Pack to a mass storage volume after the data set is closed. (14)

Direct access means the computer can process a particular record without accessing all of the preceding records. (1)

Direct access storage device (DASD) is a disk or drum. (1)

Directory is at the start of the library and points to where the various members are located in the library. (5)

Directory block is the building unit of a directory and is 256 bytes in length. In addition to pointers to the members, it contains information on how much of the block is in use. (5)

DJC network—see **Dependent job control network.** (15)

DSCB—see **Model data set control block.** (6)

Dump is a listing of the contents of main storage. A dump may be of all main storage or part of it. (4)

Dynamic allocation is allocating a data set after the job has begun. (12)

Dynamic linking is linking modules during execution. (7)

EBCDIC stands for extended binary coded decimal interchange code. The code uses one byte to express each character; thus 256 characters can be represented. (1)

Entry sequence data set (ESDS) is a VSAM data set in which the records are stored in the order in which they were entered. These data sets have only one piece—the data portion. (12)

EOD stands for end of data. (2)

ESDS—see **Entry sequence data set.** (12)

Extent consists of a group of contiguous tracks, all of which either are used by one data set or are available. (3)

External references are module or program names that are used in a module or program but are not contained in that module or program. (7)

Forward reference uses the keyword parameter DDNAME to replace the DD statement with another one that appears later in the job stream. (7)

Freespace is unused space scattered throughout a KSDS. (12)

Generation, or generation data set, is a data set within a generation data group. (6)

Generation data group is a collection or group of cataloged data sets having the same name and bearing a chronological relationship to one another. (6)

Generation data set—see **Generation.** (6)

Generation group index contains information on how many generations are to be retained and what to do when the index becomes full. (6)

Generation number distinguishes one member of a generation data group from another. The number may be absolute (G0238V00) or relative (+ 1). (6)

Hexadecimal number system is a base-sixteen number system. Two hexadecimal digits can represent the contents of a byte. (1)

Index area is the part of the ISAM data set that contains the index. If the data set is small, the index area may be at the start of the prime area. (11)

Indexed sequential access method (ISAM) uses an index to locate a record. The index is read first, and the record location is determined from the index. (1, 11)

Index sequential access method (ISAM)—see **Indexed sequential access method.** (1)

Index set is a higher-level index in the index portion of a VSAM KSDS that points to control intervals in the sequence set. (12)

Input stream data are data included in the job stream. They usually follow a DD * or DD DATA statement. (1)

Input work queue is where jobs await resources needed for execution to begin. There may be several, based on job class designation. (1)

Integrated catalog facility (ICF) is the newest type of catalog, designed for both VSAM and non-VSAM data sets. (12)

Interblock gap is the space between blocks of data on a reel of tape or a disk pack. (3)

I/O stands for input and output. (1)

IPL means initial program load. (13)

ISAM—see **Indexed sequential access method.** (1)

JCL—see **Job control language.** (1)

JES—see **Job entry subsystem.** (1)

Job consists of one or more job steps preceded by a JOB statement. (1)

Job control language (JCL) is the language used to communicate with the operating system. (1)

Job entry subsystem, JES, JES2, or JES3, is that part of the operating system that reads jobs into the system, schedules them for execution, and then handles the output. (1)

JOBLIB is the ddname of a DD statement that points to the library or libraries in which the executable load modules used in the job are found. (7)

Jobname is the name field coded on the JOB statement. (2)

Jobstep consists of an EXEC statement and its DD statements. (1)

Job stream consists of JCL statements that invoke the program or programs that are to be executed and point to the data to be operated on. (1)

Julian date is the date specified in the form of a two-digit year number and a three-digit day number—either yyddd or dddyy. (10)

K—see **Kilobyte.** (1)

Key is the field used to identify the record. (11)

Key field—see **Control field.** (9)

Key sequence data set (KSDS) is the VSAM data set that may be accessed by a key contained in the record. It consists of two parts, the index and data. (12)

Keyword parameters are identified by the equals sign that follows—for example, CLASS=A. These parameters may be coded in any order in the operand field. (2)

Kilobyte (K) is 1024 bytes. (1)

KSDS—see **Key sequence data set.** (12)

Label records precede and follow standard label data sets. They contain information about the data set such as data set name, logical record length, blocksize, recording density, and number of blocks in the data set. (3)

Library consists of groups of sequential records and a directory and is also known as a partitioned data set (PDS). (5)

Linkage editor performs the same function as the loader except that the program does not start executing. A load module is produced instead. (7)

Loader resolves external references, includes modules from the SYSLIB library, relocates address constants, and then causes the program to begin executing. (7)

Loading is re-creating a PDS or an ISAM or VSAM data set from a sequential data set that was created by an unload operation. (5)

Load module is the output of the linkage editor, which is executable, assuming there are no errors. (7)

Logical record length is the number of bytes of data in a record. (3)

Logic error occurs when the job executes but gives incorrect results. (2)

M—see **Megabyte.** (1)

Main storage is where programs and data are stored while they are being processed. (1)

Map is a list of called modules produced by either the loader or the linkage editor. (7)

Mass storage system is equivalent to 4720 3336 Disk Packs. It provides the usability of DASD at the cost of tape. (14)

Mass storage volume consists of two cartridges. (14)

Master index is the third level of indexing used with an ISAM data set. This index has an entry for each track in the cylinder index. (11)

Megabyte (M) is 1,048,576 bytes. (1)

Member is a group of sequential records in a library which may be treated as a physical sequential data set. (5)

Merging combines records from two or more sorted data sets to form one sorted data set. (9)

MFT stands for multiprogramming with a fixed number of tasks. Main storage is divided into a fixed number of partitions. The number and the size of the partitions are set when the system is installed; however, the operator can modify the partitions during execution. (1)

Model data set control block (DSCB) contains DCB information that the system will use in creating or accessing a generation data set. It must reside on the same volume as the system catalog. (6)

MSVGP is a parameter coded on a DD statement when a data set is being created on mass storage. It names the group in which the particular volume to be used will be found. (14)

Multiple virtual storage (MVS) is a virtual version of MVT. (1)

Multiprogramming means executing two or more programs at the same time. While I/O operations are being performed for one program, the computer actually executes another. (1)

MVS—see **Multiple virtual storage.** (1)

MVS/XA is a version of MVS that allows a program to use 2 billion bytes of storage. (1)

MVT stands for multiprogramming with a variable number of tasks. A part of main storage is reserved for OS programs, and the rest is available in one large pool to be used by jobs. Each job gets the amount of storage it needs. (1)

Name field assigns a system-recognized name to a JOB, EXEC, or DD statement. The name field must start in column 3 and may be from one to eight characters in length. Permitted characters are the letters A through Z, the numbers 0 through 9, and the three national characters #, @, and $; however, the first character may not be numeric. (2)

National characters are the three characters #, @, and $. (2)

Nodename is a name given by systems programmers to a particular installation. (15)

Node number is an identifier assigned by systems programmers to a particular installation. (15)

Nullify means to remove the value. Symbolic parameters are nullified by coding the symbolic parameter followed by an equals sign and nothing else. (8)

Object module is the output of the compiler or assembler and consists of machine-language instructions. (7)

Off-line refers to volumes not currently accessible by the computer, as well as devices not currently usable by the computer. (3)

On-line refers to volumes currently accessible by the computer, as well as devices currently usable by the computer. (3)

Operand field consists of one or more parameters that provide detailed information about the job, the program being executed, the data sets used, and the procedure. (2)

Operating system (OS) consists of a collection of programs that control the operation of the computer. (1)

Operation field follows the name field and specifies the kind of statement being coded. Valid values are JOB, EXEC, DD, OUTPUT, PEND, and PROC. (2)

Origin group is a group of printers defined for a local or remote site by systems programmers. (15)

OS—see **Operating system.** (1)

Output work queue is DASD space where unit record data sets are written during job execution. (1)

Overflow area is the optional third part of the ISAM data set. This is where records that do not fit in their proper place in the prime area are placed if there is no cylinder overflow or if the cylinder overflow is full. (11)

Overlay structure creates a load module that will be loaded into main storage in predefined pieces. (7)

Override statement is a DD statement in a job stream that is used to replace, in part or in totality, a DD statement from a procedure. (7)

Packed format is a method of storing numeric data that permits two digits to be stored in each byte except the rightmost byte, which contains one digit and a sign. (1)

Page is a section in which a program or data may be divided and then written to either main or auxiliary storage. (1)

Paging involves reading a page in from DASD or writing one out to DASD. When the information in a page is no longer being used by a program, it may be written out. When it is needed, it is read in. (1)

Parameter provides detailed information about the job, program, or data set being used. (2, 7)

PARM field is used to pass information to the program that is being executed. It is limited to 100 characters. (7)

Partition is a region of main storage in which a program is executed. This term is associated with MFT and other systems based on MFT. (1)

Partitioned data set (PDS) is synonymous with library. (5)

PDS — see **Partitioned data set.** (5)

Performance group is installation defined and specifies the workload-dependent processing rate at which a job or jobstep executes. If implemented, it affects turnaround time. (10)

Positional parameter is a parameter recognized by the operating system by its position in the operand field. Positional parameters must be coded before any of the keyword parameters. (2)

Prime area is that part of the ISAM data set that contains the data. It is always required. (11)

Prime key is the original key in a KSDS. (12)

Procedure is precoded JCL. (7)

PROC statement, if used, is the first statement in a procedure. It is required for in-stream procedures, but is optional for cataloged procedures. It is used to set default values for symbolic parameters. (7)

Processor ID is a single-digit identifier assigned to a CPU in a JES3 system. (15)

Procstep is an abbreviation for procedure step. (7)

Procstepname stands for procedure stepname. (7)

Queue is a list of items waiting for service. (1)

Random access refers to the ability to directly read a particular record and add a record in the middle of a data set without re-creating the data set. (11)

RBA — see **Relative byte address.** (12)

Real storage in a virtual system is main storage as opposed to auxiliary storage. (1)

Record definition field contains the length of the corresponding record in the control interval and the number of records that are of that length. (12)

Recording density is the number of bytes recorded per inch of tape. Common values currently are 800, 1600, and 6250. (3)

Relative byte address (RBA) is the byte count, starting from the beginning of the storage space. It is used to locate a particular record. (12)

Relative key position (RKP) specifies the location of the key in the record. The first byte is 0, the second is 1, and so forth. (11)

Relative record data set (RRDS) is a VSAM data set in which each record is uniquely identified by its position in the data set or its record number. (12)

Remote job entry (RJE) refers to using job entry devices (such as a card reader) that are separated geographically from the computer on which the job is executed but connected by communication lines, which frequently are supplied by the telephone company. (15)

Reorganization (ISAM) recovers space by eliminating records marked for deletion and places records from the overflow areas in their proper places in the prime area. (11)

Reorganization (PDS) reclaims unused space in a library or PDS. (5)

Return code — see **Condition code.** (2)

RJE — see **Remote job entry.** (15)

RKP — see **Relative key position.** (11)

RRDS — see **Relative record data set.** (12)

SDS — see **Sequential data set.** (4)

Segment is a piece of a load module created when overlay structure is used. (7)

Sequence set is the lowest-level index in the index portion of the KSDS. (12)

Sequential access method (SAM) requires that records be processed in the order in which they physically occur in the data set. (1)

Sequential data set (SDS) is a data set whose records are organized on the basis of their successive physical positions. (4)

Serial number consists of one to six alphameric characters and is used to identify a reel of tape or a disk pack. (3)

Sorting puts data set records into a specified order. (9)

Source code is the high-level-language program. (7)

Source module is the assembler or a high-level-language program. (7)

Special characters are characters other than letters, digits, and the three national characters. (2)

Spooling writes the input job stream to DASD and writes the printer or card punch output to DASD instead of to the printer or card punch. Spooling isolates the CPU from the slow unit record devices. Spool is an acronym for simultaneous peripheral operations on-line. (1)

Staging is the process of taking data from a mass storage volume and placing it on a 3336 Disk Pack, where it is accessible through an application program. (14)

STEPLIB is the ddname of a DD statement that points to the library or libraries in which the executable load modules used in a step are found. (7)

Stepname is the name field coded on the EXEC statement. (2)

Symbolic parameter starts with an ampersand and represents a parameter or subparameter in a procedure. (7)

Syntax is the structure of expressions in a language. (1)

Syntax error is an error that violates a JCL rule. In English such an error is called a grammatical error. (2)

Sysgen is the process by which a system is created or generated to meet the individual requirements of an installation. (1)

Task is an executable program and associated data. It is the basic unit of work performed by a computer. (1)

Temporary data set is a data set that exists only for the duration of a job. (5)

Temporary data set name consists of two ampersands followed by an unqualified data set name. (5)

Terminal consists of a typewriter device or typewriterlike keyboard and TV-like display screen connected by a communications line to a computer at a central site. (1)

Time sharing is having many terminal users employ a computer simultaneously. (1)

Time sharing option (TSO) is a feature that permits conversational time sharing from remote stations. (15)

Track is a circle on the recording surface of a disk pack upon which data are recorded. (3)

Transparent means that the user is not aware of a process. For example, in a virtual system paging is transparent to the user. (1)

TSO—see **Time sharing option.** (15)

Unit affinity characterizes two data sets that use the same physical device. (10)

Unit record device is a card reader, card punch, or printer. (1)

Unloading is copying a PDS or an ISAM or VSAM data set to a sequential data set in a way that permits the original data set to be re-created at a later time by means of a load operation. (5)

Unpacking converts packed decimal data to character format, usually for printing. (1)

Utility program performs commonly required tasks. See Chapter 13. (1)

VIO—see **Virtual input/output.** (5)

Virtual input/output (VIO) involves using the operating system's paging facility to store temporary data sets. (5)

Virtual storage treats auxiliary storage as if it were main storage. Programs are divided into small sections called pages. (1)

Virtual storage access method (VSAM) is an access method especially designed for use with virtual systems. (1)

Virtual storage operating system, VS1, is a virtual version of MFT. (1)

Volume is a reel of tape or a removable disk pack. (3)

Volume label is the first record on a reel of tape. It contains the serial number of the volume. (3)

VSAM—see **Virtual storage access method.** (1)

VTOC stands for volume table of contents. There is a VTOC on each disk pack; it is used to keep track of the data sets stored on each volume as well as the space still available for use. (3)

Workstation is an RJE station or terminal. Workstation may be written as either one or two words. (1)

Bibliography

OS/VS1 JCL Reference, GC24-5099
MVS/370 JCL User's Guide, GC28-1349
MVS/370 JCL Reference, GC28-1350
MVS/XA JCL User's Guide, GC28-1351
MVS/XA JCL Reference, GC28-1352

OS/VS1 Utilities, GC26-3901
MVS/370 Data Administration: Utilities, GC26-4065
MVS/XA Utilities, GC26-4018

OS/VS1 System Messages, GC38-1001
MVS/370 Message Library System Messages, GC28-1374 and 1375
MVS/XA Message Library System Messages, GC28-1376 and 1377

OS/VS1 System Code, GC38-1003
OS/VS Message Library: VS2 System Codes, GC38-1008

IBM OS/VS COBOL Compiler and Library, Programmer's Guide, SC28-6483
VS COBOL II Application Programming Guide, SC26-4045
OS PL/I Optimizing Compiler, Programmer's Guide, SC33-0006
OS/VS, VM/370 Assembler Programmer's Guide, GC33-4021
OS FORTRAN IV, Compiler and Programmer's Guide, SC28-6852

OS/VS Linkage Editor and Loader, GC26-3813
MVS/370 Linkage Editor and Loader, User's Guide, GC26-4061
MVS/XA Linkage Editor and Loader, User's Guide, GC26-4011

DFSORT Application Programming Guide, SC33-4035

IBM 3800 Printing Subsystem Programmer's Guide, GC26-3846

OS/VS1 Access Method Services, GC26-3840
MVS/370 Access Method Services, Reference, GC26-4051
MVS/XA Access Method Services, Reference, GC26-4019

OS/VS1 Checkpoint/Restart, GC26-3876
MVS/370 Checkpoint/Restart, User's Guide, GC26-4054
MVS/XA Checkpoint/Restart, User's Guide, GC26-4139

OS/VS MSS Services Reference Information, GC35-0017

Index

Common Abend Codes and Their Causes

001 CHECK, GET, PUT—I/O error.

An I/O error occurred during the reading or writing of a data file. Your DCB did not contain the address of an error handling routine; therefore, your program was terminated. Specify an error handling routine address. Other conditions causing this abend: the logical record length and blocksize specified in the DCB or DD statement differ from the logical record length and blocksize indicated in the data set.

0C1 Operation exception.

An operation code is not assigned or the assigned operation is not available on the particular model. In this instance the machine did not recognize the instruction or operation used. Possible reasons include a clobbered core or a subscript error. This error could be caused by an attempt to read a file that was not opened, a misspelled ddname, or a missing DD statement.

0C4 Protection exception.

In high-level languages this means that a subscript was out of range or a computed GOTO type statement took a wild branch.

0C5 Addressing exception.

An address specifies any part of data, an instruction, or a control word outside the available real storage for the particular model. A subscript error also usually causes this error (see 0C1 and 0C4).

0C7 Data exception.

With a high-level language, this code usually results from attempting a "decimal" operation on properly defined fields with invalid contents (garbage, not initialized, overwritten, etc.). The equivalent of decimal in COBOL is COMPUTATIONAL-3 and in PL/I is FIXED DECIMAL. Note that converting a zoned decimal (character) format to binary involves a decimal operation.

122 Normal operator-issued cancel and dump.

The job may have been canceled because of an endless loop or because resources were not available. Consult your operator to find out why the job was canceled and resubmit it. There may be nothing wrong with your job.

213 OPEN—I/O error.

The error occurred during execution of an OPEN macro instruction for a direct access device. In the case of disk reads, this usually means that the data set was not on the volume that was specified—or was misspelled—on the DD